CW01336661

Killing History

The False Left-Right Political Spectrum and the Battle between the 'Free Left' and the 'Statist Left'

L.K. Samuels

Copyright © 2019 by L.K. Samuels

Published by

**Freeland
Press**
P.O. Box 22231
Carmel, CA 93922
http://www.freelandpress.org/

All Rights Reserved, Published 2019

Printed in the United States
ISBN (Print): 978-0-9615893-1-8
ISBN (ebook): 0-9615893-1-0

L.K. Samuels
Killing History: The False Left-Right Political Spectrum and the Battle between the 'Free Left' and the 'Statist Left'

1. Political Spectrum 2. Political 3. History 4. Socioeconomics

Cover design by Rick at Vision Press. www.myvisionpress.com
Ebook design by Mike Dworski.

Name: Samuels, L.K.
Title: Killing History: The False Left-Right Political Spectrum

Website for author: www.lksamuels.com

First published, 2019

Acknowledgements

After six years of research and writing, I want to acknowledge some of the people who made this book possible. First, I had two editors who worked on various chapters in a valiant effort to bring order to chaos— Elizabeth Brierly and Erin Becker. Also, Mike Dworski was very helpful in formatting the ebook and print versions and cleaning footnotes. They did a great job. After that, I decided to bring in Linda Blumenthal to do the final proofing, especially since I often followed the suggestions of my editors, and rewrote some material, over and over again. Again, she did a splendid job. But the one person who came to my rescue after reworking the material when I had grammar questions, was my wife, Jane Heider, who was indispensable.

I must also acknowledge Prof. David R. Henderson, who gave suggestions and looked over my preface, and offered some revisions. It does indeed take a cooperative village of professionals to write a book.

Contents

Preface

Almost everything about the political spectrum is dead wrong. If the two polar opposites are Communism versus Fascism, what is in the middle? If the middle is halfway between Communism and Fascism then everyone not on the extreme ends must be half-communist and half-fascist?[1] Nobody believes that, but the old political spectrum prescribes that exact political scenario. There must be a better way.

The political spectrum is not only a false dichotomy, but also has been rendered contradictory and ludicrous. The American political philosopher Chispin Startwell pointed out the insanity of the positions along the left-right axis: "This spectrum stretches from authoritarianism on the one end to authoritarianism on the other, with authoritarianism in between."[2] This designation makes the left-right model of politics a confusing mess, with little or no clarity. There must be a way to discover which political sides you like or dislike. There must be a way to find the right coordinates and redraw the political map. I felt that it was my duty to become that political cartographer and produce accurate charts. And that is how I came to write my book.

But it was a long and arduous journey that started in 2013. A few years later, the political spectrum was racing ahead on steroids, exhibiting signs that its distortion of reality was expanding. When Donald Trump was elected as President of the United States in 2016, the political compass for classifying different political positions went into an uncontrollable spin and threw many people into almost uncharted territory. This may feel new to many onlookers unfamiliar with the complex history of political ideology, but the left-right categorization has actually been twisted, falsified, and distorted for some time. Why? Because a more accurate assessment would disadvantage a raft of powerful political ideologies. To less-than-ethical characters who have a reputation to protect, a muddled sense of history in the public's mind can be advantageous.

These distorters of history have been increasingly averse to providing an accurate political methodology for people to navigate the complex political mazes. In fact, they sidestep the idea of an accurate compass since it might expose their old and sullied ideological laundry. They want the populace to be led astray, or to be neutralized, politicalized or divided by simplistic and misleading linguistics and faux data. They also want the left-right model to be identified as exclusively binary—a spectrum theory of politics that is boxed in with only two sides so as to ignore gray areas. But this imprisonment to an incoherent, two-sided political position has great potential to inflame division and mistrust where "We don't need to understand those who disagree with us, we only need to destroy them."[3] Here, ideologism and tribalism are far more important than civil discourse or a thirst for knowledge; the former permit each side to judge, hate and condemn based on political labels. This trend towards dogmatic ideologism has become a "new form of acceptable bigotry."[4] This false dichotomy not only closes minds and stifles public debate, but also makes people more susceptible to a misleading, narrow-minded, and dis-informational political paradigm.

Historically, this process of disinformation went into high gear in the decades following the French Revolution. After the bourgeoisie, middle class, and merchants instigated the French Revolution and sat on the left side of the aisle in opposition to the authoritarians, their legacy was ignored. The Socialist and nationalist intelligentsia sought to consciously bury the memory of original left-wing middle class history and sitting arrangements. They mercilessly co-opted the left-wing label from the bourgeoisie revolutionary "Free Left," and denounced anyone who opposed their social revolution as reactionary or right-wing. These usurpers not only stole the left-wing designation from the bourgeoisie insurgents, but also absconded with their revolutionary ancestry. English historian William Doyle acknowledged this historical thievery, writing that after the French Revolution, the socialists were able to "appropriate the left-wing label and... lay exclusive claim to the revolutionary heritage."[5] During this brief moment of liberalism, the revolutionary epiphany gleaned from the French Revolution provided a coherent left-right dichotomy that allowed the public to locate their own true political positions relative to those of others. It did not last long. Such moments of clarity and discovery become futile when conquerors and government apologists rewrite history to favor their particular ideological causes while sabotaging others. So it should be no surprise that this kind of historical manipulation has been particularly rampant throughout the last two centuries. My purpose was and is to document such transgressions by explaining the political spectrum and its accompanying ideologies that spawned the French Revolution and climaxed in the ideological determinism of the mid-20th century. I do this with historical evidence: there are over 1,500 footnotes by major and minor historians and political scientists. In a sense, my book is a reference guide for future research on the subject.

There were other reasons why I wrote this book. First, it evolved from another unfinished book: *Government: A State of Deception*, which I had started in 2013. In one chapter, I plunged so deep into the quagmire of classifying political ideologies, positions, and movements that my writing began to take on a life of its own. I attempted to define Italian Fascism, German National Socialism and Russian Sovietism to better understand where they stood on the political continuum. What I began to uncover was shocking. It was at this moment that I began to sense something terribly wrong with the political spectrum. Most ideology did not match well with their alleged corresponding left-right designation. It was as if the political dichotomy was riddled with serious errors, and maybe even fraud and deception. I began to wonder if this was an elaborate charade and a campaign of disinformation. I'd had no idea that so much of the political spectrum had been based on conjecture, pseudo-analysis, and the cultivation of myths. The three most infamous totalitarian regimes of the 20th century appeared both misaligned and eerily similar.

As I delved deeper into ever more serious academic research, my chapter veered off course, into almost uncharted territory. I landed in a strange land of so-called polar-opposite ideologies that were instead virtual carbon copies, at first coexisting, but then coalescing until they appeared almost indistinguishable. I had entered the twilight zone, a black hole of paradoxes. What was originally considered left-wing had seemed to have become right-wing, and what was right-wing now postured as left-wing. How could this be? The people calling themselves conservatives appeared to be more in tune with Lockean and Jeffersonian liberalism, while the people calling themselves liberals cross-dressed, donning outdated English Toryism with blood-red authoritarianism and statism.

This conflicting mismatch of political genres and ideologies seemed to approach historical proportions. I could not understand why those claiming to be apostles of liberalism failed to abide by its original etymological root in the Latin word "liber," which means "free." But these so-called defenders of freedom were more concerned over security and equality, and were willing to sacrifice liberty for the sake of a government-directed orderly society.

Meanwhile, during my research, I encountered something curious in the writings of Benito Mussolini. In his famous "Political and Social Doctrine of Fascism," everything came down to one word in defining the entire modern political spectrum, the Holy Grail of words that determines political orientation. I soon discovered that a controversy had erupted over that one word in Mussolini's 26-page booklet. So, I bought a copy of the first authorized English edition, found the exact page and slid my fingers across its indented, lead-type printed page. The word was not "Right," but "Left"—not what I had expected.

This discrepancy made no sense, and for some time, I could not figure out why. But that one crucial word spelled a world of difference to the orientation of the political compass, in positioning people and ideas on the political spectrum. Most books and internet sites had Mussolini writing that he was on the "right" or "tending to the right." But that was not the phrase found in my 1933 original copy, nor in the 1934 edition, which I also bought. Then I found books and publications from the 1930s that verified that Mussolini had indeed written, "... it may rather be expected that this will be a century of authority, a century of the Left, a century of Fascism."[6]

All I could conclude was that Mussolini's explanation of fascism in his most famous work had been doctored to keep alive certain fallacies about the political spectrum; that fascism had to be the complete opposite of Marxism, despite its close ideological and historical relationship. But this anti-Marxist narrative did not jibe with direct quotes from Mussolini himself, particularly his 1932 interview with biographer Emil Ludwig. In that interview Mussolini stated for the record:

> It was inevitable that I should become a Socialist ultra, a Blanquist, indeed a communist. I carried about a medallion with Marx's head on it in my pocket... [Marx] had a profound critical intelligence and was in some sense even a prophet.[7]

This was an important quote that until recently never made it to the public spotlight, although the 230-page book *Talks with Mussolini* was published in many languages.

Such dishonest treatment of history can only be regarded as an act of historical sabotage—a ploy to kill history in order to satisfy political ends. What I had run across was the handiwork of a cadre of extremists determined to sacrifice truth at the altar of ideology. This obvious attempt to rewrite history drove me to write more on the subject, but it also made me wonder what else had been sabotaged, forged, or hidden from public view to tilt the political spectrum in someone's favor.

But another major problem soon arose over the interpretation of fascism as a left-wing movement. That left-wing designation did not correspond well to the historical spectrum of political ideas. I wanted to remain loyal to the original left-right designation of the French Revolution. Mussolini had been an avowed Marxist and revolutionary socialist for decades, associating with Lenin and Trotsky, and referred to himself as an "authoritarian communist."[8] Therefore, despite his endeavor in the 1930s to peg fascism on the "Left," he should actually be classified as a disciple of the right. Ever since the French Revolution, the sitting arrangement for authoritarians has been reserved for the right side of the table. Of course, another nagging headache immediately shot to the forefront. To remain consistent, all authoritarians would have to be grouped within the ranks of right-wing extremists, including Marx, Stalin, Lenin, Mao, Hitler and so forth. There could be no exceptions. That would be a hard sell among the radical and authoritarian left who have little knowledge of their ancestors' theft of the left moniker from the bourgeoisie. Moreover, such nuances about the left-right spectrum are rarely taught in grade school, or in universities, for that matter, or broadcast in the mainstream media. Nonetheless, it would seem logical to group authoritarians with authoritarians, despite their inherent rivalry. Logic, however, always takes a back-row seat when masters of crowd dynamics and propagandists have taken control of the political stage.

As I show in this book, totalitarian and authoritarian movements have much in common. Different dictatorships may refer to their policies by dissimilar names and vary their propaganda to befuddle their respective populaces to maintain support. But their core ideological and tactical features are practically identical: blind submission to coercive authority, a predominance of collectivism over individualism, a hostility to private-sector capitalism, and a single-party concentration of power predisposed to suppress individual freedom of speech, thought, and action.

Efforts to alter the political spectrum to favor a particular brand of authoritarianism are obvious. In the world of dog-eat-dog politics and power, consistency and logic are orphans. There is more than a whiff of politics directing a campaign of public disorientation. Darkness has always been a good friend to manipulators of politics. The politics of confusion allows the elite power brokers and "controlaholics" to do their work unimpeded. They know that to be able to navigate political and moral swamplands, one needs a faithful instrument to triangulate one's position. But, if the political compass has been deliberately broken and made meaningless, citizens cannot find their way through the contorted political maze. If people are unable to discover their own political pathway on their own, they will be lost, divided and alone—the perfect storm for Orwellian politics to control the public. Whoever commands the high ground of political classification can easily control the process of human thought. As Alexander Hamilton once warned about the stratagem of deceitful demagogues, their main "object is to throw things into confusion that he may ride the storm and direct the whirlwind."[9]

From this realization, I concluded that I had to set the record straight, engage in massive research, and write a heavy tome about why the current left-right spectrum is phony. I felt I had to get the word out to reconnect the political spectrum to its historical roots.

Around the same time, I decided that it was important to correct the Wikipedia page on "Fascism" by inserting the authentic version, showing that Mussolini considered Italian Fascism to be on the Left. Wikipedia's editors were not amused; they quickly deleted my new material. I don't blame Wikipedia; this kind of back-and-forth editorial revision is typical of crowdsourced informational platforms. So, I had Mussolini's booklet scanned, along with other well-known publications and books of the 1930s, and eventually made it available to the Wikipedia page editors and the general public. Finally, after a few editors acknowledged that the booklet had indeed read "Left," they merely scoffed, insisting that it had to have been a misprint, or mistranslated. They often referred to the 1932 Italian version but never could produce a copy from the actual *Enciclopedia Italiana* volume. Apparently, the few volumes printed had been lost or destroyed during World War II.[10] But Jane Soames from the *Times* of London correctly translated the word "left" in other sections of Mussolini's "Doctrine of Fascism," and since it was an authorized translation, someone in Mussolini's administration had to proof it and sign off on it.

To prove that Mussolini had meant "Left," I wrote a new Wikipedia page—"Controversies over Italian Fascism's Political Placement"—citing over 114 sources from historians and political scientists, who basically concluded that Mussolini's Fascism was either a heretical revision, variety, or consequence of Marxism, demonstrating that Mussolini had indeed thought of himself and his movement as left-wing social revolutionaries who opposed classical liberalism, individualism, free-market capitalism, religion, monarchies, and limited government. Prior to and during his fascist years, Mussolini repeatedly demonstrated his appetite for hardcore socialism, verifying that Italian Fascism was actually just one of many variant shades of Marxist-influenced socialism, which snuggled up to the political left. Moreover, Mussolini's dedication to his socialist comrades was such that he worked hard to make fascist Italy the first nation in the West to officially recognize the Soviet Union, in 1924. Does this sound like the mindset of an anti-communist?

In 1934, Mussolini boasted in a major speech that he had nationalized three-fourths of the Italian economy. Who but a Marxist or communist sympathizer would boast about heavily socializing his nation's economy? Isn't the true measure of a dedicated socialist his following Karl Marx's wishes to have the means of production owned by government or public entities? The Wikipedia editors continued to remove my demonstration of Mussolini's left-wing orientation of Italian Fascism. Eventually, my Wikipedia page on Italian Fascism was deleted.[11]

Many months later, I made the requested changes and resubmitted the page with more than 350 citations, still retaining Mussolini's controversial sentence. The Wikipedia editors had had enough; they refused to consider reposting it. One editor said that to display Mussolini's avowed dedication to leftism would overturn "80 years of historiography."

Yet I found an overwhelming abundance of evidence to demonstrate Mussolini's affection for Marxism and the Soviet Union, which is found in Chapter 3. He even went so far as to boast about his paternity to "communist children," metaphorically. This happened after he was first elected to Italy's Chamber of Deputies in 1921, as leader of the Fascist Revolutionary Party that later changed its name to the National Fascist Party. Richard Pipes, a Harvard University professor of history, summed it up well:

> Even as the Fascist leader, Mussolini never concealed his sympathy and admiration for Communism: he thought highly of Lenin's "brutal energy," and saw nothing objectionable in Bolshevik massacres of hostages.[12]

Pipes went so far as to claim that "Genetically, Fascism issued from the 'Bolshevik' wing of Italian socialism, not from any conservative ideology or movement."[13]

Mussolini's perspective was common among heretical Marxists. Like most Marxist revisionists, *Il Duce* had adopted a "semi-Marxist," "right-wing socialist," or what I like to call a "Marxist lite" position, which renders meaningless the antiquated circular political spectrum, in which the far right and far left almost meet, but are still touted as being polar opposites. In fact, such notions are not just nonsense, but underhandedly meaningless. I finally came to the realization that it is pure bunk, an artifice manufactured to make political designations incomprehensible and incoherent.

The main reason for sowing confusion is that the consequences would be too dreadful to even contemplate. To affix the poisonous label of "fascism" to Communism, depicting them under the same collective brotherhood, would have irrevocably damaged the status of socialism. The socialist franchise would be mortally wounded. To acknowledge a strong ideological and political link to Mussolini and Hitler would forever expose socialists and Marxists to their historical collaboration with fascist atrocities, racism, and genocide. Not only would socialists be seen as accomplices to some of the most horrific crimes in history, but also communists would also face similar scrutiny over their own atrocities, that racked up over 148 million citizens murdered in the 20th century.[14]

To socialist doctrinaires, to see Mussolini as a Fascist-Marxist partisan would make a mockery of the circular (or U-shaped) political spectrum. Of course, such pseudohistorical notions of the political divide are rubbish. Starting in 1914 with the Marxist-sounding Fasci of Revolutionary Action (*Fasci d'Azione Rivoluzionaria*, FAR), followed in 1915 with his founding of the Fascist Revolutionary Party, for six or seven years Mussolini was simultaneously a Marxist heretic and an Italian Fascist, meaning that he commingled the two into a Fascist-Marxist ideology. He supported the 1917 Communist Revolution in Russia,[15] later criticizing Lenin for not having lived up to Marx's "dictatorship of the proletariat" and for having failed to create a true socialist party.[16] In 1919, Mussolini was still calling himself "the Lenin of Italy."[17] But socialist and Marxist historians have conveniently overlooked such facts. To reveal Mussolini's fascist lineage to Marxism would complicate their scheme to magically transform Marxism and fascism into political antipodes instead of a fascist-socialist revolutionary duality. One can see why. If classified accurately, fascism and communism would easily be identified as closely related breeds of authoritarian species—albeit sprinkled with minor disparities—together with an ideology that could be trademarked as "Marxofascism."

Any reference to a Fascist-Marxist duality had to be concealed or neglected by Marxists. Any different type of narrative might expose a fictionalized and contradictory political spectrum, which denied communism's authoritarian legacy even for Stalin's ruthless regime. Even communists who acknowledged their authoritarian nature still refused to place fellow authoritarians under the same umbrella, as if authoritarians could somehow be polar opposites of each other with nothing in common. This delusional classification of left-right positions was the main reason for the spectrums' overall meaninglessness in classifying political orientation. That blame can be laid on the heads of Soviet propagandists and Marxian historians, who were directed to mastermind a campaign to distort the classification of different political positions, for political, not rational, reasons.

In addition, these falsifiers were also determined to overlook the fact that the French Revolution was organized by the bourgeoisie Left (or as I call it, "the free Left"),[18] who were eventually beheaded on October 31, 1793, by the statist Left. This slaying of the classical liberal legislators signaled the end of the original French Revolution and the beginning of the Reign of Terror, and with it, a social and national revolution that inspired the German National Socialists and the Russian Soviets.

Again, a case can be made that Italian Fascism and German National Socialism belong squarely on the right, but only if their sidekick, communism, is also classified as a proponent of extreme right-wing ideology. I make this case in Chapter 1, arguing that, in accordance with the original seating arrangement in the French National Assembly/Legislative Assembly, any ideology or movement that encompasses authoritarianism (similar to the absolute monarchy and the church) must naturally reside alongside the reactionary, authoritarian Right. Therefore, communist dictatorships have strong ties to right-wing extremists. However, since the communists and socialists still remain committed to their image as left-wing partisans, despite evidence to the contrary, I will refer to them as the "statist Left," although there is little difference between them and the "statist Right."

Yet, whether charted on the left wing or the right wing, to conjecture that Mussolini and Hitler were not socialists in good standing is to ignore the Marxist and utopian-socialist influences upon their collectivistic movements. This fairy tale may have served well as Soviet propaganda to dissociate them from their 1939–1941 alliance with Nazi Germany, but such narratives have no factual basis. National Socialism and Italian Fascism sprang from a number of socialist movements, originating first in France, which melded revolutionary socialism within a nationalistic framework of "people's community" (*Volksgemeinschaft*), similar to Stalin's nationalistic "Socialism in One Country" policy. The fascists in Italy and Germany were, in fact, wildly leftist and inspired by variant shades of Marxism and revolutionary syndicalism. Hitler has been particularly singled out as an opponent of Marxism. In fact, he volunteered to become an elected low-level leader in the Marxist-instigated 1919 Bavarian Soviet Republic, diligently working under the leadership of the Communist Party of Germany where he wore red communist armbands. After his arrest and internment in Munich, Hitler turned away from communism and "espoused the cause of Social Democracy against that of the Communists."[19] He had to disown communism. If he hadn't he would have likely been executed, imprisoned or banished from Germany.

But international socialists found it advantageous to hide both Mussolini's and Hitler's socialist, labor unionist, Marxist, and atheist pasts. One reason was that Hitler and Mussolini were independent of Moscow's direct control, and they had the audacity to oppose the Soviet Union in the Spanish Civil War. To pay for their insolence, the Soviets and their minions felt compelled to whitewash the collectivist-socialist ideology and history behind nationalistic socialism, determined to bury Hitler and Mussolini under a falsely inscribed tombstone. That is, they threw both comrades Mussolini and Hitler under the socialist bus in a campaign to relabel their Marxist-leaning collaborators as reactionary, monarchy-loving, and religious extremists who were claimed to be duty-bound to the capitalist and land-owning class. Never was there a more beautifully executed con job designed to erase and alter history in the Soviets' favor. But then again, Stalin accused the Social Democrats, who originally arose out of Marxist ranks, as "social fascists," comparing Hitler's Nazis as "twin" brothers to the Social Democrats.

To evaluate our own philosophical bearing, we all need to know who sits on which side of the aisle. We need to know who we are, where our ideas came from, and what we favor and oppose. Only through honest inquiry and dialogue can one learn and understand, but if mass deception is thrown into the mix to hide past ugliness, we will learn no meaningful lessons or introspection. This book is dedicated to exposing the erroneous historiography that was used to conceal the villains behind various socialist movements.

I believe truth will set people free, but to the politically motivated who revere Machiavelli and who hasten serfdom, truth is meaningless. Accurate records of history are vital to civilization because those records can greatly alter the course of the future. George Orwell understood this principle well, creating in *Nineteen Eighty-Four* the slogan: "Who controls the past controls the future. Who controls the present controls the past."[20] History must be preserved accurately, but such ends will not come from Machiavellian deviants, who adhere to the heavily traveled path of deceptive means.

I have redrawn the political spectrum, which can be found in Chapter 7. There are two charts. I prefer Chart A, which is based on the French Revolution, but contemporary minds might fancy Chart B. Both charts group authoritarians on one side of the political divide and the original liberals on the other. I believe this more precise interpretation will clear up the confusion.

Notes

[1] Matt Kibbe, "The Deadly Isms," Episode 1: "Up From Totalitarianism," Free The People, documentary, 2018. https://www.youtube.com/c/freethepeople.

[2] Chispin Startwell, *Entanglements: A System of Philosophy* (Albany, NY: State University of New York Press, 2017), p. 358.

[3] Hyrum Lewis, "It's Time to Retire the Political Spectrum," *Quillette*, May 3, 2017. https://quillette.com/2017/05/03/time-retire-political-spectrum/.

[4] Ibid.

[5] Doyle, *The Oxford History of the French Revolution*, p. 422.

[6] Mussolini, *The Political and Social Doctrine of Fascism*, p. 20. This was the first authorized translation into English by Jane Soames. Original 1933 scans can be found at: http://historyuncensored.wixsite.com/history-uncensored (retrieved 2-1-2017).

[7] Ludwig, *Talks with Mussolini*, p. 38. Interview between Mar. 23 and Apr. 4, 1932, at the Palazzo di Venezia in Rome.

[8] *Opera Omnia di Benito Mussolini*, E. and D. Susmel, edit., Florence, 1951–, 1/52–3, 60, 92, 251 (Mar. 26, 1904), Dinale, 36.

[9] Alexander Hamilton, "Objections and Answers respecting the Administration of the Government" letter, Aug. 18, 1792.

[10] See Mussolini's booklet and other artifacts: http://historyuncensored.wix.com/history-uncensored (retrieved 2-1-2017).

[11] The banned Wikipedia page can be found at http://fascistcontroversies.weebly.com.

[12] Pipes, *Russia Under the Bolshevik Regime*, p. 252.

[13] Ibid., p. 253.

[14] Rummel, *The Blue Book of Freedom*, p. 99.

[15] Peter Neville, *Mussolini* (Oxon, England, UK and New York, NY: Routledge, 2004), p. 36.

[16] Smith, *Mussolini*, p. 41. Original source: *Opera Omnia di Benito Mussolini*, E. and D. Susmel, edit., Florence, 1951–, 13/168 (June 4, 1919), *Opera Omnia di Benito Mussolini*, E. and D. Susmel, edit., Florence, 1951–, 15/220 (Sept. 20, 1920).

[17] Smith, *Modern Italy*, p. 284.

[18] The term "free Left" is my coinage to represent the bourgeoisie and classical liberal left.

[19] Heiden, *Hitler: A Biography*, p. 54.

[20] George Orwell, *Nineteen Eighty-Four* (New York, NY: Alfred A. Knopf, 1992), p. 37. Originally published in 1949.

1. The Political Spectrum: Altered, Revised, and Falsified

I don't like politics. I hate them! I only speak out when I think something is important. I like to consider myself a liberal, but with semantics as it is today, I seem to be running backwards—fast.

—John Wayne[1]

I don't see myself as conservative, but I'm not ultra-leftist. You build a philosophy of your own. I like the libertarian view, which is to leave everyone alone. Even as a kid, I was annoyed by people who wanted to tell everyone how to live.

—Clint Eastwood[2]

Libertarianism is rejected by the modern left—which preaches individualism but practices collectivism. Capitalism is rejected by the modern right—which preaches enterprise but practices protectionism.

—Karl Hess[3]

The reality is that the two sides of the spectrum are largely mixes of incoherent, unrelated, and constantly shifting positions lumped together by the accident of history.

—Hyrum Lewis[4]

John Locke (1632–1704) is often cited as the father of liberalism. Historians credit him with developing the first distinctly liberal philosophical framework. His theories promoted the ideals of natural rights, the consent of the governed, individualism, a limited "night watchman" government, and equal rights to "life, liberty, and property." This is the liberalism that John Wayne, the American film actor, meant when describing himself as a dyed-in-the-wool liberal back in 1972.

John Wayne didn't understand that by the early 20th century, the liberalism of Thomas Jefferson, Benjamin Franklin, Thomas Paine, and John Locke was starting to fade into the cobwebs of history. Originally, "liberal" connoted "liberty." We can trace the term *liberal*, or *libertarian*, back to its root: the Latin word "liber," which means "free."[5]

From the outset, liberalism was dedicated to maximizing individual liberty. Yet that meaning is often watered down so much that it sputters and drowns—until it finally surfaces as its polar opposite. Some even argue that liberalism, the philosophy, was co-opted by anti-liberal forces in order to neuter the essence of liberty.

One of the first to detect this liberticidal drift was Austrian economist Ludwig von Mises (1881–1973). In 1927 Mises described liberalism as displaying a much greater compatibility "in England to Toryism and socialism" than to the true liberalism of the free traders, and "nothing is left of liberalism but the name."[6] Another academician to detect this tide of illiberalism was economist Joseph Schumpeter, who in 1950 wrote that:

> The term (liberalism) has acquired a different—in fact almost opposite meaning since about 1900 and especially since about 1930. As a supreme, if unintended compliment, the enemies of the system of private enterprise have thought it wise to appropriate its label.[7]

The hijacking of the words "liberal" and "Left" have had profound effects. The patrons of this new pseudo-liberalism no longer focused on protecting the life, liberty, and property of citizens. Instead, they relegated individual rights to the back burner to make room for special privileges and benefits that could only be furnished at the expense of others. Moreover, they asserted that certain alleged rights could trump other unalienable rights, permitting one person to infringe upon the rights of another.

Originally, John Lockean liberalism embraced the concept of "negative" rights, wherein people have freedom from being aggressed upon by a person, a group of persons, or a governmental body. According to the Russian-born American novelist and philosopher Ayn Rand (1905–1982), rights impose no obligations upon one's neighbor "except of a *negative* kind: to abstain from violating his rights."[8]

This includes the right not to be threatened, kidnaped, enslaved, murdered, robbed, raped, or defrauded. It is a right to be let alone in peace, to freely partake in "inactions," without being prosecuted or imprisoned. Under this John Lockean liberalism, everyone has a right not to be subjected to the physical action of others—whether individuals or groups. Liberalism promoted individual liberty under a constitutionally bound government of extremely limited authority, where people had an inalienable right to freely choose how they want to live. In other words, liberalism made a person neither a slave nor a slave master. The ideals of liberalism were revolutionary, anti-political, anti-authoritarian, and anti-coercion.

In a nutshell, if a man cannot act unobstructed by others, he is unfree. As Isaiah Berlin, a Russian-British philosopher and social-political theorist, wrote:

> If I am prevented by others from doing what I could otherwise do, I am to that degree unfree; and if this area is contracted by other men beyond a certain minimum, I can be described as being coerced, or, it may be, enslaved.[9]

Frederick Douglass, the African-American social reformer and abolitionist, made a similar case in 1886, declaring:

> The great fact underlying the claim for universal suffrage is that every man is himself and belongs to himself, and represents his own individuality. ... And the same is true of woman... Her selfhood is as perfect and as absolute as is the selfhood of man.[10]

But 20th century collectivists sought to redesign liberalism to serve their new paradigm: redistributive politics and compulsory equalitarianism that would subordinate every action of individuals to the supremacy of the group. The modern, government-centric liberal had in essence usurped the heart and soul of anti-state liberalism. This faux liberalism, which leaped into the spotlight during Woodrow Wilson's and, later,

Franklin Roosevelt's presidencies, disowned the ideals of liberty. "Liberalism 2.0" obligated peaceful people, meaning that they could be forced to do that which they did not want to do, culminating in bureaucracies that resorted to legalizing and institutionalizing brute force and theft—an ideological construct compatible with German National Socialism, Italian Fascism, and Russia Sovietism. This altered form of liberalism assumed that people had to be saved from themselves, that they could not be trusted with their own affairs, so they must submit to micromanagement by the state.

To accomplish this herculean feat, governmental bodies captured the legal power to intrude on human affairs in the hope of fixing man's flawed nature, as though mankind were destined to live on a sterilized Planet Clorox, a land where everything could be made not only perfectly clean but free of risks. Governmental power was bulked up to launch a toxic blend of utopian and draconian measures to outlaw poverty, inequality, and injustice—supposedly. This socioeconomic jihad against liberty emerged after adherents of state-enhanced liberalism revised their ideological arsenal to include "positive rights."

Positive rights require physical force or intimidation in order to enforce these alleged "rights." In essence, they are faux rights that violate other people's rights. Positive rights actually don't exist; they are fictitious, a fraudulent tactic which subverts choice. Rights are not obligations. To physically force someone to give financial benefits to another makes a mockery of the principles of freedom of action, freedom of choice, and the right to be free from aggression. Rather, the license to institute compulsory practices leads to legalized and institutionalized aggression and robbery. Enabling political structures to plunder one in the name of others perverts the meaning of individual human rights. Positive rights grant governmental agencies the invasive authority to force citizens to surrender their earnings and property so that others may indulge in free or subsidized food, education, housing, medical care and so forth. Positive rights imposed obligations, a duty that must be fulfilled, or the violator would be arrested and jailed, thus nullifying the role of individual autonomy that was the inspiration for the American Revolution. In other words, positive rights make *society* sovereign, rather than the *individual*. As Ayn Rand wrote:

> If some men are entitled by right to the products of the work of others, it means that those others are deprived of rights and condemned to slave labor. ... There can be no such thing as the right to enslave, i.e., the right to destroy rights.[11]

What this means is that liberalism had been poisoned by a false definition of *liberty*, one characterized by an unethical authoritarian demeanor, cast in rigid conformity to authority, obedience to rules, and slave-like submission to the collective, making the individual subservient to the group. Instead of questioning authority or challenging state power, the apostles of illiberal positive rights idealize the State as a social panacea. To them, the state is everything, and almost nothing should be outside the state's jurisdiction. This variant of creeping fascization infected Germany, Italy, and Russia in the first half of the 20th century. Adolf Hitler made this crystal clear in a 1931 interview, asserting that:

> the good of the community takes priority over that of the individual. But the State should retain control; every owner should feel himself to be an agent of the State; it is his duty not to misuse his possessions to the detriment of the State or the interests of his fellow countrymen.[12]

In short, Hitler boiled down his socialism to its essential parts, exhorting to his Nazi party followers in 1920: "The common good before the individual good."[13]

Under the notion of these faux positive rights, productive citizens are made legally responsible for ensuring everyone has an equal or so-called fair, share of wealth. Of course, this "equality of outcome" is state-determined, state-imposed, and enforced by political institutions and self-serving bureaucracies, who have an exhaustive record of being underhanded, privileged-oriented, corrupt, tyrannical, and disempowering. Since the debasement of liberalism's original ideal of liberty and individualism, the positive "right" to material goods and services has overridden the natural right to be left unmolested, subjecting most citizens to, basically, "economic rape."

To the modern, statist Left, the problem is not that the government does too much, but that it does too little. For instance, modern liberals

often blame government policies for having failed to stop the enslavement of African immigrants before the Civil War. They contend that
state legislators passively allowed slavery to occur and that they should
have enacted stronger laws to prevent it. However, the statist Left completely ignores the historical fact that it was Southern legislators, mostly
Democrats, who purposely enacted strict laws to make slavery legal.
Modern leftists usually assume that slavery in America developed because of weak governmental policies; that those in government had
done too little; whereas, in fact, the governments of the Southern states
had done too much, explicitly enacting laws to make slavery the law
of the land. In fact, after Nat Turner's slave rebellion in 1831, general
assemblies in Virginia and other Southern states enacted "slave codes"
to make it unlawful to teach any slave, free black, or mulatto to read or
write,[14] while also prohibiting free blacks and mulattoes from owning
guns.

Ignorance of such history is ubiquitous among the modern left, who
exploit every opportunity to deny individuals the right to control their
own destiny, who believe that universal liberty would only lead to heinous injustices that an impotent government would be unable to stop.
Their lack of trust in people's capability to run their own lives is so pervasive that it has come to the point where most contemporary politicians
leave for the populace only one right: to let governmental bodies plunder
society in order to fund social-justice schemes.

Collectivists of all faiths—including fascists and communists—fail to
understand that theft enacted by the state turns citizens into slaves. In
truth, the modern left finds slavery acceptable, as long as the populace
belongs to a particular class or race deemed entitled to free-but-equal
services and goodies, which just so happens to make them dependent,
controllable, and obedient. As Charles T. Sprading noted, "Mere equality does not imply equal liberty, however, for slaves are equal in their
slavery."[15] F.A. Hayek (1899–1992) also took a swipe at the enigma of
equality, explaining,

> There is all the difference in the world between treating people
> equally and attempting to make them equal. While the first is the

condition of a free society, the second means, as De Tocqueville describes it, "a new form of servitude."[16]

Modern liberalism has led to roads overcrowded with flaccid serfs and overbearing foremen willing to crush the rights of others.

In order to differentiate the two, the liberalism of the 17th to 19th centuries has been dubbed "classical liberalism" (also called "*laissez-faire* liberalism"), while the more contemporary version has been labeled "modern liberalism," "social liberalism," or "nanny-state liberalism." But when this Europe-inspired modern liberalism approaches its far edge, it contorts into a mishmash of Fascist-Marxist contagion known as the "statist or progressive Left," which often battles what I call the "free Left."[17] Some writers have referred to this perverted liberalism as "liberal fascism," the Fascist Left, or informally, the "alt-left" (alternative left).

Interestingly, the foremost cause of the change in the meaning of *liberalism* in the United States was a cultural accident. During the great immigration boom of the 1880s and 1900s, thousands of German and Russian intellectuals poured into the United States. They brought with them boatloads of garden-variety socialists, national socialists, proto-fascists, social democrats, Marxist reformers, and diehard Marxists. Immediately, these intellectual outsiders set about to promote their socialist agenda, establishing newspapers and organizations. There was just one small problem: it turned out that Americans distrusted—even hated—collectivistic creeds, especially anything to do with "socialism." Unable to gain traction in their new country, these immigrants joined liberal organizations, publications, and educational institutions in order to peddle their canards about wealth redistribution, state-mandated socialism, and social justice. They worked diligently to usurp the original meaning of *liberalism*. And eventually, they succeeded. In fact, their sales pitch was so subtle that many adherents of the Nurse Ratched welfare-state still have no idea they are expounding collectivist dogma that aligns better with Niccolò Machiavelli, Benito Mussolini, and Joseph Stalin than with the American founders, who embodied the concepts of natural rights and liberal capitalism.

This slow transformation of liberalism rarely spilled over into continental Europe. Most liberal political parties in Europe are still beholden to John Locke's "classical liberal," individualist, and *laissez-faire* market economics.

Classical Liberalism: Leave Us Alone Rights

Liberalism arose as a veritable revolution, to dethrone power and uncloak the so-called divinity and privileges of despotic overlords, an emancipating movement that advanced the ideals of constitutional republics and democratic principles and opposed various forms of slavery. The original liberals were visionaries, iconoclastic, tolerant of others' opinions, open-minded, and supportive of free marketplaces, private property, the rule of law, human rationality, the need to seek the consent of the governed, freedom from restraints, and protection of civil liberties. They were skeptical of established religion, distrustful of government authority, detested taxation, and worried about democracy turning into a "tyranny of the majority," a term first used by John Adams.[18] The modern libertarian movement represents a renaissance of the original Lockean *laissez-faire* liberalism that Benjamin Franklin co-introduced to the English-speaking world in the 1774 book *Principles of Trade*.[19] The original liberals preferred a world free of obstructions, traversing a sociopolitical road that favored openness over closeness. And because of this fact, some scholars assert that the left-right spectrum is largely redundant or outdated and should be replaced by "a new political fault line: not between left and right, but between open and closed."[20]

In fact, former British Prime Minister Tony Blair came out in 2016 with a similar approach, arguing that the emerging political order should be defined less by left-right orientation and be more in tune with "open and closed," something that he has explored since 2007.[21] Blair commented that, for example, both the left and right tend to take a "closed" protectionist and anti-globalization position, while the left's anti-business and the right's anti-immigrant position are also closed, making them more aligned instead of the opposite.

Not only was the American Revolution a revolution to change the rulership of America, but a revolution against government itself. The

American colonists wanted government to be chained to a constitution with little elbow room for government intrusion, taxation, and bureaucracy. If this anti-statist aspect of the revolution had not occurred, the former colonists would have merely replaced a British king with an American king—an outcome vigorously endorsed by Alexander Hamilton.[22] Moreover, the American Revolution was also a war against taxation, especially duties. The anti-tax sentiment in America was so deeply rooted that the US federal government placed no direct taxation upon its citizenry for approximately 80 years, taxing only foreign imports. In 1816, Thomas Jefferson expressed the concept of a voluntaryist society, writing that "No man has a natural right to commit aggression on the equal rights of another, and this is all from which the laws ought to restrain him."[23] In fact, as president, it was Jefferson who rid the nation of all direct taxation, fulfilling one of his main campaign promises.[24,25] What other countries could boast of such a radical and revolutionary policy—ripping out the heart of the government's insatiable appetite to enrich itself at the expense of its citizens.

This American exceptionalism was clearly built on the idea of voluntaryist-based societies in which one man should not rule over another. John Locke fleshed this principle out in the *Second Treatise of Government* in 1689, taking up the mantle of self-ownership, writing that "every Man has a Property in his own Person. Thus, no Body has any Right to but himself."[26]

Locke's unifying principles of liberty focused on the minimization of power—where the power of authority should be so diffuse that no one man or group can gain a larger share than another. This orientation around the "parity of power" sought to "de-monopolize" society and disempower the state. This makes sense. How can political savants bother themselves with the little guy, when they spend most of their time conniving and expanding their Machiavellian power?

Adam Smith (1723–1790), considered the father of economics, held similar visions that fostered the virtue of the self-regulating nature of marketplaces and society. To him, society would operate far better under a system of cooperative production and free exchange—that is, exchanges free from coercion and manipulation—leading to increased prosperity and peace. Nobel Prize-winning economist Milton Friedman once referred to Smith's self-organizing "invisible hand" metaphor as "the possibility of cooperation without coercion."[27]

An opponent of state-chartered corporations, Smith wrote that businessmen would conspire in beer halls to fleece the most money possible from the public. He believed that this "mercantile system" would allow schemers to organize state-enforced monopolies in an effort to boost consumer prices, block competitors, and reap higher profits, exemplifying a sort of "crony mercantilism." To Smith's way of thinking, government was established to extract taxes in order to subsidize the aristocratic elite and sanctioned corporations (royal charters) akin to the East India Company and the Hudson's Bay Company. Smith acknowledged that the best way to stop swindlers from gaming society was to harbor a diffuse, unstructured marketplace and society—making it nearly impossible to squelch either competitors or individual rights through state-approved monopolies. Here, the empowered elite, who are often lavished with government favoritism and subsidies, would find it difficult to survive.

Libertarians and classical liberals have argued that genuinely free markets have the ability to weaken the politically favored business class while empowering the working class, upstarts, and underclass. Milton Friedman made that point clear, contending that "business is not a friend of the free market. ... It's in the self-interest of the business community to get government on their side."[28]

Classical liberals opposed mercantilism, which seeks to monopolize suppliers and markets by military conquest and colonization of foreign lands. Under the theory of mercantilism, the state had to keep their gold reserves safely tucked away in their vaults, and therefore it discouraged—or banned outright—trade with other nations. To the mercantilists, wealth did not grow; it was forever fixed, stagnant. Trade was viewed as a zero-sum game, in which if one person won, the other would lose—and the transfer of wealth was accomplished mainly through theft. Because colonies were bound to their home nation, they could not trade with other nations, thus ensuring that a nation's gold reserves would be locked away within a nation's borders. This linear notion of wealth creation led directly to the European colonial period, causing a plethora of economic and political disasters across the globe, and provoking the American Revolution.

Classical liberals saw the challenge of increasing wealth differently. By embracing *laissez-faire*, free-trade policies, the original liberals took a radical, antiwar stance, arguing that empire-building and militarization were unnecessary. In their judgment, open, unrestricted trade with all nations would fill the economic pool, lift all boats, expand abundance and knowledge, and instill peace. Wars of conquest and foreign military occupation were regarded as unnecessary to foster trade. That is why Europe enjoyed an unprecedented 100 years of peace following the Napoleonic wars until World War I. Europe had been influenced toward accepting various aspects of the gold standard, free trade, and *laissez-faire* capitalism.

Of course, socioeconomic changes can be difficult to accept. During the Age of Enlightenment, the upper class found itself irked by entrepreneurial upstarts and free-thinkers, seeing them as overstuffing their pocketbooks with cash. This conflict was a clash over economic interests. The privileged aristocrats and nobility were invested mostly in large, feudal estates, and were often receiving subsidies or pensions from the Crown. They kept little hard currency and hated free-wheeling upstarts who engaged in turbulent markets where consumers and workers could enjoy the freedom of mobility. Open markets and industrialization gave the underclass the means to obtain their autonomy from the tight grip of the land-rich aristocrats. Now the less privileged could escape to the towns and cities to pursue individual goals. However, this new sociopolitical climate threatened the status quo of the traditional power brokers. Not only were the peasants defying their "masters," they were jeopardizing the cheap labor market on which land-owning interests so depended. With a plethora of jobs spontaneously arising in the cities, landowners eventually had to pay higher wages to their landless peasants, which hit aristocrats hard in the pocketbook. Soon they entered the political arena to retaliate against the urban, town-dwelling entrepreneurs.

The retaliation came in the form of regulations on labor. Because the English kings were often preoccupied with fishing, hunting, or chasing loose women, the privileged classes took the initiative and enacted child-labor laws, purportedly to improve conditions for workhouse children. But this was a self-serving guise: the new laws failed to include any protection for farm-bound children who worked long hours on the estates of the upper classes. Starting in 1802, autocrats in the British parliament instituted the Factory Acts, a series of laws which regulated working hours for children in textile factories, and later, in other industrial jobs. However, working children on farms were excluded from the law and were left unprotected.

It was the land-owning class who originated labor laws, not labor-union ideologues or socialists—a fact often overlooked by many historians. As society prospered—with higher wages, better conditions, and shorter working days, early socialists saw this evolution in a different light. To them, all workers were being exploited by the emerging class of capitalist merchants, shopkeepers, artisans, and especially the Jews. Never mind that the new industrial worker had fled the farm fields to escape low-paying, back-breaking labor from sunup to sundown drudgery under inclement conditions. As men were refusing to work in the factories, viewing such jobs as degrading, factory owners resorted to hiring women, children, and a slew of starving orphans.

Many historians have failed to note the high number of workhouse children orphaned or abandoned during this period. Centuries before the miracles of modern medicine, England was awash in parentless, sick, and dying children. The average life expectancy during this period hovered around 35 years. For children, the mortality rate was worse. Mabel C. Buer, in *Health, Wealth and Population in the Early Days of the Industrial Revolution*, revealed the harsh reality of children's lifespans. But her study on the effects of the Industrial Revolution showed a bright spot when it came to children. Actually, according to Buer, life expectancy for children increased dramatically as the Industrial Revolution progressed.[29] In London, for example, the number who died before reaching the age of five decreased from 74.5 percent in 1730–1749 to 31.8 percent in 1810–1829.[30]

But the point is that without this newly industrialized economy, brimming with jobs, new technologies, increasing levels of wealth and opportunity, many young and adult workers would have starved or succumbed to sickness, as in the past. Outside of the cities, the environment was just as brutal for the young. Rural communities were still steeped in a feudal mindset that afforded little hope for advancement.

Despite the great successes of classical liberalism in boosting wealth, living standards, life spans, liberty, peace, education, and technology—

faster than ever recorded in human history—its achievements were continuously scorned by wealthy adversaries with ulterior motives, and ideologues with political ends to serve. Near the end of the Enlightenment era, skeptics of liberal capitalism argued that the accomplishments of classical liberalism were not enough. More had to be done to atone for the social and economic wrongs of the past. These social faultfinders believed that the American Founders' fears of a big government mutating into an evil leviathan was highly exaggerated. The world had changed. By the early 20th century, tyranny was considered passé.

Nonetheless, the new prototypical liberals still held a sort of wishy-washy, vacillating version of liberty. Within this context, the question that post-liberals entertained most was whether government could remain tamed and corralled even if its formidable powers were released in order to accomplish good works. David Boaz, author of *Libertarianism: A Primer*, propounded this point, explaining that as the old anti-statist liberals died off, the "younger liberals began to wonder if government couldn't be a positive force, something to be used rather than constrained."[31] Radio commentator Paul Jacob went a step further, asserting that progressives had "brought back European ideas of an aggrandized state to counter American notions of limited government."[32]

The post-liberals' agenda focused on acquiring and concentrating political power, not germinating liberty. They coveted equalitarianism, wealth distribution, and guaranteed outcomes that would be designed and managed by bureaucratic dictocrats who would officially arbitrate the meaning of fairness. But such anti-Founder policies could be accomplished only if the state could be freed from its constitutional restraints. With visions of grandeur and dreams of re-engineering mankind's shortcomings, they released the Kraken and stepped back, expecting the unbounded force of incredible power to perform wondrous socioeconomic miracles. Instead, Europeans got socialist-inspired atrocities, genocide, and totalitarian regimes that spawned World War II and the Cold War.

Despite the abject failure of statism and socialism, the post-liberal intelligentsia still agitated for a larger role and scope for government. In their minds, a virtuous commitment to economic equality would somehow overpower the impulse by those in government to take advantage of the weak. After all, they reasoned, aren't the people actually the government, anyway? Aren't government officials always looking out for the people's best interest, and never their own private gain, ambitions, and pleasure? Aren't political leaders the supermen of humanity, the standard-bearers of goodness, brotherhood, and truth? And because the state's intentions always radiate an angelic purity, shouldn't it determine what is permissible? After all, isn't the scourge of humanity their penchant to make wrong choices? Such notions have dominated the modern post-liberals' premise that politicians, bureaucrats, and technocrats are the only ones capable of expertly conjuring up a kinder, gentler society, overflowing with heavenly altruism. Maybe such purity is abundant in heaven, but on corruption-ridden terra firma, it is a rare commodity. Of course, these fallacies had a vulgarizing and eviscerating effect upon America's social and economic culture. By the time this artifice was recognized, not only had progressives and post-liberals had released the autocratic genie from the bottle, but they had thrown away the cork.

Of course, history was to repeat itself—again. By the 20th century, the governments of most civilized nations were behaving like imperial overlords, morphing into repressive states masquerading as democratic republics. The new theories that spoke of a caring government's duty to establish good socioeconomic policies and procedures soon relapsed to the old perilous, autocratic rule—the same cataclysm of bad behavior that had befallen society during the era of kings, tyrants, and monarchy-chartered corporations. One has only to glance quickly at the victimization, wars, and genocide perpetrated on society by the socialist regimes of Hitler, Stalin, Mao, and Pol Pot to be able to attest to this fact. Their slick packaging and sloganeering may have garnered mass populace appeal, but their policies resulted in a myriad of genocidal and democidal crimes against humanity.

Some of the main differences between oppressive monarchies and the modern ideological regimes entails more sophisticated hyperbole and a much higher body bag count. The ideological regimes painted themselves with an infallible equalitarian sheen to conceal empty pledges to abolish poverty, inequality, war, and injustice. But the costs were extremely high compared to monarchical rulers. The number of non-combatant, civilian deaths perpetrated mostly by ideological regimes in the 20th century, reaching across statist Left and statist Right lines, is estimated at 272 million to 400 million people.[33]

Essentially, modern and social liberals have turned their backs on John Locke and the Founders of the American republic. They have severed most of their bonds to the guiding tenets of true liberalism and of the American revolutionaries who fought and battled their own government. Ironically, as modern liberals expound extremely anti-liberal ideology, they still want to be identified as liberals, even though they "interpret liberty in more Marxist/Fascist terms than Jeffersonian."[34] Post-liberals should be branded for what they are: a resurgence of Tory-inspired anti-Founders with fascist tendencies.

Perhaps this is why the statist Left despises President Trump so much; he has disproved their theory that the voting public would never elect an unqualified cretin who basked in manic bouts of reckless immaturity. And yet, why else would progressives work so feverously to enlarge the power and scope of the state? Apparently, they thought that nobody would ever be elected to exploit expanded powers, to employ government as their little private fiefdom or to cause the abuse of power. What could possibly go wrong when the leviathan state is pumped up with full-strength steroids?

Chartered Corporate Monopolies: Mercantilism

In Europe, fortunes had traditionally been made through privileged and protected patronage via monarchs, aristocrats, and financial insiders. For instance, starting in 1600, the British East India Company was granted an English royal charter with monopolistic powers. Such state-sanctioned and often subsidized monopolies led directly to overseas military expansion, colonialism, and empire-building. It was the privileged who thrived. The only course of action for politically unconnected merchants and foreigners was to circumvent trading monopolies by engaging in smuggling. A number of American Founding Fathers, including John Hancock, made fortunes by smuggling foreign goods into the American colonies.

Adam Smith favored free trade and opposed cozy financial entanglements between the state and business. So, long before Karl Marx ever penned a screed against colonial empires, Smith had harsh words for what are now called colonialism and imperialism.[35] In sharp contrast, many collectivists supported colonialism, including the socialist British Fabians and Marxist revisionists, such as Eduard Bernstein (1850–1932).

Often bordering on the crime of collusion, the symbiotic merging of capitalists' interests with those of the nation-state is a primitive form of "mixed economy," where state planning can become entwined with the market. Political scientists have dubbed this mishmash of complex integration of government and economics "state capitalism," "state-monopoly capitalism," "crony capitalism," "crony statism," or the newest name on the block, "market socialism." During the 18th century, Adam Smith used the term "mercantilism" to describe the horrors of state-directed and subsidized capitalism. Economist Murray Rothbard (1926–1995) defined mercantilism as

> a system of statism which employed economic fallacy to build up a structure of imperial state power, as well as special subsidy and monopolistic privilege to individuals or groups favored by the state.[36]

Under extreme conditions, the coalescing of government with business interests can induce strong-arm economic politics, political repression, and wars of conquest. This economic interventionism was plainly visible under Italian Fascism and German National Socialism, where the ideological, political, and plutocratic elite had captured the state and its bureaucracy. In fact, some have called the Nazi party's capture of the German state a "government within a government." Not unlike the Soviets, the Nazi party had

> its own courts and judiciary because Party members are not bound by official laws in their activities; they are permitted and indeed required to violate the laws in order to defend the prestige and authority of the Party leaders.[37]

Under the mixed economy of state-directed capitalism, most companies had little choice but to participate in cronyism and bribery—if they wished to survive. The larger companies had a better survival rate because small businesses and private citizens often falter under the burdens of high taxes, merciless regulations, stiff penalties, and unresponsive bureaucrats. With higher concentrations of wealth and a less competitive environment, those near the bottom of society are condemned to live under a less fair, less efficient economy.

Under mercantilism, the state attempts to prevent free trade by playing a key role in protecting the economy from foreign competition. Exports are encouraged, along with generous subsidies and pensions to favored companies. Imports of foreign goods are discouraged, banned or slapped with protective high tariffs.

Mercantilism was the dominant economic ideology in Europe from the 15th to 18th centuries. Later, the theories of market liberalism became wildly popular. But the popularity and practice of mercantilism never died. The struggle between protectionism and liberal capitalism is still a hot item, but various versions of mercantilism, mixed economic, state capitalism, state socialism, fascism, or whatever it is called, command the driver's seat in most nations. In fact, because the German Nazis and the Italian Fascists argued that their economic policies represented the Third Way between *laissez-faire* capitalism and Marxian socialism, any middle point between the two could be identified as both fascist and a mixed economy. Nonetheless, at the time of this writing, there is no purely liberal market economy in existence. The closest examples would be the sovereign city-state of Singapore and the free port of Hong Kong, now under the jurisdiction of the Communist Chinese government.

Pro-Business versus Pro-Market

To be accurate, capitalists don't control capital. It is the other way around. The anarchy of capital drives capitalists and non-capitalists, alike. The market's autonomous dynamics govern the turbulent workings of capital. Further, those who engage in capitalistic ventures are not the same as the defenders of true, liberal capitalism. Most practitioners of capitalism do not support market-driven capitalism (market democracy) unless some facet of it becomes personally advantageous.

They would rather have risk-free, state-granted protection that would foil their competitors, muzzle upstart entrepreneurs, and block foreign imports. This sharp division in economic theory is best described by two irreconcilable schools of thought: "pro-business" advocates versus "pro-market" advocates.

Pro-business advocates have little interest in safeguarding or defending free-market principles. They are hard-nosed businessmen who want to make profitable deals, not become philosophers. They have no qualms about hiring lobbyists to wrangle no-bid government contracts, financial favors, and political capital that may lead them to lucrative grants or concessions. They know where the barrels of "gravy" are stored, within state and national treasuries. They know that politics, not efficiency, can offer a company a better chance of survival in the marketplace (which is a concept known as rent-seeking). They understand that under a politically driven economy, government has the power to pick winners and losers—and to be a winner, one must play by the political rule-book. To the crony capitalists' way of thinking, only a fool would refuse to participate in the state's lucrative gravy train.

One example of pro-business cronyism that harmed consumers occurred in 2014 when Gov. Rick Snyder (Michigan) signed legislation officially banning Tesla Motors, or any other car manufacturer, from selling their product directly to consumers within his state.[38] Under this law, cars could be sold legally only through networks of state-licensed auto dealers. But Tesla had developed a business plan to lower costs by cutting out the middleman (the dealerships) and selling its all-electric car directly to consumers. Unfortunately, this type of protect-established-businesses laws is not unusual in the United States. More than half the states have enacted similar laws to ban car manufacturers from competing with state-licensed dealers.[39]

In sharp contrast, free-market capitalists point out the dire consequences of crony capitalism and socialism under a state-directed economy. Monopolies and price-fixing cartels may be lucrative for the few, but for the many, a politically muzzled economy spurs higher taxes, greater inflation, unsustainable government debt, protracted poverty, and extended economic downturns. Big-government corporatists have little concern for such calamities. Whether the economy is in good or bad shape, corporate cronies profit handsomely since they have a "willingness to use the coercive powers of government to gain an advantage they could not earn in the market."[40]

Pro-market adherents champion radically free markets, often referring to them as "freed" markets, to distinguish them from economic systems riddled with statist and capitalist privileges.[41] Many of these free-marketeers welcome the moniker of left-wing market anarchists or market-oriented libertarians who take anti-hierarchal, anti-corporatist, pro-labor positions in economics, along with anti-imperialism in foreign policy. In fact, some openly classify themselves as "anti-capitalist," contending that the ultimate battle line is free-marketism versus capitalism, accenting "markets, not capitalism." These market anarchists argue that no current nation has an authentically free and open market economy and that those who tout *laissez-faire* economics are generally "vulgar libertarian apologists for capitalism" who instead defend corporate capitalism and economic inequality.[42]

According to Kevin Carson, author and research associate at the Center for a Stateless Society, it is "state intervention that distinguishes capitalism from the free market." Historically, the original term "capitalism" had little relation to free-market principles. As Europe slowly emerged from feudalism, the holders of capital and industrial production were still bound to a statist class structure where owners of private wealth "controlled the state and the state intervened in the market on their behalf."[43]

In its early stages, capitalism was neither market-friendly nor equable as it was based on state-sanctioned acts of monopolistic trade practices and conquest of other people's land. As David S. D'Amato so elegantly expressed: "When government intervenes, it frequently does so on behalf of the powerful and privileged, tipping the scales in favor of the connected, making life more difficult and expensive for the rest of us."[44] In the final analysis, state interventionism not only compromised the integrity of markets and property rights, but functioned as an enabler for the exploitation of consumers.

Collaboration between businesses and governments is hazardous to decent governance and market participation. "Politicophiles" of every stripe understand that the more regulations there are, the fewer new actors have the capital or fortitude to enter markets. The engine that drives prosperity and innovation becomes gummed up and blocked, causing economic constipation, which will likely cause economic stagnation, high unemployment, lower wages, and political corruption. For crony capitalists, a distressed economy can serve up their preferred diet of scant competitors. For the crony socialists, a distressed economy can rustle up a rich feast of state-induced nationalization, no-bid state contracts, and "authorized corruption."[45]

Crony capitalists favor perpetual crises to expand their privileges to feed at the public trough, further increasing the capacity of the corruptive state. Crony socialists, too, need perpetual crises, to usher in more self-serving socialism, further entrenching the bureaucratic-welfare state. Despite being touted as saving the public from economic malaise, its codependence on political machinations gives it all the earmarks of a crisis lying in wait. Financial crises and constraints are favorite cuisines of crony capitalists, particularly since economic calamities allow large businesses to remain big not because of their competitive merits, but because of their political clout and state-arranged marriage.

The ability to bar new entrepreneurs is bad enough, but the state's pampering of the privileged often gives business leaders carte blanche to be financially irresponsible. During the 2007 economic meltdown, any failed or bankrupt corporation joined at the hip with government was deemed "too big to fail." One would think that only crony capitalists would heap praise upon "too big to fail" policies. Not so. Left-wing economist Paul Krugman gave his blessing.[46] Not only were bankrupted and fraudulent companies too big to fail, but they were also considered "too big to jail." Attorney General Eric Holder freely confessed his belief that criminal indictments against banks and bankers could harm the economy, and were, therefore, too risky to litigate.[47]

When companies and their shareholders are no longer held responsible for their own bad or fraudulent conduct, the taxpayer plays patsy. In effect, financial-industry fraud is being treated as de facto legal mandates. Of course, this designation is usually not available for the general public. But the real crime? Under big-government corporatism, the state allows the wealthy elite to privatize their gains, while socializing their losses. What a racket. The taxpayers get stuck covering the insiders' investment (read: gambling) losses but receive little to nothing when good investment bets pay off. This construct only helps concentrate wealth and widen income disparities.[48]

Pro-business corporatists and their state partners have a history of awakening the specter of economic horrors. Ironically, progressive, modern liberals are blind to this obvious predicament. As writer Bill Frezza pointed out: "Progressives who think they can solve our problems by making government bigger and more powerful only dig the hole deeper, playing into the hands of the Crony Capitalists they claim to hate."[49]

Perhaps this is why President Obama, during his 2008 presidential campaign, raised more money from Wall Street firms than did Republican nominee Senator John McCain, despite claims that Republicans are beholden to Wall Street.[50] Not only did Obama raise about $42.8 million from Wall Street and other financial interests, compared to McCain's $31.1 million, but he voted in favor of the Wall Street bailout on October 1, 2008.[51] It is astonishing to watch a crony capitalist like Obama attacking big banks and Wall Street, while he rakes in the lion's share of his campaign contributions. Is this sheer stupidity, is it routine extortion, or is Wall Street hedging its bets by paying off anti-capitalist candidates? Perhaps all three.

Interestingly, similar bailouts, buyouts, subsidies, and guarantees were also disbursed by Fascist Italy during the Great Depression.[52,53] Under Mussolini, his state capitalist policies eventually crept into wholesale government ownership of the economy. Mussolini boasted in 1934 that "Three-fourths of the Italian economy, industrial and agricultural, is in the hands of the state."[54,55] By 1939, Italy had reached the highest number of state-owned companies in the entire world, except for the Stalin's Soviet Union.[56]

The *Washington Post*'s Ezra Klein, a left-wing progressive, recognized the difference between pro-market and pro-business orientation, writing, "It's easy for a government that partners with incumbent corporations to think it's helping 'business' when really, it's helping 'a business.' And that can be very bad for the market."[57] Klein wholeheartedly agreed with University of Chicago economist Luigi Zingales, who asserted,

> Being pro-market is being in favor of new entries into the market. If you're a businessman, you're pro-freedom of entry when you enter an industry, and as soon as you enter an industry, you want to raise the bar of entry.[58]

Even consumer advocate Ralph Nader echoed the same sentiments. In *Unstoppable: The Emerging Left-Right Alliance to Dismantle the Corporate State*, he acknowledged Adam Smith's concern that government regulations benefited special interests, writing that "such restraints favor the privileged interests that want to entrench their economic advantages through the force of law."[59,60]

Antitrust Corporatists

Not surprisingly, leaders with a pro-business but anti-market agenda were in the forefront of the antitrust movement, which encouraged legislation to squash competition, not to promote it. Samuel Gompers (1850–1924), the first president of the American Federation of Labor, strongly opposed all antitrust laws, arguing that it would damage industry and "cause injury upon the working people."[61]

As history has demonstrated, so-called pro-competition legislation has had the debilitating effect of muzzling competitive forces, hampering innovative forces, and harming consumers, especially when a government agency is captured by an industry (known as "regulatory capture"). Government is the epitome of barriers, monopolies, and privileges; they are averse to letting things evolve or self-organize on its home turf. As paradoxical as it seems, markets have no need of politically-engineered statutes. For centuries, merchants and the populace were content to defend their interests through common laws and non-state judicators when adjudicating wrongs (torts).

During the boom years following the American Civil War, when corporate laws became prominent, a running battle began to brew between David and Goliath. The older corporations sought to hamper "new kids on the block." Although smaller and financially weaker, the upstarts often took advantage of the latest technology, newer marketing techniques, and better management to keep costs down. This jeopardized the "big boys," prompting unprofitable businesses to seek relief from politicians. They would lobby congressional leaders to enact antitrust laws to prevent competitors from dumping lower-priced products on the market. In fact, according to economist Thomas DiLorenzo, the real reason behind the Sherman Antitrust Act of 1890 was to stop consumer prices from falling.[62]

For instance, John D. Rockefeller of Standard Oil had pushed down the price of kerosene from "58 cents to eight cents a gallon," putting countless oil refineries out of business.[63] Other figures show that oil prices fell "from over 30 cents per gallon in 1869, to 10 cents in 1874, to 8 cents in 1885, and to 5.9 cents in 1897."[64]

The salient point is this: consumers were harmed not by the steady decline of Standard Oil's kerosene prices, but only by inefficient oil refineries. Rather than expending the effort to improve their efficiency, those companies scamper to the political establishment to extract relief. By producing a better product at a lower price, Standard Oil had achieved a near-monopoly on kerosene, but only for so long. Years before antitrust laws broke up Standard Oil in 1911, upstarts and innovative companies had already discovered Rockefeller's successful business formula and gained market share. In 1904, Standard Oil controlled 85 percent of the market. By 1906, its share had eroded to 70 percent, and by 1911, the year the court ordered a breakup of Standard Oil, the company's market share for refining oil had dropped further to 64 percent.[65]

As pro-market capitalists have cited, the separation of business and state levels the playing field for everyone. Here, nobody is guaranteed an edge or the opportunity to obtain favoritism, corporate welfare, exclusive territory, subsidies, special tax loopholes, loan guarantees, government-issued loans, non-bid government contracts, or slush funds. Everyone is treated equally before the law. An operator with a hotdog pushcart has the same rights and legal status to engage in business as Microsoft cofounder Bill Gates does. The dynamics of unconfined competition is the spontaneous thrust that inhibits unfair political advantages. Author William W. Lewis noted the fairness arising from markets absent of cronyism, writing that when "special interests cannot gain legal privileges, competition is often fairly equal."[66]

Most endeavors should be independent of government's poisonous influence. The power to coerce is the power to corrupt. The firewalls erected between church and state in America most likely prevented the type of religious conflicts and wars that had devastated Europe for centuries. Government involvement in any sector of society can boomerang, causing serious damage, especially concerning the history of religion. This is not an argument to malign religious institutions, but to oppose their commingling with the state. The Christian faith has admirable attributes—it provides charity for the poor, hospitals for the sick, orphanages for abandoned and bereaved children, homeless centers for the displaced, soup kitchens for the hungry—but government involvement in religion has corrupted religious institutions and government, alike.

The government's commixture and intervention in the economy will always lead to a politicized economy. The reason is self-evident. If the state tries to control businesses, businesses will eventually try to control the state. This titanic struggle of two powerful interests has no other recourse but to disfigure society, commerce, and governance.

Yet, every year, governmentalists take to the airwaves and demand a crackdown on anti-competitive practices. This has always been an empty gesture. Statutory antitrust laws simply silence the self-organizing forces that release the marvels of spontaneous innovation. Such laws boomerang and bestow favors on the usual suspects: the politically connected elites with greater resources and larger staffs of costly attorneys. Perhaps this was why Rep. Ron Paul of Texas, considered one of the strongest free-market advocates in Congress, got the lowest score for a Republican from the US Chamber of Commerce in 2009. In that year, Paul voted against a bill to boost subsidies for unprofitable solar energy technology, another bill to subsidize the tourism industry, and President Obama's $787 billion stimulus bill.[67]

Slap to Classical Liberalism and Market Capitalism

In a slap across the face of classical liberalism, crony capitalists embolden the inherent DNA of government to grow bigger, bolder, and badder. Most economists and political pundits may give a thumbs-down to cozy relationships between government and private interests, but still ardently endorse regulatory policies that spawn the abuses of crony-based pseudo-capitalism.

The original Lockean liberals were opposed to government becoming involved with the economical and personal life of each citizen. They championed a decentralization of power through constitutional republics to keep government's bad habits under control. They also understood the unified theory of rights. And that is: if we let government abridge the liberty of *anyone*, then the authorities will have the legal precedent to curtail the liberty of *everyone*. If liberty is weakened for one individual or minority, then liberty is weakened for all; or put more succinctly, any threat to freedom anywhere is a threat to freedom everywhere.

During the Age of Enlightenment, classical liberals regarded government as the greatest potential for evil, a perpetual incubator of corruption and injustice. To them, the greatest enemy of humanity was the state. Thomas Paine ascribed the state as a "necessary evil." But he painted a darker picture of the states' intentions in another passage in *Common Sense*, writing that as people suffer from "the same miseries by a government, ... our calamity is heightened by reflecting that we furnish the means by which we suffer." Explained in plain English, this means that not only do the people have to endure government-devised suffering, but must also bear its expense. Through taxation, the people are financing their own misery and self-destruction.

Nonetheless, many latter-day liberals took issue with Paine's assertions about the evils residing within the coercive powers of government. They thought they could tame the beast, teach the old dog of war new tricks, and gentrify the iron-fisted hand of the political leviathan. But such notions were found wanting, even during the Enlightenment. For instance, not long after the signing of the US Constitution, Alexander Hamilton's central bank caused a 72 percent rise in price inflation in its first five years of operation (1791–1796), as cited by Murray Rothbard in *A History of Money and Banking in the United States*.[68]

Considered the father of American crony capitalism, Hamilton supported British-style mercantilism, corporate welfare, huge government debt, high tariffs, and a centralized monarchic-like government. Thomas Jefferson wrote that Hamilton's schemes were "the means by which the corrupt British system of government could be introduced into the United States."[69] One of the most deep-rooted struggles in American politics has been the battle between the ideals of Thomas Jefferson and those of Alexander Hamilton.

To classical liberals, the institution of government seemed tainted with a caustic acidity extracted from Machiavellian malevolence. To counter creeping government, argued classical liberals, government must be shackled with iron-clad constitutional chains, like the phrase in the First Amendment: "government shall pass no law respecting. ..." Furthermore, they believed that the authority to self-govern must be reserved to the individual, so that each person has discretion over how to live his or her life, peacefully, with or without the approval of a majority. Other constraints included governments being mostly restricted to adjudicating violations of individuals' rights to life, liberty, and property. Laws were not to be based upon arbitrary or political whims, but would rely on the presence of victims who believed they had been wronged. In this way, the government's primary duty is to defend the public from force and fraud, and not from victimless indiscretions or political dissent. The purpose of true governance is to protect citizens' rights and property, not to perpetrate intrusive offenses that would normally be classified as criminal. This was plainly spelled out by Thomas Jefferson who wrote: "The legitimate powers of government extend to such acts only as are injurious to others."[70] Unfortunately, most governments commit crimes of aggression while protecting government-inspired criminals. Jefferson also acknowledged that this penchant to misuse the law to carry out a ruler's resolve, writing that the "law is often but the tyrant's will..."[71]

Of course, some classical liberals—Lysander Spooner (1808–1887), Herbert Spencer (1820–1903), Henry David Thoreau (1817–1862), and Murray N. Rothbard, to name a few—opposed any initiatory coercion, and therefore opposed any type of government structure. They held to what they called the "non-initiation of aggression" principle.[72] As such, any state infrastructure and obligatory authority were seen as an affront to liberty. These individualists, voluntaryists, and market anarchists believed the state is unable and unwilling to limit itself—under any circumstance. These radical classical liberals held that any quest to limit the state was impossible to achieve or maintain.

The theory of limited government is engaging. James Madison, one of the first to explore this question, pondered how anyone could bestow limited authority to a leader without also giving him almost unlimited authority to abuse? In *The Federalist* (1788), James Madison, the father of the US Constitution, wrote:

> In framing a government which is to be administered by men over men, the great difficulty lies in this: you must first enable a government to control the governed; and in the next place obligate it to control itself.[73]

Peter Leeson, a George Mason University economist, put it more succinctly:

> An authority strong enough to constrain itself is also strong enough to break those constraints when it's convenient.[74]

Origins of the Left-Right Political Spectrum: French Revolution

So, what is the origin of the political spectrum? Originally, it revolved around the seating arrangements in the French parliament (National Assembly and Legislative Assembly)—the Estates General. It occurred near the end of King Louis XVI's reign, during the Age of Enlightenment, when the flowering of liberty was in full bloom. Before the king was completely deposed, one side of the legislative chamber was populated by the pro-royalists (*Ancien Régime*) that embodied the authoritarian culture of traditionalism and elitism. They sat smugly on the right side of the legislative chamber, which included aristocrats, monarchists, and ecclesiastical leaders who opposed capitalism, republicanism and limited government. These "statist Right" authoritarians were determined to protect the status quo, long-held privileges, political power and the caste prestige of the ruling elites. They felt entitled to live off the people's labor through high debt and almost confiscatory taxation.

During the monarchical era, not only did Europe's power-obsessed nobility engage in brutal persecution, but they drifted continuously toward centralization and nationalization of governance, especially after Napoleon's attempted conquest of Europe. These potentates believed they had been ordained by God to rule mankind in whatever way they deemed suitable. But their fundamental role was to fleece the public while retaining their supremacy. At the time, anyone brave enough to proclaim support for the-will-of-the-people republicanism were often charged with treason, jailed, and if convicted, received an appointment with the hangman's noose. The rule of law had no meaning. Legally, the law assured whatever the king decreed on a particular day. Citizens had no rights except those granted through the ruling apparatus—the antithesis of the Enlightenment principles that rights come from nature or God, but not governmental decree.

In contrast, on the opposite side of the chamber sat the left-wing revolutionaries, who congregated under the radical republican banner of the bourgeoisie Left, often identified as the anti-royalists, yeomen, and commoners (Third Estate). For the most part, they comprised a loosely affiliated group of individuals with anti-authoritarian leanings, which included the rising merchants, master artisans, shopkeepers, land-owning farmers, financiers, Jewish tradesmen, doctors, the liberal bourgeoisie (whose Old French root word literally translated as "town dweller"), and upstart capitalists who held radical Lockean and "*laissez-faire*" economic views.

Another large bloc included the less freedom-oriented judges, low-level officials, lawyers, administrators, and prosecutors. Many of these classical liberals were admirers of Thomas Paine, who quickly published his *Rights of Man* (1791), and by the end of 1793 had sold over 200,000 copies throughout Europe. In fact, Paine was elected to France's National Convention, which represented the district of Pas-de-Calais. He voted in favor of the French Republic, but opposed the execution of King Louis XVI on the grounds that capital punishment, as a form of revenge killing, was immoral. This attitude irked the more bloodthirsty and statist revolutionaries, who suspected counter-revolutionaries lurked under every bed.

The French Revolution was more than a clash between ideological battle lines; it was personal. The rising merchant class and peasants detested the granting of privileges to the noble class and their dominance of public life. Many commoners regarded the Catholic Church as having a chummy relationship with the monarchy, and thus they believed the Church was an accessory to the state's oppressive practices. As the largest landowner in France, the Church with its hierarchy was seen as strangling commoners with increased controls and almost obligatory tithing. Theocratic authority became one of the main obstacles to free thought, transparency, borrowing with interest, and open marketplaces—the factors that would eventually come to lift the poor from their plight.

But there was more to the struggle. French commoners took up arms, not only over being disempowered and dehumanized by the French political elite, but their revolt also was driven by high, regressive taxation, which rose 50 percent between 1705 and 1781.[75] The farming peasants and merchant class mainly bore the brunt of the unfairly-collected taxes where the "top decile of the population were taxed about 60 to 65 per cent to all assessments."[76] As for the nobility and the clergy, they got off easy, being mostly exempt from taxation.

Not surprisingly, the French Revolution had an anti-tax component that mirrored the motives behind the American Revolution. For instance, this anti-tax fervor was on full display just before the Bastille was attacked and overrun. Before the angry French mob and the Bourgeois Militia of Paris stormed the Bastille on July 14, 1789, they first launched an assault against the hated Paris' "tollgates," where excise taxes were collected by the state.[77] Later, in a number of areas in France, the people displayed a general animosity towards imposed levies and "denounced all taxes."[78]

It was not just high, unevenly levied taxes that agitated the French Third Estate. Despite a crushing national debt from past wars, French monarchists in the late 1700s were living high on the hog. The peasants suffered under periods of starvation, rising bread prices, and freezing weather. Upon learning that the people had no bread, Queen Marie Antoinette allegedly uttered the callous remark: "Then let them eat cake." Of course, cake was far more expensive than bread. This heartless retort, if true, illustrates the extent of the monarchy's being out of touch with the public. But at least the nobility was usually more honest about their selfish lifestyles, arrogant ways, and petty squabbles. Monarchies rarely developed propaganda machines to manipulate public opinion. Large-scale institutionalization of propaganda by government agencies arrived on the scene in the early 20th century, specifically during World War I.

In 1789, the French Revolution began as a bourgeoisie-led drive to advance political and legal equality, and equality of opportunity, for every citizen. Coupled with their emphasis on reason and science, the free-Left rebels championed liberal capitalism, civil liberties, and secularism, which means that *laissez-faire* capitalists and the merchant class were the original left-wing revolutionaries. Emulating the rebellious Americans across the pond, French radicals embraced liberal values that demanded a republic with Locke's "consent of the governed." Since there was no organized socialist movement at the time to steal the limelight, these revolutionaries were touted as the "left" and "liberal" originators of the insurrection. Indeed, most historians provide little explanation for this oddity. Andrew Knapp and Vincent Wright, in *The Government and Politics of France*, merely noted that "to be Republican was automatically to be on the Left and to identify with the heritage of the Revolution. ..."[79]

Nonetheless, one historian, Fred Siegel, pointed out that the political dichotomy present during the French Revolution was "a brief moment of political and ideological clarity."[80]

Others have clarified the left-right division that emerged from the French Revolution in this way:

> Because the political franchise at the start of the revolution was relatively narrow, the original "Left" represented mainly the interests of the bourgeoisie, the rising capitalist class. At that time, support for laissez-faire capitalism and Free markets were counted as being on the left; today in most Western countries these views would be characterized as being on the Right.[81]

Without an established socialist or collectivist movement until the 1820s and 1830s, the left-wing status of classical liberalism had few capable challengers. But decades later, when competition did come, it was the less extreme, utopian socialism of the Owenites, Saint-Simonians, and Fourierists, among others. Nonetheless, whether it was early soft-shelled utopian socialism or later impregnable Marxism, their movement was regarded as a reaction against industrial capitalism and freethinking liberalism.

Regardless of the rise of socialism, the original liberal left still had a presence in France. For instance, Frédéric Bastiat (1801–1850), the author of the libertarian classic *The Law* (1850), was elected to the French

Assembly in 1848. He sat on the left side of the hall with other liberal, *laissez-faire* market adherents, including some anarchists. Bastiat was an ardent anti-statist who publicly denounced socialism as just another form of "plunder." Nonetheless, socialists and communists began to identify themselves as belonging on the left side of the political spectrum, unable to stomach a right-wing designation that was already occupied by unpopular monarchical authoritarians. During this adjustment, socialists started to turn their gunsights on liberals, blaming them for not completely abolishing the economic inequality and grinding poverty that had festered for over 600 years of medieval feudalism.

But this narrative is more complex than that. Although the classical liberal intelligentsia instigated the revolt in France, their vanguard status was short-lived. Factionalisms and extremism soon impaired progress towards a peaceful, thriving democratic republic. Dark and violent forces interfered and eventually culminated in paranoia, civil war, the nihilistic Reign of Terror, mass executions, high inflation, shortages, price controls, economic restraints, and dictatorship. What had started out as a relatively peaceful revolution prompted by the Enlightenment under left-wing, classical liberals to topple the king's ancient order, reverted, paradoxically, to something far worse than the monarchy.

What went wrong?

The problem was that a bevy of revolutionaries was caught up in the political abyss of power plays, self-righteousness, conformity, and social revolution, believing that supremacy was the only means with which to rapidly change society and politics. For centuries, devotion to the governmentalism of physical force was incarnated by conservative autocrats, who distorted and bruised the psyche of the public. The violence inherent in rulership was not questioned—only who was ruling. Under this mindset, the French insurgents could take control and become tyrannical by merely pursuing what they thought was the "general will"—a concept made popular by Genevan philosopher Jean-Jacques Rousseau (1712–1778). By following the general will, which was thought to be infallible, these social revolutionaries could justify their ruthlessness, a concept deemed by some as "proto-communist."[82]

Ultimately, the initial meaning of the French Revolution drifted away from liberty and veered towards nationalism, socialism, centralism, and autarkic protectionism, mostly because of the collectivistic influence of the proto-socialist Montagnards' faction within the Jacobin Club, the most influential political club during the revolution. In later years, Alexis de Tocqueville (1805–1859) depicted this sudden change in the revolution as "a push towards decentralization... [but became,] in the end, an extension of centralization."[83] Although the liberal free-marketers had instigated the revolution, they were loosely organized and did not form an official political party. They were eventually called the Girondins, a name given to them by their opponents, the Montagnards, led by Maximilien Robespierre. It was Robespierre and his social revolutionary firebrands who were responsible for unleashing the Reign of Terror, which resulted in over 16,000 death sentences. The Montagnards were highly organized, close-knit, well disciplined, and determined to seize and retain power, the ultimate power-mongering collectivists who epitomize the politically-obsessed.

The Montagnards embodied a radical collectivist and nationalist demeanor that was a harbinger of the revolutionary socialism and collectivistic nationalism that came to inspire Nazism and communism. In many respects, the French Revolution could be seen as a dress rehearsal for the Russian Revolution, which, likewise, started as a peaceful movement by the bourgeoisie Left to overthrow the Czar, but climaxed in the violent takeover by socialist militants and Lenin's Red Terror. In the case of Russia, however, the body count far surpassed that of Maximilien Robespierre's Reign of Terror.

The Montagnards, like both the nationalistic socialists and the communists, engaged in xenophobic and racial violence. These French agitators and populists turned on minorities, expropriated private wealth, jailed and executed prisoners, guillotined other revolutionaries considered enemies of the revolution, and persecuted foreigners, confiscating and selling émigrés' property.

In other words, they exhibited "unmistakable communistic implications."[84] It was Marx's study of the latter part of the French Revolution and of the Montagnards' tactics to exploit and inflame popular resentment against other classes and groups that helped him develop his theory of class struggle. Because of Marx's influence, campaigns to foment social antagonism for political purposes gained "moral legitimacy" for the first time. As the Polish-American historian Richard Pipes explained, the tactic of winning mass popular support in order to topple democratic governments drove communism, fascism and national socialism to appeal to "the emotion of hate," turning conflicts over class, race, and ethnicity "into a virtue."[85] Later generations in the socialist movement emulated the violent mob mentality of the *sans-culottes* that had marred the French Revolution, discovering that they could divide nations and seize power by weaponizing the politics of envy and hate.

The Free Bourgeoisie Left: The Girondins

Originally, the Montagnards had allied with the larger, Enlightenment-inspired bourgeoisie Left, but that alliance with the Girondins was short-lived. After the monarchy completely fell, many of the Montagnards took to the streets, alongside *sans-culottic* elements and acted like mindless thugs pushing for more political power. Like Lenin's Red Terror and Stalin's purges of the old Bolshevik revolutionaries, the Montagnards orchestrated mobs who assailed anyone considered a counter-revolutionary, even their own brothers in arms. They arrested many of the Girondin revolutionary leaders and extrajudicially guillotined 22 Girondin deputies from the National Convention on October 31, 1793, taking 36 minutes to chop off 22 heads. This was the flashpoint when the statist Left rose up and sought to destroy the original bourgeois free Left near the beginning of the Reign of Terror. At this juncture, freedom-of-the-individual liberalism was assaulted by Robespierre's Reign of Terror, which later influenced both Communism and National Socialism. One notable member of the Girondin bloc who was swept up in this violent socio-political tempest was Thomas Paine, who was arrested, imprisoned, and barely escaped the executioner's blade.

As for the placement of the Montagnards' faction on the political spectrum, one could appraise them as either the statist Left or the statist Right, since they had reverted into the same authoritarian abyss of the old, absolute-power monarchists and moralistic dogma of the Church. This fact alone provides the evidence that there were two French Revolutions—the first stage instigated by free-Left elements imbued with toleration, anti-authoritarianism, secularism, individualism, liberty and the revolutionary individualism of Thomas Jefferson and Thomas Paine. The second stage of the French Revolution devolved into a bloody, terroristic dictatorship, an all-powerful state amidst a cult of personality, such as the so-called incorruptible Maximilien Robespierre, in a counter-revolution that was anti-liberal and antithetical to the *Lumières* movement, which became the Age of Enlightenment.

Here, passion for power-mongering and obedience to authority resumed their political attraction. In fact, Hitler recognized the French Revolution as influencing national socialist thought, saying: "This revolution of ours is the exact counter-part of the French Revolution."[86] As for Marxists and their colleagues, they approvingly saw Robespierre and the *sans-culottes* as quasi-Marxist heroes as defenders of the revolution by foreign and domestic enemies as expressed by the Marxist historian Albert Soboul, while others argued that the revolutionaries had to exterminate domestic enemies to defend their utopian goals. Marxists have long revered Gracchus Babeuf, a journalist and political agitator during the French Revolution, as the first revolutionary communist. In fact, the communists were ecstatic over Robespierre's revolutionary aspirations; Lenin commissioned a number of monuments to memorialize him. The first one was erected within the walls of the Kremlin in Moscow on November 3, 1918. In an edict, Lenin referred to Robespierre as a "Bolshevik *avant la lettre*" or a "Bolshevik before his time," declaring that he had reached "one of the highest summits attained by the working class in struggling for its emancipation."[87]

In the case of Mussolini, Italian Fascism and revolutionary syndicalism also developed strong ideological links to the Western radical tradition of the latter-stage French Revolution. According to Italian historian Renzo de Felice, Fascism was not tethered to an archetypical reactionism, but to the extremist Rousseauian themes of the Reign of Terror and "totalitarian democracy."[88] In other words, many scholars argue that Jean-Jacques Rousseau's thoughts led French extremists to engage in the Reign of Terror, which many consider a precursor to fascism. Such a perspective is reasonable. Italian Fascism's tendencies towards social revolution, anti-democracy, and violence could be expected since "most fascist intellectuals started out as Marxists."[89]

Nonetheless, it is no wonder that many historians cite Robespierre's

Reign of Terror as the endpoint of the Age of Enlightenment, considering that that reign had inspired subsequent national socialist and Marxist movements.

But more important, not only did the statist Left guillotine the leaders of the free Left, but ever since, the statist Left has schemed to control the future by altering the past. To accomplish that feat, they had to hide their own reactionary violence, autocracy, and racism. True to their Machiavellian upbringing, the statist Left's intelligentsia found it necessary to subvert and supplant the meaning of liberalism and democracy, frequently attempting to doctor or conceal their capitalistic and individualistic roots, while likewise undermining the historical meaning of the left-right political spectrum. They crafted semantic changes to liberalism that reflected a collectivist outlook that was actually anti-liberal. As economist Daniel B. Klein pointed out, the original language of liberalism "receded sharply during the period 1880 to 1940," losing its semantic integrity in a fog of vagueness.[90] In fact, Herbert Spencer, the old liberal of individualist anarchism and anti-imperialism heritage, lamented in 1884 about liberalism's new illiberal direction, asserting that "most of those who now pass as liberals are Tories of a new type."[91] In other words, language and its uses have the potential to determine how people think. Altering certain elements of language can affect its meaning and reshape attitudes towards political and economic institutions. It seems that the semantic content of the original language of liberalism became contaminated to the point that it readily disowned its own principles, and thereby misshaped the political dichotomy.

It is not widely known that the bourgeoisie Left and middle-class free-marketeers instigated the French Revolution. Part of the reason is that socialists and Marxist leaders schemed to alter history and cut out the left-wing middle-class narrative. When collectivists and Marxists finally leaped onto the political stage long after the French Revolution, they co-opted the "left" label from the bourgeoisie and condemned anyone who opposed them as reactionary or right-wing. But more astonishingly, the statist Left not only stole the left-wing designation from the bourgeoisie Left, but they also absconded with their revolutionary ancestry. English historian William Doyle acknowledged this historical theft, writing that after the French Revolution, the socialists "appropriate[d] the left-wing label and... lay exclusive claim to the revolutionary heritage."[92] In later years, the collectivists were also successful in eventually expropriating the term "liberalism" while completely changing its original liberty-based context. In this sense, since authoritarian socialists hijacked the "left-wing" designation from the political spectrum, they can be described as political usurpers who don "fake Left" ID badges.

If we were to fully examine the left-right demarcation from one extreme end to the other, nationally organized socialism would be perched side by side with internationally organized socialism. Where else could such strikingly similar ideologies lie? They sat in the same bleachers and rooted for the same team's goals, but because of their large and unruly numbers, subgroups moved a little more to the right or left side of the stadium. German National Socialism, Italian Fascism, and Russian Sovietism had their differences and competitive instincts, but so does everyone. Authoritarian ideologies occupy a relatively small, extremist niche on the political spectrum, compared to the wide-ranging non-authoritarian moderates, regardless of whether these monomaniacs are labeled "left" or "right." Historians constantly factionalize groups within the same political movement, postulating that one side is somehow more left-wing or more right-wing than the other. Communists famously pin different political labels on those within their own ranks, as exemplified by the hostile rivalry between the Left Opposition and Right Opposition communists in the Soviet Union. Despite dividing themselves up within left-wing and right-wing subgroups, they still considered themselves communists.

The Soviet Union's propaganda mill spun the narrative that its former allies, Nazi Germany and Fascist Italy, had suddenly come down with the "right-wing" blues, but as any historian can attest, government propaganda is rarely truthful. Consider what the Soviet Union's theoreticians were preparing to decry against Red China after their "whirlwind romance" ended in a messy divorce. Political scientist A. James Gregor did so, remarking:

> By the end of the 1960s, Soviet theoreticians were prepared to argue that the "Chinese leadership" had transformed itself into an "anti-Marxist, anti-socialist, chauvinistic and anti-Soviet...

bourgeois-nationalistic" movement of reaction... In their account, Soviet thinkers had recourse to the same list of descriptive traits that Western academics had employed for some considerable time to identify fascist political and social systems.[93]

Fascist-Marxist Sibling Rivalry

As it turned out, conservative right-wing elements had little to do with fascism or Nazism. The Polish-born Israeli historian Zeev Sternhell came to this conclusion in *Neither Right nor Left: Fascist Ideology in France*. Sternhell explores the theme of the "meaninglessness of left-right distinctions." "Fascism," he wrote, "emerges on the left while claiming to be anti-left."[94] Right-wing groups and parties had no more in common with revolutionary nationalists beholden to socialism and anti-Semitism than it had with democratic liberalism. Hitler said as much in a 1920 speech in Munich, declaring: "There comes a time when it will be obvious that socialism can only be carried out accompanied by nationalism and antisemitism."[95] So, why the confusion? It would seem to be a no-brainer. If socialist regimes work together, trade together, fight together, collaborate, and have fundamentally equivalent ideologies and tactics, they are genealogically related (a sort of Communist-Nazi brotherhood), which could be regarded as a Fascist-Marxist mindset. Of course, these socialist ideologues also fight each like rival siblings.

But to dedicated propagandists of the collective persuasion, the nasty cases of sibling rivalry between socialist regimes during World War II were too horrific to permit unmonitored public viewing. Desperate to erase embarrassing socialist atrocities, a coterie of collectivists had to place the blame elsewhere, even if it meant distorting history so that the public could not discern which political ideologies were responsible. Because the politically engaged intelligentsia was already tuned in to the mindset of "the ends justify the means," it was a piece of cake to mix, sift, fold, stir, and blend history through the use of their own ready-made recipes. To successfully cook history, they had to switch their ingredients to fit a faux narrative.

As previously mentioned, the statist Left's first move was to alter the meaning of *liberalism* so as to keep the free Left and the public in a constant state of confusion. They diluted the original principles of liberalism while firing cheap polemical shots, arguing that John Locke's liberalism had nothing to offer, that it contradicted itself. After all, if the statist Left could not win a fair fight on the philosophical battlefield, it had to resort to chicanery to gain an advantage. One way to accomplish this was to adulterate or falsify the liberal message to render it meaningless while advancing a new, redefined liberalism to replace the old. The deception was successful. The free-Left liberals and their allies had lost the semantic ammunition to defend liberty, and therefore became neutered, defanged, almost defenseless, deprived of the cognitive capability to defend the autonomy of the individual. As for the statist Left, they had to work diligently to "defascistize" historical Fascism, because to do otherwise would force them to face an ugly image in the mirror.

The Girondin's Liberalization of France

What were some of the reasons that the free-Left Girondins were treated so ruthlessly? The Montagnards resented the Girondins' liberalization of the economy, respect for property rights, deregulatory policies, Montesquieu's separation of powers, a night-watchman government, and mostly, their opposition to executing King Louis XVI. Unwilling to accept delays, the Montagnards accused the Girondins of harboring loyalty to the old order, and therefore, of conspiring with counter-revolutionaries.

Yet it was the majority-led Girondins who had spearheaded the revolution and challenged the establishment. They accomplished far more than did the Montagnards. After toppling the king, the Girondins rushed into an abolitionist spree fueled by liberty, dissolving the last vestiges of aristocratic privilege, the system of church tithes, dues owed to local landlords, and personal servitude. The radical liberals also released the peasants from the *seigneurial* (lord) dues, which helped tenant farmers buy their own private farmland. Next, they turned their abolitionist gun-sights on the guild system that blocked entry to markets, as well as "tax farming," where private individuals would be licensed to collect taxes for the state while taking a large share for themselves.

The Girondins' most lasting legacy was the ratification of "The Declaration of the Rights of Man and of the Citizen" (August 1789), which was directly influenced by Thomas Jefferson. As a US diplomat at the time, Jefferson had worked with General Lafayette to write a French bill of rights, which Lafayette introduced to the National Constituent Assembly.[96] Referring to this declaration, French historian François Furet (1927–1997) wrote:

> For this structure they substituted the modern, autonomous individual, free to do whatever was not prohibited by law... The Revolution thus distinguished itself quite early by its radical individualism.[97]

Moreover, the Girondin bloc also ratified laws ensuring equality in taxation, freedom of worship, and legal equality of punishment, and abolishing serfdom outright, including a 1791 law to emancipate Jewish citizens from unequal treatment. The Girondin-led assembly also granted free people of color full French citizenship and enacted universal voting rights for all adult males, regardless of race, religion, income, property or any other qualification. They even included a pro-gun rights provision in the French Declaration of Rights, which declared that "every citizen has the right to keep arms at home and to use them, either for the common defense or for his own defense, against any unlawful attack which may endanger the life, limb, or freedom of one or more citizens." Despite the effort, this draft did not make it into the final document.[98]

After the classical liberals had ousted state monopolies, high and unequal tax rates, specially endowed privileges, entrance barriers and stifling regulations, the economy flourished. However, with British blockades at French harbors, runaway inflation, and invasions by foreign armies, the economy soon turned the other direction, sputtering into recession.

Nonetheless, the Montagnards' expectations could not be satisfied. The revolution also had to correct social and economic wrongs. They sought immediate change, demanded that every citizen have a right to "public relief,"[99] and that the state now had to guarantee social and economic "rights" such as free education for all. For these social revolutionaries, limiting government to the protection of individual rights would hamper the state's ability to solve social and economic inequalities. Although the abstract concept of equality was bourgeois in nature, the Montagnards began to see government as an equalizer, a force which could assist the unfortunate, through the implementation of certain policies, even if its intervention would infringe on the equal rights of others. They began to look at government as an arbitrator of justice and equality, assuming the paternalistic role of a nearly autocratic overseer, with a democratic veneer. They were engaging in the welfare and social-engineering policies which, later, the German National Socialists and the Russian Soviets found so appealing.

More than that, the collectivist French revolutionaries moved toward a more utilitarian perspective, ascribing that the needs of the many could outweigh the needs of the few, which, if taken to its logical conclusion, is a recipe for legalized murder and genocide. They reverted to an anti-individualist theory of political liberty embraced by the ancient world of Rome and Greece, where each citizen could vote to go to war or remain at peace, but otherwise "was a slave in all his private relations."[100] As Benjamin Constant wrote in 1819, the collectivist French revolutionaries recycled from antiquity the enslavement mindset that called for citizens to be entirely dominated by political forces "in order for the nation to be sovereign, and that the individual should be enslaved for the people to be free."[101] In this vein, governance was not to be seen as a tyrannical edifice occupied by flawed kings and rulers, but as a societal collective which wielded a moral superiority and infallibility overshadowing the individual.

Such social precepts caused the Montagnards to push even further the envelope of government intrusiveness, deifying the state as a kind of national "collective will," imbued with the right to protect itself from all opponents. Written by the Montagnards and passed by popular vote, the revised "Declaration of the Rights of Man and Citizen" of 1793, proclaimed: "Let any person who may usurp the sovereignty be instantly put to death by free men."[102] Because sovereignty was defined as "residing in the people," it could be argued that government had the duty to kill those who objected to the actions of the collective nation-state in order to protect society—which could explain some of the motivation behind the Reign of Terror pursuit of "virtue through terror." According to François Furet, as the ringleaders of the Reign of Terror tore society apart and systematically executed opponents, the revolution descended towards a "democratic ideology to rule in a despotic manner," without regard to individual rights.[103] Moreover, many revolutionary leaders took the position that "democracy meant the power of a nation-state to defeat those who opposed its will."[104] This is a rather fascist notion, treating the nation as a collective entity that has the ultimate sovereignty to punish those who might disregard its societal will.

The Girondins had tried to hold the line against extremism and violence as well as the reactionary tide of nationalism, protectionism, coercion, and proto-socialism. But the Montagnards' waves of mob violence, power grabs, and subsequent executions were relentless, later inspiring many socialist movements to sanction nationalism, racism, genocide, atheism, and economic xenophobia. In fact, by March 1793, the Montagnards' tactics had spawned an episode of mass killings, called the War in the Vendée, which some scholars have classified genocidal. The rural French population turned against newly imposed taxation, anti-clericalism, and conscription of their unmarried sons. The peasants had had enough of the senseless violence and social revolution. On August 1, 1793, the Committee of Public Safety ordered the French Republic troops to physically destroy the insurrection, slaughtering up to a half-million peasants where "rebel prisoners—men, women, and children—were executed in mass crowds by gunfire and drowning."[105] General Westermann allegedly reported back to Robespierre's Committee of Public Safety and stated that

> The Vendée is no more. ... According to your orders, I have trampled their children beneath our horses' feet; I have massacred their women, so they will no longer give birth to brigands. I do not have a single prisoner to reproach me. I have exterminated them all.[106]

Some historians dispute the existence of Westermann's letter, but many other reports of genocidal massacres have been verified.

In retrospect, the French Revolution, which culminated in the dictatorship of Napoleon Bonaparte, could be described as a revolving door, where everything changes, but still remains the same. In this paradoxical sense, post-monarchal governments continued to behave remarkably like the old, absolute-power juggernauts of the monarchy. Little had changed. The free Left had liberated France, while the statist Left had shackled it again. So, if the statist Left was responsible for resurrecting authoritarian governance, then they should bear their right-wing moniker and ancestry. Of course, that political designation was already reserved for the extremely unpopular ancient order, and no radical worth his tricolored cockade wanted any connection to the right-wing status of aristocrats, the Church, and monarchists. Yet, despite the fact that the statist Left fiddled with age-old despotic power, terror, and sanctified dogma, its influence ultimately overran Europe and relegated free-Left liberalism to a less diminished role.

New Boss Same as the Old Boss

Providing insight into the conflict between the rising socialists and the dying aristocracy during the 1930s, a lucid example can be found in one of the most endearing films to come out of Hollywood, the "Sound of Music," based on the memoirs of Maria von Trapp.[107] While the 1965 dramatization diverges from the true story in many respects, Captain Georg von Trapp did indeed oppose the Nazis' de facto annexation of Austria (the *Anschluss*) in 1938. Besides his distaste over the persecution of Austrian Catholics by the Nazis, he understood, as did many in the upper class, that the German National Socialists would likely confiscate their land holdings and privileges. The Church and the aristocrats were the predominant statist-Right forces opposed to fascism, socialism, and communism. This epic struggle represented the power shift from the old authority to the new authority. Only if aristocrats would join the Nazi party and rise to high positions could they have any hope of saving their ancestral assets. Active participation in a regime usually provides some protection from unscrupulous party officials in the government, reinforcing the old adage, "If you are not at the table, you're on the menu."

When the socialist and communist ideologues started to stroll onto the political stage in the mid-19th century, they would often be cast in supporting roles. Almost a century later, those performers ushered in single-party regimes directed by a troupe of misfit tyrants and prima donnas whose abuses of the public surpassed those inflicted by absolute monarchies. In reality, these so-called revolutionary new bosses were simply the same old tyrannical bosses.

There are some minor differences. The collectivists, dictocrats, and central planners articulated catchier catchphrases, promised more undeliverable goodies, and commanded an ideological army of zealots who are willing to commit atrocities for the supposed betterment of mankind. They have been receptive to any means of correcting socioeconomic wrongs or mandating any social justice policies that could beget a militarized police state. This militarization of righteousness was on display at one of the first concentration camps in the Soviet Union, where a welcoming sign epitomized the communist commitment to an absolutist utopia: "With an Iron Fist, We Will Lead Humanity to Happiness."[108] That is like saying that in order to save humanity, one must slaughter humans. Under this level of myopia, any tactic is therefore acceptable to wage war on poverty, inequality, and exploitation, to the point where even mass murder can be characterized as a heroic deed. Such violent interventions to create a new man are irrelevant, because, in the minds of collectivist do-gooders, people are expendable, while unproven hypotheses are indispensable.

Again, despite propaganda to the contrary, the statist Left retained ruling methods and ideology painfully reminiscent of the old, right-wing monarchic rulers, but carried out more ruthlessly. They instigated traditional, top-down, political command structures that climaxed in epic carnage and destruction considered inconceivable under even the most brutal monarchies. Despite sweet-sounding platitudes, the new political bosses were essentially no different from the old political bosses—only the names and faces had changed. These overlords continued victimizing the citizenry, but under the guise of noble causes, like an iron fist brandished by Napoleon Bonaparte in search of new conquests.

Yet few have acknowledged that revolutionary coups d'état are mostly conservative and authoritarian by nature, especially socialist *putsches* that merely rehash variants of the same old, baneful, authority-based model. Throughout history, such actions were seen as conservative-laced uprisings provoked by ambitious political rivals. For instance, the French literary realist Gustave Flaubert (1821–1880) considered socialists as both authoritarian and boorish.[109] Wielding a pen like a scalpel, Flaubert regarded the Commune of Paris in 1871 as part of the same old story, where the commune's direction was "returning to the real Middle Ages" and the "government interferes in natural rights."[110] Lord Acton (1834–1902) had made similar observations about the rusty sword of revolution, writing: "The object of revolution is the prevention of revolution."[111]

As surprising as it may be, the politically entrenched often incited rebellions in order to preserve the status quo. They were not thirsting for revolutionary or socioeconomic change; they were merely defending their authority. After all, socialism's inherent rigidity and subordination were simply a reaction to the liberating forces of industrial capitalism that had hamstrung the authoritarian, oppressive, and slavish conditions of feudalism. Considering the abuses perpetrated by single-party, communist dictatorships, socialist states merely engage in ploys to replace one overlord with another. Nothing had actually changed; these revolutions were exercises in futility—but succeeded in hoodwinking the public.

Historically, the far more revolutionary ideas, which could topple the status quo, have resided within the context of radical individualism. This is the elixir of autonomy that empowers people to assume control of his own priorities—free choice—alongside fellow individuals in a voluntaryist society. This is the battle between choice and compulsion, which are just as diametrically opposed as are individualism and collectivism. Most classical liberals concur that the eternal struggle of humanity pits the maverick against the collectivity of the state. In modern times, that battle is often seen as libertarian versus authoritarian, but despite the different wording, it still boils down to the age-old contest between individual choice and collective servitude. Just after World War II, the English author George Orwell identified this striking, polar dichotomy. He wrote in 1948: "The real division is not between conservatives and revolutionaries but between authoritarians and libertarians."[112]

The polar opposite of individualism—collectivism—tends to hold society hostage, lumping distinct parts together, creating the bulwark of a "superorganism" dedicated to an all-encompassing unity. To many, it is a question of whether a person's life belongs to oneself (self-ownership) or to the group, society, or the state (group ownership). Is the individual sovereign and free, or is the group sovereign and can do anything it wants to individuals? This contested battle pitted the individual minority against the group majority. But it was the original liberals who first saw the individual as the quintessential minority, often treated as a nonentity who was denied life, liberty and property by everyone from monarchs and aristocrats to southern slaveholders and tribal socialists.

The classical liberal and English journalist Rudyard Kipling recognized that the rights of the individual were being compromised. He wrote that he was determined to "fight every effort to set up the tyranny of a minority over a majority," which included countering Bolshevism.[113] In a 1935 interview, Kipling expressed the concept of self-ownership in opposition to the collectivism of tribalism:

> The individual has always had to struggle to keep from being overwhelmed by the tribe. To be your own man is a hard business. If you try it, you'll be lonely often, and sometimes frightened. But no price is too high to pay for the privilege of owning yourself.[114]

Under collectivism, society is sovereign, and pesky individuals are not. Not surprisingly, a Marxist once crowed, "Marxism does not deny the role of the individual in history. It merely asserts that individuals, no matter how capable, are never free agents."[115] If people don't have free agency, they become mere chattel to the herdsman who wields the biggest horsewhip. Obviously, statists see the individual as enjoying no rights except those in service to the group. Hitler epitomized such collectivism in the 25 points of his National Socialist Programme, proclaiming in 1920 to a large crowd: "The common good before the individual good."[116] As Mussolini succinctly put it: "Liberty is a duty, not a right."[117] In fact, Mussolini attacked classical liberalism and individualism in his 1935 version of "The Political and Social Doctrine of Fascism," writing:

> Against individualism, the Fascist conception is for the State; and it is for the individual in so far as he coincides with the State. ... It is opposed to classical Liberalism. ... Liberalism denied the State

in the interests of the particular individual; Fascism reaffirms the
State as the true reality of the individual.[118]

Any modern-day leftist worth his collectivistic salt would endorse Mussolini's affirmation.

And because collectivism is methodized to pit groups against each other to achieve idealistic ends, conflict and war become inevitable. Economist Ludwig von Mises described collectivism as

> a doctrine of war, intolerance, and persecution. If any of the collectivist creeds should succeed in its endeavors, all people but the great dictator would be deprived of their essential human quality. They would become mere soulless pawns in the hands of a monster.[119]

As the heirs of classical liberalism, libertarians have been put in a difficult position; their effort to decipher the more sophisticated and autocratic varieties of collectivism brings challenges. The forces of collectivism can be found everywhere, even permeating the traditional American Right. Many so-called right-wing political parties defend many aspects of the interventionist welfare-warfare state, including a strong allegiance to nationalism, a form of national-identity collectivism. In fact, across the globe, almost every major modern political party has stuck their fingers in the political pie to control whatever they can. They aspire to become head of a mishmash of economic and social measures to retain the power in others' conformity. Few are immune from collectivism's seductive allure that promises peace, contentment, and community, only to see it extinguished in war, economic malaise, and discontentment.

Collectivism has a proclivity to bring out the worst in people because in a politically charged world, the only way to survive is to cheat the system before it can cheat you. When collective systems become increasingly unfair, except for high authority figures, people can feel compelled to seek revenge not only by cheating the system, but each other. Nobody wants to be a sucker, so nobody trusts anybody. Collectivism is the last refuge for finding peace, harmony, or justice. Ludwig von Mises remarked in *Human Action* that "collectivism cannot result in anything but social disintegration and the perpetuation of armed conflict."[120]

For instance, despite cries for a culture of peace, socialist factions have marshaled nations into conflicting warfare states, as witnessed by the militaristic adventurism of Russia's Soviet Union, Germany's National Socialists, Mao's Red China, Italian Fascism, and Pol Pot's Khmer Rouge, to name a few. Politicos of every stripe try to hide their collectivistic warts from public scrutiny, in order to either muster enough support to win elections or to amass enough armed revolutionaries to overthrow a government.

When all is said and done, deep down inside, most political leaders and movements are less interested in ideology than in obtaining and preserving political dominance. Before Mussolini gained power in 1922, he employed all sorts of connivance and deception to disarm political adversaries. One method was to declare that fascism was extremely flexible. According to English historian Denis Mack Smith, Mussolini reminded major power players that fascism "was a 'super-relativist movement' with no fixed principles, ready for almost any alliance."[121] Despite his hardcore Marxist background, Mussolini, found it easy to join and discard alliances to gain permanent power.

Modern political parties on both the left axis and right axis seek the holy grail of true political achievement: overall rulership. It does not matter whether two or three political parties of the same collectivist hydra are slugging it out, lying, cheating, or even killing one another. It is all about dominance and who can first scale the political pyramid. Such struggles and alliances between political collectivists often confuse the public, who are content to keep it simple and look for easy, black-and-white comparisons.

Historically, it has not been uncommon for collectivist parties to wrestle each other in violent death matches. Nor is it uncommon for socialist nations to invade each other. This fact alone makes it difficult, or even impossible, to determine whether a political group or movement sits squarely on the right or left side of the aisle—and if so, which—an endeavor which news reporters carelessly attempt in order to quickly identify the opponents. Considering that most political leaders and parties employ a heavy dose of deception, the political spectrum is easily compromised, which can group political participants into unambiguous and often inaccurate categories.

Could Marxism and Socialism be on the Extreme Right?

Some scholars, including economist Murray Rothbard, have suggested that Marxism and socialism actually belong on the extreme right end of the political spectrum. Obviously, since communist dictators have embraced authoritarian policies that closely resemble those of past theocratic and monarchic regimes, where else would they belong? In practice, Marx-inspired despots have employed the absolutism of power once wielded by monarchies, while preaching a moralistic ethos embraced by the Catholic Church. Even Ayn Rand hinted at the same conclusion, writing in the 1960s that "socialism is merely democratic absolute monarchy..."[122]

As evidence for this position, some historians have pointed to communist governments who have consecrated royal dynasties to rule their countries. For instance, the Democratic People's Republic of Korea (North Korea) is considered a "hereditary monarchy" that is racist, fascist, and manages to manifest a cult following. After the death of Kim Il-sung, founder of communist North Korea, his son Kim Jong-il inherited the throne in 1994. On December 17, 2011, Kim Jong-il died; within a few weeks, his son Kim Jong-un became his successor. North Korea is, no doubt, an old-fashioned hereditary monarchy, in which the crown has been passed down through three generations of a family line. Some experts see North Korea as having descended back into a pre-capitalist mode, steeped in a military hierarchal feudalism which, in historical context, resembles a "communist monarchy."[123] The Republic of Cuba followed suit with their hereditary dictatorship in early 2008, when Fidel Castro named his brother Raúl Castro to rule Cuba.

Communism has exhibited a litany of links to the feudal traditions of the monarchy and the Church. Foremost is communism's sociological determinism, which sought to impose a puritanical morality in an effort to weed out citizens' decadent and immoral behavior. Taking its cue from Christian theology, communists have adopted policies to create the perfect, unselfish "socialist man," who is noble, viceless, and gracious to a fault. For instance, most communist leaders and theorists have opposed the practice of prostitution. When communists attain control of a nation, they immediately crack down on sex workers. Hostile to the idea of divorce, Karl Marx thought of sex work as "only a specific expression of the general prostitution of the laborer." He advocated its abolishment, viewing it as the product of an evil capitalist society. Friedrich Engels, the son of a German industrialist, thought that marriage could be considered a form of prostitution.[124]

Not only did most communists oppose prostitution, but they condemned homosexuality, viewing it as one of the depraved effects of a capitalist society engaged in "bourgeois decadence."[125] Friedrich Engels despised such sexual practices and associated them with pedophilia.[126] Although Vladimir Lenin (1870–1924) decriminalized homosexuality, Joseph Stalin (1878–1953) referred to homosexuality as a disease, and revised the entire Soviet Union criminal code, enacting laws to make male homosexuality a crime punishable with up to five years' imprisonment.[127] Not long after the Cuban Revolution, Castro's government began to imprison lesbians and gay men in labor camps without charge or trial. Most members of these persecuted groups fled Cuba permanently, having been treated by the Cuban communist leaders as counterrevolutionary.[128] Castro labeled gay men as "agents of imperialism"[129] and once boasted that "there are no homosexuals" in Cuba.[130]

For instance, Reinaldo Arenas, a dissident writer and homosexual in Castro's Cuba, was imprisoned for his maverick beliefs and sexual orientation. He wrote that "Gays were not treated like human beings, they were treated like beasts... the most insignificant incident was an excuse to beat them mercilessly."[131] The Cuban prison guards called homosexuals "fairies, faggots, queens, or at best, gays."[132]

Not only was Castro's regime homophobic, but it engaged in extrajudicial executions of prisoners, banned books, and prohibited foreign periodicals. In the case of Ernesto "Che" Guevara, he actually burned 3,000 stolen books,[133] which started a long tradition of court-ordered book burnings across Cuba.[134] Such inflammatory behavior mimicked the 1933 book burning campaign at German universities coordinated by the Nazi-backed German Student Union (DSt). In fact, Che Guevara sought to ban jazz and rock-'n'-roll music (the Beatles, for instance), considering these genres "imperialist music."[135] Such atrocities should not be surprising. One exiled Cuban author and journalist, Carlos Alberto

Montaner, was clear in his evaluation of Guevara's depraved behavior, proclaiming that Che manifested "a Robespierre mentality," making "a virtue out of cruelty."[136]

According to Cuban jazz legend Paquito D'Rivera, "Che hated artists." He accused Guevara and the Castro regime of first killing an opponent, and then judged him.[137] Such anti-gay attitudes and violent behavior are indistinguishable from those demonstrated in Nazi Germany.

Most Marxist and socialist theoreticians and writers going back to Engels were noted for their extremely homophobic views. Although the Communist government of Cuba lifted some restrictions on homosexuality since 1979, the police regularly harassed and arrested gays.

In the case of people using drugs, the followers of Marxism traditionally "reject all forms of drug usage," because this would conflict with the "search for enlightenment."[138] Karl Marx expressed the view that drugs, like religion, represent the evils of self-deception. Marx wrote that drugs numb the senses, which corresponds to his famous anti-religion metaphor: "Religion is the opium of the people." Marx made it clear that he hated the drug culture, referring to it as "vile, mindless, escapism, and an 'illusory happiness.'"[139]

Another presumed evil was lending money. Mindful of the Catholic Church's ecclesiastical laws on usury, most theorists of socialism also opposed such practices, condemning money-lending and profiting as unjust and exploitive aspects of capitalism and Jewish dominance.[140] Like most disciples of socialism, Christianity regarded usury as the antithesis of compassion, generosity, and charity. The Catholic Church did not change its canon to remove usury's status as a sin until 1917.[141] Interestingly, Islamic leaders traditionally took a similar stand, prohibiting Muslims from collecting interest from the lending of money.

Marx attributed much of the capitalistic culture of usury to the Jewish culture. Some scholars have contended that Marx's argument was not that Jews merely embraced this form of money-lending capitalism, but rather that they "embodied" it.[142]

Although Marx was of Jewish ancestry who later embraced atheism, he came to see Judaism as a commercial practice, not a theology.[143] He opposed the "bourgeois values" of greed and self-indulgence as much as Christianity, which preached that egotistic practices would sentence people to eternal damnation in Hell. It is no wonder that a number of early socialists derived some of their collectivistic principles from Christian values, especially in their opposition to the profiteering from money-lending, rents, employment, and general exploitation.

Libertarians on the Left Side of the Political Spectrum

To get a clearer picture of the world's political makeup, scholars have scrutinized the forensic history of the political spectrum. Some have concluded that the entire range of authoritarian regimes—Communism, Italian Fascism, and German Socialism, to name a few—should be categorized as reactionary forces and therefore must be seen as envoys of the statist Right or alt-right. In a 2015 essay, Jeff Riggenbach took that position and more. He asserted that the traditional left-right political dichotomy was not meaningless or useless, only that people have allowed themselves to be either confused by "political fraud" or too lazy to dig deep into the red meat of political history.[144]

Proclaiming to be a "Left Libertarian," Riggenbach pored over the original meaning behind the seating arrangement of the 1791 French Legislative Assembly and noticed that those who favored authoritarian and dictatorial rule sat together on the right side of the aisle. So, under this interpretation, all authoritarians must be recognized as right-wingers, meaning that Communists, Nazis, and Fascists must occupy the same rows of pews even if they carry on like contentious, misbehaving siblings. From this revelation, Riggenbach revamped the political contours of America, writing that it is "governed by a single conservative party with two wings: the Republicans and the Democrats," who, in the tradition of Germany's Otto von Bismarck's social statism, simply quarrel over how much to expand or reduce the authoritarian weavings of its welfare canopy. In other words, the two dominant political parties in the United States epitomize the monotony of Tweedledee and Tweedledum.

So, what are the differences between liberals and conservatives? Riggenbach dealt with this conundrum by invoking Rothbard, who wrote in 1965 that liberals inhabit "the party of hope, of radicalism, of liberty, of the Industrial Revolution, of progress, of humanity," while conservatives represent "the party of reaction, the party that longed to restore the hierarchy, statism, theocracy, serfdom, and class exploitation of the old order."[145] This definition compelled Riggenbach to conclude that most political ideologues resided on the statist right because they usually demand obedience or subjugation to authority. But when he mused over who nowadays roosts on the topmost branches of the freethinking left, he proclaimed that "Libertarians are almost the only true leftists left in this country."

To supply evidence for such a claim, Riggenbach cited a 1979 interview with anarcho-communist Murray Bookchin (1921–2006), who freely confessed,

> the American left today as I know it—and believe me, I am very familiar with the American left—is going toward authoritarianism, toward totalitarianism. It's becoming the real right in the United States. We don't have an appreciable American left any more in the United States.[146]

Backtracking, Bookchin conceded that the scattering remnants of the true left represented:

> People who resist authority, who defend the rights of the individual, who try in a period of increasing totalitarianism and centralization to reclaim these rights—this is the true left in the United States. Whether they are anarcho-communists, anarcho-syndicalists, or libertarians who believe in free enterprise, I regard theirs as the real legacy of the left, and I feel much closer, ideologically, to such individuals than I do to the totalitarian liberals and Marxist-Leninists of today.[147]

Calling socialism the "authoritarian version of collectivism," Bookchin readily admitted that the self-identified leftists who sidle up to authoritarians are actually right-wing extremists only masquerading as leftists. To him, the real left-wing radicals are the anti-authoritarian defenders who uphold the virtues of individual liberty, mutual cooperation, and voluntary association.

As mentioned earlier, the best way to differentiate between the two left-wing antagonists is to designate the volitional contingent the "free

Left," and its authoritarian horde as the statist or Fascist Left. The free Left, like the Free French during World War II, comprises anti-authoritarians who felt as though their long-established realm had become occupied by foreign invaders. A logical progression would be to simply remain faithful to the original left-right classification and lump the entire menagerie of authoritarians (Nazis, Fascists, and Communists) into the reactionary ranks of the statist Right.

To put this all into historical context, Riggenbach again examined the seating arrangement of the French Assembly, but this time, 50 years later during the February Revolution (1848–52). Here, he highlighted two noteworthy legislators, Frédéric Bastiat of free-trade and open-market fame, and Pierre-Joseph Proudhon, one of the first to proclaim himself an "anarchist." These two legislators sat next to each other on the left side of the aisle. This fact alone underscores the point that free-market capitalists still considered themselves left-wingers. Proudhon, who anarchism flavored voluntaryist action, argued that he did not support "restrictions or suppressions" imposed by law on various human activities— including ground rent and interest on capital, although he personally opposed the charging of interest and rent.[148] Proudhon held socialist leanings but serenaded voluntaryism, singing of greater dedication to community—which some could nowadays categorize as "libertarian socialism," a philosophy that defends both liberty and communitarianism, but not market-based capitalism.

So, are advocates of socialism and liberty on the left or on the right? Libertarian socialists take an anti-authoritarian and pro-decentralism stance while rejecting the hierarchical, top-down model of socialism. It is complex. They are "skeptical of centralized state intervention as the solution to capitalist exploitation."[149] But they still uphold socialism since they oppose capitalism's hierarchical structure. Under his communitarian principles, Bookchin maintained that his anti-capitalist posture "does not seek to create a power center that will overthrow capitalism; it seeks rather to outbid it, outprice it, or outlast it."[150]

Like most libertarians, those regarded as libertarian socialists base their metaphysics on voluntary human relationships and cooperation. Despite that premise, however, they harbor an anti-capitalist perspective, believing that people with capital have an unfair edge over those without. They engage in the politics of envy, unaware that concentrations of wealth occur in both socialist and free-market capitalist nations, but for different reasons. Nonetheless, a belief in voluntary socioeconomic activity would still loosely fasten them to the old, classical liberalism of the 18th century. With this in mind, Riggenbach took comfort in asserting that authoritarian elements, including those found in socialism and statism, encompassed a wide range of fire-breathing dogmatists on the right. He expounded that "Fascism and socialism are the same thing, but they are both products of Right-wing thinking."[151]

This is reasonable because most collectivists and socialists cluster under one communal umbrella mounted on a rigid, obedience-to-authority pole. This non-volitional socialism was designed to protect only those few who controlled the umbrella; everyone else is left out in the rain. This exclusivity of power and officialdom has always dogged autocratic socialism. Yet such rigid stances would be indicative of a reactionary and right-wing backdrop. It is not by accident that history is littered with socialists who were considered stodgy, conservative, and cozy within the right-wing memes. One such early Utopian socialist, Henri Saint-Simon (1760–1825), exhibited a number of right-wing tendencies. He defended the ancient regime by seeking a more modern, scientific, and powerful national government to run society in the same fashion as had the old monarchy. Many early socialists had embraced rigid economic controls domestically, alongside trade-barrier protectionism against foreign imports.

Only after World War II did a host of scholars and authors seriously begin to recognize the uncanny resemblance of fascism to communism. Ayn Rand had the same epiphany, writing that

> fascism and communism are not two opposites, but two rival gangs fighting over the same territory—both are variants of statism, based on the collectivist principle that man is the rightless slave of the state.[152]

The British journalist, author, and Member of Parliament, Ivor Bulmer-Thomas, who resigned from the Labor Party due to his fear that he would increase the concentration of state power, also recognized the similarities of Nazism and communism. He wrote:

> From the point of view of fundamental human liberties there is little to choose between communism, socialism, and national socialism. They all are examples of the collectivist or totalitarian state ... in its essentials not only is completed socialism the same as communism but it hardly differs from fascism.[153]

So, if fascism and communism are within the same brotherhood of authoritarian socialism, then both have to be positioned on the same side of the political spectrum. If fascism swings to the statist Right, then communism must also veer to the statist Right. So, if the national socialist Hitler was a right-winger, then so were the communists. The only way Mussolini and Hitler can have any meaningful designation as "right-wing" is if Stalin, Lenin, and Mao are inducted also as members of that right-wing fraternity.

After all, those armed with authoritarian behavior and methods have long been classified by left-wing scholars as extremely right-wing. Yet somehow, these same scholars have failed to connect the dots, declining to correctly label so-called left-wing authoritarian regimes as abettors of the right-wing villainy. Why the exceptions? Why would so many academics flout consistency and refuse to remain consistent to affix the right-wing imprint upon political movements and dictators who goose-step with Italian Fascists or German National Socialists? Why should socialists and communists be exempt from their obvious authoritarian legacy? Why should they be deposited on the left side of the political scorecard when they exhibit attributes almost identical to those of right-wing dictators? Only deception or incompetence can explain such myopic ineptness.

Then again, many historians take exception to lump fascists with communists, arguing that an absence of class distinction differentiates the left from the right. But Hitler, too, preached equality, classlessness, and social justice—though only for racially pure Aryans. The communists preached the same, except for certain impure classes.

Even Fidel Castro, during his struggle to topple a dictator, was proclaimed by Ed Sullivan on his television show (CBS, 1959) as "the George Washington of Cuba." Castro had declared that he was "against all kinds of dictators." The left-leaning mainstream press ate it up, despite evidence that Castro and his merry band held allegiance to Marxism. Not long after having seized control of Cuba, Castro finally displayed his dark side, imposed autocratic rule, murdered hundreds of jailed prisoners without trial or jury (often under Che Guevara's supervision), executed thousands of political prisoners, and set up a single-party dictatorship. Yet many on the extreme left still accord praise for both Castro and Guevara in their so-called heroic gallop to impose the order of social equality. Still, Castro couldn't avoid all the maladies of fascism under his nationalist and socialist regime.

The Left-Right Political Spectrum Sham

Such blatant displays of hypocrisy make the left-right political spectrum a sham, a charade designed to misdirect the populace toward a flawed methodology that could instead have helped them to correctly classify different political positions. The ruse was perpetrated by historians, taxonomists, and political scientists, most endowed with socialist credentials, who altered the political axis to conceal the horrifying similarities between Fascist and Soviet authoritarianism. To these dichotomy deceivers, it did not matter whether a communist dictatorship mirrored tyranny, ideology, and terror identical to that of Hitler or Mussolini. What mattered was the political label under which such heinous atrocities were committed. To these charlatans, left-wing authoritarianism was seen as somehow different from right-wing authoritarianism. Left-wing murder was apparently distinct from right-wing murder. Left-wing atrocities could be applauded and cheered because they laid claim to noble-sounding, social-justice sloganeering and causes. In other words, if authoritarian-inspired brutalities were committed by self-avowed leftists, somehow such atrocious behavior was not identified as authoritarian or right-wing. These authoritarians were somehow "good" political activists who murdered, plundered, and committed genocide for equality and social justice. This made little sense, but then again, such nonsense seemed to be coming from so-called experts.

Another notable example of this political charade is the hostility to placing Italian Fascism next to general socialism and communism. Since Italian fascism rests on the same collective and socialist bedrock as Russian Sovietism, they should be regarded as brothers in arms, marching in lockstep on the same side of the left-right fence. After all, Mussolini had been an avowed Marxist, associating with Lenin and Leon Trotsky (1879–1940) in Switzerland in earlier years, but Mussolini's Marxist sympathies never died. He boasted about nationalizing most of Italy's industrial base in 1934. Government ownership of the means of production is the ultimate litmus test for belonging to the ranks of hardcore socialists or communists. There is no greater standard. Mussolini had followed Karl Marx's definition of socialism and communism to the letter, and therefore should share the same political homeland. Incredibly, though, some scholars still located Mussolini on the right. That is a fair political interpretation, but only if Marx, Lenin, and Stalin also bunked with their right-wing bedfellows. Either Mussolini is on the right side of the political divide with Marx or they all congregate on the left. They are inseparable; there is no other logical alternative. Of course, socialist historians will violently disagree, not by the standards of historical accuracy or logic, but because such an association is an embarrassment to their beloved ideology of communalism.

Another point should be made about Mussolini. As most historians agree, Mussolini softened his rhetorical stand once he had decided to seek power through elective processes rather than through street violence. He had ideologically shifted to be more in line with the Social Democrat movement that had originally embraced various versions of Marxism but evolved toward Bernstein's Marxist revisionism. Mussolini had also drifted away from his previous position as belonging to the "Bolshevik-wing of Italian socialism" in an effort to procure broader support among the electorate.[154] This incremental move away from full-fledged Marxism could be seen as moving toward the right. But if this was the case, then Lenin must have also turned right-wing after abandoning War Communism in his retreat from Marxism in 1921. Lenin reinstituted a number of policies that brought back more freedom and capitalism in Soviet Russia, and, as some might call it, he indulged in right-wing extremism. Strangely, few adherents of Marxism labeled Lenin's drift toward capitalism as "right-wing." Still, when considering the entire length of the political spectrum, a slight back-pedaling, or modification, does not change one's overall political designation. Lenin had simply revised his Marxism, like Mussolini, and he took another direction that softened his dedication to classical, and later to orthodox Marxism.

Furthermore, under this line of thinking, one could extrapolate that a right-wing journey would gravitate toward no government (anarchy), while a left-wing journey would navigate toward total government. This possibility calls into question the integrity of the old left-right dichotomy, meaning that the old, circular, horseshoe theory or U-turn spectrum (pitting fascism and communism as polar opposites) is either broken, a complot of historical sabotage, or simply an invention of pure fallacy. Such bending is absurd, at best, or dangerous, at worst. Why? Because if totalitarianism is positioned on the circular ends of both left and right, then "the political spectrum teaches us that opposites are the same and the same are opposites."[155] Such absurdity fogs the mind with uncertainty and confusion; reality becomes nearly impossible to identify or define. And without clarity, how can anyone determine what is true or false?

For instance, Cas Mudde, a Dutch political scientist, defined the "extreme right" as having five key features: nationalism, racism, xenophobia, anti-democracy, and the belief in a strong state. But these exact five traits are also abundant on the extreme left, especially in Marxist states like North Korea, which has been regarded as hardline Stalinist, but now is seen as a far-right, fascist state.[156] Why engage in a convoluted theory that tries to separate political extremists while at the same time touting their congruent ideological proximity? It is much simpler to explain the left-right spectrum as linear—that Italian Fascism's and National Socialism's topography stands a few yards away from Russian Sovietism, their collectivist, but rival brethren. Historically, all of these totalitarian nations were partners in crime, and after their glory was cut short, their apologists still point fingers of blame at their accomplices.

How could almost identical ideologies, armed with equivalent tactics, and former wartime allies, be considered polar opposites? Randolph Churchill, Winston Churchill's son, once remarked that his father was confident that fascism and communism stood side by side on the totalitarian line. When his son brought up the notion that they could be polar opposites, the prime minister of the United Kingdom replied: "Polar opposites—no, polar the same!"[157] Fascism and communism were so close, that Churchill repeatedly warned in 1938 that "German Militarism" would ally with "Bolshevism."[158]

In the case of libertarianism, because it opposes fraud and the initiation of force, when pursuing its hereditary linkage to original liberalism it should be classified as standing on the left side of the political divide. Some might respond that legions of capitalists have taken leading roles in authoritarian productions. True, but these so-called capitalists mostly hobnob with politicians and statists, promote rent-seeking, endogenous policies to obtain state-sanctioned monopolies. As the cronies of statists, they are barely a cut above socialism, and have little interest in letting capital and goods move freely and unrestricted between buyer and seller, for whom, in turn, they have little sympathy. They are fastened to government coffers and machinations, and they downplay the value of the dynamics of competition.

On the other hand, libertarians are pro-market, not pro-business. They oppose the Bismarckian economics of authority, oligarchy, and cartels, which are usually beholden to those politically-motivated capitalists who seek out governmental agencies and promote policies for personal gain. Many in the big business crowd, especially those in the Republican ranks, swear allegiance to a bastardized and manipulated capitalism, while openly opposing free markets. For instance, the Republican president Herbert Hoover introduced many government programs that were later taken up and expanded by Franklin Roosevelt in his New Deal.

The vast majority of libertarians see themselves as neither left nor right, especially those who are perched at the pinnacle of the Nolan Chart, David Nolan's two-dimensional chart depicting his view of the political spectrum. But Riggenbach argued that they have been "misled by a political confidence game." He traced this con game back to the 1930s, when FDR was proclaimed to represent a new type of liberalism, when in fact, he was pushing collectivist ideas akin to those of the proslavery socialists of the American south and of the right-wing authoritarians from Europe. For instance, when Grover A. Whalen traveled to Rome to ask Mussolini for permission to have an Italian pavilion at the 1939 World's Fair, the New York politician found Mussolini initially opposed to the idea.

Mussolini huffed and replied, "What, Italy compete with Wall Street? What, for example, would it accomplish?"

Whalen countered: "The American people would like to know what fascism is."

Mussolini quickly responded: "You want to know what fascism is like? It is like your New Deal!"[159]

So, what is to be made of such a twisted, paradoxical left-right continuum? Everything seems backward. To be more succinct, one could argue that by the early 20th century, the modern left had turned right, and the modern right had turned to the left in the United States. Since America was founded over 200 years ago as a liberal nation, a slew of American sociopolitical movements have evolved apart from traditional political labels. Much of the current right-wing conservatism originated from the left-wing liberalism of the American founders and British Whigs, who were not only anti-government, but anti-statist. In fact, today's conservatives still hold many of the radical liberal values of the American Revolution, to the point that unofficial militias still train in the countryside in preparation to fight Toryesque forces hostile to individual liberty. Here, they foresee the United States government evoking General Gage's 1775 orders to British troops to seize colonists' guns and powder from townships that included Lexington and Concord. And yet the modern, left-wing liberals, who find centralization and big government so appealing, feel obliged to confiscate or ban all privately-owned firearms, making them the new breed of conservative Tories.

These new Tories have a monomaniacal fondness for command structures and find it acceptable to cuddle up to bedeviled authorities to fight bad dominance with good dominance. Those who label themselves as the "progressive Left" often attempt to silence speech by using deception, cries of "hate speech," and strong-arm tactics to trample First Amendment rights. How could this ever be considered left-wing or liberal?

After the upset of Donald Trump's victory in the 2016 US presidential race, *The New York Times* and others began calling for some controls over the "digital virus called fake news" on social media platforms such as Facebook.[160] The airwaves were flooded with calls for crackdowns on and censorship of those alternative websites deemed purveyors of "fake news." Censorship is more than just muzzling those whose ideas are found to be objectionable or offensive; it is the means by which government agencies attempt to halt access to information for self-serving reasons. Since the statist Left has unwavering confidence in the state and little faith in the private sector, they see government controls as the final solution to prevent problems—meaning that government censorship would be considered a viable alternative, especially since 2015, when the Federal Communications Commission (FCC) wrested control over the Internet's infrastructure and carriage under the guise of net neutrality.

In truth, the modern American left has become the aegis of Tory conservatism, opposing property rights and free-market capitalism, while favoring security over liberty and collectivism over individualism. The modern, self-identified leftist is neither left nor liberal, but conservative and authoritarian. President Ronald Reagan once noted this transformation, remarking:

> I think conservatism is really a misnomer just as liberalism is a misnomer for the liberals—if we were back in the days of the Revolution, so-called conservatives today would be the Liberals and the liberals would be the Tories. The basis of conservatism is a desire for less government interference or less centralized authority or more individual freedom and this is a pretty general description also of what libertarianism is.[161]

Nonetheless, modern-day liberalism originated from many diverse, but mostly collectivistic movements. Those included the proslavery Democratic Party, among whose intellectual leaders included the anticapitalist stalwart George Fitzhugh (1806–1881), who declared, "Slavery is a form, and the very best form, of socialism,"[162] and that "It is the duty of society to enslave the weak."[163] Like a true socialist doctrinaire, Fitzhugh argued that "Liberty is an evil which government is intended to correct. This is the sole object of government."[164] These collectivists and authoritarians from the southern United States also contributed to the ideals of welfarism, social justice, and economic controls to stop "wage-slavery," and the ideals of government dependence to prevent economic inequalities. Those ideals are the heart and soul of modern, state-embedded liberalism.

Of course, other ideologies mingled together to forge modern liberalism, mostly from immigrating socialists and proto-national socialists from Europe during the end of the 19th century.

But the point to remember is that although political labels have flopped around, reversed, and now contradicted their original meaning, the philosophies separating the two polar political opposites remain the same. The political battle has always been, regardless of labels, a struggle between freethinking individuals and authoritarian collectivity.

Disparities between Christianity, Socialism, and Marxism

To be clear about Christianity's role in the political realm, there are some important distinctions between Christianity, socialism, and Marxism. The main contrast is their approach for improving mankind's condition and behavior. Christianity has relied mostly upon the power of persuasion and good works to advance humanity, while Marxists and most revolutionary pantheons resort to intimidation and threats of violence. Although most religions promise paradise after death, most collectivists, especially Marxists, preach paradise on Earth, but through means rarely considered heavenly. Nonetheless, Marxists are self-righteous moralists, who enforce rigid creeds just as moralistic as some of the creeds found in America's Christian Right.

In truth, most collectivists assume the role of moral arbiter, in deciding what is and what is not proper and acceptable, especially with regard to minorities with different cultural backgrounds. This is a natural consequence of collectivist norms. Because collectivists stress the priority of group goals, opinions, and rights over those of the individual, they have no aversion to imposing a group-centric archetype of morality. In the long run, collectivists cannot help but drift toward the magisterial position which holds that everything not forbidden becomes obligatory.

Although many socialist practitioners preach atheism, they do it not because they doubt there is a higher authority, but because the act of worshiping a god could eclipse a person's reverence to the state. Collectivists must eliminate everything outside the state—any and all distractions—either eliminating or absorbing labor unions, religious sects, ethnic groups, and businesses, anything that smacks of independence. To collectivists, fascists, communists, national socialists, and a slew of a-dime-a-dozen rigid ideologies, the state is god-like, the highest embodiment of an authority, and nothing must overshadow their all-encompassing Big Brother divinity. As the atheist and Marxist-spired Mussolini declared, "Everything in the State, nothing outside the State, nothing against the State." In actuality, the only thing that can be worshiped at the altar of an authoritarian regime is the almighty state. In practice, communism mimics a religious ethos, where the people are pressured to sacrifice their own will, to envisage fulfillment. Under this dogmatic metaphysics, the individual is seen as simply an empty vessel whose purpose is to genuflect in adoration. To most collectivists, it is the state's mechanics and commonality which make it possible to create virtuous men, and not the efforts of individual self-control, scrupulous attention to ethics, or self-responsibility. Even Albert Einstein remarked about communism's resemblance to a religious cult, writing, "One strength of the Communist system ... is that it has some of the characteristics of a religion and inspires the emotions of a religion."[165]

Although monarchists and collectivists attempt to control the populace in a similar fashion, there are slight differences. Autocratic regimes commonly had little or no ideological substance. Courtiers, ministers, clergy, military, bureaucrats, middlemen and aristocrats huddled at the public trough to gorge themselves at the expense of plebeians, artisans, and the bourgeoisie. These feeders dined on the largesse of the royal chef with little concern over those who actually paid for the royal feast. Monarchs were infamous for displaying clueless and apathetic attitudes towards peasantry, roosting over an inconsistent and jury-rigged system that permitted surrogates to grease the skids of corruption. And if anyone dared question the wisdom of the king, he might find himself sitting inside a Star Chamber, sentenced to hang at the gallows, ordered into exile or imprisoned at the drab Bastille.

Generally, socialists take a different approach. Neither clueless nor apathetic, they are political junkies who are never satisfied in their attempt to impose their vision of equality and perfection. They are talking heads *par excellence*, standoffish to outsiders, politicophiles with a fetish for molesting people, and believe they are on a divine mission to serve as God's atheistic vicar on Earth. They eat sugar-coated politics for breakfast, lunch, and dinner, but are never contently fulfilled. Speaking mostly in fluent politicalese, they hunger to politicalize everything imaginable, but their creed boils down to nothing more than intransigent do-goodism and old-fashioned moral arrogance. In this way, socialists have become just as rigid and conservative as right-wing religious fanatics.

The socialist brood are aesthetes, dashingly clever as the *condottieres* of politics, contemptuous of any limits on their authority. Chocked by their holier-than-thou postures, they harbor political ambitions that induce them to act like all things to all people—until they take command and learn that it is better to be a victimizer than a victim. But if they can find power in even the smallest crevice of society, they will burrow in like a tick and wait to exploit political and social divides.

Socialist partisans use an array of complex social and economic theories in their pursuit of ending poverty and inequality under a touchy-feely utopian society. They want the well-to-do to be generous to the less-well-to-do, but under the auspices of mandatory compliance—that is, forced charity. They imbue the highbrow of political engagement, absorbed in "activist government" to purportedly right all those wrongs found so readily in society. Again, if someone is stupid enough to oppose such allegedly enlightened politics, they may be arrested, put before show trials for counter-revolutionary activities, sent off to the gulag, or shot. Monarchies have done the same, but at not anywhere near the scale and intensity.

To libertarians and classical liberals, it does not matter whether the political uber-elite eschew a comprehensive ideology or embrace a fully formed ideology that purports to deliver miracles that would impress a deity. Such distinctions are irrelevant to a dissenter facing beheading by King Henry VIII's hooded executioner or the firing squad of Stalin's Red Army. It is not the particular ideology or message, or lack thereof, that matters, but the means by which the thing is implemented. One cannot use immoral means to achieve worthy goals. The classical-liberal Mahatma Gandhi (1869–1948) expressed it best in an article addressing socialism: "Impure means result in an impure end. ... One cannot reach truth by untruthfulness."[166]

Socialists have no hesitancy in promoting themselves as guardians of peace, justice, and the downtrodden plebs. Despite their heartfelt tears of compassion, the time comes when strong-arm measures must replace consensual decision-making. Like a sleazy salesman with a bad habit of cheating people, socialists must repackage their failed miracles under false pretenses. When the promised paradise fails to materialize, not only does the state flex its bulging muscles, but false narratives and pretexts are devised to disguise broken commitments. Legend has it that Lenin eluded Soviet Russia's failures when a friend voiced distaste over the growing incidents of Bolshevik atrocities. In a famous metaphor, Lenin replied: "If you want to make an omelet, you must be willing to break a few eggs." To which the responding Bolshevik asked: "Comrade, I see the broken eggs everywhere. But where, oh where, is the omelet?"[167]

Under many religious doctrines, each individual person has the option to seek out enlightenment and change through self-persuasion and self-discovery. Here, there is no promise to orchestrate or foster change. To religions based on mutual consent, change is bottom-up, self-enhanced, and easy to rescind. People are encouraged to be the change they want to see. As Alcoholics Anonymous teaches, people need the willingness and desire to change, before change can occur. In the long run, attitudes and behavior cannot be forced. Like the old adage says, "You can lead a horse to water, but you can't make it drink." But for the impatient, the politicization, weaponization, and institutionalization of society obliges people to change without consent or abrogation, and sometimes without even their knowledge.

So how has imposed change worked out? Has the collectivist agenda created a better, happier society? Not exactly. Despite their fondness for community, collaboration, and cooperation, many socialist and statist regimes, such as North Korea, Red China, and the former Soviet Union, have fallen off the peace wagon. They have grown far more dictatorial and deadly than have the old monarchy and its aristocratic ruling class.

A number of communist regimes could be described as "super-monarchists," in that they engaged in political solutions to intentionally murder their own citizens in mass kill-offs. In *The Blue Book of Freedom*, R.J. Rummel estimated that communist dictators killed "nearly 148 million people from 1917 to 1987," where almost everyone was an unarmed or disarmed non-combatant civilian. This official government policy is now called "democide" (death by government).[168] To give a perspective of the size of these democides, bear in mind that "all domestic and foreign wars during the twentieth century killed in combat around 41 million."[169] Although collectivism has an award-winning record of filling the most body bags, its adherents are still unabashed to let the body count grow higher.

Authoritarian Brothers: Similar in Ideology and Actions

During the 1920s, the statist Left embraced the fascists as one of their own, brothers in arms, lionizing both Hitler and Mussolini for championing a progressive social movement, especially Hitler's welfare society of socialized medicine and a social security program. Even W.E.B. Du Bois, the American sociologist, historian, civil-rights activist, socialist, and Pan-Africanist who in 1961 would join the Communist Party, was inspired by Nazi Germany's march toward collective empowerment and viewed Hitler as a man of the Left.[170]

So, it is easy to see why authoritarian personalities are widely spread among many political movements, from the statist Left to the statist Right. And yet for some strange reason, many psychologists found authoritarian personalities to reside only among right-wing hardliners, as if Stalin's left-wing authoritarianism was without foundation. Apparently, those on the left would not harm a fly. Maybe not a fly, but as for human beings, Stalin, Mao, Pol Pot, and lesser-known communist bosses have each left a slew of killing fields in their wake. Just the number of atrocities committed by goose-stepping Communists tells us that the hallmarks of authoritarian personalities are not exclusive to the statist Right.

Other experts in psychology have argued that most authoritarians share certain attributes, no matter their ideological differences. Hans Jürgen Eysenck (1916–1997), a British psychologist who was a pioneer in behavior therapy, discovered little contrast between authoritarians no matter their place on the political spectrum. He focused his research on the political opinions of those who had identified with the National Socialists of Germany or with Communists. This study was significant because many political scientists after World War II had revised the left-right matrix and parked the Nazis and Communists at opposite poles.

But this placement failed to explain the similarities in their authoritarian personalities. After extensive research, Eysenck released his 1954 book, *Psychology of Politics*, and argued that Fascists and Communists were distinctively linked; they permeated a tough-minded, aggressive behavior based within an authoritarian framework.[171] The champions of communism and nationalistic socialism conducted themselves as ideological brothers, competing for power as though they were members of different organized-crime families. In essence, Communists and National Socialists, like many collectivists, behave like street gangs who compete for authority over territory and power, differing little from the rivalry found between the Bloods and the Crips, in the inner cities of America.

For instance, the early tenets of Italian Fascism arose both in Italy and France, spearheaded by French Marxist theoretician Georges Sorel and the Marxist-inspired revolutionary syndicalists, who sought, through violence and general strikes, an economic system with all of the companies in an industry being owned and managed by their workers. Another factor in Italian Fascism's foment in the 1890s was the crisis in Marxist theory, which was making Marxism archaic, obsolete, and irrelevant—sparked by Marxist revisionist Eduard Bernstein, who had close personal and professional relationships with Karl Marx and Friedrich Engels. One crisis of Marxism revolved around class struggle, which classical Marxists saw as a class-based hierarchy that plagued capitalism. Unfortunately for staunch Marxists, fewer and fewer workers were interested in class struggle. Instead, the populace was drawn to the flags of nationalism, especially with the unification of Italy in 1861 and of Germany in 1871. In an attempt to save Marxism, a number of renowned Marxist intellectuals attempted to replace class struggle with revolutionary nationalism and class cooperation. Some Italian Fascist labor leaders such as Edmondo Rossoni wanted to infuse nationalism with class struggle.[172]

In "The Mystery of Fascism," a former member of the Socialist Party of Great Britain, David Ramsay Steele, explained:

> Fascism began as a revision of Marxism by Marxists, a revision which developed in successive stages, so that these Marxists gradually stopped thinking of themselves as Marxists, and eventually

stopped thinking of themselves as socialists. They never stopped thinking of themselves as anti-liberal revolutionaries.[173]

Actually, they had transformed into radicals who wanted a nationalist-flavored socialism that preferred their cultural, linguistic and historical heritage.

Because of Italian fascism's roots in revolutionary syndicalism (labor unionism) and revised Marxism, Mussolini never thought of himself as a rightist; that label was already reserved for the reactionary forces of the monarchy and the clergy. According to the *Encyclopedia Americana*, Mussolini's *Fasci di Combattimento* (combat groups) declared that they were trying to start a "leftist revolutionary program of action."[174] But like a typical politician, Mussolini wanted to appeal to a wider audience, and by 1922 he had begun to distance himself from rival Marxist and Socialist party competitors.

Nonetheless, Mussolini remained dedicated to his heretical version of Marxism. According to English historian Paul Johnson, "Mussolini was a reluctant fascist because, underneath, he remained a Marxist, albeit a heretical one."[175] Johnson also depicted fascism as "a Marxist heresy, indeed a modification of the Leninist heresy itself."[176]

Further, in "The Political and Social Doctrine of Fascism," Mussolini specified the type of liberalism he opposed, to counter the inroads that socialists had been making in corrupting the meaning of the term. To differentiate the two types of liberalism, Mussolini used the word "individualism" to connote *government-dependent* liberalism rather than the standard *government-averse* liberalism. In a telling sentence in his doctrine to describe fascism, he wrote, "If classical liberalism spells individualism, fascism spells government."[177]

Although Mussolini told the world that fascism was a revolutionary leftist movement, later generations could not accept fascism's left-wing clanship, especially the socialist and Marxist historians who dominated academia. What socialist would pinpoint Italian Fascists as first cousins to a larger socialist family? Naturally, they had to spin the story and make their unwelcome ideological kinfolk appear as far away on the political spectrum as possible. They had plenty of distorted history at their disposal. The post-World War II Soviet Union propaganda machine had cranked out reams of revised history to distance themselves from their former partners in crime, the National Socialists of Germany.

Socialist versus Socialist

There is nothing unusual about socialist revolutionaries' waging war against each other. In concert with their allegiance to conformity, most socialists envision that their own dogmatic version of utopia will alter man's behavior through governmental action. If another group or individual resists the majority's resolution, they will be branded as anti-social or condemned for traitorous motives. Historically, when such conflicts split hairs over ideological nuances, they have provoked global death matches of gladiatorial brutality. Occasionally, a socialist faction will fire potshots at liberty-minded liberals, but they reserve their greatest acrimony for other power-seeking socialists. To the shock troops of total equality, their greatest menaces are like-minded collectives, who are also willing to use any means possible to bring about their own unique, visionary endgame. This was why the most vicious battles of World War II occurred between the two ideologically totalitarian and militarized giants—Nazi Germany and the Soviet Union.

One reason for this kill-your-comrade culture is that collectivists want everyone to accept a particularly detailed and non-negotiable value system. This means that every collectivist must tote the same dogmatic, ideological line—or else. Seeing the world's problems in stark black and white, the socialistic hive mentality takes the approach that you are either part of the swarm, or you are against the swarm. There is no middle ground. In an inescapably collectivist world, individuality has no merit in a Borg-like universe of fixed, demarcated boundaries, as individual thoughts are considered subservient to group thoughts. To collectivists, the uniqueness of self is a weakness; individual choice is a bourgeois plague on mankind.

Collectivists treat the group as a single unit, not as a subset of individual voices. The uniqueness of the individual is viewed as expendable or as a threat—like a single candle eclipsing the brightness of the sun. As a consequence, the consensus-seeking characteristic of groupthink can easily foment policies harmful to minority subgroups and outsiders, and turn, for example, racist. Collectivists put little faith in people or individual identity because they oppose the liberal concepts of individualism and self-determination. Collectivists hate diversity; they desire the conformity of ideology and behavior and seek to assimilate everyone within their own one-world view. They will kill to instill and preserve their only one-way collective culture. They may speak of liberty, but it is a type of liberty reserved just for them in their activities. No one else need apply.

Anti-individualists tend to pursue dogmas of indigestible creeds that are pre-designed and spoon-fed by a hubristic elite. Here is where group-think can eclipse free governance, with a kibbutz-like hierarchy of race, nation, class, gender, and so forth. Within a collective, this conflict of power muzzles diversity and toleration, especially when rationalized conformity is challenged by a minority viewpoint. It is just a matter of time before disunity breaks out into open warfare, launching everything from xenophobia to outright racism. When collective goals collide—ever so slightly—with those of other collectivist groups holding similar fundamental dogma, vindictive, violent clashes are not far behind. Such political rivalry can burst into an eye-gouging, blood-letting, all-out street fight that runs roughshod over the innocent. Their actions are analogous to those of the almost indistinguishable rival street gangs who fight over money, turf, and power.

After the Russian Red Revolution of October 25, 1917, a host of other communistic groups, mainly the Socialist Revolutionary Party (SRs), and the Mensheviks, once led by Leon Trotsky, eventually opposed the Bolsheviks' power grab. Lenin and Trotsky, as supreme overlords, were determined to install a monolithic, one-party regime. But they ran into a problem. The nationwide elections held November 12 in 1917 to fill seats in the Russian Constituent Assembly did not go their way. The Socialist Revolutionaries proved far more popular with voters, receiving 57 percent of ballots cast. The Bolsheviks, who had limited support—mostly in a few large cities—garnered only 25 percent of the vote. Fearing the loss of power, the Bolsheviks, under Lenin's leadership, quickly disbanded the Russian assembly. Despite being unpopular, the Bolsheviks had stolen the election, and got away with it.

After having seized control of the Russian government without an electoral plurality, the Bolsheviks refused to let rival socialist-revolutionary parties share any significant power in the new, communist government. The situation became ugly. Unhappy with the Bolsheviks' refusal to share, the Left Socialists Revolutionaries instigated the Third Russian Revolution of 1918. With between 800 to 2,000 armed revolutionaries, the insurgents attacked the Kremlin with machine-guns and armored cars and bombarded the capital with artillery fire.[178]

Many other Russian cities saw anti-Bolshevik uprisings. After a few days, the *coup d'état* in Moscow failed. Many of the Left Socialist Revolutionaries were arrested, imprisoned, or shot.[179] During this intra-socialist warring, the second of two failed assassination attempts on Vladimir Lenin's life was carried out by a Socialist Revolutionary Party member, Fanya (Fanny) Kaplan. She was upset over the Bolsheviks' banishment of her party and the closing down of the Russian Constituent Assembly. Accusing Lenin of being a "traitor to the Revolution,"[180] she approached him and fired three shots. One of Kaplan's bullets struck Lenin's shoulder; another one slammed into his jaw and neck. Lenin was seriously injured but did not die. Immediately, the Bolsheviks issued a "Red Terror" decree. Within the month, the secret police (Cheka) rounded up some 800 Socialist Revolutionary Party members and other opponents of the Bolsheviks, including many Mensheviks. Most were executed without trial.

After the failed revolution against Lenin's Bolsheviks, many Socialist Revolutionaries and some Menshevik leaders allied with the White Russians or Green Armies to fight the Bolsheviks in the Russian Civil War. Further, many Black Army detachments of anarchists also fought the Bolsheviks, in 1919 bombing the headquarters of the Moscow Committee of the Communist Party.[181] In the rural regions, Green Armies of armed Russian peasants fought both the White Army and Red Army.

The Conflict Legacy of Collectivism and Socialism

Conflict is the well-worn legacy of collectivist, socialist ideology. As Joshua Muravchik wrote in *Heaven on Earth: The Rise and Fall of Socialism*, the history of socialism has been so filled with strife that the epitaph for its headstone should read: "If you built it, they will leave."

Like desolate stretches of a ghost town, socialism's stormy, gloomy outcomes mocked the communal and utopian ideals it proclaimed, causing
people to abandon its faltering prospects, and if the inhabitants cannot
leave, the people become demoralized, cynical, and frustrated.

So, what makes collectivism so violent and blustery? Primarily the
violence revolves around the self-perpetuating obstructions that riddle
centralized systems, blocking any chance for an evolutionary process. If
society is confined by the chains of groupthink and top-to-bottom command structures, frustration and anger have few outlets—leading mostly
to hopeless confrontation with the status quo. When confronted by a
wall of complex, emotional, and politically charged rifts, a powder keg of
resentment can burst into a vicious civil war of backstabbing, mistrust,
and disloyalty, especially when taking political control is the only means
by which to terminate domination by a particular ruling elite.

At the psychological level, societal structures centered on the group
will pressure their members to heed the dictates of a consensus-seeking
process, with little room for deviation or individuality. Peer pressure
intimidates individual group members to recite mantras instead of nurturing out-of-the-box thinking. Among the animal kingdom, humanity
is idiosyncratic in its rejecting of compliance to conformity. Most human beings would rather drift in favorable currents with the option to
swim towards one's own goals, but that can rarely be achieved under a
myopic, collective seawall.

The essential dilemma of collectivism is its bias towards the unanim-
ity of groupthink rather than the discord of difference. As Irving Janis wrote in *Victims of Groupthink*, the pressure applied under groupthink creates an environment where "the members' striving for unanim-
ity overrides their motivation to realistically appraise alternative courses
of action."[182] It becomes a vicious circle of accelerated reassurance: the
more desire for cohesion, the more pressure to conform. To have true
interdependency, which is a goal of horizontal collectivism, both independence and dependency must have equal footing within a consensual
framework. If independence is overcome by conformity, the sharing of
wisdom and knowledge becomes restricted by the status-maintaining collective. This is where independence is sacrificed for the sake of unity,
turning society into a sterile echo chamber—effete, impotent and isolated. This homogeneous bliss could easily descend into group social-

ization and indoctrination in which nobody feels free to question or critically evaluate the official doctrine. By this time, the whole structure could easily have faltered because there is no mechanism to enable evolution to lead to a better solution. Authoritarian socialism is simply a dead-end street.

To collectivists, homogeneity is seen as the only way to promote social harmony, not realizing that diversity does a better job. In its extreme, a rigorous conformity can forge a dictatorial class known as "bureaucratic collectivism," which was predominant in the Soviet Union. Despite claims of harmonious brotherhood, collectivist ideologies usually generate a dissonance which not only is counterproductive but provokes sectarian in-fighting.

So, it is not surprising to see the collectivistic culture of National Socialist German Workers' Party (NSDAP or Nazi) clash with the Communist Party of Germany (KPD) in the 1920s–30s. The two groups developed different socialist visions. Both wanted sole, hegemonic power by way of street violence and revolution, or, if they could gain popularity, by way of the ballot box. Under a collectivistic state, there can be only one common group, only one political party, and just one state-recognized ideology.

Only after Hitler's invasion of his partner—Stalin's Soviet Union— did the Russian propaganda machine go into high gear to reposition their old Nazi allies back to the right-wing of the political spectrum, lambasting their spurned pals as evil capitalists bent on destroying the less fortunate. This tactic was an understandable ploy. Stalin was afraid that Hitler's and Mussolini's explicitly socialist context would tarnish his own future efforts to socialize the world.

Although Stalin was repeatedly accused of belonging to the right-wing Bolshevik faction in Russia (the Right Opposition), he excelled at provoking his own intra-party conflicts. He called Communist Party troublemakers every pejorative name in the book and often denounced critics in his own ranks as right-wing counter-revolutionaries and running dogs of Yankee capitalism. One such Communist Party antagonist was Leon Trotsky, one of the main Marxist leaders involved in the famed 1917 Russian October Revolution, and the founder and first leader of the Red Army. After he was expelled from the party and deported, Trotsky began to publicly refer to Stalin as a "fascist" reactionary. Stalin returned the favor and referred to Trotskyites as "red fascists" who were cooperating with the Nazis.

It is George Orwell who is considered to have introduced the phrase "right-wing socialist" to the political lexicon. Orwell had gone to Spain to fight General Franco during the Spanish Civil War (1936–1939), but instead his unit—the Workers' Party of Marxist Unification (POUM)—fought street battles with the communist-leaning Spanish Republic. In actuality, this brutal communist infighting was a vicious clash between the more radical Trotskyists and the more conservative Stalinists. Orwell portrayed these violent firefights as a struggle between left-wing and right-wing socialist factions. In his book *Homage to Catalonia*, Orwell remarked that the "Communist viewpoint and the Right-wing Socialist viewpoint could everywhere be regarded as identical."[183] In his opinion, "the Communists had gained power and a vast increase of membership partly by appealing to the middle classes against the revolutionaries..."[184]

I remember a course in political science I took at Fullerton Junior College. The conventional wisdom of the day was that communists belonged on the extreme left, while fascists belonged on the opposite side—the extreme right. And yet, after I read this ridiculous claim in the textbook—*Living Issues in Philosophy*—the author also implied that the current "far right is opposed to all forms of collectivism." But wait. How could Hitler and Mussolini be right-wingers when they were notoriously hardcore collectivists? Was the author saying that these socialist dictators were actually individualist anarchists who had no desire to rule over anybody? How could self-avowed collectivists oppose collectivism? After all, Mussolini had come out in favor of anti-individualism and collectivism in his 1928 autobiography, writing, "The citizen in the Fascist State is no longer a selfish individual who has the anti-social right of rebelling against any law of the Collectivity."[185] I found this lack of syllogistic reasoning in a college-level textbook shocking. I knew something about Hitler's National Socialist party at the time. The fascists were anti-capitalistic, anti-classical liberal, and anti-individualistic. This was plainly evident. When Nazi politician Otto Strasser arranged a meeting with Hitler, the Führer admitted his support for socialism, declaring, "I am a Socialist, and a very different kind of Socialist from your rich friend, Count Reventlow...."[186]

To jumble the left-right division a bit more, consider the animosity between fascist regimes before World War II. Mussolini's Italy and Hitler's Germany were not always on the best of terms. In fact, after his first meeting with *der Führer* in 1934, Mussolini referred to Hitler as that "silly little monkey."[187] Their rivalry was in accordance with the collectivistic nature of strict group conformity.

In 1934, Engelbert Dollfuss, the "Austro-fascist" chancellor of Austria and strong admirer of Mussolini, feared Hitler's rise to power in Germany.[188] He established a one-party dictatorship, banning both the Austrian National Socialist Party and the Communist Party. His concentration camps were packed with Nazis, Communists, and Social-Democrats. Imagine, communists and Nazis jailed together by a so-called fascist regime. This makes a complete mockery of the argument that fascism and communism were polar opposites. Dollfuss had allied with Mussolini in order to protect Austria from Nazi Germany's aggression, determined to keep his country independent. During this time, Dollfuss saw little difference between the ideology of Hitler and that of Stalin, convinced that Austro-fascism and Italo-fascism could keep other socialist rivals at bay. Nazi agents assassinated him in 1934.

The assassination of Dollfuss was the first stage in an attempted Nazi coup d'état. Called the "July Putsch," Austrian and German Nazis engaged in an uprising across Austria. Within days, the coup was put down by policing and military units who remained loyal to the government. A few hundred men were killed, up to 223 deaths, with 500 to 600 injured.[189] Dollfuss' death at the hands of the Nazis forced Mussolini to mobilize Italian troops on the Italy-Austria border where he threatened war with Germany should Hitler invade Austria.[190,191] A northern unit of German Nazis invaded Austria's southernmost state of Carinthia but was routed, apparently by either Austrian or Italian military units. Italy's military actions apparently intimidated Hitler to the point where he decided to "end a Nazi putsch in Vienna," which helped to keep Austria independent.[192]

Of course, dictators being no strangers to distorting the truth, will— when it is politically expedient—lavish praise on each other. According to François Furet, despite some ideological differences, Adolf Hitler in many discourses, "expressed his respect, if not admiration, for Stalinist Communism and its leader."[193]   Although Hitler was arguably the most diabolical man in history, he seemed to enjoy lauding a man considered to be his nemesis, as evidenced by his monologues with friends, transcribed and compiled as "Hitler's Table Talk," which includes the following gems: "Stalin must command our unconditional respect. In his own way, he is a hell of a fellow!"[194] Further, he expounded that Stalin was "a beast, but he's a beast on the grand scale."[195] These expressions of admiration can be put into perspective when considering a joke that circulated in Berlin during the war. It went: "What's the difference between Nazi Germany and Soviet Russia? It's colder in Soviet Russia."[196]

Of course, as political contenders, Communists and National Socialists would be bitter enemies to the end—just as the Socialist Revolutionary Party members fought with the Bolsheviks for control of Russia. Politics is built on mutual advantage, not on trust. After a mutual advantage evaporates, the new impulse becomes the survival of the politically fittest: who strikes first with the most brutal force—hence, a political form of Social Darwinism. Subscribers to an ideology founded on seizing absolute power will discover, sooner or later, that everyone is a potential adversary, even those among their own ranks. Hardcore collectivists have, innately, a habit of purging and executing their own members.

Both Hitler and Stalin had horrendous purges within their own beloved echelons. Stalin slaughtered over 700,000 of his dear comrades, including his most loyal and important Old Bolshevik party leaders and military officers during 1936–1938, and he ordered the assassination of Leon Trotsky in 1940.[197] Hitler had his 1934 "Night of the Long Knives" where 85 to several hundred party leaders and opponents, mostly members of the *Sturmabteilung* (SA) brownshirts, were extrajudicially executed and up to one thousand were arrested.

The Nazi and Communist parties did indeed ally together when it was to their mutual advantage. For instance, they came together in 1931 to bring down the Prussian state government of Social Democratic Party of Germany (SPD) via a plebiscite—"the Red Referendum."[198] Obviously, as political rivals, both sides were waiting for an opportunity to take sole control of the state. But another reason for the alliance was the communist hostility toward the ruling Social Democratic Party. In 1929, the Berlin police fired upon communist workers demonstrating on May Day (Berlin's Bloody May).

A number of diehard Marxists have confirmed the mirroring of social totalitarian ideologies. Otto Rühle, a German Left communist and one of the founders of The Internationale, asserted that Bolshevism is a model for Italian Fascism and German National Socialism. In his 1939 article "The Struggle against Fascism Begins with the Struggle against Bolshevism," Rühle wrote that "Fascism is merely a copy of bolshevism," and that it was a "political and administrative terror system." Calling Russia a totalitarian state stained by brown and red fascism, Rühle wrote:

> Russia was the example for fascism. ... Whether party "communists" like it or not, the fact remains that the state order and rule in Russia are indistinguishable from those in Italy and Germany. Essentially, they are alike. One may speak of a red, black, or brown "soviet state," as well as of red, black or brown fascism.[199]

Even the Bolshevik firebrand Trotsky finally came to the realization in 1937 that Stalin's communism and fascism were "symmetrical." He asserted, "Stalinism and fascism, in spite of a deep difference in social foundations, are symmetrical phenomena. In many of their features, they show a deadly similarity."[200]

Obviously, collectivists not only have anger issues, but are determined to seize power, carry out witch hunts and inquisitions, purge the ambitious among their ranks, and torture the opposition, drenching them in their own blood. George Orwell, the author of *Animal Farm* and *Nineteen Eighty-Four*, remarked: "that collectivism is not inherently democratic, but, on the contrary, gives to a tyrannical minority such powers as the Spanish Inquisitors never dreamt of."[201]

Over in America, the adherents of collectivism echoed the anti-capitalism and anti-Semitism of the National Socialist German Workers' Party. One of the most egregious examples was Father Charles Coughlin (1891–1979), a staunch but brief supporter of President Franklin Roosevelt and his New Deal proposals. A Roman Catholic priest, Coughlin became a pioneer in radio broadcasting in the 1930s, using his weekly program to reach a mass audience of up to thirty million listeners. He told those listeners that it was "Roosevelt or ruin," and that "the New Deal is Christ's Deal." After turning against President Roosevelt for supporting capitalistic monetary policies, Coughlin attacked the "money changers" of Wall Street, proclaiming in 1935, "I have dedicated my life to fight against the heinous rottenness of modern capitalism because it robs the laborer of this world's goods."[202] It was Coughlin's belief that capitalism was a Jewish plot to enslave the people. His monetary reforms included the nationalization of the Federal Reserve System, most major industries, and the railroads.

A champion of the poor and the rights of laborers, Coughlin published a nationally circulated magazine called *Social Justice*, and set up the National Union of Social Justice, which was a nationalistic workers' rights organization. By the late 1930s, Coughlin's broadcast increasingly centered on anti-Semitic themes. He warned about "Jewish conspirators" and displayed sympathy for the fascist policies of Hitler and Mussolini.[203] For a time, Coughlin was considered a "hero of Nazi Germany," according to a *New York Times* foreign correspondent assigned to Germany. One author referred to his broadcasts as "a variation of the Fascist agenda applied to American culture."[204]

What Coughlin's confusing ideology illustrates is that such disunity among collectivists lends credence to the idea that collectivism, instead of bringing people together, is prone to tear them apart, usually fomenting conflict, ultra-nationalism, and war. Despite their call for humanitarian and social causes, they instead clash and cannibalize their own comrades, while the innocent are caught in their blood-drenched wake. A few examples vividly illustrate this communist-versus-communist carnage. In the 1979 Sino-Vietnamese War, the People's Republic of China invaded the Socialist Republic of Vietnam. The casualties on both sides are disputed, but the Vietnamese government reported that China suffered 62,500 total casualties while China reported that Vietnam suffered a loss of 127,000 combatants.

In 1978 the Socialist Republic of Vietnam's launched a full-scale invasion and occupation of communist Cambodia with estimated casualties of 25,000–50,000 Cambodians killed and 45,000–55,000 Vietnamese killed or wounded. Then there was Red China and the Soviet Union's border skirmishes against each other in the 1969 Sino-Soviet border conflict. Not many casualties were reported, but 814,000 Chinese troops faced 658,000 Russian troops. In Africa, communist-backed Somalia invaded communist Ethiopia in 1977. Then there was the 1991 civil war between two different communist parties in Ethiopia in which Marxist-Maoist Ethiopian People's Revolutionary Democratic Front rebels militarily battled and forced out the communist People's Democratic Republic of Ethiopia. Of course, who can forget the three revolutionary socialist parties—the Bolsheviks, and Mensheviks, Socialist Revolutionaries—that violently attacked each other in a struggle to control Russia in 1918.

The Bolsheviks won the war and proceeded to arrest, imprison, exile, or execute any other communist or socialist movement members who refused to obey. It was a brutal bloodbath of terror to eliminate all independent communist-socialist opposition. This was not an environment conducive to joining hands and singing "Kumbaya."

As for the political spectrum, all of this might seem a bit confusing. What it really means is that these political labels no longer match their original descriptions. The left-right axis has become antiquated because so many doctrinaires have been trying to obfuscate the true original meaning of political identifications, resolute in concealing the ugliness of manifesting their dogmatic ideology. Nonetheless, one could make the case that political dichotomies are relative to each individual's point of view. In this sense, it all depends on where a person seems to be positioned on the left-right axis depends entirely on where his observer is standing. It is all about "relativity," as Einstein would explain.

Therefore, to Marxists, everyone stands on the far right, including almost everybody from President Obama to Senator Bernie Sanders, whereas, to someone on the extreme right, wherever that is, everyone appears to be corralled within the far-left stockade. To this extent, it appears that political relativity is far more dependent on subjectivism, one's corresponding positions, and a heavy dose of myth-making than on ideological stance.

The Nolan Chart

To cut through this confusing hodgepodge, libertarians redesigned the political spectrum to better parallel reality. They had an urgent need. After their break with conservatives at the 1969 Young Americans for Freedom (YAF) convention, libertarians soon discovered their classical liberal roots and wanted little to do with conservatives. But they had a problem. For years, many libertarians had upheld Frank Meyer's concept of a conservative-libertarian fusionism, whereby libertarians were seen as part of the traditional and social conservative movement. This coalition was cobbled together in the 1950s to combat the threat from Soviet and Chinese Communism. Some refer to this marriage of convenience as "libertarian conservatism."

To combat this perception, a number of libertarians created a bi-dimensional chart to depict where libertarians belonged in political cartography. The first writers to dispel the notion that libertarians belonged on the right were Maurice Bryson and William McDill, who published their work in the *Rampart Journal of Individualist Thought* in 1968, entitled, "The Political Spectrum: A Bi-Dimensional Approach." The most famous political diagram, however, came from the main founder of the United States Libertarian Party, David Nolan. Known as the Nolan Chart, it made its debut in 1971, being presented in Society for Individual Liberty's monthly magazine, *The Individualist*.[205]

Yet author Steve Mariotti contended that the first insight behind the Nolan Chart had actually emerged after Carl Oglesby's (1935–2011) famous "Let Us Shape the Future" speech as the president of the left-wing Students for a Democratic Society (SDS). In an article for the *Huffington Post*, Mariotti recalled November 27, 1965, as that breakthrough day when Oglesby shattered the one-dimensional, left-right dichotomy before a crowd of 35,000 Vietnam War protestors in Washington, D.C. According to Mariotti, "Carl used the word 'coordinates' to describe issues on which he believed the left and the right shared common ground."[206]

It wasn't long before Mariotti realized the significance of Oglesby's speech. He could see that the traditional political spectrum was out of whack, riddled with inescapable problems. Mariotti wrote,

> Carl was trying to explain in his speech that plotting our political ideologies in this limited way had created a false left-right dichotomy that made Democratic and Republican viewpoints seem hopelessly at odds.[207]

Oglesby was not your typical SDS leader of the far-left. Although regarded as an early inspiration to the New Left, he held many classical liberal convictions. Because Oglesby had been heavily influenced by libertarian economist Murray Rothbard, he had rejected the "socialist radical, the corporatist conservative, and the welfare-state."[208] In fact, Tom Hayden dubbed him a "radical individualist" in the philosophical heritage of Henry David Thoreau. Supporting decentralism and many classical liberal ideals, Oglesby dismissed socialism as "a way to bury social problems under a federal bureaucracy." He even challenged his friends on the left to embrace "American democratic populism" and "the American libertarian right."[209] He considered the Old Right and the New Left to be morally and politically connected.[210]

Mariotti had drawn a crude cube of three dimensions, based on Oglesby's insights, and presented it to David Nolan and Murray Rothbard in 1972. However, the "Mariotti Chart" cube was deemed too complicated to summarize in a few sentences. Nolan offered Mariotti credit for the chart, but Mariotti declined, saying that Nolan "had done the work to develop the chart further and had had the courage to incorporate the Libertarian Party." In addition to Oglesby and Nolan, Mariotti attributed a number of others with having helped develop the chart, including Murray Rothbard, Ayn Rand, and F.A. Hayek.

As a tool for assessing political views, the Nolan Chart is important because it helps diverse people to clearly identify the different shades of their political views, and to find common ground. Libertarians stand at the top of the diamond-shaped diagram because they embrace total economic liberty and total personal liberty, which led them to understand that radical libertarians appear neither left nor right. Conversely, at the bottom of the diagram, the totalitarians, if they reject any iota of personal or economic liberty, also appear to get neither a left nor right rating. In this sense, as dictatorships oppose every possible variety of liberty, their statist Left or statist Right designation come into total uniformity—meaning that there is almost no difference between communist and fascist dictatorships; they are cut from the same authoritarian cloth.

The Nolan Chart was the beginning of an era that began to untangle the political spectrum and give back some of its respectability.

Notes

[1] Quote from John Wayne in *Family Weekly*, Mar. 12, 1972.

[2] Dennis McCafferty, "American Icon series: Clint Eastwood," *USA Weekend*, Jan. 25, 2004.

[3] Karl Hess, "The Death of Politics," *Playboy*, Mar. 1969. https://mises.org/library/death-politics.

[4] Hyrum Lewis, "It's Time to Retire the Political Spectrum," *Quillette*, May 3, 2017. https://quillette.com/2017/05/03/time-retire-political-spectrum/.

[5] Jonathan David Gross, *Byron: The Erotic Liberal* (Lanham: Rowman & Littlefield Publishers, Inc., 2001), p. 5.

[6] Ludwig von Mises, *Liberalism: In the Classical Tradition*, (Ludwig von Mises Institute, 2002), p. 3, first published in 1927.

[7] Joseph Schumpeter, *History of Economic Analysis*, ed. Elisabeth Boody Schumpeter (Routledge, 1954), p. 372. This book was published posthumously.

[8] Ayn Rand, "Man's Rights" in *Capitalism: The Unknown Ideal* (New York, NY: Signet Book from New American Library, 1964), p. 94.

[9] Isaiah Berlin, *Two Concepts of Liberty: An Inaugural Lecture Delivered Before the University of Oxford on October 31, 1958* (Clarendon Press, 1959), p. 7.

[10] Frederick Douglass, speech at the New England Woman Suffrage Association, (May 24, 1886). Nicholas Buccola, ed., *The Essential Douglass: Selected Writings & Speeches* (Hackett Publishing Company, 2016), p. 307.

[11] Ayn Rand, "Man's Rights" in *Capitalism: The Unknown Ideal* (New York, NY: Signet Book from New American Library, 1964), p. 96.

[12] Hitler's interview with Richard Breiting, 1931, published in Calic, *Secret Conversations with Hitler*, chapter "First Interview with Hitler, 4 May 1931," pp. 31–33. Also published under the title *Unmasked: Two Confidential Interviews with Hitler in 1931* (Chatto & Windus, 1971).

[13] The National Socialist Program or Nazi 25-Point Program: Adolf Hitler proclaimed his party's program on Feb. 24, 1920, in Munich, Germany. Lane and Rupp, *Nazi Ideology Before 1933*, p. 43.

[14] Virginia Writers' Program, *Virginia: A Guide to the Old Dominion* (Richmond, VA: Virginia State Library, 1992), p. 78.

[15] Charles T. Sprading, *Liberty and the Great Libertarians: An Anthology of Liberty, a Handbook of Freedom* (Los Angeles, CA: The Golden Press, 1913), p. 13.

[16] F.A. Hayek, *Individualism and Economic Order* (The University of Chicago Press, 1958), p. 16, first published 1948. Originally comes from the 1945 essay "Individualism: True and False."

[17] I coined the term "free Left." As far as I know, I am the first to have coined this term and put it into a context of the "free Left" versus the "statist Left."

[18] John Adams, *A Defence of the Constitutions of Government of the United States of America*, vol. 3 (London, UK, 1788), p. 291.

[19] The French concept of *laissez-faire*—"Let (people) do (as they choose)"—was co-introduced by Benjamin Franklin and George Whatley in *Principles of Trade*, reprinted in *Works of Benjamin Franklin*, vol. 2 (Boston, MA: Hilliard Gray, 1882), p. 401. Franklin presented the French maxim: *pas trop gouverner* ("not to govern too much").

[20] "The new political divide," *The Economist*, July 30, 2016. https://economist.com/leaders/2016/07/30/the-new-political-divide/.

[21] Jason Cowley, "Tony Blair's unfinished business," *New Statesman America*, Nov. 24, 2016. http://www.newstatesman.com/politics/uk/2016/11/tony-blair-s-unfinished-business/.

[22] Alexander Hamilton not only advocated that the US president should serve a life term, but that all state governors should be appointed by the president. He wanted to revert to a monarchy.

[23] Letter to Francis W. Gilmer, June 27, 1816; Paul Leicester Ford, *The Writings of Thomas Jefferson, 1816–1826*, vol. X (New York, NY: G.P. Putnam's Sons), p. 32.

[24] Gordon S. Wood, *Empire of Liberty: A History of the Early Republic, 1789–1815* (Oxford University Press, 2010), p. 293.

[25] Jeremy D. Bailey, *Thomas Jefferson and Executive Power* (Twenty-First Century Books, 2007), p. 216.

[26] John Locke, *Second Treatise of Government*, Ch. V, sec. 27, published anonymously in 1689 by Awnsham Churchill.

[27] Friedman's Introduction to "I, Pencil" essay reprint in 1998. Originally published in the Dec. 1958 issue of *The Freeman*.

[28] Russ Roberts, "An Interview with Milton Friedman," *EconTalk*, Sept. 4, 2006, sponsored by Library of Economics and Liberty. https://www.econlib.org/library/Columns/y2006/Friedmantranscript.html.

[29] Some of the higher life expectancy rates were due to lower infant mortality rates.

[30] Mabel C. Buer, *Health, Wealth and Population in the Early Days of the Industrial Revolution* (London, UK: George Routledge & Sons, 1926), p. 30.

[31] David Boaz, "Hitler, Mussolini, Roosevelt: What FDR had in common with the other charismatic collectivists of the 30s," *Reason* magazine, Oct. 2007. http://reason.com/archives/2007/09/28/hitler-mussolini-roosevelt.

[32] Paul Jacob, "Progressives' Progress," Common Sense with Paul Jacob, which is a short radio commentary feature syndicated by the Citizens In Charge Foundation, posted July 24, 2013. http://thisiscommonsense.com/2013/07/24/progressives-progress/.

[33] Rummel, *The Blue Book of Freedom*, p. 75.

[34] Christopher Taylor, "Anti-Founder," *Word Around the Net*, Jan. 7, 2011.

[35] David R. Henderson, "Adam Smith's Economic Case Against Imperialism," *Antiwar.com*, Nov. 28, 2005. http://www.antiwar.com/henderson/?articleid=8159.

[36] Murray Rothbard, "Mercantilism: A Lesson for Our Times?" *Mises Daily*, May 12, 2010. Originally published in the Nov. 1963 issue of *The Freeman*. https://mises.org/library/mercantilism-lesson-our-times/.

[37] Reimann, *The Vampire Economy*, p. 16. First published in 1939.

[38] Micheline Maynard, "Michigan to Tesla Motors: You're Not Welcome," *Forbes*, Oct. 21, 2014. https://forbes.com/sites/michelinemaynard/2014/10/21/michigan-to-tesla-motors-youre-not-welcome/.

[39] Greg Gardner, "Michigan weighs whether to bar Tesla," *USA Today*, Oct. 19, 2014. https://usatoday.com/story/money/cars/2014/10/19/michigan-tesla/17544663/.

[40] Bill Frezza, "Exactly What Is Crony Capitalism, Anyway?" *Real Clear Markets*, Dec. 21, 2011. https://www.realclearmarkets.com/articles/2011/12/12/exactly_what_is_crony_capitalism_anyway_99412.html.

[41] William Gillis, "The Freed Market," in *Markets Not Capitalism: Individualist Anarchism Against Bosses, Inequality, Corporate Power, and Structural Poverty*, ed. Gary Chartier & Charles W. Johnson (Brooklyn, NY: Minor Compositions/Autonomedia, 2011), pp. 19–20.

[42] Kevin A. Carson, *Studies in Mutualist Political Economy* (BookSurge Publishing, 2007), p. 142.

[43] Kevin A. Carson, "Carson's Rejoinders," *Journal of Libertarian Studies*, Vol. 20, No. 1 (Winter 2006): 97–136, pp. 116–117.

[44] David S. D'Amato, "The Falsehoods and Truths About Libertarianism," *The American Spectator*, Mar. 22, 2018. https://spectator.org/the-falsehoods-and-truths-about-libertarianism/.

[45] Jan Winiecki, *Resistance to Change in the Soviet Economic System: A Property Right Approach* (New York, NY: Routledge, 2011), p. 57.

[46] Paul Krugman, "Financial Reform 101," *New York Times*, Apr. 1, 2010. https://www.nytimes.com/2010/04/02/opinion/02krugman.html.

[47] Robert Borosage, "Outrage: Some Banks Are Too Big to Prosecute: Attorney General Eric Holder admits that the biggest banks are not just too big to fail, but above the law," *AlterNet*, Mar. 7, 2013. https://www.alternet.org/2013/03/outrage-some-banks-are-too-big-prosecute/.

[48] Companies do pay an assortment of local and federal taxes if revenues provide net income, but the cost of taxes is often passed onto consumers.

[49] Bill Frezza, "Exactly What Is Crony Capitalism, Anyway?" *Real Clear Markets*, Dec. 21, 2011.

[50] John Rossomando, "Obama attacks banks while raking in Wall Street dough," *The Daily Caller*, Oct. 10, 2011. https://dailycaller.com/2011/10/10/obama-attacks-banks-while-raking-in-wall-street-dough/.

[51] Amy Sherman, "American Future Fund says Wall Street 'supports President Obama' and funds him like in 2008," *Tampa Bay Times/Miami Herald PolitiFact*, May 24, 2012. https://politifact.com/florida/statements/2012/may/24/american-future-fund/american-future-fund-wall-street-obama/.

[52] Newton, *The Path to Tyranny*, p. 170.

[53] Jeffrey M. Herbener, "The Vampire Economy: Italy, Germany, and the US," *Mises Daily*, Oct. 13, 2005. http://mises.org/daily/1935.

[54] Toniolo, *The Oxford Handbook of the Italian Economy Since Unification*, p. 59; Mussolini's speech on May 26, 1934.

[55] Carl Schmidt, *The Corporate State in Action* (London, UK: Victor Gollancz LTD., 1939), pp. 153–176.

[56] Knight, *Mussolini and Fascism*, p. 65.

[57] Ezra Klein, "Where are the pro-market Republicans?" *Washington Post*, Sept. 21, 2012. https://www.washingtonpost.com/news/wonk/wp/2012/09/21/where-are-the-pro-market-republicans/.

[58] Ibid.

[59] Ralph Nader, *Unstoppable: The Emerging Left-Right Alliance to Dismantle the Corporate State* (New York, NY: Nation Books, 2014), p. 24.

[60] David Asman, "Book Review: 'Unstoppable' by Ralph Nader" *Wall Street Journal*, July 17, 2014. https://www.wsj.com/articles/book-review-unstoppable-by-ralph-nader-1405638700.

[61] "ALL ANTI-TRUST LAWS Are Strongly Opposed by Labor Leader Gompers," *Los Angeles Herald*, Oct. 11, 1899.

[62] Thomas DiLorenzo, Cato Handbook for Congress, "Antitrust," 105th Congress, #39, p. 402.

[63] Burton W. Folsom Jr., *Entrepreneurs vs. the State* (Washington D.C.: Regnery Pub., 1989).

[64] Gary Galles, "100 Years of Myths about Standard Oil," *Mises Daily*, May 13, 2011. https://mises.org/library/100-years-myths-about-standard-oil. Many of these figures come for D.T. Armentano, *The Myths of Antitrust: Economic Theory and Legal Cases* (New Rochelle, NY: Arlington House, 1972).

[65] Leslie D. Manns, "Dominance in the Oil Industry: Standard Oil from 1865 to 1911," chap. 2 in *Market Dominance: How Firms Gain, Hold, or Lose It and the Impact on Economic Performance*, ed. David Ira Rosenbaum (Westport, CT: Praeger Publishers, 1998), p. 33.

[66] William W. Lewis, *The Power of Productivity: Wealth, Poverty, and Threat to Global Stability* (University of Chicago Press, 2004), p. 289.

[67] Timothy P. Carney, "Once again, Ron Paul gets the lowest GOP score from the US Chamber of Commerce," *The Washington Examiner*, Apr. 27, 2010. https://www.washingtonexaminer.com/once-again-ron-paul-gets-the-lowest-gop-score-from-the-us-chamber-of-commerce/.

[68] Murray N. Rothbard, *A History of Money and Banking in the United States: The Colonial Era to World War II* (Ludwig von Mises Institute, 2002), p. 69.

[69] Thomas J. DiLorenzo, "The Founding Father of Crony Capitalism," *Mises Daily*, Oct. 21, 2008. https://mises.org/library/founding-father-crony-capitalism.

[70] Thomas Jefferson, *Notes on the State of Virginia*, Query XVII, (published in Paris in 1785).

[71] Thomas Jefferson's letter to Isaac H. Tiffany in 1819.

[72] The current term is called the Non-Aggression Principle (NAP) or the Zero-Aggression Principle (ZAP).

[73] James Madison, *The Federalist Papers*, No. 51, "The Structure of the Government

Must Furnish the Proper Checks and Balances Between the Different Departments," *Independent Journal*, Feb. 6, 1788.

[74] Peter Leeson, *The Invisible Hook: The Hidden Economics of Pirates* (Princeton University Press, 2009), p. 28.

[75] Sylvia Neely, *A Concise History of the French Revolution* (Lanham, MD: Rowman & Littlefield Publishers, 2008), p. 11.

[76] Christian Morrisson, Wayne Snyder, "The income inequality of France in historical perspective," *European Review of Economic History*, 4, 59–83, Cambridge University Press, 2000, p. 64.

[77] Sylvia Neely, *A Concise History of the French Revolution* (Lanham, MD: Rowman & Littlefield Publishers, 2008), p. 10.

[78] Doyle, *The Oxford History of the French Revolution*, p. 113.

[79] Andrew Knapp and Vincent Wright, *The Government and Politics of France*, 5th ed. (Routledge, 2006), p. 3.

[80] The Editors, "What is Left? What is Right? Does it Matter?" *The American Conservative*, Aug. 28, 2006. Quote from Fred Siegel as one of the commentators. https://www.theamericanconservative.com/articles/what-is-left-what-is-right/.

[81] *Political and Economic Spectrums: Twenty-one Wikipedia Articles*, posted Feb. 1, 2012, p. 4. http://www.BahaiStudies.net/asma/political_and_economic_spectrums.pdf.

[82] Hannah Malcolm, "Was the Reign of Terror Totalitarian? A Study of Hannah Arendt and J.L. Talmon," Appalachian State University, Proceedings of The National Conference On Undergraduate Research (NCUR) 2014 University of Kentucky, Lexington, KY, Apr. 3–5, 2014.

[83] Vivien A. Schmidt, *Democratizing France: The Political and Administrative History of Decentralization* (Cambridge University Press, 2007), p. 10.

[84] Pipes, *Russia Under the Bolshevik Regime*, p. 262.

[85] Ibid., p. 262.

[86] Hermann Rauschning, *Hitler Speaks* (London, UK: Thornton Butterworth, 1939), p. 230.

[87] David P. Jordan, *The Revolutionary Career of Maximilien Robespierre* (University of Chicago Press, 1989), p. 2.

[88] Michael A. Ledeen, introduction to *Fascism: An Informal Introduction to Its Theory and Practice*, by Renzo de Felice (Routledge, 2017), p. 15.

[89] Ibid., p. 16.

[90] Daniel B. Klein, "Lost Language, Lost Liberalism: Introduction to 4L," Adam Smith Institute. http://www.lostlanguage.org/introduction/.

[91] Andrew Sartori, *Liberalism in Empire: An Alternative History* (University of California Press, 2014), p. 95.

[92] Doyle, *The Oxford History of the French Revolution*, p. 113. Also see Andrew Knapp and Vincent Wright, *The Government and Politics of France*, 5th ed. (Routledge, 2006), p. 422.

[93] Gregor, *The Faces of Janus*, p. 71.

[94]David Renton, *Fascism: Theory and Practice* (London, UK: Pluto Press, 1999), p. 20.

[95]Adolf Hitler "Why We Are Anti-Semites," Aug. 15, 1920 speech in Munich at the Hofbräuhaus. Speech is also known as "Why Are We Anti-Semites?" Translated from *Vierteljahrshefte für Zeitgeschichte*, 16. Jahrg., 4. H. (Oct. 1968), pp. 390–420. Edited by Carolyn Yeager.

[96]Gregory Fremont-Barnes, *Encyclopedia of the Age of Political Revolutions and New Ideologies, 1760–1815* (Greenwood Press, 2007), p. 190.

[97]François Furet, "Night of August 4," in *A Critical Dictionary of the French Revolution* (Cambridge, MA: The Belknap Press of Harvard University Press, 1989), p. 112.

[98]Stephen Halbrook, *Gun Control in Nazi-Occupied France: Tyranny and Resistance* (Oakland, CA: Independent Institute, 2018), pp. 2–3.

[99]"The Declaration of the Rights of Man and Citizen of 1793," Article 21–22.

[100]Benjamin Constant, "The Liberty of Ancients Compared with that of Moderns," 1819 essay.

[101]Ibid.

[102]"The Declaration of the Rights of Man and Citizen of 1793," Article 27.

[103]Gary Kates, ed., *The French Revolution: Recent Debates and New Controversies*, 2nd ed. (New York, NY: Routledge, 2006), p. 5.

[104]Ibid.

[105]Dan Sanchez, "How Nationalism and Socialism Arose from the French Revolution," *FEE*, Apr. 12, 2017. https://fee.org/articles/how-nationalism-and-socialism-arose-from-the-french-revolution/.

[106]Mark Levene, "The Vendée – A Paradigm Shift?," chap. 3 in *The Rise of the West and the Coming of Genocide, Volume II: Genocide in the Age of the Nation State* (London/New York: I.B. Tauris, 2005), p. 104.

[107]Marion von Trapp, *The Story of the Trapp Family Singers* (Philadelphia, PA: J.P. Lippincott Company, 1949).

[108]Bret Wallach, *Understanding the Cultural Landscape* (New York, NY: The Guilford Press, 2005), p. 253. The camp was built on the White Sea's Solovetzky islands during the early 1920s. Reports of seeing these welcoming signs came from prisoners during the 1930s.

[109]Watson, *The Lost Literature of Socialism*, p. 11.

[110]George Sand and Gustave Flaubert, *The George Sand—Gustave Flaubert Letters* (Great Britain: Billing and Sons, LTD, 1922), p. 193.

[111]Watson, *The Lost Literature of Socialism*, p. 31.

[112]George Orwell, letter to Malcolm Muggeridge, Dec. 4, 1948. Published in Ian Hunter, *Malcolm Muggeridge: A Life* (Vancouver, Canada: Regent College Publishing, 2003), p. 107.

[113]"The Liberty League: A Campaign Against Bolshevism," *The Times of Wednesday*, letter to the editor, Mar. 6, 1920, signed by him and others.

[114]Arthur Gordon, "Interview with an Immoral," *Reader's Digest* (July 1959). Reprinted in the Kipling Society journal, "Six Hours with Rudyard Kipling," Vol.

XXXIV. No. 162 (June 1967) pp. 5–8. The Interview took place in June 1935. http://www.kiplingjournal.com/textfiles/KJ162.txt.

[115] Alan Woods, "A tribute to Hugo Chávez," *In Defense of Marxism*, Apr. 16, 2013. https://www.marxist.com/a-tribute-to-hugo-chavez.htm.

[116] Payne, *A History of Fascism, 1914–1945*, p. 246. Konrad Heiden in *A History of National Socialism*, p. 17, translated this line as "The good of the state before the good of the individual."

[117] Redman, *Ezra Pound and Italian Fascism*, p. 114. Originally cited from a speech on the 5th anniversary of the Combat Leagues, Mar. 24, 1924.

[118] Benito Mussolini, *Fascism: Doctrine and Institution* (Howard Fertig, Inc., 1968), p. 10. First published in English by Ardita, Rome in 1935. Also published in *International Conciliation*, No. 306, Jan. 1935.

[119] Ludwig von Mises, *Theory and History* (Yale University Press, 1957), p. 61.

[120] Mises, *Human Action*, p. 152.

[121] Denis Mack Smith, *Mussolini: A Biography* (New York, NY: Alfred A. Knopf, Inc., 1982), p. 48.

[122] Ayn Rand, "The Monument Builders," in *The Virtue of Selfishness: A New Concept of Egoism* (New York, NY: A Signet Book from New American Library, 1964), p. 91.

[123] Robert Kelly, "How Communist Is North Korea?" *Real Clear World*, Oct. 19, 2015. https://realclearworld.com/articles/2015/10/19/how_communist_is_north_korea_111509.html.

[124] Forrest Wickman, "Socialist Whores: What did Karl Marx think of prostitutes?" *Slate Magazine*, Nov. 4, 2011. https://slate.com/news-and-politics/2011/11/socialist-whores-what-did-karl-marx-think-of-prostitution.html.

[125] Peter Tatchell, "Gay Rights and Wrongs in Cuba," *Gay and Lesbian Humanist*, Spring 2002.

[126] Igor Kon, *The Sexual Revolution in Russia: From the Age of the Czars to Today*, English Edition (New York, NY: Simon and Schuster, 1995), pp. 52–53.

[127] Donald J. West and Richard Green, eds., *Sociolegal Control of Homosexuality: A Multi-Nation Comparison* (New York, NY: Springer Science+Business Media, 1997), p. 224.

[128] Lourdes Arguelles and B. Ruby Rich, "Homosexuality, Homophobia, and Revolution: Notes toward an Understanding of the Cuban Lesbian and Gay Male Experience," *Signs*, "The Lesbian Issue" (Summer, 1984), Vol. 9, No. 4, The University of Chicago Press, pp. 683–699.

[129] Jose Luis Llovio-Menendez, *Insider: My Hidden Life as a Revolutionary in Cuba* (New York, NY: Bantam Books, 1988), pp. 156–158, 172–174.

[130] Peter Tatchell, "Gay Rights and Wrongs in Cuba," *Gay and Lesbian Humanist*, Spring 2002. Also, in *The Guardian*, "The Defiant One," Friday Review, June 8, 2001.

[131] Reinaldo Arenas, *Before Night Falls: A Memoir* (London, UK: Serpentis Tail, 2001), p. 180.

[132] Ibid.

[133] Allison Aldrich, "Column: Che Guevara: exposing myths about a murderer," *Collegiate Times*, Mar. 11, 2008. http://www.collegiatetimes.com/opinion/column-che-guevara-exposing-myths-about-a-murderer/article_7392ebfe-329b-5736-881e-d37e10ce733f.html.

[134] "Ray Bradbury condemns Cuban book burning," *WND*, June 29, 2005. https://www.wnd.com/2005/06/31082/.

[135] "Killer Chic: Hollywood's Sick Love Affair with Che Guevara," *Reason.TV*. https://www.youtube.com/watch?v=iQcUkd1w_TY.

[136] Interview of Carlos Alberto Montaner, *Freedom Collection*, Mar. 2011. http://www.freedomcollection.org/interviews/carlos_alberto_montaner/?vidid=343.

[137] "Killer Chic: Hollywood's Sick Love Affair with Che Guevara," *Reason.TV*.

[138] Daniel Vigilante, "Drugs, Religion and Marxist Philosophy: The Contradiction Triangle," *Vigilante Citizen*, June 2, 2008.

[139] Ibid.

[140] Louis Crompton, *Homosexuality & Civilization* (First Harvard University Press, 2006), p. 189.

[141] Ibid.

[142] Derek Jonathan Penslar, *Shylock's Children: Economics and Jewish Identity in Modern Europe* (University of California Press, 2001), p. 44.

[143] Frederick M. Schweitzer and Marvin Perry, "Homo Judaicus Economicus: The Jew as Shylock, Parasite, and Plutocrat," chap. 4 in *Anti-Semitism: Myth and Hate from Antiquity to the Present* (New York, NY: Palgrave Macmillan, 2002), p. 156.

[144] Jeff Riggenbach, "Why I Am a Left Libertarian," *Liberty.me*, Aug. 6, 2015. https://jeffriggenbach.liberty.me/why-i-am-a-left-libertarian/. And Center for a Stateless Society, Aug. 8, 2015. https://c4ss.org/content/39598.

[145] Murray Rothbard, "Left, Right, and the Prospects for Liberty," originally appeared in *Left and Right*, Spring 1965, pp. 4–22.

[146] Leslee J. Newman, "Reason Interview: Murray Bookchin: A controversial anarchist talks about government, the Libertarian Party, Ayn Rand, and the evolution of his own ideas," *Reason* magazine, Oct. 1979, pp. 34–39. http://reason.com/archives/1979/10/01/interview-with-murray-bookchin/1.

[147] Ibid.

[148] P.J. Proudhon, *Proudhon's Solution of the Social Problem*, ed. Henry Cohen (Vanguard Press, 1927), p. 94.

[149] Roderick T. Long, "Toward a Libertarian Theory of Class," *Social Philosophy and Policy*, Vol. 15, No. 2, Summer 1998, p. 305.

[150] Murray Bookchin, "Thoughts on Libertarian Municipalism," keynote speech at the conference entitled "The Politics of Social Ecology: Libertarian Municipalism" held in Plainfield, Vermont, US on Aug. 26–29, 1999. The speech has been revised for publication. Originally appeared in *Left Green Perspectives*, No. 41, Jan. 2000.

[151] Jeff Riggenbach, "Why I Am a Left Libertarian," Center for a Stateless Society, *Stigmergy: The C4SS Blog*, Aug. 8, 2015, and at *Liberty.me*, Aug. 6, 2015. https://jeffriggenbach.liberty.me/why-i-am-a-left-libertarian/.

[152] Ayn Rand, *Capitalism: The Unknown Ideal* (New York, NY: Signet Book from the New American Library, 1967), p. 180.

[153] Ivor Bulmer-Thomas, *The Socialist Tragedy* (Macmillan, 1951), p. 241. He is also known as Ivor Thomas.

[154] Pipes, *Russia Under the Bolshevik Regime*, p. 253.

[155] Hyrum Lewis, "It's Time to Retire the Political Spectrum," *Quillette*, May 3, 2017.

[156] Cathy Cockrell, "North Korea's official propaganda promotes idea of racial purity and moral superiority, scholar says," *Berkeley News*, Feb. 19, 2010. https://news.berkeley.edu/2010/02/19/northkorea/.

[157] James C. Humes, *Churchill: The Prophetic Statesman* (Washington D.C.: Regnery Publishing, 2012), p. 137.

[158] Ibid., pp. 137–138.

[159] Whalen, *Mr. New York*, p. 188.

[160] The Editorial Board, "Facebook and the Digital Virus Called Fake News," *New York Times*, Nov. 19, 2016. https://www.nytimes.com/2016/11/20/opinion/sunday/facebook-and-the-digital-virus-called-fake-news.html.

[161] Manuel Klausner, "Inside Ronald Reagan: A Reason Interview," *Reason* magazine, July 1, 1975. https://reason.com/archives/1975/07/01/inside-ronald-reagan.

[162] Fitzhugh, *Sociology for the South*, pp. 27–28.

[163] Fitzhugh, *Cannibals All!*, p. 278.

[164] Fitzhugh, *Sociology for the South*, p. 170.

[165] Albert Einstein, "Atomic War or Peace," chap. 31, part II in *Out Of My Later Years: The Scientist, Philosopher, and Man Portrayed Through His Own Words*, 1950.

[166] Dennis Dalton, ed., *Mahatma Gandhi: Selected Political Writings* (Indianapolis, IN: Hackett Publishing Company, 1996), p. 140.

[167] Actually, Maximilien Robespierre is credited with coining this metaphor in 1790, in his attempt to justify earlier executions during the Reign of Terror, saying: *On ne saurait faire une omelette sans casser des oeufs*, or "One can't expect to make an omelet without breaking eggs."

[168] Rummel, *The Blue Book of Freedom*, p. 99.

[169] Ibid.

[170] Thomas Sowell, "Don't Call Obama a Socialist," *Lewrockwell.com*, June 19, 2012. https://www.lewrockwell.com/2012/06/thomas-sowell/dont-call-obama-a-socialist-2/.

[171] Hans Jürgen Eysenck, "Politics and Personality," chap. 7 in *Sense and Nonsense in Psychology* (Baltimore and London: Penguin Books, 1957). http://www.ditext.com/eysenck/politics.html.

[172] Adler, *Italian Industrialists from Liberalism to Fascism*, p. 311.

[173] David Ramsay Steele, "The Mystery of Fascism," Libertarian Alternative, 2003. Also published in *Liberty*, Vol. 15, No. 11, Nov. 2001.

[174] Drake De Kay, *The Encyclopedia Americana*, 1954, Vol. 11, p. 50.

[175] Johnson, *Modern Times*, p. 101.

[176] Ibid., p. 102.

[177]Benito Mussolini, *Fascism: Doctrine and Institution* (Howard Fertig, Inc., 1968), p. 10. First published in English by Ardita, Rome in 1935.

[178]Leon Trotsky, "THE REVOLT: Report to the Fifth All-Russia Congress of Soviets of Workers', Peasants', Cossacks' and Red Army Men's Deputies," on July 9, 1918.

[179]E.H. Carr, *The Bolshevik Revolution, 1917–1923* (W.W. Norton & Company, 1985). Also found in the 1950 London, UK edition, Vol. 1, p. 168.

[180]David Shub, *Lenin: A Biography* (New York, NY: Penguin Group, 1976), p. 362.

[181]Paul Avrich, *The Russian Anarchists* (Chico, CA: AK Press, 2006), p. 188.

[182]Irving Janis, *Victims of Groupthink: A Psychological Study of Foreign-Policy Decisions and Fiascoes* (Boston, MA: Houghton Mifflin Company, 1972), p. 9.

[183]George Orwell, *Homage to Catalonia* (New York, NY: Harvest Book, Harcourt Brace & Company, 1980), pp. 58–59, first published in 1938. See especially chapter 5.

[184]Ibid., p. 63.

[185]Mussolini, *My Autobiography*, p. 280.

[186]Strasser, *Hitler and I*, p. 106. Adolf Hitler, spoke with Otto Strasser in Berlin, May 21, 1930.

[187]Meeting of Hitler and Mussolini in Venice, Italy on June 13, 1934.

[188]Austria had simply allied with Mussolini's Italy to check the power of Nazi Germany, and was not considered to have a fascist ideology. Opponents of Dollfuss and his party coined the term "Austro-fascist."

[189]Kurt Bauer, *Elementar-Ereignis. Die Österreichischen Nationalsozialisten Und Der Juliputsch 1934* (Vienna: Czernin Verlag, 2003), p. 325.

[190]R.J.B. Bosworth, *Mussolini* (New York, NY: Bloomsbury Academic, 2011), p. 511.

[191]"Civil War Spread over Austria; Italian Army on Alert at Border," *Associated Press*, published in the *Albany Evening News*, July 26, 1934.

[192]Stoker, *Girding for Battle*, p. 181.

[193]Furet, *The Passing of an Illusion*, p. 191.

[194]Adolf Hitler, *Hitler's Table Talk, 1941–1944: Secret Conversations*, ed. H.R. Trevor-Roper (New York, NY: Enigma Books, 2013), p. 443, talks on July 22, 1942.

[195]Ibid., p. xxxvi.

[196]Brian Walden, "A Point of View," *BBC News*, June 13, 2005.

[197]N.G. Okhotin, A.B. Roginsky "Great Terror," Brief Chronology, Memorial, 2007.

[198]Leon Trotsky, "Against National Communism! (Lessons of the 'Red Referendum')," written in exile in Turkey, Aug. 25, 1931. Printed in the "Bulletin of the Opposition," No. 24, Sept. 1931.

[199]Otto Rühle, "The Struggle Against Fascism Begins with the Struggle Against Bolshevism," first appeared in the American Councilist journal *Living Marxism*, Vol. 4, No. 8, 1939. A longer text was published in French as *"Fascisme Brun, Fascisme Rouge"* by Spartacus in 1975 (Série B—No. 63).

[200]Trotsky, *The Revolution Betrayed*, pp. 237–238.

[201] George Orwell, "Review of the Road to Serfdom by F.A. Hayek, etc." *As I Please, 1943–1945: The Collected Essays, Journalism & Letters*, Vol. 30.

[202] Michael Kazin, *The Populist Persuasion: An American History* (New York, NY: Basic Book, 1995), p. 109, speech in 1935.

[203] John Shelton Lawrence and Robert Jewett, *The Myth of the American Superhero* (Wm B. Eerdmans Publishing, 2002), p. 132.

[204] Lawrence DiStasi, ed., *Una Storia Segreta: The Secret History of Italian American Evacuation and Internment During World War II* (Heyday Books, 2001), p. 163.

[205] David Nolan, "Classifying and Analyzing Politico-Economic Systems," *The Individualist*, Jan. 1971.

[206] Steve Mariotti, "Economically Conservative Yet Socially Tolerant? Find Yourself on the Nolan Chart," *Huffington Post, Business*, Oct. 23, 2013. https://www.huffingtonpost.com/steve-mariotti/find-yourself-on-the-nolan-chart_b_4152470.html.

[207] Ibid.

[208] Carl Oglesby and Richard Schaull, "Vietnamese Crucible: An Essay on the Meanings of the Cold War," in *Containment and Change: Two Dissenting Views of American Foreign Policy* (New York, NY: Macmillan, 1967), pp. 157–169.

[209] Ibid.

[210] Daniel McCarthy, "Carl Oglesby Was Right," *The American Conservative*, Feb. 24, 2010. https://web.archive.org/web/20100701073109/http://www.amconmag.com/mccarthy/2010/02/24/carl-oglesby-was-right/.

2. Modern Liberalism's Progressive-Fascist Ideology and the Abridgment of Civil Rights

The New Deal is plainly an attempt to achieve a working socialism and avert a social collapse in America; it is extraordinarily parallel to the successive "policies" and "Plans" of the Russian experiment. Americans shirk the word "socialism," but what else can one call it?

—H.G. Wells[1]

You want to know what fascism is like? It is like your New Deal!

—Benito Mussolini[2]

Fascism is not likely to be identical with the kinds on tap in Germany, Italy and Russia; indeed, it is very apt to come in under the name of anti-Fascism.

—H.L. Mencken[3]

Though it seems contradictory to the contemporary political observer, many modern historians are beginning to acknowledge that Italian fascism was either a revision or a variant of Marxism. And because of recent attempts to restore the original verity to the political spectrum, it has become evident that modern liberals and leftists, consumed by their appetite for statism, have rapidly moved towards a progressive-Fascist ideology, heavily influenced by Marxism. This movement fosters an authoritarian adaptation of Marxist dialectic with Freudian theory, seeking to instill a collective self-victimhood mentality which has unleashed forces of intolerance, hatred, and ends-justify-the-means violence. Some identify this belief system as cultural Marxism, which resembles the propaganda and ideological reification employed by National Socialists during the 1920s–40s.

Authoritarian socialists believe that the predominant approach to seizing political power in the Western world is to destroy the universal tolerance, diversity, and social harmony "glue" that holds the democratic-republics of the Western world together. To accomplish their anti-civil rights goals, they need to undermine Western democratic values, liberal capitalism, and individualism. In this struggle, it is the hard statist Left who are the shock troops at the forefront of this Fascist-Marxist Axis, primed to divide and conquer to assure an authoritarian apotheosis.

These high scorers on the authoritarian-hierarchical scale have steered statist leftism into the realm of neutralizing any opposition, or if that is impossible, destroying what they cannot control. This is where the statist Left entered the progressive Fascist-Marxist zone, mostly under the guise of anti-fascism, diversity, and equality. True to their arrogant and condescending behavior, they insist that their values are superior to the values of others. The only solution is to use the coercive powers of the state to impose their righteousness. If anyone has the audacity to object, they must be shouted down, dehumanized or criminally investigated. Here, the liberal act of free choice is shoved through the back door to accommodate "command socialism," involuntary communalization, and obligatory equality. This species of authoritarian socialism was on plain view when a leader of the socialist Fabian Society in England, George Bernard Shaw, gleefully made a case for compulsory servitude, social justice, and social Darwinism. Shaw, who had praised Hitler, Mussolini, and Stalin, wrote:

> Under Socialism, you would not be allowed to be poor. You would be forcibly fed, clothed, lodged, taught, and employed whether you liked it or not. If it were discovered that you had not character and industry enough to be worth all this trouble, you might possibly be executed in a kindly manner; but whilst you were permitted to live, you would have to live well.[4]

Of course, Marxism and fascism are so closely aligned that most socialists of today shy away from divulging this embarrassing but true political ancestry. Few of them want to discuss Hitler's and Mussolini's roles as the black sheep of the socialist-syndicalist family. The fear is pervasive.

Fearful of the disinfectant effect of sunlight, socialists have denied any relationship with fascism in an attempt to mask their own historical culpability and connection to one of the most despised ideologies known to man. From Georges Sorel's revolutionary syndicalism and myth-making precepts, Louis Auguste Blanqui's elitist and violent "putschism," to Charles Péguy's nationalistic socialism, historical fascism harbored a socioeconomic and metaphysical collectivism that is almost indistinguishable from the thinking of today's modern-statist Left. In reality, the descendant of Russian Sovietism, Italian fascism, and German National Socialism are kissing cousins who wish to keep their incestuous relationship under wraps.

The duality of this Marxist-Fascist genealogy is one of the main conclusions professed by UC Berkeley political scientist A. James Gregor. A leading academic expert on fascism, Gregor not only asserts that "Marxist theory reveals itself as a variant of generic fascism,"[5] but that the Soviet Union was "unmistakenly 'a cousin to the German National Socialism.'"[6]

Many of the features that secured Stalin's nomination to the fascist hall of fame included:

> nationalism, the leadership principle, anti-liberalism, anti-individualism, communitarianism, hierarchical rule, missionary zeal, the employment of violence to assure national purpose, and anti-Semitism.[7]

And because these characteristics of Stalin also mimicked those of Hitler and Mussolini, Gregor concluded that "both fascism and Marxism-Leninism would seem to be political products of right-wing extremism."[8] Whether Marxism and Fascism sit on the right or left side of the political spectrum, they nonetheless parallel each other with only minor discrepancies.

This makes perfect sense from a classical liberal standpoint, since both Marxists and Fascists were brutal in their condemnation of liberalism and capitalism as their primary enemy. Like father, like son. It now appears that modern-day authoritarians, especially those regarding themselves as left-wing cohorts, have devolved into predecessors of a neo-fascist movement of intolerance, dominance, and repression.

These shared aspirations also include a shift towards increased nationalism. During the US election of 2016, self-described "democratic socialist"[9] and FDR New Deal progressive Sen. Bernie Sanders combined his populist appeal with a "tough-talking economic nationalism" in his opposition to international free trade.[10] But economic nationalism was the heart of European fascism. Calling for nationalistic policies to keep jobs in America instead of going overseas, Bernie Sanders echoes the same anti-free trade "autarky" policies advocated by Hitler and Mussolini. Despite the horrific backstory on autarky, many on the statist Left are still enthusiastic over Bernie Sanders' economic nationalism. In 2017 Timothy Egan wrote a *New York Times* opinion piece encouraging "Democrats to grab the economic nationalism argument..., refine it along Bernie Sanders lines, and run with it."[11] Contrary to what is usually thought, nationalism is a type of tribal-collectivism where individual identity is subjugated to a collective group identity, making it a perfect habitat for most species of socialism and fascism.

Despite its overwhelming weaponry in its political arsenal, the statist Left is not the only threat to liberty. There are still elements of statist Right activism and extremism lurking about. However, their threat is less substantial due to their lack of widespread acceptance. Who nowadays publicly supports monarchism and the divine rights of kings? Almost nobody, except in the Middle East. Statist Right adherents are standard-bearers of an antiquated political structure thinly populated by a lingering band of aristocrats, nobility, and clergy. They have had little influence and few victories on the ideological battlefront.

One past example of a traditional right-wing dictator was General Francisco Franco (1892–1975), who backed the Spanish monarchy and the Church. By personal conviction, Franco was not a fascist; he refused to officially join the Spanish fascist party (Falange), and began the "de-fascistization" of his regime by 1942.[12] In fact, a coterie of Falangists plotted to assassinate Franco in 1940, upset over his reluctance to carry out their "national syndicalist revolution."[13]

Franco was an old-fashioned military, religious, and authoritarian dictator who was disinterested in emulating revolutionary and ideological fascism, steering clear of the socialist, syndicalist, anti-monarchical, and almost militant atheism that permeated the national socialists in

Germany and Italy. Furthermore, there was a strong anti-fascist mood among many rightists and Catholic leaders in Franco's regime, who were dismayed by Hitler's invasion of Catholic Poland. Because of these events, Hitler toyed with the idea of conspiring against Franco and replacing him with a pro-Nazi government favorable to the Falangists.[14]

As for the question of how Franco treated the Jews, he defied Hitler and saved up to 60,000 Sephardic Jews from the Holocaust, according to Rabbi Chaim Lipschitz and others.[15] Again, it was revolutionary, atheist, and socialist dictators who have been mostly responsible for genocidal mass murders in the 20th century.

The statist Left's movement towards authoritarianism is so pervasive that they have become the primary threat to individual liberty, liberalism, and a free economy. If a fascist dictatorship ever comes to the United States, it will most likely consist of those who hold progressive and statist Left credentials. In fact, the famously outspoken liberal and civil rights lawyer Alan Dershowitz spoke of this dangerous threat by the hard left in 2018, lamenting:

> My biggest enemies are the hard left. The hard left poses a far greater danger to the American future than the hard right. I'm not worried about a few dozen people with Swastikas who want to replace the Jews, because they're our past. They have no resonance on the university campuses today. But the hard, hard left? Anti-Semitism, anti-Christianity, intolerance for speech, it's the future. These are our leaders... And that's why we have to worry much more about what's going on, on university campuses, than in Charlottesville.[16,17]

This danger is magnified not only because the statist-fascist Left seeks to grow government with reckless abandon, but because of their erroneous conviction that they are polar opposites of National Socialism and Fascism, when in fact they emit a mirror image of socioeconomic and ideological fascism. After decades of living under a misaligned and doctored left-right political spectrum, most collectivists are convinced that they are the antithesis of fascism, while deeming classical liberals as extremists. In a nod to the philosophical kinship of fascism and modern leftist doctrine, Mussolini expressed disdain for liberalism's heavy reliance on the tenets of individualism in his 1935 "Doctrine of Fascism," writing:

> Against individualism, the Fascist conception ... is opposed to classical Liberalism... Liberalism denied the State in the interests of the particular individual; Fascism reaffirms the State as the true reality of the individual.[18]

When authoritarian leftists believe they have little in common with fascist and Nazi ideology, they feel free to engage in the social psychological phenomenon known as "self-licensing." Through this process they bestow upon themselves an ethical certification or subconscious license which can easily increase the probability of making less egalitarian decisions later. This self-licensing effect of purporting to be anti-fascist, although having little historical knowledge of it, can permit a person to embrace authoritarian tendencies that are extremely fascist.

The belief that one cannot be fascist in any shape or form liberates the individual to behave as fascist as possible, granting him or her the illusion of anti-fascist sainthood—as has been witnessed with the wildly violent, Fascist-Marxist organizations like the "Antifa" movement. These hateful gangs of revolutionary socialist and anarcho-statist militants are convinced that they are incapable of ever toting the baggage of fascism and therefore can freely be more violently fascist than the average fascist. Thinking they are free of fascist-socialist contamination, they can easily become what they oppose. The self-licensing effect presents groups like Antifa with the opportunity to see themselves as intrinsically anti-fascist, but who nevertheless engage in the same brownshirt and blackshirt fascism that they so vocally oppose. They foolishly have become "anti-fascist fascists," which also occurred after World War II when many former Italian blackshirts among Mussolini's ranks joined Antifa groups because their ideology was so similar.

In one alarming case at UC Berkley in 2017, jackbooted and black-clad Antifa goons beat up and kicked peaceful protesters, wielding clubs and pepper spray as they carried homemade shields that read "No Hate."[19] Apparently, these neo-Nazis are shockingly unaware of the irony of their message and who they historically represent. They also are oblivious to the fact that the original fascists had blind faith in a totalitarian worldview that sanctifies physical violence as ethically justifiable.

Other examples are plentiful. Around the time of President Trump's inauguration day in Washington, D.C. and during college campuses' anti-free speech travesties, masked rioters shattered store and bank windows, engaged in arson, vandalized buildings, threw Molotov cocktails, attacked and tear-gassed onlookers, and threw bricks at the police. And of course, absurdly, many wore shirts and buttons imprinted with so-called anti-fascist emblems, as if they had something to do with opposing historical fascism. Yet their breaking of windows of banks was reminiscent of the Nazi's paramilitary pogrom called the "Night of Broken Glass" (*Kristallnacht*) in November 1938. Not only that, but Nazi stormtroopers would violently disrupt other political groups, like the conservative German National People's Party (DNVP) in the early 1930s, by throwing "stink bombs and tear gas" at them.[20] Astonishingly, the Antifa shock-troop rioters were behaving like Nazis in order to oppose Nazism, which illustrates their complete ignorance of historical fascism and National Socialism.

This socio-psychological effect provides the fascist-socialist Left with the *faux* moral high ground to justify the initiation of aggression and to impose their monistic ideology upon others. Instead of upholding democratic pluralism, they have decided to violently foist political correctness upon every member of society, often throwing the first-blood punch against any disbeliever. Such politics of superiority and supremacy could easily spread to any human activity, even to compel everyone to buy corporate products, expand the regulatory and taxing power of the state, endorse laws to ban products, block free speech, justify acts of violence, and seek the nationalization of companies. These ruffians have been caught in an orgy of self-righteousness, and have become prisoners to an ideological purity that parallels a fascistic mindset.

Dabbling in a form of social justice praxis, Hitler exemplified a pseudo-righteous attitude in forging what he termed a "socially just state."[21] Under this approach, he planned to spawn a new species of superior men in order to depose God. Hitler explained to one of his confidants that "Man is becoming God—that is the simple fact. Man is God in the making."[22] In a quest to dethrone religion and God, fascist-socialist adherents have argued for the emergence of a "God-man," analogous to a sort of Nietzsche-prescribed *Übermensch*, or "Superman" that would develop into something beyond themselves. That something else beyond God was to be the enthronement of politically ruthless supermen equipped with tremendous state power. To them, if God was truly dead, the state was the only institution capable of rendering a pure utopia under a shiny sun. This is why most ideological dictatorships and "stateophiles" of the 20th century hewed tightly to an atheistic-inclined state that had no use for God or religion, preaching instead a distorted version of morality.

Without the restraints of religious self-discipline, idolizers of the state are free to supersize the machinations of government, aspiring to a role as quintessential lovers of government, while chanting Mussolini's "everything within the state, nothing outside the state" mantra. In doing so, they trigger a political revolution of ideocracy that becomes beholden to totalitarian patronage. Bound to compulsory governance and state theft, the modern left not only takes a pro-initiation of aggression stance for the supposed greater good but has all of the socioeconomic and metaphysical trappings of 1920–40s European socialist movements. Some of the policies supported by the fascists, Nazis, Soviets, and current crop of statist leftists include: high deficit spending (Keynesian economics), confiscatory taxes, government job creation, large public works projects, compulsory union membership, overbearing regulations, extensive welfare, government-run education, collectivist-socialist ethos, nationalization-socialization, atheism, high tariffs, centralization, government supremacy, central planning, social engineering, mandatory participation in social programs (retirement and healthcare), social justice, classlessness, equality (reserved only for certain races or classes), and a collective narcissism that echoed Hitler's decree: "The common good before the individual good."[23]

On the antithetical side, the fascist Left, along with its German and Italian comrades, detested economic liberalism (capitalism), religion, usury and financial capital (often due to their "Jewishness"), the gold standard, free trade, limited government, low taxation, night-watchman government, rule of law, decentralization, state rights, gun rights, self-ownership, free individual choice and individualism. In essence, what this means for American politics is that in socioeconomic and philosophical terms, the leaders of the Democratic Party are far more predisposed to historical fascism than the Republican Party and American conservatism.

The Suppression of Free Speech

In recent years, state-revering leftists have attempted to openly suppress free speech. They have hypocritically shouted down, blocked, or schemed to ban anyone who might spew out what they demonized as "hate speech," mostly at educational institutions, mimicking the thuggish intolerance of the Brownshirts and Blackshirts. One glaring example was the violent protest that prevented the abrasively flamboyant Milo Yiannopoulos, a Jewish gay immigrant, from speaking at UC Berkeley on February 1, 2017. Taking on the sarcasm of a stand-up comedian, Yiannopoulos's outrageous provocateur trope was staged to shock the politically correct crowd. The pushback was ferocious and led to demands for political censorship at the birthplace of the "Free Speech Movement," a sad commentary on the present state of modern liberalism. The incident exposed the true anti-free speech colors of the statist Left. To them, it appears that free speech is only meant for approved speakers, and not for anyone else. In fact, many progressive statists believe that just by allowing someone to speak with an alternative opinion is a form of violence.

This truly fascist mentality has led to other extremes, permitting the statist Left to bully those opposed to or simply neutral to their dogma. Many of them espouse the absolutist fallacy and polarizing phrase, "You're either with us, or against us." But if you are the second group, expect slander and defamation for failing to fall into line. This is what happened to teaching assistant Lindsay Shepherd at Wilfrid Laurier University in 2017. She faced censure from college administrators for showing a video clip of Prof. Jordan Peterson debating Nicholas Matte over the issue of using non-binary gender pronouns. Although Shepherd considered herself a "leftist," the statist Left began to slander her in public, denouncing her as a white, alt-right neo-Nazi. Her crime: She showed the debate to her communications class without first denouncing Prof. Jordan Peterson's views. She forgot to pre-condition her students to a particular point of view. Apparently, it is difficult to indoctrinate students if teachers are allowed to provide neutral-free educational material. Fortunately, Shepherd secretly taped the inquisition and survived.

In the case of Peterson's crime, he came out against "compelled speech" and Canadian laws that dictate which gender pronouns must be uttered around certain minorities. A Canadian clinical psychologist, Peterson's outspoken criticism often sent statist leftists into tailspins, causing them to paint him with every broad-stroke brush pejorative in the book. He has been accused of engaging in so-called "hate speech," and therefore singled out to send a message to other freethinking heretics. Amazingly, not long after Peterson refused to use government-imposed gender-neutral pronouns, he was locked out of his YouTube channel and Gmail, accounts he had maintained for at least 15 years.[24] When he contacted Google about his inability to access his account, they responded: "After review, your account is not eligible to be reinstated due to a violation of our Terms of Service." Although he eventually regained access to his accounts, there was little doubt that he had been targeted for censorship.

Ever since his clash with the Canadian language police and college administrators, Jordan Peterson has been engaged in speaking tours to expose the dangers of collectivism, tribalism, postmodernism and the anti-free speech culture. According to Peterson, postmodernists believe that everyone is oppressed, suffering under a "Hobbesian nightmare" of everyone against everyone else, which sows divisiveness and a war-like culture. Under postmodernism, Peterson describes the movement as an ideological war where:

> You're in a group and I'm in a group and all we can have is a war. Or we can talk but we don't get to talk because you can't talk to a post-modernist because speech is just chatter; so, it's just chatter that supports the people in power. That's how they think and so the whole world is this little armed war of identity group against identity group against identity group. And you shut down people who don't agree with you because why should you let them talk? You don't believe in any of the reasons why you would let someone talk.[25]

In an effort to censor or stifle speech, activists have become completely disdainful of diversity of thought, while at the same time feigning praise for diversity and equality. Sure, they sometimes called for free speech, but only for themselves. Harboring an authoritarian mindset, collectivists hold that they are the only holders of truth—no one else need apply. Anyone with an opposing viewpoint must be silenced because they are not voicing the correct opinion. Moreover, controversial or offensive speech is seen as violence, justifying a violent response. Nazi stormtroopers used the same rationale when confronting their opposition in the streets. With brute force, they stopped any speech they opposed.

It must be remembered that the National Socialist movement was very popular among German college students. In fact, "university students were the first stratum in Germany to back the Nazis."[26] Before Hitler became Chancellor of Germany, Nazi students under the leadership of Baldur von Schirach and his National Socialist German Students' League had "completely taken over student representation in Germany."[27] The young von Schirach saw himself as a radical socialist who stood close to Hitler. When the National Socialist movement began to reach its revolutionary crescendo, he bluntly declared: "A socialist and anti-capitalist attitude is the most salient characteristic of the Young National Socialist Germany."[28] Besides taking over many student unions and fraternities, Nazi students engaged in "provocative actions," the dismissal of unsupportive and Jewish professors, and the "creation of new chairs in subjects like Racial Studies and Military Science."[29] They were even able to get universities to divert their focus from the pursuit of knowledge to political and national agendas.[30] Many teachers who failed to follow along with the Nazis' campaign of political correctness were targeted, named, and finally had to endure public "shaming" by Nazi student organizations.[31]

Not surprisingly, the concept of free speech is waning on college campuses. In a Gallup and John S. and James L. Knight Foundation poll taken in 2018, students were asked what was more important, free speech or diversity and inclusion, only 46 percent of the student chose free speech.[32] In another poll in 2017 by John Villasenor, a Brookings Institution senior fellow and University of California at Los Angeles professor, the question was asked: "A student group opposed to the speaker disrupts the speech by loudly and repeatedly shouting so that the audience cannot hear the speaker. Do you agree or disagree that the student group's actions are acceptable?" The results were chilling. Fifty-one percent of all students agreed. Broken down into groups, 62 percent of Democrats, 39 percent of Republicans, and 45 percent of independents found it acceptable to silence a speaker they deemed offensive.[33]

Many school administrators have displayed similar prejudices against free speech, decreeing policies of policed or censored discourse, maintaining that students are too snowflake-fragile to challenge contrasting or offensive opinions. These public officials have become, like days of old, star-chamber judges who want to arbitrarily decide who can say what on campus, often under a wide range of dubious excuses: diversity, inclusiveness, and political correctness. Nonetheless, this illiberal movement is still just a progressive-fascist stratagem to shut down opponents with every trick and pejorative in the book. One illuminating example of this anti-free speech mindset occurred at California Polytechnic State University (Cal Poly) in San Luis Obispo, California.

In December 2017, a number of flyers were posted at Cal Poly that displayed a photo of Kate Steinle with a few simple words: "She Had Dreams Too." The flyers were posted to protest the lenient verdict given to her murderer. What happened to Steinle? On July 1, 2015, she was killed in San Francisco when she was hit by a bullet from a stolen handgun fired by Jose Ines Garcia Zarate, a seven-time felon illegal immigrant who had been released by the city of San Francisco. On November 30, 2017, Zarate was acquitted of all charges, including the lesser offense of voluntary manslaughter, except for one count of being a felon in possession of a gun. The verdict caused an uproar in the community.

Within days, flyers were put up to acknowledge the unjust jury decision, causing a stir at Cal Poly in San Luis Obispo, Steinle's alma mater. Immediately, a student filed a complaint, writing that those who were "seeking to transform [Steinle's] tragic death into a racist 'dog whistle' to be used against undocumented members" in Cal Poly's community.[34] Associate Vice President Kathleen McMahon called on campus security to investigate the culprits who created and posted the flyers.[35]

Immediately, the matter was sent to the Cal Poly "Bias Incident Response Team" to unmask the perpetrators. Teams of students roamed the streets of San Luis Obispo, knocking on neighborhood doors to glean information about the alleged crime of posting flyers about Steinle. This whole anti-free speech episode is reminiscent of the Gestapo searching for the student members of the White Rose after they had distributed and tacked up anti-fascist flyers at the University of Munich in the 1940s. Of course, their punishment was far worst; they had to face show trials by the Nazi People's Court (*Volksgerichtshof*), and eventually most were executed by guillotine.

Of course, to express one's opinion is not a crime, at least not in the United States. Nor does so-called "hate speech" trump the First Amendment as confirmed by a number of US Supreme Court decisions, including the 1992 *R.A.V. v. City of St. Paul*, the 2011 *Snyder v. Phelps*, and the 2017 *Matal v. Tam* court decisions. The US Supreme Court has repeatedly reaffirmed that there is no "hate speech" exception to the First Amendment. The attempt to criminalize speech thought to be hateful only enables progressive-fascists to muzzle political enemies. They selfishly want to be the only ones with the legal right to speak freely, while banning or censoring those they disagree with using the exact formula that led to a one-party Nazi dictatorship.

The most frightening aspect of Cal Poly's anti-liberal actions was to publicly condemn the flyer's simple and affable message as if it were inflammatory, obscene, or racist. This incident indicates that any printed or spoken words, no matter how benign, are now subject to censorship or criminalization by government officials, who are always searching for excuses to silence opponents. In an environment where academic freedom is—or should be—prized, it seems almost impossible for universities and student organizations to promote "no platform" policies to prevent the airing of diverse views in the public sphere.

Glen Greenwald, the American Pulitzer Prize-winning journalist, editorialized about the absurdity of censorship, penning that anyone "purporting to oppose fascism by allowing the state to ban views it opposes is like purporting to oppose human rights abuses by mandating the torture of all prisoners."[36]

To make matters worse, hundreds of US college campuses have instituted policies to encourage students to spy on their peers and report back to the authorities anyone who is found to have engaged in inappropriate or offensive speech. The University of Arizona has offered students cash for spying on other students, nagging them to follow their responsibilities to be a "social justice advocate."[37] If students discovered deviant action or thought, they were told to snitch on their schoolmates to a higher authority, and "report any bias incidents or claims to appropriate Residence Life staff."[38] As for non-compliant students who object to thought control, they might have to take re-education courses to replace their political thoughts with an alternative set of fixed beliefs. One columnist argued that students and taxpayers were funneling money "toward a social justice Gestapo whose primary function seems to be a combination of social justice secret police and indoctrination activities."[39]

This speech-police program echoes back to the block administrators (*blockwalter*) in Nazi Germany, whose responsibility was to spy on citizens and uncover anyone who did not tote the Nazi party line. Then again, Hitler employed the term "social justice" to promote his National Socialist agenda.[40] Mussolini did the same.

Racism and Fascism on Campus: Evergreen State College

Another case of the progressive left's plunge into fascist and racist territory occurred at Evergreen State College near Olympia, Washington, in May 2017. It all started when a professor of biology, Bret Weinstein, a left-wing Jewish supporter of Bernie Sanders, opposed the call for white faculty, staff, and students to leave the campus for a day. Ever since 1970, Evergreen State College has honored a tradition of holding a daylong event known as *Day of Absence*, which was based on a play by Douglas Turner Ward. On that day, students of color would voluntarily assemble at an off-campus site to raise awareness over racial and campus issues. In 2017, that tradition was reversed. Instead, students and administrators of color decided that only white students and faculty members should leave campus for one day, but according to Weinstein, the absence of whites was not exactly voluntary. He said that white students were *ordered* off campus, not asked.[41]

In a letter to the faculty, Weinstein argued that "On a college campus, one's right to speak—or to be—must never be based on skin color."[42] Weinstein pointed out that it was fine for a racial group or coalition to decide to gather off campus to attend a special event, but very wrong to pressure "another group to go away."[43] In other words, one group should not be telling another group what to do. Such a requirement would upend legal equality, sanctity of conscience, and self-determination. It harkens back to plain, old-fashioned racial segregation of the Deep South. In fact, Weinstein called the notion of using force and threats to divide racial groups "coercive segregation by race," and that it "is a show of force, and an act of oppression in and of itself,"[44] something that the civil rights movement and Martin Luther King were attempting to eradicate during the 1960s. So, Weinstein was essentially protesting a segregationist no-whites-allowed day.

The combination of racial demands for segregation and authoritarian pressure tactics is at the heart of a racist-fascist ideology that embraces collectivist prejudice against other groups. Here, the culture of outrage licenses collectivists and progressives to resort to any action deemed necessary. What most authoritarians on the left and right fail to comprehend is the vast difference between voluntary action and threatening action that predominantly relies on physical violence. They have no ethical bearings by which to judge the initiation of aggression as morally wrong, predatory, and uncivilized.

When Weinstein's letter and emails became public, all hell broke loose on campus. Over 50 outraged and mostly-white students disrupted Weinstein's class. They shouted epithets outside his classroom to get him to come out. When he entered the hallway, they accused him of saying "racist shit," and being a white supremacist, and demanded his immediate resignation. One screamed, "You're useless! Get the fuck out!" The agitated students had no intentions of engaging in a dialectic exchange to learn more about their disagreement. Instead, they angrily chanted: "Hey-hey, ho-ho, Bret Weinstein has got to go."[45]

During the heated uproar, a friend of Weinstein shouted, "Would you like to hear the answer or not from the professor?" The mob thundered, "No!"[46] One student yelled that Weinstein had already lost the discussion; therefore, free speech was no longer an option. The mob of students had little patience for a civil dialogue; they were there to intimidate and silence him, a tactic taken right out of the Nazi Stormtroopers' handbook. They not only tried to stop him from speaking, but they blocked him when he attempted to leave.

After the openly hostile encounter, the students marched to the library, occupied it, and surrounded the college president's office, barricading entrances with furniture. For a time, some 200 to 400 students seized control of the entire campus, arming themselves with batons, baseball bats, and tasers as they patrolled the campus buildings and grounds.[47,48] Next, the students took control of the campus parking lot and stopped all cars leaving the campus, presumably searching for Weinstein and any of his supporters.[49] Across the campus, "Fire Bret" graffiti were scrawled on campus buildings.[50]

According to Weinstein, hours after his confrontation with the student, the situation grew worse, turning surreal and anarchistic, where "people were, including me, literally being stalked and hunted."[51] A number of professors were accosted while administrators were held captive in their offices, and not permitted to leave. One professor, Nancy Koppelman, was left physically shaken after students followed her, yelling and cursing, and then accused her of ignoring people of color. They towered over her and demanded, according to Koppelman, that "The only thing they would accept was my obedience."[52]

For all practical purposes, President George Bridges and other administrators were held hostage, made to dance like a bear, until they agreed to the list of demands. Bridges was not even able to go to a bathroom without an escort of student guards. As the campus became a militarized zone, it began to display the terrifying breakdown of rules and conventions so abundantly found in *Lord of the Flies*. Like most college presidents confronted by tantrum-throwing students, President Bridges caved in to all of the students' demands.

Incredibly, during this confrontation with Weinstein, the students accused the faculty and the college of "targeting" people of color with discrimination. They accused the college of engaging in "systemic racism."[53] The dissenters believed that the college was a hotbed of white supremacy and saw victimhood and oppression at every turn. This accusation seems totally groundless since Evergreen State College was founded as an experimental liberal college with an equalitarian-progressive program of little structure, faculty autonomy, no majors or grading.

So many threats of violence were made on the part of protesters that

Weinstein had to hold his biology class in a public park.[54] Not much later, he and his wife, also a professor at the college, had to go into hiding, and finally they resigned since the school's security police force was told to "stand down" by Evergreen's president, George Bridges. Since their hands were tied, the police chief informed Weinstein that they could not guarantee his safety on campus.[55]

Three days later, the students went ballistic again when Weinstein appeared on Tucker Carlson's Fox News show. The reason Weinstein decided to speak on a conservative TV talk show was indicative of the left-wing broadcast media's attempt to ignore the simmering violence at Evergreen State College. Nobody but conservative TV hosts wanted to interview him. Weinstein wanted the public to know the full extent of the craziness, the hateful rhetoric, and condescending angst that was wreaking havoc at his college campus. But the left-wing mainstream media were not interested in his liberal narrative, although Weinstein considered himself "deeply progressive."

Weinstein was apparently unaware that the postmodern progressivists were willing to sacrifice free speech and liberalism at the altar of authoritarianism and supplant them with equality of outcome and social justice. Weinstein acknowledged this problem in a *Wall Street Journal* article:

> The plan and the way it is being forced on the college are both deeply authoritarian, and the attempt to mandate equality of outcome is unwise in the extreme. Equality of outcome is a discredited concept, failing on both logical and historical grounds, as anyone knows who has studied the misery of the 20th century. It wouldn't have withstood 20 minutes of reasoned discussion.[56]

This authoritarian groupthink and deterministic equality of outcome was epidemic at Evergreen. When a backlash of threats and hostile responses poured back from the community, offending students instead blamed it on free speech. One student stated that when threats are made to "execute every single person on campus, at that point, fuck free speech!"[57] Another white student on campus denounced Weinstein because he had "incited white supremacists and has validated white supremacists and Nazis in our community and in the nation. And I don't think that should be protected by free speech."[58]   Later, declaring that the professor was a "piece of shit," the student smiled and said, "Hopefully, in the long-term, we can weed out people like Bret."

The bullying and intimidation had a debilitating effect on the other students. In a number of interviews at the 4,000-student campus, undergrads expressed their desire to publicly support Weinstein, but felt intimated by the roving vigilante mobs of bat-wielding thought-police. Like gangs of Nazi youths roaming the streets in search of Jewish victims, these tactics were meant to terrify and terrorize others.

In the aftermath, Weinstein started to refer to the current crop of protesting students as the "authoritarian left," suggesting in one tweet that "The authoritarian left is cannibalizing the libertarian left. On the chopping block are: enlightenment values, science, merit, MLK's dream."[59] Weinstein eventually began to consider himself a left-wing "classical liberal," and advanced a strong belief that liberty puts limits on the voracity of equality. John Lockean liberals understand that equality is impossible unless the people first have the superior liberty of free speech to create it.

The lesson to be learned here is that the postmodern progressive left is willing to impose any authoritarian measures to create equality of outcome, without any reverence for individual liberty or the free-Left's conveyance of free choice. Unfortunately, free speech in a post-liberal world now plays second fiddle to a deterministic racial ideology. As the statist and progressive left gravitate closer to historical fascism, they increasingly embrace a form of ideological and biological determinism, which has been used to advocate supremacy over particular races and groups. This is the same biological determinism that was championed by German National Socialists to prove the superiority of their Aryan race.

This retreat from the free-Left's classical liberalism became shockingly visible as early as 2015 when Evergreen faculty and administrators switched from a "diversity agenda" to an "equity agenda" that required an "'equity justification' for every faculty hire."[60] The criterion for hiring new teachers was now their ability to focus on the topic of equality in every class, whether it be the humanities, science or mathematics. The college administrators were "establishing a racial hierarchy among the faculty." In his US Congressional testimony, Weinstein argued that he was being silenced because the Evergreen administration wanted payback for "violating a de facto code of faculty conduct in which one's right to speak is now dictated by adherence to an ascendant orthodoxy in which one's race, gender, and sexual orientation are paramount."[61] This situation echoed the mandatory requirement to insert the topic of racial biology and racial science into almost every school course across Nazi Germany. The Nazis even developed "social arithmetic" to peddle racial indoctrination as a central feature in their arithmetic textbooks.[62]

Michael Zimmerman, the former Vice President and Provost of Evergreen State College, reported that before the student riot, Evergreen had already

> become a place where it is acceptable for colleagues to levy personal attacks on colleagues in response to differences of opinion and even in response to calls for dialogue. It has become a place where it is acceptable to shout down those with whom you disagree.[63]

Weinstein attested to a number of these uncivil behaviors, saying that before the hallway ruckus, facility members were free to paint him as a "racist" in public meetings, mostly for questioning whether the revised changes to the Day of Absence would help racial equality.

In retrospect, Weinstein mentioned that when he discovered that a particular group wanted to segregate another group, all sorts of warning bells went off. Coming from a Jewish background, he saw this anti-freedom movement as something potentially dangerous that had happened in the not-too-distant past in Germany. When he was singled out at public meetings and berated by other faculty members for his diverse opinions, he could no longer remain silent.

In sum, trying to prohibit speech by labeling it controversial or hateful is an old tactic employed by intolerant and anti-liberal elements. Yet this is now the trend among pseudo-liberals who are averse to diversity because under their self-righteous assumptions, they are right and everyone else is wrong. And if everyone else is wrong, there is no need for a platform to allow for diversity of opinion. The National Socialists were big on treating people as subhuman creatures, especially weaker minorities. It is only a matter of time before these mobs of self-righteous crusaders don the swastika armband and storm the citadel of democracy.

Eliminating Conversation beyond the Campus

The barring and censorship of free speech have become just as relentless off campus. In fact, such invasive episodes are almost exclusively perpetrated by the statist Left, and their hordes of anti-civil rights sycophants, who are determined to shut down or eliminate debate from anyone with different perspectives. To them, it is more important to eliminate diverse dialogue and so-called offensive speech than to engage in dialectic argumentation to investigate the truth of a theory or opinion. Truth be told, the last thing the statist-progressive Left wants is an actual conversation with feedback; they would rather persecute dissenters as heretics in inquisitions that border on a modern-day book burning.

In their zeal to prohibit and police speech, these doctrinaires are increasingly turning to blackmail, intimidation, lawsuits, bullying, and boycotts to alter or vanquish diverse voices, especially on social media platforms such as Facebook, Apple, Spotify, Google, Twitter, YouTube, and others. For instance, conservative conspiracy theorist Alex Jones of *InfoWars* website fame was removed from most social media platforms for engaging in so-called "dehumanizing language" and "hate speech." Meanwhile, Antifa has been relatively free to disseminate their hateful and fascist militancy across the internet. Apparently, only those who incite hate from a statist-Left point of view can secure free speech.

So what have some politicians done to reverse this anti-openness trend? They have joined the censors. In his zeal to outdo Aldous Huxley's futurist *Brave New World*, Sen. Mark Warner (D-Virginia), sent out a memo listing all the ways the government could punish social media companies if they fail to cleanse the internet of "divisive" material.[64] Not to be outdone, Sen. Chris Murphy (D-Conn) took a potshot at the blacklisted Alex Jones, tweeting that he wanted more such banishments. Murphy argued that these big tech "companies must do more than take down one website. The survival of our democracy depends on it."[65]

Such internet sanitizing is not reserved for just fringe websites and controversial personalities. Even moderate conservative platforms such as *PragerU* had its popular videos blocked by YouTube and Facebook, despite having reached a billion views in 2018.

The problem with censorship is that when it becomes the norm, the story never ends well. The great temptation to stop most controversial issues can easily spill over and take down anyone. And this is exactly the Pandora Box that the state of New York and its governor, Andrew Cuomo, have opened. In 2018 New York officials began to engage in a political campaign to target and censor particular advocacy groups with different ideological voices. In this incident, the full force of the state of New York with its almost unlimited taxpayer resources went on a tear to banish an advocacy group through government intimidation, regulatory agencies, and legal threats. The group's only crime was to promote the Second Amendment.[66] In this case, that advocacy group is the National Rifle Association (NRA), but it could be any educational or advocacy organization that actively espouses change.

In early August, Cuomo bragged about taking down the NRA via government regulations on his Facebook post, declaring: "The regulations NY put in place are working. We're forcing the NRA into financial jeopardy. We won't stop until we shut them down."[67] Cuomo is trying to force gun-rights groups into financial ruin by pressuring banks and insurance companies to sever their business ties with them.[68] Such legal intimidation by a government body puts a chill on free expression for every group and institution, left or right. This illiberal precedent encourages all politicos to use their authority to abolish an opponent's ability for discourse, and even to erase their mere existence. When a political movement or governmental entity demands loyalty to its ideology as a condition for doing business in the community, the darkness of Fascist-Marxist totalitarianism is not far away.

The state of New York is using its vast legal and taxing power to punish political enemies. Only a narrow-minded ideologue would brag about employing the power of the state to silence private organizations they deem adversaries. They are simply outlawing their political opponents without actually legislating laws that explicitly make them illegal. Surprisingly, the ACLU has legally intervened to oppose the blacklisting of an advocacy group, asserting that "The First Amendment bars state officials from using their regulatory power to penalize groups merely because they promote disapproved ideas."

The Statist Left, the Big Lie, and Bret Kavanaugh

The Statist Left and the leadership of the Democratic Party repeatedly foster the "Big Lie" to get what they want, at any cost. Like the Big Lie strategy of Hitler, who found it a "force of credibility,"[69] the progressive Left has endorsed fascist and postmodern dogma in their incessant grab for political power. And in their thirst to take command, they have made a deal with the devil, rejecting objective truth and logic, fairness, empirical evidence, science, rationality, meaningful language, and the liberal elements of the Enlightenment.[70,71]

These unprincipled cretins have found that it is easier to spread colossal falsehoods if truth and rationality are no longer thought to exist. Many postmodernists harbor a belief in no belief; their nihilism necessitates a life without intrinsic value or meaning. This is the same nihilistic tendencies of Nazism and Marxism that Frederick Augustus Voigt elaborated on in *Pax Britannica*, explaining that "The super-abundance of false beliefs has led to unbelief."[72] This postmodern mentality, accompanied by the rise of historical fascism, came to a boiling point during Bret Kavanaugh's Judiciary Committee hearings for the US Supreme Court in 2018. Here, the nihilistic left took center stage by storm. Abandoning due process, hard evidence, and corroborating witnesses, the statist Left immediately endorsed all sexual assault allegations against Kavanaugh, without the benefit of an investigation or testimony from Dr. Christine Blasey Ford or Kavanaugh, a mode of conduct preferred by most authoritarians.

Unable to stop Kavanaugh's confirmation by legitimate means, and consumed with hate, many US Democratic Party Senators and cadres threw a political tantrum reminiscent of Hitler's legendary tirades. Mobs of Robespierrian zealots invaded the US Senate chambers and hallways where they cornered, trapped, and intimated anyone who failed to believe Dr. Ford's unproved allegations. The mob interrupted the proceedings like angry carnival barkers; they bellowed out primal screams, purposely ignored the absence of evidence, and declared Kavanaugh guilty by accusation, pushing the illiberal position that the accused are guilty until proven innocent. They were willing to toss out the old Roman law that "the burden of proof is on the one who declares, not on one who denies."

None of the women who accused Kavanaugh of sexual assault or misconduct provided any corroborating evidence, neither exact dates, times, nor locations, except that the crime occurred over 30 years ago. There was simply no evidence and no eyewitnesses. Even Dr. Ford's best friend and classmate, Leland Keyser, who was supposedly at the party, swore that she had no knowledge of the events. According to a statement by Keyser's lawyer: "Ms. Keyser does not know Mr. Kavanaugh and she has no recollection of ever being at a party or gathering where he was present, with, or without, Dr. Ford."[73] Nonetheless, the mobs, pundits, and media went out of their way to refer to Kavanaugh as a serial rapist who should not even continue to coach a girls' basketball team.[74]

As the statist Left and mainstream media spun new falsehoods by the nanosecond, truth was held hostage. Democratic Party Senators replaced judicial review with a search and destroy mission to prevent Kavanaugh's appointment to the US Supreme Court, orchestrating a political campaign of character assassination and mudslinging, even considering his beer drinking as a prelude to rape. Without hesitation, most Democratic Senators on the judicial committee believed that even without a scrap of evidence all women are honest while all men are liars, a brazenly sexist assumption. And when Kavanaugh was finally confirmed by the US Senate on October 6, 2018, a mob of young people threw their bodies against the US Supreme Court door, pounded their fists against it, and shouted "burn it down,"[75] like the Nazi students of 1933 who burned huge piles of offensive books.

What must be underscored here is that such mob-led political circuses mimic the destructive behavior of the National Socialists, who would do anything to acquire power, especially since they held dearly the doctrine that "power is its own justification."[76] These extreme fits of histrionics and nihilistic outbursts matched Hitler's Machiavellian profile. In late 1943 or late 1944, the United States Office of Strategic Service came out with a report on Hitler's psychological profile.

> [Hitler's] primary rules were: never allow the public to cool off; never admit a fault or wrong; never concede that there may be some good in your enemy; never leave room for alternatives; never accept blame; concentrate on one enemy at a time and

blame him for everything that goes wrong; people will believe a big lie sooner than a little one; and if you repeat it frequently enough people will sooner or later believe it.[77]

This profile perfectly matches the statist-fascist Left's strategy to reject truth, create crises, blame and belittle others.

Even the ACLU has abandoned its civil libertarian tradition during Kavanaugh's hearings. Michael Meyers, the nationally prominent Democrat liberal and former national vice president of the ACLU, proclaimed that the current ACLU has lost it way, trending towards fascism. Pointing to the ACLU's million dollar advertising campaign that compared Kavanaugh's sexual misconducts to those of Bill Cosby and Bill Clinton, Meyers declared, "I was proudest of the ACLU when the ACLU resisted fascism, when it stood up to the mob. Now the ACLU has become the mob."[78] Meyers contended that the ACLU never got involved in the politics of endorsing or opposing a Supreme Court nominees. The TV advertisements by the ACLU specifically argued that Dr. Ford's sexual misconduct charges were "credible," although there was no evidence of a crime. Meyers explained that the ACLU leadership has gone off the deep end and had betrayed their core civil liberties principles. He summed it up: the ACLU is "supposed to stand up to the mob, it's supposed to stand for freedom and individual liberty, it's supposed to stand for the presumption of innocence and it doesn't make assumptions."[79]

This situation has gotten to the point where it appears that the leadership of the Democratic Party is rushing headfirst towards historical fascism, embracing not only socialist interventionist ideology and collectivistic metaphysics, but encouraging uncivility that has incited mob-like violence that harkens back to Nazi street firebrands. In 2018, Hillary Clinton publicly declared that her supporters should be rude and brutish: "You cannot be civil with a political party that wants to destroy what you stand for, what you care about,"[80] which within weeks resulted in more physical attacks on candidates for political office.[81]

Other leading Democrat Party voices have urged combative and in-your-face approaches against any adversary. Calls for intimidation, harassment, and violence have come from Democrat bigwigs such as

Sen. Nancy Pelosi, Rep. Maxine Waters, and former Attorney General Eric Holder, who gleefully stated "When they go low, we kick 'em. That's what this new Democratic Party is about."[82] Numerous Republican officeholders and candidates have been targeted and attacked, including everything from the 2017 baseball shooting of US Congressmen and Senators at Eugene Simpson Stadium Park in Virginia by a Bernie Sander supporter[83] to an attempted stabbing of a Republican congressional candidate, Rudy Peters, with a switchblade in Castro Valley, California in 2018.[84]

But there is more than a moral-superiority complex within the Democratic Party leadership. They have increasingly rebutted almost every important amendment of the US Bill of Rights, implying that civil liberties and free speech are reserved only for themselves. Many moderate Democrats have either been kicked out of their own party or have abandoned it. Mark Salvas, the former executive director of the Allegheny County Democratic Party, was forced to resign his position for a remark in a year-old Facebook post, stating: "I stand for the flag, I kneel at the cross."[85,86] By 2018, it became clear to political observers that the top tier of the Democratic Party no longer had a connection to western liberal capitalism, civility and the party of President John F. Kennedy.

The Movement to Abridge Civil Rights

The statist Left's track record on civil rights has become increasingly devoid of any substance, and defiant of the US Constitution. For instance, they have had a poor history of defending the freedom of association and disassociation. Freedom of association allows any organization to make expenditures for any political activity of their choice. This principle was upheld under the landmark Supreme Court 2010 *Citizens United vs. FEC* decision. Due to the McCain-Feingold Act of 2002, Citizens United had been prohibited by the Federal Election Commission from airing a film berating Hillary Clinton. Although the law that limited free speech and freedom of association was ruled unconstitutional, instead of celebrating, the statist Left became unglued over the government's inability to retain its power to ban and restrict books, films, and funding during political campaigns. This battle over free speech occurred in 2010 and signaled future anti-Founders movements geared to assault the very core of free speech.

And then there was the issue of transparency in government, which has often led to a double standard among those who supposedly champion openness in government. For instance, *The Washington Post* has been at the forefront in defending transparency at every opportunity. They were the ones who enthusiastically supported the publication of secret government documents as essential to a free society, even if such transparency might harm national security. After *The Washington Post* published a portion of The *Pentagon Papers* in 1971, the Assistant US Attorney General William Rehnquist issued an injunction to cease its publication. *The Washington Post* initially refused, even though the publisher and the news staff feared arrest. They were dauntless in upholding transparency.

But in 2018, while the Hollywood film *The Post* with Tom Hanks and Meryl Streep was still flickering with life at the theaters, the supposed civil-liberties-minded mainstream media and *The Washington Post* opposed the release of Congressman Devin Nunes' memo that reported corruption, lying, and surveillance abuses at high levels in the FBI and Department of Justice. There was a concerted campaign to block the release of the memo by the alleged fans of government transparency. In a weasel-worded editorial, *The Washington Post* said that the release of the Nunes memo was "nothing but a hyperpartisan attempt to discredit Mueller" and his investigation as if there was nothing partisan or political about the release of the *Pentagon Papers*.[87]

The Washington Post displayed little concern over preserving transparency or letting the public decide the merits of the information released. Instead of affirming civil liberties, the statist Left worked itself into a frenzy over the Congressional release of Nunes' classified material. Many leftist media outlets and politicians opposed such transparency due to the possible damage to "national security," the identical argument employed against releasing the *Pentagon Papers*. This illustrates the hypocrisy of so-called civil liberty activists who only seek to further their own political interests, denying similar rights of transparency to others when it becomes inconvenient. The guardians of transparency have instead reverted to defenders of unaccountable, opaque government.

Incredibly, even many peace movements have been infected by progressive statists who would deny civil rights to prisoners and jailed political opponents. They seem to hold a double standard when it comes to civil liberties, and apparently find it acceptable to justify extra-judicial killings if such violent acts are committed by dedicated socialists or communists. For instance, California Senator Bill Monning (D-Carmel) spoke warmly of Che Guevara at the Monterey Peace and Justice Center fundraising function in 2015.[88] A guerrilla leader who engaged in violent and armed revolution, Che was a "cold-blooded killing machine" who extra-judicially killed hundreds of prisoners in Cuba.[89] Many scholars consider him a "mass murderer clothed in the guise of an avenging angel whose every action is imbricated in violence—the archetypal Fanatical Terrorist."[90]

Any organization dedicated to peace, justice and non-violence should expect their keynote speaker to quote Gandhi or Martin Luther King, Jr., not a pathological murderer. This case exemplifies the way in which the issue of peace has become a gateway teaser by which to introduce the glories of authoritarian socialism, which is anything but peaceful. The statist Left deceitfully conflates the concept of peace with violent ideologies, regardless of how brutal or unjust. It seems as if a belief in peace permits social activists to be violent in their quest to achieve certain socioegalitarian goals. Such an attitude takes on an Orwellian tone, in that one must be at war with society in order to bring about peace. Here, the question of peace is not whether opponents should be allowed to speak, but whether opponents should be allowed to live.

Obamacare and the Fascist Third Way

Although the statist Left struts their best "Mussolini pose" in public view, almost nobody recognizes its authoritarian effigy. One of the most stunning examples of this political makeover was President's Obama's effort to vastly increase government involvement in American's healthcare. Here, so-called "progressive" leftists forged a crypto-fascist law that commingled big-government socialism with big-government corporatism, which mimicked the Hitler-Mussolini government-run social welfare and healthcare programs.

The Patient Protection and Affordable Care Act (2009), informally known as Obamacare, included an authoritarian provision that forced the public to buy a product from a corporation—health insurance. This individual mandate, which regulates inactivity and obligates Americans to engage in commerce, represents the "Third Way" that both the German National Socialists and Italian fascists employed to describe their socioeconomic policies. Historically, Obamacare cannot get any closer to full-bodied Italian Fascism.

Obama's healthcare initiative can also be linked to other historical movements that preceded Fascist Italy. Some argued that this integration of statism with capitalism resembles Lenin's advocacy for "state capitalism" in 1921. In this case, Lenin's failed "War Communism" of mass nationalization and confiscation led to the loosening of the economic noose, allowing the private sector to co-exist with the public sector, which Mussolini in later years approvingly called "state capitalism."

Today, most nations have some modified variant of this "Third Way" state capitalism, which combines fascist-inspired syndicalism and corporatism under an umbrella of interventionism, socialism, and statism. Economist Murray Rothbard defined this type of economic system as "state-monopoly capitalism," a condition where the partnership of government and big business provides the state with the authority to intervene on the behalf of crony capitalist to the detriment of consumers.[91] This was exactly what Italian Fascism and German National Socialism had forged, and what most current governments now emulate—a sort of mixed-economic dirigisme of nationalistic and collectivistic populism that opposes individualism, free markets, and classical liberalism. Today, it is clear that this "Third Way" politics foreshadows the economics of socialistic nationalism that increasingly burdens modern America.

Nationalism, whether infused with socialism or statism, is a primitive tribalism projected on a massive scale. Matt Kibbe, an economist by training, contends that "Nationalism is another form of collectivism, putting the abstract idea of country ahead of the needs of individual citizens. 'America first' puts Americans last."[92]

In fact, such state-granted privileges and institutional barriers only incentivize the state to behave like madcap cabdrivers, who take unwary passengers on scary rides. And why not? Those trying to impose lofty goals always search for easy solutions while ignoring bad consequences. When a reckless state becomes "fascisized," it can begin to operate behind a facade of respectability and altruism, while treating the populace as cargo to be hauled around, boxed, categorized, and stacked in rows. During these negligent mishaps, politicos become agents for an authority who demands loyalty and obedience. Similar to the results of Milgram's 1961 experiment, prominent governmentalists routinely permit their political minions to act in such ways to deflect responsibility for bad consequences to those who execute the orders—the authority.[93] Obedience to authority becomes an excuse for taking advantage of others with almost assured legal immunity. It is easy to rationalize injury to others if such cruel actions are shielded by top-level authority figures. When agents of the state do something wrong and get caught, they routinely plead: "I was just following orders." This was the exact verbiage mouthed by Nazi officials during the Nuremberg Trials in 1945–46.

Compliance with Authority and State Capitalism

Compliance with an authority is ingrained in the human condition. Statists of all stripes use this psychological technique to garner support for political conquests, domestic and foreign. These conquests mimic the historical policies of Italian Fascism, German National Socialism, and Russian Sovietism, which few scholars want to expose, especially when their own ideology stands in sharp accord with Fascist-Marxist mindset. Yet many political scientists go out of their way to misidentify or ignore the roots of Mussolini's syndicalist, socialist, and Marxist ideology, perhaps because of their own closely held political beliefs. Whatever the reason, scholars have gone to great lengths to obscure Mussolini's true Marxian intentions.

This attempt to hide the truth in plain sight is analogous to Hans

Christian Anderson's "The Emperor's New Clothes," where swindlers attempt to convince the public and royal court that their special fabric is invisible to any person unfit for his position or "hopelessly stupid." This ploy prevents people from voicing the obvious—that is, until one small boy blurts out the naked truth: "But he has nothing on at all!" The concealment of the true nature of two of the 20th century's most notorious regimes seems to have followed a similar dynamic. Many historians, political scientists, and pundits have remained silent about the socialist, Marxist-leaning nature of both Italian Fascism and German National Socialism. Everything is there to see, but few are willing to point to Hitler and Mussolini and proclaim that their bodies are covered with more than fifty shades of naked Marxism.

He may be among the most notorious fascists, but Mussolini was not the first to introduce economic and political fascism to the world. After Lenin's "War Communism" produced massive famine, street riots, and economic collapse, Marxist leaders searched for an alternative "Third Way" between socialism and capitalism. In response, Lenin rolled out of his New Economic Policy (NEP) in 1921, which introduced a form of "market socialism" or what he approvingly dubbed, "state capitalism." In fact, Lenin described this change as the "development of capitalism under the control and regulation of the proletarian state (in other words, 'state' capitalism of this peculiar kind) is advantageous and necessary..." which was adopted by the Third Congress of the Communist International.[94] This means that fascism was not the "last stage of capitalism" as Marxist historians have maintained, but the first stage of a pullback from the economic and political failures of Marxism-Leninism. Lenin's reactionary policies to mitigate the defects of absolute nationalization and communism not only spawned the NEP but also ushered in the world's first modern fascist regime.

Under the NEP, markets gained greater degrees of private initiative, flexibility, and private ownership, while sanctioning the coexistence of the private and public sectors, which helped to open the Soviet Union to private capital and foreign investment. Lenin's NEP allowed some privatization of small business and farming operations that recognized market principles and profit motives. This opening of the economy permitted trade and the purchase and sale of goods between individuals for private profit. Even state-owned enterprises kept an eye on profit and loss. Lenin's NEP was turning Russia into a state-oriented "mixed economy,"[95] part socialist and part capitalist. Lenin made a big push to support state capitalism, and Mussolini did the same years later, in the 1930s. Lenin argued in 1921:

> State capitalism would be a step forward as compared with the present state of affairs in our Soviet Republic. If in approximately six months' time state capitalism became established in our Republic, this would be a great success and a sure guarantee that within a year socialism will have gained a permanently firm hold.[96]

State capitalism is simply the control or ownership of capital by the state. The state manages the economic activity of the nation under a mixture of state control and ownership of the means of production, a sort of "state monopoly capitalism" that closely parallels a mercantilist system that occurred during the pre-Industrial Revolution era.[97] Although some Marxists doubt the true socialist nature of state capitalism, they still recognize it as a social system that combines some capitalism with state ownership. This economic system is sometimes referred to as state socialism.

When Mussolini bragged about nationalizing "three-fourths of the Italian economy, industrial and agricultural" in 1934, he proposed introducing Italy to "state capitalism or state socialism, which is the reverse side of the medal."[98] When Lenin turned Soviet Russia's economy over to a "communist-lite" version of state capitalism, he inspired Mussolini to craft his own Italian-style fascism with an alleged right-wing socialist twist. With this in mind, it could be argued that Lenin's revisionism could be designated the first modern-day proto-version of fascism.

And yet, Red China, with its Lenin-like drift towards loosening up its market mechanism, invokes the same ugly specter of fascism, where much of its large industrial base is state-owned, an economy plagued by centrally-planned and state-directed edicts, a foreign policy favorable to expansionistic politics (consider the invasion of Tibet in 1950), and a xenophobic attitude towards the Japanese, Westerners, and Tibetans. Despite the socialist, nationalist, and racist policies of many of the world's nations, most political observers avoid labeling them as fascist. It does not even matter if these nationalistic socialist nations have engaged in genocide or democide; they rarely suffer the consequences of being officially listed as dues-paying members of the fascist fraternity.

Interestingly, after the fall of Russian communism in 1991, many socialist intellectuals contended that nations like the Soviet Union were not socialist in the least, but rather institutional pillars of state capitalism, where the state controlled all the industrial and financial capital, but not the people. Peter Binns, a former editor of *International Socialism* magazine, wrote in 1986 that "A proper understanding both of Russia today and of Marx's analysis of capitalism will reveal Russia to be state capitalist, not socialist." He also labeled Russia "an imperialist capitalist power."[99] The Marxist economists Richard D. Wolff and Stephen Resnick have also identified state capitalism in the Soviet Union as its dominant class system, concluding that "The USSR was the ultimate state capitalism..."[100] Others, like Max Horkheimer from the neo-Marxist Frankfurt School, pointed out that "Fascism was the less extreme [version of state capitalism], since it still allowed some private property..."[101]

Despite the melding of some capitalistic elements alongside state socialism that appeared in many 20th century fascist regimes and continue, to a degree, to this day, it is disingenuous for socialist intellectuals to claim that the Soviet Union was not socialist in the least, but rather functioned under a variant of state capitalism. Still, academics and pundits who linked state capitalism with communist Russia fail to realize that Mussolini was also a devoted enthusiast of state capitalism and state socialism. And part of state capitalism's allure to the Italian Fascists was its syndicalist-style corporatism that theoretically sought an equal partnership of employers with employees. However, Mussolini's syndicalist-style corporatism was also, in several important ways, vastly different from American-style corporatism, where shareholders, instead of political string pullers and ideologists, lorded over corporations.

By the early 1930s, Mussolini had devised twenty-two state-run holding companies (corporations), where the major decisions were being made by "party-controlled workers' unions, the autonomous employers' organization, *Confindustria*, and Mussolini."[102] In reality, the shots were being called by the National Fascist Party, as part of Mussolini's effort to supposedly move beyond both capitalism and socialism. According to Pamela D. Toler, Mussolini's "corporatism borrowed heavily from Georges Sorel's theories of revolutionary syndicalism."[103] In his 1908 book, *Reflections on Violence,* Sorel promoted violent revolution via worker's general strikes in order to end the corrupt politics of the bourgeois democracy and to destroy capitalism. Sorel was a French Marxist who advocated myth-making and bloodshed in the street. He distrusted socialist lawmakers in parliament, preaching that socialists had to seize power by force and not by the ballot box. Mussolini was impressed and declared that "Georges Sorel had been my Master" in a 1937 interview,[104] attributing the birth of Italian Fascism to a Marxist, which could easily consign Sorel to the political realm of Fascist-Marxist chauvinism.

The Fascist-Marxist History of Italy and Germany

Heavily influenced by Sorel's revolutionary syndicalism, Mussolini was attempting to create worker-empowered corporations in Italy. Nonetheless, Mussolini's administration eventually outlawed all strikes and lockouts, nationalizing the labor unions. Of course, Russian Marxist leaders had done the same earlier in the Soviet Union, taking over all independent labor unions, factory committees, and worker cooperatives and merging them within the apparatus of the state. Soviet trade unions became "subordinate to the state," to the point where one labor leader "described the unions as 'living corpses.'"[105] In fact, the first president of the American Federation of Labor, Samuel Gompers (1850–1924), was horrified by Lenin's labor practices. He referred to them as "slavery," and called the mandatory 80-hour work week as the "militarization of labor," claiming that the Bolshevist's ill-conceived labor policy where strikes were illegal as constituting "the gravest danger that has confronted labor for centuries."[106]

The reason strikes were banned was that workers were now supposedly in control of the government, making such disruptive actions unnecessary. To Russian Bolsheviks, German National Socialists, and Italian Fascists, the workers' state had been established to bring about, as Trotsky insisted, "the embryo of workers' government."[107] This meant that

there was no need for independent labor unions, and none were seen in
the Soviet Union's sphere of influence until Solidarity arose in Poland in
1980 at the Gdańsk Shipyard under Lech Wałęsa.

In fact, during one of Italy's economic downturns that started in 1926,
Mussolini's government did exactly what President Bush and Obama
undertook during America's Great Recession that started in December
2007. According to Jeffery Herbener in "The Vampire Economy: Italy,
Germany and the US," the Italian fascist state had to intervene to stop
the ill effects of its monetary problems and to expand its scope. Fascist
Italy "had to bail out big businesses and banks, fostered mergers and acquisitions, cartelized the remaining, now larger enterprises, and renewed
spending, mainly for war."[108] Interestingly, one of the outcomes of Mussolini's heavy-handed interventionism in the economy was a large unused
pool of cash; nearly one-third of capital capacity sat idle in 1934, similar
to the large stockpiling of cash by American businesses during America's
Great Recession.

Although Mussolini had merged state and corporate power, what
he eventually got was a vertical syndicalist-type corporatocracy that
harkened back to medieval guilds. Speaking about what he had done,
Mussolini explained in 1932,

> When brought within the orbit of the State, Fascism recognizes
> the real needs which gave rise to socialism and trade unionism,
> giving them due weight in the guild or corporative system in
> which divergent interests are coordinated and harmonized in the
> unity of the State.[109]

In fact, with his revolutionary syndicalist past, Mussolini himself was
a union man. Not long after taking complete control of Italy's government, Mussolini imposed mandatory unionism for all workers.[110] Of
course, workers had to join the government-controlled Fascist union,
but this policy was no different from what Lenin had imposed after the
October 1917 revolution. This fact alone provides the evidence that the
Italian Fascists were left-wing, pro-government devotees determined to
create a union-installed worker paradise under a heavily regulated and
controlled bureaucratic state. A right-wing dictator would have simply
outlawed labor unions, whether government-controlled or independent.

Both Mussolini's National Fascist Party and Hitler's National Socialist party regarded themselves as an integral part of the workers' movement. Italian Fascism arose out of Marxism and revolutionary syndicalism and resolved to nationalize all private labor organizations to better regulate, manage and protect workers and improve working conditions. The Nazi party in Germany, often known by international observers as the "National Socialist Labor Party," also promoted trade unionism in order to provide generous benefits for workers under the Nazi-controlled German Labor Front. In general, both the Fascist and Nazi regimes treated workers far better than most nations of the era, providing more favorable policies and state-supported subsidies to laborers than either Lenin or Stalin.

Nazism and unionism were virtually synonymous, where both German Communists and National Socialists attempted to outrival each other to gain working-class support. From day one, the Nazis saw themselves as the pro-labor party. In *Mein Kampf*, Hitler wrote:

> [T]rade unions... are among the most important institutions in the economic life of the nation. Not only are they important in the sphere of social policy but also, and even more so, in the national political sphere. For when the great masses of a nation see their vital needs satisfied through a just trade unionist movement the stamina of the whole nation in its struggle for existence will be enormously reinforced thereby.[111]

After studying the Nazis 25-Point Program of 1920, which demanded the right of employment (plank 7), political scientist and historian William Brustein, asserted that the Nazi Party originated as a working-class political party.[112]

As for corporatism, Mussolini also made it clear that his ideal corporatist nationalism was a top-down model of state control, writing,

> The Fascist conception of the State is all-embracing; outside of it no human or spiritual values can exist, much less have value. Thus understood, Fascism is totalitarian, and the Fascist State— a synthesis and a unit inclusive of all values—interprets, develops, and potentiates the whole life of a people.[113]

Mussolini was the quintessential left-wing governmentalist, asserting that "Government alone is in the right position to see things from the point of view of the general welfare."[114] This viewpoint perfectly explains his admiration for Machiavelli's tactics to wrestle control of society. In fact, Mussolini admitted that Machiavelli's book, *The Prince*, was "the statesman's supreme guide."[115] Furthermore, Mussolini agreed with Machiavelli's pessimistic outlook on human nature. According to Australian historian R.J.B. Bosworth, Mussolini believed that "individuals could not be relied on voluntarily to 'obey the law, pay their taxes and serve in war.' No well-ordered society could want the people to be sovereign."[116] Beyond this, Mussolini sought to use this so-called "evil nature of mankind" to do his bidding, believing that a good ruler "must suppose all men bad and exploit the evil qualities in their nature whenever suitable occasion offers."[117]

As for Hitler, he was a longtime connoisseur of undiluted Machiavellianism; the ends always justified his lethal means. He admitted to a number of Nazi confidants that he had no scruples whatsoever. Perhaps this is why he admired strongmen like Napoleon Bonaparte (1769–1821). In a rare moment of honesty, Hitler once confided that he saw Napoleon as his role model for his anti-conservative, anti-capitalist and anti-bourgeois attitudes.[118]

There were other ways, too, which Mussolini hewed closely to the ideology of the modern-day, statist Left. Calling himself a "non-believer," Mussolini saw himself as anti-bourgeois, anti-classical liberal, anti-individualist, anti-*laissez-faire* capitalist, and anti-clerical. He fancied himself as a leader of a great pro-worker state, saying: "If the 19th century has been the century of the individual (for liberalism means individualism), it may be conjectured that this is the century of the State." Under the fascist concept to oppose a "Bourgeois nation," Mussolini publicly invited Italians to mail anti-bourgeois cartoons to the newspapers to rebuke "social games, five o'clock tea, vacations, compassion for Jews, preference for armchairs, desire for compromise, desire for money" as "offensive bourgeois practices."[119]

In this way, much of modern leftism can be considered a recycled version of Italian fascism, which was itself also influenced by German Marxist revisionist Eduard Bernstein. Holding close associations to Karl

Marx and Friedrich Engels, Bernstein's revised Marxism theories could be seen as an archetypal of "proto-fascist" or "revolutionary conservative" model for Mussolini's policies on class conflict. Some have argued that Mussolini's fascism was bereft of Marxist overtones simply because he opposed Marx's theory of class struggle, but so did Marxist revisionist Bernstein, who, like Mussolini, stressed class cooperation.[120,121]

In short, Mussolini was not only a hardcore Marxist during his early years, referring to Marx as "the greatest theoretician of socialism,"[122] but most likely a closet Marxist throughout most of his life, as has been suggested by English historian Paul Johnson. In this light, the statist liberal-left could be seen not only as quasi-authoritarian with heavy fascist tendencies, but which routinely suffers from political amnesia, alongside an acute identity crisis. Of course, no upstanding pro-state leftist wishes to be associated with fascism, but as Israeli historian Zeev Sternhell contended in *The Birth of Fascist Ideology*, Mussolini had turned into a fascist long before World War I—back when Mussolini was still advocating Marxism, albeit heretically. Sternhell attributed Mussolini's fascism to "an intellectual evolution and growing awareness of European and Italian realities that existed before the war and was unconnected with it."[123] Italian fascism evolved from a movement of socialized and unpatriotic nationalism within the perimeter of revolutionary syndicalism and Marxist revisionism.

The Austrian economist Ludwig von Mises, who had his Viennese apartment ransacked by the Nazis in 1938, was an eyewitness to the surging threat from national socialism and fascism, writing that

> Fascist governments clung first to the same principles of economic policies which all not outright socialist governments have adopted in our day, interventionism. Then later it turned step by step toward the German system of socialism, i.e., all-round state control of economic activities.[124]

Mises was explaining that the mingling of socialism and corporate state was not only interventionist and aggressive, but a forged monopolistic body left free to exploit the public at will.

As for Hitler, his dying support for socialism is not hard to find. He often referred to himself and his movement as socialist, as did all the major

Nazi leaders, especially Dr. Joseph Goebbels who hated capitalism and pushed for radical socialism. Goebbels made no bones about what socialism meant. "To be a socialist," Goebbels wrote, "is to submit the I to the thou; socialism is sacrificing the individual to the whole."[125] When he was once asked about the position of National Socialism, Goebbels responded, "the NSDAP is the German Left. We despise bourgeois nationalism."[126]

According to Goebbels, National Socialists opposed Jews because they are considered exploiters and capitalists. The Nazis regarded capitalism as coming from Jewish origins; in fact, to most socialists, the Jews personified the heart of capitalism and democracy. Believing in "biological determination," Goebbels wrote in 1932: "As socialists, we are opponents of the Jews, because we see, in the Hebrews, the incarnation of capitalism, of the misuse of the nation's goods."[127] Perhaps this is one reason why Hitler commended Stalin for purifying the Communist Party of its Jewish leaders.[128]

The more left-wing Nazis like Gregor Strasser—a Nazi party (NSDAP) national propaganda leader from 1926 to 1928—did not mince words about the Third Reich's chief nemesis. In 1927, Strasser said, "We National Socialists are enemies, deadly enemies, of the present capitalist system with its exploitation of the economically weak... and we are resolved under all circumstances to destroy this system."[129]

Hitler himself was crystal-clear about his advocacy of socialism. He boisterously proclaimed in a 1927 May Day speech, "We are socialists, we are enemies of today's capitalistic economic system for the exploitation of the economically weak..."[130] Hitler believed that the Germany state did not have to nationalize every factory and blade of grass; that German socialism went deeper: "We socialize human beings."[131]

Hitler occasionally voiced support for private property to placate the middle classes, small businessmen, and industrialists, but under his interpretation, owners were to be subservient to the state. Hitler made this clear in no uncertain terms, proclaiming:

> The party is all-embracing. It rules our lives in all their breadth and depth... There will be no license, no free space, in which the individual belongs to himself. This is Socialism... Let them then

own land or factories as much as they please. The decisive factor
is that the State, through the party, is supreme over them, regardless whether they are owners or workers.[132]

Starting during the early years of the Nazi reign, the state owned a
majority of shares in big banks and other large industries. The Nazis
occasionally sold government-owned businesses, but mostly to give them
to loyal Nazi Party members. Although the German economy was not as
nationalized as Mussolini's economy, the Nazi 13th plank in their Party's
25-Point Program demanded the nationalization of all corporations.

Some historians argue that the reason for Nazi's Keynesian-like approach to economic control was to gradually introduce a stronger
version of socialism without causing too much controversy. Adolf
Hitler's economic advisor, Otto Wagener, made this case, saying that
people would eventually "find and travel the road from individualism to
socialism without revolution."[133]

When the Nazis took control of Germany in 1933, Hitler strengthened the German welfare state. Germany had already become the first
modern welfare state under the leadership of Otto von Bismarck, the
first chancellor of Germany, and the Nazi regime expanded socialized
medicine and state funding for old-age pensions, which included euthanasia programs that assisted in socially engineering society. National
Socialism called for full employment, good living wages, and "breaking
the slavery to interest."

The Nazis made "full employment an ideological tenet to which they
were fully committed before they seized power."[134] Referring to full employment as a "right to work" entitlement, this Nazi policy was considered so important that it was "almost synonymous with what they called
German socialism." Bernhard Köhler, the head of the Nazi Party Commission for Economic Policy, declared in 1932: "The National Socialist
state will guarantee that every one of our people finds work."[135] Moreover, the Nazis were able to achieve near-full employment four years later
by actively engaging in massive public work projects and deficit spending that almost bankrupted their economy in subsequent years. Yet, in
2018 Sen. Bernie Sanders, announced a similar Nazi-like jobs guarantee program that would provide work for every American "who wants

or needs one."[136] His plan entailed a large-scale government sector jobs program aimed at such priorities as "infrastructure, care giving, the environment, education and other goals."[137] This is exactly what Hitler proposed and then carried out starting in 1933 under his jobs guarantee and public works projects. Such state-funded projects were used not only for general public work jobs but were integrated into Germany's armament buildup.

The Nazis used pro-labor rhetoric, demanding limitations on profits and the abolition of rents. They actively limited competition and private ownership, under the guise of promoting the general welfare. Hitler expanded credit, subsidized farmers, suspended the gold standard, instituted government jobs programs, mandated unemployment insurance, decreed rent control, imposed high tariffs to protect German industry from foreign competition, nationalized education, enacted strict wage and price controls, borrowed heavily and eventually ran huge deficits almost to the point of financial collapse. Eventually, both Germany and Italy turned into vast welfare-warfare nations.[138]

These welfare-warfare costs almost bankrupted Germany by 1938. For this reason, Germany had to levy heavy taxes on the wealthy. By 1943, industrialists complained that the Nazis were siphoning off 80 to 90 percent of business profits.[139] Further, the Nazis had sharply increased taxes on capital gains as well as hiking taxes on corporate revenues over 1,365 percent during a six-year period.[140] Such anti-capitalist policies were no surprise from an ideology that proclaimed in its Nazi 25-Point Platform from 1920: "The Common Good Before the Individual Good."

To refinance their massive national debt, the Nazis increasingly had to rely on plunder from conquered nations and the cannibalization of Jewish assets.[141] In *Hitler's Beneficiaries: Plunder, Racial War, and the Nazi Welfare State*, German historian Götz Aly described National Socialism as a form of populist wealth-redistribution welfare-state socialism.[142] He asserted that Nazi ideology preached equality only among Germans, and no other groups. To maintain their generous welfare state at home, the Nazi regime transferred wealth from non-Germans to Germans.

This point cannot be overstated. Nazism was a tribal-egalitarian movement. The Nazis aspired to build what Götz Aly termed a "racist-totalitarian welfare state" that bribed the Germans into complacency.[143] Hitler's socialism was focused on nation and race, whereas Stalin's socialism was centered on classes and nationalistic urges with a "Great Russian chauvinism."[144] Under National Socialism, the state plundered and killed other national groups and races and use their resources to provide Germans with an unsparing welfare-warfare society. Under the alleged international socialism of Marxism, the state plundered and killed other classes to provide comrades with a welfare-warfare society. Both systems, the German's and the Soviet's, believed in equality and socialism, but for different collective groups. Although Nazism preached inequality between the races, it placed great significance on equality among true-blooded Germans (*Völkisch* equality) and the spirit of fraternity.

Author and professor of economics George Reisman echoed Ludwig von Mises' observations from the 1930s–1940s that exposed how Nazi policy treated people and their property as national resources. Much of the material came from Mises' *Omnipotent Government: The Rise of the Total State and Total War*, published in 1944, which is considered by many to be the most bitterly anti-Nazi book ever written. Mises contended that since the German National Socialists regarded the state as the supreme authority, the state assumed ownership rights to everything. Due to their complete control, Nazi administrators had little reason to officially deed over private property to state ownership; with complete control comes *de facto* ownership of all assets. With this in mind, Reisman concluded: "If the individual is a means to the ends of the State, so too, of course, is his property. Just as he is owned by the State, his property is also owned by the State."[145]

In his lecture on why Nazism was socialism, Reisman explained Mises' main points further:

> What Mises identified was that private ownership of the means of production existed in name only under the Nazis and that the actual substance of ownership of the means of production resided in the German government. For it was the German government and not the nominal private owners that exercised all of the substantive powers of ownership: it, not the nominal private owners, decided what was to be produced, in what quantity, by what methods, and to whom it was to be distributed, as well

as what prices would be charged and what wages would be paid, and what dividends or other income the nominal private owners would be permitted to receive.[146]

Similarly, *Time* magazine confirmed the Nazi policy of running rough-shod over the business community in Germany. Choosing Hitler as *Time* magazine's 1938 Man of the Year, the editor's tone was cautious and critical about the German Chancellor, writing:

> Most cruel joke of all, however, has been played by Hitler & Co. on those German capitalists and small businessmen who once backed National Socialism as a means of saving Germany's bourgeois economic structure from radicalism. The Nazi credo that the individual belongs to the state also applies to business. Some businesses have been confiscated outright, on other what amounts to a capital tax has been levied. Profits have been strictly controlled. Some idea of the increasing Governmental control and interference in business could be deduced from the fact that 80% of all building and 50% of all industrial orders in Germany originated last year with the Government. Hard-pressed for food-stuffs as well as funds, the Nazi regime has taken over large estates and in many instances collectivized agriculture, a procedure fundamentally similar to Russian Communism.[147]

Mimicking Marxism, the National Socialists also regularly combined socialism and classlessness with purity of race. In the 1935 Third Reich-released *Triumph of the Will* propaganda film, Hitler announced: "We want a society with neither castes nor ranks and you must not allow these ideas to grow within you!" Hitler's sentiments represent the key elements of the Hegelian and Marxist ideology of an equalitarian and classless society. In *Mein Kampf*, Hitler wrote: "The National Socialist State recognizes no 'classes.' But, under the political aspect, it recognizes only citizens with absolutely equal rights and equal obligations corresponding thereto."[148]

Many American politicians embraced the economic policies of National Socialism and fascism, at least in the beginning, when Mussolini was heralded as a far left-wing socialist, as was voiced by left-wing socialist George Bernard Shaw in 1927.[149]

President Franklin D. Roosevelt remarked to the US Ambassador to Italy, Breckinridge Long, that,

> There seems to be no question that [Mussolini] is really interested in what we are doing and I am much interested and deeply impressed by what he has accomplished and by his evidenced honest purpose of restoring Italy.[150]

Roosevelt was indeed impressed with Mussolini and his third-way economics, eventually championing laws to cartelize, monopolize, and impose price controls on the United States economy under the National Recovery Administration (NRA), which was later unanimously declared unconstitutional by the US Supreme Court in 1935.

British-American journalist, television personality, and broadcaster Alistair Cooke was alarmed over FDR's increased power and centralization. He described FDR's early presidency as a benevolent dictatorship.[151]

Anti-Semitism, Racism, Marxism, and Hugo Chavez

One of the ugliest aspects of collectivism is its tendency to bundle people into groups regardless of their individual traits. Novelist Ayn Rand wrote, "Racism is the lowest, most crudely primitive form of collectivism. It is the notion of ascribing moral, social or political significance to a man's genetic lineage..."[152]

Despite his Jewish background, Karl Marx's writings displayed anti-Semitism, especially in his 1843 essay "On the Jewish Question." To Marx, Jews were the money lenders, the rising bourgeois class, the very essence of capitalism and the evil it represents.[153]

Marx saw Judaism as a pseudo-religion and characterized market capitalism as "Judaized" economy. He wrote: "The God of the Jews has become secularized and is now a worldly God. The bill of exchange is the Jew's real God. His God is the illusory bill of exchange."[154]

Hyam Maccoby, a British Jewish scholar and dramatist contended that Marx's "On the Jewish Question" was an early example of his hostilities against Jews and religion. Further, Maccoby argued that because of Marx's distress over his own Jewish heritage, he felt compelled to use Jews as a "yardstick of evil."[155]

Hitler's racial policies echoed Marx's anti-Semitic mindset. Nazi propaganda regularly condemned "the materialistic Jewish spirit as the chief evil."[156] But many decades earlier, Marx's opinions were similar to those that eventually led to Nazi policies inflicting suffering on millions of Jews, Gypsies, homosexuals, and other minorities. In his essay "On the Jewish Question," Marx demands a simultaneous elimination of individualism and the Jew, writing:

> As soon a society succeeds in abolishing the empirical essence of Judaism, the huckster, and the conditions which produce him, the Jew will become impossible, because his consciousness will no longer have a corresponding object, because the subjective basis of Judaism, viz: practical needs, will have been humanized, because the conflict of the individual sensual existence, with the generic existence of the individual will have been abolished.[157]

Both the National Socialists and Karl Marx saw the Jew as part of a Jewish capitalistic conspiracy of big banking interests yearning to exploit the working class. The Soviet government in Russia followed Marx's footsteps in mistreating the Jews from the very start of the 1917 October Revolution. The Communist Party set up a Jewish section in their propaganda department (*Yevsektsiya*) to spread the progressive social message to Jews, but the agency opposed traditional Jewish culture and Zionism, considering Judaism as "bourgeois nationalism."

By 1919 the Russian Communist Party began to confiscate Jewish properties and synagogues according to new anti-religious laws. They dissolved many Jewish and Christian communities in accordance with their atheistic views. But there was more to the persecution of the Jews. As collectivists, Communist Party officials wanted everyone to be obedient Russian citizens, to act, speak and conform in the same way. But the Jews were atypical. This caused Lenin to look for systematic ways to assimilate Jews into Russian society. He feared that he could not control millions of Russian Jews who spoke their own language and lived by their own social institutions. Staffed mostly by communist-atheist Jews, the Yevsektsiya was organized as the means to convert the Jewish culture and language into something more manageable through "Russification." The Yevsektsiya program ended in 1929 under the assumption that it had accomplished its mission. Many of its members were arrested and executed in Stalin's Great Purge.

During the Soviet Union's anti-Semitic campaign of 1948–1953, Stalin attempted to destroy Jewish culture, heritage, and religion. There were mass arrests of Jewish intellectuals in an operation to suppress "rootless cosmopolitans" and Zionism. During the 1952 "Night of the Murdered Poets," thirteen prominent Jewish artisans were executed on orders from Stalin. Most Jewish periodicals, newspapers, and synagogues previously allowed to operate before 1948 were censored, halted or annihilated. Soviet anti-Semitic incidents become so rampant that human rights activists coined the phrase "Never Again!"

Many historians suggest that Stalin felt threatened by the new nation-state of Israel, which was siding with the United States. Although the Soviet Union briefly supported the creation of a Jewish state, believing it would become another socialist satellite, Israel instead allied with the West. After this, the government-controlled Soviet media took potshots at Israeli nationalism, sometimes labeling it "fascist."

I remember learning about Soviet anti-Semitism when I met several members of the Jewish Defense League (JDL) in California in the 1970s. Described in *Time* and *Life* magazines as a right-wing Jewish organization, the JDL tirelessly worked to fight racism in Russian and oppose the National Socialist White People's Party (formerly the American Nazi Party) in the United States. I can recall a JDL member showing me cartoons from Soviet newspapers depicting long-nosed Jews as swindlers who violently scooped up synagogue funds for personal use. Other caricatures portrayed Jews as religious fanatics who used brides to ensnare innocent youth into the Jewish faith. In fact, I wrote a position paper for Orange County Young Americans for Freedom in 1972, called "Soviet Jews—Political Prisoners," discussing the discrimination faced by Jewish people living in the Soviet Union.

Newsweek magazine remarked on March 23, 1970, that if the Jewish protests were to continue, "Soviet Jews might find themselves cast as the scapegoats for widespread economic difficulties now plaguing the Soviet Union." This was, of course, the same strategy employed by Hitler to deflect blame for Germany's economic woes on the Jews. The communists in Russia were using the same tactics to oppress minorities. In fact, a simple application to leave Russia and live in Israel constituted an oath of disloyalty. In a so-called classless society, the Soviet Jews were treated as second-class citizens.

By 1971, Seymour Martin Lipset, an American sociologist, was warning in *The New York Times* that many "New Leftists, black militants and anti-Zionists" were heading towards or had already reached "full-fledged anti-Semitism."[158] Called by the *Washington Post* "one of the most influential social scientists of the past half century," Lipset was sounding the alarm that a current wave of anti-Semitism was sweeping the world by "groups which are conventionally described as leftist." In that article, Lipset also reminded his readers that there was "considerable literature" that upheld "anti-Semitism in socialist and other leftist movements" that predated Hitler and his socialist movement.

Even in the late 20th century and early 21st century, little has changed to alleviate ethnic discrimination. Like clockwork, every time a statist Left regime wrestles away political power, one of its first assignments is to maltreat minorities, often targeting Jews and indigenous tribes. These fascistic and racist tactics occurred in both Chávez's Venezuela and Daniel Ortega's Nicaragua. In the case of Nicaragua, Russell Means, a prominent leader in the American Indian Movement (AIM), traveled to the Nicaraguan jungles in 1985 and 1986 to investigate reports of persecution against the Miskito Indians by the one-party dictatorship of Ortega and his Marxist Sandinistas. Here, he discovered that the Marxists were involved in the forced collectivization of the Miskito Indians, compelling them to relocate from their traditional tribal lands to concentration camps. When they resisted, the Indians were intimidated, arrested, or murdered. There were massacres, burning, and the bombing of villages with 500-pound bombs, under a "campaign of systematic violence against the Miskito Indians"[159] that perpetrated ethnic bigotry and cleansing, eventually escalating into a protracted civil war.

Means wanted to save the Miskito Indians from what he warned was "an extermination order" issued by Daniel Ortega's Sandinistas.[160] Means was himself wounded by shrapnel during a bombing raid while his team was gathering evidence of Indian atrocities.[161] In essence, the

Marxist government was treated the native tribes like the reactionary "trash people" that Engels insisted on eliminating. According to Means, Tomás Borge Martínez, the Interior Minister of Nicaragua, referred to the Miskito people as "monkeys hanging around the trees."[162]

At the end of the war, some 14,000 Indians had been imprisoned,[163] causing anthropologist Gilles Bataillon to term the abuses as "politics of ethnocide." Since the Marxist Nicaraguan government now owned all the land in the nation, they were simply obeying their dogma to evict any undesirables they deemed as either homeless or trespassers.

Venezuela has been especially hard hit by a Fascist-Marxist pogrom during the presidency of Hugo Chávez (1999–2013), who befriended the Marxist-Leninist government of Fidel Castro and later Raúl Castro. Chávez worked diligently to uphold the fascist tradition of combining socialism with anti-Semitism, alongside a bastion of nationalist chauvinism. Throughout the presidency of Venezuelan Hugo Chávez, who fancied himself a Marxist-influenced Trotskyite, the Jewish population was under attack. As leader of the United Socialist Party of Venezuela (PSUV), Chávez made a 2005 Christmas Eve address to warn that "a minority, the descendants of the same ones that crucified Christ" had now "taken possession of all of the wealth of the world."[164] Earlier, Chávez had warned oppositional leaders to avoid being "poisoned by those wandering Jews."[165]

Not surprisingly, one of Chávez's "early mentors was the Holocaust-denying Argentine social scientist Norberto Ceresole." This blatant anti-Semitism by the government resulted, perhaps inevitably, in violence. Besides the vandalism and defacement of synagogues, state security forces launched armed raids against Jewish elementary and high schools in Caracas. One Jew from Caracas confessed her horror when she saw swastikas and anti-Semitic slogans such as "Hitler didn't finish the job" plastered on her synagogue walls.[166]

A darling of statist leftists and Hollywood celebrities, Chávez and his *Chavistas* attacked synagogues after government-sponsored rallies, causing Rabbi Henri Sobel of Brazil, a leader of the World Jewish Congress, to accuse Chávez of anti-Semitism.[167] The ominous slogan "Jews go home" was carved across synagogues walls, sometimes tagged by the Communist Party of Venezuela and Chávez's socialist party. The politi-

cal environment for Jews in Venezuela turned so ugly that the American
State Department listed Chávez's socialist government as a "state spon-
sor of antisemitism as well as anti-Israel hysteria."[168]

By 2013, there were over 4,000 anti-Semitic incidents reported in Venezuela. Similar to what happened in Nazi Germany, the Jewish community began to migrate to other nations. By late 2010, over half of Jewish
Venezuelans had emigrated since Chávez's first election victory as president in 1999.[169,170]

Chávez's Marxist legacy continued under his successor, Nicolás Maduro, who watched Venezuela free fall into an economic abyss. The socialization of Venezuela resulted in a crisis where hospitals had no drugs
or basic supplies, where the poverty rate went from 30 percent in 1999
to 87 percent in 2016,[171] chronic food shortages erupted, and children
and the sick began dying from malnutrition. These ill-advised fiscal policies also led to triple-digit inflation ushering in chaos while prices, wages,
and foreign exchange controls prevented commerce, spiking nationalization and blocking domestic production. Finally, first Chávez, and then
Maduro, oversaw intense suppression of the press as well as the militarization of society where the government was spending "more money
than any other country in Latin America on military equipment in recent years."[172] In fact, following fascist doctrine, the Venezuelan socialists have expanded their military prowess. From 2011 to 2015, Venezuela has been "the 18th largest importer of military equipment in the
world."[173]

Despite his campaign to vilify opponents as fascists, Chávez had actually reincarnated Mussolini, projecting his familiar egotistical demeanor,
as well as his loud, boastful and arrogant voice, interlaced with nationalistic jingoism, military chauvinism, and socialist swagger. Both were
self-avowed Marxists who preached street violence to overthrow capitalism and create a dictatorship of the proletariat. In an attempt to imi-
tated Lenin, Mussolini threatened to take over the government of Italy
via a mass march on Rome in 1922. Violence was avoided when the
Italian king transferred power to Mussolini under a multi-party coalition government that was finally terminated in 1925. Chávez attempted
the same maneuver in 1992 when he led a violent military coup d'état
against President Carlos Andrés Pérez that saw hundreds killed in battle.

Chávez's coup was unsuccessful, and yet, like Hitler, he spent little time in prison—only two years.

Hitler's first attempt to seize power also failed. During his 1923 Beer Hall Putsch, two thousand men marched to Munich's center, confronted the police, and battled the authorities, resulting in the death of 16 Nazis and four policemen. Hitler was captured, and imprisoned, but released after a little more than a year. The attempted coup generated front-page headlines around the world. Similarly, Chávez traveled down the same Hitlerian road, where he was also "pushed into fame by his very coup and imprisonment, which fueled his shift towards propaganda rather than violence."[174]

Both Hitler and Chávez nationalized chunks of their economy, developed one-party structures, suffered food shortages,[175] and oversaw inflation serious enough to impose wage and price controls. They both damaged their governments financially by supporting policies of unsustainable welfare, large public work projects, and a military build-up that devolved into an anti-democratic police state. As one journalist warned, "you can't democratically give power to those who tried to take it by force."[176]

In reality, Chávez, Hitler, and Mussolini engaged in an anti-capitalist campaign of authoritarian populism, playing the role of socialist strongmen who promised to stop rich from stealing from the poor in order to spread the wealth out equally—but as it turned out, the economy crumbled and left the country poorer. Along with their disdain for certain races and classes, these socialists promised to make their country great again, alongside sweet-talk of free goodies, disposed to telling the public exactly what they wanted to hear—fascism at its deceptive finest.

The Legacy of Racism in the United States

A virulent strain of racism has been the hallmark of the statist Left in America, particularly the Democrat Party, which was created in the 1830s and supported John C. Calhoun's concept of "positive slavery." One of the most overlooked racists and white segregationists was President Woodrow Wilson (1856–1924). Elected as a Democrat and considered a progressive reformer, Wilson instituted a policy of officially-sanctioned segregation in most federal government departments, including the Navy and Post Office.[177]   One black federal clerk, who worked closely with whites due to his type of work, had a cage built around him.[178]   In other cases, Wilson harassed and demoted black federal employees in order to get them to resign. When some of them protested this strong-arm discrimination, Wilson retorted: "Segregation is not a humiliation but a benefit, and ought to be so regarded by you gentlemen."[179]   During his presidency, Wilson was asked to speak out against the lynching of blacks in the South, but refused, saying that he had no authority.[180]   He held a private White House screening of *The Birth of a Nation*, a film glorifying the Ku Klux Klan. Of the film, Wilson remarked: "It was like writing history with lightning. And my only regret is that it is all so terribly true."[181]   While president of Princeton University, Wilson barred blacks from enrolling, although other Ivy League colleges, were already opening their doors to people of color.[182]

Even in the 20th century, racism often rears its head within the ranks of the collectivist left. During the US presidential election of 2008, members of the New Black Panther Party intimidated voters at a polling station in Philadelphia. Caught on videotape, several men wore paramilitary-style fatigues, black berets, jackboots, with one brandishing a billy club.[183] They intimidated and blocked voters and poll watchers as they shouted racist slurs – "You are about to be ruled by the black man, *cracker*."[184]   Bartle Bull, a longtime civil rights attorney and an aide to Senator Robert F. Kennedy's 1968 presidential campaign, was an eye-witness to the incident. As one of the poll watchers, Bull signed an affidavit attesting to the intimidation, declaring:

> In all my experience in politics, in civil rights litigation and in my efforts in the 1960s to secure the right to vote in Mississippi… I have never encountered or heard of another instance in the United States where armed and uniformed men blocked the entrance to a polling location.[185]

But before the case reached a final sentencing stage, higher-ups in President Obama's Department of Justice (DOJ) ordered the civil rights attorney to dismiss the case, saying that "facts and law" did not support the case. Incredibly, the US Department of Justice was blocking justice and giving a free pass to the black equivalent of a white-hooded Klansman. Some in the media dubbed this incident as a "whitewashing of black racism," a case of unequal justice from an administration that had promised unparalleled transparency.

But the New Black Panther Party is not only anti-white. According to the leftist Southern Poverty Law Center, the black racist organization is "a hate group based on the anti-white, anti-gay, and anti-Semitic views its leaders have repeatedly expressed."[186] One of their leaders and a defendant in the DOJ voter intimidation lawsuit, King Samir Shabazz, has called for racial segregation. He wants "separate societies, segregated on the basis of skin color. Whites here, blacks there, brown-skinned, red-skinned and yellow-skinned people there and there, each in control of their own pieces of real estate." And the only way to make this fundamental change is through "armed insurrection."[187]

An ardent anti-capitalist, Shabazz displayed his bigotry at a 2009 Philadelphia street fair, shouting to a small crowd: "You want freedom? You're gonna have to kill some crackers. You're gonna have to kill some of their babies."[188]

J. Christian Adams, one of the leading voting rights attorneys at the Department of Justice prosecuting the case under the Voting Rights Act of 1965, said the case should have been a "slam-dunk" against "these armed thugs."[189] There was just so much evidence.

After resigning his position at the DOJ, Adams became a whistle-blower. He wrote that the there was a "lawless hostility toward equal enforcement of the law," suggesting that the DOJ had a hidden policy not to prosecute any more voter intimidation cases if the defendant was black and the victims were white. Obviously, this is blatant, government-sponsored racism which is providing special treatment to a group engaged in racial hate. The Civil Rights Division of the DOJ is entrusted with enforcing the Voting Rights Act equally and fairly. Instead, this watchdog agency turned the tables and became what it was supposed to stop by engaging in polities of race-based discrimination.

In a TV news interview, Bartle Bull said that the Department of Justice and Obama's administration were "protecting the abusers instead of the voters." Bull warned that DOJ's dismissal of the case was so flagrant that he believes "Obama has violated his oath of office."[190]

When I engaged a progressive radio show host on this voter intimidation story, he, like many left-wing wonks and pundits, simply disregarded the whole story. It was unimportant; they considered the case as a "non-issue." If two Tea Party leaders had donned paramilitary uniforms, carried a weapon, and spewed out racist epithets at a polling place, they would have been jailed and the story would have made nationwide front-page news. Instead, this story never made many expected inroads in the established press.

It was not until 2018 that blatant racism began to completely saturate the statist Left. For instance, blatant racism raised its ugly head within the media when Don Lemon, host of *CNN Tonight*, berated a particular racial group, declaring on his show: "We have to stop demonizing people and realize the biggest terror threat in this country is white men, ..."[191] Lemon also questioned why there was not a travel ban in place for white men. He was neither fired nor reprimanded. Apparently, as the argument goes, it is not racist if attacks of bigotry and hatred are hurtled against white people.

What if Lemon had instead accused "black men" of being the biggest terror threat, and that they should be put on a travel ban? Of course, shouts of racism would pour down from the hilltops. Obsessed with using the race card for every possible occasion, the progressive left howls against racism while lobbing racist slurs at other races. Apparently, Orwellian doublespeak is the official lingo of the statist-progressive Left.

Another example of virulent racism occurred when *The New York Times* stood by its decision to hire Sarah Jeong for their editorial board even after her racist tweets became known. A lawyer and veteran technology journalist of Korean ancestry, Jeong had tweeted racially inflammatory language against a racial group solely based on the color of their skin—white people. Some of her tweets: "Dumbass fucking white people marking up the internet with their opinions like dogs pissing on fire hydrants," "Oh man it's kind of sick how much joy I get out of being cruel to old white men," and "white men are bullshit." Another anti-white racist tirade read: "Are white people genetically predisposed to burn faster in the sun, thus logically being only fit to live underground like groveling goblins."[192,193] But despite her outright racism she was defended and hired by *The New York Times*.

Curiously, earlier in 2018, another tech specialist, Quinn Norton, was hired by *The New York Times* to join its editorial board. Although she was part of the LGBT community, years-old tweets turned up where she "used slurs against gay people and another in which she retweeted a racial slur."[194] She was immediately fired. Why the double standard? Why is one race viewed by *The New York Times* as worthier than another? This would seem to be pure unadulterated racism, officially advanced by the illiberal, or perhaps better put, the "anti-liberal" *New York Times*.

If Jeong had instead inserted the word "blacks" in her tweets, her career would have been over. It appears that racism today involves discrimination against particular races, but not against white people, at least according to the thinking of the statist-progressive Left.[195] This hypocrisy explains the thinly veiled racism found everywhere on the collectivistic Left side of the fence. To them, it is fine to engage in racism so long as the hate is directed against white people. How can such bigotry be okay against one race, but not others? Evidently, collectivists hold a core belief in the superiority of particular races or group identities over others, since they cultivate groupthink and identity politics that reject the virtues of individual character. But to take a color-blind temperament and judge people by individual character was touted by Martin Luther King, Jr. In a speech delivered to over 250,000 civil rights supporters, King dreamed that his "children will one day live in a nation where they will not be judged by the color of their skin but by the content of their character."[196] In her defense, Jeong replied that her racist rants were just jokes. Unlike Roseanne Barr, whose revived "Roseanne" TV series was canceled by ABC after one offensive tweet in 2018, *The New York Times* simply ignored Jeong's slew of bluntly racist tweets. But in the case of Roseanne Barr, she said she was unaware that Valerie Jarrett, the target of her tweet, was not Arabic, but of European and African-American descent. Barr tweeted: "Muslim brotherhood & planet of the apes had a baby=vj."[197] Immediately, she was condemned with the full force of the statist Left arsenal. She replied, "I'm not sure, but I think I spent the last 24 hours watching the party of inclusion, diversity, understanding, and acceptance, lynch a Jew."[198]

Interestingly, past unconventional antics by Barr had been usually tolerated by the mainstream media. Although she was the 2012 presidential nominee of the Peace and Freedom Party and an Occupy supporter, she turned more conservative by 2016 and voiced support for Donald Trump. In a 2018 interview, Barr suggested that her change occurred when she realized that many of her leftist friends held strong anti-Jew or anti-Israel views. Born into a Jewish family, Barr declared:

> They have called me a racist on the left for a long time ever since I said that the Jewish people have a right to live in their ancestral homeland... that is racism to the far left, which I used to be one of.[199]

Barr lost her television career in Hollywood over a misunderstanding, but Jeong will take her seat on the NYT's editorial board despite her many explicitly racist remarks.

Then there was the cancellation of the "Megyn Kelly Today" TV show in October 2018. The topic focused on a Halloween costume worn by *Real Housewives* star Luann de Lesseps, who desired to imitate the black singer Diana Ross.[200] In a lively discussion with other guests, Kelly, a former TV host on the conservative Fox News channel, stated that it is now considered racist to paint your face for Halloween, explaining that

> You do get in trouble if you are a white person who puts on blackface for Halloween or a black person who puts on whiteface for Halloween. Like back when I was a kid it was okay if you were dressing up as a character.[201]

Within 48 hours, accusations of racism shattered the airwaves and Kelly's benign comments were grounds for axing her TV show. Apparently, honest discussion about race issues and how they have changed now qualified as a firing offense. But other Hollywood stars have done more than talk about black facial makeup. Robert Downey Jr. performed an entire movie in blackface in the 2008 comedy movie *Tropic Thunder*. Jimmy Fallon, Jimmy Kimmel, and Sarah Silverman all performed in blackface during some point in their career.[202] At the 2017 Golden Globe Awards show, Jimmy Fallon showed an old 2000 *Saturday Night Live* clip of himself doing a Chris Rock impression while wearing a blackface.[203] The comedy skit bombed, but Fallon was not fired from his position as the host of NBC's *The Tonight Show.*

So, why were there so many demands for NBC to cancel Megyn Kelly's show? In their zeal to enforce political correctness, the statist Left had to silence anyone from entering into controversial or unpopular subject matter so as to prevent them from wandering off the approved pathway. Kelly was torpedoed by the current fear that almost everyone, especially whites, have become crypto-racists. Like the hysterical "red scare" that brought about the McCarthyism of 1950s, the current "racist scare" foresees all sorts of bigots and white supremacists hiding under every bed in America. And in doing so, the mainstream media like NBC erode diversity and discourse, while projecting their own biases onto others to quash commentary about issues that might stray from the populist view. The firing of Kelly was simply part of a campaign of identity politics geared to silence opposing viewpoints. They want exclusion, not inclusion, where they can treat heretics unequally in the name of equality and censor opinions in the name of free speech. What better way to shut down free speech than by eliminating anyone who might offend or disturb the status-quo?

But the mainstream media has often been complacent in silencing certain narratives they oppose, often ignoring transgressions against free speech and liberty in general, shifting from neutral observer to political actor. When NBC News reporter Cal Perry and his crew prepared to cover a peace rally in Charlottesville, Virginia, they were attacked by Fascist-Marxist Antifa protesters. They were forced to flee the scene.[204] The violent protesters were trying to shut down the free press, who were covering an important story that marked the one-year anniversary of the 2017 deadly Charlottesville protests.[205]

But NBC commentators failed to mention the attack on their own reporter and cameraman in the next day's *Sunday Today* TV show; no rebuke of fascist-like tactics by an angry mob of camera smashing vandals. NBC broadcasters only hinted that the media were simply "heckled" by protesters, appearing to cave in to Antifa's demands not to be exposed as violent street bullies.[206]

Deconstruction of Lockean Liberalism

Looking through the yellowed typewritten pages of my book that I wrote back in the early 1970s on libertarian and anarchist philosophy, I could not help but notice my questioning of the left-right dichotomy. I saw it as illogical and confusing and confessed that I needed more research material, which was fairly limited at my college library. But I was apparently dauntless in that I rediscovered an old and forgotten letter to the editor that I wrote in 1970 regarding the misconceptions about the outdated political left-right continuum taught at school. My letter clumsily spelled out the essence of the later-known Nolan Chart: that a reality-based political spectrum must be consistent and reliable. Around this time, I happened upon a scholar who was one of the first to frame the political division in the post-World War II world. As far back as 1947, J. Pepa focused on this sharp left-right division, succinctly writing: "The individual on one side, the state on the other; that is the underlying substance of this contrast."[207]

Pepa had identified the individualism versus collectivism divide, which became more apparent as liberalism continued to morph into a form of unfettered statism. This caused individualists of original liberalism to rebrand themselves under the classical liberal banner. The movement towards anti-liberalism culminated in the gradual deconstruction of Lockean liberalism, which was both a travesty and a triumph for the myth-making arsenal of socialist disinformation. At the beginning of the 20th century, the Progressive movement began to drift towards an authoritarian doctrine of "strait jacketism," a sort of early anti-capitalist postmodernism that rejected objective reality while propagating political hybrids of socialism, tribalism, fascism, and nationalism. As early as World War I, the nascent theories of cultural Marxism were causing modern liberals to abandon Western culture, learning instead to distrust truth, objectivity, and open dialogue. And without a devotion to reason and truth, most liberals were destined to alter their philosophical DNA, soon becoming almost unrecognizable from their original Lockean rootstock.

The core principles of liberalism shifted to refocus on the collectivistic culture of abstract groupthink, group rights, statism, militant equalitarianism, class conflict, redistribution of wealth, and authoritarian overtones to institute group identity. Such fundamental changes pushed group-oriented liberals towards the ugly side of racism, state-terrorism, tax-theft, moral self-righteousness, intolerance, monopolistic central banking (Federal Reserve), prohibition of alcohol, eugenic sterilization, jailing of anti-war leaders, censorship, interventionism, and gunboat diplomacy.

These pseudo-liberals became the "drill-sergeant overlords" for socially and politically acceptable processes to institutionalize violence and threats of intimidation to re-engineer society. In the early 20th century, liberalism began to almost unnoticeably morph into a collective-based dogma which subordinated individual identity to group identity. This transcending of liberalism towards the politics of group power kindled ideologies that fostered honeycomb-like structures that compartmentalize society into conflicting socioeconomic classes and racial interest groups, which abetted in segregating and destabilizing society—the tyranny of identity politics. For American collectivists, this uncharted territory offered an opportunity to divide and conquer society before ossifying or assimilating people into a new world order.

To the utopian-driven modern liberal, individuals no longer existed, only groups within groups. Modern, social liberals had mutated into "Machiavellians in drag," Jacobin-inspired provocateurs, and overbearing babushkas with red scarves and espial eyes, all smug with the satisfaction that the deployment of state violence would solve most of the basic problems of humanity.

What this all means is that the political spectrum has radically shifted, mostly due to fabricated data, obfuscation, and historical sabotage. Meanwhile, the statist Left embarked on an ideological voyage towards Marxist-inspired Italian Fascism (Marxism-lite) which, if its exploratory route remains steadfast, will likely disembark at the shores of communism. It is almost a preordained journey. When a society decides to mingle do-goodism with coercion, they can often justify control over every aspect of human action, intervening in both the personal and economic lives of the plebs. Within no time, the organizing power of politics can transform into an orgy of servitudal dominance and criminalization.

Such statist journeys are often self-fulfilling prophecies, a sort of never-ending odyssey that searches for the truth but gets swayed by the false. Flourishing under a reign of errors, these political jesters intentionally plant falsehoods, disguising untruths to persuade others to yield to their political agenda. These falsehoods are dressed up so seductively that the unsuspecting public will lust after them like Paris for Helen of Troy.

In their deliberately fabricated fiction, these illiberal charlatans flip-flop the meaning of words and make what was once completely erroneous appear genuinely truthful. And by their doing so, the mind envisages truth where it once only saw self-evident fallacies. For deeply rooted in the stateophiles' psyche is the Machiavellian principle of power that embellishes deceit and treachery in order to retain the people's faith in government. Under this strategy to maintain legitimacy, politicos popularize glorious visions of the future, manifesting a journey worth killing or dying for, even if predicated on monstrous lies. The adaptability of dishonesty has been the statists' main weapon of choice and their most valuable currency. Even the German philosopher Friedrich Nietzsche recognized the true nature of the prevaricative state, writing: "Everything the state says is a lie."[208]

Extreme collectivists are always rushing ahead to impose a brave new world of visionary utopian delights that are fictitious to the fidelity of human nature. To come within sight of their communal vision, they must be willing to enter the half-way mark of nanny-state liberalism, the gateway ideology. Then, if unsatisfied, they move to the borders of National Socialism and Italian Fascism, and, if still wanting, take the last steps to the futile worker's paradise state under communism.

The journey is everything to the dedicated interventionist. Mussolini was eager to provide such directions to this dreamland, offering his vision of "communalville." He even identified the economic tenets of John Keynes with fascist economics. Modern leftists have supported civil liberties in the past, but that claim had been undermined by President Obama's anti-civil liberties history. The statist Left has been losing its pro-civil rights credentials and moral high ground for reasons that are clear. With President Obama's support for the USA Patriot Act, NSA's mass spying on US citizens, FISA's secret courts, secret judges, secret laws, secret warrants, and secret rulings,[209] the 2012 National Defense Authorization Act (NDAA), which permits indefinite detention without trial, drone killings of US citizens overseas without trial or jury, it turns out that, state-centric, authoritarian liberalism has more in common with Mussolini, Hitler, and Stalin than with Jefferson, Madison, and Paine. The contemporary statist Left has self-circuited itself, disdained the true origins of liberalism and free markets, and veered towards the collectivism of both national and international socialism. The statist Left has transformed itself into a formidable anti-Founders movement.

The most disturbing tragedy in the debasement of original liberalism was the ease by which its adherents were willing to surrender to the insidious gifts of an overreaching fascist-like authority. They no longer wished to reduce the size of aggressive predators—the scaly leviathans; they instead sought to pump up the beastie with performance-enhancing steroids. Limiting the scope of government was no longer considered sacrosanct by the early 20th century. Instead of defending the cause of liberty, which is the accepted dictionary definition of liberalism, post-liberals instead march in lockstep with statist-enriched agendas, dead set on releasing stormtroopers and parity-pushers to impose their "social justice-for-all" ideology. As philosopher Tibor R. Machan spelled out in *Private Rights and Public Illusions*:

> While the expansion of government may be motivated by concerns for justice and human well-being, it instead institutionalizes the use of invasive force against the liberties and privacy of the innocent, the very people it allegedly exists to protect.[210]

The original liberals simply wanted to be free to engage in their own virtues or vices. They abided by a "live and let live" approach to life, trusting that the cooperative and mutual behavior of people is far more beneficial than applying nightsticks, jackboots, and bullets to accomplish good deeds. They sought to protect individual autonomy from imposed social obligations and perpetual wars, fearful that the state would usurp society's self-governance authority. As individualists and free-thinkers, the true free-Left liberals were extremely skeptical of authority and were favorable towards decentralizing decision-making. Often endowed with a logical and scientific inclination, these liberals believed that each person knew how to improve his own affairs better than a gaggle of bureaucrats thousands of miles away. To their way of thinking, governments usually lacked moral and political legitimacy, which reinforced the original liberals' conviction that people, not government, should run society.

Although John Lockean liberals sought to mind their own business, they placed great emphasis on having everyone work together to assist the community during thick and thin times. Free societies are inherently interdependently connected with each other in a mutualism of beneficial association. Adam Smith addressed this issue in his 1759 book *The Theory of Moral Sentiments*, but this classical liberal stressed that people must want to help each other, and not be compelled to be charitable. A thousand points of light burning with voluntarism bring the community together under an independence and interdependence duality. To physically force people to help others can only impart animosity. A community is best forged with the tools of cooperation and collaboration. This exemplified the Age of Enlightenment and the "velvet liberal" who was divergently-minded, a free-thinker, scientifically inclined, who did not want anybody lording over him or his fellow man; that would be tantamount to being under the yoke of slavery.

Interestingly, such ideas of self-governance unknowingly put the original liberals in league with the anarcho-individualist camp—Lysander Spooner, Henry David Thoreau, William Godwin, and Herbert Spencer to name a few. Even Thomas Jefferson has been seen by some scholars as a "philosophical anarchist."[211] Nonetheless, both anarchists and minarchists had no desire to hold the reins of political power to alter humanity towards perfection, understanding that such busybodyness is a fool's game. The more far-sighted sages realized that real change only comes from within, not from without.

Unfortunately, original liberalism of the free-Left was seduced by the tribal and vague notions of the common good and utilitarianism, a sort of collectivized conformity that ultimately requires forced interventionism to carry out some mandate of undefined equality of outcome. These theories hold that an individual can be sacrificed for the good of the whole—like a lamb to the slaughter. In Dostoevsky's *Crime and Punishment*, the anti-hero protagonist suggests that the murder of one person could be justified if the perpetrator were to help many others. Did it matter if one person was put to the sword if that act saved hundreds? Is there not redemption in numbers? Of course, this rationalization leads to the slippery slope where any unethical behavior can be justified. But the most serious problem of the common good is this: Who will be the arbitrator in determining the one killed? Who is to decide the criteria for putting one innocent person to death? And who is to say that only one murder will be enough? When liberals begin to believe that an individual can be justly sacrificed for the good of others, true liberalism dies and genocide becomes an acceptable option.

A host of collectivist theories, from the common good, utilitarianism to paternalism, had a crippling effect on the soul of liberalism. Nanny-statists would naturally disagree, except when the issue involves something that lets them freely convey their statist opinions—the right to free speech. Until recently, these champions of state interventionism seem to have an aversion to regulating the unfettered exercise of free speech. Why the inconsistency? Why not come out in favor of meddling in everything? Shouldn't the state impose heavy regulations and licensing on every journalist, editor, and author, similar to what other professions must lawfully endure? Apparently, that is what has happened. Those who see themselves as broad-minded liberals have finally realized how dangerous it is to permit unfettered speech for everyone. They are now eager to snap shackles over the hands of universal free speech. They have weaponized into legions of intolerant bigots who feel the urge to control everything in life. That is not the true nature of liberalism.

Usually, control-maniacs have a messianic passion to shove everyone through the regulatory thickets, believing that uncontrollable chaos would ensue without the disciplinary fist of government. To ask for no government control or oversight over speech and press is the equivalent of believing that anarchy should reign supreme forever. How could the denizens of the collective deep support the lawlessness of anarchy in any form, especially the marketplace of information? They cannot. Historical figures from Lenin to Mussolini publicly embraced free speech until they seized power. Most politicians give lip-service to the concept of liberty while secretly attempting to conspire against it.

But modern statist leftists have taken up the assumption that they are "absolutely morally superior" to all other peoples. They are without a scintilla of self-doubt or skepticism, affirming that their noble goals are inevitable. Such scary total moral certainty fails to allow for errors, and in doing so, unleashes the Kraken of totalitarian dictatorship that can obliterate all traces of civil rights and liberties.

Superiority vs. Inferiority Bias

Collectivism provides the social mechanics to rationalize racist attitudes or actions. Since the group is more important than the individual, individuals can be persecuted, and competing groups can be attacked or praised without regards to the diversity of their individual members. As an example of the latter, if a particular group has a collective tendency to cheat people in financial dealings, every member will likely be painted with the same wide, stereotypical brushstroke. Group character becomes more important than individual character.

The danger of collectivism is that it treats the individual as irrelevant baggage, believing that only the aggregate opinion of the group matters. In a way, collectivists perceive society as something independent and separate from the human actions of individuals. This stereotypical construct relegates the individual subordinate to the group. Thus, it judges people according to the social, cultural and economic norms to which they belong. This leads to an anti-diversity mentality, with collective groups understood as only being based on their congruent identity.

This kind of discrimination often has little to do with a person's skin color, dress, religion, age, or nationality. The real culprit is the arrogance of feeling superior to another human being or group. Most people want to associate with bright and witty people, which is another way of saying that they try to avoid the opposite—dull and half-witted plebs.

A case in point is the strained relationship between West and East Germans. For 40 years, East and West Germans were unable to communicate with each other until the Berlin Wall fell in 1989. When the borders opened up, the two German sides had the opportunity to greet each other and compare notes. These encounters soon turned unpleasant. The westernized Germans, the "Wessi," regarded the easternized Germans, the "Ossi," as lazy, unskilled, and provincial. On the other hand, the Ossis saw the Wessi as arrogant know-it-alls. These acts of discrimination were serious. For decades, there were few marriages between the West and East Germans. They simply did not get along. Nonetheless, this hostility was not based on ethnic discrimination—they both came from the same Germanic ancestry and language. Because West Germany was based on market economics, their citizens became more educated, technical, and sophisticated. Meanwhile, East Germans vegetated under an outdated and backward socialist economy incapable of keeping up with a fast-changing world.

The political divide between capitalist and socialist systems caused a societal rift. Still, the discrimination is based on groupthink—one group feeling superior to another group. The important point to remember is that nationality, race, religion, or gender are not the real determinate for the specters of hatred and intolerance; it is usually the yearning to feel far superior to another person or group.

Positive and Negative Racism of the Statist Left

Although modern leftists bathe in a whirlpool of collectivism, many of them were active in the 1960s Civil Rights Movement. These liberals, including civil libertarians, stood firmly next to Martin Luther King, Jr. in his fight against state-sponsored Jim Crow Laws, forced segregation, and officially mandated and institutional racism. And yet, while still duty-bound to a collectivistic bias, they racked up a solid record against racial discrimination. Or did they?

Consider this. Nanny-state liberals were correct in their opposition to state-instituted "*negative* racism," but did they also support state-instituted "*positive* racism?" Unfortunately, yes. Many modern liberals strongly advocated "force racial integration" of public schools through forced busing court orders and mandates. After the passage of the Civil Rights Act of 1964, leftists turned the tables and dabbled in positive racism. Just as Alabama's Governor George Wallace tried to block desegregation at the University of Alabama, left-wing judges and politicians used National Guardsmen, police, guns, tear gas and jail to forcibly bus children to mostly *de facto* segregated schools. Of course, since public institutions of learning are funded by all citizens, such segregation is not only illegal, but morally corrupt.

Still, forced integration is just as racist as forced segregation. Statist liberals have believed that forcing the races together at gunpoint would cause more harmony and less racial tension. Of course, compelling people to do anything frequently leads to distasteful unintended consequences. For every force, there is a counterforce. To bring about social change by threats of physical violence can cause deep resentment and a climate of injustice. So, no matter how noble the intentions of government may be, many people will have the inclination to do the exact opposite. Nobody likes to have a gun shoved in their face and be told what to do. Most people want to make their own decisions.

To believe that equality, community, and fraternity will surge by forcing races or any group together or apart is not only lunacy but racially intolerant. This is like saying that black people or other minorities cannot advance unless they associate with so-called smarter races, and many black American parents understood this racist point. In the case of forced busing, some black parents and leaders disclosed that they were insulted by the notion that their child could only academically excel if he or she sat next to a white child. Naturally, racial tensions in these schools escalated. Racial identity became more pronounced and, therefore, a barrier to better understanding between races. Even a supporter of busing for desegregation purposes, Nancy St. John, came to the same shocking conclusion after studying 100 cases of urban busing in the north, finding no significant black academic improvement, and that forcefully-integrated schools had worse interracial relations than non-integrated schools.[212] And yet, although 96 percent of whites and 91 percent of blacks opposed forced busing outside of their neighborhood, the practice remained intact for almost 30 years.[213]

So, what did modern, social liberal politicians do? Very little. Many US Senators made solemn promises that the Civil Rights Act of 1964 would not trigger forced busing. Senator Hubert Humphrey, citing the 1963 *Bell v. School City of Gary, Indiana* decision, remarked that the ruling "makes it clear that while the Constitution prohibits segregation, it does not require integration."[214] Two years later, the Department of Health, Education, and Welfare made these promises worthless and ordered a slew of cities to forcibly integrate their government-run schools.

In another example of positive racism (sometimes dubbed reverse racism), by the 1960s the modern liberal started to campaign for all sorts of special race-based policies of affirmative action and quotas for minorities. Certainly, this is better than legislation designed to harm, damage, or block opportunities to groups of people, but such legislation should still attempt to be equally colorblind to everyone. No racial group should receive an advantage over another racial group, especially in tax-supported institutions. Unfortunately, the statist Left has demanded that people be hired or promoted according to race or gender, and not by merit. This perspective is the very definition of racial and gender discrimination. Furthermore, this racist attitude can be characterized as

> racial determinism, where individuals cannot hope to succeed outside the stereotyped behavior of their racial background, their skin color and physical features determining their performance, except when Government steps in to save them (this is statist messianism).[215]

Fearless of limitless government action, these statist leftists got caught up in the politics of racial favoritism. Under their plans to impose equality, they favored one group over another in order to overcome racial imbalance. This is understandable. Many minorities have been gravely injured by past government legislation, especially state-enacted slavery and segregation laws in the Democrat Party south, but state-driven discrimination was not imposed on just one group or minority. Such discrimination was rampant and ubiquitous for anyone outside of the majority.

Libertarians were appalled over the Southern states' legislative efforts to strip minorities of their "equal justice" and individual rights before the law. After all, the abolitionist movement came out of classical liberalism. Many of the free-Left classical liberals and civil libertarians were active in the Civil Rights movement. Racial discrimination is a clear example of the dangers of majority rule. Southern white governments represented a "tyranny of the majority" over the liberty of the weaker minority. Obviously, the white majority felt justified in abusing the minority black population, but this is what majority-based democracy has repeatedly imposed in the past. Discrimination against a powerless minority is the normal operating procedure in a system that puts group rights above individual rights.

So, what is so wrong with promoting positive racism policies? These well-intended measures attempt to help underprivileged minorities. However, the danger is the dosage. Too much political power granted to a particular group leads to polarization, political hardball, and the rationalization for more control over society. Further, when group rights are substituted for individual rights, collectivists can easily flip-flop from a positive mindset to a negative stereotype. Remember, to collectivists, it is all about identity politics of the group. If a few members of a group engage in nefarious acts, everyone in that group could be tarnished with the same negative image—creating a hard-to-remove stigmatic image.

But the overwhelming problem with identity politics is that it defines individuals by the group he or she belongs to, and therefore creates division, not inclusion. Under this illiberal social construct, similar to the racist tactics used by the National Socialists of Germany, people are classified within a particular group: race, gender, ethnicity, sexual orientation, religion, culture, and nationality. This formula collectivizes and segregates society to the benefit of the political elites who are often solely motivated by power-seeking agendas.

During the Nazi era, the concept of political identity was used to strong-arm German citizens to distrust and hate other groups, notably the Jewish community. People were compelled to become what their group represented, often leading to stereotyping which made it easier to divide, attack, and persecute outsiders. Here, the populace is expected to assume, for instance, that if a person is white, he or she has to condone white supremacy. The Nazis expertly used the tyranny of identity politics to make German citizens believe that anyone from another identity group could be regarded as enemies of the people and treated as traitors, subhuman and entirely expendable.

An example of this identity politics occurred after the Japanese military-government attacked Pearl Harbor in 1941. Many Americans suddenly turned against US citizens of Japanese heritage and supported their forced relocation and incarceration in concentration camps, believing that they would be traitors. But the primary responsibility of a free government is to protect the rights of all citizens, not just some. Instead, FDR's administration blamed the war policies of the Imperial Japanese government on the American citizens of Japanese ancestry, who came to America to escape the injustices of Japan's dictatorship.

One of the few newspapers in the United States that publicly opposed the forcible internment of 110,000 Japanese-American citizens during World War II was the *Santa Ana Register*, (now known as the *Orange County Register*) owned by R.C. Holies, one of the last remaining classical liberal-libertarians of his day.

In sharp contrast to the collectivists, the individualist sees everyone through a transparent, character-driven prism. To him, what the group thinks is not very relevant. Those caught up within a groupthink vacuum find it difficult to break free of an already established paradigm that treats people, not as individuals, but as a subset segment of society.

I can still remember an incident where I had business dealings with a black couple. Someone asked me whether my clients were black, wondering if he knew them. I could not remember. I did not think in terms of race. My powers of observation have always concentrated on personal character, and less on outward appearances. I see people as unique individuals. I do not adjust my treatment of a person because of their ethnicity—negative or positive. That is just not a factor.

Modern, social leftists often bend over backward to help minorities. This is what community is all about, but exclusive favoritism can quickly reverse to a negative side effect. I observed an incident where a modern liberal had been caught in a whirlwind of violent ghetto crime—beaten senseless by a gang of minorities and almost died. After the experience, her positive racism switched 180 degrees into hateful invectives that bordered on negative racism. One negative incident spurred her to condemn a minority group as violent thugs and thieves, suggesting that they were all that way. Groupthink can easily backslide into group intolerance and discrimination fixated against an entire ethnicity or class.

A collectivistic mindset is often primed to explode into a discriminatory rant by judging a person by the uncivil activities of a few members of the group. This is what occurred in National Socialist Germany with different races and in Soviet Russia with different classes—a sort of ideological determinism combined with identity politics. The results were horrific.

Besides engaging in positive racism, the progressive left is fearful that swift change will not come about unless government becomes involved. They would rather use the brass knuckles of government to impose their beliefs than attempt to facilitate change through voluntary, Gandhi-like action. The free-Left libertarians have been chastised for believing too strongly in the principles of voluntary and peaceful activities to correct wrongs. They shy away from government mandates and instead support boycotts, sit-ins and peaceful civil disobedience as originated by Henry David Thoreau and practiced by Gandhi and Martin Luther King, Jr. Progressives and statists often seek shortcuts by unleashing the guard dogs of state repression on what they disfavor, believing that racial discrimination cannot be curtailed without violent intervention by authorities. This attitude is framed to imply that American citizens are completely useless in stopping an injustice. Historically, Americans have self-organized into mass movements to stop political injustice—the anti-slavery abolitionists, the women's suffrage and civil rights movements, to name the more familiar ones.

The grassroots civil rights movement came about because Americans were willing to risk their lives and liberty to protest against "whites only" bathrooms, restaurants, drinking fountains, schools, hospitals, etc. Sheldon Richman in *The Christian Science Monitor* writes:

> Starting in Greensboro, North Carolina, in 1960, lunch counters throughout the South began to be desegregated through direct but peaceful confrontation—sit-ins—staged by courageous students and others who refused to accept humiliating, second-class citizenship. Four years before the Civil Rights Act passed, lunch counters in downtown Nashville were integrated within four months of the launch of the Nashville Student Movement's sit-in Campaign.

City and state police often reacted violently by beating up and jailing many of the protestors. But with Gandhi-style tactics, civil rights activists were beginning to shame bigots and southern society into seeing the injustice of an apartheid-like society. The Greensboro protest eventually spread to a nationwide boycott of all segregated department stores.[216]

Actions do speak louder than words. Senator Barry Goldwater, the Republican presidential nomination in 1964, worked hard to desegregate the Arizona National Guard and the Senate cafeteria. In fact, he got his family to end segregation in their Phoenix department store. Goldwater, however, opposed a small anti-property rights portion (Title II) of the Civil Rights Act of 1964, saying "You can't legislate morality." He believed that privately-owned shops should able to serve whomever they please, without government-imposed mandates. A supporter of past Civil Rights legislation in 1957 and 1960, Goldwater believed that it was wrong to legally mandate racial equality to remedy discrimination.[217] Additionally, a large number of Democrats and modern liberals did not support the Civil Rights Act of 1957. Senator John F. Kennedy voted against this groundbreaking civil rights legislation, as did Senator Al Gore, Sr. President Kennedy actually opposed Martin Luther King, Jr.'s 1963 March on Washington.

Another habit of the statist Left's culture is an eagerness to level charges of racism against anyone who dares to question its authority or policies. This is pure politics of the worse sort. In today's Western world of increased tolerance towards others, to cry "racism!" at the drop of a hat is the last refuge of a scoundrel who has lost his or her argument.

The Statist Left and the Arab-Muslim World

There is a strange relationship that is increasingly difficult to comprehend between the modern statist Left and the Arab-Muslim world. The statist Left clearly ignores the medieval cultural climate that permeates most Arab-Muslim societies. These societies are still ruled by monarchists or dictators, oppose democratic values, engage in anti-Semitic behavior and patriarchal privileges, adhere to a theocratic state, foster hostility towards gays, feminism and tolerance, oppose individualism, admire nationalism, and favor a type of tribal socialism that suffocates the liberty of human action. This narrative has no linkage to the liberalism of plurality, individual liberty, freedom of conscience and belief. Strangely, the statist Left trivializes such nightmarishly reactionary beliefs, and panders to fundamental Islamic movements and leaders. Moreover, they rarely protest directly against Muslims' staunch opposition to the separation of church and state or criticize their defense of Sharia law, which is totally incompatible with secular governance, freedom of thought and action, the 1948 United Nations' Universal Declaration of Human Rights, and particularly women's rights.

For instance, the *Hisbah* doctrine holds that every Muslim is obliged to report any violation of Sharia or acts of apostasy to the authorities. When someone disrespects Islam by converting to another religion or blasphemy, the offender can be "subject to the death penalty, forfeiture of property, nullification of marriage" or other legal punishment.[218] The death penalty is rare in legal proceedings, but Islamic terrorists outside of state law are prone to use it. Sharia law also authorized the institution of slavery, but due to pressure from England and France, most Muslim lands had outlawed or suppressed slavery by the early 20th century. However, there was no ideological debate among the Muslim populace, as compared to the Abolitionist movement in America, to challenge slavery since it was so profoundly anchored to Islamic law.[219]

In spite of the harshness of Sharia law, the statist Left often turns a blind eye to Islamism's marriage of a monotheistic church to a despotic state, while firing a broadside of lawsuits and campaigns of intimidation at Judeo-Christian groups if they attempt to retain religious symbols on public land or buildings. To them, somehow the classical liberal tenet that calls for the separation of church and state is relevant for everyone except Islamic nations.

But it appears to be worse than that. Despite the extremely anti-liberal nature of Islamic fundamentalism, the statist Left appears to be enthralled with the current status of the Arab-Muslim world and tends to look the other way when extremist Islamists go on killing sprees. Instead of holding Muslims accountable to Mohammad's concepts of peace as found in the beautifully written *Quran*, they denounce the Judeo-Christian community, who have evolved past their state-religion days and have accepted most of classical liberalism's tenets by the 20th century.

Interestingly, a number of young libertarians from the Muslim Liberty Caucus once revealed to me that the Prophet Mohammad and the early Islamic communities were more liberal in their understanding of religious human rights.[220] Apparently, such plurality is supported by "scriptural Islamic sources."[221] For instance, one line in the *Quran* states: "There shall be no compulsion in religion."[222] These libertarians asserted that government, legal, and bureaucratic creep suffocated Mohammad's original intent in respect to the universality of human rights and freedom of belief. It was heartening, but that is not the current state of affairs in most Islamic regions.

The Arab-Muslim world shares much in common with other authoritarian and monistic political systems. Not surprisingly, a cozy relationship developed between the National Socialists and the Arab-Muslim political elite, starting in the 1930s, which revealed a strong ideological commonality between the two. Within a few weeks of Hitler's rise to Germany's Chancellorship in 1933, the German Consul-General in Jerusalem for Palestine, Heinrich Wolff, touted Mohammed Amin al-Husseini's eager support of the Nazis, especially of their anti-Jewish boycott across Germany. Wolff relayed to Berlin that Amin al-Husseini, the Grand Mufti of Jerusalem since 1921, had asserted that the Muslims in Palestine "looked forward to the spread of Fascism throughout the region."[223]

To many in the Middle East, Nazi Germany was considered the natural ally of the Arab and Muslim world. When Amin al-Husseini finally traveled to Europe in 1941, he first met with Mussolini in Italy and declared his intentions to ally with the Axis. A number of high-level Nazi leaders learned of this encounter and invited the Palestinian leader to visit Hitler in Berlin. Hitler was interested in the Arabic nations and their rising animosity towards Jews and the British and agreed to meet with Amin al-Husseini on November 28, 1941. In that meeting, Al-Husseini pressed for Arab independence, particularly the liberation of Palestine from the British. He also sought to prevent the establishment of a Jewish national home in Palestine, as had been proposed by the British government. This might look like normal political negotiations between nations, but al-Husseini had a darker side. He began to work for the Nazis and became involved in the Arabic-language service broadcast program. He made a series of propaganda broadcasts from Berlin in an effort to "foment unrest, sabotage, and insurrection against the Allies."[224] Obviously, al-Husseini was a Nazi collaborator and used his influence to turn Arabs against the Jews and Western Allies. In a Nazi-sponsored radio broadcast in 1944, he asked Arabs to rise up and "Kill the Jews wherever you find them."[225] In his supervision of pro-Nazi radio broadcasts out of Zeesen, Athens, and Rome, al-Husseini was considered more effective than any other Arab leader at "promoting hatred of the Jews among Muslims."[226]

But the Nazis did more than broadcast messages to the Middle East by Arabic National Socialists. There was a drive to give students from Arab countries German scholarships, to have business firms take in Arab apprentices, and invite Arab party leaders to "Nuremberg party rallies and military chiefs to Wehrmacht maneuvers."[227] In fact, the Nazis established an "Arab Club" in Berlin as the "center for Palestine-related agitation and Arabic-language broadcasting." Some Nazi leaders, such as Heinrich Himmler, talked about the "ideology closeness" of National Socialism and Islam, coming up with the concept of *Muselgermanen* or "Muslimo-Germans."[228]

As for creating an Arab-Nazi army, Amin al-Husseini by 1943 helped to arrange the creation of the 13th *Waffen-SS* Mountain Division (also called the "*Handschar*"), mostly manned by Bosnian Muslims, to fight the Allies. Some 24,000 to 27,000 Arab recruits signed up to fight with the Nazis.[229] Because of his collaboration with the Nazis, the American Jewish Congress (AJC) has described Amin al-Husseini as "Hitler's henchman."[230]

But oddly, anyone today who dares to criticize the ideological and theological dimensions of Islam becomes an object of scorn for supposedly hating Muslims. This happened to Ayaan Hirsi Ali, a Somali-born Dutch-American woman who abandoned Islam and advocates the self-determination of people to decide their own religious or non-religious beliefs. She opposes honor killings, stoning, forced marriage, female genital mutilation, blasphemy laws, child marriage, and acid-in-the-face attacks, and in doing so has been designated by the left-wing Southern Poverty Law Center (SPLC) as an "anti-Muslim extremist."[231] Although the SPLC is supposedly committed to seeking justice, that apparently "doesn't include civil rights in the Muslim world or among Muslims living in the US."[232] Somehow, to the statist Left, Muslim reformers and civil rights advocates do not deserve to be defended. Instead, time and money are spent to go after Judeo-Christian symbols and displays of historical documents such as the Ten Commandments and monuments, all criticized as crossing the line between church and state. Where are the outcries over Islam's blatant marriage of church and state where almost 2 billion people suffer under the rule of its theocratic dictatorships?

To illustrate this hypocrisy and prejudice, consider what happened to Ayaan Hirsi Ali when Brandeis University in Massachusetts offered her an honorary degree in 2014. Within a month or two, Brandeis University rescinded the offer after 85 faculty members and several Islamic students' groups accused her of "intolerance" and hate speech.[233] The president of the Brandeis, Frederick M. Lawrence, an American lawyer and civil rights scholar, said that Hirsi Ali's core values were "Islamophobic." With several death-threat Fatwas hanging over her head, she once declared that "Islam is part religion, and part a political-military doctrine," and that the Muslim's "political doctrine contains a world view, a system of laws and a moral code that is totally incompatible with our constitution, our laws, and our way of life."[234]

In 2017, Hirsi Ali was prevented from speaking in Australia by a coalition of far leftist and radical Islamist women. They were akin to the statist Left in America, engaged in unethical practices to silence dissenting voices. Her distractors threatened mass demonstrations at her speaking ventures, while condemning her in the media as voicing the language of white supremacists, hate mongering, and profiting from "an industry that exists to dehumanize Muslim women."[235]

In response, Hirsi Ali denounced those who wanted to shut down the debate and sabotage her speaking tour, declaring: "Today you have this horrible alliance between the far left and the Islamists and they're using the modern media tool to shut people like me out by smearing us."[236] This is just another example of the authoritarian Left's sometimes militant tactics to snuff out free speech, nullify civil liberties and reverse liberal rights to self-determination, often in partnership with other fascist-like or autocratic doctrinaires.

The Power to Do Good and Bad

The power to do good is also the same power to do bad. This is one principle that statist leftists have never fully understood. They feel entitled to engage in all sorts of dangerous endeavors that could retrogress the Western World back to the imperialist, mercantilist, and monarchical dark days of the past.

For instance, the power to prohibit segregation of the races is also the power to impose segregation. In the early years after the American Revolution, many blacks in the South enjoyed the equal right to vote and own property. In fact, a community of interracial marriage had developed in the colony of Virginia before the British authorities quenched the Bacon Rebellion of 1676.[237] After the British regained control of burned-out Jamestown, the political elite obtained the authority to begin the institution of slavery—slowly violating the rights of blacks and legislating draconian laws to protect the white race. At this point, interracial marriage in the colony of Virginia ended abruptly. The passage of these new laws affected the social configuration of how races were to interact with each other. These laws were not only discriminatory, but they changed the moral conditions of society.

The expansion of slavery in America is a classic example of government creep that slowly arrogated citizens' rights. After a number of individual rights were suspended for blacks in the lawmaker's chamber, the loss of other liberties inevitably followed. The restrictions became harsher and harsher as southerners eventually codified and regulated slavery. In fact, they did more. They codified race. At this point, many blacks fled to the North.

Libertarians are well-known for their dutiful opposition to the initiation of private or public aggression against another. The whole idea of threatening peaceful people with violence so as to force them to comply with a political directive is seen as repulsive. To the free-Left classical liberals, people can only be free when they are allowed to use their rational faculties to seek their own peaceful ends, so long as their means do not infringe upon the equal rights of others, but this is exactly what most legislators fail to do. They impose victimless-based laws to compel instead of allowing alleged victims adjudicate wrongful claims (the torts of common law). In fact, politically-enacted statutory laws often require no decisive evidence that anyone has been harmed by alleged wrongful activity. In other words, adherents of governmentalism on either side of the statist left and right dichotomy are simply legislating morality—to forcibly change people's behavior. Such legislation puts politicians in a position to tell a peaceful citizen what he or she can and cannot do—readily turning lawful people into lawbreakers.

Although it may be reckless and ill-advised, everyone has a right to make wrong and stupid decisions. People have a right to act foolhardy and discriminate against whomever or whatever they please, providing they initiate no physical harm against another. If a black organization wishes to exclude South Koreans from a group or commercial enterprise, although imprudent, such a policy is their prerogative. If a member of a woman's association voted to ban men from their privately-held meetings, that action would come under the scope of freedom of association. Everyone should have the choice to ask someone to leave their property—for whatever reason. What if a skinhead walked into to a Jewish-owned deli with a swastika tattooed on his forehead? What if a KKK white-hooded man wanted to eat at a black-owned lunch counter? Why can't the owner tell the customer to leave?

Sure, nobody should ever discriminate on the superficial basis of race, age, culture, nationality and so forth; to do so is sheer stupidity. But stupidity has a price. As Elbert Hubbard, an American writer and publisher, wrote, "We're not punished *for* our sins, but *by* them."

Just as in the case of free speech, each person has a right to make a babbling fool of himself and to opine degrading, disgusting, and discriminatory expressions. Just because someone supports free speech for bigots, racists, communists or Nazis does not mean that they agree with their loony causes. In 1977 the American Civil Liberties Union (ACLU) defended the rights of Neo-Nazis to demonstrate and preach their racist-spewing hatred in Skokie, Illinois, which has a high Jewish population. The ACLU won the case. A local ordinance, which had outlawed the right of a Neo-Nazis group to express their opinions in public, was overturned. But who would argue that the ACLU is a racist, anti-Semitic, or white supremacist organization?

However, in 2018 the ACLU reversed course and decided that free speech was no longer for everyone. They apparently have reneged on the civil libertarian idea that if any one person is denied free speech, then anyone can be refused the right to speak freely. In a leaked memo, the ACLU said that they would no longer defend "others whose views are contrary to our values," meaning that even these so-called civil libertarians are drifting towards the authoritarian left.[238]

Free speech is not about content or context; it is about having no blockage in saying what one thinks in public. After all, rights come from individuals, not government. No level of government can legislate or grant someone the right to free speech; we already have this unalienable right. The responsibility of lawmakers is to make sure nobody, including themselves, can stop others from expressing their opinions in a peaceful manner. Unfortunately, governments are usually the main culprit in inhibiting people from expressing divergent viewpoints.

Historical Struggles

There have been slews of epic struggles between the state-granted privileged and the underprivileged commoners, spanning back to ancient Greek days. One of those struggles occurred early in American history. After the American War of Independence, two groups quickly pitted themselves against each other—the Federalists, back by the Alexander Hamilton, and the Anti-Federalists, supported by the more plebeian-friendly Jeffersonian-Republicans.

Like many political conflicts, the battle was over power. The Hamiltonians wanted more government spending, taxation, capacity and control while the Jeffersonians desired less. The Anti-Federalists viewed the Articles of Confederation as a decentralizing influence that would curb political power so as to inhibit the spread of despotism. Under the Articles of Confederation, which were ratified by the states, the President was elected to his position by Congress and was limited to only a one-year term. Similar to the 1848 Swiss Federal Constitution, the Articles restricted the role of the executive branch in order to prevent it from overstepping its authority. After all, almost all tyrants of history have emerged from the executive branch.

This was the first political struggle that I studied as a youth. For some reason, I was always impressed by Thomas Jefferson. I favored decentralization and rights of the individual. It seemed to me that the average citizen was better able to understand and handle his own affairs than his next-door neighbor or political busybodies. I thought citizens should be empowered by their own actions. Unbeknownst to me, I was supporting the classical liberal heritage. At the time, that would have surprised me. As a political activist in high school, publisher of an underground student newspaper and a leader in Young Americans for Freedom, I thought I was a conservative.

A few years later, I came into contact with a cadre of hardcore libertarians, most from Rampart College in Santa Ana, California. They provided plenty of reasons to dislike the Federalists. Many of the delegates to the 1787 Constitutional Convention were told that they were going to just revise the Articles of Confederation. The proceedings were conducted in secrecy, the windows boarded-up and posted with several guards near the entrances.[239] I discovered that the anti-Federalists had been victims of a conspiracy-like movement that marginalized their effects to retain and reform the Articles of Confederation.

As it turned out, the anti-Federalists were right all along—the US Constitution had indeed bestowed too much power to the executive branch. This was plain to see early on. The executive branch had gotten out of control—especially, for instance, during President Woodrow Wilson's administration. Sometimes called the first fascist-like US administration, Wilson had arrested and imprisoned thousands of American citizens for speaking out against US involvement in World War I. Wilson even imprisoned a presidential candidate that opposed him in the election of 1912. Up to 75 periodicals were shut down by the government.[240] Over 400 publications had their postal privileges revoked by US officials.[241] Wilson continued his assault on civil rights by introducing the Sedition Act of 1918 to suppress criticism of America's war policies, which forbade Americans to

> willfully utter, print, write, or publish any disloyal, profane, scurrilous, or abusive language about the form of government of the United States or the Constitution of the United States, or the military...[242]

It has been estimated that some 175,000 citizens were arrested for violating the various anti-freedom and pro-patriotism laws; most were punished and many were jailed.

By the early 1970s, I could see that the US Constitution had failed in its mandate. The Federalists had been in error. The Federalist-sponsored Constitution eventually unleashed the rampaging leviathan upon the public. Some argued that this expansion of the power beyond its original mission was unintentional. Maybe, but many American leaders had been warned about the consequences of forging a strong centralized government. Thomas Jefferson once put this threat into historical perspective: "The natural progress of things is for liberty to yield and government to gain ground."

Of course, the supporters of the US Constitution promised that such mission creep would not occur. After reading the sordid annals of history, I feel safe in saying that government always remakes itself into the current politician's own image. Considered as the "Father of the Constitution," Madison ignored the pleas of Jeffersonians and the Anti-Federalists, who warned that a centralized government could easily violate prior limitations. Madison tried to dispel such fears, writing: "The power delegated by the proposed Constitution to the Federal Government, are few and defined." I suppose "few" and "defined" have now become ambiguous words.

Many of the signers of the US Constitution were intelligent men, but Alexander Hamilton had led many astray with sweet political talk of a strong central government and national banking system. He proposed to have the US president serve for life, similar to the kings. And in that capacity, the president would appoint the governors of each state. Returning to a monarchy was not in the cards, but unfortunately, delegates at the Constitutional Convention in 1787 ignored the travesties that had befallen all past great republics, which always terminated in economic collapse, debased by an overbearing centralized government and Caesar-like dictator, along with financial mismanagement, and a privileged-driven society. In fact, some libertarians refer to the Constitutional Convention as a bloodless counter-revolution against the Declaration of Independence. Nonetheless, only a fool believes that the state can actually limit itself. Although the anti-Federalists have been proven correct about the flawed US Constitution, few politicians want to revisit that graveyard.

My first encounter with this age-old struggle occurred in high school. I can still remember my civics teacher trashing the Articles of Confederation. This teacher warned about the terrible bickering and chaos resulting from the Articles' weak, decentralized structure. She implored us to understand that Americans needed a powerful state. Moreover, she found it inconceivable that the Articles of Confederation gave Congress no authority to levy taxes (funding came from the states). Finally, she asserted that if the US Constitution had not been ratified, war would eventually erupt between the states. Of course, as I realized later, that was a ridiculous statement. America had experienced a massive civil war between the states from 1861 to 1865 under the US Constitution. What she also failed to include in her monologue was the fact that not long after the ratification of the US Constitution, a number of states talked seriously about secession.

According to economist Thomas J. DiLorenzo,

> From 1800 to 1815, there were three serious attempts at secession orchestrated by New England Federalists, who believed that the policies of the Jefferson and Madison administrations, especially the 1803 Louisiana Purchase, the national embargo of 1807, and the War of 1812, were so disproportionately harmful to New England that they justified secession.[243]

These confederate-seeking northern Yankees believed that the southern states were getting too wealthy and influential. They argued for states' rights and worried over an overreaching federal government.

New England's secession threats were backed up with threats and detailed plans. One politician from Connecticut, US Senator James Hillhouse, spoke glowingly about secession, saying, "The Eastern States must and will dissolve the Union and form a separate government."[244] When the former President Jefferson was confronted with calls for secession, he said: "If any state in the Union will declare that it prefers separation... to a continuance in union... I have no hesitation in saying, 'let us separate.'"[245]

New England's confederates were not the only secessionists. During the Andrew Jackson's presidency, South Carolina threatened to break away from the Union because of high tariffs and in 1833 Congress gave Andrew Jackson the authority to use violence to prevent South Carolina from seceding.

Let us not forget that during the American Revolutionary War, the thirteen colonies voted and warred to secede from the English motherland and forged a new nation. And secede they did. The historical tradition of America is deeply rooted in the secession of self-determination. This fact alone is rarely mentioned in government-owned schools, to the point where a number of political leaders and pundits argued that succession was "un-American" after Texas Governor Rick Perry broached the succession issue in 2009.

The Conservative Contingency

Modern conservatism can be traced back to a philosophical break between two distinctive personalities—Thomas Paine and Edmund Burke. In the intellectual sense, Burke is considered by many as the philosophical founder of current-day conservatism. An Anglo-Irish member of the House of Commons, Burke represented the conservative wing of the Whig Party, who opposed the French Revolution. Nonetheless, he supported self-rule for the colonists during the America War of Independence, lamenting about a king with German blood fighting "our English Brethren in the Colonies." At the time, Burke was considered a classical liberal intellectual who defended constitutional limitations and religious tolerance.

Basically, Burke's blunt attacks centered on the radical principles and violence that came to the forefront in the French Revolution, as published in his *Reflections on the Revolution in France* in 1790. In his mind, the French were moving too fast in destroying the monarchy and should take their time to gradually restructure government wisely. Paine fired back with his *Rights of Man* in 1791. He supported a faster pace towards self-governance and republicanism, to quickly abolish the hereditary privileges that were so offensive to the French. Despite his support of the French Revolution, Paine was arrested and imprisoned in Paris, only narrowly escaping the guillotine.

Yet Burke was worried not about the threats to monarchy, but about the ugly side of revolution. He was convinced that the French Revolution would merely transfer power from the monarchy to starry-eyed elitists who would employ more violence and abuse than even the upper classes. He was right. He correctly predicted France's slippage into a state of terror. As one of the most influential figures of the French Revolution, Robespierre advocated state terrorism, with the post-revolution government becoming the first government to make terror an official policy. Robespierre and his Committee of Public Safety sent thousands to the guillotine before he himself was beheaded. Before his own execution, he was determined to protect the revolution by any totalitarian means possible, rationalizing:

> There are only two parties in France: the people and its enemies. We must exterminate those miserable villains who are eternally conspiring against the rights of man... we must exterminate all our enemies.

With the later rise of Napoleon Bonaparte, liberty was itself extinguished as France entered not only an age of dictatorship but of massive military buildup, perpetual wars, proto-nationalism, and empire building.

Burke deeply favored liberty. But this liberty had to come through a slow process of shifts in customs and traditions. Many moderate libertarians found Burke's message appealing. Slow change is better than change for change's sake. Hardcore American conservatives were even more impressed. Intellectual conservatives flocked to William Buckley, Jr. and Burke's writings, prepared to re-cast his anti-French Revolution critique into a 20th century battle against socialism and communism.

Even so, the more radical libertarians were impatient with Burke's respect for "cautious expediency."[246] To the radical libertarian way of thinking, in times of crises, traditionalism, order, and the status-quo have often been seen as the worst possible weapons. Radical libertarians frequently feel more attuned to Gandhi's tactics of peaceful civil disobedience and non-violent resistance than they are to the slow and steady progress called for by Burke. The state, in their mind, must be actively opposed. Libertarians sought to free up more rights to expand liberty, not to wait for the impossibility—a government voluntarily loosening up its tight grip. Such a miracle was not going to happen on its own.

However, after World War II, most conservatives had become blinded to their obsession with a strong foreign military to defeat or delay Soviet expansionism. Before the war, the Old Right, which emerged in the

1930s and 1940s to oppose FDR's collectivist policies, sought a non-interventionist foreign policy overseas and opposed statism at home. Nonetheless, the last vestiges of the Old Right died with the failed presidential bid by Republican US Senator Robert Taft in 1952. After that defeat, the new conservatism threw its weight behind a military build-up that eventually saw over 800 military bases in over 130 countries. Of course, modern liberals had joined the conservatives in transforming the American republic into a military-bound empire. By the 1950s, conservatives and liberals alike had embarked on an odyssey to forge a vast military-industrial complex. Ironically, these same conservatives continuously call for a return to constitutional principles of limited government while supporting a massive expansion of government to engage in nation-building and unconstitutional foreign wars.

Still, as I have often maintained, there seems to be little difference between moderate, modern liberalism and conservatism. Here is the litmus test: What modern liberal would refuse to support Medicare, Social Security, Medicaid, SBA loans, FHA-backed loans, subsidized housing (section 8), government schools, food stamps, and so forth? None. And yet, modern-day conservatives also support these state-run programs, although reluctantly and with some limitations. Surely, conservatives attempt to reform them when they become too costly, bankrupt, or corrupted, but so have some modern liberals. As the author and journalist Jacob Hornberger contends, conservatives

> never challenge the nature or existence of the programs themselves. They have come to believe that it is an important role of government to the use force of government to take from Peter to give to Paul.[247]

The conservative forces that wanted to keep America's traditional values of economic liberty and non-interventionism alive simply surrendered by the end of FDR's administration. When the battle between principle and expediency started to rage, conservatives usually opted out for expediency, arguing that principles are both vague guidelines and unsustainable. So, in the long run, conservatives do what they do best—they work to preserve the status quo. If total socialism ever reached the

American shore, conservatives would be there to begrudgingly defend it. And defend it they did, especially the neo-conservatives. Nobody should have been surprised when President George W. Bush touted his right-wing leviathan state under the ensign of "big-government conservatism."

Hornberger concluded:

> So, here we have the confluence of liberalism and conservatism. Liberals are still promoting their socialist-interventionist schemes under the banner of "reforming" free enterprise. Conservatives are doing the same thing under the banner of their old mantra "free enterprise, private property, and limited government."[248]

As author and newspaper columnist Mark Steyn has repeatedly echoed, political leaders in America "invoke the Constitution for the purpose of overriding it."[249]

* * * * *

Almost all political ideologies have one thing in common: they want to use government intervention to impose their values on all citizens in order to enforce a particular agenda. Some ideologies want to intervene more, some less. Only the classical liberals and their libertarian offspring take a different approach by advocating that each person should make his or her own choices in running their lives. They take the neutral position, contending that citizens have more localized information and better incentives in pursuing their self-directed goals. Political spectrums help to provide a crude road map to discovering where a given person's opinions are positioned, in relation to others' opinions. But such maps can also lead people down unwanted, confusing, and treacherous roads, which can make it difficult to find one's true home. In the case of the statist-progressive Left, however, they are prone to switch around the road signs to mislead the public and conceal their real fascist persona. And their *modus operandi* will not change; they will only become less effective when their deceptive tactics become better known.

Notes

[1] H.G. Wells, *The New World Order* (Filiquarian Publishing, 2007), p. 46. Originally published in 1940.

[2] Whalen, *Mr. New York*, p. 188.

[3] H.L. Mencken, "Of The People, By The People," *The Baltimore Sun*, Nov. 6, 1938, p. 8.

[4] George Bernard Shaw, *The Intelligent Woman's Guide: To Socialism and Capitalism* (New York, NY: Brentano, 1928), p. 670. Book title was changed by Shaw in the 1930s to *The Intelligent Woman's Guide to Socialism, Capitalism, Sovietism, and Fascism.*

[5] Gregor, *The Faces of Janus*, p. x.

[6] Ibid., p. 5.

[7] Ibid., pp. 4–5.

[8] Ibid., p. 5.

[9] Democratic Presidential Debate in Las Vegas, NV, Oct. 13, 2015.

[10] Stephen Collinson, "How Trump and Sanders tapped America's economic rage," Mar. 9, 2016, *CNN Politics*. https://www.cnn.com/2016/03/09/politics/sanders-trump-economy-trade/.

[11] Timothy Egan, "What if Steve Bannon Is Right?" *New York Times*, Aug. 25, 2017. https://www.nytimes.com/2017/08/25/opinion/bannon-trump-polls-republican.html.

[12] Payne, *A History of Fascism, 1914–1945*, pp. 430, 435.

[13] Ibid., p. 431.

[14] Ibid., p. 435.

[15] Chaim Lipschitz, *Franco, Spain, the Jews, and the Holocaust* (Ktav Pub & Distributors Inc., 1984), p. 142. Also in *Newsweek* magazine, Mar. 2, 1970, p. 53. Lipschitz is from Brooklyn's Torah Vodraath and Mesivta Rabbinical Seminary. Other claims have Franco and his diplomats saving 30,000 Sephardic Jews. Also see "Franco's Spain and the Jewish Rescue Effort during World War Two," Gena Olan, thesis, Apr. 2013, Duke University.

[16] Interview of Alan Dershowitz by Dennis Prager in *No Safe Spaces* 2019 documentary. Clip from interview published on Feb. 12, 2018. https://www.youtube.com/watch?v=Gc86fPirz3A.

[17] "Surprise! Dershowitz 'Biggest Enemies' Not Who You Think: Harvard Prof Says Group Poses 'Great Danger to the American Future,'" *WND*, Feb. 12, 2018. https://www.wnd.com/2018/02/surprise-dershowitz-biggest-enemies-not-who-you-think/.

[18] "The Doctrine of Fascism" Firenze: Vallecchi Editore (1935 version), p. 13.

[19] Marc A. Thiessen, "Yes, antifa is the moral equivalent of neo-Nazis," *Washington Post*, Aug. 30, 2017. https://www.washingtonpost.com/opinions/yes-antifa-is-the-moral-equivalent-of-neo-nazis/2017/08/30/9a13b2f6-8d00-11e7-91d5-ab4e4bb76a3a_story.html.

[20] Back, *The Fateful Alliance*, pp. 72–75.

[21] Hitler's speech to workers at Berlin's Rheinmetall-Borsig factory, Oct. 10, 1940. Published in Aly, *Hitler's Beneficiaries*, 2007, p. 13.

[22] Rauschning, *The Voice of Destruction*, p. 246.

[23] The Nazi 25-Point Program speech by Adolf Hitler, who proclaimed his party's platform on Feb. 24, 1920, in Munich, Germany. Lane and Rupp, *Nazi Ideology Before 1933*, p. 43.

[24] Rob Shimshock, "Google and YouTube Ban Prof Who Refused to Use Gender-Neutral Pronouns," *The Daily Caller*, Aug. 1, 2017. https://dailycaller.com/2017/08/01/google-and-youtube-ban-prof-who-refused-to-use-gender-neutral-pronouns/.

[25] Jordan Peterson, "Freedom of Speech/Political Correctness," Part 2, Jan. 22, 2017. https://www.youtube.com/watch?v=aDRgMUoEvcg.

[26] Seymour Martin Lipset, "'The Socialism of Fools,'" *New York Times*, Jan. 3, 1971. https://www.nytimes.com/1971/01/03/archives/-the-socialism-of-fools-the-new-left-calls-it-antizionism-but-its.html.

[27] Evans, *The Coming of the Third Reich*, pp. 214–215.

[28] Heiden, *The Führer*, p. 501.

[29] Evans, *The Coming of the Third Reich*, pp. 214–215.

[30] Ibid., p. 215.

[31] Evans, *The Third Reich in Power, 1933–1939*, p. 292.

[32] Jeffrey J. Selingo, "College students support free speech—unless it offends them," *Washington Post*, Mar. 12, 2018. https://www.washingtonpost.com/local/college-students-support-free-speech--unless-it-offends-them/2018/03/09/79f21c9e-23e4-11e8-94da-ebf9d112159c_story.html.

[33] Catherine Rampell, "A chilling study shows how hostile college students are toward free speech," *Washington Post*, Sept. 18, 2017. https://www.washingtonpost.com/opinions/a-chilling-study-shows-how-hostile-college-students-are-toward-free-speech/2017/09/18/cbb1a234-9ca8-11e7-9083-fbfddf6804c2_story.html.

[34] Brendan Pringle, "Where is the outrage at Cal Poly over alumna Kate Steinle?" *Washington Examiner*, Dec. 12, 2017. http://www.sanluisobispo.com/news/local/education/article188894069.html. Note: there was a second flyer with Steinle's photo and a three-line depiction of what happened to her on the day of the shooting.

[35] Andrew Sheeler, "Cal Poly investigates anti-undocumented immigrant flyers mentioning Kate Steinle death," *The Tribune*, Dec. 8, 2017. https://www.sanluisobispo.com/news/local/education/article188894069.html.

[36] Glen Greenwald, "The Misguided Attacks on ACLU for Defending Neo-Nazis' Free Speech Rights in Charlottesville," *The Intercept*, Aug. 13, 2017. https://www.theintercept.com/2017/08/13/the-misguided-attacks-on-aclu-for-defending-neo-nazis-free-speech-rights-in-charlottesville/.

[37] David Krayden, "University Pays Students To Spy On Peers For 'Bias Incidents,'" *The Daily Caller*, May 10, 2017. https://dailycaller.com/2017/05/10/university-pays-students-to-report-bias-incidents-of-peers/.

[38] Ibid.

[39] Tom Knighton, "Campus SJWs Get Paid by the Hour at the University of Arizona," *PJ Media*, May 10, 2017. https://pjmedia.com/trending/2017/05/10/campus-sjws-get-paid-by-the-hour-at-the-university-of-arizona/. Eventually, the university backed down on establishing social justice advocates.

[40] Adolf Hitler, "Why We Are Anti-Semites," Aug. 15, 1920 speech in Munich at the Hofbräuhaus. https://carolynyeager.net/why-we-are-antisemites-text-adolf-hitlers-1920-speech-hofbr%C3%A4uhaus.

[41] Katie Herzog, "Evergreen Ranks as One of the Worst Colleges in the US for Free Speech," *The Stranger*, Feb. 14, 2018, Rashida Love was the head of the campus diversity office—First Peoples Multicultural Advising Services. Equity Council meeting. http://www.evergreen.edu/sites/default/files/Minutes_Equity%20Council%20Regular%20Meeting_01-11-17.pdf.

[42] Susan Surluga, Joe Heim, "Threat shuts down college embroiled in racial dispute," *Washington Post*, June 1, 2017. https://washingtonpost.com/news/grade-point/wp/2017/06/01/threats-shut-down-college-embroiled-in-racial-dispute/.

[43] Eugene Volokh, "Opinion: 'Professor told he's not safe on campus after college protests' at Evergreen State College," *Washington Post*, May 26, 2017. https://www.washingtonpost.com/news/volokh-conspiracy/wp/2017/05/26/professor-told-hes-not-safe-on-campus-after-college-protests-at-evergreen-state-university-washington/.

[44] Bret Weinstein, "The Campus Mob Came for Me," *Wall Street Journal*, May 30, 2017.

[45] YouTube segment of the incident: "Bret Weinstein Tries To Reason With Angry Student Mob As They Call For His Resignation." https://www.youtube.com/watch?v=LTnDpoQLNaY.

[46] Ibid.

[47] Katie Herzog, "Evergreen Ranks as One of the Worst Colleges in the US for Free Speech," *The Stranger*, Feb. 14, 2018.

[48] Michael Zimmerman, "The Evergreen State College Implosion: Are There Lessons To Be Learned?" *HuffPost*, July 5, 2017.

[49] Katie Herzog "After Evergreen: One Year Later, Bret Weinstein and Heather Heying Look Back," *The Stranger*, May 23, 2018. https://www.thestranger.com/features/2018/05/24/26472992/after-evergreen.

[50] Bari Weiss, "When the Left Turns on Its Own," *New York Times*, June 1, 2017. https://nytimes.com/2017/06/01/opinion/when-the-left-turns-on-its-own.html.

[51] Dave Rubin, *The Rubin Report*, "Live with Bret Weinstein: Evergreen State College Racism Controversy?" May 30, 2017.

[52] Mike Paros, "The Evergreen Meltdown," *Quillette*, Feb. 22, 2018. https://quillette.com/2018/02/22/the-evergreen-meltdown/. Paros is a biology professor at Evergreen State College.

[53] Editorial: "The Evergreen State College: No safety, no learning, no future," *Seattle Times*, June 5, 2017. https://www.seattletimes.com/opinion/editorials/the-evergreen-state-college-no-safety-no-learning-no-future/.

[54] Bret Weinstein, "The Campus Mob Came for Me," *Wall Street Journal*, May 30, 2017. https://wsj.com/articles/the-campus-mob-came-for-meand-you-professor-could-be-next-1496187482.

[55] Bari Weiss, "When the Left Turns on Its Own," *New York Times*, June 1, 2017.

[56] Bret Weinstein, "The Campus Mob Came for Me," *Wall Street Journal*, May 30, 2017.

[57] "Campus Argument Goes Viral As Evergreen State Is Caught In Racial Turmoil (HBO)," *Vice News/HBO*, published on June 16, 2017. https://www.youtube.com/watch?v=2cMYfxOFBBM.

[58] Ibid.

[59] Bret Weinstein. Twitter post. Nov. 26, 2017, 11:53 AM. https://twitter.com/BretWeinstein/status/934872752405716992.

[60] Bret Weinstein, "The Campus Mob Came for Me," *Wall Street Journal*, May 30, 2017.

[61] "Bret Weinstein Testifies to Congress on The Evergreen State College riots, Free Speech & Safe Spaces," United States House of Representatives, May 22, 2018. https://www.youtube.com/watch?v=uRIKJCKWla4.

[62] Evans, *The Third Reich in Power, 1933–1939*, p. 265.

[63] Michael Zimmerman, "The Evergreen State College Implosion: Are There Lessons To Be Learned?" *HuffPost*, July 5, 2017.

[64] Justin Raimondo, "Challenging the Lords of the Internet," *Antiwar.com*, Aug. 9, 2018. https://original.antiwar.com/justin/2018/08/08/challenging-the-lords-of-the-internet/.

[65] Joseph Farah, "Don't Doubt Me: Democrats Love Censorship," *WND*, Aug. 24, 2018. https://www.wnd.com/2018/08/dont-doubt-me-democrats-love-censorship/.

[66] Declan McCullagh, "ACLU Sticks Up for the NRA?!" *Reason* magazine, Aug. 24, 2018. https://reason.com/archives/2018/08/24/aclu-teams-up-with-nra.

[67] John Steele Gordon, "Andrew Cuomo's Mafia Tactics," *Commentary*, Aug. 27, 2018. https://www.commentarymagazine.com/politics-ideas/andrew-cuomo-mafia-tactics-nra-aclu/.

[68] Matt Ford, "Andrew Cuomo's Trumpian War on the NRA," *The New Republic*, Aug. 28, 2018. https://newrepublic.com/article/150933/andrew-cuomos-trumpian-war-nra.

[69] Hitler, *Mein Kampf, Vol. One*, chap. X, "Causes of the Collapse."

[70] David Detmer, *Challenging Postmodernism: Philosophy and the Politics of Truth* (Humanity Books, 2003), pp. 31, 111, 314.

[71] See "Why Postmodernists Reject Logic & Evidence," Jordan Peterson. https://www.youtube.com/watch?v=CTBOU77czpY.

[72] Frederick Augustus Voigt, *Pax Britannica* (London, UK: Constable & Company LTD., 1949), p. 28.

[73] Rowan Scarborough, "Blasey Ford's lifelong friend to tell FBI she has no knowledge of Kavanaugh or party," *Washington Times*, Sept. 29, 2018.

[74]Mairead Mcardle, "*USA Today* Amends Article Saying Kavanaugh Shouldn't Coach Basketball," *National Review*, Sept. 30, 2018. https://www.nationalreview. com/news/usa-today-amends-article-saying-kavanaugh-shouldnt-coach-basketball/.

[75]*Tucker Carlson Tonight* show, Oct. 8, 2018. https://www.youtube.com/watch? v=TAZYa0bJKlQ also https://www.youtube.com/watch?v=fUu1hFUGaEg.

[76]Drucker, *The End of Economic Man*, pp. 14–15.

[77]Walter C. Langer, *A Psychological Analysis of Adolph Hitler: His Life and Legend*, Office of Strategic Services (OSS) Washington, D.C. With the collaboration of Prof. Henry A. Murr, Harvard Psychological Clinic, Dr. Ernst Kris, New School for Social Research, Dr. Bertram D. Lawin, New York Psychoanalytic Institute, p. 219.

[78]Sam Dorman, "Former ACLU Exec Blasts Organization as It Breaks Policy to Oppose Kavanaugh: They've 'Become the Mob,'" *IJR*, Oct. 6, 2018. Originates from Meyers's interview on *The Sean Hannity Show*, Oct. 4, 2018. https://dailycaller.com/ 2018/10/04/aclu-kavanaugh-partisan-resistance/.

[79]Ibid.

[80]Rachel Ventresca, "Clinton: 'You cannot be civil with a political party that wants to destroy what you stand for,'" *CNN*, Oct. 9, 2018. Clinton declared in an interview with *CNN*'s Christiane Amanpour: "You cannot be civil with a political party that wants to destroy what you stand for, what you care about," https://www.cnn.com/ 2018/10/09/politics/hillary-clinton-civility-congress-cnntv/index.html.

[81]Cheryl K. Chumley, "Minnesota Republicans attacked in streets show true colors of left," *The Washington Times*, Oct. 16, 2018. https://www.washingtontimes.com/ news/2018/oct/17/minnesota-republicans-attacked-streets-show-true-c/.

[82]Aaron Blake, "Eric Holder: 'When they go low, we kick them. That's what this new Democratic Party is about,'" *Washington Post*, Oct. 10, 2018. https://www. washingtonpost.com/politics/2018/10/10/eric-holder-when-they-go-low-we-kick-them-thats-what-this-new-democratic-party-is-about/. Later, Holder claimed that he was not suggesting anything illicit.

[83]Oliver Laughland and Jon Swaine, "Virginia shooting: gunman was leftwing activist with record of domestic violence," *The Guardian*, June 15, 2017. https: //www.theguardian.com/us-news/2017/jun/14/virginia-shooting-suspect-james-t-hodgkinson-leftwing-activist.

[84]Megan Cassidy, "Castro Valley man allegedly cursed Trump, tried to stab GOP congressional candidate," *San Francisco Chronical—SFGate*, Sept. 11, 2018. http: //www.sfgate.com/crime/article/Castro-Valley-festival-stab-attempted-rudy-peters-13221444.php.

[85]Avery Anapol, "Pennsylvania Dem claims he was forced to resign from local party over 'Stand for the flag' Facebook post," *The Hill*, Oct. 15, 2018. http: //thehill.com/homenews/state-watch/411385-pennsylvania-dem-forced-to-resign-from-local-party-over-stand-for-the.

[86]Nicole Rojas, "Democratic Official asked to Resign After 'Stand for the Flag,' 'Kneel at the Cross' Facebook Posts Surface," *Newsweek*, Oct. 15, 2018. https://

www.newsweek.com/dem-official-forced-resign-local-party-after-posts-standing-flag-support-1170407.

[87]"'#ReleaseTheMemo' is nothing but a hyperpartisan attempt to discredit Mueller," editorial board of the *Washington Post*, Jan. 30, 2018. https://www.washingtonpost.com/opinions/releasethememo-is-nothing-but-a-hyperpartisan-attempt-to-discredit-mueller/2018/01/30/cf5d6000-05ec-11e8-b48c-b07fea957bd5_story.html.

[88]State Senator Bill Monning Speech at the Hyatt Hotel in Monterey, CA in support of the Monterey Peace and Justice Center, May 15, 2015. His quote: "The true revolutionary is guided by great feelings of love." I attended this event as a representative of the local Libertarians for Peace.

[89]Alvaro Vargas Llosa, "The Killing Machine: Che Guevara, from Communist Firebrand to Capitalist Brand," The Independent Institute, July 11, 2005, also published in *The New Republic*.

[90]Peter McLaren, *Che Guevara, Paulo Freire, and the Pedagogy of Revolution* (Rowman & Littlefield, 2000), p. 7.

[91]Murray N. Rothbard "A Future of Peace and Capitalism," chap. 28 in *Modern Political Economy: Radical and Orthodox Views on Crucial Issues* by James H. Weaver (Boston, MA: Allyn and Bacon, 1973), pp. 419–430.

[92]Matt Kibble, "The Country vs. The Individual," YouTube short, *Free the People*, posted Aug. 8, 2017.

[93]Stanley Milgram, *Obedience to Authority: An Experimental View* (London, UK: Tavistock Publications, 1974).

[94]*Theses and Resolutions Adopted at the Third Congress of the Communist International, June 22nd to July 12th, 1921* (New York, NY: The Contemporary Publishing Association, 1921), p. 125.

[95]V.N. Bandera, "New Economic Policy (NEP) as an Economic System," *The Journal of Political Economy*, Vol. 71, No. 3, 1963, p. 268.

[96]V.I. Lenin, "The Tax in Kind," written Apr. 21, 1921, Lenin's *Collected Works*, 1st English Edition, Progress Publishers, Moscow, 1965, Vol. 32, pp. 329–365. http://www.marxists.org/archive/lenin/works/1921/apr/21.htm.

[97]Murray N. Rothbard "A Future of Peace and Capitalism," chap. 28 in *Modern Political Economy: Radical and Orthodox Views on Crucial Issues* by James H. Weaver (Boston, MA: Allyn and Bacon, 1973), pp. 419–430.

[98]Toniolo, *The Oxford Handbook of the Italian Economy Since Unification*, p. 59. Mussolini's speech to the Chamber of Deputies on May 26, 1934.

[99]Peter Binns, "State Capitalism," from the collection, Marxism and the Modern World, *Education for Socialists No. 1*, Mar. 1986. Published by the Socialist Workers Party (Britain).

[100]Stephen A. Resnick and Richard D. Wolff, *Class Theory and History: Capitalism and Communism in the USSR* (London, UK: Routledge, 2002), pp. 115–117.

[101]Ibid., p. 114.

[102]Christopher Duggan, *Fascist Voice: An Intimate History of Mussolini's Italy* (New York, NY: Oxford University Press, 2013), pp. 239–240.

[103]Toler, *The Everything Guide to Understanding Socialism*, section: "Mussolini Rises to Power," p. 186. https://web.archive.org/web/20130527163952/http://netplaces.com/understanding-socialism/chapter-15/mussolini-rises-to-power.htm.

[104]Donald Parkinson, "Sorel's reflections on violence and the poverty of voluntarism," libcom.org, Mar. 8, 2014. https://libcom.org/library/sorels-reflections-violence-poverty-voluntarism.

[105]Rod Jones, "Factory committees in the Russian revolution," libcom.org, Aug. 7, 2005. https://libcom.org/library/factory-committees-russian-revolution-rod-jones.

[106]Gompers and Walling, *Out of Their Own Mouths*, p. 79.

[107]Tony Cliff, "The 1905 Revolution," chap. 7 in *Trotsky: Towards October 1879–1917* (London, UK: Bookmarks, 1989). Transcribed by Martin Fahlgren, July 2009.

[108]Jeffrey M. Herbener, "The Vampire Economy: Italy, Germany, and the US," *Mises Daily*, Oct. 13, 2005. http://mises.org/daily/1935.

[109]Benito Mussolini, "The Doctrine of Fascism" ("*La dottrina del fascism*"). The 1935 edition from Vallecchi Editore Firenze, p. 15.

[110]Salvemini, *The Fate of Trade Unions Under Fascism*, p. 35.

[111]Hitler, *Mein Kampf, Vol. Two*, chap. XII, "The Trade-Union Question."

[112]William Brustein, *The Logic of Evil: The Social Origins of the Nazi Party, 1925–1933* (New Haven, CT: Yale University Press, 1996), p. 141.

[113]Benito Mussolini, copied directly from an official Fascist government publication, *Fascism: Doctrine and Institutions* (Rome: Ardita Publishers, 1935), pp. 7–42.

[114]Jim Powell, "The Economic Leadership Secrets of Benito Mussolini," *Forbes*, Feb. 22, 2012. http://www.forbes.com/sites/jimpowell/2012/02/22/the-economic-leadership-secrets-of-benito-mussolini/.

[115]Robert Bingham Downs, *Books That Changed the World* (New York, NY: Penguin Group, 2004), p. 201.

[116]R.J.B. Bosworth, *Mussolini* (Bloomsbury Academic, 2002), p. 192.

[117]Flynn, *As We Go Marching*, p. 45.

[118]Peter Conradi, *Hitler's Piano Player: The Rise and Fall of Ernst Hanfstaengl: Confidant of Hitler, Ally of FDR* (New York, NY: Carroll & Graf Publishers, 2004), p. 284.

[119]"LIFE on the Newsfronts of the World," *LIFE* magazine, Jan. 9, 1939, p. 12.

[120]Jackson J. Spielvogel, *Western Civilization, Vol. C: Since 1789*, Ninth ed. (Stamford, CT: Cengage Learning), p. 713.

[121]Berman, *The Primacy of Politics*, p. 2.

[122]Sternhell, Sznajder, and Asheri, *The Birth of Fascist Ideology*, p. 197.

[123]Ibid., p. 195.

[124]Mises, *Human Action*, p. 814.

[125]Erich Fromm, *Escape from Freedom* (Farrar & Rinehart, 1941), p. 233.

[126]*Der Angriff* (*The Attack*) was the official newspaper of the Nazi-Sozi party in Berlin, according to author Erik von Kuehnelt-Leddihn, Dec. 6, 1931.

[127]Joseph Goebbels and Mjölnir, *Die verfluchten Hakenkreuzler. Etwas zum Nachdenken*, English translation: "Those Damn Nazis. Something to Consider/Think About/Reflect Upon," Munich: Germany, Verlag Frz, Eher, 1932.

[128] Furet, *The Passing of an Illusion*, p. 191.

[129] Alan Bullock, *Hitler: A Study in Tyranny*, Abridged edition (Harper Perennial, 1991), p. 175.

[130] Toland, *Adolf Hitler: The Definitive Biography*, p. 224. Hitler's speech on May 1, 1927.

[131] Rauschning, *The Voice of Destruction*, pp. 191–193. Hitler's conversation with Hermann Rauschning.

[132] Ibid., p. 191.

[133] Wagener, *Hitler—Memoirs of a Confidant*, p. 14.

[134] Barkai, *Nazi Economics*, p. 168.

[135] Ibid., p. 169.

[136] Jeff Stein, "Bernie Sanders to announce plan to guarantee every American a job," *Washington Post*, Apr. 23, 2018. https://www.washingtonpost.com/news/wonk/wp/2018/04/23/bernie-sanders-to-unveil-plan-to-guarantee-every-american-a-job/.

[137] Ibid.

[138] Harold H. Titus, *Living Issues in Philosophy*, fifth ed. (New York, NY: Van Nostrand Reinhold Company, 1964), p. 487.

[139] Aly, *Hitler's Beneficiaries*, 2007, p. 68.

[140] Germà Bel, "Against the mainstream: Nazi privatization in 1930s Germany," first published online: Apr. 27, 2009, p. 19. Source on Internet: http://www.ub.edu/graap/nazi.pdf. Also published in *The Economic History Review*, Vol. 63, issue 1, pp. 34–55, Feb. 2010. The years were between 1932/33 and 1937/38.

[141] Aly, *Hitler's Beneficiaries*, 2007, p. 41.

[142] Ibid., pp. 43–47.

[143] Ibid., pp. 2–4.

[144] Robert C. Tucker, *Stalin in Power: The Revolution from Above, 1928–1941* (W.W. Norton & Company, 1990), p. 41.

[145] George Reisman, "Why Nazism Was Socialism and Why Socialism Is Totalitarian," an Oct. 8, 2005 lecture delivered at the Mises Institute's "The Economics of Fascism: Supporters Summit 2005" in Auburn, Alabama. https://www.youtube.com/watch?v=XsaG-pJ_4RA&list=PLOCWSOHhjJPUQ9kkhBKV9js9tFJTPp3yC&index=3&t=0s.

[146] Ibid.

[147] "Man of 1938: From the unholy organist, a hymn of hate," *Time* magazine, Jan. 2, 1939. http://content.time.com/time/magazine/article/0,9171,760539-6,00.html.

[148] Hitler, *Mein Kampf, Vol. Two*, chap. XII, "The Trade-Union Question."

[149] Bernard Shaw wrote, Mussolini was "farther to the Left in his political opinions than any" of his socialist rivals. Griffith, *Socialism and Superior Brains*, p. 253. Shaw made this statement in the *Manchester Guardian* in 1927.

[150] Schivelbusch, *Three New Deals*, p. 31.

[151] Alistair Cooke, *Memories of the Great & the Good* (New York, NY: Arcade Publishing, 1999), p. 65.

[152] Ayn Rand, *The Virtue of Selfishness: A New Concept of Egoism* (New York, NY: A Signet Book from New American Library, 1964), p. 126.

[153] Edward H. Flannery, *The Anguish of the Jews: Twenty-Three Centuries of Anti-semitism* (Paulist Press, 2004), p. 168; Marvin Perry and Frederick M. Schweitzer, *Antisemitism: Myth and Hate from Antiquity to the Present* (New York, NY: Palgrave Macmillan, 2005), pp. 154–157.

[154] Dagobert D. Runes, ed., *Karl Marx: A World Without Jews*, (New York, NY: Philosophical Library, 1959), p. 41. Source: https://www.resist.com/Onlinebooks/Marx-WorldWithoutJews.pdf.

[155] Hyam Maccoby, *Antisemitism and Modernity: Innovation and Continuity* (New York, NY: Routledge, 2006), pp. 64–66.

[156] Gottfried Feder, *Hitler's Official Programme and its Fundamental Ideas* (New York, NY: Howard Fertig, Inc., 1971), p. 71. First printed in English in 1934.

[157] Karl Marx, *Selected Essays*, "On the Jewish Question," trans. H.J. Stenning (New York, NY: International Publishers (Soviet publication outlet), 1926), p. 97. First printed in the *Deutsch-Französische Jahrbücher*, Paris, 1844. Marx was co-editor of this periodical.

[158] Seymour Martin Lipset, "'The Socialism of Fools,'" *New York Times*, Jan. 3, 1971. https://www.nytimes.com/1971/01/03/archives/-the-socialism-of-fools-the-new-left-calls-it-antizionism-but-its.html.

[159] Jeane J. Kirkpatrick, *Legitimacy and Force: Political and Moral Dimensions* (New Brunswick, NJ: Transaction Books, 1988), p. 188.

[160] Dennis McLellan, "Russell Means dies at 72; American Indian rights activist, actor," *Los Angeles Times*, Oct. 23, 2012. http://articles.latimes.com/2012/oct/23/local/la-me-russell-means-20121023.

[161] Russell Means and Marvin J. Wolf, *Where White Men Fear to Tread: The Autobiography of Russell Means* (New York, NY: St. Martin's Griffin, 1995), p. 470.

[162] Ibid., pp. 462–463.

[163] Mike Arayuwa Wilkie, "Ortega names wife as vice," *New Telegraph*, Aug. 11, 2016.

[164] Douglas Schoen and Michael Rowan, *Hugo Chávez and the War Against America: The Threat Closer to Home* (New York, NY: Free Press, 2009), pp. 117–118.

[165] The 2004 Annual Report of the Stephen Roth Institute.

[166] Natasha Mozgovaya and Shlomo Papirblat, "In Venezuela, Remarks Like 'Hitler Didn't Finish the Job' Are Routine," *Haaretz*, Nov. 20, 2010. https://www.haaretz.com/jewish/1.5141994.

[167] Marc Perelman, "Venezuela's Jews Defend Leftist President in Flap Over Remarks," *Forward.com*, Jan. 13, 2006. https://forward.com/news/1874/venezuela-e2-80-99s-jews-defend-leftist-president-in-fla/.

[168] Robert S. Wistrich, *From Ambivalence to Betrayal: The Left, the Jews, and Israel* (University of Nebraska Press, 2012), p. 583.

[169] Natasha Mozgovaya and Shlomo Papirblat, "In Venezuela, Remarks Like 'Hitler Didn't Finish the Job' Are Routine," *Haaretz*, Nov. 20, 2010.

[170]Gil Shefler, "Jewish community in Venezuela shrinks by half," *The Jerusalem Post*, Sept. 1, 2010.   https://www.jpost.com/Jewish-World/Jewish-News/Jewish-community-in-Venezuela-shrinks-by-half.

[171]Nicholas Casey, "Hungry, Venezuelans turn to pillaging," *International New York Times*, June 21, 2016, front page.

[172]Ernesto Londoño, "Venezuela's Military in the Spotlight," *New York Times*, May 24, 2016. https://takingnote.blogs.nytimes.com/2016/05/24/venezuelas-military-in-the-spotlight/.

[173]Ibid.

[174]Rodolfo Chacin, "Quora Question: What Can We Learn From Chávez and Venezuela's Crisis?" *Newsweek*, Oct. 10, 2016. https://www1.newsweek.com/quora-question-what-can-we-learn-venezuela-508990.

[175]Kershaw, *Hitler 1889–1936: Hubris*, 2000, pp. 577–578.

[176]Rodolfo Chacin, "Quora Question: What Can We Learn From Chávez and Venezuela's Crisis?" *Newsweek*, Oct. 10, 2016.

[177]Nancy J. Weiss, "The Negro and the New Freedom: Fighting Wilsonian Segregation," *Political Science Quarterly*, 1969, Vol. 84 (1): pp. 61–79.

[178]W.E.B. Du Bois, "Another Open Letter to Woodrow Wilson," Sept. 1913.

[179]John R. MacArthur, "The Presidency in Wartime: George W. Bush discovers Woodrow Wilson," *Harper's Magazine*, Sept. 30, 2008.   https://harpers.org/blog/2008/09/the-presidency-in-wartime-george-w-bush-discovers-woodrow-wilson/.

[180]Bruce Bartlett, *Wrong on Race: The Democratic Party's Buried Past* (Palgrave Macmillan, 2008), p. 109.

[181]Ibid., p. 109.

[182]Ibid., p. 98.

[183]Charlie Savage, "Racial Motive Alleged in a Justice Dept. Decision," *New York Times*, July 6, 2010. https://www.nytimes.com/2010/07/07/us/07rights.html.

[184]Jesse Washington, "Ex-Justice Dept. lawyer says whites' rights ignored," *Associated Press*, July 1, 2010.

[185]Jerry Seper, "EXCLUSIVE: Career lawyers overruled on voting case," *The Washington Times*, May 29, 2009.

[186]Southern Poverty Law Center, "Feds Investigate Dropping of Panther Case – Black Separatists," *Intelligence Report*, Winter 2009, No. 136.

[187]Nancy Kaffer, "A New Breed of Panther," *Detroit Metro Times*, May 4, 2005. https://www.metrotimes.com/detroit/a-new-breed-of-panther/Content?oid=2181373.

[188]Greg Chapman, "Going Inside the New Black Panther Party," National Geographic Channel, Jan. 9, 2009.

[189]J. Christian Adams, "ADAMS: Inside the Black Panther Case," *The Washington Times*, June 25, 2010. https://www.washingtontimes.com/news/2010/jun/25/inside-the-black-panther-case-anger-ignorance-and-/.

[190]Megyn Kelly's interview of Bartle Bull on American Live, "Bartle Bull Reacts to FMR DOJ attorney on Black Panther case," *Fox News*, July 1, 2010.

[191] Shawn Langlois, "CNN's Don Lemon doesn't apologize for calling white men 'biggest terror threat,'" *MarketWatch*, Nov. 1, 2018, segment aired on Oct. 31, 2018.

[192] Jack Crowe, "Newest Member of NYT Editorial Board Has History of Racist Tweets," *National Review*, Aug. 2, 2018. https://www.nationalreview.com/news/sarah-jeong-new-york-times-hires-writer-racist-past/.

[193] Andrew Sullivan, "When Racism Is Fit to Print," *Daily Intelligencer*, Aug. 3, 2018. http://nymag.com/intelligencer/2018/08/sarah-jeong-new-york-times-anti-white-racism.html.

[194] Jim Windolf, "After Storm Over Tweets, The Times and a New Hire Part Ways," *New York Times*, Feb. 13, 2018. https://www.nytimes.com/2018/02/13/business/media/quinn-norton-new-york-times.html.

[195] Robby Soave, "Call out hypocrisy, but don't join the lynch mob," *Reason: Hit and Run*, Aug. 2, 2018.

[196] Martin Luther King, Jr., "I Have a Dream" speech, Aug. 28, 1963 at the Lincoln Memorial, Washington D.C.

[197] Tweet on May 29, 2018.

[198] Roseanne Barr: "Hey Lefties... I'm a Jew, Quit Lynching Me!" *TMZ*, May 31, 2018.

[199] "One on One with Roseanne Barr," redemption interview with Sean Hannity, *Fox News*, July 26, 2018.

[200] Carlos Greer and Ian Mohr, "How Megyn Kelly blew her megadeal with NBC," *New York Post*, Oct. 25, 2018.

[201] Scott Morefield, "FLASHBACK: Jimmy Fallon, Jimmy Kimmel And Sarah Silverman All Wore Blackface," *The Daily Caller*, Oct. 25, 2018. See interview: https://www.youtube.com/watch?v=qu8lK3Stuws.

[202] Ibid.

[203] Fallon's mimicking Chris Rock at Golden Globes Awards: https://www.youtube.com/watch?v=E37BSMRA7-o.

[204] Emily Zanotti, "WATCH: ANTIFA Protesters Attack NBC News Reporter In Charlottesville," *The Daily Wire*, Aug. 12, 2018. https://www.dailywire.com/news/34396/watch-antifa-protesters-attack-nbc-news-reporter-emily-zanotti.

[205] Avi Selk, "Antifa protesters couldn't find any fascists at Unite the Right—and harassed the press instead," *Washington Post*, Aug. 14, 2018. https://washingtonpost.com/news/local/wp/2018/08/13/antifa-protesters-couldnt-find-any-fascists-at-unite-the-right-and-harassed-the-press-instead/.

[206] Nicholas Fondacaro, "NBC Ignores Own Reporter and Crew Assaulted By Antifa in Charlottesville," *NewsBusters*, Aug. 11, 2018. https://www.newsbusters.org/blogs/nb/nicholas-fondacaro/2018/08/12/nbc-ignores-own-reporter-and-crew-assaulted-antifa.

[207] J. Pepa, essay "Etudes Materiales," No. XIV, Sept. 1947. Sourced in Max Eastman, *Reflections on the Failure of Socialism* (New York, NY: Devin Adair, 1955), pp. 70–71.

[208] Thus Spoke Zarathustra: A Book for All and None. Part I, Chapter 11, "*Vom neuen Götzen*" ("The New Idol"). Published in four parts between 1883 and 1891,

another translation: "But the state lieth in all languages of good and evil; and whatever it saith it lieth; and whatever it hath it hath stolen."

[209] Ben O'Neill, "FISA, the NSA, and America's Secret Court System," *Mises Daily*, Feb. 22, 2014. https://mises.org/library/fisa-nsa-and-america%E2%80%99s-secret-court-system.

[210] Tibor R. Machan, *Private Rights and Public Illusions* (New Brunswick, NJ: Transaction Publishers, 1994).

[211] Mortimer Jerome Adler, *The Great Ideas: A Lexicon of Western Thought* (Chicago, IL: Open Court Publishing, 2000), p. 378.

[212] David Frum, *How We Got Here: The '70s* (New York, NY: Basic Books, 2002), p. 262. Figures from a 1970 Gallup poll.

[213] Ibid., pp. 252–264.

[214] Ibid., p. 252.

[215] Paul Jacob, "Degrading Expectations," *Common Sense* radio program, June 15, 2018.

[216] Sheldon Richman, "Rand Paul and the Civil Rights Act: Was he right?" *The Christian Science Monitor*, May 26, 2010. https://www.csmonitor.com/Commentary/Opinion/2010/0526/Rand-Paul-and-the-Civil-Rights-Act-Was-he-right.

[217] Cathy Young, "Racism, Civil Rights, and Libertarianism," *Real Clear Politics*, blog-magazine, June 11, 2010. http://www.realclearpolitics.com/articles/2010/06/11/racism_civil_rights_and_libertarianism_105934.html.

[218] Abdullahi A. An-Na'im, "Islamic Foundations of Religious Human Rights," in *Religious Human Rights in Global Perspective: Religious Perspectives*, eds. John Witte and Johan David van der Vyver (Martinus Nijhoff Publishers, 1996), p. 341.

[219] Murray Gordon, *Slavery in the Arab World* (New York, NY: New Amsterdam Press, 1989). Originally published in French by Editions Robert Laffont, S.A. Paris, 1987, pp. 44–45.

[220] Muslim Liberty Caucus, Libertarian Party, 2016.

[221] Abdullahi A. An-Na'im, "Islamic Foundations of Religious Human Rights," in *Religious Human Rights in Global Perspective: Religious Perspectives*, eds. John Witte and Johan David van der Vyver (Martinus Nijhoff Publishers, 1996), p. 341.

[222] *Quran*, (2:256)

[223] Francis R. Nicosia, *The Third Reich and the Palestine Question* (Transaction Publishers, 2000), pp. 85–86.

[224] "Hajj Amin al-Husayni: Wartime Propagandist," United State Holocaust Memorial Museum. https://www.ushmm.org/wlc/en/article.php?ModuleId=10007667.

[225] Moshe Pearlman, *Mufti of Jerusalem; the Story of Haj Amin El Husseini* (London, UK: Victor Gollancz, University of Michigan, 1947), p. 51.

[226] Matthias Küntzel, "National Socialism and Anti-Semitism in the Arab World," *Jewish Political Students Review*, Spring 2005.

[227] Ibid.

[228] Ibid.

[229]"Hajj Amin al-Husayni: Wartime Propagandist," United State Holocaust Memorial Museum. https://www.ushmm.org/wlc/en/article.php?ModuleId=10007667.

[230]Norman G. Finkelstein, *The Holocaust Industry: Reflections on the Exploitation of Jewish Suffering* (New York and London: Verso, 2003), p. 25.

[231]"Branding Moderates as 'Anti-Muslim': The American left tries to stigmatize Muslim reformers," *Wall Street Journal*, Oct. 30, 2016.

[232]Ibid.

[233]"Brandeis University's Disgraceful Act," *Frontpage Mag*, Apr. 13, 2014. http://frontpagemag.com/fpm/223408/brandeis-universitys-disgraceful-act-jeffrey-herf.

[234]Hearings at Homeland Security & Governmental Affairs Committee, June 14, 2017, 10:00 AM, SD-342, Dirksen Senate Office Building.

[235]Emily Ritchie, "Ayaan Hirsi Ali slams protesters who prevented her visit to Australia," *The Australian*, Apr. 5, 2017.

[236]Ibid.

[237]Robert M.S. McDonald, "Fredrick Douglass: The Self-Made Man," *Cato's Letter*, Fall 2011, Vol. 9, No. 4.

[238]Robby Soave, "Leaked Internal Memo Reveals the ACLU Is Wavering on Free Speech," *Reason.com* "Hit & Run," June 21, 2018. The memo was leaked by former ACLU board member Wendy Kaminer.

[239]Mark J. Rozell, *Executive Privilege: The Dilemma of Secrecy and Democratic Accountability* (Baltimore, MD: John Hopkins University Press, 1994), p. 26.

[240]H.C. Peterson and Gilbert C. Fite, *Opponents of War, 1917–1918* (Seattle and London: University of Washington Press, 1957).

[241]Barbara Kay, "Fascism in America? Sure, but not because of You Know Who," *National Post*, Jan. 31, 2017. https://nationalpost.com/opinion/barbara-kay-fascism-in-america-sure-but-not-because-of-you-know-who.

[242]Sedition Act of 1918, United States, Statutes at Large, Washington, D.C., 1918, Vol. XL, pp. 553 ff; approved, May 16, 1918.

[243]Thomas J. DiLorenzo, "Yankee Confederates: New England Secession Movements Prior to the War Between the States," in *Secession, State and Liberty*, ed. David Gordon (Transaction Publishers, 1998).

[244]Claude G. Bowers, *Jefferson in Power: The Death Struggle of the Federalists* (Boston, MA: Riverside Press, 1936), pp. 235, 243.

[245]Paul Leicester Ford, *The Writings of Thomas Jefferson, 1816–1826*, vol. X (New York, NY: G.P. Putnam's Sons), p. 35; Thomas Jefferson's letter to William H. Crawford, Secretary of War under President James Madison, on June 20, 1816.

[246]Russell Kirk, *The Conservative Mind* (New York, NY: Avon Books, 1968), p. 45.

[247]Jacob G. Hornberger, "The Confluence of Left and Right," *Hornberger's Blog*, May 25, 2010, Future of Freedom Foundation. https://www.fff.org/2010/05/25/confluence-left/.

[248]Ibid.

[249]Mark Steyn, "Obamacare made legal by a lie," *Orange County Register*, July 1, 2012.

3. Italian Fascism's Political Spectrum Controversies

> ... it may rather be expected that this will be a century of authority, a century of the Left, a century of Fascism.
>
> —Mussolini, "The Political and Social Doctrine of Fascism," 1933[1]

> It was inevitable that I should become a Socialist ultra, a Blanquist, indeed a communist. I carried about a medallion with Marx's head on it in my pocket.
>
> —Mussolini, 1932 interview[2]

> If the Fascist ideology cannot be described as a simple response to Marxism, its origins, on the other hand, were the direct result of very specific revision of Marxism. It was a revision of Marxism and not a variety of Marxism or a consequence of Marxism.
>
> —Zeev Sternhell[3]

> The further a society drifts from truth the more it will hate those who speak it.
>
> —Selwyn Duke[4]

Since the end of World War II, the conventional view held by most historians concerning Mussolini's political and social creed was that he exhibited features that would place him on the right side of the political

---

NOTE: I originally submitted a Wikipedia page in November 2014 that was posted, but later banned for, among other things, refusing to remove the word "Left" in which Mussolini used to describe his fascist movement in his 1933 "Doctrine of Fascism." I later submitted another version with more footnotes and evidence from historians of why Mussolini would have referred to himself and fascism as left-wing. That larger version was rejected. The material in this chapter is from that Wikipedia page, but has been revised and expanded since the rejection.

spectrum. But this view has come under closer scrutiny in recent years. A number of historians and political scientists argue that fascism is a doctrine which mixes the philosophies of the left and right into a confusing maze.[5,6] However, others argue that there is little evidence that much right-wing impetus rose from monarchists, reactionaries or the clergy that could have led to the founding of fascism. Even the nationalist vigor of fascism was untraditional, compressed within revolutionary, unpatriotic and anti-conservative confines—a "revolutionary nationalism" espoused by fascist theoreticians as a cultural and racial vessel to hold the precious cargo of socialism, akin to Stalin's national communism that was embedded within his "Socialism in One Country."

Some political sociologists, such as Seymour Martin Lipset, argued that fascism is actually "extremism of the center." Lipset contended that fascism was not on the right because Mussolini (1883–1945) did not plan to restore monarchical or aristocratic privilege.[7] Arthur M. Schlesinger, Jr., American historian and a Pulitzer Prize winner, asserted that the "Fascists were not conservative in any very meaningful sense... The Fascists, in a meaningful sense, were revolutionaries."[8]

Ernst Nolte argued in his acclaimed work, *Three Faces of Fascism*, that fascism was neither on the far right nor was it a kind of conservatism, since politicians of a conservative mindset were usually antagonistic towards fascism.[9]

Others, like Israeli historian and political scientist Zeev Sternhell, viewed fascism in its early years as "an anti-Marxist form of socialism,"[10] and compared fascism's origins to revolutionary far-left French movements, creating a branch that he referred to as the "revolutionary right." Considered one of the world's leading experts on Fascism, Sternhell contended that the essence of fascism represented "a synthesis of organic nationalism with the antimaterialist revision of Marxism."[11] Sternhell concluded that the fascist ideology manifested

> a variety of socialism which, while rejecting Marxism, remained revolutionary. This form of socialism was also, by definition, anti-liberal and anti-bourgeois and its opposition to historical materialism made it the natural ally of radical nationalism.[12]

As for the left-right political spectrum, Sternhell argued that in

France the sources of the fascist movement, as well as its leaders, were to be found as much on the left as on the right of the political spectrum, and often more to the left than to the right. To be sure, this was also the case elsewhere in Europe.[13]

By the late 20th century, the general consensus among most historians attributed the origins of fascism to one of the numerous branches of heretical Marxism that had developed into dictatorship, nationalization, welfarism, and militarism. Later, Sternhell, in *The Birth of Fascist Ideology*, took the position that the "origins" of Franco-Italian fascism ideology was "Marxism," or to be more precise, from "a very specific revision of Marxism."[14] Giovanni Gentile (1875–1944), an Italian fascist politician, academic, and the philosopher of Fascism, affirmed in 1929 that "Fascism [is] a consequence of its Marxian and Sorelian patrimony."[15] In his 1925 essay "What is Fascism?" Giovanni Gentile openly acknowledged that Fascism emerged from Marxism, particularly from the French Marxist Georges Sorel, writing: "It is well known that Sorelian syndicalism, out of which the thought and the political method of Fascism emerged—conceived itself the genuine interpretation of Marxist communism."[16]

To state it bluntly, both Italian and French fascism emerged out of Marxism. The Marxist-inspired "Italian revolutionary syndicalism became the backbone of fascist ideology,"[17] which also implies that a large strain of the trade labor movement was involved in spawning Italian fascism. In fact, "most syndicalist leaders were among the founders of the Fascist movement," and many held key positions in Mussolini's administration.[18] According to UC Berkeley political scientist A. James Gregor,

> What some of the revolutionary syndicalists proceeded to do was to identify the "communality" of man not with *class*, but with the *nation*. The first intimations of a "revolutionary nationalism" made their appearance among the most radical Marxists.[19]

This would indicate that Mussolini's fascism, although heretical, could be identified as part of a "Fascist-Marxist Axis."

There were hardly any noteworthy theoreticians or leaders of Italian or French fascism who did not, at one point in their lives, embrace variants of Marxism, Revolutionary Syndicalism or socialism, including Giovanni Gentile, Georges Valois, Paul Marion, Georges Sorel, Hubert Lagardelle, Angelo O. Olivetti, Gustave Hervé, Nicola Bombacci, Cesare Rossi, Roberto Farinacci, Sergio Panunzio, Alfredo Rocco, Gabriele D'Annunzio, Cario Silvestri, Ottavio Dinale, Edmondo Rossoni, Paolo Orano, Agostino Lanzillo, Armando Casalini, Paolo Mantica, Marcel Déat, Adrien Marquet, Michele Bianchand, Massimo Fovel, Ugo Spirito, Émile Janvion, Walter Mocchi, Giuseppe Ungaretti, Pierre Renaudel, Henri de Man (from Belgium), Pierre Drieu La Rochelle, *ad nauseam*, along with Mussolini himself.

Robert Michels, a sociological positivist, revolutionary syndicalist, and radical socialist, joined the National Fascist Party in 1924, claiming that Fascism was "the revolutionary nationalism of the poor."[20] Once a member of the Social Democratic Party of Germany, Michels understood the close connection between fascism and Marxism, writing: "Fascism cannot be comprehensively understood without an understanding of Marxism."[21]

According to *World Fascism*, Bolshevism and fascism had many similarities, including a "revolutionary ideology," a vanguard "elitism," a "disdain for bourgeois values," and a penchant for "totalitarian ambitions."[22] Author and publisher Roger Kimbal contends that

> Mussolini began as a disciple of Lenin and did not so much repudiate Marxism-Leninism as become a self-declared "heretic." Thus, one of Mussolini's groups of thugs called itself the Cheka, after Lenin's secret police.[23]

The Italian syndicalist Giuseppe Prezzolini saw fascism as a movement populated by an elite cadre, similar to what Lenin realized in 1902—that the workers would never desire a revolution. This realization called for a small group of dedicated revolutionaries "to play a more decisive role than Marx had imagined."[24] To facilitate this social revolution, the type of proletarian violence advocated by French Marxist Georges Sorel in his *Reflections on Violence* would be required. As an admirer of Mussolini, Prezzolini wrote an optimistic article ("The *Fascisti* and the Class Struggle") concerning Mussolini's 1922 coup in Italy. Republished in the Socialist Labor Party's *Weekly People*, Prezzolini lauded that fact that the "Fascisti" were seizing private estates "on the pretext that unused land must be brought under cultivation." And if owners refused, they would be punished "under penalty of military occupation of their property." In his article, Prezzolini discounted the intimidation employed by Mussolini's forces and appeared pleased that the "Fascisti have just occupied a factory that was not paying wages on time," and that "squadrons of 'Black Shirts' compelled employers to cancel wages reductions."[25]

When Georges Valois, founder of the French Fascist political party (*Le Faisceau*) in 1925, attempted to explain fascism in relationship to Marxism, he wrote, "that since it was a total conception of national, political, economic and social life...,"[26] "fascism had precisely the same aim as socialism."[27] Valois insisted that Fascism, "which has a foothold both on the left and on the right, is in fact much closer to what is called the left than to what is called the right in that it builds the authority, the state, on the needs of the people in order to defend them against the great and the mighty,"[28] and that "there could be no greater mistake than to regard fascism as an extreme right-wing movement..."[29] Further, Valois praised Georges Sorel and his revolutionary syndicalist theory of the trade union movement "as the intellectual father of fascism."[30] Near the end of the 1920s, "Valois defined fascism and Marxism as 'varieties of socialism.'"[31]

In *Fascism: Theory and Practice*, David Renton agrees with Sternhell's assertions, writing that "One of Sternhell's consistent themes is the meaninglessness of left-right distinctions. Fascism, he says, emerged on the left while claiming to be anti-left."[32] The Italian philosopher Augusto del Noce interpreted "Italian Fascism as the competitor of Leninism" and "a revolutionary form of certain European nationalism during the 'first age of secularization.'"[33] When trying to explain fascism, the French monarchist Charles Maurras replied: "What is Fascism? It is socialism emancipated from democracy"—that is, fascist socialism.[34]

In fact, this was the term that a number of proponents of fascism in the 1930s used to describe their ideology—"Fascist Socialism." Sympathetic to surrealism and communism, Pierre Drieu La Rochelle eventually drifted towards favoring the merging of French fascism with socialism. In 1934, he wrote a book in which he explained his dissatisfaction with Marxism and his enthusiasm for Georges Sorel, Fernand Pelloutier, and the earlier works of French socialism that included Charles Fourier, Saint-Simon, and Proudhon. La Rochelle titled his book *Socialisme Fasciste* (*Fascist Socialism*).

When it comes to the challenges of defining fascism, however, there is not a better source than Mussolini's "The Political and Social Doctrine of Fascism."[35] In 1933, Mussolini wrote:

> For if the 19th century was the century of individualism (Liberalism always signifying individualism) it may be expected that this will be the century of collectivism, and hence the century of the State.[36]

Most political scientists have identified collectivism as synonymous with the idea that the group's goal should be superior to the individual's so as to advance the "greater good." The German economist Herbert Giersch contended that "collectivism is on the left, individualism is on the right."[37]

The Doctrine of Fascism

An admirer of Karl Marx and Georg Wilhelm Friedrich Hegel, Giovanni Gentile had a hand in writing the 1927 essay for Mussolini known as "The Political and Social Doctrine of Fascism."[38] The first authorized English translation by Jane Soames in 1933 has language that varies greatly from the 1935 version. One controversial sentence was: "... it may rather be expected that this will be a century of authority, a century of the Left, a century of Fascism."[39] A number of other books and publications of the era also used all or parts of Soames's translation, including President Herbert Hoover in his 1934 book *The Challenge to Liberty*.[40] Hoover went on to describe Mussolini's Fascism as having features in common with socialism, communism, and Nazism.[41]

The Controversy

Most historians agree that historical Italian Fascism was a mixed bag of rightwing and left-wing socioeconomic policies. Nevertheless, recent evidence has shed new light on the underpinnings of Italian Fascism, discovering that this totalitarian state had embodied a far more collectivistic, socialist, and progressive ideology, placing it squarely on the left side of the political dichotomy, that is, only if Marxism is also considered to be on the Left.

Influenced by various factions of syndicalism, Italian Fascism borrowed its ideology and terminology from socialism.[42]   The British journalist Frederick Augustus Voigt, a correspondent for the *Manchester Guardian* in Berlin during the 1920s and 1930s, concluded that "Marxism has led to Fascism and National-Socialism, because, in all essentials, it is Fascism and National Socialism."[43,44]

Historically, Italian Fascism was founded as a Marxist-leaning party, which some have classified as a form of Fascist-Marxist ideology. From 1914 to at least 1921, Mussolini simultaneously proclaimed himself a Fascist while still adhering to Marxist doctrines and Marxist leaders such as Lenin.   In 1914, Mussolini created the Marxist-sounding organization—the Fasci of Revolutionary Action (*Fasci d'Azione Rivoluzionaria*, FAR).[45] Mussolini's first Fascist party—the Fascist Revolutionary Party (*Partito Fascista Rivoluzionario*, PFR)—was founded in 1915.[46] Two years later, Mussolini still considered himself within the Marxist camp, praising the Bolshevik's 1917 October Revolution,[47] boasting of his camaraderie with Lenin and violent revolution. In the Italian elections of 1919, he publicly compared himself to Lenin, bragging that he was the "Lenin of Italy."[48] In his seminal work, *Three Faces of Fascism*, the German historian Ernst Nolte acknowledged that in 1921, Mussolini was still proudly claiming his "paternity" of the communist movement, declaring as a newly elected Fascist Deputy, that "I know the Communists. I know them because some of them are my children..."[49] Richard Pipes in *Russia Under the Bolshevik Regime* concurred, writing:

> Even as the Fascist leader, Mussolini never concealed his sympathy and admiration for Communism: he thought highly of Lenin's "brutal energy," and saw nothing objectionable in Bolshevik massacres of hostages. He proudly claimed Italian Communism as his child.[50]

Eventually, Mussolini toned down his radical socialist rhetoric and his praise for Lenin in an effort to gain control of the Italian government via electoral politics, substituting "National" for "Revolutionary" in his party's name in late 1921. Still, for Mussolini to concurrently adhere to fascism and Marxism for over six years invalidates the theory of a political spectrum tied to the notion that these two collectivist ideologies are considered polar opposites. Italian Fascism was just an offshoot of a revised Marxism.

Historically, Mussolini's fascist movement had little to do with the anti-socialist right-wing and their reaction to the various communist or socialist movements. Mussolini tried to take control of the rural, anti-socialist *squadristi* chieftains, but they turned on him when he signed the Pact of Pacification with the Italian Socialist Party in early August 1921. During this struggle, Mussolini condemned conservative landowners and the middle class, saying that provincial Fascism was "no longer liberation, but tyranny; no longer protector of the nation, but defense of private interests and of the dullest, deafest, most miserable cast that exists in Italy."[51] Mussolini wanted to lead a populist movement, but not at the expense of his left-wing philosophy and credentials, although eventually, he found it necessary to succumb to bourgeoisie elements until his dictatorship in 1925.

He would denounce rival socialist leaders and movements, but according to the Polish-American historian Richard Pipes,

> Given the opportunity, Mussolini would have been glad as late as 1920–21 to take under his wing the Italian Communists, for whom he felt great affinities, greater, certainly, than for democratic socialists, liberals, and conservatives. Genetically, Fascism issued from the "Bolshevik" wing of Italian socialism, not from any conservative ideology or movement.[52]

In "The Manifesto of the Fascist Struggle" (June 1919), Mussolini's cohorts called for radical policies of the times, including: a heavy progressive tax on capital that would truly expropriate a portion of all wealth; the seizure of all the possessions of the religious congregations and the abolition of all the bishoprics; the nationalization of all the arms and explosives factories; reduction of retirement age from 65 to 55; women's suffrage; a minimum wage; eight-hour workday; participation of workers' representation in the functions of industry commissions; and pro-labor policies.[53] In addition, the manifesto advocated "forcing landowners to cultivate their land or have them expropriated and given to veterans and farmers cooperatives,"[54] and demanded "participatory democracy on the factory floor."[55] The Manifesto was written by national syndicalist Alceste De Ambris and Futurist movement founder Filippo Tommaso.[56]

Mussolini was adamant that his anti-capitalist agenda be implemented. Mostly directed towards banking and the financial sector, Mussolini wrote in his fascist newspaper *Il Popolo d'Italia* that: "This is what we propose now to the Treasury: either the property owners expropriate themselves, or we summon the masses of war veterans to march against these obstacles and overthrow them."[57]

Even in his early years as a child, Mussolini was nurtured on Marxist and socialist revolutionary ideology. Some referred to him as the "original red-diaper baby."[58] His father, Alessandro Mussolini, often cited as a socialist revolutionary militant, was an admirer of Karl Marx and became a member of the First International.[59] When Benito Mussolini was a boy, his father would read passages from Karl Marx's *Das Kapital* aloud to his entire family at night.[60] Beginning at age six, Mussolini would accompany his father to socialist "committee meetings and political assemblies."[61]

A former member of the Socialist Party of Great Britain, David Ramsey Steele described Mussolini in his early years as

> the Che Guevara of his day, a living saint of leftism. Handsome, courageous, charismatic, an erudite Marxist, a riveting speaker and writer, a dedicated class warrior to the core, he was the peerless *duce* of the Italian Left. He looked like the head of any future Italian socialist government, elected or revolutionary.[62]

According to Steele, "Fascism began as a revision of Marxism by Marxists..."[63] In other words, many strands of Marxism had devolved into Italian Fascism. A. James Gregor concurred in his book, *The Faces of Janus: Marxism and Fascism in the Twentieth Century*, writing: "The first Fascists were almost all Marxists—serious theorists who had long been identified with Italy's intelligentsia of the Left."[64]

A political scientist at UC Berkeley and known for his research on fascism and Marxism, A. James Gregor asserted that fascism is a Marxist heresy, explaining that "Mussolini was a Marxist 'heretic.'"[65] In *Young Mussolini*, Gregor attempted

> to establish that Fascism was a variant of classical Marxism, a belief system that pressed some themes argued by both Marx and Engels until they found expression in the form of "national syndicalism" that was to animate the first Fascism.[66]

Zeev Sternhell takes a different approach and sees fascism as "a revision of Marxism and not a variety of Marxism or a consequence of Marxism."[67]

Richard Pipes summed up fascism's affinity with socialism by arguing that both "Bolshevism and Fascism were heresies of socialism."[68] Sense of community and socialization were important aspects of many 20th century movements and regimes, including the theory of "social fascism," which was initiated by the Soviet government and the Comintern to stigmatize social democracy as a variant of fascism.[69] Referring to social fascism, Joseph Stalin described fascism and social democracy (democratic socialism) as "not opposites, but twin brothers."[70] Apparently, Stalin felt confident that comparing social democracy with fascism was an easy sell.

Cornell University sociologist Mabel Berezin suggested that despite fascism's inchoate mishmash of contradictory ideas, "a belief in community unites Fascism and Marxism."[71] Some contemporary historians have referred to fascism in general as "folk socialism."[72] By the 1930s, many Marxists and non-Marxists noted the "convergence" of fascism and Stalinism, where Soviet Russia was seen as transforming into a developmental nationalism that had abandoned its earlier anti-nationalism, anti-statism, and anti-militarism tenets.[73] Nikolai Bukharin, who spent six years in exile with fellow exiles Lenin and Trotsky, alluded to the "fascist" features of the emerging Soviet system.[74] Referring to the "bureaucratic collectivism" that captivated Stalinism and Fascism, the Italian Marxist, Bruno Rizzi, who years later became a Trotskyite, remarked, "that which Fascism consciously sought, we [Marxists] involuntarily constructed."[75] Even Mussolini made a similar comparison in 1938, confidently attesting that "in the face of the total collapse of the system [bequeathed] by Lenin, Stalin has covertly transformed himself into a Fascist."[76]

In Gregor's discussion of the origins of fascism, he wrote: "Fascism's most direct ideological inspiration came from the collateral influence of Italy's most radical 'subversives'—the Marxists of revolutionary syndicalism...,"[77] and that "by the early 1930s, the 'convergence' of fascism and Stalinism struck Marxists and non-Marxists alike."[78] Eventually, Leon Trotsky developed serious misgivings about the political and socioeconomic directions of Soviet Russia and Stalin, writing that "Stalinism and fascism, in spite of a deep difference in social foundations, are symmetrical phenomena. In many of their features they show a deadly similarity."[79]

Other writers have come to the same conclusion, including Italian historian Renzo De Felice, who is best known for his 6,000-page biography of Mussolini. According to A. James Gregor, De Felice has reached the conclusion that Mussolini was a revolutionary modernizer in domestic issues, while "Mussolini's fascism shared considerable affinities with the traditional and revolutionary left."[80,81] A former member of the Italian Communist Party (PCI), Felice conceded that he saw "in fascism a manifestation of that left-wing totalitarianism."[82]

Gene Edward Veith, Jr., who examined fascism from a Judeo-Christian viewpoint, writes:

> The influence of Marxist scholarship has severely distorted our understanding of fascism. Communism and fascism were rival brands of socialism. Whereas Marxist socialism is predicated on an international class struggle, fascist national socialism promoted a socialism centered in national unity.[83]

Observing that the Soviets were often "ambivalent" about early fascism, Stanley G. Payne concluded that "Fascism was sometimes perceived not inaccurately as more of a heresy from, rather than a mortal challenge to, revolutionary Marxism."[84] In fact, at the 1923 Twelfth Party Congress in Moscow, Karl Radek, briefly the Secretary of the Comintern, pointed out that the Nazis had "inherited Bolshevik political culture exactly as Italian Fascism had done."[85]

Right-Wing Socialism and Petty-Bourgeoisie Socialism

Other scholars have preferred to interpret both National Socialism and Fascism as "right-wing socialism" or "petty-bourgeoisie socialism." Economist Murray Rothbard considered Bismarckism and later fascism and Nazism as examples of "right-wing socialism."[86] Rothbard further wrote:

> There were from the beginning two different strands within Socialism: one was the Right-wing, authoritarian strand, from Saint-Simon down, which glorified statism, hierarchy, and collectivism...[87]

Right-wing socialism may have surfaced due to a convergence of the authoritarian left and right. Historian George L. Mosse noted that by the early 20th century "the radical Left and the radical Right were apt to demand control of the whole man, and not just a political piece him."[88]

Karl Radek, a Marxist theoretician and international communist leader, also described fascism as the "socialism of the petty bourgeoisie."[89] He was one of the passengers traveling on the "sealed train" that carried Vladimir Lenin and other Russian revolutionary leaders to Russia in 1917.[90]

The Italian Catholic priest known as the "clerical socialist," Luigi Sturzo, portrayed Bolshevism in 1926 as "left Fascism" and fascism as "right Bolshevism."[91]

Nobel laureate in economics F.A. Hayek conjectured that within the socialist movement there were rival right-wing and left-wing factions. In *The Road to Serfdom*, Hayek wrote:

> There are bound to arise rival socialist movements that appeal to the support of those whose relative position is worsened. There is a great deal of truth in the often-heard statement that Fascism and National Socialism are a sort of middle-class socialism—only that in Italy and Germany the supporters of these new movements were economically hardly a middle class any longer.[92]

In his essay "Spilling the Spanish Beans," George Orwell may have been the first to coin the term "right-wing Socialism" in his story about his days fighting General Franco's forces in Spain.[93] During the Spanish Civil War, Orwell had found himself caught in the middle of street-fighting waged between left-wing Communists and right-wing Communists. In his 1938 book *Homage to Catalonia*, Orwell documented how "The Communists had gained power and a vast increase of membership partly by appealing to the middle classes against the revolutionaries..."[94] He also noted that the "Communist viewpoint and the Right-wing Socialist viewpoint could everywhere be regarded as identical."[95] Orwell's fighting unit, the POUM (Workers' Party of Marxist Unification), was accused by the Communist press the world over of both being fascist and collaborating with the fascists.[96,97]

Disillusioned over his experience in the Spanish Civil War, Orwell speculated that the Second Spanish Republic (1931–1939) might be even more fascist than General Franco's regime. Referring to the leaders of the Second Spanish Republic as "right-wing socialists," Orwell wrote that the regime will be fascist, and

> It will not be the same as the fascism Franco would impose, it will even be better than Franco's fascism to the extent of being worth fighting for, but it will be Fascism. Only, being operated by Communists and Liberals, it will be called something different.[98]

In essence, Orwell saw Stalinists as right-wing socialists because of their repressive policies in the liquidation of Trotskyites, anarchists, and revolutionary Communists in Spain to "prevent any elements of the Spanish far Left... from fomenting social revolution."[99] The Stalin-backed Communists in Spain became a "bulwark against revolution, collectivization and social disorder, while seeking to manipulate and control events for their own ends."[100]

Another description of right-wing socialism has come from economist Jesús Huerta de Soto, who referred to this anti-market, paternalistic ideology as a type of socialism "in which institutional aggression is employed to maintain the social status quo and the privileges certain people or groups enjoy." Soto continues, "In this sense, conservative socialism and democratic socialism differ only in the motivations behind them and in the social group each aims to favor."[101]

Both Karl Marx and Friedrich Engels were highly critical of those who would ignore Marxism and embrace a form of "petty-bourgeois social-ism." In *The Communist Manifesto*, Marx and Engels attempted to dis-tinguish their version of socialism and communism from other versions of socialism, including "petty-bourgeois socialism" and "conservative or bourgeois socialism."[102]

Engels was particularly concerned with avowed socialists who devi-ated from Marxist theory, writing in 1877: "Even in the Social-Demo-cratic Party, petty bourgeois Socialism has its defenders."[103]

Pejoratives and Marxist Terminology

The words "fascist" or "right-wing fascist" are sometimes used to deni-grate people, institutions, or groups that have no connection with his-torical or ideological fascism. Many of these claims are historically mean-ingless, but still remain a popular polemical sport to defame others.

Near the end of World War II, George Orwell, author of *1984* and *Animal Farm*, attempted to define fascism. He found it difficult. He wrote that the word "fascism" is almost entirely meaningless, arguing that it is recklessly flung around in every direction.[104] Gregor concurred, writing: "By and large, the term 'fascism' has only pejorative uses. It is employed to disparage and defame."[105] Historian Richard Griffiths has argued that "fascism" is the "most misused, and over-used, word of our times."[106]

Marxists have employed the terms "reactionary," "counter-revolu-tionary," "bourgeoisie," "fascist," or "right-wing" to clarify ideological differences and identify common denominators. In other cases, right-wing designations and other pejoratives have been used to disparage both non-Marxist opponents and pro-Marxist heretics. Historically, Marxists who stray from classical Marxism or have been caught up in a political power struggle or ideological disputes, such as Marxist revi-sionism, have resorted to using pejorative terms less for clarification and more for defaming.

Such pejorative adjectives were regularly applied during the 1920s when a power struggle erupted between Trotsky and Stalin after the death of Vladimir Lenin. In 1924, the ruling communist triumvirate denounced "Trotskyism" as "petty bourgeois deviation."[107]   Soon after Trotsky was stripped of his authority, a wider schism developed between the left-wing Bolsheviks and right-wing Bolsheviks—referred to as the Left Opposition and the Right Opposition.   In those years both Stalin and Trotsky hurtled charges of fascism or "Bonapartism" at each other.[108]   Communist parties worldwide jumped at the opportunity to condemn Trotsky's own organization as "being a crypto-fascist organization in Nazi pay."[109]

In response to Stalin's power plays, the Left Opposition within the Bolshevik Party fought back from 1923 to 1927, headed *de facto* by Trotsky.   It was destroyed by Stalin when he aligned himself with right-wing Bolsheviks who wanted to continue Lenin's New Economic Policies (NEP) and restore "concessions to the capitalist system favored by the party's right wing," which included opening up the Russian economy to private capital and foreign investment.[110]   In short order, Stalin then "demolished" the right-wing communists.[111]

The pejorative war escalated during the 1937 Moscow show trial (Great Terror).   Trotsky responded sarcastically to charges of collaboration with fascism, espionage, and capitalism.   Trotsky wrote:

> How could these Old Bolsheviks, who went through the jails and exiles of Tsarism, who were the heroes of the civil war, the leaders of industry, the builders of the party, diplomats, turn out at the moment of "the complete victory of socialism" to be saboteurs, allies of fascism, organisers of espionage, agents of capitalist restoration?[112,113]

Stalin and other Marxist leaders habitually used pejoratives to slanderously attack opponents.   "Charges of rightism, fascism and Nazism were leveled at countless victims of Stalin's purges."[114]

Other accusations leveled against supporters of Trotsky and Stalin centered on the pejorative "Red fascism," but even some non-Marxists found the term appropriate to describe Stalin's regime.   *The New York Times* dubbed Stalinism "red fascism"[115] after National Socialist Germany and Soviet Russia allied in 1939 and invaded Poland.

Allegations by communists against communists perceived as embracing fascist convictions intensified after Nikita Khrushchev rebuked

Stalin in 1956. According to A. James Gregor, "by the mid-1970s, Soviet thinkers had discovered that Chinese Maoism, for all its pretended
left-wing convictions, was actually of the 'right,' a variant of European
fascism."[116] Soviet theoreticians had concluded that "Maoists were, in
fact, neofascists."[117] Likewise, Chinese Communist leaders targeted the
Soviet Union as a reactionary regime riddled with "Red Fascist" dogma,
especially during the Sino-Soviet split (1960–1989).[118]

In *Russia Under the Bolshevik Regime*, Richard Pipes maintained that
what kept historians from inquiring into the

> influence of Bolshevism on Fascism and National Socialism was
> the insistence of Moscow to banish from the vocabulary of "pro-
> gressive" thought the adjective "totalitarian" in favor of "Fascist"
> to describe anti-communist movements or regimes.[119]

For dedicated Marxists, "any form of government other than the 'dictatorship of the proletariat' was reactionary, counterrevolutionary, and
fundamentally irrational."[120] The party line of the Soviet Union was
so stringent that many hardline Marxists held the position that there
was "no essential difference between parliamentary democracy and 'Fascism.'"[121] The practice did not stop until the advent of Mikhail Gor-
bachev's *glasnost* (openness).

The Politics of Mussolini

Mussolini got the nickname "Il Duce" after he was released from jail
for organizing violent workers' revolts during protests over Italy's "imperialistic" invasion of Ottoman Libya. During a celebratory banquet, a
Marxist veteran praised Mussolini, announcing: "From today you, Benito, are not only the representative of Romagna Socialists, but Il Duce of
all revolutionary Socialists in Italy."[122] This is not surprising since, beginning in 1903, he had called himself an "authoritarian communist"[123]
and an "aristocratic" socialist.[124]

As a union organizer and agitator, Mussolini instigated strikes and violent riots against Italy's invasion of Ottoman Libya in 1911–1912, which
got the attention of various Marxist, syndicalist, and socialist leaders.[125]

When interviewed by Emil Ludwig in March and April 1932, Mussolini confessed that he was "indeed a communist."[126] In that same interview Mussolini remarked that Marx "had a profound critical intelligence" and was "even a prophet."[127] Mussolini's reputation grew rapidly and eventually became a leading force in the Italian Socialist Party. Even as a teenager, Mussolini had joined the Italian Socialist Party in 1900.[128]

During this time, Mussolini displayed his militancy for socialist and communist insurrections, writing:

> The law of socialism is that of the desert: a tooth for a tooth, an eye for an eye. Socialism is a rude and bitter truth, which was born in the conflict of opposing forces and in violence. Socialism is war, and woe to those who are cowardly in war. They will be defeated.[129]

In 1908 Mussolini professed his loyalty to Marxism by saying, "Marx was the greatest of all theorists of socialism,"[130] and referred to Marx as "the magnificent philosopher of working class violence."[131] Sternhell concurred and noted that:

> Like all self-respecting revolutionaries, Mussolini considered himself a Marxist. He regarded Marx as the "greatest theoretician of socialism" and Marxism as the "scientific doctrine of class revolution."[132]

In 1910 Mussolini founded the newspaper, *La Lotta di Classe* (*The Class Struggle*). Later in 1913, he established a theoretical Marxist journal, *Utopia*. Lasting until 1914, *Utopia* attracted "many of the most important young theoreticians of socialism."[133] Three of his writing collaborators went on to found the Italian Communist Party and the German Communist Party.[134] The future Communist leaders were Amadeo Bordiga, Angelo Tasca, and Karl Liebknecht.[135] Contrary to earlier historians' description of Mussolini as an unaccomplished simpleton, he was actually a prolific and influential journalist and essayist. After four decades of writing, his collected works amounted to 36 volumes.[136]

In 1912 Mussolini was elected to the National Executive Committee of the Italian Socialist Party and appointed editor of their party newspaper, *Avanti!* (*Forward*).[137,138] He brought a radical Marxist strand to the newspaper, soon doubling its circulation. With a growing audience,

Mussolini redoubled the urgency of his utopian propaganda; "private property is theft" and should be abolished as Italy moved through the phase of collectivism forwards to the ultimate goal of communism.[139]

Mussolini's election and appointment to the Italian Socialist Party was considered a victory by the diehard Marxist left.[140] When he took an interventionist stand for Italy's involvement in the First World War, he was expelled from the Italian Socialist Party on November 25, 1914, which was meeting in Milan. At that contentious moment, Mussolini shouted to his comrades: "You cannot get rid of me because I am and always will be a socialist. You hate me because you still love me."[141] Mussolini promised that he "would never abandon the principles of socialism."[142] In his closing remarks before the Milan's Socialist Assembly that determined his expulsion, Mussolini said:

> Do not believe, even for a moment, that by stripping me of my membership card you do the same to my Socialist beliefs, nor that you would restrain me of continuing to work in favor of Socialism and of the Revolution.[143]

The crowd at the Milan's People's Theatre applauded.

Mussolini reversed his prior anti-war position when he realized the "great importance to war as a catalyst for revolution."[144, 145] In fact, this about-face occurred after many of his socialist colleagues quoted Karl Marx's aphorism that most social revolutions usually supersede war.[146] Mussolini was impressed by Marx's argument. However, another issue that drove Mussolini to support the Great War in 1914 was his hatred of the Hohenzollern and Hapsburg monarchies in Germany and Austria-Hungary, who he claimed had mistreated his socialist comrades for over 40 years.[147] The leaders of the Italian Socialist Party saw it differently and condemned Mussolini's band of socialist interventionists as "Marxist renegades."[148]

After deciding to support Italy's entry into World War I, "Mussolini joined with pro-war leftists outside the Socialist party and launched a new socialist newspaper, *Il Popolo d'Italia* (*People of Italy*)," which became the official newspaper of the fascist movement.[149] By February of 1915, Mussolini was defining himself and his followers in *Il Popolo d'Italia* as "we, interventionists and fascists,"[150] and was considered as a major force behind the "interventionist Left."[151] Up until August 1918, the tagline "socialist" was displayed daily on the newspaper's masthead, which sought to attract followers to "his idea of a 'revolutionary war.'"[152,153] But Mussolini kept a quotation by Louis Auguste Blanqui (1805–1881) that read: "He who has iron, has bread," which some have "interrupted as the birth cries of Fascism."[154] Blanqui was a revolutionary socialist who became a legendary figure of French radicalism, imprisoned for nearly half his life. Blanqui inspired an uprising in Paris in May 1839 in which the League of the Just participated. Later that organization merged with the Communist Corresponding Committee to form Karl Marx's Communist League. Not long after Blanqui's death, a concord was established between the Marxists and the Blanquists, which led to the founding of the Central Revolutionary Committee in 1881 and to the Revolutionary Socialist Party in 1898.[155] *Il Popolo d'Italia* was founded as a socialist newspaper and may have been subsidized by Italian industrialists and the French government, who were attempting to persuade Italy to join the Allied war effort.[156]

After Mussolini's expulsion from the Italian Socialist Party, he joined a splinter group of revolutionary syndicalists who wanted Italy to side with the Allied Powers and declare war on the Central Powers. This organization of labor union activists marked the beginning of the Marxist-inspired *Fasci d'Azione rivoluzionaria internazionalista*—later known as the Fascists—which resulted in a breach between pro-war socialists and anti-war socialists.[157] Similar breaks occurred within communist and socialist communities across Europe. As Vladislav Zubok and Constantine Pleshakov noted in their book, *Inside the Kremlin's Cold War*, "The Socialists of France and Germany and even of Russia supported World War I as a war between nation-states."[158] The Social Democratic Party of Germany (SPD), which coalesced into a Marxist party earlier in 1875, eventually lent its support to World War I.[159] Not long after Germany declared war on France,

Section Française de l'Internationale Ouvrière (SFIO), which eventually morphed into the French Communist Party, dropped its antimilitary, internationalist stand and replaced it with French patriotism, fully supporting the war.[160]

The Encyclopedia of World War I: A Political, Social, and Military History maintain that "once the war began, Austrian, British, French, German, and Russian socialists followed the rising nationalist current by supporting their country's intervention in the war."[161] In fact, most socialist parties had discarded internationalism for nationalism and national identity. At the start of World War I, "almost all the socialist parties of the Second International abandoned their commitment to internationalism and supported their national government."[162] The Second International soon dissolved over the crisis because so many members had supported the position that "nation triumphed over class" and "nationalism overrode internationalism."[163] Not only had the concept of nationalism and socialism achieved popularity among socialist intellectuals, but Lenin agreed that Marxist strategy "should take all available forces into consideration, including the force of nationalism."[164] Even Mussolini acknowledged this migration towards nationalistic socialism by most socialist party leaders. As he explained:

> During my whole life I was an internationalist socialist. When the Great War broke out I saw that all our parties that were internationalists became nationalist socialists, that happened to me and that is fascism.[165]

Mussolini opposed any socialist who refused to support what he and Italian nationalist intellectual, Enrico Corradini, called "proletarian nationalism," including the Italian Socialist Party, which he considered "reactionary." In his March 23, 1919, speech to announce the first *Fasci di Combattimento* (League of Combat), he proclaimed:

> We declare war against socialism, not because it is socialism, but because it has opposed nationalism. Although we can discuss the question of what socialism is, what is its program and what are its tactics, one thing is obvious: the official Italian Socialist Party has been reactionary and absolutely conservative.[166]

Further, during hostile exchanges with opposing socialist factions, he would retort that if anyone depicted him and his comrades as "conservatives or reactionaries," they were "downright imbeciles."[167,168]

In their first election, Italian fascists proclaimed to Italian voters that they were part of the left-wing movement. During the parliamentary elections of 1919, "fascist candidates presented themselves as part of the Left not only in their beliefs, but also in their willingness to ally with other leftist parties."[169] Mussolini and his party garnered few votes, due mostly to an incoherent message of left-wing issues and nationalistic appeals that the voters found unappealing. Apparently, Italy was awash with too many competing socialist left-wing parties, forcing Mussolini to engage in a futile attempt to "out-socialist the socialists."[170] According to historian Denis Mack Smith, the 1919 election was an indication that "the prevailing sentiment in the country was to the left and Mussolini acknowledged this fact by still in 1920 calling himself a socialist, albeit a dissident."[171] During this time, Mussolini continued to call for nationalization of land, limited confiscation of capital, and pro-worker policies to give workers a voice in operating factories.[172]

While Mussolini continued to liken himself to Lenin under his Fascist Revolutionary Party banner, he adopted the black shirts of the "anarchists and *Giovinezza* (Youth)" to create paramilitary armed squads.[173,174] In a way, this was not surprising, since Mussolini, as an unorthodox Marxist with bohemian proclivities, flirted with anarcho-syndicalist theories that "crossed anarchism with syndicalism."[175] During this time period, Mussolini was still billing himself "as a left-wing extremist," who publicly "applauded the strikes" in factories.[176] In January 1919, he agitated for an illegal strike of postal workers and proposed that employees "seize factories," while in mid-1919, he demanded in *Il Popolo d'Italia* that profiteers should be "strung up on lampposts."[177] He was simply following the examples of other trade union organizations and began to engage in numerous occupations of Italian factories, but under conditions that he characterized as not "interrupting production."[178] Referring to his occupation of factories as "creative strikes," Mussolini considered such union tactics as truly "revolutionary" actions, demanding that all workers "have the right to 'parity' with employers," but contingent upon employees possessing "the 'collective capacity' to maintain production."[179]

Along with Edmondo Rossoni's newly founded *Unione Italiana del Lavoro* (UIL) labor union in 1918, Mussolini and his squads of blackshirts were involved in the factory occupation of the metallurgical plant *Franchi e Gregorini* at Dalmine in March 1919. He delivered his "Dalmine speech" on March 20, when over 2,000 steelworkers had occupied the factory. During other strikes in 1920, Mussolini arranged secret meetings with labor representatives and hinted that he would lead them to victory, suggesting that they could seize control of the Italian state.[180] But workers and union representatives balked at his idea of violent revolution, whereupon Mussolini became frustrated, and discerned union officials and other socialists as revolutionaries only in name. Such weak response to the idea of mounting a Lenin-style revolution in Italy forced Mussolini to move closer to the interests of the middle class and industrialists.

This realization forced Mussolini to be more ambiguous in describing the meaning of fascism. Trying to be all things to all people, he compromised his past principles, and entered into political alliances to achieve parliamentary success. For several years, this pragmatism was the hallmark of Mussolini's strategy to obtain power. As Peter Neville wrote: "Mussolini [was] always the pragmatic, when it suited him..."[181] Mussolini had to transform himself into a pragmatic socialist, the kind of wishy-washy cretin he opposed and hated during his early years. At this low point in his political career, Mussolini allied himself and his political party with Giovanni Giolitti's Italian Liberal Party (PLI), the Italian Social Democratic Party (PDSI), and the Italian Nationalist Association (ANI) under the National Bloc (NB) for the May 15, 1921 general election, where his Fascist Revolutionary Party won 35 seats in the Italian parliament.[182]

Mussolini had slowly drifted away from his Marxist-based Fascism after his disastrous 1919 election under the Fascist Revolutionary Party banner, searching for a populist movement that could catapult him towards a high position of power. An opportunity arose in 1919–1921, when socialists and communists turned violent, seizing farms, factories, companies and even private homes in attempts to "coerce smallholders [farmers]... as well as laborers into Socialist unions,"[183] that would engage in riots, strikes, and political assassinations. The violent agitators often expelled owners and engineers from their factories; in some cases they rounded up owners and their families and took them hostage.[184] They set up Soviet-style "committees of workmen" to facilitate a Dictatorship of the Proletariat on a large scale.[185] In one case, a socialist deputy named Cagnoni publicly lauded a group of revolutionary terrorists for planting a bomb in a Milan theater that killed 20 patrons.[186] The public was incensed, which helped to recruit a diverse group of people from ex-servicemen, landowners, businessmen, farmers and the general public. Even many students were willing to join action squads to even the score, attack, or club the perpetrators or make them swallow castor oil or live frogs.[187]

Across Italy "trains and barracks, banks and public buildings were attacked by mobs," while entire cities and areas were proclaimed to be under the control of Communist militants.[188] Believing that only greater violence would stop the transgressions, many middle-class defense leagues were formed to fight the revolutionary socialists. The propertied classes organized paramilitary organizations, especially in rural areas, called *squadrismo*, where "local groups or *fascio* knew little about Mussolini and tended to follow their own immediate leader."[189]

The most prominent anti-socialist militia, the conservative Italian Nationalist Association (ANI), organized the first wave of anti-socialist counter attacks in 1919 with their blue-shirted *Sempre Pronti* (Always Ready) militias.[190] They were simply reacting to the socialist-led violence towards the middle class, farmers and the wealthy, and had little ideology or vision to spearhead a mass movement.[191] Their opposition included Mussolini's Fascist party. The ANI opposed Mussolini's 1922 March on Rome, assuring King Victor Emmanuel III that "their own *Sempre Pronti* militia was ready to fight the Blackshirts," if the fascists were foolish enough to enter the city.[192] King Emmanuel instead offered Mussolini the position of Prime Minister of Italy. In fact, many *squadristi* leaders (the *ras*) were suspicious of Mussolini, due to his "lingering leftist loyalties,"[193] especially his Marxist and socialist background.

Mussolini courted them nonetheless, discovering that the *squadristi* were highly diverse, independent and loosely organized. "One *ras* could be on the political left, his neighbor on the right"; some were anti-clerical, some republican, some monarchical, some simply "no better than gangsters."[194]   In fact, in 1921, a slew of leading *ras* urged Gabriele D'Annunzio, a popular and radical nationalist rival of the Duce, to "replace Mussolini" as Italy's Fascist leader.[195]   Despite the difficulties, Mussolini successfully latched onto the *squadristi* militias for opportunistic reasons, as well as to settle a score with the Italian Socialist Party, which had purged Mussolini from their leadership position in 1914, an insult he neither forgot nor forgave. After all, when Mussolini led the Italian Socialist Party, he was the one who took delight in condemning and purging more moderate socialists from the party's ranks.

After becoming Prime Minister, Mussolini kept warm relations with the Soviet Union and its leaders. In spite of the worldwide fear of the Red Army's offensive in Poland after World War I (the Polish-Soviet War of 1919–1921), Mussolini's National Fascist Party welcomed the Bolsheviks with open arms. Mussolini was first to take the initiative by urging parliament to formally recognize the USSR in a speech on November 20, 1923.[196]   On February 7, 1924, the Italians did more than make overtones for closer ties with Lenin's Russia; they actually signed their Italo-Soviet treaty to recognize the USSR. According to Stanley G. Payne, *A History of Fascism, 1914–1945*, "Not only was Italy the first Western country to recognize the Soviet Union in 1924, but the new Soviet art first appeared in the West that year at the Venice *Biennale*, Italy's premiere art show."[197]   The British, who also sought closer ties with Soviet Russia, were still involved in heavy negotiations, and their treaty with the Soviets was not signed until August 8, 1924.[198]   Mussolini's government was first to officially sign a treaty with the USSR for full *de jure* recognition.

To further cement relationships with the Soviet Union, Fascist Italy signed the 1933 "Treaty of Friendship, Nonaggression, and Neutrality" (Italo-Soviet Pact) which helped to provide technical assistance and supplies to Moscow from numerous slew industries, including aviation, automobile, and naval.[199]   Italy received oil in exchange. Italian shipbuilders even produced a number of vessels for the Soviet fleet in 1933.[200]   Some authors have contended that this treaty with Italy was essential to Russia's ability to develop its oil industry, and later to its industrialization and armament capabilities.[201] The close relationship between Soviet Russia and Fascist Italy was the talk of Rome in the early 1930s, where many Italians referred to their mutual friendship as the "revolutionary affinity."[202] Many soviet military leaders soon arrived in Italy to show their respect. While a cortege of Soviet military brass convened with Italian military leaders, one Italian general stated that "the Italian Army has feelings which go deeper than the usual professional ones toward the Red Army. These feelings have been strengthened as a result of the Italo-Soviet Pact."[203]

One well-known Fascist leader, Sergio Panunzio (1886–1944), took the position that the Soviet Union was adopting more and more Fascist features, and that "Moscow bows before the light radiating from Rome."[204] Mussolini found many opportunities to display his sympathy for Soviet Russia, professing in 1932 that "In the whole negative part, we are alike. We and the Russians are against liberals, against democrats, against parliament."[205,206]

Even though Mussolini had harsh criticism for Italian Socialist Party leaders and ineffective socialism, he still retained great admiration for Lenin. Denis Mack Smith writes in *Mussolini*:

> Mussolini had once belonged to the Bolshevik wing of the Italian Socialist Party and still in 1924 confessed admiration for Lenin, while Trotsky was quoted as saying that Mussolini was his best pupil.[207]

Years later, after associating with Mussolini in Switzerland, Trotsky said, "He was the only man who could have brought about the revolution of the proletariat in Italy."[208]

After Mussolini's march on Rome in 1922, a disappointed Lenin remarked: "What a waste that we lost Mussolini. He is a first-rate man who would have led our party to power in Italy."[209] Earlier, during a reception at the Kremlin in Moscow, Lenin told Nicola Bombacci, an Italian Marxist revolutionary, that "In Italy, comrades, in Italy there was but a Socialist able enough to lead the people through a revolutionary path, Benito Mussolini."[210] Instead, Mussolini forged a Fascist revolution that accented national socialism instead of international socialism.

Lenin once deemed Mussolini one of the five greatest Marxist theo-reticians of the 20th century. While traveling through Marxist circles in Switzerland in 1902–1904,[211] Mussolini took classes from Russian-Italian communist Angelica Balabanoff and apparently met Lenin,[212] once remarking that "Lenin knew me better than I knew him."[213] Ap-parently, it was Balabanoff who first introduced Mussolini to Lenin.[214]

Mussolini was deeply impressed by the French Marxist and revolution-ary syndicalist Georges Sorel, who helped him formulate the core princi-ples of Italian fascism[215] and "fused socialism with nationalism."[216] In fact, Sorel is considered to be a hero to both Marxists and Italian Fas-cists alike. Mussolini claimed: "What I am, I owe to Sorel."[217] In 1921, Sorel returned the favor, calling Mussolini "a man no less extraordinary than Lenin. He, too, is a political genius, of a greater reach than all the statesmen of the day, with the only exception of Lenin..."[218] Sorel had gone through many ideological stages, but "his final ideological incar-nation appeared to be a Bolshevist praising Lenin,"[219] referring to the leader of the Russian Bolshevists in 1920 as "the greatest theoretician of Socialism since Marx..."[220] To most revolutionary socialists, syndical-ism represented a form of collective economic corporatism that would replace capitalism with socialism through trade union organizations.

Calling fascism a "political religion," Emilio Gentile, Italy's foremost historian of fascist ideology and totalitarianism,[221] regarded Mussolini's purpose to be developing, through syndicalism, a quality-based "social-ization" where Mussolini, the country, and the state would become one.[222] Gentile wrote:

> For Mussolini, syndicalism was the most modern embodiment
> of the *spirit* of Marxist doctrine, which he added to the myths
> of his Nietzschean aristocratic philosophy to reach a socialism of
> *quality* rather than *quantity*.[223]

In front of big crowds, "Mussolini frequently claimed to advocate a kind of 'socialism of the trenches,' in which the final victors would be workers, peasants, or veterans (depending on his audience)."[224] In the late 1930s, Mussolini launched a nation-wide campaign against Italy's bourgeoisie, denouncing them as more interested in private gain than national victory.[225]

Just before the end of World War II, Mussolini spoke to a socialist journalist and complained bitterly about the bourgeoisie, declaring in the interview, "I bequeath the republic to the republicans and not to the monarchists, and the work of social reform to the socialist and not to the middle class."[226] When Mussolini was shot by partisans in 1945, one of his long-term aides, Nicola Bombacci, a former student of Vladimir Lenin and a founder of the Italian Communist Party, shouted out, "Long live Mussolini! Long live socialism!"[227]

Some scholars consider Bombacci, who authored the economic theory of socialization in 1943 for Mussolini, as an example of a fascist-Marxist concord. In the journal *La Verità* (1936), Bombacci confessed "his adhesion to Fascism but also to Communism," writing:

> Fascism has made grandiose Social Revolution, Mussolini and Lenin, Soviet and Fascist corporate state, Rome and Moscow. Several stands already taken had to be rectified, we have nothing of which to ask pardon for as both in present and past, we are impelled by the same ideal: the triumph of work.[228,229]

Further, the supporters of revolutionary fascism argued that "the enemies of Bolshevism and Fascism were the right wing pluto-monarchist."[230] In his *La Verità* journal, Bombacci invoked the cause of "social justice" to describe the struggle against the western Allied forces as "a proletarian Italy locked in struggle with capitalist imperialism."[231]

During its early years from 1914 to 1921, the essence of fascism hinged on its attachment to socialism and social revolution. In his book *Revolutionary Fascism*, Erick Norling asserts that "Fascist Socialism is rooted in the very tradition of Fascism as a revolutionary movement, being that Socialism and Revolutionary Syndicalism decisively contributed to its foundation."[232]

The Supreme Opportunist

A master of propaganda, Mussolini was a Machiavelli-inspired politician and a "supreme opportunist."[233] He viewed himself as a Machiavellian and wrote an introduction to his honorary doctoral thesis for the University of Bologna entitled "Prelude to Machiavelli," explaining: "I have wished to put as few intermediaries as possible between Machiavelli and myself, so that I might not lose direct contact between his teachings and my life experience."[234] As for mastering the art of politics, Mussolini described Machiavelli's *The Prince* as "the statesman's supreme guide."[235] He saw Machiavelli's political ideals as "more alive now than ever," an Italian politician and philosopher who believed that so-called noble ends justify almost any violent and deceptive means.

Other dictators of the 20th century held similar views about Machiavelli. "Stalin... saw himself as the embodiment of Machiavellian *vertù*."[236] Lenin was "very much influenced by *The Prince* as well, keeping a copy of it on his nightstand," as did Hitler.[237]

Myth of Mussolini's Anti-Communism

In his 1936 *Under the Axe of Fascism*, Italian historian Gaetano Salvemini noted that Mussolini was an unabashed creator of mythology, especially his myth that he and his Italian Fascism had slain the Red Dragon of communism, a fable he soon abandoned when it "had outlived its usefulness."[238] The Prime Minister of Italy, Francesco Saverio Nitti (1919–1920), concurred with Mussolini's efforts to fool the public, writing in 1927 that Mussolini "has always retained a great admiration for Bolshevism, though he presented himself to the public as an antidote to Bolshevism."[239]

Despite his deceptive methods, Mussolini eventually acknowledged this myth, contending "that Italy had never been neither on the verge of ruin nor under the menace of a Communist Revolution."[240] Mussolini

> agreed that the danger of bolshevism was no worse than in England or France and, although strikes and inflation were as serious a problem in Italy as elsewhere, they were less so in 1921 than in 1920.[241]

He readily admitted this fact in his July 2, 1921, *Il Popolo d'Italia* newspaper, explaining: "To maintain *that the Bolshevist danger still* exists in Italy is to mistake fear for reality."[242] Covering the Italian turmoil, journalist George Seldes reported that there had been "no Bolshevik revolution in

1920," and was amazed in 1925 to hear "Mussolini propagate the claim that he had 'saved Italy from Bolshevism.'"[243] Nonetheless, at one point in November 1921, Mussolini made a threat that if the Italian government outlawed his fascist party, he "might move to the other extreme and join the communists in revolutionary action."[244]

Still, Mussolini kept a watchful eye on the Russian Revolution. He was disheartened to discover the Bolsheviks were advancing a "tyranny worse than that of the tsars."[245] By June 1919, Mussolini was criticizing Lenin's handling of the communist revolution in Russia, concerned that he was straying from the tenets of Marxism. Distressed that Lenin was not Marxist enough, Mussolini wrote that his old comrade was "'the very negation of socialism' because he had not created a dictatorship of the proletariat or of the socialist party, but only of a few intellectuals who had found the secret of winning power."[246] Despite Mussolini's sympathies towards Marxist ideology, he "carefully promoted the legend of a communist danger in Italy against which he would be in the frontline of attack."[247] When trade union workers occupied factories in Northern Italy in September 1920, Mussolini was quick to use the event to frighten Italians about "communist barbarianism."[248] Not long after spreading fear of a communist threat by striking workers, he orchestrated secret talks with union leaders and suggested that he could win them a victory.[249]

After World War I, Italy experienced serious economic and civil disorder and rapidly become ungovernable. As head of the Fascist Revolutionary Party (PFR), Mussolini exploited the political and economic chaos, forging, realigning, and breaking alliances with liberals, nationalists, conservatives, and socialists. Around the time Mussolini officially changed his party's name to the National Fascist Party (PNF) at the Third Fascist Congress in Rome on November 7–10, 1921,[250] he forged a temporary electoral coalition with the other political parties, including the Italian Liberal Party.[251] The turbulent alliance lasted until it afforded little advantage to the Fascists.

Another notable alliance created by Mussolini was a peace agreement—the "Pact of Pacification"—with the Italian Socialist Party (PSI) and the General Confederation of Labor (CGL) to end the violence between the socialists and *squadristi* militias, along with the Socialists' refusal to recognize the anti-fascist militia, *Arditi del Popolo*.[252,253] Mussolini was adamant about honoring the Pact, remarking that, "I shall defend this pact with all my strength, and if Fascism does not follow me in collaboration with the Socialists, at least no one can force me to follow Fascism."[254,255]

At this point in time, Mussolini wavered as to which political direction to take—stay with the left or gravitate towards the right. According to historian Stanley G. Payne, Mussolini wanted to assimilate the violent, but mostly independent, *squadrismo* into his fascism movement, but "did not want to lose his position on the left," still hoping to create a "Fascist Labor Party" or "National Labor Party."[256] Signed on August 2, 1921, the peace pact with the socialists angered the leading *squadristi* leaders, especially Dino Grandi and Italo Balbo. Branding Mussolini's agreement as an "Appeasement Pact,"[257] most *ras* leaders denounced the revolutionary socialists, who had originally sparked the violence against the middle class. The nationalistic militias also condemned Mussolini, saying that he "had not created the movement" and that they could "get along without him."[258] Posters plastered on walls in the city of Bologna condemned "Mussolini as a traitor to Fascism."[259] Moreover, many *squadristi* leaders and members abandoned their chapters to "protest against the Pact and Mussolini's leadership."[260] Mussolini resigned his position on this issue, but Fascist National Council rejected his resignation.

Mussolini was infuriated by the *squadristi* leaders' refusal to follow his directives, lashing out at them. He accused the agrarian militias and landowners of representing "the private interests of the most sinister and contemptible classes in Italy."[261] Another Fascist party leader, Cesare Rossi, the party's deputy-secretary, followed suit, arguing that the rural *fasci* militias were pushing fascism towards a "pure, authentic and exclusive movement of conservatism and reaction."[262] Mussolini, however, had been desperate after his election losses in 1919, with his family almost broke, his mouthpiece publication leaking red ink, and his *fasci* movement stillborn. The socialists garnered 40 times as many votes as the Fascist Revolutionary Party, and Mussolini's home villages of Predappio did not provide a single vote for the fascists.[263] Instead, Mussolini found it necessary to go after the larger *squadristi* movement by embracing "entryism," a political strategy in which a smaller group attempts to take over a larger group through subversion and chicanery. He had little to lose except his long-held socialist ideology, which he was willing to momentarily sacrifice until better political conditions presented themselves.

The Pact of Pacification was officially denounced months later in Rome at the Third Fascist Congress (November 7–10, 1921) where the *squadristi* activists, representing the majority of delegates, forced Mussolini into officially changing the name of the Fascist Revolutionary Party to the National Fascist Party (PNF).[264] Interestingly, a few weeks before the conclave, Mussolini was still clinging to the idea of adopting the name "Fascist Labor Party," if he could acquire the backing of the leftist General Confederation of Labor, but had to pull back and drop the word "labor" due to pressures by the more nationalistic leaders such as Grandi and Balbo.[265]

Although it appeared that Mussolini's dreams of heading a "coalition of labor syndicalists"[266] had failed, he still continued to entertain the concept, allowing Edmondo Rossoni (1884–1965) and other fascist syndicalists (considered the "left Fascists") a major voice in his regime.[267] In fact, commenting on Mussolini's march on Rome decades later, Alessandro Pavolini, who led a squad of black-shirted fascists in 1922, revealed that Mussolini still held a pro-socialist attitude towards labor unions. On the twenty-first anniversary of the March on Rome, Pavolini disclosed:

> By order of the Duce, in a closed Party meeting, the programmatic directives concerning the most important state problems and those concerning the developments with respect to labor were specified. They can be characterized; I have no hesitancy in saying, most appropriately as socialists rather than social.[268]

To further his ambitions and confuse squabbling factions, Mussolini often denied that he had any fixed program because Mussolini "wanted to appeal simultaneously to 'aristocrats and democrats, revolutionaries and reactionaries, proletarians and anti-proletarians, pacifists and anti-pacifists.'"[269] Mussolini would remind the various political parties that fascism "was a 'super-relativist movement' with no fixed principles, ready for almost any alliance."[270] In *Mussolini and Italian Fascism*, Giuseppe Finaldi contends that "Mussolini was too astute a politician to tie himself down to a detailed set of dogmas."[271] Christopher Lehmann-Haupt wrote in *The New York Times* that Mussolini's

> Fascism was less a coherent philosophy than simply a technique for winning power. He never took a stated position—on war, on foreign policy, on the class struggle, on the Roman Catholic Church, on nationalism, on press censorship, on freedom, on the state—that he didn't eventually contradict completely.[272]

The confusion generated over Mussolini's tactics and policies provided the leverage needed to gain national attention, prompting some to compare the situation to the "magic mirror in which everyone, whether militaristic reactionary or extreme pacifist on the left, could see his heart's desire."[273] Mussolini was a quick learner when it came to the deception required to succeed as an opportunist. Even when he seated himself on the extreme right of the amphitheater, where he was rarely seen, he railed against the Pope, attacked Christianity as "detestable" and demanded that the Pope depart Rome for good.[274] Later, after his belligerent anti-clerical tirades concluded, he would completely change his position, believing it would now be an advantage to have an alliance with the church, recommending that "government should subsidize churches and religious schools."[275]

Mussolini's Disillusionment with Socialism and Bolshevism

Mussolini often wrote about his displeasure with socialism, referring to it as a "fraud, a comedy," arguing in "The Doctrine of Fascism": "When the war ended in 1919, Socialism as a doctrine was already dead; it continued to exist only as a grudge." There were a number of factors for his disappointment. After the general strike of 1919 and 1920, Mussolini was distressed by the Italian Socialist Party's inability to take advantage of the chaotic times and overthrow the Italian government. Mussolini saw the Socialists and their trade unionists as revolutionaries only in name, who could not even stand up to fascist armed squads if they clashed.[276]

Mussolini further found fault with socialism because its adherents typically opposed nationalism.[277] To the early fascist theorists, revolutionary syndicalists, and fascist-socialist reformers, the collectivity of a workers' nation, not the individual proletariat, was seen as the means by which to overthrow liberal democracy and a capitalist social order. Nationalism and "the nation was seen as the foremost agent of revolution."[278] But the fascist concept of nationalism was devoid of traditional right-wing nationalism; it was a form of "anti-conservative nationalism."[279] Mussolini was an adherent of what is called "revolutionary nationalism."

Historian A. James Gregor explained Mussolini's concept of nationalism, writing:

> Mussolini's revolutionary nationalism, while it distinguished itself from the traditional patriotism and nationalism of the bourgeoisie, displayed many of those features we today identify with the nationalism of underdeveloped peoples. It was an anticonservative nationalism that anticipated vast social changes; it was directed against both foreign and domestic oppressors; it conjured up an image of a renewed and regenerated nation that would perform a historical mission; it invoked a moral ideal of selfless sacrifice and commitment in the service of collective goals; and it recalled ancient glories and anticipated a shared and greater glory.[280]

By 1909, Mussolini was dispersing "large dose of nationalism into working class internationalism," meaning that this "was not a 'patriotic' nationalism that was traditional, monarchic and conservative—which Mussolini always rejected."[281]

Besides the lost opportunities to install a social revolution in Italy, Mussolini became increasingly disillusioned with the progress of the Russian Revolution. Although Mussolini had originally praised the 1917 October Revolution, he eventually turned against it.[282] In his writings, Mussolini chastised Lenin for suppressing labor strikes, curtailing freedom of the press, ignoring socialism's principles and engaging in a "policy of terror."[283] Mussolini and fascist syndicalists were repelled by the Bolsheviks' handling of their revolution, which left a serious stigma on the image of socialism and a worker state.

A number of renowned socialists and communist leaders reflected Mussolini's criticisms. Angelica Balabanoff, secretary of the Communist Third International in 1919, who befriended Mussolini in Switzerland, openly criticized the authoritarianism of the Bolshevik regime, especially the "corrupt and manipulative tactics of Lenin and Zinoviev."[284] She resigned her post with the Bolsheviks' regime and left Russia in 1921.

The collapse of Russia's economy under the Lenin's "War Communism" caused further consternation with Mussolini and other Fascist leaders, who came to reject the radicalism of "Bolshevism on the ground that it was 'ahistoric' in its attempt to introduce, in a totally unsuited economic environment, a socialism predicated on the availability of a mature industrial base."[285] After all, the collapse of the Russian economy in 1921 signified that the Soviet Union was no longer a worker state; there was almost no economic activity, no jobs, no food, and few workers. To many within the Marxist ranks, socialism and communism had indeed failed, as Russia increasingly turned into an authoritarian dictatorship whose cities resembled industrial ghost towns.

Karl Marx, Friedrich Engels, and Georges Sorel taught that only an advanced industrial system could provide the productive capacity for the proletariat to bring about their historical worker-state destiny.[286,287] Marx argued that the "material conditions necessary for the emancipation of the proletariat" must be "spontaneously generated by the development of capitalism,"[288] and that the "productive forces are the result of man's practical energy," which "engenders a relatedness in the history of man."[289] This concept of productive forces influenced Fascist intellectuals and syndicalists to strive for increased production rather than redistributive economics in an effort to follow Marxian theory. Engels echoed the same sentiment, but in starker terms. Engels warned that communism could only survive in advanced industrial societies where the economy could provide the material abundance required to support a classless and egalitarian society. Without an advanced industrial system established by capitalism, Engels warned that a socialist revolution would reproduce all the "'old filthy business' of inequitable distribution of limited goods, endemic poverty, invidious class distinctions, and systemic oppression."[290]

The Italian Marxist and Fascist leader Angelo O. Olivetti rejected the claim that Lenin's revolution in the economically backward Russia had the "remotest connection with classical Marxism."[291] He contended that the Bolshevik revolutionaries had "undermined the productive forces that were not only necessary for the ultimate attainment of socialism, but essential to the very foundation of collective life."[292] It was Olivetti and three others who published the manifesto *Fasci d'Azione rivoluzionaria internazionalista* (roughly, revolutionary international fascist activism) on October 5, 1914, which Mussolini quickly joined and of which he promptly took a leadership role.

But economics became the primary concern for Italian Fascists operating in a nationalistic proletarian state. In part because of the Bolsheviks' failure to recognize their historical obligations to full industrial development, many nationalist syndicalists came to oppose class struggle as a component of their revolutionary strategy, although the more Marxist-leaning fascist syndicalists, such as Edmondo Rossoni, called for "class struggle" within a national identity. The national syndicalists supported the collaboration of all classes and origins to forge productivist socialism where "a proletariat of producers" would be critical to the revolutionary political thought and social revolution.[293] This was the point where the revolutionary syndicalists, especially Sergio Panunzio, a major theoretician of Italian Fascism, realized that "Syndicalists were productivists, rather than distributionists."[294] They were fearful of Lenin's socialization policies, which had led to the total economic collapse, starvation, and chaos, along with massive unemployment of workers. Unemployment under Lenin's Soviet Russia did not merely skyrocket; it was a catastrophe. One professor of history, Patrick M. Patterson, indicated an "unemployment rate of near 85% in Russia and its satellites."[295]

Usually hesitant to reveal their failures, Stalin and a slew of Bolshevik party leaders did just that in 1938, acknowledging the plight that War Communism had inflicted upon the Soviet Russian economy. They publicly declared:

> Even worse was the plight of industry, which was in a state of complete dislocation. The output of large-scale industry in 1920 was a little over one-seventh of pre-war. Most of the mills and factories were at a standstill; mines and collieries were wrecked

and flooded. Gravest of all was the condition of the iron and steel
industry. The total output of pig-iron in 1921 was only 116,300
tons, or about 3 per cent of the pre-war output.[296]

Such fears of a total economic collapse of production under absolute
communism forced many Fascist intellectuals to rethink or abandon the
class struggle theories of classical and orthodox Marxism. Their socialism would instead bring workers, employers, and society together within
a classless environment of cooperation. Under what they termed "disciplined socialism," national syndicalists sought to advance workers' income and benefits, produce wealth and security, through common purpose efforts between all classes and factions,[297] without employing Bolsheviks' means of confiscating and redistributing wealth according to political criteria. Not only were European Marxists, Marxist reformers, syndicalists and socialists horrified by Lenin's economic disaster, but they
were equally shaken by the Bolsheviks' policy of arrest, imprisonment,
and execution of rival socialist and Marxist political parties and organizations (e.g., Socialist Revolutionary Party, Mensheviks, and anarchists).

The economic politics of fascism were intended to resolve class
conflict through collaboration among the classes.[298] Correspondingly,
many Marxist revisionists also displayed serious misgivings about the
theories of class struggle. They denied the necessity of class conflict and
believed that socialism could be achieved through cooperation among
people without regard to class.[299] The German Marxist theorist Eduard
Bernstein (1850–1932), who many consider as an heir apparent to Marx
and Engels, argued that class conflict was not only decreasing, but could
be considered part of Marx's outdated accessories—inaccurate or obsolete.[300,301] In his 1899 book *Evolutionary Socialism: A Criticism and
Affirmation*, Bernstein argued that Marxism had fundamental flaws
and that "socialists needed to stress cooperation and evolution rather
than class conflict and revolution."[302,303] Bernstein further asserted that
socialism would be achieved by capitalism, not by capitalism's destruction.[304]

The luster of socialism was further tarnished when serious peasant,
worker, and farmer riots erupted across Russia due to food shortages,
malnutrition, and requisition of farmers' crops (*prodrazvyorstka*). This
was in tandem with the government's ban on private trade, closure of

factories, and "numerous arrests and suppressing several labor organizations," which lead to the Kronstadt Rebellion.[305] Mussolini was disheartened to see the failure of Lenin's policies of socialization in the Soviet Union, and accused Bolshevism as having "ruined" and "totally paralyzed" Russia's economy.[306] For a time, Mussolini questioned the viability of Bolshevism, particularly after Lenin decided to replace "War Communism" in 1921 with his New Economic Policy (NEP), which ushered in what Lenin approvingly called "state capitalism," or what has recently been labeled market socialism.[307]

Proletarian Nationalism

Mussolini, fascist syndicalists, and fascist theoreticians came to the conclusion that, because Bolshevism in a primitive economy could not capture the equality and prosperity assured by the teachings of Karl Marx, revolutionaries would have to be "Fascists, not Marxists."[308] Instead, "Fascism," as fascist theoreticians argued, "was the socialism of 'proletarian nations.'"[309]

The concept of proletarian nationalism was a big issue with both German National Socialists and Italian Fascists, especially Enrico Corradini, who was appointed to the Italian Senate by Mussolini. Corradini professed that, "We are the proletarian people in respect to the rest of the world. Nationalism is our socialism."[310]

Mussolini took up the proletarian mantle and, according to A. James Gregor, "insisted that Fascism was the only form of 'socialism' appropriate to the 'proletarian nations' of the 20th century."[311] Weighing in on the importance of both proletarian nationalism and social justice, Mussolini declared on March 20, 1945, in one of his last interviews, that: "We are fighting to impose a higher social justice. The others are fighting to maintain the privileges of caste and class. We are proletarian nations that rise up against the plutocrats."[312] In the early 1930s, Mussolini spoke about equality, social justice, and his admiration for the labor movement, declaring in a speech to workers in Milan:

> Fascism establishes the real equality of individuals before the nation... the object of the regime in the economic field is to ensure higher social justice for the whole of the Italian people... What

does social justice mean? It means work guaranteed, fair wages, decent homes, it means the possibility of continuous evolution and improvement. Nor is this enough. It means that the workers must enter more and more intimately into the productive process and share its necessary discipline... As the past century was the century of capitalist power, the twentieth century is the century of power and glory of labour.[313]

Not only did Mussolini confess to his commitment to social justice and trade unionism, but proclaimed that he had always been a socialist. In his same March 20, 1945, interview by Ivanoe Fossani, Mussolini stated:

For this I have been and am a socialist. The accusation of inconsistency has no foundation. My conduct has always been straight in the sense of looking at the substance of things and not to the form. I adapted *socialisticamente* to reality. As the evolution of society belied many of the prophecies of Marx, the true socialism folded from possible to probable. The only feasible socialism *socialisticamente* is corporatism, confluence, balance and justice interests compared to the collective interest.[314]

Cesare Rossi, director of Mussolini's Press and Propaganda who fled Italy in 1924 and became a critic of fascism in his exile, agreed that Mussolini had "remained transfixed, throughout his entire political life, by socialism."[315]

Fascist Syndicalism

Fascist syndicalism was populated by "left Fascists" who were hostile to the business community, sought worker control over factories, and favored class struggle within a national framework. Edmondo Rossoni was their main leader, who was once imprisoned for his labor-related activism as a revolutionary syndicalist in 1908. He was heavily involved in the socialist trade unionism, fascist syndicates and was seen as both controversial and a favorite ideologue of Mussolini. As a union organizer with the syndicalist *Federazione Socialista Italiana* (FSI) for six years (1910–1916),[316] "Rossoni sought to make the Fascist unions genuine vehicles of working-class interests, and he did not hesitate to criticize business in surprisingly outspoken terms; his position, then, was leftist and syndical-ist. ..."[317]

When Rossoni traveled to the United States, he became an organizer for "Big Bill" Haywood of the Industrial Workers of the World (IWW).[318] Returning to Italy at the outbreak of World War I with the purpose of "fusing Nationalism with class struggle," Rossoni was a big supporter of Sorel and Mussolini's Fascist syndicate state, and professed that "by dictatorship of the proletariat, we mean a government of workers' syn-dicates."[319] By 1922, he became the first leader (secretary-general) of the Italian Fascist labor confederation—the General Confederation of Fascist Syndical Corporations,[320] under the auspices of Mussolini's administration, and held other important positions. Rossino and his Fascist syndicalist followers were vehemently anti-capitalist, arguing that capitalism "depressed and annulled production rather than stimulating and developing it" and that industrialists were "apathetic, passive, and ignorant."[321] In one incident, Rossino verbally attacked industrialists in 1926 as "vampires" and "profiteers."[322]

Similarly, harsh language caused industrialists to no longer be content with Mussolini. Considered by historians as adherents of "left fascism," Rossoni and his Fascist syndicalists created so much trepidation among industrialists, due to their support of "labor's autonomy and class con-sciousness,"[323] that a circle of industrialists voiced the opinion that "it might now be wise to pay the Communists to fight the Fascists!"[324]

Despite Rossoni's loyalty to fascism and Mussolini, he was none-theless dismissed in 1928 from his position for being too protective of workers' rights.[325] He had accomplished much in successfully creating a large Fascist syndicate movement, increasing membership from 250,000 to 1.8 million from 1920 to 1924, where he outshone every other labor organization.[326] His fascist syndicate even exceeded the membership of the National Fascist Party, which had 650,000 members in 1924, which alarmed Fascist leaders. Despite his labor union radicalism, Rossoni was appointed to high leadership positions, becoming a member of the Grand Council of Fascism from 1930 to 1943, also serving as undersec-retary of state, from 1932 to 1935, and as the minister of agriculture and forestry from 1935–1939.[327]

Lenin's NEP and Mussolini's Fascist-Marxist Adjustments

Considered a strategic retreat from socialism, Lenin's NEP policies enacted a more capitalist-oriented policy of economic management,[328] which, like the national syndicalists of Italy, concluded that productivity was a "critical condition for revolutionary struggle."[329] In 1921 Nationalization was partially removed and supplanted by a mixed economy with less strict regulations to allow small-scale private ownership, minor privatization, profit-orientated markets, and retail trade. The state still commanded the heights, retaining control of heavy industry, banks, transport, and foreign trade.[330] Lenin also pursued international financing and investments by European and American companies. Despite classical Marxism's hostility towards finance capitalism, Lenin sought financial assistance from the capitalist West.[331]

Lenin decreed that state-operated enterprises must be self-reliant and operate on profit/loss principles.[332] Searching for greater economic efficiency, Lenin moved towards a state-oriented economy that would allow private initiative as well as the ability for peasants to pursue their self-interests.[333] Lenin wrote in 1921:

> State capitalism would be a step forward as compared with the present state of affairs in our Soviet Republic. If in approximately six months' time state capitalism became established in our Republic, this would be a great success and a sure guarantee that within a year socialism will have gained a permanently firm hold.[334]

Lenin characterized "state capitalism" as a system that entailed "a free market and capitalism, both subject to state control," where state agencies and enterprises will operate on a "profit basis."[335] Lenin also allowed the privatization of small, formerly state-owned companies or new enterprises to be owned and operated by individuals.[336] During this crisis, Lenin confessed to his Bolshevik comrades-in-arms that "socialism is inconceivable without large-scale Capitalist engineering... and planned organization."[337]

One apparent reason for Lenin's decision to back-peddle from communism and strive for state capitalism can be seen in something that Mussolini's feminist mistress wrote about Lenin in 1926. Margherita Sarfatti, considered the woman who birthed Fascism alongside Mussolini, wrote in *The Life of Benito Mussolini*, that Lenin acknowledged his failure to bring socialism to Russia and was crestfallen over the economic collapse of his socialist republic. According to Sarfatti, Lenin had admitted in late 1920 that:

> The economic basis for a true Socialist Republic does not yet exist... Communism is failing. Russian expectations are not towards communism, but towards capitalism. ... The capitalist classes are advancing in serried ranks towards the promised land, destined to become in a few decades one of the greatest productive forces in the world.[338]

Historically, Lenin's state capitalism policies closely represented many of the defining properties of Fascism. According to A. James Gregor,

> by 1925, both Leninism and Fascism, variants of Marxism, had created political and economic systems that shared singular properties... Both sought order and discipline of entire populations in the service of an exclusivistic party and an ideology that found its origins in classical Marxism... Both created a kind of "state capitalism," informed by a unitary party, and responsible to a "charismatic" leader.[339]

Lenin, like Mussolini, had to revise his Marxist theories in order to "increase production first and foremost and at all costs," which caused him to abandon all the socialist pretensions of war communism—which were the core components of implementing communist economics.[340]

It appears that Mussolini had simply based Italy's economic policies eventually on Lenin's NEP examples that had permitted market mechanisms, privatization of small companies and the pursuit of profit. However, by 1934 Mussolini embraced a policy of increasing state-ownership of companies. He had not only nationalized a sizable chunk of Italy's economy, but abandoned some of Lenin's NEP economic policies, "reiterat[ing] that capitalism, as an economic system, was no longer viable."[341] At this point, Mussolini made it clear that fascist economics were "based not on individual profit but on collective interest."[342]

Lenin was also impressed with the militarized economics of "war socialism" that had developed in Germany through the efforts of General Erich Ludendorff.[343] Lenin hired German experts to advance the economic methods of German state capitalism.[344] Other historians have referred to war socialism as a form of militarized state socialism.[345]

Some have argued that Lenin's NEP, which conjoined socialism with capitalism, fostered an economic structure that might be classified as the first modern-day fascist regime, which helped to motivate Mussolini to abandon full-blown economic socialism.[346] Some interpretations of Bolshevism are seen, especially its Stalinist transmutation, "as belonging to the family of fascist ideology."[347] Noam Chomsky considered a progressive and anarcho-syndicalist, reaffirmed this view in 1989, arguing that both Lenin and the Bolsheviks were "right-wing" deviations, describing their authoritarianism in terms that caused some to interpret the Soviet Union as fascist.[348]

Like Lenin, Mussolini supported the concept of state capitalism. He declared in his 1933 "On the Corporate State" speech that fascism could be considered a form of "state capitalism." He claimed that if fascism were to follow "this latest phase of capitalist development, our path would lead inexorably into state capitalism, which is nothing more nor less than state socialism turned on its head."[349] Mussolini argued that whether the outcome was state capitalism or state socialism, state intervention became "even more necessary."[350]

In that same November 14, 1933 speech on corporatism, Mussolini reminded listeners that he still held to his promise of achieving a social revolution in Italy. He proclaimed the end of capitalism, declaring:

> To-day we can affirm that the capitalistic method of production is out of date. So is the doctrine of *laissez-faire*, the theoretical basis of capitalism... To-day we are taking a new and decisive step in the path of revolution. A revolution, in order to be great, must be a social revolution.[351]

Mussolini further asserted that "Italy is not a capitalist country according to the meaning now conventionally assigned to that term."[352] After pronouncing a death sentence to capitalism in Italy, critics asserted that Mussolini had "gone to the Left," while the Hearst newspaper chain ran the headline "Mussolini Abolishes the Capitalist System."[353]

By the late 19th century, the realization for a preceding mature industrial-capitalism had caused many syndicalists, including Angelo O. Olivetti, to support some free trade policies because they believed it would stimulate the growth of industry and fulfill Marx's dreams.[354,355] By the first decade of the 20th century, the socialist-national synthesis of syndicalism had caused many former adherents of classical Marxism to descend into heresy, which eventually led to the rationale behind fascism and its socioeconomic policies.[356]

Economic Policies of Fascist Italy

Some of the components of fascist interventionist economics, especially during the 1930s, were central planning, heavy state subsidies, protectionism (high tariffs), steep levels of nationalization, rampant cronyism, large deficits, high government spending, steep taxes, bank and industry bailouts, overlapping bureaucracy, massive social welfare programs, crushing national debt, bouts of inflation and "a highly regulated, multiclass, integrated national economic structure."[357] This ultimately led to economic stagnation. On numerous occasions, Mussolini identified his economic and corporate policies with "state capitalism" and "state socialism," which were comparable to economic dirigisme, where governments exercise strong directive influence, and seek to effectively control production and allocation of national resources.[358] Despite Italy's economic problems, a number of political leaders in America expressed admiration for Italy's corporatism. *The New York Times* reported in 1933 that there was a mood in FDR's administration that "envisaged a federation of industry, labor, and government after the fashion of the corporative State as it exists in Italy."[359]

The Jewish economist Ludwig von Mises, who fled the Nazi conquest of Europe, referred to the economics of Italian fascism as a system that

> clung first to the same principles of economic policies which all not outright socialist governments have adopted in our day, in-

terventionism. Then later it turned step by step towards the German system of socialism, i.e., all-round state control of economic activities.[360]

Further, Mises contended that the "economic program of Italian Fascism did not differ from the program of British Guild Socialism as propagated by the most eminent British and European socialists," which were detailed in Sidney and Beatrice Webb's 1920 *A Constitution for the Socialist Commonwealth of Great Britain*.[361,362] In *Politics of Eugenics: Productionism, Population, and National Welfare*, Alberto Spektorowsik referred to the economic fascism of both Mussolini and Hitler as representing a form of "nationalist productivist socialism," despite their denunciation of Marxism, international socialism and parasitical capitalism.[363]

When it came to industry, banking, and fascist syndicalism, Mussolini saw the state as taking over the "imposing tasks" to "control all forces of industry, all forces of finance, and all forces of labor."[364] In addressing labor's position in Italy, Alfredo Rocco, a former Marxist in the Radical Party and one of the foremost theoreticians of national syndicalism under Mussolini, wanted to assure that all of the collective energy of the working class, the syndicate, be integrated. He stated that "the syndicate must necessarily be subject to the control of the state. The syndicate [must become] an organ of the state."[365] In a 1925 speech, Rocco delved further into the concept that the individual in socioeconomic matters had to subordinate himself to the group, proclaiming:

> For liberalism, the individual is the end, and society the means. ...
> For Fascism, society is the end, individuals the means, and its whole life consists in using individuals as instruments for its social ends.[366]

In *The Concise Encyclopedia of Economics*, Sheldon Richman succinctly states: "As an economic system, fascism is socialism with a capitalist veneer."[367] He contended that socialism seeks to abolish capitalism totally, while fascism gave the appearance of a market-based economy even though it relied heavily upon central planning for all economic activities. According to authors Roland Sarti and Rosario Romeo, "under

Fascism the state had more latitude for control of the economy than any other nation at the time except for the Soviet Union."[368]

Both Hitler and Mussolini referred to their economic policies as "The Third Way," which was to synthesize the best of two extremes—"liberal capitalism and Marxist socialism."[369] Mussolini's middle way approach has often been viewed as a propaganda device to counteract the flaws and contrast the rashness "between the failed anarchy of capitalism and the oppressive command economy favoured by the communists."[370] Most economists treat the economic policies of Italian Fascism as the proverbial "mixed bag," especially during its early years. However, by the 1930s, Italy increasingly centralized its economy under state-directed mandates, nationalization, and protectionism. According to University of Oxford historian Cyprian P. Blamires,

> Fascism advocates a state-controlled and regulated mixed economy; the principal economic goal of fascism is to achieve national self-sufficiency and independence, sometimes through protectionist and interventionist economic policies.[371]

Many theorists of Italian Fascism, as well as the Nazis, admired John Maynard Keynes' economic theories, especially his advocacy of big government spending and deficit financing. One British disciple of Mussolini, James Strachey Barnes, found the economics of Keynes congruent with fascism, writing:

> Fascism entirely agrees with Mr. Maynard Keynes, despite the latter's prominent position as a Liberal. In fact, Mr. Keynes' excellent little book, *The End of Laissez-Faire* (1926) might, so far as it goes, serve as a useful introduction to fascist economics. There is scarcely anything to object to in it and there is much to applaud.[372]

Despite his admiration for Keynes, Barnes took liberalism to task for its economic chaos, writing in his 1928 book that "liberalism can propose but an unstable equilibrium. It is a gloomy edifice built upon the shifting sands."[373]

However, early on, Italy engaged in economic liberalism and some privatization before Mussolini installed a one-party dictatorship in 1925.

During the years he ruled constitutionally under a multiparty parliamentary coalition, Mussolini appointed a classical liberal economist, Alberto De Stefani, a former stalwart leader in the Center Party as Italy's Minister of Finance.[374] During the 1922–1925 coalition years, only three out of the thirteen cabinet positions were held by Fascist party members.[375]

Before he was fired by Mussolini in 1925, De Stefani managed to simplify Italy's tax code, reduce taxes, do away with rent controls, cut spending, and reduce trade restrictions by liberalizing foreign trade barriers.[376] The Italian economy prospered, growing more than 20 percent while unemployment fell 77 percent. During De Stefani's administration, Italy privatized some public enterprises, telephone networks, match sales, life insurance, the metal machinery firm Ansaldo—and gave concessions for a number of tolled motorways along with state subsidies. Railways were considered for privatization, but "strong opposition from the Fascist railwaymen's union," prevented it.[377]

After the Great Depression spread internationally, Mussolini became more vocal in his claims that fascism explicitly rejected the capitalist elements of economic individualism and *laissez-faire* liberalism.[378] In one version of "Doctrine of Fascism," Mussolini posits:

> The Fascist conception of life accepts the individual only in so far as his interests coincide with the State... Fascism reasserts the rights of the state. If classical liberalism spells individualism, Fascism spells government.

In the 1935 version, Mussolini writes that Fascism

> ... is opposed to classical Liberalism... Liberalism denied the State in the interests of the particular individual; Fascism reaffirms the State as the true reality of the individual.[379]

In his 1928 autobiography, Mussolini made clear his dislike for liberal capitalism, writing: "The citizen in the Fascist State is no longer a selfish individual who has the anti-social right of rebelling against any law of the Collectivity."[380] In his 1937 *The Good Society*, Walter Lippmann, winner of two Pulitzer Prizes, remarked on Mussolini's anti-individualism and reflected that Fascist Italy's "full-blown collectivist order" was essentially the same absolutism found in Russia and Germany, which were also refusing to recognize the rights of the individual.[381]

As the effects of the Great Depression lingered, Italy's government promoted mergers and acquisitions, bailed out failing businesses, and "seized the stock holdings of banks, which held large equity interests."[382] The Italian state took over bankrupt corporations, cartelized business, increased government spending, spurred monetary inflation, and boosted deficits.[383] Unlike the United States, the Italian government promoted heavy industry by "nationalizing it instead of letting the companies go bankrupt."[384]

The Great Depression in Italy indirectly resulted in the "nationalization [of] a great part of Italian industry," which came the under control of the socialist financier, Alberto Beneduce, head of Italy's *Istituto per la Ricostruzione Industriale* (IRI) in 1933.[385,386]

Italy had enacted legislation that instituted twenty-two state-directed corporations, "which acted as a cover for cartelization."[387] With the power in 1932 to mandate cartels, monopolies emerged and "created a vast bureaucracy operating controls, granting licenses, manufacturing paperwork and all too often simply providing jobs for party members."[388] Other systematic problems plaguing Fascist Italy were cronyism, a "mass-party patronage machine," and "bureaucratic elephantiasis," as well as "inept and corrupt intervention in the economy."[389]

Italian cartels were often obligatory and monopolistic, a type of purportedly "revolutionary" corporatism that would "guarantee economic progress and social justice."[390] Italian Fascist theories of corporatism arose out of revolutionary and national syndicalism (workers' rule) via trade unions, craft guilds, and professional societies, which continuously acknowledged its socialist roots and influences, including Sorel and French Marxist and revolutionary syndicalist Hubert Lagardelle.[391] Under fascist terminology, corporatism signifies an all-encompassing organization, which includes "not only associations of employers and the unions of employees but also those bodies which are supposed to stand above the association and the unions" to coordinate all their activities.[392]

Under the fascist corporate state, "planning boards set product lines, production levels, prices, wages, working conditions, and the size of firms. Licensing was ubiquitous; no economic activity could be undertaken without government permission," which restricted new business from forming or expanding.[393,394] In addition to all this, "levels of consumption were dictated by the state, and 'excess' incomes had to be surrendered as taxes or 'loans.'"[395]

By the mid-1930s, corporate statism and regulatory concentration had caused the Italian credit system to be put "under the control of the state and parastate agencies," and by the late 1930s, "approximately 80 percent of the credit availability" was "controlled directly or indirectly by the state."[396] As war with Ethiopia approached, Italy imposed price controls, production quotas, and higher tariffs. A large trade deficit swelled, which led to more restrictions on imports, tighter controls on foreign exchange, and greater controls over the distribution of raw material.[397] As Mussolini moved towards "autarky" or self-sufficiency and imposed more protectionist laws, Italy's "budget deficit increased sevenfold between 1934 and 1937."[398,399] To help with budgetary deficits, in 1936 the government required the Italian citizenry to "spontaneously" donate their gold, which included many women's wedding rings—which were replaced by rings of tin.[400]

With the passage of the Bank Reform Act in 1936, "the Bank of Italy and most of the other major banks became public institutions."[401] One year earlier, the confiscation of capital began when state edicts mandated that all banks, businesses, and private citizens had to surrender their foreign-issued stocks and bonds and convey them to the Bank of Italy.[402]

Like most industries in Italy, Italian newspapers were also controlled through state funding. Not only were newspapers state-subsidized, but its editors were personally chosen by Mussolini, who provided "paychecks for many journalists,"[403] effectively controlling the political narrative in Italy. State subsidies were pervasive, distributed to many industries, including farmers, landowners, and especially shipbuilders.

Mussolini doubled the number of Italian bureaucrats under an enormous bureaucracy of committees. By 1934, one Italian in five worked for the government.[404] There was a labyrinth "of overlapping bureaucracies where Mussolini's orders were constantly being lost or purposely mislaid."[405]

In May 1934, as the government-operated Institute of Industrial Reconstruction (IRI) was taking over bank assets, Mussolini declared,

> Three-fourths of the Italian economy, industrial and agricultural, is in the hands of the state. And if I dare to introduce to Italy state capitalism or state socialism, which is the reverse side of the medal, I will have the necessary subjective and objective conditions to do it.[406,407]

Other scholars have noted Italy's head-long rush towards nationalization, professing that the "Institute for Industrial Reconstruction (IRI)" had "became the owner not only of the three most important Italian banks, which were clearly too big to fail, but also of the lion's share of the Italian industries."[408]

As Mussolini increasingly espoused anti-capitalist rhetoric, he further stated that anyone engaged in capitalism who resisted his economic structure would "be replaced without hesitation by a new, entirely different and more worthy force."[409] Since most of Italy's industry was state-owned, Italian Fascism could be described as a watered-down version of Marxism, a throwback to Bernstein revisionism—in essence, a sort of Marxist-lite knockoff.

Despite the fact that three-fourths of Italy's economic sector was owned by the government by the mid-1930s, most scholars routinely ignored Italian Fascism's slide into pure Soviet-style socialism, a concentration of state ownership so large that it was only eclipsed by Stalin's Soviet Union. The conventional definition of socialism is described as a social and economic system characterized by "public ownership" of the "means of production." On the other hand, fascism is often explained as a social and economic system characterized by "public control" over the "agents of production." But Mussolini's regime eventually morphed into Fascist socialism as its means of production was placed under public ownership. On the other hand, Hitler's German National Socialism was more attune to the industrialism and socialism of Henri de Saint-Simon (1760–1825) who viewed industrialists and private property as an important component of an enlightened industrial class.

By January 1934, IRI had gained "48.5 percent of the share capital of Italy," and a few months later acquired the capital of the banks themselves.[410]   Interestingly, *The Oxford Handbook of the Italian Economy Since Unification* also noted that Mussolini's May 26, 1934, speech at Italy's Chamber of Deputies was dramatic and "seemed to come back to the anticapitalist rhetoric of the early days of Fascism." According to Patricia Knight in *Mussolini and Fascism*, a number of years later, in 1939, Italy saw the highest rate of state-owned enterprises in the entire world outside of the Soviet Union.[411] The professor of Modern European History, Martin Blinkhorn, echoed the same theme, writing that "This level of state intervention greatly surpassed that in Nazi Germany, giving Italy a public sector second only to that of Stalin's Russia."[412] By 1939, the state "controlled over four-fifths of Italy's shipping and shipbuilding, three-quarters of its pig iron production and almost half that of steel."[413] In addition, Mussolini had "nationalized nearly all war-relevant industries."[414]

As the Italian economy struggled due to military expenditures and accelerating inflation, Mussolini imposed wage and price controls through the Permanent Committee of Price Control, along with his plans to impose autarky politics to increase tariffs on foreign trade. In 1936, the Fascist Party in Italy imposed a royal decree that "fixed commodity prices, utility rates and rents."[415,416] During his 1940 speech declaring war on France and England, Mussolini denounced both Western democracy and capitalism, proclaiming that: "We go to battle against the plutocratic and reactionary democracies of the West," explaining that

> this gigantic struggle is nothing other than a phase in the logical development of our revolution; it is the struggle of peoples that are poor but rich in workers against the exploiters...[417]

After Mussolini headed a Nazi-like puppet state, now referred to as the Italian Social Republic (RSI) in 1943, which he originally wanted to call the "Italian Socialist Republic,"[418] he proposed the policies of "economic socialization" (fascist socialism), displaying a renewed interest in his earlier Marxist radicalism. Wishing to destroy the independent power base of the capitalist class, "Mussolini attempted to impose socialism on Italy from the top."[419] Claiming he had never abandoned his earlier socialist and left-wing ideals,[420] "he returned to a type of socialism which once again attacked capitalism," in an effort to "annihilate the parasitic plutocracies."[421] He wrote anonymous articles stating that he was correct in 1910 to have "called on the proletariat to capture power from the capitalists by a bloody revolution."[422] In another case, Mussolini boasted that his fascist Social Republic of Italy, sometimes known as Republic of Salò, was the "only truly socialist government in existence—with the possible exception of Soviet Russia."[423] To offset the domestic threat from communist insurgents, the RSI emphasized Mussolini's commitment to a "variety of fascist egalitarianism and an amplified fascist welfare state."[424] In *The Ideology of Fascism*, A. James Gregor pointed out that the program manifesto of the Fascist Republican Party of Verona included a plank to "abolish the capitalist system and to struggle against the world plutocracies..."[425] During this time, Mussolini decreed that all companies with over 100 employees had to be nationalized.[426]

But more than that, the constitution for the Italian Social Republic—the Manifesto di Verona—was also drafted by Bruno Spampanato (1902–1960), who was a proponent of "left-wing fascism."[427] In 1930 Spampanato wrote "Revolutionary Equations: from Bolshevism to Fascism," which argued that the Russian Revolution's fullest phase would lead to a sort of oriental fascism.[428] Other left-wing fascists in Italy, like Sergio Panunzio, went further and saw the Italian move toward fascism and the October Russian Revolution as "the diagonal of the historical contact of the two great modern revolutions."[429] Part of the socialization plan also called for cultivated and uncultivated lands to be "divided among day laborers or handed to farmer cooperatives" if property owners failed to use their land productively.[430]

In February 1944, a "socialization law" was devised and called for more nationalization of industry, where "workers were to participate in factory and business management," along with collectivized land reform.[431] One section of the socialization law proclaimed: "Enforcement of Mussolinian conception on subjects such as much higher Social Justice, a more equitable distribution of wealth and the participation of labor in the state life."[432] The Italian Social Republic "obsessively emphasized" commitments to socialization and a "variety of fascist equalitarianism and an amplified fascist welfare state."[433]

When Mussolini addressed the Milanese Fascists and Black Brigade "*resega*" officers on October 14, 1944, he announced the basis for his new proletarian and syndical state:

> Some still ask of us: what do you want? We answer with three words that summon up our entire program. Here they are... Italy, Republic, Socialization... Socialization is no other than the implantation of Italian Socialism...[434]

Social Welfare and Public Works

Fascist Italy had one of the most advanced welfare states long before the beginning of World War II. As early as 1927, Italian fascists had pledged themselves to a policy of complex social welfare, insurance, and assistance programs that Werner Sombart, a German economist and sociologist, described as the most "audacious" in Europe.[435] In *My Autobiography*, Mussolini boasted of his social welfare accomplishments, writing that "Italy is advanced beyond all other European nations." He listed, among others, the eight-hour workday, old age pension, assistance and benefits, adult education, and efforts to enact minimum wage laws.[436] A. James Gregor professed that Italy spent considerable funds on elaborate social welfare programs, which were "motivated by the 'moral' concern with abstract 'social justice.'"[437] He wrote: "Fascist social welfare legislation compared favorably with the more advanced European nations and in some respect was more progressive."[438]

By 1939, twenty million Italians were covered by old age and general disability insurance. Other social welfare programs included maternity insurance and assistance, unemployment benefits, medical benefits, general family assistance, child welfare programs, paid vacations, indemnities in event of job loss, food-supplemental assistance, occupational disease insurance, and recreational centers.[439] Like Hitler, Mussolini engaged in "social engineering" schemes, especially after the conquest of Ethiopia (1935–36).[440] A former schoolteacher, Mussolini was determined to improve Italy's educational system. Substantial funding was provided to public education; the "total expenditure on education rose from 922.4 million lire in the financial years 1922–23 to 1,636 million lire for 1936–37."[441] Between 1930 and 1935, over 16,000 new elementary schools were constructed in Italy.

Fascist Italy's spending on public works dwarfed that of most developed nations. English historian Christopher Hibbert wrote that Mussolini

> instituted a programme of public works hitherto unrivalled in modern Europe. Bridges, canals, and roads were built, hospitals and schools, railway stations and orphanages; swamps were drained and land reclaimed, forests were planted, and universities were endowed.[442]

In fact, the outlays for public works tripled between 1929 and 1934, "overtaking defense for the first time as the largest item in total government expenditure."[443]

Despite his promises to the contrary, Mussolini never balanced Italy's budget, proceeding to spend profusely on public works after entering the office.[444] Italy experienced massive deficits and ever-rising national debt. When Mussolini took office in 1922, Italy had a national debt of 93 billion lire. One historian and writer, Gaetano Salvemini, suspected that Mussolini's figures were wrong and estimated Italy's national debt at 148,646,000,000 lire by 1934.[445] *The New York Times* put Italy's national debt in 1943 at 405,823,000,000 lire.[446] Most of the long-term debt was hidden from the treasury books and the public through yearly installment plans that did not show up in the official Italian budget.[447]

Mussolini's aim to forge a totalitarian corporate worker-state lent itself to centrally-planned strategies to dominate almost every facet of human existence, including the economy. The effort to nationalize most of Italy's industry was in keeping with efforts to politicize everything spiritual and human under Mussolini's creed: "Everything within the state, nothing outside the state, nothing against the state."[448] His formula for a corporatist, totalitarian state was proclaimed as: "We control the political forces, we control the moral forces, we control the economic forces. Thus, we are in the midst of the corporative fascist state."[449]

What Contemporaries Thought of Mussolini and Fascism

After he was purged from the Italian Socialist Party, Vladimir Lenin later expressed his feeling that Mussolini was the only true revolutionary in Italy.[450] Lenin also sent a note to the Italian Socialists and Communists, berating them for ousting Mussolini, writing: "Why have you allowed Mussolini to leave your ranks?"[451] According to Margherita Sarfatti, a well-known Jewish socialist, journalist, and feminist who became Mussolini's main mistress, Lenin had also remarked, "Mussolini? A great pity he is lost to us! He is a strong man, who would have led our party to victory."[452] Trotsky expressed the same sentiment: "You have lost your trump card; the only man who could have carried through a revolution was Mussolini."[453]

In the early 1920s, the Comintern weighed in on the prospect of Mussolini's movement. They were considered the first "to grasp the full potential for political stigmatization of the new terms 'fascism' and 'fascist' arising from Mussolini's government in Italy," and "recognized certain key similarities between such a movement and Communist parties."[454]

Upon learning of Mussolini's ascent to Prime Minister of Italy, "Stalin supplied Mussolini with the plans of the May Day parades in Red Square, to help him polish up his Fascist pageants."[455]

The founder of the British Union of Fascists (BUF), Sir Oswald Mosley, had been the Chancellor of the Duchy of Lancaster in the left-wing Labor Government of 1929–1931. A committed member of the socialist Fabian Society during the 1920s and 1930s,[456,457] during his Labor Party days, Mosley called for state nationalization of the larger industries as well as a public works program that would solve unemployment. When the Labor party ignored Mosley's recommendations, he resigned and founded the New Party. After traveling to Italy at the behest of Mussolini during a study tour of "new movements," Mosley referred to Mussolini and his movement as "hard, concentrated, direct—in a word 'Modern.'"[458] Mosley "instantly felt a kinship with Mussolini," and inspired, he returned to England and launched the BUF in 1932. Considering himself as a socialist, Mosley argued: "If you love our country you are national, and if you love our people you are a socialist."[459] In 1968, Mosley confessed that he was never a man of the "right," explaining: "I am not, and never have been, a man of the right. My position was on the left and is now in the centre of politics."[460]

Opposed to the impacts of free trade, Mosley proposed protectionist policies of high tariffs in order to prevent "cheap slave competition from abroad."[461] As for his economic policies, Mosley was captivated by economist John Maynard Keynes. "Mosley created the British Union of Fascists as a vehicle for his economic vision of Britain as a Keynesian economic state, with an emphasis on deficit spending."[462]

Other Fabian Society members, including socialist and science fiction writer H.G. Wells, embraced not only Mussolini's fascism, but Hitler's National Socialism and Stalin's communism.[463] In a speech entitled "Liberal Fascism," Wells told the Young Liberals Club at Oxford (1932) that young people should transform themselves into "Liberal Fascisti" and have the "foresight for enlightened Nazis."[464] He wanted to use "fascist means to serve liberal ends by way of a liberal elite as 'conceited' and as power-hungry as its rivals."[465] Wells proposed that liberals "consider the formation of a greater Communist Party as a western response to Russia."[466]

Irish playwright George Bernard Shaw, a leading member of the socialist Fabian Society, "held Lenin, Mussolini and Hitler in high regard and felt that Sir Oswald Mosley and his Fascist Party offered the only solution to Britain's problems."[467] Defending Sir Oswald Mosley's British Union of Fascists, Shaw wrote in *The News Chronicle* of January 1934, "As a red hot Communist, I am in favour of fascism. The only drawback to Sir Oswald's movement is that it is not quite British enough."[468]

Shaw particularly extolled Mussolini in 1927, writing that fellow "socialists should be delighted to find at last a socialist who speaks and thinks as responsible rulers do."[469] Applauding his domestic policies, Shaw pointed out that Mussolini was "farther to the Left in his political opinions than any of his socialist rivals."[470] He wrote in the *Sunday Dispatch* in June 1933 that Hitler was a fellow National Socialist, penning: "The Nazi movement is in many respects one which has my warm sympathy, ..."[471] Given Shaw's views, George Orwell felt compelled to dub

Shaw as a man who "declared Communism and Fascism to be much the same thing, and was in favour of both of them."[472]

Shaw also wrote a 1927 "Defence of Mussolini" letter clarifying his support for both Mussolini and Stalin despite their violent coup d'état methods. He deplored the abuse by the press against "my fellow Socialists in Italy," writing that "the campaign of abuse against the Mussolini dictatorship is just as stupid as the campaign against the Soviet dictatorship in Russia." Further, he admiringly writes: "Some of the things Mussolini has done, and some that he is threatening to do go further in the direction of Socialism than the English Labour Party could yet venture if they were in power."[473] Such opinions fueled Shaw's reputation as a "proto-fascist."

Shaw was also a firm believer in Mussolini's corporatism. He saw the corporate state as "clearly a necessary part of socialism," claiming that this was "precisely what the Fabian Society wants, ..."[474] To Shaw, it was clear that "the ideal corporate state could only be achieved through communism..."[475] Many historians have pointed out that corporatism emerged in Europe as a

> vogue word to represent any and every form of collectivism: "the civilized way of getting along is the way of corporate action, not individual action; and corporate action involves more government than individual action." This was the old Fabian message.[476]

Actually, the type of corporatism that Mussolini and the revolutionary syndicalists supported were worker-based societies founded on medieval-style guilds, collective-based with monopolistic cartel-like authority to control the practice of their craft in particular geographical locations, sometimes referred to as "guild socialism."

Although Mussolini regularly criticized members of the Italian Socialist Party and Bolshevism, he told friends and foreign visitors that fascism and Bolshevism were similar. A number of book authors and historical figures attest to Mussolini's sympathies towards Russian Bolshevism, for example in 1931, when Alfred Bingham, the son of a conservative US Republican Senator from Connecticut, visited Italy, he met Mussolini in person. "Mussolini told the young man of his admiration for Communism, stating, 'Fascism is the same thing' [as Communism]."[477] According to author Arthur M. Schlesinger, President Franklin D. Roosevelt understood the close relationship between Italian Fascism and Russian Sovietism, writing: "Roosevelt had no illusions about revolution. Mussolini and Stalin seemed to him 'not mere distant relatives' but 'blood brothers.'"[478]

The former Prime Minister of Italy, Francesco Saverio Nitti, said the same thing in his 1927 book entitled *Bolshevism, Fascism and Democracy*. Considered as a prominent left-liberal, Nitti was an opponent of both fascism and communism, stating: "There is little difference between the two, and in certain respects, Fascism and Bolshevism are the same."[479] Nitti continued this theme in his chapter "Bolshevism and Fascism are Identical." In that chapter Nitti voiced his alarmed over Fascist Italy's fervent coziness with Soviet Russia, writing: "In Italy today one finds that greater tolerance is shown toward Communists affiliated with Moscow than to Liberals, democrats, and Socialists."[480]

Considered a classical liberal by today's standards, Nitti argued that "Fascism and Bolshevism are not two opposing principles, they are both the negation of the same principles of freedom and order."[481] Calling Mussolini a "revolutionary agitator," Nitti wrote:

> Fascism in Italy was the work of the revolutionary Socialists, who, after opposing the war, were converted to its support as an extreme Radical movement, actually favourable to the cause of Socialism.[482]

In another example, when Mussolini wanted to show his support for the Nazi-Soviet Pact of 1939, he told fellow Fascist official Giuseppe Bottai that the internal differences between fascism and Bolshevism were minor, arguing that both Italian fascism and Russian Bolshevism opposed the "demo-plutocratic capitalism of the western powers."[483]

Many intellectuals of the era supported both Mussolini and Lenin. For instance, Ezra Pound (1885–1972), an expatriate American poet who lived in Italy, not only idealized Mussolini, but also Lenin. He had a private meeting with Mussolini in 1933 and remarked that he had "never met anyone who seemed to GET my ideas so quickly as the boss."[484] By 1935, Pound professed in his book *Jefferson and/or Mussolini* that communism and fascism were comparable. According to Tim Redman in *Ezra Pound and Italian Fascism,*

> Pound's ideas about Russian communism developed in two directions. First, he felt that there were basic similarities between the Russian and the fascist revolutions. Second, he felt a great deal of admiration for Lenin as a man of action in the mold of his hero, Mussolini.[485]

This was not an entirely accidental comparison, for the contemporary figure most admired by Mussolini was Lenin.

Two well-known Americans who had been swept up in communist euphoria, John Reed and Lincoln Steffens, were both enamored of Mussolini and his socialist-based strong man image, but eventually, according to political sociologist John Hollander, switched their "admiration of Mussolini to Stalin."[486]

President Franklin D. Roosevelt found Mussolini and his accomplishments impressive, commenting in 1933 that, "I don't mind telling you in confidence that I am keeping in fairly close touch with that admirable Italian gentleman."[487] In a 1933 letter to Ambassador Breckinridge Long in Italy, Roosevelt continued to explain his admiration for Mussolini, writing:

> There seems to be no question that [Mussolini] is really interested in what we are doing, and I am much interested and deeply impressed by what he has accomplished and by his evidenced honest purpose of restoring Italy.[488]

Mussolini returned the favor in 1939 by giving a thumbs-up to FDR's New Deal, explaining to a prominent New York City politician, Grover A. Whalen, that, "You want to know what fascism is like? It is like your New Deal!"[489]

A number of famous Americans felt the same way, arguing that FDR's New Deal policies matched well with Mussolini and other European dictatorships. The well-known novelist and journalist Theodore

Dreiser, who joined the Communist Party in 1945, classified FDR with Hitler, Stalin, and Mussolini, explaining that they all were using the concepts of Karl Marx.[490] The socialist Norman Thomas openly declared what many Americans were already thinking of Mussolini and Hitler by the mid-1930s asserting that "The similarities of the economics of the New Deal to the economics of Mussolini's corporative state or Hitler's totalitarian state are both close and obvious."[491] One progressive writer, Roger Shaw, attempted to explain why mechanics of Mussolini's policies were so applicable, opining that the New Dealers "have been employing Fascist means to gain liberal ends."[492]

Since his days as a youth, Mussolini had been an admirer of Lenin and considered Stalin a "fellow Fascist."[493] He had called Stalin, at least up until 1938, a "cryptofascist."[494] Not long after the signing of the Hitler-Stalin Pact in August 1939, Mussolini was overjoyed and praised Stalin for replacing Bolshevism with "a kind of Slavonic Fascism."[495,496] To some Italian fascist intellectuals, Stalin's Bolshevism was moving towards a nationalized and socialist version of fascism. Gabriele D'Annunzio, regarded as a folk hero and the John the Baptist of Italian Fascism, said that the Italian "State was something of a Latinized, National Bolshevism."[497]

In March 1945, Nicola Bombacci, editor of the Fascist newspaper *La Verità* and special counselor of Mussolini, told a crowd in Genoa in 1945 that "Stalin will never make socialism; rather Mussolini will."[498] Nicknamed "The Red Pope," Bombacci had participated in the Fourth Communist International Congress (1922) as a representative of Italy. It was Bombacci who perceived "Fascism as the only viable form of Marxism for economically retrograde communities."[499]

Mussolini and Fascist Jews in Italy

There is a common belief that all fascists harbored deep-seated animosity towards the Jews, but perception can cloud facts. Early on, Mussolini disagreed with Hitler over many political, economic and racial issues. In reality, the relationship between Mussolini and Hitler was turbulent, especially after the Nazi assassination of the Austro-fascist dictator of Austria, Engelbert Dollfuss, in 1934, an ally of Mussolini; the event almost provoked a war between Fascist Italy and Nazi Germany.[500,501] As for the Jewish question, Mussolini thought little of Hitler's preoccupation with racial purity and his hatred of Jews. He acknowledged that the Jewish minority had lived in Italy since the days of the Roman emperors and should "remain undisturbed,"[502] instead concentrating on "Italianizing" those areas planned for his future empire.[503]

When asked about his opinions on race, Mussolini replied "Race! It is a feeling, not a reality: ninety-five percent, at least, is a feeling. Nothing will ever make me believe that biologically pure races can be shown to exist today."[504]

Up until 1938, Mussolini had "warm relations with Jews" on multiple levels.[505] In 1933, Mussolini was selected by the American Jewish Publishers as among one of "the world's 'twelve greatest Christian champions' of the Jew."[506] Jewish members were welcomed into the National Fascist Party, which had a "disproportionately high" Jewish participation in comparison to the general population of Italy.[507] Up to one-third of Jewish adults had been a member of the Fascist party.[508] A number of high-profile Jews were deeply involved in the National Fascist Party, including Ettore Ovazza, an Italian Jewish banker who in 1935 founded the Jewish Fascist paper *La Nostra Bandiera* (*Our Flag*). Ovazza founded the paper in "an effort to show that the Jews were among the regime's most loyal followers."[509] The Jewish-Italian politician Aldo Finzi was one of the nine Jewish deputies elected to parliament for the *Fasci italiani di combattimento* in 1921 and remained in Mussolini's Chamber of Deputies until 1928.[510] Another Jewish Italian, Giuseppe Volpi, served as Italy's Financial Minister from 1925 to 1928.

In late 1935, Mussolini declared a national day of faith to show national solidarity over worldwide criticism over Italy's invasion of Ethiopia. Almost every Italian synagogue participated in the celebration and played songs during the service, including the fascist song "Giovinezza."[511]

Due to Italy's signing of the Anti-Comintern Pact in 1937 and pressure from Nazi leaders, Mussolini finally relented and enacted the Manifesto of Race of 1938 to officiate the enforcement of racial discrimination. The harsh conditions, which were modeled after the Nazi Nuremberg laws, caused a number of Fascist Jews to leave Italy.[512] Although some Jewish fascists continued to defend Mussolini, his Jewish mistress, Margherita Sarfatti, left Italy in 1938 for Argentina and Uruguay. Interestingly, in recent years, Sarfatti has been referred to as the "Jewish Mother of Fascism" for her early assistance in helping Mussolini establish the Italian Fascist movement.[513]

The mandate was so unpopular that ordinary Italians, military officials, and fascist leaders often refused to participate. After Italy became a puppet state of Nazi Germany in 1943, an estimated 8,529 Jews were arrested and 6,806 deported to concentration camps.[514] Mussolini and the Italian military in occupied regions openly opposed efforts by the Germans to deport Italian Jews.[515] Approximately, only 10 percent of the deported Jews survived.[516]

The Church and the Monarchy

During his years as a young man, Mussolini was an avowed anti-cleric who "proclaimed himself to be an atheist and several times tried to shock an audience by calling on God to strike him dead."[517] He likened Roman Catholic priests to "black germs."[518] He once announced during a speech that "Religion is a species of mental disease."[519] According to English historian Denis Mack Smith, Mussolini believed that any socialist who was Christian or who accepted religious marriage should be expelled from the party, condemning the Catholic Church for "its authoritarianism and refusal to allow freedom of thought..."[520] Once, while debating a Protestant clergyman in Lausanne, Switzerland, he conjectured: "God does not exist—religion in science is an absurdity, in practice an immorality and in men a disease."[521]

During his youthful years, Mussolini advocated for the state to confiscate all of the church's land, threatening to end the reign of Papacy. Later, the Fascists were more than just hostile to the church; they were violent, participating in assaults where "several priests were assassinated and churches burned by the Fascists."[522] In the fall of 1920, squads of young fascists (*squadristi*) roamed the country, targeting Catholic labor organizations and using force to disperse them.[523] However, Fascist attacks against the Pope and the Catholic religion were damaging Mussolini's popularity within a deeply religious nation, forcing him to tone down his invective after rising to Italy's Prime Minister. The church was considered too strong and institutional "to be confronted head-on."[524] According to Mussolini's widow, Rachele, her husband continued to be "basically irreligious until the later years of his life."[525]

When the Fascist *Balilla* organization attempted to "control and indoctrinate the youth of Italy," the "church put up stout resistance."[526] Eventually, "Rivalry between the Catholics and Fascist Youth organizations led to the banning of the Catholic Scout movement in 1928."[527]

To consolidate his power, Mussolini eventually made peace with the Vatican and signed the Lateran Treaty in 1929, granting the Church official recognition as a sovereign state. A number of years after his truce with the Vatican, the National Fascist Party's alliance with the Church faded and turned turbulent, especially after Mussolini instituted his new anti-Semitic policy in 1938.[528] Pope Pius XI condemned both Mussolini and Hitler as adherents of "stupid racialism" and "barbaric Hitlerism."[529] The Church was also "wary of the claims by some Fascists to be creating a new religion and morality..."[530] The Pope publicly condemned the ugly specter of "racism as imitative of German Nazism and a sign of the fascist regime's pagan 'totalitarianism.'"[531]

But Mussolini could not refrain from criticizing the Pope. Not long after signing the Lateran Treaty, his offenses were considered so serious that he was almost excommunicated by the Catholic Church.[532] Not only were Mussolini's hostilities denounced as "intractable," but he sent his cohorts on raids that "confiscated more issues of Catholic newspapers in the next three months than in the previous seven years."[533]

During the mid-to-late 1930s, Mussolini repeatedly chided the Catholic Church, declaring that the "papacy was a malignant tumor in the body of Italy and must 'be rooted out once and for all,' because there was no room in Rome for both the Pope and himself."[534] During one round of anticlerical rants against the papacy, Mussolini announced that he hoped that death would soon overcome the Pope.[535] Referring to himself as an "outright disbeliever," Mussolini once "told a startled cabinet that Islam was perhaps a more effective religion than Christianity."[536]

Mussolini attempted to substitute the state for a spiritual god, considering "the state as the creator of the nation, the Italian Fascist discourse aimed at the construction of a new man, a man of the future: 'the *Homo fascistus.*"[537] Mussolini displayed his irreligious nature in his "Political and Social Doctrine of Fascism," writing, "The fascist concept of the state... is all-embracing, and outside of the state no human or spiritual values can exist, let alone be desired."

Mussolini was furious with Pope Pius XII after learning about secret messages sent to the Allies warning of Germany's planned invasion of Holland, Luxembourg, and Belgium in May 1940. Taking it as a personal affront, Mussolini denounced the papacy as "a disease wasting away the life of Italy," promising to "rid himself of this turbulent priest."[538]

Embracing a form of secular religion, Mussolini sought his people to make self-sacrifices to an omnipotent state. Sociologist George Ritzer noted this behavior in Mussolini, contending that the Italian dictator viewed the "state as an institution on whose behalf its people should sacrifice themselves."[539]

Mussolini was so enamored with the greatest of the Roman Empire that he considered reintroducing ancient Roman paganism. In *Roads and Ruins*, Paul Baxa revealed "Mussolini's 'pagan' view of history" led him to "retrieve what had been lost in the intervening centuries." Baxa contended that Mussolini's fascination with uncovering pagan Roman temples "was an attack on the Christian heritage of the city."[540]

Mussolini had similar disrespect for the weak Italian monarchy and the more powerful Hapsburgs. Most fascists favored ending the monarchy. In order to win Caesarian glory, Mussolini thought he "would gain him the prestige necessary to abolish the monarchy and create a truly totalitarian state."[541] On July 24, 1943, not long after Allies launched an attack on the Italian mainland, Mussolini was arrested by the Italian King Victor Emmanuel III. Soon, Italy announced an armistice and declared war on Germany.

Left and Right Criticism

Many political commentators view the conventional left-right spectrum as problematic. Contending that the "Right-Left spectrum is increasingly useless as a way of talking about many issues," David McKnight writes that it is also confusing and "inadequate" and "has changed dramatically."[542]

A number of historians argue that Mussolini's Marxist-leaning background has little importance due to the changing and confusing nature of political ideology. Some point to the communist North Korean government, which has enshrined an absolute monarchy within a hereditary dictatorship. Three generations of the same family line have ruled North Korea, starting with Kim Il-Sung in 1948.[543,544] In *The Cleanest Race*, B.R. Myers argues that North Korea is an extreme right-wing state since it exudes intense nationalism, xenophobia, race-based rhetoric, militaristic, and an almost religious glorification of current and past communist leaders.[545,546] That exclusive ideology of North Korea is linked more to Japanese-colonial fascism, than any variant of communism. Despite North Korea's reputation as a hardline Stalinist nation, a communist dynasty with such right-wing policies would be the antithesis of classical or orthodox Marxism and much more in line with the ideology of a fascist state.

Italian Fascism is often considered to be reactionary due to its glorification of ancient national history. Although Mussolini looked backward to the glory of the Roman Empire, so did the Cambodian communist leader Pol Pot, who sought to mix elements of Marxism with Khmer nationalism and a desire to idealize the Angkor Empire (802–1431).[547] Not only did he support nationalism and expansionism, but xenophobic racism as well. During a May 10, 1978, broadcast, Pol Pot exhorted his listeners to "Exterminate the 50 million Vietnamese... and purify the masses of the Cambodian people."[548] The Khmer Rouge army hunted down and exterminated every one of the remaining 10,000 or so Cambodian citizens of Vietnamese ancestry in the nation, a genocidal spree that eventually killed over a million Cambodians and disproportionally targeted ethnic minorities.[549]

Mussolini's nationalistic overtones have been cited as evidence of right-wing extremism, even though Stalin had no qualms about utilizing Russian nationalism during the Great Patriot War of WWII. Contending that the Bolsheviks in the Soviet Union had eventually rationalized a sort of "autarchic nationalism," A. James Gregor noted that, "By 1934, the Red Army was no longer swearing allegiance to the 'international proletariat,' but to the 'Socialist Fatherland.'"[550] Moreover, "Political reality motivated Stalin to exploit Russian Nationalism."[551] Political scientist Cheng Chen argued that "Slavic solidarity, instead of proletarian internationalism, was invoked to fight against the Germans."[552] He continued, "During the 1920s, a series of episodes heralded the forthcoming marriage of nationalism and Marxism."[553] Some have claimed that the works of Karl Marx tacitly supported proletarian nationalism or "left-wing nationalism" as a means to develop a proletarian rule over a nation, which would evolve in stages towards a true revolutionary communist society.[554] This was often expressed by Stalin's famous dictum, which could have been easily expressed by Mussolini or Hitler: "Nationalist in form; socialist in context."[555]

Historically, Marxist leaders have supported nationalist movements if they adhered to socialism and class struggle.[556] Joseph Stalin, who promoted a civic patriotic concept called "revolutionary patriotism," supported the use of proletarian nationalism when nationalistic movements fought for class struggle within an internationalist framework.[557,558] Marxism had also been moving towards nationalism in other nations. Near the end of the nineteenth century, "Marxism in Western Europe was becoming more and more national, and was being transformed into the Social-Democratic projects of a welfare nation-state."[559]

Left-wing nationalism has been described as a form of nationalism centered upon equality, popular sovereignty, and national self-determination with origins dating back to Jacobinism of the French Revolution.[560,561] Another form of left-wing nationalism, known as "National Bolshevism," incorporates elements of extreme nationalism (especially Russian nationalism) and Bolshevism.[562] According to journalist Martin A. Lee, the origins of National Bolshevism surfaced from German politician Ernst Niekisch and German writer Ernst Jünger during World War I, who were willing to accept communism if Marxists would embrace nationalism and reject internationalism.[563]

Italian fascism was not the only collectivistic ideology that favored nationalism within a wide or narrow scope. Leading Marxist revisionists flirted with both nationalism and colonialism. Marxist reformer Eduard Bernstein, who held a close association with Karl Marx and Friedrich Engels, came to believe that the state had a critical role to play in nation-building and "opposed the anti-national rhetoric of the radical left."[564] He coined the phrase "sociological nationalism," and described it as a way to socially restructure population groups into larger units, which he praised as "progressive and forward-reaching."[565] Upholding a Euro-centric perspective, Bernstein suggested that socialists should be "strong advocate[s] of colonialism" to assist in the development of industrial so-cieties.[566]

As for Mussolini's militaristic and authoritarian behavior, there seems to be little distinction between left-wing and right-wing regimes. As Stanley Milgram's experiment contended concerning obedience to au-thority figures, people simply doing their jobs, without any particular hostility, "can become agents in a terrible destructive process."[567] In *Planned Chaos*, Ludwig von Mises cited Mussolini's fanatical appetite for war and new territory, but also noted that in all the other European nations, "most of the Marxians longed for war and conquest."[568]

Some psychologists have argued that most authoritarians have similar attributes despite varying ideological differences. Hans Jürgen Eysenck, a British psychologist who was a pioneer in behavior therapy, discovered little contrast between authoritarians, no matter where they were placed on the political spectrum. This is what Eysenck discovered during his extensive research which he published in his 1954 book *Psychology of Poli-tics*. He found that both fascists and communists had a tough-minded ag-gressive behavior within an authoritarian framework.[569] In other words, fascist and communists were authoritarian brothers-in-arms who were political rivals drawn from different mob-like crime families. They have some ideological and political differences, but nothing big enough to put them on opposite ends of a political spectrum. Depending on one's point of view, they might be positioned on either the left or right side of the political axis, but they have to be grouped together to maintain ideological, political, and historical continuity.

There have been a number of other studies on the authoritarian per-sonalities. Social psychologist Arlin James Benjamin, Jr. contends that "a number of psychologists have argued that authoritarianism has been endemic in both fascist and socialist societies (e.g. McColskey & Chong, 1985; Ray, 1979)."[570] Behavioral Scientist J.J. Ray has conducted stud-ies on authoritarian behavior and concluded "that half of all authoritarians measured by the Fascism (F) Scale (Adorno et al., 1950) are left-ists."[571,572] The F-scale was designed by Theodor W. Adorno in 1947 to measure authoritarian personality.

The Nolan Chart, a political view assessment diagram, shows a left-right convergence at the bottom of their diamond-shaped chart with those identified with authoritarian or totalitarian regimes.[573] Under this interpretation of the political spectrum, those who advocate almost total government control over the economy and over personal lifestyles generally display similar practices, goals, and ideologies, causing the left and right to melt into one another.

Socialist-Fascist Corporatism

Many contend that corporatism has a traditional right-wing component. In the case of Italy's corporatist political system, the economy at the national level was collectively managed from the top down.[574] According to the fascists, the economy was centralized to bring harmony among social classes.[575] In "The Political and Social Doctrine of Fascism," Mussolini wrote that

> Fascism recognizes the real needs which gave rise to socialism and trade-unionism, giving them due weight in the guild or corporative system in which divergent interests are coordinated and harmonized in the unity of the State.[576]

The socialist-fascist corporatism in Mussolini's Italy was very dissimilar to America's independently-operated, shareholder-driven corporations.[577] In the early 1930s, Mussolini fashioned twenty-two state-run holding corporations headed by a top official of the government or by members of the National Fascist Party.[578] They were completely controlled and operated by the Italian state in Mussolini's effort to move beyond capitalism and socialism. Mussolini's "corporatism borrows heavily from Sorel's theories of revolutionary syndicalism," an ideology that promoted the virtues of trade unionism and socialism.[579]

The Italian government had developed a strict worker-state corporate structure where trade unions and employer associations were subordinate to the state. When the Syndical Laws were enacted in 1926, it "made the existence of non-Fascist-syndicates virtually impossible."[580] Non-Fascist unions were outlawed, and membership in the state-run fascist union organization became mandatory.[581] Mussolini had nationalized all independent trade unions in accordance with Marxist-Leninist theory that opposed privately operated and independently owned organizations outside of the state. A leading anti-fascist politician in Italy, Gaetano Salvemini wrote in 1937:

> In [Fascist] Italy and [Nazi] Germany the official unions have been made compulsory by law, while in the United States, the workers are not legally obligated to join the company unions but may even, if they so wish, oppose them.[582]

Mussolini's administration also made strikes illegal, as had Lenin and Stalin in the Soviet Union. Before he had acquired power, Mussolini had often been critical of Lenin's regime for "refusal to permit strikes" in Russia.[583,584]

Both the Soviet Union and Fascist Italy enacted similar policies to prohibit independent labor unions. Although Lenin called for "every cook to govern," he shut down the factory committees and made the unions "subordinate to the state," a policy that had been approved at the first All-Russian Congress of Trade Unions.[585] Unhappy over the banning of all independent trade unions, one delegate at the event "described the unions as 'living corpses.'"[586] Lauding the benefits of "one-man management" (versus democratic factory committees) Lenin and Trotsky abolished the right to strike and implemented compulsory labor (mandatory overtime) that saw workers labor up to 80 hours a week.[587,588] Samuel Gompers, first president of the American Federation of Labor, derided the Soviet Union's labor policies as "slavery," and the "militarization of labor" which "constitutes the gravest danger that has confronted labor for centuries."[589]

Trotsky was particularity adamant that the State should fully control the unions. When the Bolsheviks broke up factory worker strikes in Petrograd, the conflict led to the Kronstadt Rebellion of 1921. The Kronstadt insurrectionists called for, among other things, "the right of assembly, and freedom for trade union and peasant associations."[590] Russian

Bolsheviks, German Nazis, and Italian Fascists took the position that the workers were now in charge of the government, making strikes and independent labor unions unnecessary.

* * * * *

Mussolini was a Marxist of varying degrees and evolving schisms for at least two decades, and a closet Marxist thereafter. He always thought of himself as socialist who had to unfortunately bend with the trending winds. He never thought of himself as reactionary or a right-wing partisan, since he had nothing but contempt for the monarchy and Church. If he were alive today, he would have been totally shocked to see himself positioned on the political spectrum as the icon for right-wing extremism.

Notes

[1] Mussolini, *The Political and Social Doctrine of Fascism*, p. 20. Jane Soames's translation was widely published in major journals of the time, including "The Political Quarterly," London, Vol. 4, Issue 3, pp. 341–356 (quote on p. 351), July 1933 and in "The Living Age," Nov. 1933, New York City, (quote on p. 241) entitled "The Doctrine of Fascism." Original 1933 and 1934 English translation posted at http://historyuncensored.wixsite.com/history-uncensored.

[2] Ludwig, *Talks with Mussolini*, p. 38. Interview between Mar. 23 and Apr. 4, 1932, at the Palazzo di Venezia in Rome.

[3] Sternhell, Sznajder, and Asheri, *The Birth of Fascist Ideology*, p. 5.

[4] Has been attributed to George Orwell, but no record of it can be found. The first record of its public use was in 2009 by writer and columnist Selwyn Duke.

[5] Roger Griffin, "The Palingenetic Core of Fascist Ideology," in *Che cos'è il fascismo? Interpretazioni e prospettive di ricerca*, ed. Alessandro Campi (Rome: Ideazione editrice, 2003), pp. 97–122.

[6] Roger Eatwell, "A Spectral-Syncretic Approach to Fascism," chap. 4 in *The Fascism Reader*, ed. Aristotle A. Kallis (London/New York: Routledge, 2003), pp. 71–80.

[7] Seymour Martin Lipset, "Fascism: Left, Right, and Center," chap. 5 in *Political Man: The Social Bases of Politics* (Garden City, NY: Doubleday and Company, Inc., 1960), p. 133. This award-winning book was highly influential.

[8] Arthur M. Schlesinger, Jr., "Not Right, Not Left, But a Vital Center," *New York Times Magazine*, Apr. 4, 1948.

[9]Nolte, *Three Faces of Fascism*, p. 313. Reference is to the fascism of German National Socialism, but the principle also applies to Italian Fascism.

[10]Stephen D. Shenfield, *Russian Fascism: Traditions, Tendencies, Movements* (Armonk, NY: M.E. Sharpe, Inc., 2001), p. 14.

[11]Sternhell, Sznajder, and Asheri, *The Birth of Fascist Ideology*, p. 6.

[12]Sternhell, *Neither Right nor Left*, p. 268.

[13]Ibid., p. 14.

[14]Sternhell, Sznajder, and Asheri, *The Birth of Fascist Ideology*, p. 5.

[15]Giovanni Gentile, *Origini e dottrina del fascismo*, Rome, 1929, p. 58, also in Gregor, *The Ideology of Fascism*, p. 317.

[16]*"Che cosa è il fascismo: Discorsi e polemiche"* ("What is Fascism?"), Florence: Vallecchi, (1925) *Origins and Doctrine of Fascism*, A. James Gregor, translator and edit., Transaction Publishers, 2003, p. 59.

[17]Sternhell, *Neither Right nor Left*, p. 21.

[18]Sternhell, Sznajder, and Asheri, *The Birth of Fascist Ideology*, p. 33. *Syndicat* is the French word for trade union.

[19]A. James Gregor, *Giovanni Gentile: Philosopher of Fascism* (New Brunswick, NJ: Transaction Publishers, 2004), p. 55.

[20]Gregor, *The Faces of Janus*, p. 133.

[21]Gregor, *Young Mussolini and the Intellectual Origins of Fascism*, p. 1.

[22]Blamires, *World Fascism: A Historical Encyclopedia*, pp. 95–96.

[23]Roger Kimball, "The Death of Socialism," *The New Criterion*, Apr. 2002. https://www.newcriterion.com/issues/2002/4/the-death-of-socialism.

[24]David Ramsey Steele, "The Mystery of Fascism," first published in *Liberty*, Vol. 15, No. 11, Nov. 2001. http://www.la-articles.org.uk/fascism.htm.

[25]Diggins, *Mussolini and Fascism*, p. 213. *Weekly People*, Nov. 18, 1922. Prezzolini's article was first published in the *New Republic*, Nov. 1, 1922, pp. 242–244.

[26]G. Valois, "Erreurs et véritsé sur le fascisme," *Le Nouveau Siécle*, Apr. 24, 1926. See also Valois, *Le Fascisme*, pp. 15–16.

[27]Sternhell, *Neither Right nor Left*, p. 105.

[28]G. Valois, *"Le Fascisme, conclusion du mouvement de 1789,"* *Le Nouveau Siècle*, July 14, 1926. Quoted in Sternhell, *Neither Right nor Left*, p. 106.

[29]Ibid.

[30]Neocleous, *Fascism*, p. 10.

[31]Sternhell, *Neither Right nor Left*, p. 226.

[32]David Renton, *Fascism: Theory and Practice* (London, UK: Pluto Press, 1999), p. 20.

[33]Stanley G. Payne, *Fascism: Comparison and Definition* (Madison, WI: University of Wisconsin Press, 1980), p. 184. Original source: Augusto del Noce, *L'Epoca della secolarizzazione* (Milan, 1970), 111–135; and *"Per una definizione storica del fascismo,"* in *Il problema storico del fascismo* (Florence, 1970), pp. 11–46.

[34]Pipes, *Russia Under the Bolshevik Regime*, p. 240.

[35]See Footnote 1 of this chapter.

[36] Mussolini, *The Political and Social Doctrine of Fascism*, p. 20.

[37] Herbert Giersch, "Preliminary Reflections on Economics as a Public Good," chap. 3 in *Exemplary Economists: Europe, Asia and Australasia, Volume II*, eds. Robert Backhouse and Roger Middleton (Cheltenham, UK: Edward Elgar Publishing, Limited, 2000). p. 80.

[38] First published in 1932 in the fourteenth volume of the *Enciclopedia Italiana*. All copies of this edition had allegedly been destroyed before the end of World War II. For more information on the English translation, see Footnote 1 of this chapter.

[39] Mussolini, *The Political and Social Doctrine of Fascism*, p. 20.

[40] Herbert Hoover, *The Challenge to Liberty* (New York/London: Charles Scribner's Sons, 1934), p. 66. Source cited in book is from *The Political Quarterly*, London, Vol. 4, Issue 3, pp. 341–356, July 1933.

[41] Ibid., p. 74.

[42] Roger Griffin, *The Nature of Fascism* (New York, NY: St. Martin's Press, 1991), pp. 222–223.

[43] Voigt, *Unto Caesar*, p. 95.

[44] "Current Literature: Render Unto Caesar," book review of F.A. Voigt's *Unto Caesar* book, *The Sydney Morning Herald*, Aug. 20, 1938.

[45] This organization was renamed in 1919 to The Italian Fasci of Combat (*Fasci Italiani di Combattimento*, FIC).

[46] Mussolini, *The Political and Social Doctrine of Fascism*, p. 7. Note that Mussolini's first political party has also been translated as the "Revolutionary Fascist Party."

[47] Peter Neville, *Mussolini* (Oxon, England, UK and New York, NY: Routledge, 2004), p. 36.

[48] Smith, *Modern Italy*, p. 284.

[49] Nolte, *Three Faces of Fascism*, p. 154, quoted in Italian on p. 489 37n: "Conosco i communisti. Li conosco perché alcuni di loro i miei figli..." Speech presented on June 21, 1921, in Italy's Chamber of Deputy.

[50] Pipes, *Russia Under the Bolshevik Regime*, p. 252.

[51] Elazar, *The Making of Fascism*, p. 141. Also found in Paul Corner, *Fascism in Ferrara, 1915–1925* (New York, NY and London, UK: Oxford University Press, 1975), p. 193n5.

[52] Pipes, *Russia Under the Bolshevik Regime*, p. 253.

[53] Vox Day, "Flunking Fascism 101," *WND.com*. Jan. 8, 2008. http://www.wnd.com/2004/06/25291/.

[54] Goldberg, *Liberal Fascism*, p. 46.

[55] Bosworth, *Mussolini's Italy*, p. 118.

[56] Elazar, *The Making of Fascism*, p. 73.

[57] Daniel Guerin, *Fascism and Big Business* (New York, NY: Monad Press, 1973), p. 83. First edition published in 1939. Originally from Mussolini's article in his fascist newspaper *Il Popolo d'Italia*, June 19, 1919.

[58] Muravchik, *Heaven on Earth*, p. 144.

[59]Brenda Haugen, *Benito Mussolini: Fascist Italian Dictator* (Minneapolis, MN: Compass Point Books, 2007), p. 17.

[60]Toler, *The Everything Guide to Understanding Socialism*, p. 179.

[61]Roberto Olla, *Il Duce and His Women* (London, UK: Alma Books, 2011), p. 27.

[62]David Ramsey Steele, "The Mystery of Fascism," first published in *Liberty*, Vol. 15, No. 11, Nov. 2001.

[63]Ibid.

[64]Gregor, *The Faces of Janus*, p. 20.

[65]Gregor, *Young Mussolini and the Intellectual Origins of Fascism*, p. xi.

[66]Ibid.

[67]Sternhell, Sznajder, and Asheri, *The Birth of Fascist Ideology*, p. 5.

[68]Pipes, *Russia Under the Bolshevik Regime*, p. 253.

[69]Klaus Hildebrand, *The Third Reich* (London, UK: Routledge, 1991), p. 106.

[70]Larry Ceplair, *Under the Shadow of War: Fascism, Anti-Fascism, and Marxists, 1918-1939* (Columbia University Press, 1987), p. 50.

[71]Mabel Berezin, *Making the Fascist Self: The Political Culture of Interwar Italy* (Ithaca, NY: Cornell University Press, 1997), p. 19.

[72]Nigel Copsey, *Contemporary British Fascism: The British National Party and the Quest for Legitimacy* (New York, NY: Palgrave Macmillan, 2004), p. 11.

[73]Gregor, *The Faces of Janus*, pp. 144–146.

[74]Kenneth Murphy, *Retreat from the Finland Station: Moral Odysseys in the Breakdown of Communism* (New York, NY: Free Press, 1992), pp. 73–76.

[75]Gregor, *The Fascist Persuasion in Radical Politics*, p. 132.

[76]Ibid.

[77]Gregor, *The Faces of Janus*, p. 130.

[78]Ibid., p. 144.

[79]Trotsky, *The Revolution Betrayed*, pp. 237–238.

[80]Gregor, *Young Mussolini and the Intellectual Origins of Fascism*, p. xi.

[81]Renzo De Felice, *Fascism: An Informal Introduction to Its Theory and Practice* (New Brunswick, NJ: Transactions Publishers, 1976), pp. 67ff.

[82]Ibid., p. 106.

[83]Gene Edward Veith Jr., *Modern Fascism: Liquidating the Judeo-Christian Worldview* (Concordia College, 1993), p. 26. Prof. Gene Edward Veith is a professor of English at Concordia University, Wisconsin.

[84]Payne, *A History of Fascism, 1914–1945*, p. 126.

[85]Mikhail Agursky, *The Third Rome: National Bolshevism in the USSR* (Boulder, CO: Westview Press, 1987), p. 301.

[86]Murray Rothbard, "Left and Right: The Prospects for Liberty," *Left and Right: A Journal of Libertarian Thought*, Spring 1965, pp. 4–22. http://mises.org/daily/910.

[87]Ibid.

[88]George L. Mosse, "Towards a General Theory of Fascism," chap. Nine in *Masses and Man: Nationalist and Fascist Perceptions of Reality* (Detroit, MI: Wayne State University Press, 1987), p. 163.

[89]Blamires, *World Fascism: A Historical Encyclopedia*, p. 136.

[90]Pierre Broue, *The German Revolution: 1917–1923* (Chicago, IL: Haymarket Books, 2006), p. 87.

[91]Luigi Sturzo, *Italien und der Faschismus*, (Cologne: Gilde Verlag, 1926).

[92]F.A. Hayek, *The Road to Serfdom* (New York, NY: George Routledge and Sons, 1944), p. 120.

[93]George Orwell, "Spilling the Spanish Beans," *New English Weekly*, July 29 and Sept. 2, 1937. http://www.english.illinois.edu/maps/scw/orwell2.htm.

[94]George Orwell, *Homage to Catalonia* (New York, NY: Harvest Book, Harcourt Brace & Company, 1980) p. 63, first published in 1938. See especially chapter 5.

[95]Ibid., pp. 58–59.

[96]John Newsinger, "Orwell and the Spanish Revolution," *International Socialism Journal*, Issue 62, Spring 1994. http://pubs.socialistreviewindex.org.uk/isj62/newsinger.htm.

[97]Geoffrey Gorer, "*Time and Tide*, April 30, 1938," chap. 36 in *George Orwell*, New Ed ed., ed. Jeffrey Meyers (New York, NY: Routledge, 1997), pp. 599–600.

[98]George Orwell, "Spilling the Spanish Beans," *New English Weekly*, July 29 and Sept. 2, 1937.

[99]Ronald Radosh, Mary R. Habeck, and Gregory Sevostianov, eds., *Spain Betrayed: The Soviet Union in the Spanish Civil War* (Yale University Press, 2001), p. xxx.

[100]Ibid.

[101]Jesús Huerta de Soto, *Socialism, Economic Calculation and Entrepreneurship* (Glos, England and Northampton, MA: Edward Elgar Publishing Limited, 2010), pp. 79–80.

[102]Karl Marx and Friedrich Engels, *Communist Manifesto*, ed. D. Ryazanoff (New York, NY: Russell and Russell, Inc., 1963), Part III, pp. 54–68.

[103]Friedrich Engels, "Preface to The Housing Question," *Selected Works*, Moscow Edition, Vol. I, p. 498.

[104]George Orwell, "What is Fascism," first published: *Tribune*—GB, London, Mar. 24, 1944.

[105]A. James Gregor, *Mussolini's Intellectuals: Fascist Social and Political Thought* (Princeton, NJ: Princeton University Press, 2004), p. 4.

[106]Richard Griffiths, *An Intelligent Person's Guide to Fascism* (London, UK: Duckworth Publishers, 2001), p. 1.

[107]Pipes, *Russia Under the Bolshevik Regime*, p. 486, occurred in May 1924 at the Thirteenth Party Conference.

[108]Leon Trotsky, "The Workers' State, Thermidor and Bonapartism," Feb. 1935. http://www.marxists.org/archive/trotsky/1935/02/ws-therm-bon.htm.

[109]George Orwell, "What is Fascism," first published: *Tribune*—GB, London, Mar. 24, 1944.

[110]Donald C. Hodges, *The Bureaucratization of Socialism* (University of Massachusetts Press, 1981), p. 131.

[111]Ibid.

[112]David Evans, *Understand Stalin's Russia*, 1st ed. (McGraw-Hill, Teach Yourself series, 2012), p. 89.

[113]Rob Sewell, "Leon Trotsky: The Man and His Ideas," *In Defense of Marxism* website, Aug. 20, 2012. http://marxist.com/leon-trotsky-the-man-and-his-ideas.htm.

[114]Goldberg, *Liberal Fascism*, p. 77.

[115]Richard M. Fried, *Nightmare in Red: The McCarthy Era in Perspective* (Oxford University Press, 1991), p. 50. "Editorial: The Russian Betrayal," *New York Times*, Sept. 18, 1939.

[116]A. James Gregor, *The Search for Neofascism: The Use and Abuse of Social Science* (Cambridge University Press, 2006), pp. 18–19.

[117]Ibid., p. 19.

[118]Claudio Quarantotto, *Tutti Fascisti* (Rome: Il Borghese, 1976).

[119]Pipes, *Russia Under the Bolshevik Regime*, p. 242.

[120]Gregor, *The Faces of Janus*, p. 26.

[121]Pipes, *Russia Under the Bolshevik Regime*, p. 242.

[122]Gregor, *Young Mussolini and the Intellectual Origins of Fascism*, p. xi.

[123]*Opera Omnia di Benito Mussolini*, E. and D. Susmel, edit., Florence, 1951–, 1/52–3, 60, 92, 251 (Mar. 26, 1904), Dinale, 36.

[124]Gregor, *Young Mussolini and the Intellectual Origins of Fascism*, p. 57. Original: Mussolini, "Sebastian Faure," *Opera Omnia di Benito Mussolini*, 1, 47.

[125]David Ramsey Steele, "The Mystery of Fascism," first published in *Liberty*, Vol. 15, No. 11, Nov. 2001.

[126]Ludwig, *Talks with Mussolini*, p. 38. Interview between Mar. 23 and Apr. 4, 1932, at the Palazzo di Venezia in Rome.

[127]Ibid.

[128]Santi Corvaja, *Hitler & Mussolini: The Secret Meetings* (New York, NY: Enigma Books, 2008), p. 299.

[129]Kemechey, *Il Duce*, p. 56.

[130]Smith, *Mussolini*, p. 7. Original source: *Opera Omnia di Benito Mussolini* 1/102–3 (Mar. 14, 1908), 135, 142.

[131]Johnson, *Modern Times*, p. 57. Original source: Benito Mussolini, *Opera Omnia di Benito Mussolini*, 36 Vols. (Florence 1951–63) II 32, 126.

[132]Sternhell, Sznajder, and Asheri, *The Birth of Fascist Ideology*, p. 197. Original source: Vero Eretico [Mussolini], "Socialismo e socialisti," *La Lima*, May 30, 1908, *Opera Omnia*, Vol. 1, p. 142.

[133]Gregor, *Young Mussolini and the Intellectual Origins of Fascism*, p. 138.

[134]David Ramsey Steele, "The Mystery of Fascism," first published in *Liberty*, Vol. 15, No. 11, Nov. 2001.

[135]Brenda Haugen, *Benito Mussolini: Fascist Italian Dictator* (Minneapolis, MN: Compass Point Books, 2007), pp. 31–34.

[136]Giuseppe Finaldi, *Mussolini and Italian Fascism* (London and New York: Routledge, 2013), p. 159.

[137]Gregor, *Young Mussolini and the Intellectual Origins of Fascism*, p. 53.

[138] Smith, *Mussolini*, p. 8.

[139] Ibid., p. 23.

[140] David Ramsey Steele, "The Mystery of Fascism," first published in *Liberty*, Vol. 15, No. 11, Nov. 2001.

[141] Smith, *Mussolini*, p. 8.

[142] Jasper Ridley, *Mussolini* (New York, NY: St. Martin's Press, 1998), p. 67.

[143] Norling, *Revolutionary Fascism*, p. 88.

[144] Richard Pipes, *Three "Whys" of the Russian Revolution* (New York, NY: Vintage Books, 1997), p. 38.

[145] Benito Mussolini, "The War as a Revolution," 1914, in Roger Griffin, edit., *Fascism*, 1995, pp. 26–28.

[146] Hibbert, *Mussolini: The Rise and Fall of Il Duce*, p. 21. First published in 1962 as *Il Duce: The Life of Benito Mussolini*.

[147] Emil Ludwig, *Nine Etched from Life* (R.M. McBride & Company, 1934), p. 321.

[148] Gregor, *The Faces of Janus*, p. 20.

[149] Patrizia Acobas, "*Margherita Sarfatti 1880–1961*," Jewish Women's Archive, Encyclopedia, posted at http://jwa.org/encyclopedia/article/sarfatti-margherita.

[150] R.J.B. Bosworth, *Mussolini* (New York, NY: Bloomsbury Academic, 2011), pp. 100–111.

[151] Roberts, *The Syndicalist Tradition and Italian Fascism*, p. 177.

[152] Morgan, *Fascism in Europe*, p. 27.

[153] *Opera Omnia di Benito Mussolini*, E. and D. Susmel, edit., Florence, 1951–, XI, pp. 241–243.

[154] Hibbert, *Mussolini: The Rise and Fall of Il Duce*, p. 21.

[155] Jean Bruhat, "Auguste Blanqui: French socialist," *Encyclopædia Britannica*. http://www.britannica.com/biography/Auguste-Blanqui.

[156] Federico Finchelstein, *Transatlantic Fascism: Ideology, Violence and the Sacred in Argentina and Italy, 1919–1945* (Durham, NC: Duke University Press, 2010), p. 20.

[157] Sternhell, Sznajder, and Asheri, *The Birth of Fascist Ideology*, pp. 140, 214.

[158] Vladislav Zubok and Constantine Pleshakov, *Inside the Kremlin's Cold War: From Stalin to Khrushchev* (Cambridge: MA, Harvard University Press, 1996), p. 3. Constantine Pleshakov is a professor of Russian and Eurasian Studies. Vladislav Zubok is a professor of history.

[159] Lawrence Sondhaus, *World War I: The Global Revolution* (Cambridge, UK: Cambridge University, 2011), p. 177.

[160] L.K. Samuels, "Hitler and Mussolini: History's Dirty Little Secret," Feb. 28, 2014. http://www.lksamuels.com/?p=156.

[161] Spencer Tucker and Roberts Priscilla, eds., *Encyclopedia of World War I: A Political, Social, and Military History*, 5 vols. (Santa Barbara, CA: ABC-CLIO, 2005), p. 884.

[162] Chen, *The Prospects for Liberal Nationalism in Post-Leninist States*, p. 37.

[163]Yannis Sygkelos, *Nationalism from the Left: The Bulgarian Communist Party During the Second World War and the Early Post-War Years* (Brill Academic Pub, 2011), p. 13.

[164]Chen, *The Prospects for Liberal Nationalism in Post-Leninist States*, p. 37.

[165]David Muñoz Lagarejos, "*Socialism in Fascism,*" *Neuronaliberal*, Oct. 29, 2015. Cites historian César Vidal as source, from interview of Mussolini by a foreign journalist.

[166]Stanislao G. Pugliese, ed., *Fascism, Anti-Fascism, and the Resistance in Italy: 1919 to the Present* (Lanham, MD: Rowman & Littlefield Publishers, Inc., 2004), p. 43.

[167]*Opera Omnia di Benito Mussolini*, E. and D. Susmel, edit., Florence, 1951–, XXI, p. 309.

[168]Bosworth, *Mussolini's Italy*, p. 116.

[169]Toler, *The Everything Guide to Understanding Socialism*, p. 184.

[170]Smith, *Modern Italy*, p. 297.

[171]Smith, *Mussolini*, p. 40.

[172]*Opera Omnia di Benito Mussolini*, E. and D. Susmel, edit., Florence, 1951–, 14/287 (Feb. 5, 1920), 342, 381 (Mar. 26, 1920).

[173]David Ramsey Steele, "The Mystery of Fascism," first published in *Liberty*, Vol. 15, No. 11, Nov. 2001.

[174]Hibbert, *Mussolini: The Rise and Fall of Il Duce*, p. 29.

[175]"Benito Mussolini," *Encyclopedia.com*, The Gale Group, Inc., 2004. http://www.encyclopedia.com/people/history/italian-history-biographies/benito-mussolini.

[176]W. William Halperin, *Mussolini and Italian Fascism* (Princeton, NJ: D. Van Nostrand Company, 1964), pp. 32–33.

[177]Pipes, *Russia Under the Bolshevik Regime*, p. 251.

[178]Gregor, *Italian Fascism and Developmental Dictatorship*, p. 179.

[179]Ibid.

[180]Smith, *Mussolini*, p. 41.

[181]Peter Neville, *Mussolini* (London, UK: Routledge, 2001), p. 47.

[182]Thomas Streissguth and Lora Friedenthal, *Isolationism (Key Concepts in American History)* (New York, NY: Chelsea House Publishers, 2010), p. 57.

[183]Payne, *A History of Fascism, 1914–1945*, p. 95.

[184]Sarfatti, *The Life of Benito Mussolini*, p. 278.

[185]Ibid.

[186]Martin Clark, *Mussolini* (London, UK and New York, NY: Routledge, 2014), p. 49.

[187]Hamish Macdonald, *Mussolini and Italian Fascism* (Cheltenham, UK: Stanley Thornes Publishers, LTD, 1999), p. 17.

[188]Hibbert, *Mussolini: The Rise and Fall of Il Duce*, p. 28.

[189]Smith, *Mussolini*, p. 40.

[190]Payne, *A History of Fascism, 1914–1945*, p. 95.

[191]Ibid.

[192]Ibid., p. 108.

[193] Ibid., pp. 100–101.

[194] Smith, *Mussolini*, p. 40.

[195] Townley, *Mussolini and Italy*, p. 31.

[196] Zara S. Steiner, *The Lights That Failed: European International History, 1919–1933* (Oxford University Press, 2005), p. 172.

[197] Payne, *A History of Fascism, 1914–1945*, p. 223.

[198] Xenia Joukoff Eudin and Harold Henry Fisher, *Soviet Russia and the West, 1920–1927: A Documentary Survey*, p. 261.

[199] Stoker, *Girding for Battle*, p. 180.

[200] Payne, *A History of Fascism, 1914–1945*, p. 230.

[201] Stoker, *Girding for Battle*, p. 116.

[202] Payne, *A History of Fascism, 1914–1945*, p. 230.

[203] Stoker, *Girding for Battle*, p. 180. See esp. chap. 9, "Italo-Soviet Military Cooperation in the 1930s," by J. Calvitt Clarke III.

[204] Payne, *A History of Fascism, 1914–1945*, p. 230.

[205] Yvon de Begnac, *Palazzo Venezia: Storia di un Regime* (Rome, 1950), p. 361.

[206] Pipes, *Russia Under the Bolshevik Regime*, p. 252.

[207] Smith, *Mussolini*, p. 96.

[208] Kemechey, *Il Duce*, p. 47.

[209] Carlos Rangel, *Third World Ideology and Western Reality: Manufacturing Political Myth* (Transaction Publishers, 1986), p. 15. Quote from Vladimir Lenin when he addressed a delegation of Italian socialists in Moscow not long after Mussolini's march on Rome.

[210] Norling, *Revolutionary Fascism*, p. 28.

[211] Gregor, *The Ideology of Fascism*, p. 100.

[212] Kemechey, *Il Duce*, p. 47.

[213] Richard Pipes, *Three "Whys" of the Russian Revolution* (New York, NY: Vintage Books, 1997), p. 37.

[214] John Gunther, *Inside Europe* (Harper & Brothers, 1936), p. 172.

[215] Delzell, *Mediterranean Fascism 1919–1945*, p. 3.

[216] Sternhell, *Neither Right nor Left*, p. 107.

[217] Neocleous, *Fascism*, p. 10. Other source: Jean Variot, *Propos de G. Sorel*, Paris, 1935, p. 219.

[218] Jacob L. Talmon, *The Myth of the Nation and the Vision of Revolution: The Origins of Ideological Polarization in the 20th Century* (University of California Press, 1981), p. 451. Sorel's conversations with to Jean Variot, *Propos de Georges Sorel*, pp. 53–57, 66–86 passim, conversation in Mar. 1921. *Propos de Georges Sorel*, is a collection of Sorel's pronouncements published in Paris, 1935.

[219] Jan-Werner Müller, *Contesting Democracy: Political Ideas in Twentieth-Century Europe* (Yale University Press, 2011), p. 94.

[220] Georges Sorel, "For Lenin," *Soviet Russia*, Official Organ of The Russian Soviet Government Bureau, Vol. II, New York: NY, Jan.–June 1920 (Apr. 10, 1920), p. 356.

[221] Anthony L. Cardoza, "*Il Culto del Littorio: La Sacralizzazione della Politica nell'Italia Fascista*," by Emilio Gentile (book review). *The American Historical Review* 99 (5): 1721–1722, Dec. 1994, JSTOR 2168494.

[222] Emilio Gentile, *The Origins of Fascist Ideology* (New York, NY: Enigma Books, 2005), p. 248.

[223] Ibid., p. 11.

[224] Blamires, *World Fascism: A Historical Encyclopedia*, p. 136.

[225] Smith, *Modern Italy*, p. 394.

[226] Muravchik, *Heaven on Earth*, p. 170.

[227] Ibid., p. 171. Nicola Bombacci was one of the founding fathers of the Italian Communist Party.

[228] Norling, *Revolutionary Fascism*, p. 30.

[229] Arrigo Petacco, *Il comunista in camicia nera: Nicola Bombacci tra Lenin e Mussolini*, Italian Edition (Milan, Italy: Mondadori, 1996), p. 115.

[230] "Tributo al grande Nicola Bombacci, vero Rivoluzionario" – Italian song in tribute to Nicola Bombacci. http://www.youtube.com/watch?v=4kRyxSPZYNU.

[231] Bosworth, *Mussolini's Italy*, pp. 510–511.

[232] Norling, *Revolutionary Fascism*, p. 82.

[233] Marvin Perry, Myrna Chase, James R. Jacob, Margaret C. Jacob, Theodore H. Von Laue, eds., *Western Civilization: Ideas, Politics and Society, Volume II: From 1600*, Tenth Edition (Boston, MA: Wadsworth Cengage Learning, 2012), p. 750.

[234] Benito Mussolini, "Prelude to Machiavelli," *The Living Age*, Vol. 323, No. 4194, Nov. 22, 1924. Originally published in the Italian journal *Gerarchia* in 1924, edited by Mussolini and Margherita Sarfatti. Mussolini's thesis was titled "Comments of the year 1924 on the Prince of Machiavelli," University of Bologna, 1924.

[235] Robert Bingham Downs, *Books That Changed the World* (New York, NY: Penguin Group, 2004), p. 201.

[236] Robert Service, *Stalin: A Biography* (UK: Macmillan Publishers, LTD., 2004), p. 343.

[237] Laura LeFae, "Political Philosophy: History Machiavelli Hitler Mussolini Fascism Socialism," *Humanities 360°*, Nov. 25, 2010. http://archive.is/mT5Xs.

[238] Salvemini, *Under the Axe of Fascism*, p. 9.

[239] Nitti, *Bolshevism, Fascism and Democracy*, p. 73.

[240] Salvemini, *Under the Axe of Fascism*, p. 9.

[241] Smith, *Mussolini*, p. 41. Original source: *Opera Omnia di Benito Mussolini*, E. and D. Susmel, edit., Florence, 1951–, 15/171 (Aug. 27, 1920), 188; *Opera Omnia di Benito Mussolini*, E. and D. Susmel, edit., Florence, 1951–, 16/44 (Dec. 7, 1920); Opera Omnia di Benito Mussolini, E. and D. Susmel, edit., Florence, 1951–, 17/21 (July 2, 1921); *Opera Omnia di Benito Mussolini*, E. and D. Susmel, edit., Florence, 1951–, 35/68 (Sept. 21, 1920); *Opera Omnia di Benito Mussolini*, E. and D. Susmel, edit., Florence, 1951–, 44/3 Pomba, *La Civiltà fascista*, 13 (Vople).

[242] Payne, *A History of Fascism, 1914–1945*, p. 100.

[243] George Seldes, "The Fascist Road to Ruin: Why Italy Plans the Rape of Ethiopia," The American League Against War and Fascism, 1935. http://fascism-archive.org/books/fascistroadtoruin.html.

[244] Smith, *Mussolini*, p. 47. *Opera Omnia di Benito Mussolini*, 17/295 (Dec. 1, 1921); Bonomi, *Dal socialismo*, p. 117.

[245] *Opera Omnia di Benito Mussolini*, E. and D. Susmel, edit., Florence, 1951–, 14/455–6 (May 20, 1920); *Opera Omnia di Benito Mussolini*, E. and D. Susmel, edit., Florence, 1951–, 15/274, 300.

[246] Smith, *Mussolini*, p. 41. Original source: *Opera Omnia di Benito Mussolini*, E. and D. Susmel, edit., Florence, 1951–, 13/168 (June 4, 1919), *Opera Omnia di Benito Mussolini*, E. and D. Susmel, edit., Florence, 1951–, 15/220 (Sept. 20, 1920).

[247] Ibid.

[248] *Opera Omnia di Benito Mussolini*, E. and D. Susmel, edit., Florence, 1951–, 14/206, 219, 231.

[249] Sources from Italian publications: *Corriere della Sera*, Milan, Mar. 21, 1944; M.D. Tuninetti, Squadrismo, *squadristi piemontesi*, Rome, 1948, pp. 304–308; De Begnac, *Palazzo Venezia: storia di un regime*, Rome, 1950, p. 210; C. Silvestri, *Mussolini, Graziani, e l'antifascismo* (1943–45), Milan, 1949, p. 349.

[250] Delzell, *Mediterranean Fascism 1919–1945*, p. 26.

[251] Alexander J. De Grand, *The Hunchback's Tailor: Giovanni Giolitti and Liberal Italy from the Challenge of Mass Politics to the Rise of Fascism, 1882–1922* (Westport, CT: Praeger Publishers, 2001), p. 242.

[252] Antonio Sonnessa, "Working Class Defence Organization, Anti-Fascist Resistance and the Arditi Del Popolo in Turin, 1919–22," Goldsmiths' College, University of London, in the *European History Quarterly*, 2003, Vol. 33, No. 2, 183–218. http://ehq.sagepub.com/content/33/2/183.short.

[253] Payne, *A History of Fascism, 1914–1945*, p. 100.

[254] Denis Mack Smith, *Italy: A Modern History* (University of Michigan Press, 1969), p. 352.

[255] Hibbert, *Mussolini: The Rise and Fall of Il Duce*, p. 31.

[256] Payne, *A History of Fascism, 1914–1945*, p. 99.

[257] Alessio Ponzio, *Shaping the New Man: Youth Training Regimes in Fascist Italy and Nazi Germany* (University of Wisconsin Press, 2015), p. 30.

[258] Payne, *A History of Fascism, 1914–1945*, p. 100.

[259] Elazar, *The Making of Fascism*, p. 142.

[260] Ibid.

[261] Ibid., p. 93.

[262] Bosworth, *Mussolini's Italy*, p. 175.

[263] Smith, *Mussolini*, p. 38.

[264] Delzell, *Mediterranean Fascism 1919–1945*, p. 26.

[265] Ibid.

[266] Ibid.

[267] Roberts, *The Syndicalist Tradition and Italian Fascism*, p. 289.

[268] Gregor, *The Ideology of Fascism*, p. 307. Source: Ermanno Amicucci, *I 600 giorni di Mussolini* (Rome, Italy: Faro, 1949), p. 143.

[269] Smith, *Mussolini*, p. 45.

[270] Ibid., p. 48.

[271] Giuseppe Finaldi, *Mussolini and Italian Fascism* (London and New York: Routledge, 2013), p. 66.

[272] Christopher Lehmann-Haupt, "Book of the Times," *New York Times*, July 12, 1982.

[273] Smith, *Mussolini*, p. 40.

[274] *Opera Omnia di Benito Mussolini*, E. and D. Susmel, edit., Florence, 1951–, 14/193 (Dec. 12, 1919) 223; Margiotta Broglio, *Italia e Santa Sede*, 80.

[275] *Opera Omnia di Benito Mussolini*, E. and D. Susmel, edit., Florence, 1951–, 16/444 (June 12, 1921); *Opera Omnia di Benito Mussolini*, E. and D. Susmel, edit., Florence, 1951–, 18/17.

[276] *Opera Omnia di Benito Mussolini*, E. and D. Susmel, edit., Florence, 1951–, 20/321.

[277] Stanislao G. Pugliese, ed., *Fascism, Anti-Fascism, and the Resistance in Italy: 1919 to the Present* (Lanham, MD: Rowman & Littlefield Publishers, Inc., 2004), pp. 43–44.

[278] Sternhell, *Neither Right nor Left*, pp. 20–21.

[279] Roger Griffin, "The Palingenetic Core of Fascist Ideology," in *Che cos'è il fascismo? Interpretazioni e prospettive di ricerca*, ed. Alessandro Campi (Rome: Ideazione editrice, 2003), pp. 97–122.

[280] Gregor, *Young Mussolini and the Intellectual Origins of Fascism*, p. 99.

[281] "An Exchange on Fascism" by A. James Gregor, Anthony James Joes, and David D. Roberts, reply by Denis Mack Smith, *The New York Review of Books*, Nov. 6, 1980, quote from Domenico Settembrini's review of *Young Mussolini* by A. James Gregor, *il Giornale dei libri*, Feb. 14, 1980.

[282] Peter Neville, *Mussolini* (Oxon, England, UK and New York, NY: Routledge, 2004), p. 36.

[283] Bosworth, *Mussolini's Italy*, p. 115.

[284] Martha Ackelsberg, "Angelica Balabanoff: 1878–1965," Jewish Women's Archive Encyclopedia. Source: http://jwa.org/encyclopedia/article/balabanoff-angelica.

[285] Gregor, *Italian Fascism and Developmental Dictatorship*, p. 128.

[286] Bob Jessup and Russell Wheatley, *Karl Marx's Social and Political Thought: Critical Assessments of Leading Political Philosophers*, Second series (New York, NY: Routledge, 1999), p. 640.

[287] Ludwig von Mises, *Socialism: An Economic and Sociological Analysis* (Auburn, AL: Ludwig von Mises Institute, 2009), p. 546. First published in 1951.

[288] Marx to Carlo Cafiero, July 29, 1879, *Werke*, XXXIV, p. 384.

[289] Karl Marx, Letter to P.V. Annenkov, Dec. 28, 1846, Selected Correspondence, p. 7. Also published in *Marx Engels Collected Works*, Vol. 38, p. 95, International Publishers, 1975.

[290] Gregor, *The Faces of Janus*, p. 132.

[291] Ibid., p. 133.

[292] Ibid.

[293] Gregor, *Italian Fascism and Developmental Dictatorship*, pp. 59–60.

[294] Ibid., p. 60.

[295] Patrick M. Patterson, teaching course: "World History Since 1500," Chapter: "Stalin's Solution: Interwar Russia."

[296] *History of the Communist Party of the Soviet Union (Bolsheviks)*, Chapter Nine: "The Bolshevik Party in the Period of Transition to the Peaceful Work of Economic Restoration (1921–1925)." This book, which sold millions of copies in the Soviet Union, was commissioned by Stalin in 1935. The main authors were Vilhelms Knoriņš, Yemelyan Yaroslavsky and Pyotr Pospelov, with the chapter on dialectical materialism written by Stalin, who considered himself the general edit. It was first published in 1938. https://www.marxists.org/reference/archive/stalin/works/1939/x01/ch09.htm.

[297] A. James Gregor, *Mussolini's Intellectuals: Fascist Social and Political Thought* (Princeton, NJ: Princeton University Press, 2004), p. 78.

[298] John Whittam, *Fascist Italy* (Manchester, UK: Manchester University Press, 1995), p. 160.

[299] Manfred B. Steger, *The Quest for Evolutionary Socialism: Eduard Bernstein and Social Democracy* (Cambridge, UK: Cambridge University Press, 2006), p. 98, 133.

[300] Walter G. Moss, *A History of Russia, Vol. II: Since 1855*, 2nd ed. (London, UK: Anthem Press, 2005), p. 59.

[301] Manfred B. Steger, *The Quest for Evolutionary Socialism: Eduard Bernstein and Social Democracy* (Cambridge, UK: Cambridge University Press, 2006), pp. 133, 146.

[302] Jackson J. Spielvogel, *Western Civilization, Vol. C: Since 1789*, Ninth ed. (Stamford, CT: Cengage Learning), p. 713.

[303] Berman, *The Primacy of Politics*, p. 2.

[304] "Eduard Bernstein: biography" (1850–1932), FAMpeople.com. http://www.fampeople.com/cat-eduard-bernstein_3.

[305] Alexander Berkman, "The Kronstadt Rebellion," Berlin: Der Sindikalist, 1922. http://www.marxists.org/reference/archive/berkman/1922/kronstadt-rebellion/.

[306] Maurice Parmelle, *Bolshevism, Fascism, and the Liberal-Democratic State* (New York, NY: John Wiley and Son, Inc., 1935), p. 187.

[307] Julan Du (Chinese University of Hong Kong) and Chenggang Xu (London School of Economics), "Market socialism or Capitalism? Evidence from Chinese Financial Market Development," Apr. 2005, International Economic Association, 2005 Round Table on Market and Socialism, Apr. 2005.

[308] Rossoni, *Le idee della ricostruzione*, pp. 82–83, and Sergio Panunzio, *Che cos'tè il fascism*, Milan: Alpes, 1924, pp. 24–25.

[309] Gregor, *The Faces of Janus*, p. 135.

[310] Jacob L. Talmon, *The Myth of the Nation and the Vision of Revolution: The Origins of Ideological Polarization in the 20th Century* (University of California Press, 1981), p. 484. Declaration that came from a 1910 meeting of the Italian Nationalist Association.

[311] A. James Gregor, *Phoenix: Fascism in Our Time* (New Brunswick, NJ: Transaction Press, 2009), p. 191n26.

[312] Benito Mussolini quoted in "Soliloquy for 'freedom' Trimellone island," on the Italian Island of Trimellone, journalist Ivanoe Fossani, one of the last interviews by Mussolini, Mar. 20, 1945, *Opera Omnia*, Vol. 32. Interview is also known as "Testament of Benito Mussolini," or *Testamento di Benito Mussolini*. Also published under "Mussolini confessed to the stars," Publishing House "Latinitas," Rome, 1952, *Intervista di Ivanoe Fossani, Soliloquio in "libertà" all'isola Trimellone, Isola del Trimellone, 20 marzo 1945*.

[313] Mussolini, *Four Speeches on the Corporate State*, pp. 39–40. Eric Jabbari, *Pierre Laroque and the Welfare State in Postwar France* (Oxford University Press, 2012), p. 46.

[314] Benito Mussolini quoted in "Soliloquy for 'freedom' Trimellone island," on the Italian Island of Trimellone, journalist Ivanoe Fossani, Mar. 20, 1945.

[315] Gregor, *The Ideology of Fascism*, p. 307.

[316] John J. Tinghino, *Edmono Rossoni: From Revolutionary Syndicalism to Fascist* (New York, NY: Peter Lang International Academic Publishers, 1991), p. 239.

[317] David D. Roberts, *The Syndicalists and Italian Fascism* (University of Northern Carolina Press, 1979), p. 206.

[318] Adler, *Italian Industrialists from Liberalism to Fascism*, p. 311.

[319] Ibid., pp. 311–312, Ferdinando Cordova, *Sindacati fascisti*, p. 87.

[320] Roland Sarti, "Italian Fascism: Radical Politics and Conservative Goals," chap. 2 in *Fascists and Conservatives: The Radical Right and the Establishment in Twentieth-Century Europe*, ed. Martin Blinkhorn (London and New York: Routledge, 2001), pp. 22–23.

[321] Adler, *Italian Industrialists from Liberalism to Fascism*, p. 312.

[322] *Lavoro d'Italia*, Jan. 6, 1926.

[323] Roberts, *The Syndicalist Tradition and Italian Fascism*, pp. 289–290.

[324] Adler, *Italian Industrialists from Liberalism to Fascism*, p. 311.

[325] Peter Neville, *Mussolini*, second edition (New York, NY: Routledge, 2015), p. 87.

[326] Roland Sarti, "Italian Fascism: Radical Politics and Conservative Goals," chap. 2 in *Fascists and Conservatives: The Radical Right and the Establishment in Twentieth-Century Europe*, ed. Martin Blinkhorn (London and New York: Routledge, 2001), p. 23.

[327] Roland Sarti, *Italy: A Reference Guide from the Renaissance to the Present* (New York, NY: Facts on File, Inc., 2004), p. 534.

[328] "New economic policy and the politprosvet's goals," *Lenin V.I. Collected Works*, v. 44, p. 159.

[329] Gregor, *Italian Fascism and Developmental Dictatorship*, p. 62.

[330] Elisabeth Gaynor Ellis and Anthony Esler, "Revolution and Civil War in Russia," in *World History: The Modern Era* (Boston, MA: Pearson Prentice Hall, 2007), p. 483.

[331] Gregor, *Marxism, Fascism & Totalitarianism*, p. 55.

[332] V.N. Bandera, "New Economic Policy (NEP) as an Economic System," *The Journal of Political Economy*, Vol. 71, No. 3, June 1963, 265–279: p. 268.

[333] Ibid.

[334] V.I. Lenin, "The Tax in Kind," written Apr. 21, 1921, Lenin's *Collected Works*, 1st English Edition, Progress Publishers, Moscow, 1965, Vol. 32, pp. 329–365. http://www.marxists.org/archive/lenin/works/1921/apr/21.htm.

[335] V.I. Lenin, "The Role and Functions of the Trade Unions under the New Economic Policy," LCW, 33, 184. Decision Of The C.C., R.C.P.(B.), Jan. 12, 1922. Written by Lenin Dec. 30, 1921–Jan. 4, 1922. Published in *Pravda* No. 12, Jan. 17, 1922; *Lenin's Collected Works*, 2nd English Edition, Progress Publishers, Moscow, 1965, Vol. 33, pp. 184–196. https://www.marxists.org/archive/lenin/works/cw/pdf/lenin-cw-vol-33.pdf Also at: https://www.marxists.org/archive/lenin/works/1921/dec/30.htm.

[336] Peter Kenez, *History of the Soviet Union from the Beginning to the End* (Cambridge, England: Cambridge University Press, 2006), pp. 47–48.

[337] Gregor, *Marxism, Fascism & Totalitarianism*, p. 267.

[338] Sarfatti, *The Life of Benito Mussolini*, p. 261. https://archive.org/stream/in.ernet.dli.2015.173841/2015.173841.The-Life-Of-Benito-Mussolini_djvu.txt.

[339] Gregor, *Marxism, Fascism & Totalitarianism*, p. 293.

[340] Ibid., p. 268.

[341] Gregor, *The Ideology of Fascism*, p. 299.

[342] Berend, *An Economic History of Twentieth-Century Europe*, pp. 102–103. Original source: Mussolini, *Four Speeches on the Corporate State*, p. 38.

[343] Robert O. Paxton, *Europe in the Twentieth Century* (Harcourt Brace College Publishers, 1997), p. 106.

[344] Johnson, *Modern Times*, p. 90.

[345] Robert G.L. Waite, *The Psychopathic God: Adolf Hitler* (Da Capo Press, Inc., 1977), pp. 304–305.

[346] L.K. Samuels, "Hitler and Mussolini: History's Dirty Little Secret," Feb. 28, 2014. http://www.lksamuels.com/?p=156.

[347] Blamires, *World Fascism: A Historical Encyclopedia*, p. 96.

[348] Noam Chomsky – speech on "Lenin, Trotsky and Socialism & the Soviet Union," Mar. 15, 1989. https://www.youtube.com/watch?v=yQsceZ9skQI.

[349] Benito Mussolini, "Address to the National Corporative Council, Nov. 14, 1933," referred to as his "On the Corporate State." Schnapp, *A Primer of Italian Fascism*, p. 158.

[350] Benito Mussolini, "Address to the National Corporative Council (Nov. 14, 1933) and Senate Speech on the Bill Establishing the Corporations (abridged; Jan. 13, 1934)." Schnapp, *A Primer of Italian Fascism*, p. 158.

[351] Salvemini, *Under the Axe of Fascism*, p. 131.

[352] Benito Mussolini, "Address to the National Corporative Council (Nov. 14, 1933)," Schnapp, *A Primer of Italian Fascism*, p. 160.

[353] Salvemini, *Under the Axe of Fascism*, p. 132.

[354] Gregor, *Italian Fascism and Developmental Dictatorship*, p. 59.

[355] Enrico Leone, *Il sindacalismo*, 2nd revised edition (Milan: Sandron, 1910), pp. 143ff.

[356] Gregor, *Italian Fascism and Developmental Dictatorship*, p. 63.

[357] Payne, *A History of Fascism, 1914–1945*, p. 7.

[358] Berend, *An Economic History of Twentieth-Century Europe*, p. 93.

[359] Anne O'Hare McCormick, "VAST TIDES THAT STIR THE CAPITAL; Behind the Tremendous Activity and the Revolutionary Experiments in Washington There Is an Impetus That Derives Directly from a People Demanding Immediate Steps to Meet the Crisis THE STIRRING TIDES OF WASHINGTON," *New York Times*, May 7, 1933.

[360] Mises, *Human Action*, p. 814.

[361] Sidney and Beatrice Webb, *Constitutions for the Socialist Commonwealth of Great Britain* (London, UK and New York, NY: Longmans, Green & Co., 1920).

[362] Mises, *Planned Chaos*, p. 73.

[363] Alberto Spektorowski and Liza Ireni-Saban, *Politics of Eugenics: Productionism, Population, and National Welfare (Extremism and Democracy)* (New York, NY: Routledge, 2013), p. 33.

[364] Mussolini "La legge sindacale," *Opera Omnia di Benito Mussolini*, E. and D. Susmel, Florence, edit., 1951–, XXII, pp. 92f.

[365] Alfredo Rocco, "Discorso alla Camera dei deputati," *Scritti e discorsi politici*, III, 991, 995.

[366] Alfredo Rocco, "The Political Doctrine of Fascism," speech delivered at Perugia, Aug. 30, 1925. Copy of speech printed in Schnapp, *A Primer of Italian Fascism*, p. 112.

[367] Richman, "Fascism." http://www.econlib.org/library/Enc/Fascism.html.

[368] Adler, *Italian Industrialists from Liberalism to Fascism*, p. 347; original source: Rosario Romeo, *Breve Storia della grande industria in Italia 1861/1961*, Bologna, 1975, pp. 173–174; Roland Sarti, *Fascism and the Industrial Leadership in Italy, 1919–40: A Study in the Expansion of Private Power Under Fascism*, 1968, p. 214.

[369] Steve Bastow and James Martin, *Third Way Discourse: European Ideologies in the Twentieth Century* (Edinburgh, Scotland: Edinburgh University Press LTD., 2003), p. 36.

[370] Townley, *Mussolini and Italy*, p. 202.

[371] Blamires, *World Fascism: A Historical Encyclopedia*, pp. 188–189.

[372] James Strachey Barnes, *Universal Aspects of Fascism* (London, UK: Williams and Norgate, 1928), pp. 113–114. This book bears the imprimatur of Benito Mussolini.

[373] Ibid., p. 113.

[374] Howard M. Sachar, *The Assassination of Europe, 1918–1942: A Political History* (Toronto, Canada: University of Toronto Press, 2015), p. 48.

[375] Payne, *A History of Fascism, 1914–1945*, p. 110.

[376] Jim Powell, "The Economic Leadership Secrets of Benito Mussolini," *Forbes*, Feb. 22, 2012. http://www.forbes.com/sites/jimpowell/2012/02/22/the-economic-leadership-secrets-of-benito-mussolini/.

[377] Germà Bel, "The First Privatization: Selling SOEs and Privatizing Public Monopolies in Fascist Italy (1922–1925)," Universitat de Barcelona (GiM-IREA), 2009. https://ideas.repec.org/p/bar/bedcje/2009235.html.

[378] Salvemini, *Under the Axe of Fascism*, p. 134.

[379] There are a number of versions of the "Doctrine of Fascism." The original and authorized version was translated into English by Jane Soames in 1933. Another version came out in 1935. This quote is apparently from the 1935 version from published by Firenze: Vallecchi Editore, p. 13.

[380] Mussolini, *My Autobiography*, p. 280.

[381] Walter Lippmann, *The Good Society* (New Brunswick, NJ: Transaction Publishers, 2009), p. 51. First published in 1937.

[382] Newton, *The Path to Tyranny*, p. 170.

[383] Jeffrey M. Herbener, "The Vampire Economy: Italy, Germany, and the US," Mises Institute, Oct. 13, 2005. http://mises.org/daily/1935.

[384] Newton, *The Path to Tyranny*, p. 171.

[385] De Grand, *Fascist Italy and Nazi Germany*, p. 52.

[386] Franco Amatori, Robert Millward, and Pier Angelo Toninelli, eds., *Reappraising State-Owned Enterprise: A Comparison of the UK and Italy* (New York, NY: Routledge, 2011), p. 49.

[387] De Grand, *Fascist Italy and Nazi Germany*, p. 52.

[388] Townley, *Mussolini and Italy*, p. 77.

[389] John Pollard, *The Fascist Experience in Italy* (New York, NY: Routledge, 1998), p. 140.

[390] Martin Blinkhorn, *Mussolini and Fascist Italy* (New York, NY: Routledge, 1991), p. 22.

[391] Sternhell, *Neither Right nor Left*, p. 203.

[392] Salvemini, *Under the Axe of Fascism*, p. 11.

[393] Richman, "Fascism."

[394] Salvemini, *Under the Axe of Fascism*, p. 418.

[395] Richman, "Fascism."

[396] Gregor, *Italian Fascism and Developmental Dictatorship*, p. 158.

[397] De Grand, *Italian Fascism: Its Origins & Development*, p. 106.

[398] Newton, *The Path to Tyranny*, p. 173.

[399] De Grand, *Italian Fascism: Its Origins & Development*, p. 108. Italy's deficit "ballooned from two to sixteen billion lire between 1934 and 1937."

[400] Paul Corner, *The Fascist Party & Popular Opinion in Mussolini's Italy* (Oxford, UK: Oxford University Press, 2012), p. 200.

[401] De Grand, *Fascist Italy and Nazi Germany*, p. 52.

[402] Jeffrey M. Herbener, "The Vampire Economy: Italy, Germany, and the US," Mises Institute, Oct. 13, 2005.

[403] Jim Powell, "The Economic Leadership Secrets of Benito Mussolini," *Forbes*, Feb. 22, 2012.

[404]George Seldes, "The Fascist Road to Ruin: Why Italy Plans the Rape of Ethiopia," The American League Against War and Fascism, 1935.

[405]Jim Powell, "The Economic Leadership Secrets of Benito Mussolini," *Forbes*, Feb. 22, 2012.

[406]Toniolo, *The Oxford Handbook of the Italian Economy Since Unification*, p. 59; Mussolini's speech to the Chamber of Deputies was on May 26, 1934.

[407]Carl Schmidt, *The Corporate State in Action* (London, UK: Victor Gollancz LTD., 1939), pp. 153–176.

[408]Costanza A. Russo, "Bank Nationalizations of the 1930s in Italy: The IRI Formula," *Theoretical Inquiries in Law*, Vol. 13:407 (2012), p. 408.

[409]Toniolo, *The Oxford Handbook of the Italian Economy Since Unification*, p. 59.

[410]Ibid.

[411]Knight, *Mussolini and Fascism*, p. 65.

[412]Martin Blinkhorn, *Mussolini and Fascist Italy* (New York, NY: Routledge, 1991), p. 26.

[413]Ibid.

[414]Karin Priester, "Fascism in Italy between the Poles of Reactionary Thought and Modernity," chap. 4 in *Routes into the Abyss: Coping with Crises in the 1930s*, eds. Helmut Konrad and Wolfgang Maderthaner (Berghahn Books, 2013), p. 67.

[415]Hugh Rockoff, *Drastic Messages: A History of Wage and Price Controls in the United States* (New York, NY: Cambridge University Press, 1984), p. 86.

[416]Claire Giordano, Gustavo Piga, Giovanni Trovato, "Fascist price and wage policies and Italy's industrial Great Depression," p. 15, Nov. 18, 2011, Dipartimento di Economia e Istituzioni, Universitҳa di Roma "Tor Vergata," Via Columbia 2, 00133 Rome, Italy.

[417]Mussolini: Speech on June 10, 1940, Declaration of War on France and England.

[418]Gregor, *The Ideology of Fascism*, p. 307.

[419]Gregor, *The Fascist Persuasion in Radical Politics*, p. 312.

[420]Smith, *Mussolini*, p. 311.

[421]Stephen J. Lee, *European Dictatorships 1918–1945*, 3rd ed. (New York, NY: Routledge, 2008), p. 17.

[422]Smith, *Mussolini*, p. 311. (*Corriere della Sera*, Apr. 9, 1944; Carlo Silvestri, *Mussolini*, 339).

[423]Smith, *Mussolini*, p. 312, *Opera Omnia di Benito Mussolini* 32/57, Mar. 3, 1944.

[424]Bosworth, *Mussolini's Italy*, p. 523.

[425]Gregor, *The Ideology of Fascism*, pp. 356f, 388.

[426]Smith, *Mussolini*, p. 312.

[427]Giuseppe Parlato, "The fascist left," Il Mulino, Bologna, 2000, p. 76.

[428]Luke Leonello Rimbotti, "the left-wing fascism," Editions Seventh Seal, Rome, 1989, p. 121.

[429]Ibid., p. 122.

[430]De Grand, *Italian Fascism: Its Origins & Development*, p. 134.

[431] Stephen J. Lee, *European Dictatorships 1918–1945*, 3rd ed. (New York, NY: Routledge, 2008), pp. 171–172.

[432] Norling, *Revolutionary Fascism*, p. 103. Mussolini's cabinet council approved the "Socialization" bill of laws for Italy's new economic structure on Feb. 12, 1944.

[433] Bosworth, *Mussolini's Italy*, p. 523.

[434] Norling, *Revolutionary Fascism*, pp. 119–120. Speech given by Mussolini to a group of Milanese Fascist veterans and Black Brigade "Resega" officers on Oct. 14, 1944.

[435] Cf. Michaels' report, "Le *leggi sociali del Fascismo giudicate all'estero*," *Lavoro d'Italia*, Nov. 14, 1928.

[436] Mussolini, *My Autobiography*, p. 277.

[437] Gregor, *Italian Fascism and Developmental Dictatorship*, p. 257.

[438] Ibid., p. 263.

[439] Ibid., pp. 256–263.

[440] Davide Rodogno, *Fascism's European Empire: Italian Occupation during the Second World War* (Cambridge University Press, 2006), p. 44.

[441] Gregor, *Italian Fascism and Developmental Dictatorship*, p. 260.

[442] Christopher Hibbert, *Benito Mussolini: A Biography* (Geneva, Switzerland: Heron Books, 1962), p. 56.

[443] Nicholas Farrell, *Mussolini: A New Life* (London, UK: Phoenix, 2004), p. 233.

[444] Flynn, *As We Go Marching*, pp. 49–50.

[445] Ibid., p. 51. Also see Gaetano Salvemini, "Twelve Years of Fascist Finance," *Foreign Affairs*, Apr. 1935, Vol. 13, No. 3, p. 463.

[446] Ibid., p. 50. See *New York Times*, Aug. 8, 1943.

[447] Ibid., pp. 50–51.

[448] Pipes, *Russia Under the Bolshevik Regime*, p. 243. Speech to Chamber of Deputies on Dec. 9, 1928.

[449] *Scritti e discorsi di Benito Mussolini* (Writings and Discourses of Mussolini, 5: 168), 12 Volumes, Milano, Hoepli, 1934–1940. Johnson, *Modern Times*, p. 101.

[450] Goldberg, *Liberal Fascism*, p. 34.

[451] Margherita Sarfatti, *My Fault: Mussolini As I Knew Him*, ed. Brian R. Sullivan (Enigma Books, 2014), p. 41.

[452] Sarfatti, *The Life of Benito Mussolini*, p. 278. According to Sarfatti, Lenin had spoken these words in "addressing a deputation of Italian Socialists who visited Russia in 1919 and 1920." https://archive.org/stream/in.ernet.dli.2015.173841/2015.173841. The-Life-Of-Benito-Mussolini_djvu.txt.

[453] Ibid.

[454] Stanley G. Payne, "Soviet Policy and the Comintern in the Early Years 1917–1925," chap. 1 in *The Spanish Civil War, the Soviet Union, and Communism* (New Haven, CT: Yale University Press, 2004), p. 5.

[455] David Ramsey Steele, "The Mystery of Fascism," first published in *Liberty*, Vol. 15, No. 11, Nov. 2001.

[456] Fabian Society Annual Report 1929–31.

[457]The Fabian Society-Aquilion, extracts from Pierre de Villemarest's book *Facts & Chronicles Denied to the Public*, Vol. 1.

[458]Bret Rubin, "The Rise and Fall of British Fascism: Sir Oswald Mosley and the British Union of Fascists," *Intersections, (Journal of the Comparative History of Ideas)*, University of Washington, Seattle, Vol. 11, No. 2, Autumn 2010, p. 346. https://depts. washington.edu/chid/intersections_Autumn_2010/Rubin.html.

[459]Michael Mann, *Fascists* (New York, NY: Cambridge University Press, 2006), p. 7.

[460]Letter to *The Times* of London, Apr. 26, 1968, p. 11.

[461]Oswald Mosley, *Tomorrow We Live* – British Union Policy 3d, 1938.

[462]Bret Rubin, "The Rise and Fall of British Fascism: Sir Oswald Mosley and the British Union of Fascists," *Intersections, (Journal of the Comparative History of Ideas)*, University of Washington, Seattle, Vol. 11, No. 2, Autumn 2010, p. 323.

[463]John S. Partington, "H.G. Wells: A Political Life," Journal article in *Utopian Studies*, Vol. 19, 2008.

[464]Philip Coupland, "H.G. Wells's 'Liberal Fascism,'" *Journal of Contemporary History* 35, No. 4, Oct. 2000, p. 549.

[465]Fred Siegel, "The Godfather of American Liberalism," *City Journal*, Vol. 19, No. 2, Spring 2009.

[466]Ibid.

[467]Martin Kitchen, *Europe Between the Wars*, second ed. (New York, NY: Routledge, 2013), p. 25.

[468]Griffith, *Socialism and Superior Brains*, p. 264. Originally from Bernard Shaw, *The News Chronicle*, "The Blackshirt Challenge," Jan. 1934.

[469]Richard Griffiths, *Fellow Travellers of the Right: British Enthusiasts for Nazi Germany, 1933-39* (London, UK: Trinity Press, 1980), p. 259.

[470]Griffith, *Socialism and Superior Brains*, p. 253. Shaw made this statement in the *Manchester Guardian* in 1927.

[471]Ibid., p. 266.

[472]Ibid., p. 263.

[473]Ibid., p. 253. Also see "Bernard Shaw's Defence of Mussolini," Letter from G. Bernard Shaw to a friend Feb. 7, 1927.

[474]Griffith, *Socialism and Superior Brains*, p. 256. From a 1933 lecture by Shaw.

[475]Ibid.

[476]Ibid., p. 255.

[477]Arthur M. Schlesinger Jr., *The Politics of Upheaval: 1935-1936 (The Age of Roosevelt, Vol. III)* (New York, NY: Mariner Book: Houghton Mifflin Co., 2003), p. 147.

[478]Ibid., p. 648.

[479]Nitti, *Bolshevism, Fascism and Democracy*, p. 130.

[480]Ibid., p. 162.

[481]Ibid., pp. 126-127.

[482]Ibid., pp. 72-73.

[483]MacGregor Knox, *Mussolini Unleashed, 1939-1941: Politics and Strategy in Italy's Last War* (New York, NY: Cambridge University Press, 1982), p. 63.

[484]John Tytell, *Ezra Pound: The Solitary Volcano* (New York, NY: Anchor Press, 1987), p. 254.

[485]Redman, *Ezra Pound and Italian Fascism*, p. 108.

[486]John Hollander, *Political Pilgrims: Western Intellectuals in Search of the Good Society* (New Brunswick, NJ: Transaction Publishers, 1998), p. 169n. First published in 1981 by Oxford University Press.

[487]Schivelbusch, *Three New Deals*, p. 31. FDR's comments on Benito Mussolini in 1933.

[488]Diggins, *Mussolini and Fascism*, pp. 279–281.

[489]Whalen, *Mr. New York*, p. 188.

[490]"Says Roosevelt Uses Karl Marx's Ideas; Theodore Dreiser Adds That So Do Hitler and Stalin," *New York Times*, Aug. 22, 1938, p. 3.

[491]Schivelbusch, *Three New Deals*, pp. 28–29.

[492]Roger Shaw, "Fascism and the New Deal," *The North American Review*, Vol. 238, No. 6, Dec. 1934, pp. 559–564.

[493]Bruce Walker, "Fascists and Bolsheviks as friends," *Canada Free Press*, Jan. 31, 2008. https://canadafreepress.com/article/fascists-and-bolsheviks-as-friends.

[494]Payne, *A History of Fascism, 1914–1945*, p. 230.

[495]Anton Antonov-Ovseyenko, *The Time of Stalin: Portrait of a Tyranny*, trans. George Saunders (New York, NY: Harper and Row, 1981), p. 257.

[496]MacGregor Knox, *Mussolini Unleashed, 1939–1941: Politics and Strategy in Italy's Last War* (New York, NY: Cambridge University Press, 1982), pp. 63–64. Also noted in MacGregor Knox, *To the Threshold of Power 1922/33*, vol. 1 (New York, NY: Cambridge University Press, 2007), p. 11. Knox's original source cited is *Galeazzo Ciano Diario, 1937–1943* (Milan, 1980), entry for Oct. 16, 1939.

[497]Kemechey, *Il Duce*, p. 133.

[498]R.J.B. Bosworth, *Mussolini* (New York, NY: Bloomsbury Academic, 2011), p. 511. Original source: The Fascist newspaper *La Verità*, Mar. 1945.

[499]Gregor, *The Faces of Janus*, p. 168. This observation comes from Fabio Gabrielli, *"La Verità" e la sua avventura* (Milan: n.p., 1984).

[500]"Civil War Spread over Austria; Italian Army on Alert at Border," *Associated Press*, published in the *Albany Evening News*, July 26, 1934.

[501]"Engelbert Dollfuss: biography," FAMpeople.org. http://www.fampeople.com/cat-engelbert-dollfuss.

[502]Ethan J. Hollander, *Italian Fascism and the Jews* (PDF), University of California, 1997. Mussolini rejected biological racism (particularly Nordicism and Germanicism).

[503]P.V. Cannistraro, "Mussolini's Cultural Revolution: Fascist or Nationalist?" *Journal of Contemporary History* (SAGE Journals Online) 7 no. 3 (Apr. 1972): 115–139. http://jch.sagepub.com/content/7/3/115.full.pdf+html.

[504]Aaron Gillette, *Racial Theories in Fascist Italy* (New York, NY: Routledge, 2002), p. 44. Original source: Ludwig, *Talks with Mussolini*, pp. 69–70.

[505] Alexander Stille, "The Double Bind of Italian Jews: Acceptance and Assimilation," chap. 1 in *Jews in Italy under Fascist and Nazi Rule, 1922–1945*, ed. Joshua D. Zimmerman (New York, NY: Cambridge University Press, 2005) p. 26.

[506] Paxton, *The Anatomy of Fascism*, p. 166.

[507] Peter Egill Brownfeld, "The Italian Holocaust: The Story of an Assimilated Jewish Community," Fall 2003 issue. The American Council for Judaism. Source: http://www.acjna.org/acjna/articles_detail.aspx?id=300.

[508] Mark Godfrey, *Abstraction and the Holocaust* (New Haven, CT: Yale University Press, 2007), p. 194.

[509] Peter Egill Brownfeld, "The Italian Holocaust: The Story of an Assimilated Jewish Community," Fall 2003 issue. The American Council for Judaism.

[510] Franklin Hugh Adler, "Why Mussolini turned on the Jews," *Patterns of Prejudice*, Vol. 39, Issue 3, 2005, pp. 285–300.

[511] Peter Egill Brownfeld, "The Italian Holocaust: The Story of an Assimilated Jewish Community," Fall 2003 issue. The American Council for Judaism.

[512] Paxton, *The Anatomy of Fascism*, p. 166.

[513] Saviona Mane, "The Jewish Mother of Fascism," *Haaretz* newspaper in Israel, July 6, 2006. https://www.haaretz.com/1.4856144.

[514] Joshua D. Zimmerman, ed., *Jews in Italy under Fascist and Nazi Rule, 1922–1945* (New York, NY: Cambridge University Press, 2005), p. 2.

[515] Bernhard R. Kroener, Rolf-Dieter Müller, and Hans Umbreit, *Germany and the Second World War: Volume V/II: Organization and Mobilization in the German Sphere of Power* (New York, NY: Oxford University Press, Inc., 2003), p. 273.

[516] "Milan Marks Holocaust Memorial Day on Platform 21," *Italy Today*, Jan. 27, 2013. https://www.italymagazine.com/italy/history/milan-marks-holocaust-memorial-day-platform-21.

[517] Smith, *Mussolini*, p. 8.

[518] Murray R. Thomas, *Religion in Schools: Controversies Around the World* (Westport, CT: Praeger Publishers, 2006), p. 111.

[519] James A. Haught, *2000 Years of Disbelief: Famous People with the Courage to Doubt* (Amherst, NY: Prometheus Books, 1996), p. 256.

[520] Smith, *Mussolini*, p. 15.

[521] "Religion: Benito a Christian?" *Time* magazine, Aug. 25, 1924.

[522] Maurice Parmelle, *Bolshevism, Fascism, and the Liberal-Democratic State* (New York, NY: John Wiley and Son, Inc., 1935), p. 190.

[523] Roberts, *The Syndicalist Tradition and Italian Fascism*, p. 187.

[524] Morgan, *Fascism in Europe*, p. 151.

[525] Rachele Mussolini, *Mussolini: An Intimate Biography* (New York, NY: Pocket Books, 1977), p. 131. Originally published by William Morrow in 1974.

[526] John Whittam, *Fascist Italy* (Manchester, UK: Manchester University Press, 1995), p. 76.

[527] Hamish Macdonald, *Mussolini and Italian Fascism* (Cheltenham, UK: Stanley Thornes Publishers, LTD, 1999), p. 28.

[528]"Pius XI; POPE," *Encyclopaedia Britannica Online*; web Apr. 2013. http://www. britannica.com/EBchecked/topic/462393/Pius-XI.

[529]Joseph Bottum and David G. Dalin, eds., *The Pius War: The Responses to the Critics of Pius XII* (Lexington Books, 2004), p. 118, in chapter of "An Annotated Bibliography of Works on Pius XII, the Second World War and the Holocaust" by William Doino Jr. Original source: *Tablet*, Feb. 18, 1939, p. 205, a Catholic weekly published in Great Britain.

[530]Knight, *Mussolini and Fascism*, p. 49.

[531]Morgan, *Fascism in Europe*, p. 151.

[532]Smith, *Mussolini*, p. 162.

[533]Ibid.

[534]Ibid., pp. 222–223.

[535]Ibid.

[536]Ibid.

[537]Montserrat Guidbernau, "Nationalism, Racism and Fascism," chap. 4 in *Nationalisms: The Nation-State and Nationalism in the Twentieth Century*, 1st ed. (Polity Press, 1996).

[538]Ion Mihai Pacepa and Ronald J. Rychlak, *Disinformation: Former Spy Chief Reveals Secret Strategies for Undermining Freedom, Attacking Religion, and Promoting Terrorism* (Washington D.C.: WND Books Inc., 2013), pp. 62–63. Ion Mihai Pacepa was the highest-ranking Soviet bloc intelligence official to defect to the West.

[539]George Ritzer, *Introduction to Sociology* (Los Angeles, CA: Sage Publishers, Inc., 2013), p. 455.

[540]Paul Baxa, *Roads and Ruins: The Symbolic Landscape of Fascist Rome* (Toronto: University of Toronto Press, Inc., 2010), p. 130.

[541]Robert Cowley and Geoffrey Parker, eds., *The Reader's Companion to Military History* (New York, NY: Houghton Mifflin Harcourt Publishing Company, 1996), p. 316.

[542]David McKnight is Associate Professor, Journalism and Media Research Centre at UNSW Australia. See chap. 1 in David McKnight, *Beyond Right and Left: New Politics and the Culture War* (Sydney, Allen & Unwin, 2005). http://www.davidmcknight. com.au/archives/2005/09/beyond-right-and-left-introduction.

[543]Charles Armstrong, "One-Family Rule: North Korea's Hereditary Authoritarianism," *World Politics Review*, Feb. 18, 2014.

[544]Young W. Kihl and Hong Nack Kim, eds., *North Korea: The Politics of Regime Survival* (Armonk, NY: M.E. Sharpe, Inc., 2006), pp. 55–56.

[545]B.R. Myers, "The Cleanest Race," *New York Times*, Jan. 2, 2010.

[546]B.R. Myers, *The Cleanest Race: How North Koreans See Themselves and Why It Matters* (New York, NY: Melville House Publishing, 2010).

[547]Albert J. Jongman, ed., *Contemporary Genocides: Causes, Cases, Consequences* (Leiden: Programma Interdisciplinair Onderzoek naar Oorzaken van Mensenrechtenschendingen, 1996), p. 61. See esp. "The Case of Cambodia."

[548] BBC *Summary of World Broadcasts*, FE/5813/A3/2, May 15, 1978. May 10, 1978 broadcast from Pol Pot in Phnom Penh.

[549] Ben Kiernan, "External and Indigenous Sources of Khmer Rouge Ideology," chap. 8 in *The Third Indochina War: Conflict Between China, Vietnam and Cambodia, 1972–79*, eds. Odd Arne Westad and Sophie Quinn-Judge (London and New York, 2006), pp. 189–190.

[550] Gregor, *The Fascist Persuasion in Radical Politics*, pp. 131–132.

[551] Chen, *The Prospects for Liberal Nationalism in Post-Leninist States*, p. 61.

[552] Ibid., p. 63.

[553] Ibid., p. 18.

[554] Erik van Ree, *The Political Thought of Joseph Stalin: A Study in Twentieth-Century Revolutionary Patriotism* (London, UK and New York, NY: RoutledgeCurzon, 2002), p. 49.

[555] Lenore A. Grenoble, *Language Policy in the Soviet Union* (New York, NY: Kluwer Academic Publishers, 2003), p. 41.

[556] Nimni, *Marxism and Nationalism*, p. 4.

[557] Erik van Ree, *The Political Thought of Joseph Stalin: A Study in Twentieth-Century Revolutionary Patriotism* (London, UK and New York, NY: RoutledgeCurzon, 2002), p. 49.

[558] Nimni, *Marxism and Nationalism*, pp. 14, 16.

[559] Vladislav Zubok and Constantine Pleshakov, *Inside the Kremlin's Cold War: From Stalin to Khrushchev* (Cambridge: MA, Harvard University Press, 1996), p. 3.

[560] Anne Sa'adah, *Contemporary France: A Democratic Education* (Lanham, MD and Oxford, UK: Rowman Littlefield & Publishers, Inc., 2003), pp. 17–20.

[561] Angel Smith and Stefan Berger, eds., *Nationalism, Labour and Ethnicity 1870 1939* (Manchester, UK and New York, NY: Manchester University Press, 1999), p. 30.

[562] Klemens Von Klemperer, "Towards a Fourth Reich? The History of National Bolshevism in Germany," *Review of Politics* 13 (2): 1951, pp. 191–210.

[563] Martin A. Lee, *The Beast Reawakens* (New York, NY: Warner Books, 1998), p. 315.

[564] Nimni, *Marxism and Nationalism*, p. 63.

[565] Ibid., p. 63.

[566] Ibid., p. 64.

[567] Eva Fogelman, *Conscience and Courage: Rescuers of Jews During the Holocaust* (New York, NY: Anchor, 1995).

[568] Mises, *Planned Chaos*, p. 71.

[569] Hans Jürgen Eysenck, "Politics and Personality," chap. 7 in *Sense and Nonsense in Psychology* (Baltimore and London: Penguin Books, 1957). http://www.ditext.com/eysenck/politics.html.

[570] Arlin James Benjamin, Jr., "Chasing the Elusive Left-Wing Authoritarians: An Examination of Altemeyer's Right-Wing Authoritarianism and Left-Wing Authoritarianism Scales," *National Social Science Journal*, Vol. 43 (1), 7–13, 2014. Benjamin is associate professor of social psychology at the University of Arkansas-Fort Smith. http://www.nssa.us/journals/pdf/NSS_Journal_43_1.pdf.

[571] Ibid.

[572] J.J. Ray, "Half of all authoritarians are Left-wing: A reply to Eysenck and Stone," *Political Psychology*, 4, 139–144, 1983. http://jonjayray.tripod.com/halfauth.html.

[573] Advocates for Self-Government version of the Nolan Chart. http://theadvocates.org/quiz/quiz.php.

[574] Peter Jonathan Davies and Derek Lynch, *The Routledge Companion to Fascism and the Far Right* (UK: Routledge, 2002), p. 143.

[575] Mark Mazower, *Dark Continent: Europe's Twentieth Century*, new ed. (New York, NY: Penguin Group, 1999), p. 29.

[576] Benito Mussolini, "The Doctrine of Fascism" (*"La dottrina del fascism"*). The 1935 edition from Vallecchi: Editore Firenze, p. 15.

[577] L.K. Samuels, "Hitler and Mussolini: History's Dirty Little Secret," Feb. 28, 2014. http://www.lksamuels.com/?p=156.

[578] Roberts, *The Syndicalist Tradition and Italian Fascism*, p. 297.

[579] Toler, *The Everything Guide to Understanding Socialism*, p. 186.

[580] Adler, *Italian Industrialists from Liberalism to Fascism*, p. 351.

[581] Salvemini, *The Fate of Trade Unions Under Fascism*, p. 35.

[582] Ibid.

[583] *Opera Omnia di Benito Mussolini*, E. and D. Susmel, edit., Florence, 1951–, 14/455–6 (May 20, 1920); *Opera Omnia di Benito Mussolini*, E. and D. Susmel, edit., Florence, 1951–, 15/274, 300.

[584] Smith, *Mussolini*, p. 41.

[585] Rod Jones, "Factory committees in the Russian revolution," libcom.org, Aug. 7, 2005. https://libcom.org/library/factory-committees-russian-revolution-rod-jones.

[586] Ibid.

[587] Edmund Clingan, *Introduction to Modern Western Civilization* (Bloomington, IN: iUniverse, 2011), p. 207.

[588] Gompers and Walling, *Out of Their Own Mouths*, p. 76.

[589] Ibid., p. 79.

[590] Ida Mett, "Petrograd on the Eve of Kronstadt," chap. 2 in *The Kronstadt Commune*. Originally written in 1938, published in *Solidarity Pamphlet 27*, Nov. 1967. http://flag.blackened.net/revolt/russia/mett/petro_eve.html.

4. National Socialism and Marxism

> Marxism has led to Fascism and National-Socialism, because, in all essentials, it is Fascism and National Socialism.
>
> —Frederick Augustus Voigt[1]

> It is not Germany that will turn Bolshevist, but Bolshevism that will become a sort of National Socialism. Besides, there is more that binds us to Bolshevism than separates us from it... The petit bourgeois Social-Democrat and the trade-union boss will never make a National Socialist, but the Communist always will.
>
> —Adolf Hitler[2]

> If you love our country you are national, and if you love our people you are a socialist.
>
> —Sir Oswald Mosley, founder of the British Union of Fascists[3]

> [T]here is a difference between the theoretical knowledge of socialism and the practical life of socialism. People are not born socialists, but must first be taught how to become them.
>
> —Adolf Hitler[4]

The current political spectrum is not only faulty but fundamentally backward. German National Socialism and Marxism are closely aligned on the same side of the political dichotomy—whether one wants to peg them on left or right. These two authoritarian monstrosities have so many ideological and political credentials in common that it is ludicrous to treat them as complete polar opposites on any political compass. I have provided a plethora of historical data, facts, and quotations that demonstrate German National Socialism as a shifting and shadowy movement, strongly influenced by Marxism, while reflecting the left-wing collectivism of the early utopian socialists.

Just the terms from which the German acronym comes—the National Socialist German Workers' Party—imply a nationalist version of socialism. Founded in 1920, most members of the Nazi party (also known outside of Germany in the 1920s as the National Socialist Labor Party)[5] proudly self-described themselves as socialists and even radical revolutionaries, eager to destroy capitalism, Jewish banking interests, the greedy bourgeois class, classical liberalism, individualism, parliamentary process and the international aspect of Marxism. Nazis believed in a centralized "classless" socialist state embodied with egalitarian values and policies of "social justice," but reserved its demands for equality for only the racial purity of German-Aryan blood. According to professor of history, Andrei A. Znamenski, egalitarianism and socialism were like two peas in a pod, writing:

> Strictly speaking, the message of National Socialism was not radically different from that of other forms of egalitarianism and socialism: strong antibourgeois sentiments expressed through a radical empowerment of a selected group of people at the expense of other groups... What made National Socialism novel and different from earlier forms of socialism was an attempt to blend the ideas of social justice and revolutionary nationalism.[6]

As for its origins, Nazism evolved from a mixed-matched bag of utopian socialist, Marxist, and neo-socialist theories, mostly from France, along with the collectivity of a "people's community" (*Volksgemeinschaft*) where citizens within a national family would sacrifice themselves for the greater good. Nazism, like its cousin, Italian Fascism, was a socialist alternative to the socioeconomic tornadoes that had swept destruction across the communist Russian landscape. But Hitler's political party was not the first one to have electoral success under the moniker "National Socialist." On December 14, 1918, John Joseph "Jack" Jones of the National Socialist Party was elected to the British House of Commons.[7] A little later another English National Socialist politician, D.D. Irving, was elected to the British Parliament with the help of the Labor Party.[8]

There were earlier National Socialist parties, mostly confined to the Austro-Hungarian Empire, where the Czech National Socialist Party came into the spotlight in 1898. Another, the German Workers Party, which became established in Bohemia in 1903, was renamed the German National Socialist Workers' Party in May 1918, one splitting into an Austrian branch and the other into a Sudetenland branch in the territories of Bohemia.[9] This nationalistic socialism ideology had been gaining strength for decades before the Nazis came along. This nationalistic-tribal impulse caused the Second International to dissolve in 1916. Many of its members, consisting of European socialist and labor parties, decided to abandon internationalism in order to support their countries' nationalistic causes in the Great War. Nationalism was seen as a way to maintain a particular culture and language within a socialist framework. It had become popular among the socialist political elites and theoreticians, shattered the solidarity of international socialism, and added the outbreak of nationalistic socialist movements.

Some experts argued that the marriage of nationalism with socialism started to crystallize after the crisis of liberalism came to the forefront during the 1873 crash of the Vienna Stock Exchange. Others point to the "crisis of Marxism" and Eduard Bernstein's revisionist movement in the late 1890s that drove socialists towards a socialism within a one-nation paradigm.

Despite the party's long socialist heritage, some still contend that the Nazis were not socialists. Adolf Hitler (1889–1945) once displayed some regret for selecting the word "Socialist" to describe his party's ideology. However, he also mused that he would rather have inserted the communist-inspired phrase "social revolutionary" into the Nazi party's name.[10] This should not be surprising, given that fact that Hitler in 1919 took a position in the Communist run Bavarian Soviet Republic, wearing in public a red armband, according to a number of historians including Thomas Weber.[11] And a little later after the Bavarian Soviet Republic was defeated, Hitler claimed to be a "social democrat."[12]

The definition of socialism can vary dramatically among individuals, but many have argued that the core of socialism entails state *control* of the means of production, whereas, under communism, the state *owns* the means of production. This distinction makes sense, since many socialists themselves argued that, "according to Karl Marx, only when workers control the means of production for their own benefit can exploitation be abolished."[13] By the mere fact that Hitler's Nazi regime imposed strict state controls over Germany's economy and private ownership, including partial nationalization, Nazism pitched its tent in the socialist camp, also huddling next to statist, modern-day leftism, communists and social democrats. And within this collectivist menagerie, German Nazism and Italian Fascism had simply strayed a little to the right side of Russian Sovietism, and a little to the left of the Social Democracy.

Hitler and the Nationalistic Socialists

Many historians, including Conan Fischer, have concluded that the Hitler and Nazi leaders were sincere over their usage of the word "socialist" in their namesake, believing that it was inseparable from nationalism.[14] In his book, *The Rise of the Nazis*, Fischer referred to Nazism as a "form of socialism" which "could appeal across class barriers with far greater ease than could Marxist Socialism."[15] In the *Lost Literature of Socialism*, English historian George Watson asserted that "It is now clear beyond all reasonable doubt that Hitler and his associates believed they were socialists, and others, including democratic socialists, thought so too."[16] In *Adolf Hitler: The Definitive Biography*, Pulitzer Prize-winning historian John Toland described Hitler as both a socialist and an opportunist explaining:

> Hitler's socialism was his own and subordinate to his secret aims. His concept of organized economy was close to genuine socialism, but he would be a socialist only so long as it served the greater goal. He had the bohemian's rather than the revolutionary's disdain for private property and wanted only enough capital to rebuild the army and restore the economy so that he could lead Germany to its proper destiny.[17]

Hitler himself repeated his desire to achieve socialism many times. In his famous 1920 "Why We Are Anti-Semite" speech, Hitler declared that his principles were clear and inseparable:

> Socialism as the final concept of duty, the ethical duty of work, not just for oneself but also for one's fellow man's sake, and above all the principle: Common good before own good, a struggle

against all parasitism and especially against easy and unearned income.[18]

Renowned German historian Götz Aly laid out the socialist ancestry and appeal of Nazism, writing:

> Another source of the Nazi Party's popularity was its liberal borrowing from the intellectual tradition of the socialist left. Many of the men who would become the movement's leaders had been involved in communist and socialist circles.[19]

One of those socialists was Adolf Eichmann, who was in charge of implementing the Holocaust. In his memoirs, he recalled: "My personal political feelings lay towards the left, at least emphasizing the socialistic aspect as much as the nationalistic."[20] In addition, Eichmann commented that many of his comrades saw "National Socialism and the Communism of the Soviet Republic" as "sort of 'siblings.'"[21]

Earlier in 1944, economist F.A. Hayek clearly identified the socialist roots behind the ideology that forged Nazism, writing:

> It is significant that the most important ancestors of National Socialism—Fichte, Rodbertus, and Lassalle—are at the same time acknowledged fathers of socialism. ... From 1914 onward there arose from the ranks of Marxist socialism one teacher after another who led, not the conservatives and reactionaries, but the hard-working laborer and idealist youth into the National Socialist fold.[22]

Of course, Hitler had repeatedly called himself a socialist in public as well as in private conversations but was more forthcoming and outspoken during his earlier years. For instance, in a major speech in 1927, Hitler quickly identified himself as a socialist while brandishing his anti-capitalist credentials. This event occurred during a celebration of the Marxist May Day holiday where Hitler spoke to a crowd of 5,000 at the Clou restaurant center:

> We are socialists, we are enemies of today's capitalistic economic system for the exploitation of the economically weak, with its unfair salaries, with its unseemly evaluation of a human being

according to wealth and property instead of responsibility and performance, and we are determined to destroy this system under all conditions.[23]

A year earlier, Gregor Strasser (1892–1934), leader of the Nazi party's national organization, composed a one-page talking-point letter. Hitler was so impressed that he plagiarized much of it for his 1927 speech. Strasser wrote:

> We are Socialists, enemies, mortal enemies of the present capitalist economic system with its exploitation of the economically weak, with its injustice in wages, with its immoral evaluation of individuals according to wealth and money instead of responsibility and achievement, and we are determined under all circumstances to abolish this system![24]

In private, as well, a number of Hitler's confidants told of his commitment to non-Marxist socialism. One was Otto Wagener (1888–1971), Hitler's economic advisor and later major general who fought on the front. In Wagener's *Hitler—Memoirs of a Confidant*, Hitler confessed many times that he was an ardent socialist who wanted to craft a nationalist and socialist nation. Hitler explained to Wagener that the Nazi party must "convert the German *Volk* to socialism without simply killing off the old individualists."[25] Moreover, Hitler insisted that the Nazis had to "find and travel the road from individualism to socialism without revolution."[26] This indicated that the business class was regarded as servicing the needs of socialism by providing the state with revenues, and more, importantly, as Hitler declared, "we will come to liberate the individual from the domination of capital and all its institutions," which he believed would benefit workers.[27]

But socialization of the *Volk* had to be forged in a way that would not ensure societal turmoil. Since the era of classical liberalism, private commerce and private property had been fixtures of life in Germany, making it difficult for the Nazis to completely destroy the old liberalism of the individual. Rather, the Nazis believed they could still socialize society under a command-and-control economy without formally imposing too much state ownership and without eliminating the propertied classes or engaging in perpetual revolution. Hence, Hitler was convinced that he could advance the socialization of Germany, remarking: "What Marxism, Leninism and Stalinism failed to accomplish, we shall be in a position to achieve."[28]

One way to achieve socialization was state controlled interventionism and planning of the economy. Like Mussolini in Italy, Otto Wagener was impressed with the state-interventionist policies of economist John Maynard Keynes and encouraged Hitler to study his anti-*laissez-faire* economics. Otto Wagener remarked to Hitler:

> A few days ago, I read a very interesting treatise by the Englishman Keynes. Over here, he is regarded as the greatest scholarly expert in the area of monetary and fiscal systems. He is also recognized elsewhere. If one follows his thinking, one has the feeling that he is moving steadily in our direction...[29]

In another instance, Hitler told Wagener flat-out that he was a socialist. The issue came up when Wagener worried that business interests might intrude upon the Nazi's party dedication to socialism. To dispel Wagener's concerns, Hitler affirmed his socialist fidelity, saying: "It is true that I am a socialist. But you know that, at the present time, political reasons also force me to take into account the businessmen."[30] In another narrative, Hitler revealed to Wagener the meaning behind Nazism, clarifying that:

> After all, that's exactly why we call ourselves National Socialists! We want to start by implementing socialism in our nation among our Volk! It is not until the individual nations are socialist that they can address themselves to international socialism.[31]

But one of the most interesting comments made by Hitler concerned his hatred of classical liberals and his sympathy for the Bolsheviks' way of getting rid of the guardians of individualism. He explained to Wagener:

> Aren't these liberals, those reprobate defenders of individualism, ashamed to see the tears of the mothers and wives, or don't these cold-blooded accountants even notice? Have they already grown so inhuman that they are no longer capable of feeling? It is understandable why bolshevism simply removed such creatures.

They were worthless to humanity, nothing but an encumbrance to their Volk. Even the bees get rid of the drones when they can no longer be of service to the hive. The Bolshevik procedures are thus quite natural.[32]

Another of Hitler's confidants was Hermann Rauschning (1887–1982), a Nazi leader who was elected president of the Senate of the independent port city of Danzig. Rauschning knew Hitler before and after his ascendancy to Chancellor of Germany in 1933, but he turned against Hitler and Nazism by 1934. In the quote below, Hitler takes the position that socialism had to be taken directly to the people and that the people themselves had to be socialized. Hitler told Rauschning:

The party is all-embracing... Each activity and each need of the individual will thereby be regulated by the party as the representative of the general good... This is Socialism—not such trifles as the private possession of the means of production. Of what importance is that if I range men firmly within a discipline they cannot escape? Let them own land or factories as much as they please. The decisive factor is that the State, through the party, is supreme over all, regardless of whether they are owners or workers... Our Socialism goes far deeper... [the people] have entered a new relation... What are ownership and income to that? Why need we trouble to socialize banks and factories? We socialize human beings.[33]

In another passage, Hitler explained to Rauschning his debt to Marxist ideology:

I have learned a great deal from Marxism as I do not hesitate to admit... The difference between them and myself is that I have really put into practice what these peddlers and pen pushers have timidly begun. The whole of National Socialism is based on it... National Socialism is what Marxism might have been if it could have broken its absurd and artificial ties with a democratic order.[34]

According to Joshua Muravchik, a professor of international relations, "What was repugnant to Hitler about Marx was not his philosophy but his Jewishness."[35] To Hitler and other socialists, capitalism was a Jewish conspiracy of moneylenders, bankers, and financiers who were trying to control the world. In an April 1922 speech, Hitler clearly targeted the Jew as "this capitalistic people, which was brought into existence by the unscrupulous exploitation of men."[36]

In this sense, anti-Semitism is simply a hatred of liberal capitalism and the merchant class that the Jews were seen to represent. After all, traditionally Jews believed that wealth was a sign of God's favor. To socialists, however, a return on investment—profit—was not only exploitative, but it was seen as the Jewish way to institutionalize usury under capitalist greed. Hitler followed this line of logic, but stopped at the Marxist version of a "fatherless" socialism. To Hitler, international socialism had all the trappings of ideology that supported international financing, which only further convinced him that "Marxism was a Judaic doctrine." At a private gathering to celebrate his official recognition as Führer of the German Reich, Hitler reportedly said: "My Socialism is not the same thing as Marxism. My Socialism is not class war, but order."[37]

Unfortunately, Rauschning's private conversations with Hitler have been tarnished by Holocaust deniers and Hitlerite apologists, especially Mark Weber, director of the Institute of Historical Review (IHR), a well-known Holocaust denier and apologist for Nazi Germany, who asserted that "The Holocaust hoax is a religion."[38][39] Moreover, in 1983, an obscure Swiss researcher Wolfgang Häne spoke at historical revisionist association *Zeitgeschichtliche Forschungsstelle Ingolstadt* (ZFI), where he attacked the authenticity of Rauschning's writings on Hitler. Through gatherings and conference, the ZFI and the Institute for Historical Review have denounced Allied atrocities against the Germans, trivialized Nazi genocide and the dangers of Nazism, and denied Germany's guilt for starting World War II. The now-disgraced British Historian David Irving, around whom "revisionist historians gathered," led the charge against Rauschning's reputation.[40] In a 2000 libel lawsuit, Irving was found to have falsified historical facts in pursuit of his theory that the Holocaust was a hoax.[41] In that case, Judge Charles Gray ruled that Irvine was "an active Holocaust denier; that he is anti-Semitic and racist and that he associates with right-wing extremists who promote neo-Nazism."[42]

Holocaust deniers have impugned Rauschning's reputation in order to invalidate Hitler's early racist remarks and overt genocidal plans. Even before Hitler became Germany's chancellor, Hitler confided in Rauschning about his hatred of Jews and that "all the Jews had to be removed."[43] Regarding them as simply biological entities, Hitler threatened to seize all of the Jew's property, and then "hold their lives in the palm of his hand; their precious Jewish lives." Next, he joked with other Nazi leaders, that maybe the Jews should be taken hostage, made into human shields and "driven ahead of our attaching defense lines" during the next war.[44]

But Hitler's most chilling statement fixated on the depopulation of Jews, Slavs, and other inferior races. Hitler divulged to Rauschning:

> We are obligated to depopulate as part of our mission of preserving the German population. We shall have to develop a technique of depopulation. If you ask me what I mean by depopulation, I mean the removal of entire racial units. And that is what I intend to carry out... Nature is cruel, therefore we, too, may be cruel. ... I have the right to remove millions of an inferior race that breeds like vermin![45]

Hitler did indicate that his depopulation plans might be "comparatively painless" in his effort to cause "undesirable races to die out." Hitler's reference to a "painless" racial die-off might correspond to his eugenic plans to remedy genetically defective people—plans that were implemented by 1933. Nonetheless, Rauschning's book has been an affront to Holocaust deniers because it provides clear evidence of Hitler's early intentions to conduct a genocidal war against the hereditary "less valuable" or "racially foreign." The Holocaust did not start until 1941, but Rauschning's book was written in the late 1930s, and taken from conversations with Hitler in the early 1930s. Most Holocaust deniers refuse to recognize any evidence of Hitler's premeditated designs to exterminate the Jews. One wonders why anyone would trust Holocaust deniers in their quest to discredit Rauschning when they purposely disregard the mountains of evidence that attest to the validity of the Holocaust.

Joseph Goebbels: The Fascist-Marxist Ideologue

Hitler was not the only Nazi who explicitly praised socialism in public and private. Others, like Dr. Joseph Goebbels (1897–1945), the Reich Minister of Propaganda, excelled at espousing hardcore Fascist-Marxist ideas. Goebbels was often the leading cheerleader for socialism in the Nazi movement, sounding the loudest death knell for capitalism. He would talk about "the money pigs of capitalist democracy,"[46] while describing the Berlin police as "the pimp of capitalism."[47] Saying that "Capitalism is the immoral distribution of capital,"[48] Goebbels sharply proclaimed that

> The bourgeoisie has to yield to the working class... Whatever is about to fall should be pushed. We are all soldiers of the revolution. We want the workers' victory over filthy lucre. That is socialism.[49]

According to William L. Shirer, an American correspondent based in Berlin, the early entries of Goebbels' diary were "full of expression of sympathy for Communism"; both Goebbels and the Strasser brothers wanted to "nationalize the big industries and the big estates."[50] Considered one of Hitler's closest and most devoted associates, Goebbels "was happy to describe himself as a 'German Communist'" during his college days.[51,52] In fact, Goebbels had a soft spot for Marxism, considering that "he persistently attempted to convert Communists to National Socialism," determined to erect "the bridge from left to right over which those willing to sacrifice came together."[53] Goebbels had high hopes that he could convince Hitler that the "only thing separating the Communists and Nazis was the Red's dedication to internationalism."[54] As a former Marxist, he understood "how thin the dividing line between the two philosophies" of communism and Nazism.[55] In his diary, Goebbels admitted that if he had to choose between Bolshevism and capitalism, "it would be better for us to go down with Bolshevism than live in eternal slavery under capitalism."[56] Further, when asked whether Nazism stood on the left or right of the political spectrum, Goebbels responded that "the NSDAP [Nazi Party] is the German Left. We despise bourgeois nationalism."[57]

It was not only Goebbels and his revolutionary socialist cohorts who saw Russian communism as more appealing to Nazis than Western capitalists. In a rebuttal of nationalistic socialism, Aurel Kolnai, a classical liberal philosopher and political theorist who studied under Ludwig von Mises, wrote in *The War Against the West* that "National Socialism is at bottom incomparably more anti-Western than Bolshevism."[58] Hannah Arendt, who is regarded as one of the most influential political philosophers of the twentieth century, went further, arguing that "Hitler never intended to defend 'the West' against Bolshevism but always remained ready to join 'the Reds' for the destruction of the West, even in the middle of the struggle against Soviet Russia."[59] Arendt was personally affected by the terror of Nazism. She was a secular Jew living in Nazi Germany in the early 1930s. She was imprisoned by the Gestapo and immediately fled her nation upon release. She could not help but notice that the totalitarian regimes of both Nazi Germany and Soviet Russia were "essentially identical systems which were clearly growing constantly more alike."[60]

Remarkably, a 1925 *New York Times* article revealed just how Marxist Goebbels' outlook really was. In the news story, Dr. Goebbels is identified as the man who declared to a crowd in Chemnitz that "Lenin was the greatest man, second only to Hitler, and that the difference between communism and the Hitler faith was very slight."[61] At the time, Goebbels' excelled at such collaborative discourse in appealing to Marxists. In his January 31, 1926, diary entry, Goebbels wrote: "I think it is terrible that we [the Nazis] and the Communists are bashing in each other's heads... Where can we get together sometime with the leading Communists?" In an earlier article on June 14–15, 1925 entitled "Idea and Sacrifice," he was eager to make the case that the Nazi party should be "a party of class struggle."[62]

In another example, Goebbels was the author of a widely distributed Nazi pamphlet first published in 1929. This time he referred to his "true socialism" as anti-Marxist. He wrote:

> We are against the political bourgeoisie, and for genuine nationalism! We are against Marxism, but for true socialism! We are for the first German national state of a socialist nature! We are for the National Socialist German Workers' Party![63]

In the same flyer, which was distributed by the hundreds of thousands, Goebbels penned an anti-capitalist screed that any socialist would find appealing:

> The worker in a capitalist state—and that is his deepest misfortune—is no longer a living human being, a creator, a maker. He has become a machine. A number, a cog in the machine without sense or understanding. He is alienated from what he produces.[64]

The Nazis' proclivity towards hardcore socialism was substantial. Goebbels freely spoke about the Third Reich's socialist and revolutionary prospect to bolster Germany's morale during the Stalingrad crisis. He declared in his June 5, 1943, speech:

> If Germany stays united and marches to the rhythm of its revolutionary socialist outlook, it will be unbeatable. Our indestructible will to life, and the driving force of the Führer's personality guarantee this.[65]

After the invasion of Poland in 1939, Goebbels framed the war between capitalist England and socialist Germany with this observation: "England is a capitalist democracy. Germany is a socialist people's state."[66] Here, Goebbels proclaimed that the capitalists in England are the "richest men on earth. The broad masses, however, see little of this wealth." In that same "England's Guilt" speech, he throws more jabs at England's tightfisted plutocracy as compared to Nazi Germany's lavish support of social welfare programs, declaring:

> It is also why English capitalists want to destroy Hitlerism. They see Hitlerism as all the generous social reforms that have occurred in Germany since 1933. The English plutocrats rightly fear that good things are contagious, that they could endanger English capitalism.

To the Nazis, wealth inequality was a horrendous injustice that had to be solved. Both German Nazis and Italian fascists worked feverishly to strengthen and enlarge their socialized safety nets via social justice programs.

Nonetheless, the German public began to worry over the Nazis' propensity to march in lockstep with communists. According to Richard Pipes in *Russia Under the Bolshevik Regime*, both Joseph Goebbels and Otto Strasser (1897–1974) were seen as "National Bolsheviks," or the Nazi left, who wanted closer ties with Stalin's Russia. Their plan was to bolster the Soviet Union's economy so that the communists and Nazis could take down Britain and France. Goebbels explained this Nazi-Communist alliance in 1925, writing: "We can see the commencement of our own national and socialist survival in an alliance with a truly national and socialist Russia."[67] In addition, Goebbels and Strasser favored workers' strikes and the nationalization of most banks and industry.[68]

Taking a fervently anti-Semitic stand, Goebbels regarded capitalism and its international banking systems as under the control of the Jewish upper-class and therefore the ultimate enemy of the Nazis. Goebbels was frustrated that the Nazis and Communist Party of Germany (KPD) had to be rivals, forced to go after the same constituency, like "two rabid dogs fighting for one bone."[69]

This irritation caused Goebbels to offer an olive branch to the communists. Writing an open letter to "My Friends of the Left," he expressed their common goals of fighting their common enemy—the bourgeoisie. "You and I, we are fighting each other but we are not really enemies... Maybe the final extremity will bring us together. Maybe."[70] In that letter, according to William L. Shirer, Goebbels was trying to assure his red comrades "that Nazism and Communism were really the same thing."[71]

A New German Socialism

But sometimes Hitler had to curb the Nazi party's extreme left-wing socialists, once lecturing Otto Strasser over the meaning of his socialism, saying:

> I am a Socialist, and a very different kind of Socialist from your rich friend, Count Reventlow. ... What you understand by Socialism is nothing more than Marxism.[72]

Even anti-Fascists before World War II could not help but recognize the national socialism of fascism in Italy as a sort of militarized socialism.

This was the opinion of Harold Nicolson, a Democratic Socialist, who later became a Member of the House of Commons in England. After examining Italian Fascist literature in Rome in 1932, he expressed in his diary that

> it is certainly a socialist experiment in that it destroys individuality. It destroys liberty... I admit that under this system you can attain a degree of energy and efficiency not reached in our own island.[73,74]

In 1934 Richard Crossman, who was involved with the Fabian Society and later became a Labour Party cabinet minister, commented on a BBC radio show that many students in Germany thought that Hitler's Nazis were "digging the foundations of a new German socialism."[75]

Others, like Julian Huxley, who later became the first director-general of UNESCO, saw Nazis and the fascists as black sheep of the broad, big-tent socialist family. An admirer of the Soviet system, Huxley believed that fascism would be an unwelcome distraction, "a short cut towards the unified Socialised State which should be our goal," and that "its methods are so crude that it is likely to land us in war and social disaster while delaying real progress." Later, Huxley confessed that Hitler's Nazism was "a despairing attempt to find a short cut to the Promised Land."[76]

In 1940, Winston Churchill clearly saw that Nazism and Sovietism were cut from the same cloth, remarking that "Nazis despotism [is] an equally hateful though more efficient form of the communist despotism."[77] Later in 1948, he further reflected in his first volume of *The Second World War* series that:

> Fascism was the shadow or ugly child of communism... As Fascism sprang from Communism, so Nazism developed from Fascism. Thus were set on foot those kindred movements which were destined soon to plunge the world into more hideous strife, which none can say has ended with their destruction.[78]

A passive attitude towards national socialists by the left changed by 1936 when the Third Reich became involved in the Spanish Civil War on the opposite side from the Soviet Union. Suddenly, the crude Nazis, who had been earlier accused of giving socialism a bad name, magically became right-wing extremists instead of a being seen as another rival offshoot of socialism. But then, of course, Joseph Stalin (1878–1953) was legendary for accusing anyone not beholden to his interpretation of Marxism-Leninism as right-wing fanatics and fascists, including Leon Trotsky (1879–1940), the founder of the Bolshevik's Red Army.

The Early Socialists of Nationalism and Anti-Semitism

Starting in the 1820s, early socialists, prior to the debut of Marxist theory, tended to be far more moderate, tolerant, and less authoritarian towards the new industrial society that was being forged by the private capital of industrial capitalism. Mostly from France, the original social-ists sought a hodgepodge of socioeconomic controls that would ensure an economic "Third Way" between hated capitalism of individualism and beloved socialism of a communal collectivism. Nevertheless, most of the pre-Marxist socialists manifested a collectivity that would today be considered rather distasteful and ominous, promulgating varying degrees of anti-Semitism, racism, blood-and-soil nationalism, protec-tionism, a mercantilism-like mixed economy, state-directed planning and management, limited public ownership, and selective equality, which made them role models for Nazism.

Many historians regard German National Socialism as an unortho-dox and ahistorical redefinition of socialism that emerged not only in reaction to the violence and tumult of Lenin's communist revolution, but also as an alternative to liberalism and capitalism. Still, the ideas of the early origins of socialism, Nazism, and Fascism generally align with pre-Marxist socialism in Europe, which spoke of community, solidarity, proto-nationalism, brotherhood, and cooperation, but usually not out-right state ownership of all means of production or private property.

One of the most important early socialist theorists was mutualist, an-archist, and anti-Semite Pierre-Joseph Proudhon (1809–1865). Similar to many Nazi theorists, Proudhon opposed direct state ownership of land and workplaces, and instead favoring worker cooperatives and associations. Proudhon, according to author Robert LeFevre,

> distinguished between *ownership* and *proprietorship*, contending that man had a right to what he was *using*, as a proprietor, but those things in one's possessions which are not being used, may be used by others.[79]

Proudhon defined socialism as "every aspiration towards the amelioration of society," but some scholars see him as an early advocate of what is now known as market socialism. Although very critical of capitalism, he opposed policies that would over-dominate economic activity. However, he viewed capitalists as stealing the profits from laborers who were under a permanent condition of obedience and sought to emplace reasonable economic controls to socialize commerce and the state. In his support of small-time craftsmen, well-to-do farmers and merchants, Proudhon regarded meager holdings of private property as the basis of his socialist utopia. Proudhon, however, unlike Marx and Friedrich Engels (1820–1895), was opposed to violence and dictatorship to bring about a social revolutionary agenda.

Again, like the German National Socialist's hostility towards other races, Proudhon had a profoundly anti-Semitic streak, calling

> for the expulsion of the Jews from France... The Jew is the enemy of the human race. This race must be sent back to Asia, or exterminated. ... By steel or by fire or by expulsion the Jew must disappear.[80]

The anarcho-socialist Mikhail Bakunin (1814–1876), who knew and lionized Proudhon, espoused blatantly anti-Semitic views, referring to the Jews as "a kind of blood sucking people, a kind of organic destructive collective parasite."[81] Bakunin also upheld a left-wing form of national-identity collectivism during his pre-social anarchist years.

Like most anti-capitalist socialists of the day, Proudhon viewed Jews as exploiters of labor who charged high usury rates on loans to the detriment of workers. To socialists and collectivists, interest-bearing loans exemplified the depredation of finance capital and capitalism, but Proudhon went further on his racist rant. Convinced of the inferiority of certain races, he claimed that they are "badly born and bastard races."[82]

Moreover, Proudhon took a racist-nationalist tone by linking blood to soil, just as the Nazi party had promoted under their blood and soil (*Blut und Boden*) doctrine. Proudhon wrote: "Land belongs to the race of people born on it, since no other is able to develop it according to its need."[83] Furthermore, Proudhon's egalitarian beliefs were limited to the patriarchy of certain ethnicities of men. This meant that egalitarian rights were unavailable to women, who he insisted had the role of either "courtesan or housekeeper."

Some consider Proudhon's thinking to be a forerunner to the merging of nationalism with socialism that emphasized the racial hatred of anti-Semitism. A proto-fascist study group was founded around Proudhon's ideas, honoring their organization with his name. Georges Valois (1878–1945) and Édouard Berth established "Cercle Proudhon" in 1911 in an effort to synthesize socialism and nationalism into a new movement. Valois claimed that the group would "unite nationalists and left-wing anti-democrats" around an offensive against "Jewish capitalism."[84]

But Valois was no ordinary socialist. He regarded fascism as a revolt against "bourgeois rule," which reflected his influence and inspiration by Marxism. He designated fascism and Marxism as "varieties of socialism."[85] His claim to fame was his admiration of Mussolini and his founding of the French Fascist political party (*Le Faisceau*) in 1925, which "supported trade union strikes and talked about improving worker conditions."[86] Identifying himself with the socialist left, Valois wanted to create a "revolutionary national movement," but he and his French Fascist party were opposed by communists from the left as well as by monarchist conservatives in Action Française from the right.[87] Valois' mission seemed to have been to turn the proletariat away from Marxist internationalism and embrace the homogenized collectivity of the nation-state, but Valois' early fascist and socialist links go deeper. It was French Marxist and revolutionary syndicalist Georges Sorel who inspired Valois to establish the Cercle Proudhon organization.[88]

According to Benito Mussolini, Sorel was his mentor who assisted in birthing an ideology that became known as Italian Fascism, and yet this story continues. After the French Fascist party dissolved in 1928, Valois established the Republican Syndicalist Party as a left-wing movement. In 1934, he set up the *Le Nouvel Age* (*The New Era*) and advertised it as a left-wing journal. When Nazi Germany invaded France, he joined the French Resistance.

Some might question how Proudhon and other pre-Marxist socialists could be regarded as precursors to the nationalistic socialism and Italian Fascism. Some historians, including Zeev Sternhell, argued that Proudhon's mutualism had been coupled with Charles Maurras' (1868–1952) "integral nationalism," which then spawned the neo-socialist movement in France and Belgium, which culminated in their allegiance to Nazism and Hitler-controlled Vichy France (Régime de Vichy). Maurras' integral nationalism fit the fascist pattern well, sporting a mixture of corporatism and trade unionism which treated a nation as a singular organic unity where the nation-state was a morally good end, rather than a means.[89] In this sense, Nazism can be seen as a revised version of pre-Marxist French socialism.

Another prominent early socialist from France who crossbred anti-Semitism with anti-capitalism was Pierre Leroux (1797–1871). Considered the originator of the term "socialism" in 1833, Leroux was seen as identifying the "Jews with the despised capitalism, and regarded them as the incarnation of *mammon*, who lived by exploiting others."[90] Defining socialism "as opposed to individualism," Leroux remarked: "When we speak of the Jews, we mean the Jewish spirit—the spirit of profit, of lucre, of gain, of speculation; in a word, the banker's spirit."[91] Like most socialists of the day, Leroux blamed the poor condition of society on the high interest-rates charged by money-lenders and the profit motivate of finance capital. In his mind, the Jews and their hoarding of capital caused most social and economic evil.

Due to the influence of the French Revolution and Napoleon, the concept of nationalism was seen as a sort of collective identity that flourished throughout Europe. It was regarded as a revolutionary force that would liberate mankind. In fact, in France, the concept of nationalism was originally considered left-wing, perceived as an "uncompromising nationalism" for France's "revolutionary expansion."[92] This quest for a fatherland affected the early socialist movement, especially in France.

Here, the socialists favored theories and policies that would protect their nation from foreign invaders and economic competition. Known as protectionism, socialists found favor with the economic counterpart of absolute monarchies—mercantilism—which was heavily criticized by Adam Smith and classical liberals. Under mercantilism, a jingoistic attitude arose among collectivists who saw the liberalization of trade and *laissez-faire* doctrines as a threat to national identity, state control, and the rights of the working class.

Indeed, throughout history, most socialists have preferred economic policies of national self-sufficiency within racial-ethnic borders, free of foreign capital and clout, enacting bans or high tariffs on imports in an effort to become economically insulated, and to support regulations and subsidies designed to safeguard domestically made products. In this way, protectionism resembles a symbiotic relationship, where the state secures the prosperity of national businesses, while national businesses, in turn, ensured the prosperity and security of the nation-state—a cozy relationship that Proudhon thought could bring about the "the socialization of commerce and the State."[93]

Protectionism has been vital to the nationalistic elements of mercantilism, which leads to special interests, monopolies, oligarchies, economic interventionism, territorial expansion, and nationalistic self-interest. Economist Michael A. Heilperin, who earned his doctorate in economics from the University of Geneva in 1931, defined mercantilism as a subspecies of "economic nationalism," which repeatedly damages world prosperity and peace.[94] Heilperin coined this term to describe ultra-nationalistic economies that he saw spreading throughout Europe in the 1920s and 1930s, especially in Fascist Italy and Nazi Germany.

It can be argued that the early socialists were the forerunners of socioeconomic nationalism that advanced doctrines to protect one's own national interests against another. For instance, articles in the *Revue Indépendante* (1841–1848) edited by socialists Pierre Leroux and George Sand argued that "British free trade [is] incompatible with France, 'the country of democracy and equality.'"[95] As in Mussolini and Hitler's anti-free trade "autarky" of economic self-sufficiency, the early French socialists opposed free trade under the belief that it would not only lower worker's salaries and damage national unity, but make them subject to foreign and Jewish money-lenders. To these socialists, it was the state's role to drive the economy, rather than the role of foreigners bearing low-priced wares and finance capital.

Although Karl Marx (1818–1883) confided that he derived many of his philosophical ideas from the French utopian socialist movement, he also knew that he was adopting an ideological movement rife with xenophobia. Anti-Semitism was so profuse in the French socialist community that historian Zosa Szajkowski concluded in an exhaustive study that he "could not find a single word on behalf of Jews in the whole of French socialist literature from 1820 to 1920."[96] In fact, in *Why the Jews?*, Dennis Prager and Joseph Telushkin asserted that "two main ideological sources, Marx and the early French socialists, developed anti-Semitism ideals that have characterized much of the Left to this day."[97] The anti-communist socialist philosopher Sidney Hook came to the same conclusion, contending that "anti-Semitism was rife in almost all varieties of socialism."[98]

One of the two main founders of the socialist movement in France, Charles Fourier (1772–1837), was particularly hostile to Jews, considering them "parasites, merchants, usurers."[99] Contending that poverty and not inequality was the society's biggest problem, Fourier's socialism was based upon his confidence in voluntary association and social cooperation, rather than some form of state ownership.

The socialist who popularized the term "anti-Semitism," Wilhelm Marr (1819–1904), was once expelled from Zurich for alleged communist activities. Although later in life he backed away from his radical socialist roots, he wrote that "Anti-Semitism is a Socialist movement, only nobler and purer in form than Social Democracy."[100] A proponent of German unification under Prussian leadership, Marr became involved in the *Burschenschaften*, a nationalistic movement that sought a unified state of territories inhabited by the German-speaking people. Marr blamed the emancipation of Jews on German liberalism, which allowed the liberty of Jews to control the financial and industrial sectors of Germany. However, Marr became a primary ideological link that led to Germany's embracement of racism and nationalism that later spawned the Nazi era.

Furthermore, many socialist newspapers were adamantly anti-Semitic, including the French newspaper *La Libre Parole*, founded by Édouard Drumont in 1892. Like many socialists of the day, Drumont "shifted the traditional socialist focus on class struggle to questions of race."[101] Virulently anti-capitalist, *La Libre Parole* denounced Jews for engaging in corrupt capitalist activities that were believed to result in the destruction of France.

These anti-Jewish bigotries among socialists and Marxists continued into the 20th century. The well-known French Marxist and supporter of Lenin's Bolshevik Revolution, Georges Sorel, engaged in a long anti-Semitic campaign, starting just prior to World War I. He praised the most famous living anti-Semite, the socialist journalist Urbain Gohier (1862–1951), encouraging him to defend French customs and ideas "against the Jewish invaders who wanted to dominate everything."[102] Sorel made many threats against the Jews and blamed them for the decadence he thought was befalling France.

One of the few early socialists who refrained from vilifying the Jews was Henri de Saint-Simon (1760–1825), later identified by Marx and Engels as belonging to the category of "utopian socialists." Saint-Simon's socialism did not call for either class conflict or public ownership of the means of production. Neither did he "condemn outright the institution of private property," nor did he oppose the practice of charging interests on loans.[103] Instead, like the Nazis, he advocated for state controls and management "of property through central planning, in which scientists, industrialists, and engineers would anticipate social needs and direct the energies of society to meet them."[104] Unlike Marx, Saint-Simon bore no ill will towards capitalists in general, instead considering them to be vital components of the industrial class as the producers of wealth.[105]

Saint-Simon also did not consider private ownership a problem. Instead, he considered private management, not private ownership, to be the real societal ill.[106] Saint-Simon and many other utopian socialists did not believe a political revolution would accomplish their goals. Rather, they were beholden to cooperative socialism that would usher in a better future for all classes. The theories of early socialism ran the gamut, but it was Marx and Engels who demanded that true socialism could not be achieved unless all means of productions were community-state owned.

Social Justice and Hitlerian Socialism

Hitlerian socialism was also less demanding. It was a form of socialism that resembled a combination of utopian socialism and the socialist market economy found in communist China. Echoing the essences of Nazism, some Chinese communists have referred to their economic system as "birdcage" socialism, where "the market sector should be as free to fly as a bird in a cage—the cage of a state-commanded economy."[107] Nevertheless, under market socialism, the private sector creates 90 percent of new jobs in China.

From the outset, Hitler spoke of "socialism [as] a sense of community, putting the common good before self-interest."[108] He told Otto Wagener that

> In socialism of the future... what counts is the whole, the community of the Volk. The individual and his life play only a subsidiary role. He can be sacrificed—he is prepared to sacrifice himself should the whole demand it.[109]

Moreover, Hitler elucidated why life was a struggle and that socialism was more important than humanitarian beliefs, clarifying that "We are to act, not from humanitarian points of view, but from socialist ones!"[110]

Other authors and journalists who lived during the interwar years in Europe witnessed the rise of Nazism upfront as a frightening movement tinted with large pigments of Marxism. The English journalist Frederick Augustus Voigt, a Berlin correspondent for the *Manchester Guardian*, expounded the striking similarities between Nazi Germany and Soviet Russia. He wrote in his 1938 book *Unto Caesar* that

> Marxism would be a phenomenon of little more than historical interest, seeing that it has failed even in its principal stronghold, were it not so closely akin to National Socialism. National Socialism would have been inconceivable without Marxism.[111]

Born in Vienna, Austria, social scientist and management expert Peter Drucker echoed the same sentiment in 1939, writing that "Fascism is the stage reached after communism has proved an illusion..."[112] Max Eastman (1883–1969), Lenin's old friend and editor of America's leading socialist periodical, *The Masses*, was mesmerized by the allure of communism. After spending over two years in the Soviet Union in the 1920s, Eastman's enthusiasm waned. Eastman was probably taken aback by Lenin's fleet of nine Rolls-Royces and a staff of servants that might have rivaled the Russian Czar, making a total mockery of communism's egalitarian ideas.[113] Eventually, he conceded the frightening parallels between Nazism and communism, writing that "instead of being better, Stalinism is worse than fascism, more ruthless, barbarous, unjust, immoral, anti-democratic, unredeemed by any hope or scruple," and that it could be "better described as superfascist."[114]

Walter Lippmann (1889–1974), a twice-winning Pulitzer Prize journalist and author who was considered one of the earliest opponents of fascism, set forth a recurrent theme that fascism and communism were strikingly similar due to their "authoritarian collectivism" and totalitarian dictatorship. Personally interviewing Mussolini several times in Italy, Lippmann wrote in his 1937 book, *The Good Society*, that

> the totalitarian states, whether of the fascist or the communist persuasion, are more than superficially alike as dictatorships, in the suppression of dissent, and in operating planned and directed economies. They are profoundly alike.[115]

In an earlier book, Lippmann mused over the monopoly of force by government and concluded that "The modern State claims all of these powers, and, in the matter of theory, there is no real difference in the size of the claim between communists, fascists, and democrats."[116]

Still, what made the Nazi movement different from earlier versions of socialism was its "drive to couple social equality with national homogeneity, a concept that was popular not only in Germany."[117] Considering their propensity for using street violence to shut down opponents, Hitler and his SA Stormtroopers might be considered as the ultimate social justice warriors of their era. From the very start, Hitler made it plain that social justice was an important attribute to a healthy state. In one of his 1920 speeches, Hitler proclaimed to thousands of Nazi party followers: "[W]e do not believe that there could ever exist a state with lasting inner health if it is not built on internal social justice..."[118]

The advocacy for social justice was combined with the Nazis' contempt for Jewish capitalism. A propaganda poster from 1933 revealed this ethnically-segregated equality against Jews, which read: "Because Adolf Hitler's Third Reich wants social justice, big Jewish capitalism is the worst enemy of this Reich and its Führer."[119] Usually it was the Nazi's revolutionary nationalism that was regarded as the main catalyst to ensure anti-Semitism.

A number of socialist theorists reframed the concept of nationalism and asserted that it was an inseparable component of socialism in which to forge a national collectivity. Werner Sombart (1863–1941), the prominent Marxian historian and Marxist social theorist, who was later drawn to Nazism, argued for a type of social nationalism disposed to a sort of collective and homogeneous group identity, embodied within the *Volksgeist* (national spirit).[120] Referring to himself as a "convinced Marxist," Sombart blamed the Jews for breaking up the old economic guild system and replacing it with modern capitalism, where competition was unlimited and pleasing the customer became the law of the land. By 1934, Sombart was praising German Nazism because it placed the "welfare of the whole above the welfare of the individual,"[121] and that it would affect a "total ordering of life" within a "planned economy in accordance with state regulations."[122] In fact, in his 1934 book, *German Socialism*, Sombart spelled out his definition of socialism as "social regulationism," where the political community determined the behavior of the individual through social constraints.[123] Finally succumbing to the idea of merging nationalism with socialism, Sombart traveled down the typical anti-capitalist and anti-Semitic road, arguing that the antithesis of the German spirit was the Jewish spirit and most importantly the capitalist spirit, and therefore the German people and Nazism had to crush them.[124]

Another radical socialist who turned nationalistic was Johann Plenge (1874–1963), a German sociologist and a professor of political economics at the University of Münster. Considered a great authority on Marx and Hegel, Plenge's scholarly research "marked the beginning of the modern Hegel-renaissance among Marxist scholars."[125] He claimed that the spirit of the tightly-knit racial community—*Volksgemeinschaft*—would supplant class division, and cause "racial comrades" to unite and erect a socialist society of proletarian Germany against "capitalist" Britain.[126] Rejecting the "idea of boundless freedom," in his 1911 book *Marx and Hegel*, Plenge initiated a new theory of society which he referred to as "organizational socialism."[127] He favored a hierarchical technocratic state,[128] which was expected to promote social justice via a strong centralized form of state socialism. He is also noted for his "ideas of 1914" which sought to overturn the original classical liberal ideas of 1789 from the French Revolution (the free-market, free-Left Girondin faction), rejecting individualism, democratic republicanism and the liberalism of the bourgeois class. Liberal ideas were to be replaced by the obligatory German values that emphasized duty, discipline, law, and order.[129] But like so many left-wing socialists, social democrats, and Marxists, Plenge gravitated towards a collectivized nationalism that spoke of the "idea of German organization" and "the national unity of state socialism." Not surprisingly, Plenge's convictions are reputed to have been a major intellectual forerunner of German Nazism.[130]

A more elegant phrase to explain the merging of socialism with ultra-nationalism came from German historian Arthur Moeller van den Bruck (1876–1925), who declared: "To socialize is to nationalize."[131] Arthur Moeller's theories "shaped the Nazis' desire to create a new order in Europe," a "New Germany" known as the "The Third Reich," a term that he coined.[132] In his 1918 book *Das Recht der jungen Völke*, Arthur Moeller came out with an explicitly anti-Western philosophy which sought to merge nationalism with social justice.

Others, like Maurice Barrès coined the term "socialist nationalism" in 1898 "to describe the integration of the proletariat into the nation," while Marcel Déat asserted that workers' conditions would degrade "unless the state becomes a tool for the liberation of the proletariat, a process which would in turn enable the proletariat to arrive at the idea of the nation."[133] Here, fascist intellectuals were advancing the premise for the proletarian nation embodied within a socialist and nationalist framework, designed to avoid the socioeconomic collapse that had befallen Soviet Russia and its workers, and to "integrate the class into the nation through the nationalization of the masses."[134] The proletarian nation was to harness all social forces and produce a national synthesis that would "provide the basis for social justice" wherein "the state is to belong to all classes and will unite the nation with socialism."[135]

Similar to the ideology of the early utopian socialists, national socialization for the Nazis did not require commonly owned property on a massive scale. State ownership of all means of production was never the original definition of socialism prior to Marx's theories. Even George Orwell (1903–1950) recognized this fact. Considering himself a democratic socialist, Orwell wrote that the "'common ownership of the means of production' is not in itself a sufficient definition of Socialism."[136] In his 1941 essay "The Lion and the Unicorn," Orwell treated the Nazis as part of the socialist clan, writing that "Internally, Germany has a good deal in common with a socialist state." He did admit that Nazi Germany had capitalist elements, but that they were thin-layered veneers, writing:

> ... the State, which is simply the Nazi Party, is in control of everything. It controls investment, raw materials, rates of interest, working hours, wages. The factory owner still owns his factory, but he is for practical purposes reduced to the status of a manager. Everyone is in effect a State employee.[137]

Although the early socialists originated much of the Nazis' doctrines and tactics, they did not identify with the reactionary right. Not surprisingly, nearly all nascent socialists self-identified with the left, determined not to be associated with the right-wing abuses so prevalent with the Church and the monarchies, and yet their ideological positions closely matched those of the Church and the monarchies. Like the Church, the early socialists opposed interest-bearing loans, self-indulgent capitalism, unsavory races, iconoclastic heretics, uncivilized foreigners, self-absorbed individualism, and free-trading markets. They embraced the Christian socialism of equality, brotherhood, and people's community that they believed would forge a new, unselfish man of virtue. But by the later part of the 19th century, neither the Church nor utopian socialists sought to impose their moralistic value system upon the populace; rather, they resolved to resort to persuasion over the sword. This sense of free-will choice within socialist precepts eventually vanished, however, after Marxism became the dominant strain of socialism. Despite its vision of a perfect future, Marxism had moved to the dark side, corrupted by authoritarian socialism and debased with dictatorial intolerance. In this sense, Marxism could be regarded as manifesting the moral fortitude of Church while imposing the absolute authority of a monarchy, all garnished under the deceptively disguised trademark of revolutionary socialism.

What is Socialism?

Since the ideals of early socialists match fairly closely with later-day Nazism and Italian Fascism, the question becomes this: What is socialism? This question has haunted the socialist community since the beginning. Socialist ideology has embodied so many varieties under an almost infinite spectrum of colors, that few can answer that question. Peter Lamb, the author of the *Historical Dictionary of Socialism*, asserts that there is no single definition clearly defining socialism.[138] In fact, in the book's foreword, the editor confesses that socialism "seems to have never ceased evolving." Even so, many historians and academics still refuse to identify Nazism or fascism as a descent of socialism's genealogy.

Part of the reason why involves the political game of multiple rivalries. After Germany and Italy allied with Franco in the 1936 Spanish Civil War, many socialists decided to disinherit Hitler and Mussolini from their socialist fraternity. That attitude changed briefly after the Nazi-Soviet Pact (Molotov-Ribbentrop Pact) was signed in 1939, making Nazis and Communists brothers-in-unity under a solemn compact. But after Hitler stabbed his partner in the back, no communist worth his red hammer and sickle insignia wanted to acknowledge Nazism as a branch affixed to the socialist tree. The mere thought of Hitler and Mussolini occupying similar ideological and political ground with communism was abhorrent. Therefore, the two years of Nazi collaboration with Stalin's Soviet Union had to be buried under reams of propaganda, which attempted to ignore their comrade's pro-socialist brotherhood and instead condemn them as the final right-wing stage of decaying capitalism.

Since a political spectrum is a continuum, it must have two extreme opposite ends in an effort to establish categorical variations and patterns. One extreme would be total government; the other would be no government (anarchy). Since the communists were totalitarian and authoritarian and boast of their extreme left-wing orientation, naturally, Hitler would follow in the same totalitarian-authoritarian footsteps. This means that Hitler and his minions were extreme left-wing socialists determined to socialize, nationalize, welfarize, and militarize society, just as Lenin and Stalin had attempted in the Soviet Union. In fact, in the early 1920s Hitler pointed out that the political contour of his movement included communists, boasting:

> In our movement the two extremes come together: the Communists from the Left and the officers and students from the Right. These two have always been the most active elements, and it was the greatest crime that they used to oppose each other in street fights... Our party has already succeeded in uniting these two utter extremes within the ranks of our storm troops. They will form the core of the great German liberation movement, in which all without distinction will stand together when the day comes to say: "The Nation arises, the storm is breaking!"[139]

However, many socialists nowadays refuse to even recognize Stalin, Lenin, or Soviet Russia as socialist. The Socialist Party of Great Britain still maintains that "Russia was never socialist."[140] Although the Soviet Union abolished all private property in fulfillment of Marx's wish for state ownership of all the means of production, Noam Chomsky, an American philosopher, historian, and linguist who aligns with anarcho-syndicalism and libertarian socialism, was still not satisfied with its status as a socialist state. Chomsky asserted back in 1986 that the Russian Soviet State had "destroyed every vestige of socialism."[141] In a 1989 speech, Chomsky also took a similar stand: "There was nothing remotely like socialism in the Soviet Union... [Lenin] didn't believe that it was possible to have socialism in the Soviet Union."[142] George Orwell remarked: "In my opinion, nothing has contributed so much to the corruption of the original idea of socialism as the belief that Russia is a socialist country..."[143] Even a dying Lenin in 1923 echoed this narrative, declaring that Russia had reverted to "a bourgeois tsarist machine... barely varnished with socialism."[144]

On the contrary, the Soviet Union was heavily nationalized. How can a political party or movement be considered non-socialist if they have nationalized every piece of property and business in the land, from outhouses to cathouses? What is the measuring stick? Hitler repeatedly identified himself as a "socialist," so that should count for something.

The 13th plank of the Nazi's 25-Point Program demanded the "nationalization of all corporations (trusts)." Government ownership of the means of production has always been the ultimate litmus test for Marxist socialism. So, how can an avowed socialist with nationalist credentials not be included within the scope of socialist historiography? Even so, Hitler has often been barred from joining the socialist brotherhood, despite a policy of big-tent socialism.

Hitler had talked about the nationalization and socialization of all corporations, both public and private. In an angry exchange over the ownership of securities and corporations, Hitler grumbled to Albert Speer that these owners "bring in high earnings without work. One of these days I'll sweep away this outrage and nationalize all corporations."[145] Such talk is Marxist in origin, and therefore would make national socialists or international socialists worthy of their names. Then again, Stalin branded any person or socialist who failed to take his marching orders as a right-wing reactionary. Even the various Marxist-leaning social democrat and democratic socialist parties had to endure the same "fascist" and "right-wing" vilification by Stalinists.

The Social Democrats were willing to work with capitalists, but through a gradualism that gravitated towards socioeconomic interventions, welfarism, state ownership, and the redistribution of income. Yet, to staunch Marxists, Social Democrats did not represent true socialism, and therefore they were repeatedly berated as reactionary mongrels who were expounding pseudo-socialism or crypto-fascism. During his exile in Zurich, Lenin echoed similar criticism against the Social Democratic Party (SPD) in Germany, denouncing them for abandoning class warfare, proletarian internationalism, and switching over to a "new nationalist ideology" that was later "to form the basis of National Socialism."[146] Yet, since the Social Democrats were ideologically so similar to Hitler's nationalistic socialism, why were they not also labeled "revolutionary conservatives" or "right-wing revolutionaries"?

By the early 20th century, Lenin was alarmed by the plethora of socialists and communists who sought a collective identity that infused socialism within a national character, convinced that a socialist community bound by a national framework might harm their overall communal goals. And yet the Communist Party of Germany, usually obedient to Moscow directives, declared itself in 1923 to be in favor of "National Bolshevism." *Die Rote Fahne*, the Communist Party of Germany's mouthpiece, created by Karl Liebknecht and Rosa Luxemburg in Berlin in 1918, stated: "Strongly to emphasize the nation is a revolutionary deed."[147] Stalin's interpretation of socialism moved in the same direction, encouraging him to adopt a nationalistic outlook that favored a Russian-style national Bolshevism soon after he codified a state policy endorsing "Socialism in One Country."

Those who had fallen under the spell of the nationalistic socialist movement were, like the Social Democrats, gradually moving towards a greater socialization and centralization of society. This was especially true after the Second International dissolved in 1916 over a clash about whether to embrace a nationalistic or internationalistic socialism. The conflict was tearing the European socialist movement apart. Hitler had been caught in this shifting windstorm that divided socialists and caused an overwhelming wave of embitterment.

But the objective of advancing a strong social safety net was never in question by the various National Socialist and Social Democratic parties throughout Europe. Germany had already established the first modern welfare state by the 1880s and Hitler's administration continued to strengthen it, developing a robust social safety net, larger massive public works projects, higher centralization of a state-planned economies, and larger doses of socialized medicine. The Nazi's 25-Point Program enshrined a multitude of demands for the public good, including "an expansion on a large scale of old age welfare," "the state be charged first with providing the opportunity for a livelihood and way of life for the citizens," "education at the expense of the State," and the "nationalization of all trusts" (corporations). Widely circulated Nazi posters assured that nobody would be left behind, claiming: "No one shall go hungry! No one shall be cold!"[148] One poster advertised Nazi charity thusly: "Health, child protection, fighting poverty, aiding travelers, community, helping mothers: These are the tasks of the National Socialist People's Charity. Become a member!"

Written by Adolf Hitler, Anton Drexler, and Gottfried Feder (1883–1941), the Nazis' 25 planks were staunchly anti-capitalist. An early key leader of the Nazi Party, Feder has been credited with inspiriting Hitler's opposition to "Jewish finance capitalism." Appointed as under-secretary at the ministry of economics of the Third Reich in 1933, Feder's opinions were often regarded as the official Nazi position on financial politics, which frequently "called for thoroughgoing state socialism."[149]

But earlier, Hitler first felt compelled to court other socialist groups in search of a new ideological home. In mid-1919, Hitler approached the German Socialist Party (DSP) and asked its founding chair, Georg Grassinger, to write for the *Völkischer Beobachter*, the future newspaper of the National Socialists. The DSP was not interested in Hitler, although when it later dissolved, many of its members joined the Nazi Party. But Hitler's disappointment did not last long. He soon found something more promising when he attended a meeting of Munich-based German Workers' Party on September 12, 1919. Here, he listened to Gottfried Feder, who delivered a blistering anti-capitalist speech entitled "How and By What Means Can Capitalism Be Eliminated?"[150] Hitler was overjoyed with Feder's anti-capitalist speech and rose up to voice his own resentments against capitalism. Feder, soon to become Hitler's mentor in finance and economic, pushed for the nationalization of large companies and banks. In his 1934 book *A History of National Socialism*, Konrad Heiden explained the extent of Feder's extreme socialist views that invigorated the Nazi Party. He wrote:

> Gottfried Feder gave the Nazi Party an ideology. Its essential points were paramount State ownership of land and the prohibition of private sales of land, the substitution of German for Roman law, nationalization of the banks and the abolition of interest by an amortization service. It was he, too, who inspired the Party with its doctrine of the distinction between productive and non-productive capital and of the necessity for destroying the "slavery of profits."[151]

All of these socialists and unionists were ardent leftists, who opposed clericalism, monarchism, and capitalism. Even Konrad Heiden had to agree, readily admitting in 1934 that in their earlier days the "Nazi Party was still a Party of the Left."[152] In fact, Heiden asserted that as the German Worker's Party morphed into the Nazi Party, its party members considered themselves as belonging on the Left, arguing that this "youthful Party still felt itself to be a Party of the Left."[153] But somehow many historians still want to refer to these hardcore socialists and labor activists as "right-wing."

A few years later in 1922, Hitler spelled out his hatred of capitalism and its business-minded Jews, declaring:

> Capitalism as a whole will now be destroyed... We are not fighting Jewish or Christian capitalism, we are fighting very capitalism: we are making the people completely free.[154]

Hitler's rant against capitalism would have warmed the cockles of most socialists' hearts, whether inclined to engage in democracy or revolution. To the Nazis, the Jew was the typical representative of capitalist-bourgeoisie exploitation who engaged in conspiratorial work to profit from fomenting class strife. In 1931 Hitler made it clear why he hated the middle class in Germany, remarking: "The bourgeoisie rules by intrigue, but it can have no foothold in my movement because we accept no Jews or Jewish accomplices into our Party."[155] Hitler then delved a little deeper into his distaste for the bourgeoisie, declaring in a confidential interview:

> Today's bourgeoisie is rotten to the core; it has no ideals any more; all it wants to do is earn money and so it does me what damage it can. The bourgeois press does me damage too and would like to consign me and my movement to the devil.[156]

Hitler also hated the traditional German politician of the Weimar Republic. He lashed out at them, calling them "highbrows," and said that their old laws and traditions were "born in individualist thinking." But he saved his biggest rebuke for politicians, saying "most of them have never even read Marx" and regarded the "Bolshevik revolution as a private Russian affair."[157]

Following in the footsteps of the social democrats, the Nazis also publicly advocated for democratic institutions and popular suffrage, although history eventually demonstrated that representative democracy was not the Nazis' long-term goal. Nonetheless, resting on their communitarian socioeconomic laurels, the Nazis could easily be incorporated with the various social democratic gradualist movements of Europe in the 20th century. The one major fault of this comradely classification concerns the Nazi's propensity for violent street confrontations, which corresponded more closely to the violence perpetrated by the German communists, some who fancied themselves as violent Blanquists.[158] These revolutionary socialists were simply following Marx's anti-democratic instructions. Marx once explained to Engels that his objective "was at bottom nothing but a plan of war against democracy."[159] Engels enthusiastically agreed, referring to Marx's strategy as the "Plan of Campaign against Democracy."[160]

In this sense, Hitler was following his own heretical version of Marx's dream of a dictatorship established by workers, but, like Lenin, had instead decided to alter the formula and attain power through a dictatorial vanguard of political elites. This was a type of elitist revolution that Hitler saw promising; using his party organization to obtain power by violent or democratic means in an anti-democratic quest to obliterate any remaining vestige of liberal democracy in Germany. Hitler had simply found Lenin's revolutionary methodology more appealing.

Strasserism and National Bolshevism

Ever since the beginning of the Nazis movement, a powerful radical socialist coterie pressured Hitler to maintain a momentum towards socialism and revolution. Indeed, this revolutionary socialist wing of the Nazis included Otto Strasser, once a Social Democratic Party of Germany member, and his brother Gregor Strasser, considered the "undisputed right-hand man by [Nazi] party officials." The Strassers sought a nationalist form of socialist revolution.[161] Early on, Otto Strasser identified himself as left-wing student, writing in his 1940 book *Hitler and I* that he "was a young student of law and economics, a Left Wing student leader, and a leader of ex-soldier students."[162] Otto Strasser was a member of the Socialist Party and considered himself "Red" when he fought against the "reactionary Whites" in the 1920 Kapp Putsch in Berlin.[163] As Otto Strasser continued to push National Socialism towards Marxism, one scholar referred to him as "the Trotsky of the Nazi Party."[164]

It was Gregor Strasser who excelled the most during his political career, and achieved popularity and power second only to Hitler. Considered the head of the Nazi party's left-wing faction, Gregor Strasser declared in a November 1925 Reichstag speech:

> We National Socialists want the economic revolution involving the nationalization of the economy... We want in place of an exploitative capitalist economic system a real socialism, maintained not by a soulless Jewish-materialist outlook but by the believing, sacrificial, and unselfish old German community sentiment, community purpose and economic feeling. We want the social revolution in order to bring about the national revolution.[165]

These far left-wing Nazi adherents of "Strasserism" were disappointed that Hitler did not closely follow in the footsteps of a Marx-like social and worker-based revolution to achieve a national rebirth. Referring to himself as a "national revolutionary," Otto Strasser published his *Nationalsozialistische Briefe* in 1925. It addressed the ideas of redistributing wealth, class struggle, and a potential future alliance with the Soviet Union. Otto Strasser suggested a "German Central Europe—fighting against the West, with temporary support from the East."[166]

By 1930, Hitler's NSDAP was experiencing internal conflicts that were pushing the party further towards a Marxist interpretation of socialism. In a party leadership speech in Munich on April 27, 1930, Hitler tore into Otto Strasser's *Kampfverlag*[167] publishing house for the Nazis of Berlin. Hitler denounced the *Kampfverlag* and its writers as "salon Bolsheviks."[168] Otto Strasser's political views, along with those of other hardcore socialist doctrinaires, were seen as comprising a "heady brew of radical mystical nationalism, strident anti-capitalism, social reformism, and anti-Westernism," where their rejection of a bourgeois social order was producing "admiration for the radical anti-capitalism of the Bolsheviks."[169] Eventually, both brothers had to resign their positions in the Nazi party. Gregor Strasser was later shot to death in 1934 in a prison cell by the *Schutzstaffel* ("Protection Squadron," SS), over an ideological and personal rivalry with Hitler.

Despite his disdain for Strasserism, Hitler still manifested an anti-wealth posture when confronted about his personal assets. Like the typical socialist, especially Marxist dictators of later years, Hitler would brag in speeches about his wealth-deprived condition, despite living in splendor at his mountain villa at Berchtesgaden or the Chancellery in Berlin. Speaking in 1936 to the Krupp Locomotive factory workers in Essen, Hitler declared:

> Whenever I stand up for the German peasant, it is for the sake of the Volk. I have neither ancestral estate nor manor... I believe I am the only statesman in the world who does not have a bank account. I hold no stock, I have no shares in any companies. I do not draw any dividends.[170]

Goebbels held similar radical views, repeating the public message that "We are not a charitable institution but a Party of revolutionary socialists."[171] Despite Hitler's occasional reprimands, Goebbels pushed hard in the 1920s for a nationalist-style communism (a movement later known as "National Bolshevism"). Goebbels wrote in the1920: "Therefore, Russia is our natural ally against the devilish temptations and corruption of the West."[172] According to historian Gerhard Hirschfeld, Goebbels was "praising Russia for taking the path to socialism against all odds."[173]

After his expulsion from the Nazi Party in 1930, Otto Strasser continued to call for the state-imposed breakup and confiscation of large estates, more socialist-based policies, profit participation, class struggle, and stronger economic planning by the Third Reich.[174] The radical left wing of the Nazi party wanted to dislodge the wealthy German elite and finish the social revolution. They regarded Hitler's ascendancy to Chancellor as a "half-revolution," which had to someday be concluded.[175] Fiercely anti-capitalist, Otto was the guiding force behind his alternative new party—the Combat League of Revolutionary National Socialists—later known as the Black Front, which some historians have labeled as "national Marxism" or a "National-Bolshevik group."[176]

Fierce political infighting and factionalism are usually rampant among revolutionary movements, often becoming one of their most defining characteristics. Historically, most revolutions are plagued by extremist factions trying to push the revolutionary envelope to its most radical edges, usually with utopian and social justice goals. Lenin's communist revolution had to retract its "War Communism" policies after food riots and labor strikes erupted due to mass confiscation of Russian farmers' grain supply (*Prodrazvyorstka*) in addition to rationing, forced labor, a militarization of industry, and nationalization. Lenin's reaction was to appease his more conservative constituencies by accommodating a more liberal, capitalistic, and mixed economy under his New Economic Policy (NEP) in 1921, which he approvingly referred to as "state capitalism."

Hitler experienced a similar political crisis when confronted by Nazi revolutionary socialists who constantly challenged the Führer's ideological leadership. Hitler had to back away from stronger socialist measures in order to appease conservative elements, just as Lenin had done. When the hardcore Nazis continued to push for revolutionary socialism after Hitler's ascent to Chancellor, however, the regime carried out purges and political murders in 1934, in an event referred to as the "Night of the Long Knives" or the "Röhm-Putsch."

The Marxist-leaning dichotomies within Hitler's ranks had grown large, powerful, and demanding. They would settle for nothing less than unadulterated socialism. For example, the co-founder of the Nazi party's SA "brownshirts" Stormtroopers (*Sturmabteilung*) Ernst Röhm (1887–1934), pushed for fully implementing socialism, and a "second revolution" after Hitler seized power. In his 1944 book *The Fuhrer*, Konrad Heiden wrote, "Röhm coined the slogan that there must be 'second revolution,' this time, not against the Left, but against the Right." According to his diary, Goebbels found this agreeable.[177] In a diary entry on April 18, 1933, he wrote:

> Everyone among the people is talking of a second revolution which must come. That means that the first revolution is not at an end. Now we shall settle with the *Reaktion*. The revolution must nowhere come to a halt.[178]

In that second revolution, Röhm foresaw a purging of the "Reaktion"— the term used by the Nazis to identify conservative factions. During the second revolution, Röhm, Goebbels and other "radicals" demanded that Hitler liquidate the old aristocracy, big business and finance, Prussian generals, and Junker landlords,[179] and also that he "nationalize more industries, worker control of the means of production, and the confiscation and redistribution of property and wealth of the upper classes"[180]—

a type of militant revolutionary Bolshevism that would have made Lenin proud. In fact, some of these radical socialist Nazis talked about engaging in "permanent revolution," similar to what Trotsky had advocated. Naturally, Hitler was alarmed by Röhm's fiery advocacy "to redistribute wealth and to fulfill the Socialist goals of the NSDAP."[181] Hitler delivered a speech to counter the Nazi revolutionary socialists' push towards Lenin-style communism, proclaiming, "Revolution is not a permanent condition."[182] This struggle ended in "Night of the Long Knives," also known as the "Röhm-Putsch."

To maintain power, Hitler took extrajudicial action to eliminate both outside opponents and the radical left threats rising from Marxist-leaning Nazi party leaders. He could ill afford to antagonize his broad base, especially since Germany was soaked in classical liberal values of property rights and industrial capitalism. He also desperately needed some version of capitalism to assure the innovation and productivity necessary to rebuild Germany's depleted military. Even Marx recognized the benefits of industrial capitalism operated by the bourgeoisie. Writing in the *Manifesto of the Communist Party*, Marx remarked: "The bourgeoisie has... accomplished wonders far surpassing Egyptian pyramids, Roman aqueducts, and Gothic cathedrals."[183] As one socialist scholar noted, Marx was "inclined to give capitalism more credit than it deserved for developing the backward areas of the world."[184]

Hitler was well aware of the vivid accounts by Russian expatriates regarding the miserable living conditions in the Soviet Union. The socialist community of European understood the unsettling consequences that occurred after the Russian communists started to completely nationalize its industrial and agricultural base. They eventually learned that after the Soviets had nationalized all firms with five or more employees, industrial production ground to a crawl under their bureaucratic and administrative weight. As the ruble collapsed, shortages became chronic and raw material almost impossible to secure. Worst of all, tens of thousands of workers and engineers fled to the countryside in search of food. By 1920, "foreign trade had virtually ceased, and industrial production had fallen to a small fraction of its prewar quantity."[185] One source calculated that by "1921 industrial output was only 18% of its 1916 level. By 1922, it was only 27% of pre-war levels."[186] Moreover, by 1921, wages for city workers had plummeted an estimated two-thirds in just three years. Lenin could no longer brag about his communist worker state, since there were almost no workers employed in the Soviet Union.

To socialists and Marxists in other lands, such devastating economic data were frightening. For decades they had represented themselves as the true vanguard and protectors of industrial workers and labor in general. But with Lenin's almost complete nationalization of the economy and abolishment of capitalism, by 1921 the Bolsheviks had effectively destroyed Russia's industrial capacity and working class. Hitler was correct in fearing the same catastrophic outcome if he implemented the 13th planks of his 25-point Nazi Program to nationalize all corporations. He understood that without some remaining capitalist components in Germany, it would be impossible to militarily avenge the injustices of France and England and their Treaty of Versailles. He desperately needed productive workers and war factories to build his massive military machine. Hitler made this point in his declaration of war on the Soviet Union (the Barbarossa Proclamation): I "have tried for two decades to build a new socialist order in Germany, with a minimum of interference and without harming our productive capacity."[187]

Nazi SA Stormtroopers and Beefsteaks

Hitler not only had to handle disgruntled Nazi leaders who pushed for more social radical changes, but also faced two to three million SA paramilitary members of the Nazi Stormtrooper (SA) units, who had a cult-like loyalty to their leader Ernst Röhm. Most of the SA's bullyboys came from the working class and unemployed and often sympathized with a Marxist-leaning socialism. They expected Hitler and the Nazi party to remain committed to fulfilling the Nazis' official 1920 socialist program.[188] Evidence of this socialist contempt for capitalism could be seen in Nazi posters plastered throughout working-class neighborhoods, reading: "The maintenance of a rotten industrial system has nothing to do with nationalism. I can love Germany and hate capitalism."[189] In fact, Röhm, who was often portrayed as a populist demagogue, wanted his plebeian army to engage in permanent revolution, conquering Germany's conservative elements and begetting hardcore socialism via insurrection. He felt an affinity for the communists, expressing in his memoirs that "Many things are between us and the Communists, but we respect the sincerity of their conviction and their willingness to bring sacrifices for their own cause, and this unites us with them."[190]

Not only were Röhm and other SA leaders bordering on the edge of communism, but many of them were also openly homosexual, appearing fearless and confident within Hitler's vanguard of authority.[191,192] Hitler was well aware of his longtime friend's homosexuality; it was no secret by the mid-1920s. The point here is not Röhm's sexual orientation, but that Hitler, whose regime persecuted homosexuals, allowed such lifestyles among his own high-ranking leaders for so long. Röhm was no neophyte; he was a member of the German Workers' Party (DAP) before Hitler arrived on the scene to revamp and rename the party. To some scholars, Hitler was considered "to a substantial extent, Röhm's protégé."[193]

Of course, this attitude towards Röhm's and other Nazis' unconventional sexual orientation for over a decade might be due to Hitler's own possible indiscretions. A number of books, including Lothar Machtan's *The Hidden Hitler*, claimed that Hitler was a homosexual and had sexual relations with August Kubizek, Ernst Schmidt and a number of male prostitutes during his tender years.[194]

The radicalization of SA Nazi leaders and members came to light when a phenomenon arose in Germany where Nazis and communists were constantly changing their party affiliation. These party switchers were known as "Beefsteaks," or "Beefsteak Nazis." Understandably, this occurrence worried both Nazi and communist partisans. Since Nazi and communist ideology and tactics appeared similar to so many, especially the working class, side-switching between Nazis and communists become increasing popular, especially inside SA ranks. This phenomenon became most predominant in late 1932, when the Nazis' prospects for political power were high. The Nazis had accumulated 196 seats in the Reichstag compared to 100 seats for the communists.

In his 1936 book *Hitler: A Biography*, the German historian and journalist Konrad Heiden acknowledged this serious problem, writing that "there were large numbers of Communist and Social Democrats among them," Röhm *Sturmabteilung* (SA) ranks,[195] often "called beefsteaks." In fact, there were so many communists and non-Nazis within the stormtroopers that a common jest went: "one S.A. man says to another: 'In our storm troop there are three Nazis, but we shall soon have spewed them out.'"[196]

The Nazis encouraged German communists to join them, regarding them as excellent new recruits. Of course, the communists did the same, since their ideological makeup was so interchangeable. This practice became a well-known joke in the 1930s, where the Nazis were said to be "brown on the outside and red on the inside."[197] Another phrase went, "Nazi brown outside, Moscow red inside."

This Nazi-communist attraction had actually started much earlier. According to Stanley G. Payne, Nazis and communists wanted to join each other to fight "Jewish capitalists" and embrace "national liberation" as early as 1923. Payne wrote:

> At the Twelfth Party Congress in Moscow in 1923, Nikolia Bukharin stressed that the Nazi Party had "inherited Bolshevik political culture exactly as Italian Fascism had done." On June 20, 1923, Karl Radek gave a speech before the Comintern Executive Committee proposing a common front with the Nazis in Germany. That summer several Nazis addressed Communist meetings and vice versa, as the German Communist Party took a strong stand for "national liberation" against the Treaty of Versailles and inveighed against "Jewish capitalists." It is said that a few of the more radical Nazis even told German Communists that if the latter got rid of their Jewish leaders, the Nazi would support them.[198]

Not only did many members of Hitler's SA join the Communist Party of Germany, but the German communists produced a Nazi newspaper (*Der Freiheitskämpfer*) of their own to "compete with bloodthirsty rhetoric and anti-Semitic stereotypes."[199] The publication of the newspaper was carried out under a climate of a shared "culture of radicalism" for those in the local ranks of street militants.[200] Still, this convergence between the Nazi SA and communist KPD members indicated that the cohesiveness between the two totalitarian and socialist ideologies was much more closely aligned than originally thought. In fact, the SA and the KPD often formally and semi-officially cooperated with each other, blurring the ideological boundaries that should have politically separated them in their pursuit to outmuscle each other.

The similarities between Nazism and communism might explain why the diehard Marxist historian Eric Hobsbawm (1917–2012) was so impressed by the vibrancy of Nazism in Berlin during the early 1930s. Here is where he joined the Socialist Schoolboys, which was considered a *de facto* limb of the communist movement. Leaving Germany for England in 1933, Hobsbawm became a lifelong communist in the late 1930s after reading Karl Marx. Nonetheless, he confessed in a 2002 interview that the Nazi's ideology was enticing when Hitler came to power. He clearly saw the resemblances between communism and Nazism, writing:

> Liberalism was failing. If I'd been German and not a Jew, I could see I might have become a Nazi, a German nationalist. I could see how they'd become passionate about saving the nation. It was a time when you didn't believe there was a future unless the world was fundamentally transformed.[201]

Generally, during the early years, Nazis and communists were seen as budding revolutionary parties, often recognized as left-wing political competitors. For instance, an early and lifelong force within the socialist left-wing Fabian Society, George Bernard Shaw was captivated by Hitler, remarking that he was "a very remarkable, very able man," who understood that "Germany had been kicked long enough."[202] Not only that, but Shaw found time to heap praise on Stalin, proclaiming: "Stalin is a good Fabian and that's the best that can be said of anyone."[203]

Such a reply might classify Shaw and others who shared a similar fondness for fascism and communism as "Fascist-Marxists." After all, long after Mussolini founded the Fascist Revolutionary Party in 1915, he still remained loyal to Lenin, the October 1917 Russian Revolution, unionism, and various revisions of Marxism.

Imprecise Nature of the Political Spectrum

But due to the imprecise and subjective nature of political classification, one faction would be considered less or more leftist than another, meaning that one branch was going to be seen as representing right-wing socialism and the other the left-wing socialism, similar to the Soviet Russians' dueling Left Opposition and Right Opposition during Stalin's regime. Hitler was actually only a few notches to the right of Stalin's authoritarian, nationalistic and anti-Semitic excesses, but many western intellectuals spellbound by the aura of Marxism eventually decided to peg Nazism on the far right. What this really meant was that Nazis and Italian fascists were merely seated in a right-wing row of the left-wing aisle, in a similar position to that of the social democrats and democratic socialists. Relative to contemporary political, economic, and tactical policies, fascism and Nazism were still very firmly planted within the extreme socialist left, mainly due their heavily ideological and tactical influences by Marxists and revolutionary socialists who had earlier classified themselves as left-wing.

Again, this designation of left or right is a package deal. To be the polar opposite, one must actually be the exact antithetical to the other. That is how it works. Only the classical liberal bordering on individual anarchism fits the bill as complete antipodes to the authoritarian species. Since communism, Nazism and fascism are so closely aligned to each other, how could they not be regarded under same group-collective canopy?

Examples of the Nazi-Communist parallels are endless. Vera Micheles Dean, considered a leading authority in international affairs, wrote in 1939 that

> Fascism and Communism represented the urge of the lower middle class to complete the French Revolution—which had signalized the victory of the "Third Estate" over the Church, the monarchy, and the feudal aristocracy—by destroying, in turn, the privileges of the new capitalist class brought into being by the Industrial Revolution.[204]

She found few differences between the two rival socialist ideologies of communism and Nazism.

Other well-respected historians have made the same claim. French historian François Furet, a former communist intellectual, not only wrote that "Nazism was a German form of Bolshevism,"[205] but that:

> It was in Nazi Germany that Bolshevism was perfected; there, political power truly absorbed all spheres of existence, from the economy to religion, from technology to the soul. The irony, the tragedy, of history was that both totalitarian regimes, identical in their aim for absolute power over dehumanized beings, presented themselves as protection from the danger presented by the other.[206]

The stauncher classical liberals were not fooled by rivalry, propaganda, and militaristic ethos of socialist egalitarians. Generally, they understood that the Nazis, fascists, and communists were blood brothers beholden to the same collective banner, exhibiting a penchant for similar abstract notions to dominate society, including that the "common good" must always trump the "individual good." This communitarian position of a classless society was supposedly endowed with perfectible socioeconomic equality that was to foreordain harmony, but instead harbored the conflict-riddled features of paternalism, militarism, and authoritarianism—dangerous under any cosmetic label.

Even *The New York Times* acknowledged the close similarities between Nazism and communism after their non-aggression pact was signed and their armies had invaded Poland together in 1939, editorializing that the issue remained clear: "Hitlerism is brown communism, Stalinism is red fascism."[207] *The New York Times* continued by affirming that "The world will now understand that the only real 'ideological' issue is one between democracy, liberty and peace on the one hand and despotism, terror and war on the other."

The Wall Street Journal also joined the ranks of those who compared Nazis and Stalinists as evil twin comrades, observing: "The American people know that the principal difference between Mr. Hitler and Mr. Stalin is the size of their respective mustaches."[208] Some socialist leaders echoed the same sentiment about Stalin's fascist communism, including Norman Thomas, who wrote that "Such is the logic of 'totalitarianism' that 'communism,' whatever it was originally, is today Red fascism."[209,210] In fact, in a February 24, 1941, speech, as reported by *The Bulletin of International News*, Hitler said that "basically National Socialism, and Marxism is the same."[211]

Even the slight differences of intra-political ideologies do not change the fact that Nazi and communist fundamentals and tactics relied on state authority to socially re-engineer society by emasculating the individual means of self-determination and consent. To the original liberals, sacrificial collectivism inevitably leads to serfdom, the Gulag, the Holocaust, the Pol Pot Killing Fields, and mass genocide in general. To classical liberals, political labels did not matter as much as what a political ideology and movement embraced as its core philosophy. Whether touted as left-wing or right-wing, the philosophical context has always been more important than arbitrary, deceptive, and often-confusing political classifications.

Similarities among authoritarian dogmas have caused many Marxists to be lured to the socialism, anti-capitalism and revolutionary nationalism of the Nazis, since their disparities were so minor. This explains the reason why historians concede that Röhm's SA was Marxist-leaning and further left than Hitler and other Nazi party officials. Röhm and the devotees of Strasserism could be more actually described as equivalent to a strand of Hitlerite-Marxist diehards who were motivated by anti-capitalist rage and overwhelmed with a desire for a socialized nirvana.

The evidence was plain to see: Rudolf Diels, head of the Gestapo in 1933–34, remarked in 1933 that in the city of Berlin, around "70 percent" of fresh SA recruits were former communists.[212] According to political scientist Peter H. Merkl, both the SA and SS were saturated with socialists and Marxists, asserting that "The utopians and those who speak of a Marxist republic have the highest membership in the SA and SS (77.6 and 63 percent respectively)."[213]

To the pundits and humorists, the "beefsteaks" name was a pejorative to acknowledge the fact that underneath the ostensibly Nazi's brownshirt lurked a red-blooded communist. Others in the political arena saw the same Nazi-communist parallelism. For instance, in the 1920s the German chancellor Hermann Müller of Social Democratic Party of Germany (SPD) employed the beefsteaks analogy when he remarked that "red equals brown."[214] This term referred to the conviction that Communists and Nazis posed an equal danger to liberal democracy. Later, another leading German social democratic politician, Kurt Schumacher, caused a media stir when he derided communists as "red-painted Nazis," while accusing the two political movements of enabling each other.[215] In fact, after the World War II, Schumacher argued that the Soviet Union had not pursued internationalist, world-revolutionary goals, but instead "nationalist and imperialist" ones that paralleled Nazism.[216]

In another case, Alfred Hugenberg (1865–1951), the main leader of the conservative German National People's Party (DNVP), finally had enough with his short-lived coalition with Hitler's NSDAP. He concluded that the Nazis were the "main enemy" of Germany. By the fall of 1932, conservative leaders stated that they saw no difference between the "red Bolshevism" of the communist KPD and the "brown Bolshevism" of Hitler's Nazi party.[217] The Nazis retaliated by branding the conservatives as being reactionary and bourgeois.

To Hugenberg and other conservative, nationalist, and reactionary parties, Hitler's true socialist colors were starting to stain Germany red. The main bone of contention that perturbed German conservatives was Hitler's decision to come out in favor of a labor strike in Berlin by transport workers in November 1932. To make matters worse, Hitler had allied with the Communist Party of Germany against the Social Democrats in support of a workers' wage dispute.[218] In that labor dispute, Hitler's "brownshirts" and red-flag-waving communists marched side by side through the streets of Berlin and damaged any buses whose drivers had failed to participate in the worker's strike. Alongside the communists, Nazis ripped up tram lines, stood together, "shouted in unison," and "rattled their collecting tins" to get donations for their strike funds in support of the Revolutionary Trade Union Opposition (RGO) for the communists and National Socialist Factory Cell Organization (NSBO) for the Nazis.[219]

Many middle-class and rural Germans voted against Hitler to display their disgust over the Nazi-communist collaboration.[220] Other DNVP members like Count Ewald von Kleist-Schmenzin attacked Hitler and his Nazi party as entertaining neo-pagan tendencies. Many German voters had detected the "pronounced socialist image of the NSDAP that had come across strongly during the campaign," where the "Nazis had seemed to many little different from the class-warfare of the Communists. The similarity of 'red' and 'brown' varieties of 'Bolshevism' appeared proven..."[221] Many middle-class Germans suspected that "Hitler was arm in arm with Marxism," and "thought Hitler far on the Left."[222]

A number of liberal political parties attempted to impede the advancement of the National Socialists in the early 1930s, such as the German People's Party (DVP) and the German State Party (DSP). They forewarned their party members that the National Socialists represented "a party of the radical left."[223] One DVP publication denounced the socialist elements of the Nazis, warning: "Whether national or international, it is still socialism, indeed, ... of the most radical type."[224] The DVP leadership argued that the Nazis "have nothing in common with the bourgeois parties which stand on the foundation of the capitalist Weltanschauung." To DVP and DSP way of thinking, the Nazis "would make a more compatible ally of Communism," rather than liberal or conservative-based parties.[225] In fact, the DVP worked diligently to link National Socialism with Marxism. They believed that since the National Socialists were attacking capitalism, engaging in "ruthless proletarian phrases," and proposing the abolishment of "interest capital," the German economy would fail as did the Soviet economy in 1921. The DVP told their party constituents that the Nazis "socialistic programs, are not one penny better than other Socialists."[226]

These national liberal parties accused the Nazi deputies in the Reichstag of backing:

> ... the most incredible Communist-sponsored proposals. But, of course, they don't tell the middle class and the peasants about this. In front of them they portray themselves as "anti-Marxists" ... beware of wolves in sheep's clothing.[227]

According to British historian Ian Kershaw, just before Hitler gained power, most Catholics saw Hitler as "the head of a 'godless,' anti-Christian movement."[228] As for the "nationalist-conservative Right," which had some sympathies toward Hitler at first, they "had given way to hostility." Here,

> Hitler was portrayed for the most part as intransigent and irresponsible, a wild and vulgar demagogue, not a statesman, an obstacle to political recovery, the head of an extremist movement with menacing socialistic tendencies.[229]

A number of political ventures, including the Harzburg Front, were composed of conservatives, nationalists, anti-socialists, monarchists, traditionalists and Hitler's NSDAP party, all mostly brought together due to their common animosity towards the Weimar Republic. It was a marriage of convenience, with everyone harboring mutual distrust. Hitler considered the Harzburg Front as tactical, since there were too many substantial differences with Hugenberg's conservative DNVP. Goebbels saw it as a temporary alliance. Not surprisingly, the Nazi propaganda apparatus described the conservatives in the DNVP as their bourgeois arch-enemy while the Nazis were advocating an anti-bourgeois stance. In another incident, the Nazis condemned the DNVP as "an insignificant heap of reactionaries" who could not build a mass movement.[230]

By the time of the fall 1932 election, the Nazis were almost at war with the conservative DNVP—where "the Nazis broke up German National election meetings with stink bombs and tear gas" and heckled a DNVP deputy and called him "Jew boy."[231] The German national press retaliated with charges of Nazism awash in socialism, violent behavior, and stern warnings of the economic doom if the Nazis were to gain power.[232] The DNVP and German conservatives took the view that Nazism "appeared leftist" and denounced Hitler's ideology as "bolshevism in nationalist wrapping."[233]

Many historians blame the various nationalist conservative parties for releasing Hitler upon the world, but there was another side. What actually facilitated the Nazis' rise to political power at the voting booth was the Stalin-controlled Communist International (Comintern), which demanded that the Communist Party of Germany treat the Social Democratic Party of Germany as their arch-enemies—referring to them as the party of "social fascists," which splintered the opposition against Hitler on the socialist left.

Ironically, the SPD was founded as a Marxist party in 1875, but later softened its socialist policies. Attempting to intervene in German politics, Stalin opposed any independent socialist movement not directly under his thumb. He proclaimed in 1924 that "Social democracy is objectively the moderate wing of fascism... These organisations (i.e. Fascism and social democracy) are not antipodes, they are twins."[234] The Russian communists publicly stated that "The aims of the fascists and the social-fascists are the same."[235,236] This also means that Stalin considered Hitler and his Nazi allies almost identical to the left-wing social democrats. This comparison has validity except for Hitler's adherence to anti-democratic politics, violence and the ideological determinism that also imbued Marxism. In a sort of hierarchical pecking order on the political spectrum, National Socialism has all the evidential earmarks of being tightly sandwiched between Social Democracy and Marxism.

Essentially, Hitler and his National Socialist party leaders were economic social democrats. They held the typical socialist anti-Semitic and anti-capitalist mindset, but engaged in Marxist "revolutionary terror" in an effort to sabotage and mock democracy after the acquisition of power. But before that, Hitler exploited democracy to elect the largest party in Germany's parliament in the 1932 elections that resulted in Hitler's chancellorship. This was in sharp contrast to the Russian Bolshevists, who lost the 1917 election but kicked out the winning Socialist Revolutionary Party.

Historically, Hitler's beliefs were close to social democracy. After the military defeat of the Communist-organized Bavarian Soviet Republic in early May 1919, Hitler had taken off his red armband, turned against communism, and developed "Social Democratic feelings," telling comrades that he favored a nationalistic version of Social Democracy.[237] Also at the time, Erhard Auer, chairman of the Social Democratic Party of Germany parliamentary group, resisted international socialism and cooperated with other parties, which appealed to Hitler.[238] In fact, many years later, Hitler was recorded as saying on February 1, 1942, that "The only problem for the Social Democrats at the time was that they did not have a leader."[239] On the ideological level, Hitler could have become a powerful leader in the Social Democratic Party of Germany. Because of Hitler's penchant for nationalistic Social Democracy and Marxian revolutionary violence, Nazism could be easily identified as a militant Social Democratic movement.

Still, this begs the question of whether the social democracy and Marxist revisionist movements were the primary precursors to Italian Fascism and Nazism. Bernstein and social democrats not only broke with classical Marxism over revolutionary militarism, but signaled a much friendlier attitude towards capitalism, arguing that "capitalism was overcoming many of its weaknesses, such as unemployment, overproduction, and the inequitable distribution of wealth."[240] In fact, Bernstein took the position of class collaboration, an idea advocated by Mussolini, believing that "success for socialism depended not on the continued and intensifying misery of the working class but rather on eliminating that misery."[241]

Not only was Stalin accusing Nazism of being a marching partner of the social democrats and democratic socialism, but he was also saying that German Nazism was part of a wide, left-wing political movement. Interestingly, in 1921, Hitler felt compelled to defend early Nazi supporter Hermann Esser from internal Nazi party attacks, remarking, "Everyone was at one time a Social Democrat."[242] Ernst Toller, President of the Bavarian Soviet Republic for only six days in 1919, reported that a fellow prisoner also interned for his involvement in the socialist republic, and according to historian Ian Kershaw, "had met Hitler in a Munich barracks during the first months after the revolution, and that the latter had then been calling himself a Social Democrat."[243] Konrad Heiden also remarked that during this time, in heated discussions, Hitler had "espoused the cause of Social Democracy against that of the Communists."[244] During his years as a correspondent for the *Frankfurter Zeitung*, Heiden wrote that "Hitler had supported the SPD" (Social Democratic Party of Germany) and he "talked about joining the party."[245] At an early meeting of a political group that eventually turned into the Nazi Party, Hitler told Friedrich Krohn, an early supporter of the party, that he preferred a type of "socialism" he referred to as "national Social Democracy" that was not dissimilar to nations like Scandinavia, England, and prewar Bavaria.[246] One wonders if Stalin had it correct all along; that the social democrats and the Nazis were "twins" birthed by the same socialist mother.

There were a number of other reports from Germans that supported the claim that Hitler endorsed Social Democracy. One newspaper, the liberal daily *Berliner Tageblatt*, wrote in October 29, 1930, that Hitler had identified himself "as a supporter of Social Democracy," although he still expressed some reservations.[247] Not only that, but the German historian Thomas Weber asserted that "Hitler supported the left during the revolution," leaving open only the question of "what kind of left-wing ideas and groups he supported or at least accepted."[248]

Hitler's favorable backing for the Social Democrats was short-lived. His later feelings of animosity towards the Social Democrats was not over socioeconomic theories or a sudden dislike of socialism, but that the

SPD was directly responsible for approving a punitive peace treaty that made Germans realize that Germany had actually lost the war. Most Germans were traumatized from this sudden epiphany. During this juncture, Hitler experienced his own road-to-Damascus conversion when the newly-formed SPD-led government, which included the Catholic Central Party, signed and ratified the Treaty of Versailles on July 9, 1919, signifying the total defeat of Germany.[249] Hitler saw the SPD as traitors to Germany's national interests and ethnic identity. This represented Hitler's political transformation towards a militant-racial radicalization, and away from the moderate social democracy and Catholicism. He would never forgive the Social Democrats for surrendering Germany to foreigners.

It appears that Hitler's involvement with the communist-run Bavarian Soviet Republic (*Bayerische Räterepublik* in German) demonstrates some type of commitment to communism. After all, Hitler held an elected position during the red *Räterepublik* government that was under the complete control of the Communist Party of Germany. He did not flee or resign his position. Moreover, Hitler was "arrested" and interned on May 1, 1919, a few days before the Bavarian Soviet Republic was completely crushed.[250] Apparently, he found it necessary to defend himself against accusations of being a communist along with other suspects.[251] When Konrad Heiden acknowledged that there were "heated discussions" among his barracks comrades, it could mean that Hitler was under duress; that he felt compelled to defend himself and support the "Social Democracy against that of the Communists."

Hitler was not the only future Nazi leader to be drawn to socialist revolution and Marxism. Sepp Dietrich, a Waffen-SS general and head of Hitler's SS-*Leibstandarte*, held the elected position of chairman of a Soldiers' Council by November 1918.[252] Then there was Julius Schreck, who was not only the first leader of the *Schutzstaffel*, but later Hitler's chauffeur. Schreck served in the Red Army of the German Communist Party that controlled the Bavarian Soviet Republic.[253] Hitler's future deputy, Rudolf Hess, was actively serving in the Bavarian Red Army, writing home to his parents on April 23 that his unit had not experienced "any unrest at all. Yesterday we had an orderly march with red flags, nothing else out of the ordinary."[254] Another Nazi leader strongly attracted by revolutionary fever was one of Hitler's closest wartime friends, Balthasar Brandmayer, who recounted "how he at first welcomed the end of the monarchies," and the establishment of the socialist republic in Bavaria.[255] Moreover, Gottfried Feder, the Nazi's economic theoretician, was so fascinated by the revolution that he sent papers to Kurt Eisner, leader of the People's State of Bavaria, to explain his ideas.[256]

There were a number of incidents of collaboration between the National Socialists and communists before Hitler's chancellorship, including short-term accords and friendship between leaders of the Nazi party and the German Communist Party. For instance, in 1931, the communist Prussian party welcomed the Nazis with open arms, touting them as "working people's comrades" who were assisting them in pulling down their common enemy, the Social Democratic Party of Germany.[257] The Nazis and the communist Prussian party had organized a united front to overthrow the Socialist Democratic government of Prussia, as ordered by Stalin's Comintern. This Nazi-communist plebiscite became known as the "Red Referendum." Nonetheless, their referendum failed to obtain a majority.

The KPD repeatedly courted Nazi followers. In early November 1931, the German communists came out with praise for "National Socialist workers" and "proletarian supporters of the Nazi Party," referring to them as "honest fighters against the system of hunger."[258]

Ironically, under this thin contour of love-hate relationships, the German Communist Party often denied any fundamental disparity between the Hitlerites and the Social Democrats. This was an old political ploy. The German communists were waiting for their turn. First, they planned to defeat their archenemies, the Social Democrats, and then turn their gun sights on the Nazis. Ernst Thälmann, leader of the Communist Party of Germany at the time, came up with the catchphrase: "After Hitler, our turn!" Leaders of the KPD believed that "Nazi successes were not in the long run unfavorable for the communists," since it might weaken the Weimar Republic.[259] The Executive Committee of Comintern (ECCI) was furious and denounced the "passivity of the left-opportunists in the KPD who regarded fascism as an inevitable stage in the development towards a proletarian dictatorship."[260]

Unfortunately for the world, Hitler was able to outfox liberals, conservatives, and communist parties to eventually reach the chancellorship, and thus destroying parliamentary rule, banning all political parties, mandating a government-run labor union, and ushering in a plebeian-populist dictatorship with military ambitions, just like Lenin in Soviet Russia. At least the Nazis did not steal the election of 1917 as Lenin's Bolsheviks had done.

Then again, as historian Hermann Beck pointed out, the Nazis apparently had contingencies to acquire power outside of the electoral process. In 1931, documents were uncovered that detailed a counter-revolution by the Nazis if the communists were to facilitate a coup against the Weimar Republic. Coined as the "Boxheimer documents," local Nazi leaders prepared a plan for a swift attack on the government if a communist coup was defeated. In that scenario, the SA was instructed to assume all power and immediately implement the death penalty on anyone who refused to comply. If civil servants refused to resume their duties, they would be shot without trial. One of the most telling instructions was the provision where "Private property was to be abolished until further notice."[261] Written by Werner Best, a future Gestapo leader, the plan also included a section calling for "registration of all firearms and the confiscation thereof, if required for 'public safety.'"[262]

The Nazi party acknowledged the existence of the documents, but retorted that they were drawn up by a local Nazi chapter. The Boxheimer documents made front headlines in newspapers across Germany, and many began to draw comparisons between the communists and Nazis, alluding to the possibility of an approaching dictatorship. Except for mainstream liberals, the public paid little heed to the meaning behind the story, viewing such a possible catastrophe as overblown. Of course, as history has shown, the Boxheim affair was a perfectly drawn blueprint for a future totalitarian state.

Marxist and Socialist Influences on Hitler: the Bavarian Soviet Republic

Although Hitler often voiced opposition to Marxism's cold, rootless internationalism, he was nonetheless struck by the populist appeal of Marxism, mostly in his earlier years. Hitler told Rauschning that "even in the first years of my Munich period after the war, I never shunned the company of Marxists of any shade."[263]

During his formative years, Hitler has been described as a vagabond, living the Bohemian lifestyle, aimless and displaced, who roamed Austria and southern Germany as a watercolor artist, sometimes selling his paintings in beer halls. Much of this time was spent living in boarding houses for men. But then World War I arrived and altered that lifestyle. He volunteered and served four years in the Bavarian Army, advancing no higher than rank of lance corporal.

After the war, Hitler's battalion got absorbed into the "People's State of Bavaria"[264] (Bavarian Council Republic), which established a democratic socialist republic in Bavaria from November 8, 1918, to April 6, 1919, spearheaded by Jewish Marxist reformist leader, Kurt Eisner (1867–1919). A leader of Independent Social Democratic Party of Germany (USPD), Eisner and other political groups organized a large march and rally on November 7, 1918, a date which just happened to be the first anniversary of the Russian Revolution, though some have argued this was coincidental.[265] An estimated crowd of up to 60,000 workers and soldiers was addressed by Kurt Eisner at the open area (Theresienwiese), who afterward led a second march of organizers and admirers to the Mathäserbräu beer hall. There, the marchers founded the Council of Workers and Soldiers and designated Eisner as its "first chairman."[266] After King Ludwig III of Bavaria fled his kingdom, Eisner and a band of armed soldiers and supporters entered the deserted Landtag building's lower house chamber and declared the "end of the Wittelsbach dynasty and the foundation of the Bavarian Republic."[267] A red flag was hoisted up a pole at the Frauenkirche tower to proclaim the success of their bloodless Munich putsch.

Under a coalition government, the new socialist republic was organized as a workers' council republic, and sought complete independence from the Weimar Republic, designating Munich as its national capital. Eisner publicly stated that his "socialist republic" of Bavaria would keep its distance from the Russian Bolsheviks, promising that his government would protect private property. Declaring his allegiance to pacifism, Eisner voiced support for democracy and anti-militarism, and was noted as a moderate Marxist reformer compared to the violence-prone Bolsheviks, although at times he called himself a "Left Radical" (*Linksradikale*). However, taking a stand for free speech was not one of Eisner's guiding principles. Eisner and his party supporters decided to suppress freedom of the press by ordering hundreds of soldiers to take over the newspaper offices of "conservative, liberal and moderate SPD" (Social Democratic Party of Germany).[268] Even as a moderate socialist with an affinity for cooperation, Eisner found little use for individual rights and diversity of opinion.

Following in the footsteps of Eduard Bernstein, Eisner desired a role for parliamentary democracy in achieving socialist goals, gradually converting the capitalist economy over to a socialist one, echoing the same agenda of most Social Democrats. At this moment in time, Hitler probably fell under the influence of Marxist reformists and Social Democrats, since the future Führer had indirectly admitted in 1921 to once being a Social Democrat.[269] In fact, Hitler's decision to serve in his military unit loyal to Eisner was "in effect siding with the Bavarian revolution leader" rather than with Obermaat Konrad Lotter, who led a brief February 18, 1919, coup that failed to remove Eisner from power. Backed by 600 sailors, Lotter's Putsch was unable to occupy the parliament building nor did it succeed in the subsequent firefight at Munich's central train station.[270]

Hitler's attraction to social democracy would have been considerable, since most social democrats upheld an evolutionary process to institutionalize moderate socialism. They turned a skeptical eye towards Russia and its Bolshevism, although Lenin's party was predicated on social democracy, and was originally known as the Russian Social Democratic Labor Party (RSDLP) up until 1918. Eisner, like many Germans, regarded Russia as primitive compared to the "sophisticated and culturally superior Germany."[271] Disavowing Russian Bolshevism, Eisner declared that, "We have neither used Russian methods nor are we pursuing Russia objectives. There is no Russian Bolshevism in Germany, with the exception of a few visionaries."[272]

Bernstein was no outsider. He had worked with Marx and Engels in England and came to perceive that violence and even class struggle was counterproductive. Although considered a major heir to Marxism, he worked towards reforming Marxism in order to save it. Bernstein agreed with the later thinking of Karl Marx, and especially Friedrich Engels, who begrudgingly agreed that electoral means might be more successful in bringing about a Marxist world. This was a big game-changer. In earlier works, both Marx and Engels had preached that only revolutionary violence could overthrow capitalism and the power of the middle class and wealthy elite.

Another factor to consider regarding Hitler's interest in Eisner and his People's State of Bavaria was the influence generated by other leaders, such as Ernst Niekisch (1889–1967), who briefly held effective power over the regime as chairman of the central executive of Bavarian councils after Eisner's death.[273] According to Thomas Weber in *Hitler's First War*, Hitler could have been easily "attracted to Niekisch's idiosyncratic anti-Western National Bolshevism that promised to merge nationalism with socialism."[274] In fact, Weber suggested in his book that Hitler's "politics were fluid and that he could even have become a Communist if the chaotic situation in post-war Munich had tended that way."[275] Considered a left-wing Social Democrat, Niekisch took the position that Marxism and ultra-nationalism were inseparable and promoted a German-Soviet alliance against the "decadent West."

Niekisch believed that the future of Germany lay in the East and that the combined spirit of Prussia and Russia would bring about a golden age for Germany and Russia.[276] Although harboring anti-Semitic views and favoring a totalitarian state, Niekisch thought that German Nazism was too moderate in its socialist outlook. During a visit to Rome in 1935, Niekisch met with Benito Mussolini, who proceeded to tell Niekisch that he regarded Hitler's aggressive plans towards the Soviet Union a foolish venture. Since the German-Italian relationship was strained at the time, Mussolini remarked that he would contact and confer with opposition groups and make that information known to the Italian Consul General in Germany.[277] Despite his public criticism of the Nazi policies and Hitler, Niekisch was not arrested until 1937.

But the German Social Democrats were being pushed hard by the more violent socialist elements within its own ranks. The radicals, impressed by Lenin's communist revolution, wanted violent social change and split from the Social Democratic Party of Germany in 1917, eventually renaming themselves the Communist Party of Germany. The majority of SPD members remained faithful to gradual social reforms, which, in the eyes of classical and orthodox Marxists, were apologists for a right-wing party beholden to capitalists.

Meanwhile, shocking news about communist brutality in Russia began to circulate across Western Europe by mid-1918. There was nothing democratic about the atrocities committed by Bolsheviks. Lenin had turned dictatorial against other rival socialist leaders and Marxist parties, banning, jailing, or executing them. The unaligned and banned socialists and Marxists fought back with arms in what is known as the "Third Russian Revolution." His secret police (CHEKA) carried out an onslaught of mass repression and killings, mostly sparked by the attempted assassination of Lenin by a Socialist Revolutionary Party member on August 30, 1918. This episode launched a wave of state terrorism, known as the "Red Terror." Such widespread violence and socioeconomic upheaval frightened European socialists and Marxists alike. Without democratic process or electoral approval, Lenin's Bolshevik regime banned independent labor unions, closed down workers' councils, essentially nationalized the labor unions, forced workers to labor up to 80 hours a week,[278] abolished the free press, set up concentration camps, stole the November 25, 1917 election, and violently seized private property. The Bolsheviks had become the militant "bad boys" of the socialist movement that generally sought gradual means to achieve social change.

Naturally, this original gradualist position had long irked classical and orthodox Marxists who criticized the "social democracy" movement as watered-down Marxism, treasonable revisionism, or the abandonment of Marxism itself. In later years, Stalin and Grigory Zinoviev attacked the social democrats as an appendage of fascism—"social fascism"—a sort of crypto-Fascism, and as such, the foremost foe of communists.[279] Of course, since Marxist-Leninists considered themselves as far left as one could possibly go, anyone who refused to adhere to their hardline dogma was automatically vilified as a right-wing counter-revolutionary. In fact, across the world, an ideological arms race broke out among Marxist militants, pitting various factions against each other in attempts to outflank or overthrow those considered not radical or Marxist enough, as well as engaging in extrajudicial show trials, executions, and assassinations against those socialist deemed unworthy. Leon Trotsky, one of the seven members of the first 1917 Politburo, became one of the casualties in this ideological brawl, eventually exiled and then assassinated on Stalin's orders.

Despite his efforts to create a limited socialist republic, Kurt Eisner's reign was stormy and short-lived. His promises to provide better services for the populace were left unfulfilled, causing Eisner's party to be soundly defeated in the January 12, 1919, elections. A month later, he was assassinated, just before he had planned to resign. At this point, Hitler, who was stationed in nearby barracks, made his appearance on the public stage. In a clip from archival film footage Hitler was found to have displayed his solidarity with Eisner by attending his funeral and wearing a black armband of mourning on one arm and the red communist armband on the other.[280,281] Hitler is seen with some of his men from the barracks walking behind Eisner's coffin.[282] A secondary still film photo by Heinrich Hoffmann, who was to become Hitler's future court photographer, also depicted Hitler at the funeral, was snapped just before Eisner was eulogized.[283] Hoffmann's photograph is grainy, but both he and his son have confirmed that the photo depicts Hitler. In fact, an arrow had been affixed to the photo's negative that points directly to Hitler, added by Hoffmann, his son, or his grandson. In the early 1980s, Hoffmann's son publicly confirmed that the man in the photo was indeed Hitler.[284] It should also be noted that even English historian Richard J. Evans, noted for his Third Reich trilogy series, revealed Hitler's communist activities during the Bavarian Soviet Republic, penning that Hitler was "taking part in demonstration, wearing a red armband along with the rest of his comrades."[285]

The flaunting in public of Hitler's communist brassard suggests that Hitler's opinions about nationalism, socialism, and Marxism had not yet crystallized. In fact, Ian Kershaw contended that Hitler likely "wore, along with almost all the soldiers of the Munich garrison, the revolutionary red armband" during the short-lived German Communist Party Räterepublik dictatorship from April 6, 1919, to May 3, 1919.[286,287] This would make sense, given that Hitler earlier had also been "elected to the Soldier's Council of his military unit,"[288] a leadership position in the Ersatz Battalion of the Second Infantry Regiment.

Furthermore, since he was the Ersatz Battalion's representative for the regime, he was obliged to obey his higher-ups. This is where the wearing of the red communist armband is indisputable. At some point in time, just before or during the Bavarian Soviet Republic regime, all soldiers were required to wear the red brassard.[289] According to Thomas Weber, under this rigid political climate, "all Munich-based military units, and thus Hitler's regiment, too, were part of the Red Army of Bavaria. In that sense, Hitler served in the Red Army," although most Munich regiments did not actively support or oppose the communist regime.[290]

Furthermore, Hitler's outward views had to endure a left-wing socialist perspective by the mere fact of the political makeup of the soldiers in Hitler's unit, which ranged from moderate left to radical left; there were almost no conservative or monarchist elements within Hitler's barracks.[291] The struggle in the barracks oscillated between the moderate left Social Democrats and the radical left of the diehard Marxist revolutionaries, not between left-wing and right-wing ideology. The figures are stunning: more than 90 percent of these soldiers had voted for moderate or radical leftists in the January 1919 Bavarian elections in Hitler's unit. In fact, the men of the Second Demobilization Company, to which Hitler belonged, voted overwhelmingly for Josef Seihs as their representative in the Soldiers Council. Seihs eventually joined the Red Army.[292] The political composition of Hitler's barracks provides a glimpse into a world devoid of any significant right-wing counter-revolutionary activity until sometime later. According to Weber, in late 1918 and early 1919, the main threat to liberal democracy in Germany did not come from the right, rather "It came from the left."[293]

Many historians have argued that Hitler's opinions were probably vacillating during this chaotic time period. He could have been influenced by a confluence of Marxist, nationalist, and socialist ideologies and leading figures. For instance, various social democratic parties in Germany were also proposing "to merge nationalism, anti-materialism, and socialism,"[294] including some centrist social democrats who "advocated the importance of both patriotism and socialism."[295]

Marxism had a lot to offer Hitler. Largely saddled with an unmovable, single-mindedness, hardcore Marxism allowed proponents to see themselves as noble crusaders saving humankind. Here too, Hitler could identify with such closed-mindedness, political messianism, and authoritarian tactics that licensed him to see himself as the savior of the world. A lover of the power of politics, Hitler's hidebound views pushed him into the unshaded world of white and black antipodes, a battleground where you were either with him or undoubtedly against him, leaving no luxury of neutrality. Such exacting standards of political absolutism likely blinded him to other alternatives, or at least to the possibility of subjective objectivity that would allow the people to freely display their own diversity of opinions.

Marxists have always displayed a doctrinaire and opinionated mindset of moral superiority. To Marxists and Leninists, the unaligned, such as Social Democrats, German Nazis, Italian Fascists, or any other deviant political organization, were branded as adversaries and were repeatedly accused of lining up with other right-wing teammates. According to this logic, if one did not get pre-approved by the monolithic praxis of the Communist Party in Russia, due to a different interpretation of socialism, one had to be subjected to charges of blasphemy, betrayal or counter-revolutionary activities. This lack of Marxist-Leninist certification has driven many faithful socialists into the ranks of heretical or adversarial socialist movements. In this sense, these heretical deviants might be better classified as "socialist-lite," "moderate socialists," or as economist Murray Rothbard dubbed fascists and Nazis, "right-wing socialists."

Noam Chomsky treated his version of the left-right continuum in a similar light, claiming that even Lenin and his Bolshevik allies were actually right-wing extremists because they did not adhere to classical Marxism. Exposing this insight in a 1989 speech, Chomsky said, "Lenin was a right-wing deviation of the socialist movement and he was so regarded... by the mainstream Marxists... Bolshevism was a right-wing deviation."[296] In that same speech, Chomsky claimed that Lenin was not socialist at all, and had forged an oppressive and anti-worker totalitarian state that could lead many to visualize Lenin as a right-wing fascist.

And yet, despite the difficulty of defining socialism, many academics still object to the inclusion of fascists among the socialist lineup of usual suspects. But in recent years, a number of well-respected historians now acknowledge that both Italian fascism and German Nazism originated from left-wing, socialist rootstock. According to Thomas Weber, "the intellectual origins of Fascism share central tenets with the Non-Marxist Left."[297]

In spring of 1919, Hitler had little time to think about these philosophical quandaries. The political scene in Bavaria had dramatically turned volatile. Not long after the assassination of Kurt Eisner on February 21, the Communist Party of Germany seized power under a coterie of hardcore and violent communists. Under the leadership of the Russian-born Eugen Leviné (1883–1919), a cadre of mostly Jewish radicals took control of Bavaria from April 6, 1919, until May 3, 1919. These Moscow-directed Russian communists were disinterested in due process, open elections, and parliamentary procedures to reach consensus and make changes. They had been instructed to achieve Marxist-Leninist ends by violent means, using Lenin's blueprint for revolutionary communism.

In short order, Eugen Leviné established a dictatorship of the proletariat and an alleged Red Army of 20,000 workers and soldiers to defend the revolution, confiscated private homes, cash, food, and factories, promising to outlaw money and seize all private land. Following the written advice of Lenin, Leviné ordered his Red Army to round up hostages of anyone considered hostile to the new regime, including notable elites. They executed the hostages on April 30, 1919, which included Prince Gustav of Thurn and Taxis, and Countess Hella von Westarp. When a small squad of Spartacist revolutionaries arrived in late April at the extraterritorial building that housed the papal nunciature, a diplomatic representative of the pope, they confronted Eugenio Pacelli, the future Pope Pius XII, threatening him with "guns, daggers, and even hand grenades."[298] Pacelli was hit with a revolver to the chest. The force of the assault was so violent that it damaged the metal cross that Pacelli wore around his neck.[299]

During this time, food shortages became both critical and political, especially in the case of milk. The people of Munich were demanding something be done. Instead of trying to solve the problem, the communist rulers berated many Munich citizens who belonged to the wrong class, declaring:

> What does it matter?... Most of it goes to the children of the bourgeoisie anyway. We are not interested in keeping them alive. No harm if they die—they'd only grow into enemies of the proletariat.[300]

Most Bavarians were in an uproar. To the general public, Leviné's revolutionary socialists were seen as a foreign entity that was hammer-and-sickling the German populace into a bloody pulp.

But where was Hitler? Did he oppose the hardcore Marxists? No, on the contrary, he almost immediately joined the Communist Party of Germany's government of Eugen Leviné. When the Bavarian Soviet Republic conducted elections among various Munich soldier councils, Hitler threw his hat into the ring again, and within one or two days after the founding of the Bavarian Soviet Republic, he was elected "Deputy Battalion Representative," determined to support the revolutionary socialist *Räterepublik*.[301,302,303] Hitler earned the second-highest number of votes (19 votes) in his unit and was elected to the *Ersatz-Bataillons-Rat* position, becoming a "more significant cog in the machine of Socialism" and therefore helping to "sustain the Soviet Republic."[304]

Hitler not only supported Germany's communist regime during this brief time period, but also bestowed his blessings to a government that had pledged allegiance to Lenin's Soviet Russia in Moscow.[305] Hitler apparently displayed few qualms over the international (or supposedly Jewish) aspects of Marxism. The significance of Hitler's elected posts cannot be overstated. By serving under both the socialist, and later communist, governments, Hitler "held a position that existed to serve, support and sustain the left-wing revolutionary regime."[306] One wonders, given this, why Hitler would be regarded as more of a right-wing socialist or revolutionary conservative than a left-wing socialist. Social Democrats have considered themselves left-wing and favored similar socialist policies that corresponded well to Hitler's own collectivist visions and socioeconomic ideology. As mentioned previously, Hitler proposed calling his socialism a type of "national Social Democracy."

Racial intolerance against Jews plays little part in the question of whether Hitler's own beliefs were more right-wing or left-wing, since historically the socialist movement from day one has been hostile to the Jews and their capitalist-merchant culture. According to Thomas Weber, "The question is not whether Hitler supported the left during the revolution, which he clearly did, but what kind of left-wing ideas and groups he supported or at least accepted."[307] After all, Hitler had served in every left-wing regime during the various soviet republics in Munich from the more moderate leftist Eisner to hardcore communist Leviné.

During the time of the Bavarian Soviet Republic, Hitler's duties included liaising with the new soviet republic's Department of Propaganda. Some historians speculate that Hitler might have briefly shared similar views with the leaders of the communist coup, since Hitler "remained in the post for the entire lifespan of the Soviet Republic."[308] It is no wonder that Hitler remarked to Rauschning in the early 1930s that he "never shunned the company of Marxists."

Despite his subsequent reputation for anti-Marxist tirades, Hitler did not fight or oppose the communists during this time, as some might presume. He was serving them, although he later shared few details about this period in his life. One thing seems certain: Hitler did not try to escape from the political thicket in Munich, nor did he join the anti-Bolshevik armed forces of General Franz Ritter von Epp. Because he had failed to join the anti-communist forces to overthrow the *Räterepublik* red government, Hitler later suffered "scornful reproaches from Nazi leader Ernst Röhm."[309] Otto Strasser also criticized Hitler for failing to join the armed forces of General von Epp to "fight the Bolsheviks in Bavaria," asking: "Where was Hitler that day?"[310]

To counter this violent communist upheaval, the German army from the Weimar Republic and militia-organized *Freikorps* troops, under the command of General von Epp, marched into Munich with armored vehicles, heavy artillery, flame-throwers, and aircraft to face the Bavarian Red Army in street battles, leading to the death of between 600 and 1,000 revolutionaries.[311]

Interestingly, a number of *Freikorps* units considered themselves "left-wing and were reluctant to fight."[312] In one incident, Julius Friedrich Lehmann, commander of the *Freikorps* "white troops" from the southwest Germany state of Württemberg, claimed that many of his own armed men were "true Red believers."[313] According to Lehmann, his men were steadfast and "refused to shoot" on their red Bavarian comrades until they heard about the Red Army's murdering of hostages.[314] Moreover, the Jewish composition of the *Freikorps* was "not out of proportion with the overall ratio of Jews among the Bavarian population."[315]

In theory, Hitler and his military unit could be considered as having served in the Bavarian Red Army, but most regiments in Munich took a more neutral stand towards the Soviet Republic. New military units were formed for those who wanted to actively fight against invading counterrevolutionaries. It appears that Hitler's unit attempted to take a mostly disinterested position, like most military units in the city. Near the end of the communist Republic, there were mass desertions among the Red Army, but Hitler did not defect. When the anti-Bolshevik forces overran the military compound, a few shots rang out from Hitler's barrack, causing the invading soldiers to storm the building and take every man prisoner.[316] Hitler and his men from the Karl Liebknecht Barracks were made prisoners and locked up in the Max Gymnasium cellar.

According to his close friend Ernst Schmidt, Hitler's arrest and internment on May 1 were short-lived, interrupted by the intervention of a military officer, probably Karl Buchner, who had likely encountered Hitler during the war.[317] Hitler had been a dispatch runner and associated mostly with military officers. Taking advantage of past military contacts and the chaotic situation in Munich, Hitler decided to desert his red comrades and become a "turncoat," volunteering to become an "informant" and supplying the authorities with damaging information.[318] By May 9, Hitler was set to serve on the Investigation and Decommission Board of the Second Infantry Regiment, giving him the opportunity to testify about the radical activities within his own regimental peers.[319] In court trials, Hitler accused a number of military leaders of being radical rabble-rousers who recruited soldiers into joining the Red Army. In his capacity as a turncoat, Hitler had been incredibly lucky to not only escape decommissioning but to avoid "deportation to his native Austria, imprisonment or even death" for his leadership position in the Bavarian Soviet Republic.[320]

His snitching against his fellow revolutionaries gave Hitler the resume needed to become an educational officer in the German military in September 1919, which was set up to combat dangerous ideas. It was under this official position that Hitler investigated the tiny German Workers' Party, a small, pitiful party he took over and transformed into the infamous German National Socialist Workers' Party. Some historians believe that the destabilizing and bloody violence that occurred under the Bavarian Soviet Republic, organized mostly by Jewish communists, primarily Russian-born, caused Hitler to see Marxism in a different light, perhaps concluding that to be Jewish automatically meant a fanatical allegiance to foreign-led revolutionary communism that might culminate in violently upending society.

Still, Hitler's view of the Jewish connection to Marxism was rather narrow-minded. Most of the Jews dedicated to revolutionary communism were atheists, militants who despised the traditional and religious values of the Jewish faith, often viewing their brethren as greedy capitalists and bourgeoisie who should fade with history. These anti-Jewish Marxists were willing to commit any type of violence and terror to bring about a political world that substituted the state for an all-knowing deity. To them, salvation did not come from God, but from the people's humanity—via a militarized state beholden to bureaucratic collectivism, that, in practice, crushed people like bugs, something Trotsky validated years later, claiming that the Stalin's version of communism had betrayed the revolution.

Still, the question of when Hitler's anti-Semitism rose to the forefront seems ambiguous. Not until the publication of the 1999 book *Hitler's Vienna* by Brigitte Hamann did evidence appear that Hitler's hatred of the Jews surfaced after World War I. It would seem that some of his anti-Semitism must have developed in Austria when he became familiar with the anti-Jewish, nationalist, and socialist-leaning Christian-Social Party, co-founded by Karl Lueger, mayor of Vienna. Known as the "Christian Socialists" movement, Hitler cited Lueger's influence decades later as an inspiration for his own opinions on Jews. One could argue that Lueger also instilled in Hitler a favorable view towards some bastardized form of Christian-style anti-Marxist socialism.

Interestingly, the cheers for anti-Semitism and socialism were so loud in Vienna that political success was considered impossible without an anti-Semitic platform. This phenomenon led historian Léon Poliakov to note, "It was at that time that a well-known phrase was coined in Vienna: 'Anti-Semitism is the socialism of fools.'"[321] Lueger railed against the Jews as the harbingers of capitalist individualism that "masquerade[d]" their liberalism. But as the Jewish leaders of the Social Democratic movement made electoral gains, Lueger felt he had to fight "Red" Socialism with his forces of "Black" Socialists.

In fact, Hitler once distinctly explained the difference between his version of socialism and Marxist socialism, contending that "German socialism is directed by Germans; international socialism is an instrument of the Jews."[322] Hitler obviously perceived that his most powerful political rivalry would be the communists. In *Mein Kampf*, he spelled out this rivalry in simple terms. Without the "significance of race," his "National Socialist Movement... would really do nothing more than compete with Marxism on its own ground."[323] Taking this problem into account, Hitler wrote: "As National Socialists we see our program in our flag. In the red we see the social idea of the movement."[324] According to John Toland, "Hitler insisted upon a party flag that could compete with the flaming red Communist banner."[325] Ever since the French Revolution, the background red color in flags has been universally regarded as the symbol of socialism, collectivism, and revolution.

Furthermore, the ancient religious image of the swastika also inspired political meaning. Some historians argue that the swastika's hooked cross represents two crossed "S" letters that epitomize socialism. Not surprisingly, that ancient symbol was employed by both the Union of Soviet Socialist Republics and the National Socialist German Workers' Party. Apparently, the swastika was appealing to many socialists from across Europe, having been used in Soviet banknotes, Red Army shoulder patches, and official Soviet party badges that sported the hammer and sickle inside a red star that rested upon a large swastika. Hitler also indicated that the swastika symbolized the victory of the Aryan man and the idea of creative labor.

Hitler was probably impressed by the violent tactics applied by communist revolutionary leader Eugen Leviné, who took control of Bavaria by storm. Four years later, in 1923, Hitler and his new Nazi party followed the communist's example and led their own violent insurrection in Munich. During Hitler's Beer Hall Putsch, two thousand men marched towards the center of Munich, alongside SA brownshirts. The battle was short-lived, resulting in the deaths of 16 Nazis and four police officers. A bullet narrowly missed Hitler.

Just like the communists, Hitler decided on a policy of taking hostages. The first taken at gunpoint were Bavarian State Commissioner Gustav von Kahr, the Bavarian state police chief Colonel Hans Ritter von Seisser, and General Otto von Lossow, who formed a ruling triumvirate. Later, Hitler ordered the capture of Bavarian Prime Minister Eugen von

Knilling and members of Munich city council, but Hitler's plans failed, as the Bavarian government swiftly reacted to the coup with more police units, military armed forces, and determination.

For his leadership role in the bloody coup, Hitler was sentenced to five years in Landsberg Prison, but released after eight months. What Hitler learned from his failed coup was that violence and anarchy were inadequate methods to gain political power. From then on, the Nazis employed more traditional and legitimate tactics of electoral politics and propaganda to obtain power. Nonetheless, Hitler the politician changed little of the process by which violence is applied. When Hitler became Germany's leader, he simply employed state-institutionalized violence from the Chancellery rather than revolutionary violence from the streets.

The People's Community: The *Volksgemeinschaft*

According to Israelite historian Zeev Sternhell,

> Fascism extolled the values of the group, of the collectivity, of the national community, producing a "new conception of living community, where abstract brotherhood is replaced by a relationship of the blood."[326]

This is a close approximation to the Nazis' vision of *Volksgemeinschaft* (People's Community), which closely follows the German social principle of "communal use before personal use."

The *Volksgemeinschaft* construct was a perfect match for a socialism based on a racial, social and shared nationalism that affirmed societal conformity as opposed to the individualism, independence, and diversity championed by classical liberalism. Nazism was a collectivistic endeavor for a new *Volksgemeinschaft* society of a populist welfarism that sought to correct economic injustice and to abate the egotistical and self-reliant nature of individualism found in liberal democracies. Hitler proclaimed:

> ... every activity and every need of every individual will be regulated by the collectivity represented by the party. There is no longer any arbitrary will, there are no longer any free realms in which the individual belongs to himself. ... The time of personal happiness is over.[327]

Through a culmination of various social collectivist trends, the Nazis threw their weight behind the socially inclusive ideology of *Volksgemeinschaft*.[328] Promising equality and prosperity, the Nazis treated this idea of a communality of all German people as "class-transcendent *Volkspartei*" that "did not seek to represent any particular interests but rather the *Volksgemeinschaft* as a whole."[329] Vigorously promoted by the regime, *Volksgemeinschaft* became the "unifying blueprint for National Socialist social engineering initiatives at all sorts of levels."[330]

But truth be told, the Nazis borrowed and adapted *Volksgemeinschaft* to suit their own needs. The concept of *Volksgemeinschaft* was originally developed under the sociologist Ferdinand Tönnies and the Social Democratic Party of Germany (SPD), one of the first Marxist-influenced parties in the world. The Nazis added to this social ideology the concept of Germanic fatherland of identical blood, culture, and language under a collectivity of national solidarity. Any individual rights or equal treatment available in the Third Reich were intended only for those with the right blood; anyone else in the people's community was excluded. This legal exclusion mimicked the common-law meaning behind the court-designated declaration of "an outlaw," who, if ruled such, had no legal shelter and was fair game to be killed, robbed, raped, or whatnot with immunity. Those not of the community—the undesirables, unfit, and racially impure—had no legal protection under the *volksstaat* (people's state), which epitomized the ruthlessness found in totalitarian nations.

The German populace was drawn to Nazism because of its social and political fervor for national solidarity and focus on the "common good before the individual good." To the German public, *Volksgemeinschaft* was appealing "because it seemed to offer more social equality," and "it showed a path to integrate workers into national life, to break down the caste mentalities of middle-class Germans, and to disarm the deference demanded by the country's elites."[331]

Nonetheless, to demonstrate their commitment to *Völkisch* equality and a classless society, the German authorities would organize bonfires and instruct school children to throw their caps of varying colors into the fire to signify their absence of class differences.[332] That being said, it is difficult to assess these parents' true commitment to the Nazi ideology, as they were essentially compelled to support Hitler's agenda. On June 18, 1933, Hitler threatened to take children away from any parent who "did not cooperate with the Nazi regime."[333]

Early on, the Nazis adopted the idea of *Volksgemeinschaft* to convey a national unity of comrades, but only under the exclusivity of a German ethnic community. *Volksgemeinschaft* was envisioned to achieve a new German society that would reject old religions, ideologies and class divisions, and instill a united German identity based on the purity of race.[334] This classless concept where nobody is born into a permanent social order was on full display in the 1935 Nazi propaganda film *Triumph of the Will*, in which Hitler declared at a massive Hitler Youth rally: "We want a society with neither castes nor ranks and you must not allow these ideas to grow within you!"

Upholding the social-political ideal of *Volksgemeinschaft* was seen as having central importance to practical socialism. In a pamphlet celebrating the tenth anniversary of the Nazi welfare programs, Hitler declared: "This German *Volksgemeinschaft* is truly practical socialism and therefore National Socialism in the best sense of the word. Here everyone is obligated to carry his load."[335] By load, both the Nazis and the Italian Fascists took this to mean that citizens had duties, not rights. As Mussolini once proclaimed, "Liberty is a duty, not a right."[336]

When it came to defining his form of socialism, Hitler referred to it as "living, creative socialism." In a 1934 interview by the Nazi playwright Hanns Johst, Hitler was asked whether he represented the "bourgeois right-wing." Hitler responded that Nazism did not favor any particular class, nor did it belong on either the left or the right. Instead, Nazism sought to sustain both groups.[337] Hitler's exact reply was that "National Socialism derives from each of the two camps the pure idea that characterizes it, national resolution from bourgeois tradition; vital, creative socialism from the teaching of Marxism."[338] For some scholars, Hitler's reply signifies his confession to have been an heir to Marxism's legacy.

In that same interview, Hitler broached the subject of *Volksgemeinschaft*, telling Johst that "My Movement, as an expression of will and yearning, encompasses every aspect of the entire *volk*. It conceives of Germany as a corporate body, as a single organism." Hitler further remarked:

People's community: that means a community of all productive labor, that means the oneness of all vital interests, that means overcoming bourgeois privatism and the unionized, mechanically organized masses, that means unconditionally equating the individual fate and the nation, the individual and the people.[339]

Although the concept of *Volksgemeinschaft* could be perceived as all things to all people, Hitler's "emphasis was on Nazi Germany as a classless society with a shared ideology."[340] What is important to understand, however, is that the Nazi's concept of equality was similar to those in Soviet Russia: both opposed universality. Each of these dogmas of ideological determinism excluded some people from their equalitarian values. Under Nazism, those deemed biologically inferior had to be excluded, while under communism, the people deemed "class inferior" also had to be excluded. Both failed to uphold a universal equalitarian belief in equal political, economic, social, and civil rights for all people.

The concept of *Volksgemeinschaft* was in full swing when the Nazis came to power in 1933 and desired to solidify their support among German workers, which they hoped would heal the hostility between workers and burghers. The Nazi regime declared May Day of 1933 a paid national holiday and threw elaborate celebrations with songs, speeches, marches, and fireworks. The Nazi's slogan for this people's community celebration was "Germany honors labor." The prospect of national unity under the Nazis seemed so high that even the German Free Trade Unions encouraged their members to participate in the activities.[341] It was about this same time that the Nazi party required its members to address each other as *Genossen*, or "comrades."[342]

Another favorite ethos of the Nazis was *Gemeinutz vor Eigennutz*, which translates to "common interest before self." The Nazi 25-Point Program of 1920 framed this creed into a succinct slogan: "Common good before individual good" (*Gemeinutz geht vor Eigennutz*),[343] a phrase that was stamped on numerous Nazi Germany coins (Nazi Germany's coins read "*Gemeinutz vor Eigennutz*"). Stalin espoused similar dedication to the collective virtue of self-sacrifice for the collective good, writing in 1929: "True courage consists in being strong enough to master and overcome oneself and subordinate one's will to the will of the collective, the will of the higher party body."[344]

The Socialism of Anti-Semitism, Racism, and Nationalism

Some argue that Hitler could not have been a socialist because of his advocacy for massing killings of the racially unfit. Yet, according to George Watson in *The Lost Literature of Socialism*, "Only Socialists in that age advocated or practiced genocide, at least in Europe, and from the first years of [Hitler's] political career he was proudly aware of that fact."[345] Watson also attested that

> In the European century that began in the 1840s, from Engels's article of 1849 down to the death of Hitler, everyone who advocated genocide called himself a socialist, and no exception has been found.[346]

Not only that, but as it turns out, "Ethnic cleansing was orthodox socialism for a century or more."[347] Even Lenin got into the genocidal mindset, declaring in 1906 that

> We would be deceiving both ourselves and the people if we concealed from the masses the necessity of a desperate, bloody war of extermination, as the immediate task of the coming revolutionary action.[348]

This might explain why Stalin's Soviet Russia beat Hitler to the genocidal punch. The communist regime was the forerunner of holocaustic policies to terminate unwanted classes and nationalities, killing up to an estimated 7 to 11 million Ukrainians in what became known as the "Famine-Genocide."

These acts of "classicide" conformed to ideological determinism which claims that "the individual is not free to choose" since human behavior is totally achieved by "factors over which we have no control."[349] In other words, the richer classes were incapable of changing their behavior; they could not be reeducated. Similar to the biological determinism of the Nazis, particular groups of people were seen as destined to remain steadfast to their behavioral nature, and therefore had to be eliminated. In late 1929, Stalin demanded the liquidation of the Kulaks as a class. He defined wealthy kulaks as "peasants with a couple of cows or five or six acres more than their neighbors."[350] Earlier, Lenin condemned the affluent peasant farming class as "bloodsuckers, vampires, plunderers of the people and profiteers, who fatten on famine."[351]

Both the communists and Nazis were determined to forge a classless and casteless society through the cleansing of trash races, nationalities, undesirable classes and counter-revolutionaries. To Hitler, socialists were the anti-Semitic shock troops, the advanced brigade equipped with social and racial engineering policies in order to bring about social revolution and socialist racialism. Even historian Ian Kershaw recognized that socialism and anti-Semitism went together like bread and jelly, particularity in Germany, writing that "'German' socialism came to be wholly associated with the extreme anti-liberal politics of the antisemitic and *völkisch* movement."[352] Hitler clearly connected the dots between socialism and anti-Semitism in a 1920 speech, declaring:

> Since we are socialists, we must necessarily also be anti-Semites because we want to fight against the very opposite: materialism and mammonism... How can you not be an anti-Semite, being a socialist![353]

In that same speech, Hitler continued to hammer the point that anti-Semitism was the heart of socialism and nationalism, proclaiming to thousands at the great hall of the Hofbräuhaus in Munich, Germany: "There comes a time when it will be obvious that socialism can only be carried out accompanied by nationalism and antisemitism." Further, Hitler asserted that only the Aryan nations and races go together with socialism like peas in a pod, uttering:

> We are convinced that socialism in the right sense will only be possible in nations and races that are Aryan, and there in the first place we hope for our own people and are convinced that socialism is inseparable from nationalism.[354]

Such discourse was common for socialists of the era, even revolutionists of Jewish blood, who sought to belittle Jews or other allegedly unsavory and backward races and nationalities. There was a bevy of famed socialist intellectuals and atheists who engaged in racist and genocidal diatribes. In fact, when the 1891 Socialist International introduced a motion to condemn anti-Semitism, it was soundly rejected.[355] Such racial bigotry and genocidal threats often flowed from the mouths of Marxists, especially from Friedrich Engels in his 1849 essay "The Magyar Struggle." Engels wrote:

> All the other large and small nationalities and peoples are destined to perish before long in the revolutionary holocaust [world storm]. For that reason, they are now counter-revolutionary. ... these residual fragments of peoples always become fanatical standard-bearers of counter-revolution and remain so until their complete extirpation or loss of their national character... [A general war will] wipe out all these racial trash [or ethnic trash] down to their very names. The next world war will result in the disappearance from the face of the earth not only of reactionary classes and dynasties, but also of entire reactionary peoples. And that, too, is a step forward.[356]

Engels identified the trash races (*Voekerabfall*) as, among others, German and Polish Jews who constituted the "dirtiest of all races, neither by its jargon nor by its descent, but at most only through its lust for profit."[357] Although the Jewish influence within the Marxist and socialist movement was substantial, most of these revolutionaries were secular or atheist Jews themselves—the apostate Jews—which induced a "self-loathing Jew" syndrome. Jewish historian Isaac Deutscher, a dedicated atheist and communist, labeled this contrasting trait in 1954 as the "non-Jewish Jew." These Jewish-born "apostasists" had little interest in preserving the Jewish faith, religion, and culture, and favored the assimilation of all Jews into a homogeneous and communalistic society. Marx suggested a similar fate for the two-stages behind reactionary races, writing in 1853: "The classes and the races, too weak to master the new conditions of life, must give way."[358]

This viral antisemitic socialism could not help but spill over into Lenin's Soviet Russia. By the fall of 1918, Lenin had set up the *Yevsektsiya* program to abolish the essence of Jewishness in a government-mandated process to forge an atheist Russia. Under such religious and social oppression, the historical Jew was expected to die out. Lenin even

dispatched orders in November 1919 to "Treat the Jews and urban inhabitants in the Ukraine with an iron rod, transferring them to the front,
not letting them into government agencies."[359]

The *Yevsektsiya's* stated mission was to bring about the "destruction of
traditional Jewish life, the Zionist movement, and Hebrew culture."[360]
Cases have been recorded where Jews who tried to protect the sanctity of
Judaism in public were "arrested on the spot." In mock trials, they were
sentenced with a "death verdict."[361] Across Soviet Russia, communist
officials developed policies to have Jews "removed from the category of
'unsolid,' 'floating' people" in order to have them "disappear as soon
as assimilation was intensified."[362] After Joseph Stalin emerged as the
ruler of the Soviet Union, anti-Semitism became more visible, although,
on paper, the communist government had denounced anti-Semitism.
Khrushchev and other communist leaders later confessed that Stalin
had harbored resentment against Jews before the 1917 Revolution.[363]
Even Stalin's secretary Boris Bazhanov revealed that Stalin repeated made
crude anti-Semitic remarks long before Lenin's death in 1924.[364]

Hitler even congratulated Stalin for purifying the Russian Communist Party of its Jewish influences, especially among the old Bolshevik
guard, such as Karl Radek, Grigory Zinoviev, and Lev Kamenev.[365] According to author and former Marxist Eugene Lyons, Stalin came to "abhor intellectuals in general and Jewish intellectuals," and during Hitler's
alliance with the Soviet Union, he expelled "virtually all Jews from high
office in the diplomatic and military services and from the higher reaches
in the Soviet elites."[366]

Not only was Engels an advocate of genocide, racism, and revolutionary socialism, but clearly emulated the Nazis' jingoism and nationalism
in the conquest of foreign lands. Engels wrote:

> For I am of the opinion... that the reconquest of the German-
> speaking left bank of the Rhine is a matter of national honour,
> and that the Germanisation of a disloyal Holland and of Belgium
> is a political necessity for us. Shall we let the German nationality
> be completely suppressed in these countries, while the Slavs are
> rising ever more powerfully in the East?[367]

In an 1851 letter to Marx, Engels exhibited a sort of nationalistic pan-

Germanism, writing that there is "no more reason for Poland to exist," and that what should be done is to take "from the western part of Poland anything that can be taken, to let the Germans occupy their fortresses under the pretext of 'protection,' use the people for cannon fodder and devour their country."[368]

Marx also manifested chauvinistic and racial-nationalist sentiments in his disparagement of Slavic Russians, writing that "I do not trust any Russian"[369] and that "as soon as a Russian worms his way in, all hell breaks loose."[370] Favoring every war in Europe, even if it caused a world war, Marx agitated in 1848 "more violently than anyone for a war which would further the creation of the German Empire."[371] According to Christopher Hollis, a British university teacher and politician, Marx had no faith in the equality of nations, and was instead a "through and through... pan-German nationalist" where discourse "about the higher and the lower races was language that came most naturally to his pen."[372] Instead of standing up for internationalism, in 1848, both Marx and Engels campaigned for the unification of Germany, publishing a short Communist Party of Germany pamphlet demanding that the "whole of Germany shall be declared a united, indivisible republic."[373]

In one screed illustrating his penchant for German honor, superiority, and conquest, Marx wrote: "The only possible solution which will preserve Germany's honor and Germany's interest is, we repeat, a war with Russia."[374] Both nationalism and socialism were companions of Marx's ideology. Despite his advocacy for an international proletarian movement, Marx's ardent embracing of German nationalism and socialism puts him in close proximity to Nazism. Some scholars have asserted that when Marx founded nationalistic communism, he also laid the groundwork for Nazism, and that without Marx, there could have never been a Mussolini or Hitler. With Marx's blatant advocacy of a racist-nationalist-war agenda, some speculate that Hitler could have easily become one of his communist sidekicks or disciples.

Nationalist sentiments arising from Engels or Marx should not be surprising. Similar sentiments blossomed under Stalin's regime when the Soviet Union adopted the state policy of "Socialism in One Country," thereby abandoning the Marxist idea of international communism. Starting in 1926, Stalin shifted towards a form of "National Communism," while opposing Trotsky's theory of permanent revolution. Some historians regard the Russian Bolsheviks as implementing the first "nationalized communism" when compared to the more proletarian internationalism still found among the various European social democratic parties, which followed internationalist precepts more faithfully. In addition, if the communist leadership in Russia were actually opposed to nationalism, why did they engage in "Russification" of Ukraine, the Baltic nations, Crimean Tatars and a slew of other nationalities?

According to the American political scientist and historian Robert C. Tucker, Stalin held a "radical version of Russian national Bolshevism, a blend of Bolshevik revolutionism with the Great Russian chauvinism that Lenin correctly perceived in him in 1922."[375] Tucker's research also revealed the striking similarities between tsarist and Stalinist nationalism and patrimonialism, and that Stalin held anti-Semitic prejudices. Yet, Stalin's shift to a nationalistic communism did not bode well for the Nazis. After Nazi officials detected a rising tide of nationalism in Russia, they worried that a nation "regarded as a future enemy was adopting a nationalistic outlook that was very 'potent' as they knew from Nazi experience."[376] Stalin's brand of fascist communism illustrates the close similarities between Stalin's nationalistic communism and Hitler's nationalistic socialism.

Journalist Dorothy Thompson observed the excesses of Russian nationalism during her travels across Soviet Russia in 1927. In her 1928 book, *The New Russian*, Thompson commented on the nationalistic overtones exhibited in most communist theatrical plays, writing that the theme of Russian plays focused solely on "revolution, with all the patriotic and nationalistic connotations which have grown up around it," alongside "heroism" and "sacrifice for the nation and class."[377]

As for Karl Marx, he was no saintly egalitarian or communitarian, and seemed to be as inconsistent as Engels. Despite his praise for fellowship and communal harmony, his treatment of other revolutionary socialist intellectuals of the time bordered on anti-social behavior, including in-your-face confrontations and scornful reactions to other people's opinions and accomplishments. He was often verbally abusive and obsessed with the idea of a forthcoming doomsday. British historian Sir Arthur Bryant characterized Marx as someone who would not shy from "the ruthless criticism of everything that exists." When it came to Jews, Marx saw himself as an expert in citing their character flaws. Marx wrote in 1844:

> Let us consider the actual, worldly Jew—not the Sabbath Jew, as Bauer does, but the everyday Jew. ... What is the worldly religion of the Jew? Huckstering. What is his worldly God? Money... Money is the jealous god of Israel, in face of which no other god may exist. Money degrades all the gods of man—and turns them into commodities. The bill of exchange is the real god of the Jew. His god is only an illusory bill of exchange. The chimerical nationality of the Jew is the nationality of the merchant, of the man of money in general.[378]

Moreover, Marx asserted in the same 1844 letter that "In the final analysis, the emancipation of the Jews is the *emancipation of mankind from Judaism*." Here, Marx flaunted his radical anti-Semitism by saying that Jews can only become emancipated if they abandon their cultural and ethnic identity and become assimilated into the mainstream.

In another rant, Marx accused the Jews of belonging to a worldwide Jewish conspiracy, a charge that Hitler repeated many decades later. Marx wrote:

> Thus we find every tyrant backed by a Jew, as is every pope by a Jesuit. In truth, the cravings of oppressors would be hopeless, and the practicability of war out of the question, if there were not an army of Jesuits to smother thought and a handful of Jews to ransack pockets.[379]

Not to be outdone by the racist rhetoric of other socialist doctrinaires, Marx launched a barrage of insults towards a German Jewish socialist colleague, Ferdinand Lassalle. He penned a letter that accused Lassalle of being of mixed race, writing:

> ... the Jewish Nigger, Lassalle... it is now completely clear to me that he, as is proved by his cranial formation and his hair, descends from the Negroes from Egypt, assuming that his mother or grandmother had not interbred with a nigger. Now this union

of Judaism and Germanism with a basic Negro substance must produce a peculiar product. The obtrusiveness of the fellow is also nigger-like.[380]

When Marx focused on the small great men (*petits grands hommes*) within his socialist and communist ranks, his invectiveness was overflowing, believing that they were either outshining his work or defying his authority, denouncing many as "emigrant scum."[381] Often ridiculing friend or foe in public gatherings, Marx spewed out a barrage of hate against these dedicated comrades, branding them as "toads,"[382] or "the rabble,"[383] or the "European emigrant mob,"[384] or "the rotten emigrant swine who wallow in the filth of newspapers."[385]

Considering Marx's narcissistic personality, uncompassionate behavior, character assassination against his own devotees, ideological dishonesty, and obsession with twisting his words around to suit his own agendas, Marxism agitated for a fallacious metaphysical vision of the world. In essence, Marxism became a paradox masquerading as a resolved contradiction.

Marx's dedicated sidekick Engels turned his contemptuous scorn towards the proletariat. In private, he had nothing but contempt and ridicule for workers. He referred to the proletariat as "those asses"[386] or "those stupid workers who believed everything."[387] In another letter to Marx, he questioned the workers' intelligence, accusing them of bad character and finding their "drowsiness and petty jealousy" disgusting.[388]

Engels also had issues with Mexicans. In his advocacy of supporting progressive nations over primitive nations, Engels "had justified the North American conquest of Texas on the grounds that it had wrested the land from the 'lazy Mexicans who did not know what to do with it.'"[389] Marx took his own racist stab at other nationalities when he compared Mexicans with Spaniards, writing:

> The Spaniards are completely degenerated. But in the presence of a Mexican, a degenerated Spaniard constitutes an ideal. They have all the vices, arrogance, thuggery and quixotism of the Spaniards to the third degree...[390]

The Marxist legacy of racism still thrives around the world today. In an Anthony Bourdain's *Parts Unknown* episode, a black woman in

Cuba in 2015 remarked that racism in Cuba still loomed everywhere. Although the communist authorities routinely declare racism to be eradicated, she stated that the first people the police stop are black.[391]

Not only was Marx a bigot and anti-Semitic, but he exhibited a bizarre social Darwinist attitude when championing black slavery in North America. Hitler would have probably been elated with Marx's pro-slavery stance, considering that forced labor in Nazi Germany was conducted on an unprecedented scale by abducting and enslaving approximately 12 million foreigners. Marx bluntly stated in 1846:

> The only thing requiring explanation is the good side of slavery. I do not mean indirect slavery, the slavery of proletariat; I mean direct slavery, the slavery of the Blacks in Surinam, in Brazil, in the southern regions of North America.
>
> Direct slavery is as much the pivot upon which our present-day industrialism turns as are machinery, credit, etc. Without slavery there would be no cotton, without cotton there would be no modern industry. It is slavery which has given value to the colonies... Slavery is therefore an economic category of paramount importance. Without slavery, North America, the most progressive nation, would be transformed into a patriarchal country. Only wipe North America off the map and you will get anarchy, the complete decay of trade and modern civilisation. But to do away with slavery would be to wipe America off the map.[392]

Summarizing his deficiencies, Karl Marx was neither progressive nor enlightened; he was a racist, anti-Semite, a German nationalist, a warmonger, autocratic, anti-freedom proponent, Machiavellian, pro-Black slavery, petty, homophobic, megalomaniac, a bully and slanderer, anti-choice, and a reactionary against liberalism and industrial capitalism. In almost every sense, Marx fit the quintessential image of Hitler like a tight glove, both appearing almost indistinguishable. Like father and son, Marx and Hitler were two social justice warriors, determined to weaponize intolerance, racism, and nationalism for what they call the greater good. In so many ways, considering their almost identical political and social makeup, metaphorically speaking, Hitler could easily be regarded as the son of Marx.[393]

Like Hitler, it was Marx's collectivist-based racism that aided him in fomenting conflict, pitting people against people, a sort of identity politics that aroused politicization, deep divisions, and hate. The racism of Marx and Engels was the epitome of hatred and superiority, mostly directed against the middle class. Marx wrote: "Bourgeois society continuously brings forth the Jew from its own entrails."[394] However, historians have speculated that some socialists might have employed anti-Semitism simply as a means to advance their anti-capitalist doctrine. This was an easy sell. For centuries, the Europeans saw the capitalism of the Jews as a moral evil, especially usury.

To many Europeans, the Jew represented everything wrong with society. They saw Jews as money-grubbing merchants, heartless financiers, and speculators, reeking of capitalist and bourgeois decadence, who exploited society and community to maximize private profit. Under the spell of equalitarian values, socialists perceived Jews as the predatory capitalists of the commercial class, reactionary to the core, unfairly privileged, unproductive parasites, and unjustly wealthy because they lived off the workman's labor. Such attacks were not only against Jewish-inspired capitalism. Liberalism was also a key target. For instance, the socialist reformers in Germany, like the Christian Social Party in the late 19th century, "attacked *laissez-faire* economics and the Jews as part of the same liberal plague."[395] What this all boiled down to was an anti-Semitism fueled by hatred of capitalism.

But other factors fed the socialist culture of anti-Semitism. The Jewish traditions of liberal individualism, commercialism, ethical values, religious faith, and inclusivity of universalism are the antithesis of an integrated society that must, due to its socializing-collectivist nature, be completely homogenous. Since economic performance promised by the political elite rarely materializes, someone has to be blamed for reoccurring economic woes; somebody has to be assigned the role of moneyed scapegoat.

It is no coincidence that fascist-socialism has pursued policies to consolidate nationalism, collectivism, and protectionism in order to assimilate the populace within a fixed, homogeneous boundary. This stratification of social and cultural uniformity is supposed to beget a pure, classless, and egalitarian society, absent of diversity. For millennia, traditional Jews have refused to surrender their culture, language, and religion to assimilation, making them enemies of conformity-fixated ideologies. The socialist's desire for social-racial uniformity led to wide-spread segregation, discrimination, and persecution of the Jews in Nazi Germany, Soviet Russia, and other intolerant nations.

Ironically, Hitler was probably unaware that Karl Marx was half-Jewish by birth, reared by a Christian family, and later embraced atheism. Then again, according to Rauschning, "it may be that under the Nuremberg racial legislation Hitler himself is not entitled to be classed as 'Aryan.'"[396] Some historians have argued that Hitler may have been driven to extreme anti-Semitism by his fear that he shared some Jewish ancestry. The evidence is not conclusive, but Hitler, out of fear that one of his grandparents was Jewish, made sure that the Nazi laws defining Jewishness excluded both Jesus Christ and himself. It is entirely possible that, like Karl Marx, Hitler was himself a self-hating Jew?

This Marx-Hitler animosity against Jews, along with the men's fervor to wipe out archaic, counter-revolutionary races, came to a head before World War II. Here, the Nazis and the communists coalesced and cooperated to persecute unwanted minorities and defend their xenophobic message. Detailed records were found that confirmed the Gestapo-NKVD collaboration in a secret campaign to destroy the Jewish race. Starting as early as 1937, archival records were uncovered that listed thousands of German Jews who were captured, trucked to German territory by NKVD (People's Commissariat for Internal Affairs), and handed over to Gestapo or SS officials.[397] Most ended up in concentration camps that later led to death camps. This collaboration began years before the 1939 Nazi-Soviet treaty (Molotov-Ribbentrop Pact).

One of those forcibly transported back to Nazi Germany was Margarete Buber-Neumann, a member of the Communist Party of Germany who had been previously married to a Jew. She fled Germany to escape persecution but was arrested in Russia. The Soviets charged her with the crime of being a "wife of an enemy of the people."[398] She was convicted and interned in the Soviet Gulag of Karaganda, and later handed to the Gestapo in 1940. She ended up at the Nazi death camp Ravensbrück in northern Germany. She survived and wrote her accounts of the Soviet and Nazi concentration camps in *Under Two Dictators: Pris-*

oner of Stalin and Hitler, arguing that Nazism and communism were in practice almost identical, while speculating whether communism or Stalinism had spawned the virus of fascism. She wrote:

> Between the misdeeds of Hitler and those of Stalin, in my opinion, there exists only a quantitative difference. ... I don't know if the Communist idea, if its theory, already contained a basic fault or if only the Soviet practice under Stalin betrayed the original idea and established in the Soviet Union a kind of Fascism.[399]

Much of this information was revealed in the 2008 award-winning documentary film *The Soviet Story.* The film, which was sponsored by the UEN Group within the European Parliament, stated:

> Officially, Moscow portrayed itself as an epic anti-fascist fighter. Many people believed it. Many Jews fled to the USSR to be protected from Hitler. And then Stalin did something unimaginable. He rounded them up and delivered them back to the Gestapo as a gesture of friendship.

Not only did the USSR deport Jews and other nationalities back to Nazi Germany, they also did the same with German Communist Party members. For instance, after the Nazi-Soviet Pact, NKVD agents would deport German Jews and communists directly to the Nazi-occupied city of Kraków in Poland and dump them into the Kraków's Jewish ghetto. There was even a written and signed document by Lavrenty Beria, head of the NKVD, spelling out the details. Under the 1938 agreement,

> The NKVD will propose to the Soviet Government a programme to reduce the participation of Jews in state bodies and to prohibit Jews and Jewish offspring of mixed marriages from the areas of culture and education.[400]

The Soviet Story documentary disclosed that Soviet police trained the Gestapo while conferring over how to solve the "Jewish question" in occupied Poland. After the Nazis defeated Poland, the NKVD extradited Polish Jews to the Gestapo, which makes the Soviet Union an accomplice of the Nazi Holocaust. Additionally, both nations engaged in a large amount of trade during the alliance. The Soviet Union became the main supplier of raw material to Nazi Germany, transporting trainloads of Russian wheat to the German army. In return, the Soviets received commercial and industrial machinery.

But where did this intellectualized national identity of exclusivity against minorities arise? Some point to the efforts by Marxist reformers to save Marxism. During the fledgling years of socialism, the relationship between socialism and nationalism was in flux. By the 1890s, Marxists and socialists were struggling with the theoretical crisis of Marxism, where almost every prediction proclaimed by Karl Marx had failed to materialize. Marxists were struggling to make sense of a world where laborers' pay increased, living standards improved, technology advanced, profits boomed, the number of industrialists swelled, ownership of capital diffused, and nationalism was being praised. Class struggle was passé; national identity was in vogue. Many Marxists felt obligated to preserve the integrity of Marxist theory, but they thought they could only accomplish this feat through revisionism. This is where Eduard Bernstein, the foremost intellectual heavyweight of Marxism, came to the forefront.

Bernstein sought an evolutionary type of socialism through reforms within capitalism and parliamentary means. It was Bernstein who supported class cooperation, imperialism and limited nationalism similar to the revolutionary and national syndicalists that would later morph into Italian Fascism and still later beget German Nazism. This merger of socialism with nationalism occurred across Europe, which conceived the nation-state as a collectivity of people who would be empowered with a common language, culture, and race. They saw nationality as the bond to unite the members of a socialized and uniform community with generous levels of well-being and social welfare financed by the state. To these heretic Marxists and socialists, the common bond of nationhood was to be shared by all citizens, where national designation was assumed to be superior to class designation. Bernstein actually proposed that "the proletariat had an interest in their national community," meaning that he was not averse to the idea of "proletarian nationalism."[401]

Fascist and Nazi theorists argued that their nationalism was not of the "Old Right," but something new, a sort of collective nationalism based on community-based tribalism which praised the "honor of labour."[402]

Many Marxists were lured to a socialistically-inclined nationalism. The Polish-born Israeli historian Zeev Sternhell noted this pattern, writing that "Marxists could be converted to national socialism, as indeed quite a number were."[403]

The Neo-Socialists' Link to Nazism

All sorts of socialists and Marxists from France and Belgium were eventually drawn to the ideals of nationalistic socialism by the 1930s. They called themselves the "Neo-Socialists" and eventually found themselves embracing Nazism and the Vichy regime during World War II.

In 1933, Marcel Déat (1894–1955) a self-proclaimed French Marxist, called for a "revision of Marxism that he labeled Neo-Socialism," along with René Belin, Pierre Renaudel and the "neo-Turks" found in the Radical Socialist Party.[404] In Belgium, the movement was spearheaded by Henri de Man, president of the Belgian Workers' Party, who introduced an ideology called "planisme" which proposed a "command economy" to be centrally controlled by the government.

Déat wrote for *La Vie Socialiste*, the journal of the French Section of the Workers' International (SFIO), a French socialist political party. He abandoned classical socialism for neo-socialism. At this juncture, he began to advocate class collaboration, social-based corporatism, and an anti-democratic sentiment that would replace parliamentarianism with a technocratic state.[405] As Déat began to move towards a form of social proletarian nationalism, he wondered "whether it was a question of socializing the nation or nationalizing socialism."[406] By September 1940, Déat was writing:

> All things considered, I think it comes down to this one observation: the driving force of Revolution has ceased to be class interest, and has become instead the general interest; we have moved on from the notion of class to that of the nation.[407]

When the neo-socialist school shifted its emphasis towards social nationalism, many of its adherents were expelled from the SFIO. In reaction, Marcel Déat and his disciples founded the *Parti Socialiste de France-Union Jean Jaurès* in 1933. Many of the neo-socialists, like Henri de Man, later became Nazi collaborators. Marcel Déat was appointed Minister of Labor and National Solidarity under the Nazi-backed Vichy regime in France. Gaston Bergery, known as a "Radical-Bolshevik" who founded the *Front Commun* (Common Front), went over to Vichy France, becoming its ambassador to the Soviet Union. Others, like French socialist Pierre Drieu La Rochelle, became involved with Nazism. La Rochelle wrote the 1934 book *Socialisme Fasciste* (*Fascist Socialism*). Drieu recognized the socialist aspect of fascism, writing about "socialism in fascist costume," "Bolshevik fascism," "socializing fascism," and that "Fascism is always a party of the left." He remarked that "A mere nationalist cannot be one, because he has not the slightest idea of socialism."[408] Thierry Maulnier, author of 1932 book *La Crise est dans l'homme*, wondered how a person could be both national and social, asking whether "being social, was also national and, being national, was also social."[409] He was noted for his opinion that the right and left should unite to overthrow the two.[410]

Many well-known communists turned towards nationalistic socialism. Jacques Doriot (1898–1945), for instance, was a major leader in the French Communist Party (PCF) and a member in the Presidium of the Executive Committee of Comintern. Doriot founded the fascist and anti-Semitic political party *Parti Populaire Français* (French Popular Party—PPF) in 1936, along with a host of other French communists, including Henri Barbé (1902–1966) and Paul Marion (1899–1954). The PPF is considered by most historians as the French party that was the most in collaboration with Nazi Germany.

And then there was the French Marxist and revolutionary syndicalist Hubert Lagardelle (1874–1958), who became Minister of Labor in the Vichy government. Additionally, the French socialist Gustave Hervé founded the national socialist party (*Parti Socialiste National*—PSN) in 1919 and started up the magazine *La Milice Socialiste* in 1932. He was famous for heaping praise upon Mussolini, touting the Italian dictator as "my courageous Italian comrade." Another French party whose members later became important Nazi collaborators was the French National Communist Party (*Parti Français National Communiste*), founded by journalist Pierre Clémenti in 1934. After the Germany army overran France in 1940, German authorities objected to the word

"Communist," and forced party leaders to rename the pro-Nazi party to the French National-Collectivist Party.

Despite their support for the Nazis of Germany, Robert Soucy in his book *French Fascism: The Second Wave, 1933–1939*, still referred to Marcel Déat and Gaston Bergery (1892–1974) as "The Fascist Left."[411] Many of his opponents accorded the epithet of "radical Bolshevik" to Bergery. Other scholars argued that neo-socialists "were genuinely left-wing in their goals (at least until 1940...)."[412]

Starting in the late 1920s and early 1930s, even Comintern had come to the conclusion that all moderate left-wing parties (especially social democratic movements) were actually variants of fascism, that is, "social fascists." Communist parties around the world were urged to destroy all social and socialist democratic movements, including communist dissidents. The Comintern, under the oversight of Joseph Stalin and Rajani Palme Dutt, declared that independent Progressive movements were blockades to the full and final transition to true communism. The pressure was so great that the international communist movement referred to social democrats, progressive socialists, and communist dissidents as "wreckers" and "traitors," in addition to outright "fascists."

After Hitler took power in Germany, Comintern reversed its condemnation of the social fascist and instead sought to create "popular fronts" to aid in the fight against Nazism. However, the anti-Nazism campaign abruptly ended in 1939 when the Soviet Union and Nazi Germany joined forces as united allies. For almost two years, communists and Nazis worked together as brothers in arms, forcing many communist parties around the world to collaborate with other National Socialist parties. One example of this Nazi-Soviet cooperation occurred when anti-Germany protests broke out in Prague. Comintern pressured the Czech Communist Party to intervene and use its organization to disable the protesters, referring to the anti-German demonstrators as "chauvinist elements."[413]

Still, the world was shocked by the Nazi-Soviet treaty. *Time* magazine nicknamed the alliance the "Communazi Pact" and its bedfellows as "communazis."[414] In an attempt to calm Germans concerned about the Nazi-Soviet Pact, Soviet foreign minister Vyacheslav Molotov told journalists that "fascism is a matter of taste."[415] He went so far as to proclaim that fighting Nazi ideology was actually "a crime."[416] What appealed to many European socialists was that Hitler favored a socialist revolution by absorption rather than violent means. He had witnessed the social and violent upheaval during the last stage of a communist revolution, where Russian agitators under Lenin's orders attempted to convert Bavaria "into a genuine Soviet."[417] Like Bernstein's evolutionary socialism, Hitler, too, was looking for a gradual social revolution. Hitler told a state governor in 1933 that "The stream of revolution released must be guided into the safe channel of evolution."[418]

The ideology of Nazism included many of the same tenets of the social democrat and socialist democratic gradualists, today and in the past. The Nazis took gradualist positions to bring about socialism, social welfare measures, socioeconomic equality (known as *Völkisch* equality), classless society, public work projects, mandatory labor union membership, and class cooperation previously found appealing to Marxist heretics and reformers. Prior to World War II, most socialists and socialist parties of Europe held strong anti-Semitic opinions and railed against the capitalistic middle class and wealthy, especially money-lending Jews who engaged in usury. Their schemes called for wealth-confiscation and redistribution to create a truly equal society.

Nevertheless, Marxist-Leninists have and continue to tarnish social democrats and socialist democrats with other pejoratives than "social fascists." Today, the term "right-wing renegades" or "capitalist collaborators" is still lobbed by Marxist-Leninists at any gradualist socialist organization that is seen as colluding with non-Marxist-socialists and capitalists. In order words, Marxists have discredited any independent socialist political party or movement as reactionary. Hitler's social nationalist movement would also fit these same parameters and should attain the same classification as left-wing socialists who had also failed to reach their targeted socialist endgame.

The Anti-Capitalist Economics of Nazism

According to British historian R.J. Overy, when Hitler became Chancellor in 1933, "the role of the state in regulating and directing economic life increased sharply."[419] Hitler was not only devoted to central planning and economy interventionism, but he promulgated anti-capitalist rhetoric and policymaking across Germany. The Romanian-born American historian Eugen Weber, who was one of the earliest scholars to emphasize this anti-capitalist mentality among fascists, attested that, "If there is one thing all Fascists and National Socialists agreed on, it was their hostility to capitalism."[420]

As Germany's new chancellor in 1933, Hitler inherited a welfare state, which he strengthened, fundamentally transforming Germany into a utopian-style welfare-warfare state that imposed price and wage controls, rent controls, progressive income taxes, corporate taxes, redistribution of wealth, onerous regulations, and deficit spending, which led to shortages and rationing under the disincentive effects of "high taxes."[421] Hitler and the National Socialists were able to ramp up Germany's welfare system to the point where it became the largest, most massive, all-encompassing social service system of its time, even, according to some, rivaling the Soviet Union's inadequate socialist safety net. And in an effort to provide more healthcare services, the Nazi regime enhanced what was essentially a universal single-payer healthcare system fully owned and operated by the Third Reich.

As for the regulatory state, German businessman were buried under "mountains of red tape," and ordered "as to what they could produce, how much and at what price, burdened by increasing taxation and milked by steep and never-ending 'special contributions' to the party."[422] In short, the Nazis' economic policies could be easily identified as variants of current-day market socialism and interventionism found among communist nations who retain some market mechanisms to allocate capital goods, economic coordination, and means of production. The Nazis, like all the other ideological dictatorships of the 20th century, engaged in confiscatory taxation, expropriation, debt expansion, and a rapine economy as a means to redistribute wealth within society that greatly benefited the bureaucratic apparatus and the party-based political elite. Under this kleptocracy, the Nazis developed an entrenched deep state that elevated "the party machine" to a state-within-a-state, preserving the vested power of its leadership.[423]

Like almost all socialists, the National Socialists upheld the principle of full employment as one of their key economic objectives under the advocacy of "right to work." In 1932 Bernhard Köhler, the head of the Nazi Party Commission for Economic Policy, declared: "The National Socialist state will guarantee that every one of our people finds work."[424] By 1936 when jobs were more plentiful, Köhler wrote:

> For the German people the battle for work is the turning point from capitalism to socialism because its intention is to provide every member of the nation once again with a job. ... When he [Adolf Hitler] said "We will liquidate unemployment by our own strength," capitalism received its death blow.[425]

One example of that vested power included a July 1933 Nazi law that authorized the "confiscation of property of 'enemies of the people and the state'" as well as to denaturalize emigrants,[426] which were used mostly against Jews, political opponents, and minorities. By 1939 there were over 400 decrees and regulations which led to a massive program of state-sponsored theft, to which the Nazis dutifully attempted to give the appearance of legitimacy. Not only that, but German tax officials were able to levy a lien up to 250,000 Reichsmarks by 1936 on anyone, mostly Jews, suspected of planning to flee Germany.[427]

Also in July 1933, the "Compulsory Cartel Laws" were enacted, which empowered the Minister of Economics to forge new cartels or to compel already established firms to enter into cooperative agreements with other cartels.[428] Nazi administrators also had the power to dissolve any cartel agreement if they thought such action would serve the general welfare.

Furthermore, Nazi socialism advanced domestic social policies that "were remarkably friendly towards the German lower classes, soaking the wealthy and redistributing the burdens of wartime to the benefit of the underprivileged."[429] In other words, the Nazis secured revenues that "amounted to a state-sponsored campaign of grand larceny" whereby they expropriated the assets of those deemed enemies of the state.[430] In fact, the Nazis were so anti-business and anti-capitalist that on June 18, 1933, they issued a threat to "raid business houses that don't contribute sufficiently to party funds."[431] Earlier on February 28, 1933, the Nazis essentially abolished property rights under a decree that nullified Article 153 of the Weimar Constitution, "which guaranteed private property in accordance with certain legally defined conditions."[432]

While the Third Reich imposed a myriad of high taxes on businesses from a "windfall profit tax" to a "real estate inflation tax," the German citizenry received supplemental benefits for insurance, coal, rent, potatoes, and other daily needs for family maintenance such as dental bills and children's education costs.[433] Similar to farm policies later enacted in many nations, including the United States, the Nazi state "handed out billions in price subsidies to farmers."[434] The treatment of farmers was so preferential that one Nazi financial administrator grumbled that the practices were "so grotesque that it can scarcely be kept a secret from the rest of the populace, segments of which are being called on to make real sacrifices."[435]

The National Socialists engaged in a centrally planned, welfare-infused economic model alongside a military buildup. In an effort to rapidly advance their generous social welfare programs, the Nazis banned all private welfare institutions so that the government could control the distribution of welfare benefits and thereby socially engineer society.[436] As Hitler had promised in a 1940 speech, his goals for society were "the creation of a socially just state, a model society that would continue to eradicate all social barriers."[437] Additionally, "the Nazis also introduced a progressive income tax that shifted a far greater tax burden onto corporations and the very rich," a policy that has been extremely popular among left-wing social liberals and progressive policy wonks.[438] Taxes were so high and complex that there were cases where taxes were based on the gross amount, not on the net profit. One such case was a Berlin hotel owner and wine wholesaler, Lorenz Adlon, who paid "taxes equivalent to 40 percent not of his firm's profits but of its annual turnover of 5.7 million Reichsmarks."[439] One levied tax required German property owners "to pay ten years of the tax in advance in a single lump sum."[440]

However, just as Lenin's economy sputtered and then collapsed in 1921, by 1936, Nazi Germany's socialist economy was struggling with a number of economic maladies, some asserting that its economy was finally teetering on the verge of bankruptcy by 1938. For instance, take-home pay to workers kept shrinking, not only due to inflation, but due to the soaring costs of Germany's rearmament and social programs, including national labor service, government-provided healthcare, and social security-type pensions,[441] whereby Nazi administrators, by 1941, were forced to make health insurance mandatory.[442]

In this way, the Nazi economy was a disaster waiting to happen. From the very beginning, the Third Reich's economy was put under a wartime economy binge, running low on raw materials, monetary reserves, and options, yet continuing to spend money with abandon. As food supplies dwindled due to price controls and regulations, Germany had to import products like milk and butter from other nations. In fact, Nazi Germany often had difficulties reimbursing its military contractors, taking up to "well over a year" to pay them.[443]

A cursory look at what happened to Germany's stock and bond markets after the Nazis acquired power was anything but capitalistic, as revealed by Caroline Fohlin in *Finance Capitalism and Germany's Rise to Industrial Power*. Eager to establish their socialist credentials, the Nazi regime quickly manifested an "anticapitalist mindset that dictated 'the abolition of income not earned by work or toil' and distinguished between 'rapacious' and 'productive' capital."[444] Some Nazi leaders even proposed a ban on any and all trading of bonds and stocks, attributing international trade and security markets to "Jewish capital." Nazi administrators discouraged the issuance of new shares of stocks while at the same time delisting some companies' stocks that were already trading on the German stock exchange.[445] The Nazis closed many stock exchanges, reducing them "from twenty-one to nine in 1935."[446] As they continued to nationalize commercial banks, the government demanded registration of stock ownership. Wary of the speculative nature of stocks, the Nazi regime "limited the distributed of dividends to 6 percent."[447] In 1936, laws were enacted to "prohibited the quotations of foreign stocks on German stock exchanges" and later "blocked foreign exchange dealing at the stock exchanges completely."[448]

Nazi ideologues, especially Gottfried Feder, saw banks as parasitic moneylenders and dividend-drawers that had no duties to the community. Not surprisingly, in this anti-capitalist climate, the Nazis "favored public-sector banks, as a less 'capitalistic' way of managing money."[449] Before the National Socialists came to power, there were already some state-owned banks, but in accordance to their socializing bluster, "the Nazi state added more for particular investments in connection with the new military and economic priorities."[450]

When it came to limiting the authority of government, the Nazis were adamant about placing no constraints whatsoever on state power. According to Fritz Nunnenbruch, financial editor of the *Völkischer Beobachter*, "there is no law which binds the state. The state can do what it regards as necessary, because it has the authority." Nunnenbruch also added that "The next stage of National-Socialist economic policy consists of replacing capitalist laws by policy."[451] The principle of limited government has always been anathema to socialist movement.

Furthermore, many of the Nazis' anti-capitalist ideals were championed by communists in the Reichstag before Hitler rose to chancellor. On behalf of the Nazi Party, Feder, Gregor Strasser, and Wilhelm Frick introduced a bill in the Reichstag in 1931 to impose a ceiling of 4 percent on interest rates, to expropriate the holdings of "the bank and stock exchange magnates" and of all "Eastern Jews" without any compensation, and to nationalize all the big banks.[452] Fearful that the bill's Bolshevist approach would harm the Nazi Party's image, Hitler ordered it to be pulled. After Hitler had the bill withdrawn, the Communist Party of Germany stepped forward and took the Nazi Party's exact verbiage and reintroduced the bill, word for word.[453] In many cases, the communists and Nazis were legislative buddies, often voting together under Stalin-provided motto "First Brown, Then Red."

Another way the German National Socialists were able to quickly control financial markets was to discard the state-rights tenets of federalism. With the passage of the Enabling Act on March 24, 1933, Hitler was given absolute power (plenary authority) that enabled him to centralize the German state by dissolving state governments (*diets*), effectively making the Reichstag impotent.[454] But an earlier act, which came in February 1933, the "Reichstag Fire Decree" or as commonly known the "Decree of the Reich President for the Protection of People and State," is considered to have destroyed most of the civil liberties in Germany and actually started the process of transferring much of the local power of the German state provinces to the Reich central government. By 1934, Hitler's administration had "transferred many functions of individual state (*Länder*) to the Reich,"[455] destroying the semi-autonomous federalism of the German states and turning Nazism into the quintessential anti-state rights ideology. Not only were German state governments "being overthrown" by Hitler's "Nazification" policies, but so were local governments, in accordance with a January 30, 1934, law that "abolishes all states' rights."[456] With the support of armed SA Stormtroopers and SS units, local Nazis occupied town halls, "terrorizing mayors and councils into resigning" and replacing them with Nazi-loyal selections.[457] If local government officials refused to obey, they were arrested and imprisoned. The Nazis had, in essence, banned state rights as well as any sense of local autonomy.

The National Socialists were not the only major political party in Germany opposed to the concept of states' rights and mutual sharing of government power. During the short-lived Weimar Republic, the Social Democratic Party of Germany, which was originally rooted in Marxist dogmatism, took positions that were averse to sharing governance between national and provincial-state governments. According to Maiken Umbach in *German Federalism: Past, Present, Future*, "Democrats and Social Democrats were ideologically opposed to federalism... and tended to prefer a centralized Reich."[458] This anti-states' rights stance by German social democrats provides another example of the close philosophical alignment of Nazism with social democracy and the heavy influence of Marxist doctrines.

The Nazis were belligerent towards small businesses and trade associations. In an effort to eliminate small corporations, Hitler's government issued a decree in October 1937 that "dissolved all corporations with a capital under $40,000 and forbade the establishment of new ones with a capital less than $200,000." which resulted in the quick disposal of one-fifth of all small companies.[459] In an earlier law, from July 15, 1933, the Third Reich made membership in cartels mandatory, while a year later, all business and trade associations "were reorganized" and "put under the control of the state."[460]

By the late 1930s, many regional stock exchanges were subservient to adherents of Nazi ideology and had "largely become an instatement of capital mobilization by the state."[461] In other words, the stock and bond market became the state's piggy bank. Companies were routinely strong-armed and forced to make loans to the Third Reich. Some business associations initially refused to cooperate with the new Nazi regime in 1933, prompting Otto Wagener, Hitler's economic advisor, to "forcibly" occupy "the headquarters of the Reich Association of German Industry, with the clear intention of closing it down."[462] Most associations and businesses quickly capitulated in an effort to stop "intimidatory extortions exacted from business by local SA and Party groups."[463] Up to 30 million Reichsmarks went into Party coffers from industrialists in the first year of Hitler's chancellorship, but this failed to prevent extortion of smaller sums of money from small businesses by "lesser Party and SA bosses."[464]

To illustrate the Nazis' hostility towards the business community, in 1934, the Deputy Commissar in the Ministry of Economics warned an audience of businessmen that: "Any organization that represents the interests of the employer will be regarded as illegal and disbanded and the guilty parties will be prosecuted."[465] Even bonuses were controlled by the government agencies. Companies were allowed to grant bonuses if they had made so-called "voluntary social contributions" to employees, thus giving the Nazis' union German Labor Front (DAF) an indirect stake in corporate dividends.[466] Laws—like the Law for the Protection of Retail Trade of May 1933—were enacted that made it illegal for the creation or expansion of chain stores and other types of businesses. In 1935, it was illegal for department stores to have lending libraries. A few years later, all independent artisans were mandated to buy either private or public insurance.[467]

To push the business community towards *Gleichschaltung*, a Nazi German term referring to a system of totalitarian control and coordination over every aspect of society, small business "had to be bullied" while "big business was bribed."[468] This crony-statism was summed up by a Nazi official who proclaimed, "The economy is a partial expression of the *Volksgemeinschaft* subordinate to the function of the state."[469]

Many industrialists did not fare well under the Hitlerites. Fritz Thyssen, a steel magnate who was of the few industrialists who financially backed Hitler's rise to chancellor, later had second thoughts about the Nazis' policies, bemoaning in 1940:

> Soon Germany will not be any different from Bolshevik Russia;
> the heads of enterprises who do not fulfill the conditions which

the "Plan" prescribes will be accused of treason against the German people, and shot.[470]

Thyssen's change of heart started when his associates and a relative were imprisoned. In 1935, the director of Thyssen's Institute for Corporate Affairs was arrested and sent to the Dachau concentration camp; while in 1938, the Nazis imprisoned his sister's son-in-law, who was an Austrian monarchist. When Hitler invaded Poland, Thyssen bitterly complained about it to Hermann Göring (1893–1946) in a telegram. That action got him expelled from the Nazi party and saw his entire fortune nationalized by the Gestapo. Not long after fleeing to France, Thyssen was captured by the Vichy French in 1940 and spent the war in German concentration camps, mostly at Dachau.[471]

During World War II, the exiled German social scientist Fritz Pollack came to define Germany's economic system as "state capitalism," the exact term that Lenin and Mussolini had espoused.[472] Both Nazis and the communists were anti-capitalist, opposed to economic individualism, profiteering, financial capital, free markets, interest charging, and the profit motive, even though in the early 1920s, Lenin had to permit some free market mechanisms and "profit basis" in order to revive a lifeless Soviet Russian economy. Marxist-Leninists still had a visceral hatred of liberal capitalism, but their poorly producing economic policies had turned Soviet Russia into an economic basket case. Hitler was no different, eliciting the same resentment towards capitalism. He once called for "a radical removal... of all unrestricted economic liberalism," and told Mussolini that "Capitalism has run its course."[473] Expressing disgusted with bourgeois elites, the Führer stated that they "know nothing except their profit,"[474] while calling such exploitative profiteers "cowardly shits."[475] During a 1940 speech in Berlin, Hitler targeted capitalists as the enemy, declaring: "They are, after all, plutocracies in which a tiny clique of capitalists dominates the masses, and this, naturally, in close cooperation with international Jews and Freemasons."[476] Displaying his bitter hatred for the bourgeois, Hitler wrote in *Mein Kampf*:

> In 1919–20 and also in 1921 I attended some of the bourgeois meetings. Invariably I had the same feeling towards these as towards the compulsory dose of castor oil in my boyhood days....

And so it is not surprising that the sane and unspoiled masses shun these "bourgeois mass meetings" as the devil shuns holy water.[477]

Interestingly, a number of Nazi officials, including Joseph Goebbels and Heinrich Himmler (1900–1945), remarked in private that they thought Nazism was more revolutionary than Italian Fascism, pointing out that Mussolini displayed too much support towards capitalism.[478] After all, the Nazis had promoted profit-sharing programs for workers that would carry the weight of law.[479]

Hitler was not satisfied with just taking potshots at bourgeoisie industrialists and capitalist financiers. He wanted to make sure that everyone understood who exemplified the biggest enemies of the Third Reich. In an April 6, 1941, statement, Hitler pinpointed the exact enemy of the Nazis. Bragging about his victorious 45-day battle against the western Allies, Hitler declared that, "It is already war history how the German Armies defeated the legions of capitalism and plutocracy."[480] The Führer was framing World War II as a war between the socially-just proletariat nations and the Western capitalist nations, thus demonstrating the extent to which Hitler sought to destroy liberal capitalism. The German military were also exposed to this message. During the lead-up to Operation Barbarossa in 1941, many ideological lectures were given to German soldiers, such as one entitled: "Socialism against Plutocracy."[481]

In the case of businesses making profits, Nazi officials had, like the communists, an aversion to the profit motive and usury. The Nazis, however, recognized the practicality of the profit principle; it worked and kept production running smoothly, although Nazi propaganda literature referred to usury as "interest slavery,"[482] and that "unearned income" had to "be abolished."[483]

Lenin discovered this same truth about economics the hard way and was forced to re-legalize private profit and some privatization after the Russian economy collapsed in 1921. Lenin's restoration of the profit motives notwithstanding, such private pecuniary gains haunted the Nazis, and they decreed extensive government regulations to mitigate its effect. One Viennese-born economist Peter Drucker noted this hostility towards the profit motive in his 1939 book *The End of Economic Man*.

He reported that the profit motive had lost its autonomy as an objective of economic activity in Fascist Italy and Nazi Germany; that the government treated profit as more of a management fee.[484] He wrote:

> profits are so completely subordinated in Germany and Italy to requirements of a militarily conceived national interest and of full employment that the maintenance of the profit principle is purely theoretical.[485]

In other words, although Nazi administrators and intellectuals abhorred the profit motive, they realized it was vital in maintaining an innovative and productive economy. Instead, they had to find ways to leech off of market energy without killing it.

One tactic used to retaliate against privately-operated companies was to force businessmen to make loans to the Nazi government. In his 1937 book, *The House That Hitler Built*, Stephen Roberts claimed that "compulsory loans" were routinely extracted from banks and insurance companies. The situation grew so grave that armament industrialists grumbled that they could no longer afford such extracting policies and other assessments fostered upon them.[486]

Compulsory loans are not only an integral component of a corrupt and authoritarian state, but one that is dependent on the "thievocracy of socialism." The Nazis were addicted to stealing other people's and other nations' assets. Most of the mandatory loans to the Nazis were never paid back to the private creditors and companies; the loans were simply a government ploy to extort and shakedown businessmen for cash, equivalent to President Obama's Department of Justice (DOJ) demands for billions of dollars in fines from big banks. These machinations came to light in 2012 when the federal government required five big banks to cough up $25 billion in mortgage settlements.[487] This was in spite of the fact that juries in all DOJ court cases convicted only one investment banker of wrongdoing for the 2007–2008 financial meltdown, a small fry who was neither a mortgage executive nor the CEO of a bank. Juries acquitted all other bank defendants; there were no arrests.[488]

Despite an almost unanimous record of failed court prosecutions of bank executives, the DOJ went ahead and demanded money from banks, an action more worthy of a kleptomaniac banana republic than an institution of justice. In fact, what the federal authorities did was to threaten public disclosure of bank "behavior that look[ed] criminal and then, in exchange for keeping it sealed, extract a huge financial settlement."[489] These actions were textbook examples of extortion and blackmail, tactics that were perpetrated by the Nazis in order to swindle German companies.

When the Obama administration demanded that J.P. Morgan Chase handover billions of dollars, *The Wall Street Journal* repeatedly labeled it nothing short of a "Shakedown," editorializing:

> The tentative $13 billion settlement that the Justice Department appears to be extracting from J.P. Morgan Chase needs to be understood as a watershed moment in American capitalism. Federal law enforcers are confiscating roughly half of a company's annual earnings for no other reason than because they can and because they want to appease their left-wing populist allies.[490]

Whether regarded as either compelled loans or extortion, the statist Left has been unabashed in employing socialist and anti-capitalist policies reminiscent of the criminally-minded National Socialists.

Other anti-capitalist and anti-private property measures employed by the Third Reich included its agrarian policies. Nazi laws attempted to bind farmers to their land by prohibiting the selling of most agricultural land.[491] The Hereditary Farm Law of 1933 (the *Reichsnährstandsgesetz*) treated every farm up to 308 acres as a hereditary estate (family farm) that could "not be sold, divided, mortgaged or foreclosed on for debt."[492] Although nominally privately owned, German farmland was controlled by marketing boards to set production and fix prices under a quota system.[493] Farms were organized into cartels, which were regulated by a government body known as the *Reichsnährstand* (RNST), where the Nazi state decided "everything from what seeds and fertilizers were used to how land was inherited."[494,495]

As a result of Nazi attempts to regulate food production, a critical shortage of farm laborers arose, causing many workers to leave for the cities. Up to 440,000 farmers deserted agriculture between 1933 and 1939.[496] Battered by a command economy that had to heed to strict price controls, it is no wonder that Germany suffered serious food shortages.

Besides stiff taxes imposed upon redistribution income, German workers had to pay for "compulsory contributions to sickness, unemployment and disability insurance, and German Labor Front (union) dues."[497] Not only that, but workers were "required to contribute to various Nazi charities," and could be fired if the donations were too small.[498] One estimate of what the average worker paid for taxes and forced contributions by the mid-1930s was 15 to 35 percent of his or her gross wage.[499]

When Hitler became chancellor in 1933, after receiving the largest vote total in the 1932 elections, he was determined to stimulate the German economy while at the same time aggressively engaging in rebuilding Germany's military might. This was a tall order. The Great Depression had decimated the German economy, but Hitler was "wholly ignorant of any formal understanding of the principles of economics."[500] Hermann Göring, who "knew little about economics," still managed to be placed in charge of Hitler's Four Year Plan of 1936.[501] Such deficiencies did not stop the Nazis from moving full steam ahead to stimulate and deficit-spend the economy into massive indebtedness, while secretly building up Germany's re-armament industry and military.

Revealing the true economic past of Nazism, Llewellyn H. Rockwell explained that Hitler

> ... embarked on huge public-works programs like autobahns, protected industry from foreign competition, expanded credit, instituted jobs programs, bullied the private sector on prices and production decisions, vastly expanded the military, enforced capital controls, instituted family planning, penalized smoking, brought about national healthcare and unemployment insurance, imposed education standards, and eventually ran huge deficits. The Nazi interventionist program was essential to the regime's rejection of the market economy and its embrace of socialism in one country.[502]

Hitler's toxic brew of crony-socialism invited all sorts of distortions. In May 1933, Nazi Germany defaulted unilaterally on its foreign debt, imposing full-fledged capital controls that resulted in a state monopoly on foreign exchange.[503] Not surprisingly, by 1934 Nazi Germany imposed some of the strictest foreign exchange controls in the world. Soon, Germany started to become economically isolated and placed a high priority on self-reliance, since few nations were willing to make loans to the debt-defaulting Nazi regime.

To find other sources of money that would not leave a paper trail, Hjalmar Schacht (1877–1970), president of the German Central Bank, introduced MEFO (Metallurgical Research Corporation) bills to satisfy Hitler's rearming ambitions for Germany. The MEFO was set up as a dummy company. Actually, there were no MEFO bills in existence; it was merely a balance sheet entity, completely off the books. Originally in May 1933, four large companies pooled resources (around 1 billion Reichsmarks) and issued five-year promissory notes due in 1938, all guaranteed by the German government. When these notes came due, the Nazis were hard-pressed to repay the firms and "forced banks to buy government bonds, seized money from savings accounts and insurance companies," and eventually resorted to printing more Reichsmarks to meet the cash shortage, which resulted in inflation while exacerbating the shortage of raw materials.[504]

None of these financial instruments ever entered public circulation. By 1938, over 12 billion MEFO notes were in ledger-book circulation. Because of the Treaty of Versailles, Hitler felt he had to conceal this daring, but questionable, credit policy not only from the other Western nations but from the general public. By the late 1930s, more and more of these MEFO notes were coming due, which gave Hitler the choice of increasing exports—which was difficult, because of Germany's high exchange rate (Hitler refused to devalue the Mark)—or, sending Nazi Germany to war and plundering conquered nations under a form of colonialism or neo-mercantilism. Hitler feared that if inflation or high unemployment befell Germany again, social unrest might topple his regime. His high deficit spending and stimulation programs were systematically wrecking the economy and painting him into a corner. A war of conquest seemed to be his only hope.

Although the public was led to believe that Hitler could perform economic miracles—he once proclaimed that "the basic feature of our economic theory is that we have no theory at all."[505] Nonetheless, he still pressed towards an economy of statism, where financial capital was controlled by government agencies and sovereignty was vested in the leader and the nation-state, not the people. Taking a cue from the interventionist policies of John Maynard Keynes, Hitler and his anti-capitalist policies were revolutionary, but culminated in economic hardships and a devastated war economy. Many modern-day left-wing economists often applaud Hitler's Keynesian economics. For instance, Harvard University economists John K. Galbraith wrote: "From 1933, Hitler borrowed money and spent—and he did it liberally as Keynes would have advised... The results were all a Keynesian could have wished."[506]

Other economic policies included the self-sufficiency policies of "autarky" which levied high tariffs on agricultural goods and other imports, central planning and the nationalization of key industries, which included banking, steel production, shipbuilding, transportation, education, and more. The results were mixed. Unemployment was enormously reduced through government stimulation policies and fudging on the official numbers—failing to count Jews, opponents, refugees, women who got marriage allowances, and other minorities, while upping the amount of jobs by counting those in labor-service camps, army recruits, and Nazi party apparatchiks.[507] According to Dan P. Silverman in *Hitler's Economy*, "Unemployment was reduced in Germany from 34 percent or about 6 million people, in January 1933, to 14 percent, or 2.5 million people, in January 1936."[508][509] This is a good drop in joblessness, but nothing close to what some have argued was full employment. Additionally, real wages had declined by approximately 25% between 1933 and 1938.[510]

A host of economic side effects surfaced. After suspending what remain of the gold standard, Nazi Germany pressured its central bank to keep interest rates low and government budget deficits high, causing the economy to overheat and triggering higher prices. By November 1936, the Nazi regime issued a price stop decree that prohibited increases in prices and wages. Despite the fact that more waves of inflation continued to occur, prices were still kept artificially low.[511] Although Germany's economy was floundering, the Nazi administration pursued more centralization of its domestic and foreign economy and international trade continued to slow, which resulted in serious food shortages and rationing of key consumer goods like produce, butter, and many "consumables."[512] Even gasoline and fuel needed to operate cars were rationed, preventing many German citizens from owning or driving vehicles. As for shortages, one American magazine reported in 1937 that Germany was having the "most serious food shortage since the war."[513] German restaurants were ordered to limit their menus. A popular Germany ditty exposing the discontent went: "Hitler has no wife; the farmer has no sow [seeds]; the butcher has no meat; that is the Third Reich."[514]

By 1936, Germany's reckless spending, foreign-exchange controls, and anti-free trade policies had reached a crisis point. This precipitated a shortage of foreign currency and reduced imports of raw materials to the point where manufacturers had in-house supplies "sufficient for only two months."[515] This self-induced economic crisis presented Germany with the choice between either producing guns or butter. Without a sharp drop in rearmament expenditures, many believed that there had to be sharp reductions in living standards or a big increase in exports.[516] Yet the government feared that reducing living standards and consumer goods might unleash social discontent if it were to reignite higher inflation. Hjalmar Schacht, who became Germany's Economics Minister, was alarmed, warning that the high deficits would damage the economy. He strongly encouraged Hitler to slam the brakes on rearmament, but military officials disagreed, and Schacht's prestige and power slowly began to wane.

To combat this economic crisis, in 1936, Hitler issued a Four-Year Plan that was reminiscent of the Soviet Union's Five-Year Plans, which embarked on a series of economic measures to rearm the nation and increase factory production. The plan was primarily designed to get Germany ready not only to be self-sufficient but to be prepared for war. The plan never achieved its goals, and instead heightened serious shortages and rationing for the average German citizen. However, Hitler was so fearful of industrialists and financers revolting over the rising nationalization of Germany that he included in his 1936 "Four-Year Plan Memorandum" a directive for the Reichstag to pass "A law providing the death penalty for economic sabotage."[517]

A year after Hermann Göring was appointed "Plenipotentiary for the Four-Year Plan" in 1936, Schacht resigned as Minister of Economics and remained President of the Reichsbank until Hitler dismissed him in 1939. The high deficit spending and rearmament hawks had won control. Many historians argued that by 1938–39, Germany's economy was approaching a financial meltdown that tottered on the edge of financial ruin, which could have persuaded Hitler to veer towards war in order to plunder foreign lands and to nationalize Jewish property along with the property of other disfavored minorities.[518]

Military spending in 1936 had exceeded 10% of gross national product (GNP), which was higher than any other European country, causing the crowding out of private investment for consumer products.[519] By 1938, the German military budget had risen rapidly, "consuming 17 percent of GNP."[520] As for the proportion of national income, "private consumption fell from 71 percent in 1928 to 59 percent in 1938, a fall of exceptional magnitude in the economy the size of Germany's."[521] As for overall spending, the government's share of the GNP rose dramatically from "17 present of GNP in 1932 to 33 percent in 1938," effectively controlling the supply of credit.[522]

Also disastrous for Germany's economy was the crowding out of financing for private, consumer-based ventures. Government financing via the central bank dominated the investment process that saw some tax rates on corporations reach levels of as high as 98 percent on profits during the war years. Hitler had predicted this with uncanny accuracy, stating that if war came, "higher incomes would be squeezed."[523] By the time war broke out, the corporate tax rate had doubled from 20 percent in 1936 to 40 percent in 1939.[524] Even so, while some favored corporations were given exemptions from taxes, financial restrictions by the state left them as the mere "shell of private ownership."[525] During Göring's efforts to re-militarize Germany,

> the Third Reich state ownership expanded into the productive sectors, based on the strategic industries, aviation, aluminum, synthetic oil and rubber, chemicals, iron and steel, and army equipment. Government finances for state-owned enterprises rose from RM 4,000m in 1933 to RM 16,000m 10 years later; the capital assets of state-owned industry doubled during the same period; the number of state-owned firms topped 500.[526]

This amount of nationalization might appear small, but Germany is not a large country, comparable in geographical size to the state of Montana, thus making the United States 28 times larger than Germany. Although the nationalization of key industries continued, there was some minor privatization, but this accounted for only 1.4 percent of total fiscal revenues in 1937–38.[527] Nonetheless, some historians maintain that the limited privatization was adopted solely to improve cash flow, since the treasury had been depleted due to the rapidly expanding military buildup.

In Germany, during 1933–1938, approximately "45 percent of all investment was supplied by the state."[528] Even Albert Speer, Hitler's Minister of Armaments and War Production, worried about a complete government takeover of the private sector in Germany, warning that "a kind of state socialism seemed to be gaining more and more ground, furthered by many of the [Nazi] party functionaries." He was fearful that Germany's industry and "war production could easily become the framework for a state-socialist economic order," which would be the "instruments for the doom of private enterprise."[529] This was a legitimate concern that dogged German industrialists, since many Nazi party radicals favored "nationalization of industry," or what was also regarded as "state socialism."[530]

When Göring and the Nazi regime wanted additional industry capacity or raw resources, they would either establish a new state-operated company or seized a privately-owned one. For instance, in 1937 Göring decided to nationalize private deposits of iron ore, "taking control of all privately owned steelworks and setting up a new company, known as the Hermann Göring Works."[531] As one historian put it, Göring and the Nazis' military-industrial empire represented "one of the major steps towards restricting private industrial capitalism and substituting a 'völkisch,' state-run industrial economy."[532] A state-owned holding company, Göring Works (Reichswerke) was able to obtain "huge sums of money" in efforts to seize, organize, or forcibly merge industries, whereas funding for private-sector companies in other areas, like the Ruhr region, was "curtailed."[533] Despite the rush for state ownership, many of the industries still remaining within the private sphere were showered with grants, subsidies, or general state assistance. Other companies that managed to remain private came under the specter of a bureaucratic mentality that was easy transferable "between the state economic apparatus and that of industry," leading, for instance, to the "'Nazification' of IG Farben," one Germany's leading chemical and pharmaceutical companies.[534] This Nazification process spilled over into all areas of public life in order to make sure everything was in alignment with Nazism.

Despite this state assistance, businesses were also crippled by an economy that was politically organized and directed. In fact, the socialist economic policies of the Nazis closely matched those of President Franklin D. Roosevelt, strangling the middle class and small businesses with high taxation, regulations, cartels, and central planning. These policies of mixed-economy "dirigisme" closely corresponded to both Italian Fascist and National Socialist economics. Hungarian historian Ivan T. Berend referred to economic dirigisme as an inherent aspect of fascist economies,[535] wherein the state took a heavy-handed and often socialist-lite approach to directly control economic activity. Berend was also aware of the relationship between a warfare and a welfare state, professing that "'warfare' and 'welfare' were thus not isolated from each other but combined in state economic dirigisme."[536] Berend's narrative dovetails with R.J. Overy's assertion in *War and Economy in the Third Reich* that Hitler was not only "an enemy of free-market economics," but a "reluctant *dirigiste*."[537]

R.J. Overy characterized the Nazis as committed

> to a position in which the economic New Order would be controlled by the Party through a bureaucratic apparatus staffed by technical experts and dominated by political interests, not unlike the system that had already been built up in the Soviet Union.[538]

Hitler's regime had rejected economic liberalism, become stalwart enemies of liberal capitalism, embraced closed economy blocs of protectionism under autarky, and warmed up to the "idea of seizing 'living space' and resources by force."[539] In increments, Hitler established a planned and command economy of centralized hierarchical decision-making that was strikingly similar to many nations after World War II. According to Overy, Nazi Germany had transformed into a "command economy, governed by military priorities, but run by a coalition of state officials, soldiers, party hacks, and industrial technocrats."[540]

Historian Adam Tooze described Nazi economic policies as statist and socialist, emphasizing that the Third Reich imposed greater economic controls than any other non-communist regime in modern history.[541] According to German-born Israeli historian Avraham Barkai, Hitler's regime also opposed free competition and the idea that markets could self-regulate.[542] Moreover, Barkai insisted that Nazi officials presumed that economics was a zero-sum game among nations, whereby any expansion of wealth was at the expense of another nation. Under this mercantilist doctrine, wealth building could only occur by annexation or conquest of other nations.

Analogous to the current Red Chinese-style market socialism, the Nazis sought the benefits of economic efficiency and innovation to grease their warfare-welfare machine. In his 1944 book, economist Otto Nathan argued that the Nazis had imprisoned market economics within the four walls of despotism, remarking that the Hitlerites had created "a totalitarian system of government control within the framework of private property and private profit... But the traditional freedom of the entrepreneur was narrowly circumscribed."[543]

The Nazis' Welfare State and Socialization

As for the Nazis' capabilities to provide for an elaborate and generous welfare state, in *Hitler's Beneficiaries: Plunder, Racial War, and the Nazi Welfare State*, Götz Aly remarked that the Nazi leadership's "aim was clearly to soak the rich and 'neutralize big spenders,'" since they harbored "hostility towards the wealthy."[544] In essence, Nazi Germany had become a redistributive regime that sought to rob the rich to pay the poor to fashion a universal social utopia—a sort of social justice mecca that has been dubbed a "racist-totalitarian welfare state."[545] In fact, the Nazis' "policies were remarkably friendly toward the German lower classes, soaking the wealthy and redistributing the burdens of wartime to the benefit of the underprivileged."[546] Aly detailed how, besides plundering conquered territories and undesirable minorities, Hitler's regime financed its lavish social safety net for Germans with the proper racial pedigree, writing that to

> achieve a truly socialist division of personal assets, Hitler imple-
> mented a variety of interventionist economic policies, including
> price and rent controls, exorbitant corporate taxes, frequent
> "polemics against landlords," subsidies to German farmers as
> protection "against the vagaries of weather and the world mar-
> ket," and harsh taxes on capital gains, which Hitler himself had
> denounced as "effortless income."[547]

The German public was hit particularly hard by the effects of rent control. To gain popularity among the people during the early years of Hitler's dictatorship, the Nazis froze wages, prices and rents.[548] The results were unfavorable to the public. State-controlled rent only exacerbated the problems for German renters since "very few houses were built" during the 12-year Nazi era.[549] The Nazis did strengthen tenants' rights and provide some government rent subsidies for the poor, but by 1938 minorities, especially Jewish renters, were no long entitled to these programs.[550]

To achieve socialism, the Nazis had to engage in extensive social welfare programs. According to Michael Burleigh in *The Third Reich: A New History*, "charity" was "integral to National Socialism." He explained that their social welfare policies were an "uncomplicated reflection of human altruism" that "became a favoured means of mobilizing communal sentiment, that most underrated, but quintessential, characteristic of Nazi Germany."[551]

Joseph Goebbels once applauded the generosity of Hitler's welfare state, boasting in a 1944 editorial, "Our Socialism," that "We and we alone [the Nazis] have the best social welfare measures. Everything is done for the nation... the Jews are the incarnation of capitalism."[552] After all, in addition to old age insurance (social security) and universal socialized single-payer healthcare, the Nazi administration provided a plethora of social safety net benefits: rent supplements, holiday homes for mothers, extra food for larger families, over 8,000 day-nurseries,[553] unemployment and disability benefits, old-age homes, and interest-free loans for married couples, to name just a few. But there was more: under the Third Reich's redistributive-like policies, the main social welfare organization—the "National Socialist People's Welfare" (NSV)—was not only in charge of doling out social relief but "intended to realize the vision of society by means of social engineering."[554] In other words, the Nazi welfare system ushered in a menagerie of welfare programs: aid to poor families and pregnant women, nutrition programs, welfare for children, *ad nauseam*. The Nazis also put energy into "cleansing of their cities of 'asocials,'"[555] which ushered in a no-welfare-benefits-for-the-unfit program, based on a welfarism that was committed to a sort of social Darwinist collectivism. Other "asocials" and underperforming workers were housed in Gestapo-operated "labor education camps," a new category that, by 1940, encompassed two hundred camps that held 40,000 inmates.[556]

Established in May 1933, the NSV deemed that they had created the "greatest social institution in the world." To keep it that way, Hitler ordered its new chairman, Erich Hilgenfeldt, to "see to the disbanding of all private welfare institutions,"[557] which began the Nazis' effort to both nationalize charity and control society by determining who received social benefits. And yet, the banning of privately-operated welfare organizations implied far more. Such social engineering policies meant that the Nazis were entrenched in their statist, left-wing beliefs that government had to be the sole provider of welfare services. By socializing welfare in Germany, the Nazis exhibited their true red-revolutionary colors, following in the socialist footsteps of the Soviet Union. Even today, most American left-wing progressives would be hard-pressed to deny Non-Government Organizations (NGOs) the opportunity to do charity work for the community. So, does this place American progressives on the far right because the Nazis' social welfare programs were so extremely left-wing?

Nevertheless, the German welfare safety net was extensive and massive, covering almost every aspect of life, even providing "free access to higher education."[558] There was a number of little-known social welfare organizations that flourished under NSV's expanding umbrella. One was the Office of Institutional and Special Welfare, which was responsible

for travelers' aid at railway stations; relief for ex-convicts; "support" for re-migrants from abroad; assistance for the physically disabled, hard-of-hearing, deaf, mute, and blind; relief for the elderly, homeless and alcoholics; and the fight against illicit drugs and epidemics.[559]

The Office of Youth Relief, which had 30,000 branch offices in 1941, was responsible for supervising "social workers, corrective training, mediation assistance," and dealing with judicial authorities to prevent juvenile delinquency.[560] For instance, in the space of "only three budgetary years, the subsidies needed by Germany's social welfare system had more than doubled," from 640.4 million marks in 1938 to 1,395.3 marks in 1941.[561]

The NSV, second in size only to the German Labor Front, employed over eighty thousand workers, and over a million unpaid volunteers.[562] There were eight thousand community nurses throughout Germany, who were nicknamed "brown sisters." One better-known program was the NSV's "Winter Relief of the German People," which organized an annual drive to collect charity for the poor under the slogan: "None shall starve or freeze." Donations were said to be voluntary, but anyone who refused was punished or became quickly unemployed. These social welfare programs were a Hitlerian effort to place the community above the individual and advance the well-being of all citizens. As Hitler told a reporter in 1934, he was determined to give Germans "the highest possible standard of living."[563]

It is no wonder the well-respected economist and economic historian Peter Temin described the Nazi socioeconomic system as a certain "brand of socialism." Temin focused on three distinguishing properties of socialism—state-owned or regulation of big industry, government control of wages, and a universal welfare system of "social dividends," a litmus test the Nazis clearly met.[564] Initially, Temin described the Nazi economy in the 1930s as resembling a Western-style mixed economy, but after more research, he later pegged it closer to the economy of the Soviet Union.[565]

In an effort to solve Germany's economic problems, Hitler composed a secret memorandum in 1936, stating his future intentions thusly:

> We are overpopulated and cannot feed ourselves from our own resources... The final solution lies in extending our living space,

that is to say, extending the sources of raw materials and food-
stuffs of our people.[566]

In a nutshell, Hitler was saying that to obtain self-sufficiency, Germany
had to go to war and take over adjacent nations. Hitler's Keynesian policies had reintroduced a sort of neo-mercantilism, where trade could only
be conducted in the home nation or in one of its conquered colonies. If
Hitler had embraced free-trade capitalism, Germany could have simply
engaged in cooperative trade for vital raw materials instead of sending
troops across borders. But socialists have historically favored state interventionism in the marketplace where it enviably motivates all sorts of
distortions that can foster special interests, subsidies, monopolistic privileges, shortages, rationing, conflict, and war. In other words, the Nazis'
socialist economy of high taxes, crony government, social welfare, stifling
regulations, partial nationalization, large military expenditures, and high
debt damaged the economy to the point where Hitler had to resort to
military adventuring just to prop it up. Indeed, after years of Keynesian-
fueled deficit spending and "borrowing gigantic sums of money," the
Third Reich's national debt by 1939

> had reached 37.4 billion marks... Even Goebbels, who otherwise
> mocked the government's financial experts as narrow-minded
> misers, expressed concern in his diary about the exploding
> deficit.[567]

It is no wonder why most capitalists and business leaders did not support Hitler—they knew a socialist and political troublemaker when they
saw one. Conservative adversaries such as the Industrial Employers Association portrayed the Nazis as "totalitarian, terrorist, conspiratorial, and
socialist."[568] Hitler acknowledged this animosity by ultra-reactionary elements, once telling Otto Wagener that

> For *we* [National Socialists] too are considered "upstarts" and
> "leftists" by those same reactionaries. They are only too eager to
> apply such terms as "enemies of the fatherland," "Bolsheviks,"
> and "inferiors."[569]

Historians like R.J. Overy have asserted that "Hitler and the Nazi
movement were anything but the tools of the German Big Business,"

that "businessmen were wary of the closet anti-capitalism of the rank-and-file Nazis."[570] In *German Big Business and the Rise of Hitler*, Henry Ashby Turner provided evidence that "Hitler received relatively little support from big business before coming to power in January 1933."[571] Even Norman Thomas (1884–1968), the six-time presidential candidate for the Socialist Party of America, admitted, "In no way was Hitler the tool of big business. He was its lenient master. So was Mussolini except that he was weaker."[572] Thomas also conceded that Nazism and communism manifested state capitalism, writing that "both the communist and fascist revolutions definitely abolished *laissez-faire* capitalism in favor of one or another kind and degree of state capitalism."[573]

In *Hitler 1889–1936: Hubris*, Ian Kershaw was adamant that big business did not want the Nazis running the nation, writing:

> Intensified anti-capitalist rhetoric, which Hitler was powerless to quell, worried the business community as much as ever. During the presidential campaign of spring 1932, most business leaders stayed firmly behind Hindenburg, and did not favour Hitler.[574]

The Munich-born Konrad Heiden, who was a member of the Social Democratic Party of Germany and witnessed firsthand the rise of Hitler in Germany, told the same story: that big industrialists "did not, for the most part, encourage National-Socialism."[575] Why would the National Socialists support the business community and the institution of private property when they "absolutely and aggressively rejected any notion of economic liberalism" and "had no use for a *laissez-faire* free market"?[576] Hitler himself pointed this out, declaring in 1927 at a NSDAP provincial congress in Stuttgart that "We reject the political aims of the industrialists."[577]

Similarly, according to Chis Whetton in *Hitler's Fortune*, during the 1920s, "the perception at the time was that Big Business was not interested in Hitler and that his attempts to enlist its aid were more in the nature of blackmail."[578] Those in the business community who refused to temper their support of the Nazi party were often sacked, such as Robert Ley, a chemist with IG Farben, who was fired, but later headed the Nazi regime's German Labor Front.

As early as 1921, Paul Reusch, a leading Ruhr industrialist, was adamantly opposed to the Nazi party. He replied back to an NSDAP fundraising letter with the message: "... We have no reason to support our own gravediggers."[579] Despite Hitler's early cries to rearm Germany, even the Krupp family, involved heavily in the arms business, supported Paul von Hindenburg in 1932 elections, not Hitler.

German industrialists and capitalists were deeply worried that the Nazis would confiscate their assets and factories. Hermann Rauschning warned about the expropriation of the bourgeoisie's property, writing: "But the National Socialist work of revolutionary demolition goes, of necessity, yet further. ... The expropriation of property will inevitably follow, as well as the complete abolition of private enterprise."[580] Dorothy Thompson, who interviewed Adolf Hitler in 1931 and later in 1934, was the first American journalist to be expelled from Nazi Germany. She reported in 1939 that, "Having first robbed the Jews, the Nazis are beginning to rob the Church, and later will almost certainly expropriate what is left of the bourgeoisie property."[581] According to economist Dietrich Orlow, such persecution against the business community was prevalent as the Nazi party repeatedly poured "propagandistic venom on the capitalists and decadent bourgeoisie."[582]

In 1931, Hitler revealed what he thought of the bourgeoisie and their place within his new world order, declaring in an interview with journalist Richard Breiting that

> [W]e will do what we like with the bourgeoisie... We give the orders; they do what they are told. Any resistance will be broken ruthlessly... You just tell the German bourgeoisie that I shall be finished with them far quicker than I shall with Marxism.[583]

In the same interview, Hitler brought up the 13th plank of his Nazi 25-Point program, explaining that it "demands the nationalisation of all public companies, in other words, socialisation, or what is known here as socialism."[584] And yet he insisted he did not have to instigate complete socialization of industry, remarking that, "It does not mean that all these concerns must necessarily be socialised, merely that they can be socialised if they transgress against the interests of the nation."[585]

This confidential, off-the-record interview of Hitler by Breiting was never published until 1968. The shorthand notes from the interview were considered so damaging to the Nazis that the Gestapo was ordered to seize them in 1934. Although all of Breiting's personal papers were stored with his sister near Hamburg, he told the authorities that they were destroyed, even after enduring several Gestapo interrogations. As rumors persisted that the notes might still exist, two Gestapo agents in 1937 took him to a restaurant, where he died shortly afterwards, most likely poisoned.[586] The Nazis refused to allow an autopsy.

Günter Reimann (1904–2005), the author of *The Vampire Economy*, who resided inside Nazi Germany as a communist underground resister, documented the corrupt, abusive, and frightening conditions that businessmen faced under the Third Reich. In a letter to Reimann, one German businessman confided,

> Business friends of mine are convinced that it will be the turn of the "white Jews" (which means us, Aryan businessmen) after the Jews have been expropriated... The difference between this and the Russian system is much less than you think, despite the fact that we are still independent businessmen.[587]

The same businessman also expressed his feeling that most German businessmen "fear National Socialism as much as they did Communism in 1932" and that "these Nazi radicals think of nothing except 'distributing the wealth.'" He bemoaned the fact that if a businessman makes a "sale at a higher price" he might be "denounced as a 'profiteer' or 'saboteur,' followed by a prison sentence." He further declared that, "Some businessmen have even started studying Marxist theories, so that they will have a better understanding of the present economic system."[588] Evidently, many Nazi doctrinaires radiated an air of arrogance and entitlement in opposition to the business community, similar to how the bourgeoisie were maltreated in communist or socialist nations.

From another source, a German manufacturer grumbled about high confiscatory fines for the slightest mistakes. "A fine of millions of marks was imposed for a single bookkeeping error."[589] Reimann also asserted that because of rigid and far-reaching decrees "hundreds of thousands of small businessmen and their customers are forced to violate the law daily, and a whole army of policemen has been subsidized to catch these lawbreakers."[590] In other words, Nazi Germany had morphed into bureaucratic tyranny aimed to legally disenfranchise and discriminate against the merchant class.

But Germany was also turning into an informant-surveillance state. Small business owners had to provide daily reports to the local Nazi officials on what was "discussed in Herr Schultz's bakery and Herr Schmidt's butcher shop."[591] If shopkeepers grumbled too much, they would be considered "enemies of the state," and could suffer the loss of their business license or lose quotas for often scarce goods. Similar to what the Communist Party implemented after seizing power in Russia, the Nazi Party imposed an administrative program of housewatchers (*Blockleiter*—block warden, or *Blockwalter*—block administrator), which encouraged low-level Nazi officials to keep watchful eyes on their assigned commercial or neighborhood city blocks, reporting to authorities anyone who might be a "dangerous element."[592] The duty of the *Blockleiter* was to spy on the general public and report to the Gestapo who failed to give the "Heil Hitler" greeting, befriended Jews, voiced dissent or engaged in any anti-Nazi activities.[593]

As for taxes, the business community had to silently bear the burdens. Many citizens were horrified by the multitudes of newly-imposed taxes. Reimann writes: "You cannot imagine how taxation has increased. Yet everyone is afraid to complain." Shopkeepers paid up to 28 percent of their net income in taxes, which included a turnover tax, income tax, trade tax, municipality tax, citizen tax, church tax, guild contribution, Winter Help, contributions for the chamber of artisans, and health insurance.[594]

Vera Micheles Dean, a Russian American political scientist, noted in her 1939 book *Europe in Retreat*, that the same expropriation of private property charges levied against the Soviet Union could be made against Nazism. Dean asserted that both Nazi Germany and Soviet Russia had established a "monopoly of political and economic power" to mutilate the "liberties of individuals and dissident groups" under a similar totalitarian state.[595] She concluded that,

> What the Nazis have introduced in Germany is a form of graduated Bolshevism, directing their first assault upon Jewish capitalists—bankers, industrialists and businessmen—but posed to train their guns on the Catholic Church and Aryan capitalists.[596]

She warned that there is no "reason to expect that the Nazis will stop" with only abusing the Jewish population.

As for the legality of private property, Hitler made it clear that the state must have immense control over private property. Hitler stated:

> I want everyone to keep what he has earned subject to the principle that the good of the community takes priority over that of the individual. But the State should retain control; every owner should feel himself to be an agent of the State. ... The Third Reich will always retain the right to control property owners.[597]

The Nazis did not need to officially convey title to all private property to the state; that was unnecessary. If the state controls the use of private property, it has *de facto* acquired full ownership.

A hero of the far left-wing, President Hugo Chávez (1954–2013) of Venezuela, exemplified the social, revolutionary nationalism of Germany. He, like Hitler, retained limited property rights as well as refusing to nationalize his entire economy. According to one source, although Chávez was an avowed "socialist, his model even includes a respect for private property,"[598] while promoting social property too.[599] The adherents of Hitler felt the same way. They engaged in many socialist policies that paralleled Chávez's regime, nationalizing hundreds of German businesses while championing state-augmented welfare, compulsory unionism, social equality (only among Germans), a classless society, collectivistic populism, currency-capital controls and authoritarian-style rule. How could Hugo's left-wing "Chavismo" movement respect property rights without earning a "right-wing" moniker?

Historically, a nation has to first trudge through a fascist gradualism of nationalization before reaching a communist society of absolute state ownership of the means of production. As the saga under President Nicolás Maduro's regime attests, Venezuela's fascio-socialization of society was a transitional phase of mayhem that resulted in total economic collapse; the same calamity that had befallen Lenin's "War Communism" in 1921. Such left-wing nationalism and fascism plagued the economies of both the Nazis of Germany and the Fascists of Italy, causing them to drift from state capitalism to a more extreme state socialism. As private assets were coercively converted into public assets, their economies sputtered and faltered, leading to the aggressive plundering of other nations.

Governmentalists may boast of the wonders of full socialization, but the price paid by society is not only economic collapse but the abandonment of socialist principles. Fascio-socialization of an economy induces an inverse effect, meaning that as one moves closer to the edge of undiluted socialism, the more it devours the integrity of theoretical socialism, equity, and community. At this point, unforeseen consequences sabotage reality in a seemingly calculated effort to disproportionally injure society.

Unabridged nationalization must inevitably devolve into totalitarian nightmares, since central planners dictate the definition and policies of the state, and if someone objects, jobs, housing and food become bargaining chips to get people to obey the authorities. Trotsky made this point clear about Stalinism in *The Revolution Betrayed*, writing:

> In a country where the sole employer is the state, [opposition] means death by slow starvation. The old principle: "who does not work shall not eat," has been replaced with a new one: "who does not obey shall not eat."[600]

Still, Marxist theoreticians contended that socialism would never come to glorious fruition until all means of production come under direct state or worker ownership. Despite this theory, German Nazism had accomplished a form of government ownership feat without officially confiscating every parcel of private land or enterprise. Leonard Peikoff in *The Ominous Parallels* maintained that the "unqualified right" to control property is still a form of state ownership, writing:

> If "ownership" means the right to determine the use and disposal of material goods, then Nazism endowed the state with every real prerogative of ownership. What the individual retained was merely a formal deed, a contentless deed, which conferred no rights on the holder. Under communism, there is collective ownership of property *de jure*. Under Nazism, there is the same collective ownership *de facto*.[601]

In other words: if you don't control the use of your property, you don't own it. Period. Ownership means control over what you own.

The Nazis had no intentions of allowing individual control over their estate or assets, proclaiming many times that under a command economy, the national interest supersedes individual interest. It was the Nazi political and party-controlled state that determined the national or common interest. At any moment, individual or company property could be expropriated and taken over by the state or given to someone else, all without any semblance of due process. This is why German businessmen were studying Marxism; they wanted to know what to expect.

Hitler and the Nazis were so proud of their command economy that they heaped praise on others who they thought might emulate them. The chief Nazi newspaper, *Völkischer Beobachter*, found much in Franklin D. Roosevelt's proposed economic policies to commend, applauding "Roosevelt's adoption of National Socialist strains of thought in his economic and social policies" and "the development toward an authoritarian state" based on the "demand that collective good be put before individual self-interest."[602]

German Labor Front

Nazi Germany can easily be regarded as the quintessential worker state, since many Nazi leaders identified Germany as a "proletarian nation" that would struggle against "plutocratic nations."[603] Hitler's worker state was predicated on replacing individual class struggle with a "class struggle between nations."[604] After all, Hitler repeatedly glorified workers and lauded the virtues of labor, pronouncing in the *Völkischer Beobachter* that "I only acknowledge one nobility—that of labour."[605] Yet such platitudes and theories were the standard under Lenin's so-called Russian worker state and Mussolini's Italian worker state, meaning that all of these regimes nationalized their labor unions. In other words, Lenin, Hitler, and Mussolini did not just outlaw independent labor unions under their regime; they nationalized them as would any good socialist. Of course, such nationalizing effort would be in accordance with Marxist doctrines, which demanded state ownership and control over all independently private organizations. Lenin's Bolsheviks closed down all independent labor associations, factory committees, and worker cooperatives, banning strikes, walkouts, and lockouts. Under Sovietism, workers had no real representation or bargaining rights and were treated like industrial serfs chained to their factories. Hitler and Mussolini merely followed in Lenin's footsteps.

One day after a huge Nazi-sponsored 1933 May Day celebration, Hitler mimicked Lenin's labor policies and both nationalized and outlawed all autonomous labor unions, compelling every German worker to join the German Labor Front (DAF), headed by Robert Ley, who pledge "to create a true social and productive community of all Germans."[606] Political promises are rarely kept, but the Nazis actually provided far more benefits for their workers than the Soviet Union. In their pro-labor zeal, DAF got employers to allow more free time for workers and, by 1939, the standard vacation had gone up to "twelve days, the number of annual paid holidays per worker."[607] Nazi General Leon Degrelle asserted that it rose to 21 days of paid vacation after 10 years with a company and that employers "had to give four weeks' notice before firing an employee, who then had up to two months to appeal the dismissal."[608]

Hitler also supported a mandatory labor service program for the youth, declaring in a 1933 interview with Louis P. Lochner of the *Associated Press* that, "As a National Socialist, I also see in the compulsory Labour Service a means of producing respect for labour. Our young people will learn that labour ennobles man."[609] The Nazis finally decreed a compulsory labor service law by 1935, and eventually partially militarized it.

From the start, wages were set high, overtime pay was generous, and dismissal of workers by employers was difficult to execute, but inflation and stricter labor laws eroded much of that advantage. The German Labor Front preferred nationalized enterprises over privately-owned companies. Hitler and other Nazi officials displayed the same bias and were "accustomed to rant in their public speeches against the bourgeois and the capitalist and proclaim solidarity with the workers."[610] They did far more than just rant and rave. Under a special decree issued by the Office of the Four-Year Plan (June 22, 1938), the Nazis instituted "labor conscription," which "obligated every German to work where the state assigned him."[611] Even more chilling were the rules that prevented businessmen from firing bad workers. Before an owner could dismiss a worker, he had to first get permission from the regime's "government employment office," which William L. Shirer, author *The Rise and Fall of the Third Reich*, indicated was a type of job security "rarely known during the [Weimar] Republic."[612]

In any event, following socialist dogma, all sorts of revolutionary social and entertainment programs were provided to German workers via the "Strength Through Joy" program (*Kraft durch Freude*, or KdF), considered the world's biggest tour operator. The KdF was designed to provide affordable leisure activities, including subsidized domestic or foreign vacations, parks, ocean cruises, construction of worker canteens that provided subsidized hot meals, factory libraries and gardens, sport facilities and swimming pools, adult education courses, periodic breaks, orchestras during lunch break, tickets to concerts and operas, no-cost physical education, and gymnastics and sports training. The DAF-subsidized holiday vacations were so popular that by 1938 over 10.3 million Germans had signed up.[613]

The Nazi trade union even financed the building of ocean liners for its members so that most of the ocean liner vacations were not just low-cost bargains, but some were actually "all-expense paid cruises."[614] By the beginning of the war in 1939, participants in KdF trips came to 45 million, which included 31.5 million excursionists, 6 million hikers, 0.7 million cruises aboard the KdF fleet, and other activities.[615] According to Louis P. Lochner, chief of the Associated Press in Berlin for 14 years until his arrest by the Gestapo, a whole fleet of ocean vessels were planned exclusively for the DAF, and that "six steamers, in fact, were already in use when the war began." The ticket price for workers was minimal, almost dirt-cheap, somewhere between twelve to sixteen marks for "a full week on such a steamer."[616] For stay-at-home vacationers, the DAF built spas and summer resorts. One of the largest was at the German city of Sassnitz on the island of Rügen, where the National Socialists erected a "summer resort with 20,000 beds."[617] To the Nazis, cheap vacations were regarded as a way to break the travel privilege of the bourgeois. They touted it as the centerpiece to what they called "Socialism of Deed."[618,619]

As one of the largest Nazi organizations, with over 35,000 full-time employees by 1939,[620] the DAF had to arrange the building of automobiles for its workers. Hitler had decreed that every German worker must have an affordable car at $396 per vehicle. Since the private sector could not build an automobile for the paltry sum of $396, "Hitler ordered the

state to build it" and put the DAF in charge.[621] To pay for the automobile factory and other expenses, the DAF subsidized the cheap car
(Volkswagen—the People's Car) via payroll deduction. None were ever
delivered because the Volkswagen factory had to shift to wartime production in 1939. The DAF was about to engage in such expensive ventures
because it also operated one of the largest financial institutions, the Bank
of German Labor, along with providing occupational training, legal services and medical screening, and it campaigned to improve working en-
vironments.[622]

As for workplace misconduct, workers' councils were set up to regulate business practices, working hours and wages, disciplining both employers and workers. In one year alone in 1934, over 50 workers were
dismissed while 13 employers had their businesses confiscated.[623] These
"Courts of Social Honor" (*Soziale Ehrengerichte*) were established, according to law, to prevent owners and managers from the "abuse of their
position of power in the firm, having maliciously exploited the workers
or insulted their honor."[624]

Essentially, Hitler pursued a type of "dictatorship of the proletariat"
through an ideological vanguard that mimicked the elitism of Lenin's
Bolsheviks. Whether it was Italian Fascists, German Nazis or Russian
Bolshevists, every one of these regimes felt compelled to prohibit independent trade unions while imposing mandatory union membership
upon all workers. As noted by Italian historian Gaetano Salvemini,

> In [fascist] Italy and [Nazi] Germany the official unions have
> been made compulsory by law, while in the United States, the
> workers are not legally obligated to join the company unions but
> may even, if they so wish, oppose them.[625]

If a hardline right-wing or conservative regime had come to power,
they would have surely outlawed any type of unionism, private or state-
operated. As for classical liberals, they would have taken the middle
ground, and upheld the Lockean tradition of "freedom of association,"
which would let workers join whatever organization they chose, and
labor unions would not have the coercive power to fire workers who
refused to join a private, third-party organization (the union).

Some scholars contend that the Nazis were just using trade unions to
lower wages, weaken working conditions and increase production, but

Stalin had treated the trades unions just as poorly as Lenin. According to the Socialist Party of Great Britain, the "Stalin government" brought

> the unions under complete State control. In the 1930s, the unions became organs of the state, whose function was not to try to improve wages and working conditions, but rather to reduce cost, keep wages down, and increase production. As a result, wages began to fall and working conditions to deteriorate.[626]

Considering the Nazis' nationalization, central planning, social welfare programs, military Keynesianism economics, and collective devotion to the public good before the individual good, historians should have summarily pegged Nazism as a radical left-wing movement bordering on Marxian tenets and tactics.

How can the American Democratic Party or its leaders, like President Obama, Senator Hillary Clinton, or Senator Bernie Sanders be labeled left-wing when the Nazis had achieved far greater advances towards left-wing statism and socialism? For instance, Bernie Sanders, who has described himself as a socialist, said: "I don't believe government should take over the grocery store down the street or own the means of production."[627] Given that the Nazis nationalized over 500 fairly large German companies and Mussolini nationalized three-fourths of the "Italian economy, industrial and agricultural" sector, if we are calling Nazis right-wing, Sanders should logically be considered even further to the right of Hitler or Mussolini's ostensibly "right-wing" movements. Under their own interpretation of the political spectrum, progressives, Democrats, and moderate socialists, due to their basic policies, must be placed to the right of Hitler and Mussolini. Yet those same groups often term the latter as bearers of right-wing extremism prone to hate and violence.

When socialist doctrinaires propose state ownership over private property, they march in tandem down the same socioeconomic road of Nazism and fascism. Naturally, if Hitler and Mussolini are to be relegated to the extreme right-hand side of the political dichotomy, they must share their political spectrum designation with Lenin, Stalin, and Mao. The political spectrum makes no sense unless this motley crew of authoritarians and socialists are standing alongside each other in the same police lineup.

Some critics have argued that today's socialists have shifted away from their past anti-Semitic views, and therefore cannot be considered right-wing. However, given the rising left-wing hostility towards Israel, it appears that American progressives, democratic socialists, and nationalistic socialists continued to display a high degree of their old ideological baggage—whether it is labeled left or right. Whatever the case, this all serves to highlight how political classifications have been used as tools of propaganda in an effort to obscure the strong historical linkage between Nazism, Fascism, and Sovietism. As I have repeated before, whoever commands the high ground of political classification can easily control the modes of human thought.

But of course, there are always minor disparities and gray areas between similar ideologies. For instance, the communists in Soviet Russia treated their workers like disposable tools, in comparison to the German National Socialists. By almost all measures, the Hitler's German Labor Front carried out most of their pro-labor promises while Lenin and Stalin ran roughshod over their proletariat subjects. Conditions for workers and peasants alike plunged after Lenin nationalized independent labor unions and the economy. Violent labor strikes paralyzed Russian cities while, in the countryside, over one hundred peasant revolts erupted during early 1921 alone. Unlike Hitler's Germany, thousands of striking Russian workers were shot, imprisoned, or executed, particularly during the blood-soaked saga of the Kronstadt rebellion in March 1921.

The dissatisfied and starving workers and peasant farmers discovered that they had no voice in the revolution or the Russian government. Lenin had created an elitist core of middle-class intellectuals, rather than a union of workers, peasants, and farmers, to bring about his social revolution. In fact, in his 1904 pamphlet, "Our Political Tasks," Trotsky contended "that Lenin despised the people and the working class and was trying to substitute the party for the proletariat."[628] Many other contemporary Marxists denounced Bolshevism's political elitism and centralized power grab. For instance, this grievance

was the same premise for Rosa Luxemburg's criticism of Lenin: the idea of a centralized hierarchic party of professional revolutionaries was contrary to the fundamental Marxist principle that the working class can only be liberated by its own efforts.[629]

In other words, Lenin had bureaucratized the revolution, clashed with classical Marxism, and left workers out in the cold.

Luxemburg (1871–1919) was a Marxist theorist and revolutionary socialist within the Communist Party of Germany who argued that Karl Marx did not adhere to a monolithic, single-party state, but supported a radical democracy organized under local workers' councils and militias. She wrote that Lenin's Bolsheviks had bureaucratized the communist state, starved the cities, abandoned Marx's teachings of a proletariat society, and failed to allow active participation of the masses and workers.[630] Taking a position heretical to classical Marxism, Lenin held the opinion that workers could not organize a revolution any more than they could organize their thoughts.

Even Benito Mussolini echoed Luxemburg's critiques concerning Lenin's actions during the October Russian Revolution. Chiding Lenin for not being Marxist enough, Mussolini argued that his old friend was "'the very negation of socialism' because he had not created a dictatorship of the proletariat or of the socialist party, but only of a few intellectuals who had found the secret of winning power."[631] As Trotsky and other communist leaders later lamented, the Soviet Union had betrayed the revolution and transformed into a "degenerated workers' state" that treated the proletariat like political cannon fodder.

The Church under Nazi Germany

As for the plight of religion and the churches in Germany, the Nazis were far more favorable towards atheism and paganism than Christianity. Otto Strasser revealed in *Hitler and I* that Hitler "was profoundly imbued with German paganism, more so, perhaps" than other Nazi leaders such as pagan worshiper Erich Ludendorff or anti-Christian Alfred Rosenberg, who proposed to cease the publication of the Bible and to remove all Christian crosses and replace them with swastikas.[632] Otto Strasser even claimed that "Hitler is an atheist."[633] In one of his 1939 diary entries, Goebbels confessed that "The Fuhrer is deeply religious, though completely anti-Christian. He views Christianity as a symptom of decay. Rightly so. It is a branch of the Jewish race."[634]

Another early intimate friend and confidante of Hitler was Ernst Hanfstaengl, who was placed in charge of the Nazis' Foreign Press Bureau in Berlin. In his memoirs, Hanfstaengl revealed that Hitler "was to all intents and purposes an atheist by the time I got to know him, although he still paid lip-service to religious beliefs and certainly acknowledged them as the basis for the thinking of others."[635]

Although Hitler delivered a plethora of speeches placating Christians, mostly due to his anxiety over their powerful influence, he held an anti-clerical and pagan stance that aimed to worship a nation-like deity, once remarking: "We do not want any other god than Germany itself. It is essential to have fanatical faith and hope and love in and for Germany."[636] Hitler has been described as a "materialist," without "feeling or understanding for either the spiritual side of human life or its emotional, affective side,"[637] who had contempt for the German Protestant clergy, arguing that they were "insignificant little people, submissive as dogs, and they sweat with embarrassment when you talk with them."[638] Hitler was recorded to have said during his Table Talks that "In the long run, National Socialism and religion will no longer be able to exist together."[639] Other historians like Geoffrey Blainey simply described Hitler as atheistic, a man for whom his Nazi party was a religion, "a pagan religion," of which Hitler served as "high priest."[640]

Anti-Christianity permeated Nazi Germany from the very beginning of Hitler's chancellorship. For instance, on May 9, 1933, Nazi students in Berlin burned 25,000 volumes of books, including the Bible.[641] A few months later, on July 30, Wotan, a major deity in German and Anglo-Saxon paganism, was revived to replace the Christian god at a Nazi convention at Eisenach.[642]

Hitler did not frequently make his general anti-clericalism publicly known; however, he did occasionally venture out and publicly attack the Catholics. At a 1935 party congress announcement, Hitler proclaimed that "The enemies of National Socialism," were not only the "Jewish Marxists" and "certain elements of an incorrigible, stupid reactionary bourgeoisie," but also Catholics.[643] In a nutshell, British historian Michael Burleigh explained this antagonism: "The Nazis despised Christianity for its Judaic roots, effeminacy, otherworldliness, and universality."[644] Burleigh also noted that "One would have to visit the Reformation or the extremes of liberal anti-clericalism in the modern era to find anything analogous to their vicious and vulgar attacks on priests."[645]

It was no secret that Hitler and most Nazis abhorred Christianity. Albert Speer, a member of the Führer's inner circle, revealed Hitler's anti-Christian stance in his book *Inside the Third Reich: Memoirs*. Hitler told Speer:

> You see, it's been our misfortune to have the wrong religion. Why didn't we have the religion of the Japanese, who regard sacrifice for the Fatherland as the highest good? The Mohammedan religion too would have been more compatible to us than Christianity. Why did it have to be Christianity with its meekness and flabbiness?[646]

One reason for this view was Hitler's belief that a person could not simultaneously be a German and a Christian. Hitler's personal secretary, Martin Bormann, who was strongly anti-Christian, advised Nazi officials in 1941 that "National Socialism and Christianity are irreconcilable."[647] Bormann's efforts to destroy Christianity included banning members of the clergy from joining the Nazi party and removing those who were members and preventing any new churches from being built in Berlin. As the Nazi anti-Christian campaign moved into high gear, hundreds of monasteries in both Germany and Austria were seized by the Gestapo and clergymen and laymen alike were removed.[648] Starting in 1935, over 2,720 clerics were arrested and incarcerated in Germany's Dachau concentration camp, resulting in over 1,000 deaths. Over 94 percent were Roman Catholic clergymen.[649] In fact, according to Rabbi David G. Dalin, Hitler had planned to kidnap Pope Pius XII in 1943 and jail him in upper Saxony, threatening to enter the Vatican and "pack up the whole whoring rabble."[650]

The Nazi's hatred of Christianity spilled over into the Hitler Youth. During the 1934 Nuremberg Party rally, the Hitler Youth gleefully sang:

> No evil priest can prevent us from feeling that we are the children of Hitler. We follow not Christ, but Horst Wessel. Away with incense and holy water. The Church can go hang for all we care. The Swastika brings salvation on earth. I want to follow it step by step. Baldur von Schirach, take me along![651]

In addition, one of the perennial and popular verses of an SA's ditty to show their disdain for Catholic priests resounded: "Storm Trooper comrades, hang the Jews and put the priests against the wall."[652]

In his acclaimed book, *Hitler: A Study in Tyranny*, Alan Bullock writes:

> In Hitler's eyes, Christianity was a religion fit only for slaves; he detested its ethics in particular. Its teaching, he declared, was a rebellion against the natural law of selection by struggle and the survival of the fittest.[653]

According to many historians, Hitler's ultimate goal under his *Kirchenkampf* policy was not only a power struggle over ideology, but the total destruction of the Protestant and Catholic churches, including other sects such as the Seventh Day Adventists, Jehovah's Witnesses, Salvation Army, and Bahá'í Faith, which were either banned outright or disappeared. Roger Griffin, the British professor of modern history concurred, explaining that

> There is no doubt that in the long run Nazi leaders such as Hitler and Himmler intended to eradicate Christianity just as ruthlessly as any other rival ideology, even if in the short term they had to be content to make compromises with it.[654]

In their pursuit to eradicate Christianity, the Nazi party line pushed a conformity and subservience to a Nazi ideology that proclaimed, "there was to be no law but Hitler, and ultimately no god but Hitler."[655] One reason for the bitter conflict was that the Nazi government demanded that all Catholics pledge their undying loyalty to the German state, which only escalated the hostility.[656]

Joseph Goebbels exemplified this state-worshiping paganism, proposing a Nazi party religion. In his October 16, 1928, diary entry, he wrote:

> National Socialism is a religion. All we lack is a religious genius capable of uprooting outmoded religious practices and putting new ones in their place. We lack traditions and ritual. One day soon National Socialism will be the religion of all Germans. My Party is my church... That is my gospel.[657]

By the mid-1930s, the Nazis started to implement their anti-Christianity plan, arresting hundreds of clergy members, lay leaders and even nuns, usually on fabricated charges.[658] All sorts of restrictions were levied on churches. Public meetings organized by Catholics were limited and Catholic periodicals not only suffered censorship, but whole issues were often banned. The Nazi regime diminished the Catholic press steadily, "forcing a decline from 435 periodicals in 1934 to just seven in 1943."[659] To keep an eye on dissenting clergy, the authorities installed "Nazis into editorial positions in the Catholic press."[660] In other cases, crucifixes were taken down from state buildings such as mortuaries and replaced with swastikas. In some areas, the Nazis demanded that the crucifix also be removed from parish buildings and schools. Many Christians rebelled against Nazi plans to radically alter or eradicate Christianity. Thousands of Christians went underground (in a movement called the Confessing Church) and hundreds were arrested and confined in concentration camps. One vocal critic of Hitler and the genocidal persecution of the Jews was Dietrich Bonhoeffer, a German Lutheran pastor, author, and a founding member of the Confessing Church. He was arrested by the Gestapo in 1943 and eventually transferred to a Nazi concentration camp. He was executed in 1945.

There were hundreds of cases where Brownshirts "closed down Catholic lay organizations" and "confiscated money and equipment."[661] In attempts to resist the onslaught, church leaders would harshly denounce the Nazis in sermons and publicly condemn the swastika as the "Devil's Cross." Church youth organizations were banned and accused of disseminating "writings hostile to the state." Most were absorbed into the Hitler Youth (*Hitlerjugend*). In most regions, "more than a third of Catholic priests in Germany were subject to some form of disciplining by the police and state authorities."[662]

As the World War II intensified, Hitler's anti-clericalism grew stronger. On October 19, 1941, Hitler slammed Christianity. Revealed through his recorded Table Talks, the Führer declared, "The reason why the ancient world was so pure, light and serene was that it knew nothing of the two great scourges: the pox and Christianity."[663] In another exchange, Hitler once boasted:

> Nothing will prevent me from tearing up Christianity, root and branch. ... We are not out against a hundred-to-one different kinds of Christianity, but against Christianity itself. All people who profess creeds... are traitors to the people. Even those Christians who really want to serve the people... we will have to suppress. I myself am a heathen to the core.[664,665]

Like Lenin and Stalin, Hitler had decided to eliminate all Christian churches, however, he postponed terminating Christianity until after the war, concerned over the political fallout.[666] Hitler, like Stalin and Mussolini, felt compelled to discredit the Church since it obstructed their usurpation of absolute power. During another part of *Hitler's Table Talk* monologues, he clamored that "The best thing is to let Christianity die a natural death... Gradually the myths crumble... then the Christian doctrine will be convicted of absurdity."[667]

Even President Franklin D. Roosevelt attested to Hitler's aims to exterminate religion. In FDR's case, he had acquired evidence of the Nazis' plan to abolition all religious institutions. In a speech on October 27, 1941, Roosevelt declared:

> Your Government has in its possession another document, made in Germany by Hitler's Government... It is a plan to abolish all existing religions—Catholic, Protestant, Mohammedan, Hindu, Buddhist, and Jewish alike. The property of all churches will be seized by the Reich and its puppets. The cross and all other symbols of religion are to be forbidden. The clergy are to be forever liquidated, silenced under penalty of the concentration camps, where even now so many fearless men are being tortured because they have placed God above Hitler.[668]

None of this should be surprising. Earlier, according to Otto Wagener, Hitler confided that: "We must seize the evil in Germany by the root and tear it out, to make way for true socialism, for the new faith, for the new religion."[669]

* * * * *

The adherents of the German Nazi movement reflected a profoundly left-wing footprint not only as social revolutionaries, secularists of political theodicy, and diehard collectivists, but as brothers posturing and fighting for alpha-male dominance. As Nazism developed, it was heavily influenced by the early Utopian socialists, the neo-socialists, and various movements to reform Marxism, opposing any independent political or religious movement that might eclipse its own authority. Extremely hostile towards the aristocracy, Christianity, and capitalism, Nazis considered themselves revolutionaries—radicals determined to bring about a classless society of superior racial egalitarianism bathed in *volk* socialism. There was nothing traditionally conservative about their movement. The American historian Thomas Childers asserted that the "The Nazis were not conservatives. They were radicals, they were revolutionaries, and conservatives in Germany understood this."[670] Nazism arose out of the ashes of early socialist movements that commenced with Pierre-Joseph Proudhon. This was the period in which socialist and anarchist intellectuals described nations as belonging to single ethnic groups held together by a collectivity framework of socioeconomic controls.

In his 1974 book, *Leftism: From de Sade and Marx to Hitler and Marcuse*, Erik von Kuehnelt-Leddihn (1909–1999) referred to the Nazis as a part of the left-wing brotherhood, distant bedfellows of the communists in an ideological movement rooted in the French Revolution. An Austrian-born polymath, Kuehnelt-Leddihn classified Hitler as an "identitarian," in the sense that the Nazis clung to racial identity theories that matched the collective identity-based politics found among most socialist revolutionaries. Such identitarian values have been employed to capture the plebeian's self-identity in order to embolden revolutionary demagogues in their campaign to destroy individualism, market capitalism, and free trade.

Kuehnelt-Leddihn saw this collectivity of identity—social, racial, national, linguistic, or ethnic—as the theoretical backbone of totalitarian regimes. As in the case of the Soviet Union, this identity-based conformity led the Nazis to enforce their particular brand of racial collectivism, thus cementing the bricks of racism and chauvinism into the walls of statist leftism. This should not be surprising since Nazism combined national identity, biological determinism, and social radicalism, while

Marxist theory leavened international identity and sociological determinism within its social radicalism. Both systems failed in practice, but many of their philosophical tenets are still influential.

To contextualize Nazism and Fascism within our current political framework, the United States ceaselessly lurches towards a left-wing statism that is reminiscent of 1920–1940s fascist regimes. The US Democratic Party increasingly emulates the economic and metaphysical collectivism of Nazism and fascism, while the Republican Party echoes the fascistic militarism and expansionism of the Third Reich. Obama's landmark Affordable Care Act represents Italian fascism to its deepest core, forcing citizens to buy a "corporate" product—health insurance—which harkens back to the state-directed corporative policies favored by Mussolini. As for President George Walker Bush's invasion of Iraq in 2003, he pursued the invasion of a nation that never directly attacked the United States, and therefore engaged not in national self-defense, but the military conquest reminiscent of Hitler's infamy. That being said, a majority (58%) of Democratic senators voted for the Iraq War Resolution that authorized that invasion, demonstrating that this conquest was approved by both parties.

In truth, the socialist-welfare economics and collectivistic metaphysics advanced by the American statist Left and Democratic Party leadership have more commonality with German Nazism and Italian Fascism than the US Republican Party. These radical politicos strive to grow the state, empower government, and socialize the citizenry while taxing, politicalizing, borrowing, spending, and regulating with recklessness, as had all the 20th century socialist dictatorships. Frighteningly, there are increasingly few socioeconomic and metaphysical dissimilarities between the statist Leftists in the US Democratic Party and historical fascism. The statist-progressive left's approach to cede more fascist-authoritarian power to the national-state can only align with Mussolini's supreme motto: "Everything in the State, nothing outside the State, nothing against the State."

In an ironic twist, statist Leftists believe that their fascist-like policies will somehow prevent future fascism, in the mistaken assumption that they have no relationship to the policies of Hitler and Mussolini. This fallacy is pervasive. Wearing blinders to block out the history of fascism, the statist Left works diligently to collectivize America under the ideological determinism that permeated post WWI Germany, Italy and Russia, all the while accusing adversaries of harboring fascist dogma. This is the same brand of hypocrisy perpetrated by the Nazi collaborator, Joseph Stalin, who accused any opponent of communism as beholden to fascist sympathies, when he himself was the personification of the national socialist quintessential archetype.

In the final analysis, if the historical evidence of German Nazism and Italian Fascism are ignored or obfuscated, history will repeat itself to the further detriment of human liberty—most assuredly under an innocent-sounding namesake that conceals fascism's true identity and purpose.

Notes

[1] Voigt, *Unto Caesar*, p. 85.

[2] Rauschning, *The Voice of Destruction*, p. 131.

[3] Michael Mann, *Fascists* (New York, NY: Cambridge University Press, 2006), p. 7.

[4] "German *Volksgenossen!*" Hitler's opening speech at the new Winterhilfswerk, Deutschlandhalle, Berlin, Oct. 5, 1937.

[5] Robert Hessen, ed., *Berlin Alert: The Memoirs and Reports of Truman Smith* (Hoover Institute Press, 1985), p. 62.

[6] Andrei A. Znamenski, "From 'National Socialists' to 'Nazi:' History, Politics and the English Language," *The Independent Review*, Oakland, CA, Vol. 19, No. 4, Spring 2015, p. 545.

[7] Weber, *Becoming Hitler*, p. xiii.

[8] Ibid., p. 345n1.

[9] Ibid., pp. xiii–xiv.

[10] Heiden, *A History of National Socialism*, p. 76.

[11] Weber, *Hitler's First War*, p. 251.

[12] Heiden, *Hitler: A Biography*, p. 54.

[13] Gary Lapon, "What do we mean by exploitation?" SocialistWorker.org, Sept. 28, 2011. Also see Bonnie G. Smith, Marc Van De Mieroop, Richard von Glahn, Kris Lane, *Crossroads and Cultures: A History of the World's People* (Boston/New York: Bedford/St. Martin's, 2012), p. 817.

[14] Conan Fischer, *The Rise of the Nazis* (Manchester University Press, 2002), p. 53.

[15] Ibid., p. 54.

[16] Watson, *The Lost Literature of Socialism*, p. 71.

[17] Toland, *Adolf Hitler: The Definitive Biography*, p. 314.

[18] Adolf Hitler's "Why We Are Anti-Semites," an Aug. 15, 1920 speech in Munich, Germany, at the great beer hall of the Hofbräuhaus. Hitler may have given this speech a number of times since the date is also listed as Aug. 13. This speech is also known as "Why Are We Anti-Semites?" Translated and published in *Vierteljahrshefte für Zeitgeschichte*, 16. Jahrg., 4. H. (Oct., 1968), pp. 390–420. This speech can also be found in Jäckel, *Hitler: Sämtliche Aufzeichnungen 1905–1924*, pp. 200–201. This is a collection of around 600 primary documents of Hitler speeches and writings in the period from 1905–1924. This book seemed to be published only in the German language. The book's title translated into English reads: *Hitler: All Recordings 1905–1924*. Edited by Carolyn Yeager. https://carolynyeager.net/why-we-are-antisemites-text-adolf-hitlers-1920-speech-hofbräuhaus.

[19] Aly, *Hitler's Beneficiaries*, 2005, p. 16.

[20] Adolf Eichmann, *False Gods: The Jerusalem Memoirs* (London, UK: Black House Publishing, 2015), p. 75.

[21] Ibid.

[22] F.A. Hayek, *The Road to Serfdom* (New York, NY: Routledge, 2005), p. 173. First published in 1944.

[23] Toland, *Adolf Hitler: The Definitive Biography*, p. 224. Hitler's speech on May 1, 1927.

[24] Gregor Strasser, "Thoughts about the Tasks of the Future," June 15, 1926.

[25] Wagener, *Hitler—Memoirs of a Confidant*, p. 17.

[26] Ibid., p. 14.

[27] Ibid., p. 148.

[28] Ibid., p. 149.

[29] Ibid., p. 262.

[30] Ibid., p. 324.

[31] Ibid., p. 288.

[32] Ibid., pp. 16–17.

[33] Rauschning, *The Voice of Destruction*, pp. 191–193.

[34] Ibid., p. 186.

[35] Muravchik, *Heaven on Earth*, p. 164.

[36] Heiden, *A History of National Socialism*, p. 58.

[37] Rauschning, *The Voice of Destruction*, p. 175.

[38] Stephen E. Atkins, *Holocaust Denial as an International Movement* (Westport, CT and London, UK: Praeger, 2009), p. 170.

[39] Mark Weber, "Swiss Historian Exposes Anti-Hitler Rauschning Memoir as Fraudulent," *The Journal of Historical Review*, Fall 1983 (Vol. 4, No. 3), pp. 378–380.

[40] Milan Hauner, *Hitler: A Chronology of His Life and Time* (Palgrave Macmillan, 2008), p. 84.

[41] Peter Wyden, *The Hitler Virus: The Insidious Legacy of Adolf Hitler* (New York, NY: Arcade Publishing, 2001), p. 164.

[42] "Hitler historian loses libel case," *BBC News*, Apr. 11, 2000. http://news.bbc.co.uk/2/hi/uk_news/709128.stm.

[43]Rauschning, *The Voice of Destruction*, p. 87.

[44]Ibid., p. 89.

[45]Ibid., p. 137.

[46]Orlow, *The Nazi Party 1919–1945*, p. 61, Goebbels' article, "Nationalsozialisten aus Berlin und aus dem Reich," *Voelkischer Beobachter*, Feb. 4, 1927.

[47]Dietrich Orlow, "Asschnitt aus Wochenbericht Nr. 157," May 18, 1927, HA, roll 70 folder 1516. Additional sources.

[48]Goebbels' "Lenin or Hitler" speech first delivered on Sept. 17, 1925.

[49]Roger Manvell and Heinrich Fraenkel, *Doctor Goebbels: His Life and Death* (New York, NY: Skyhorse Publishing, 2010), p. 25, conversation with Hertha Holk.

[50]Shirer, *The Rise and Fall of the Third Reich*, pp. 126–127.

[51]Read, *The Devil's Disciples*, pp. 141–142.

[52]Gianluca Mezzofiore, "Joseph Goebbels' Journey from Dreamy Socialist to Ardent Nazi Chronicled in Archive," *International Business Times*, Sept. 25, 2012.

[53]Toland, *Adolf Hitler: The Definitive Biography*, p. 215.

[54]Ibid., p. 215.

[55]Read, *The Devil's Disciples*, pp. 320–321.

[56]Ibid., p. 142.

[57]*Der Angriff* (*The Attack*), Dec. 6, 1931. *Der Angriff* was the official newspaper of the Nazi-Sozi party in Berlin, Germany. First published on July 4, 1927 by the Angriff Press under Joseph Goebbels.

[58]Aurel Kolnai, *The War Against the West* (New York, NY: The Viking Press, 1938), p. 18.

[59]Hannah Arendt, *Totalitarianism: Part Three of the Origins of Totalitarianism* (New York, NY: A Harvest Book, 1985), p. 7.

[60]Hannah Arendt, *The Origins of Totalitarianism* (New York, NY: Harcourt, Brace & Company, 1951), p. 429.

[61]"HITLERITE RIOT IN BERLIN: Beer Glasses Fly When Speaker Compares Hitler and Lenin," *New York Times*, Nov. 28, 1925, p. 4.

[62]Toby Thacker, *Goebbels: Life and Death* (New York, NY: Palgrave Macmillan, 2009), p. 52.

[63]Joseph Goebbels and Mjölnir, *Die verfluchten Hakenkreuzler. Etwas zum Nachdenken* (Munich: Verlag Frz. Eher, 1932 version). Translated as "Those Damned Nazis," (propaganda pamphlet). http://research.calvin.edu/german-propaganda-archive/haken32.htm.

[64]Ibid.

[65]Joseph Goebbels, "The Winter Crisis is Over" speech on June 5, 1943, at the Berlin Sport Palace, "*Überwundene Winterkrise. Rede im Berliner Sportpalast,*" *Der steile Aufstieg*, Munich: Zentralverlag der NSDAP, 1944, pp. 287–306.

[66]Joseph Goebbels, "Englands Schuld," *Illustrierter Beobachter*, Sondernummer, p. 14. The article is not dated, but is from the early months of the war, likely late fall of 1939. Joseph Goebbels' speech was titled "England's Guilt." http://research.calvin.edu/german-propaganda-archive/goeb47.htm.

[67] National Socialist Letters, *Nationalsozialistische Briefe (NS-Briefe)*, Nov. 15, 1925.

[68] Pipes, *Russia Under the Bolshevik Regime*, p. 259.

[69] Read, *The Devil's Disciples*, p. 141.

[70] Ibid., p. 142.

[71] Shirer, *The Rise and Fall of the Third Reich*, p. 126.

[72] Alan Bullock, *Hitler: A Study in Tyranny*, unabridged edition (New York, NY: Bantam Books, 1961), p. 125; spoken to Otto Strasser in Berlin on May 21, 1930. Originally in Strasser, *Hitler and I*, p. 106.

[73] Watson, *The Lost Literature of Socialism*, p. 80.

[74] Harold Nicolson, *The Harold Nicolson Diaries: 1919–1964*, 2004, pp. 87–88. Diary entry, Jan. 6, 1932.

[75] Anthony Howard, *Crossman: The Pursuit of Power* (Jonathan Cape LTD., 1990), p. 42.

[76] Watson, *The Lost Literature of Socialism*, p. 81.

[77] "Excerpts from Churchill's Manchester Speech," *New York Times*, Jan. 28, 1940.

[78] Winston S. Churchill, *The Second World War, Volume 1: The Gathering Storm* (Mariner Books, 1985), pp. 13–14. First published in 1948.

[79] Robert LeFevre, *The Fundamentals of Liberty* (Santa Ana, CA: Rampart Institute, 1988), p. 389.

[80] "Carnets de P.J. Proudhon, Paris, M. Rivière, 1960," translator, Mitchell Abido, Carnets, Vol. 2, p. 337: No VI, 178. Written in 1847.

[81] Verlag von Julius Kittls Nachfolger, *Historia Judaica*, Volumes 12–14, 1950, p. 101. Also see Francis Wheen, *Karl Marx: A Life* (London, UK: Fourth Estate, 1999), p. 340.

[82] Peter Marshall, *Demanding the Impossible: A History of Anarchism* (Oakland, CA: PM Press, 2010), pp. 256–257.

[83] Ibid., p. 257.

[84] Paxton, *The Anatomy of Fascism*, 2005, p. 48.

[85] G. Valois, "*Les Socialistes découvrent le socialism*," *Le Nouveau Siècle*, Jan. 15, 1928.

[86] Payne, *A History of Fascism, 1914–1945*, p. 292.

[87] Ibid., pp. 292–293.

[88] The Cercle Proudhon organization published under the name of *Cahiers du Cercle Proudhon*.

[89] Wilbur W. Caldwell, *American Narcissism: The Myth of National Superiority* (Algora Publishing, 2006), pp. 22–24.

[90] Prager and Telushkin, *Why the Jew?*, p. 127.

[91] Lewis S. Feuer, *Ideology and the Ideologist* (New Brunswick, NJ: Transaction Publishers, 2010), p. 141. In his Essay: "*Les Juifs, Rois de Vepoque.*"

[92] Doyle, *The Oxford History of the French Revolution*, p. 417.

[93] Sternhell, Sznajder, and Asheri, *The Birth of Fascist Ideology*, p. 101.

[94] Michael A. Heilperin, *Studies in Economic Nationalism* (Ludwig von Mises Institute, 2011). First published in 1960.

[95] David Todd, *Free Trade and Its Enemies in France 1814–1851* (Cambridge University Press, 2015), p. 217.

[96] Prager and Telushkin, *Why the Jew?*, p. 128. The research paper was called "The Jewish Saint-Simonians and Socialist Anti-Semitism in France."

[97] Prager and Telushkin, *Why the Jew?*, p. 123.

[98] Sidney Hook, "Home Truths About Marx," *Commentary*, Sept. 1978, reprinted in *Marxism and Beyond* (Totowa, NJ: Rowman and Littlefield, 1983), p. 117.

[99] Jacob Katz, *From Prejudice to Destruction: Anti-Semitism 1700–1933* (Harvard University Press, 1982), p. 121.

[100] Peter Pulzer, *The Rise of Political Anti-Semitism in Germany and Austria*, revised ed. (Harvard University Press, 1988), p. 45.

[101] Lawrence D. Kritzman, ed., *The Columbia History of Twentieth-Century French Thought* (New York, NY: Columbia University Press, 2006), p. 151.

[102] Sternhell, Sznajder, and Asheri, *The Birth of Fascist Ideology*, p. 85.

[103] Arthur Birnie, *An Economic History of Europe 1760–1930* (London, UK and New York, NY: Routledge, 2010), p. 113. First published in 1930.

[104] Heather M. Campbell, ed., *The Britannica Guide to Political and Social Movements That Changed the Modern World* (New York, NY: Britannica Educational Publishing, 2010), p. 130.

[105] Arthur Birnie, *An Economic History of Europe 1760–1930* (London, UK and New York, NY: Routledge, 2010), p. 113. First published in 1930.

[106] Alan Ryan, *On Politics: A History of Political Thought from Herodotus to the Present* (Liveright, 2012), pp. 647–651.

[107] George F. Will, "China's deeply flawed ascent," *Washington Post*, Jan. 20, 2016. https://www.washingtonpost.com/opinions/chinas-deeply-flawed-ascent/2016/01/20/94bdf1ae-bed5-11e5-83d4-42e3bceea902_story.html.

[108] Jäckel, *Hitler: Sämtliche Aufzeichnungen 1905–1924*, p. 190.

[109] Wagener, *Hitler—Memoirs of a Confidant*, p. 16.

[110] Ibid., p. 284.

[111] Voigt, *Unto Caesar*, p. 35.

[112] Drucker, *The End of Economic Man*, pp. 245–246.

[113] "Lenin and his nine Rolls-Royces," *The Telegraph*, Nov. 30, 1996. https://www.telegraph.co.uk/culture/4706414/Lenin-and-his-nine-Rolls-Royces.html.

[114] F.A. Hayek, *The Road to Serfdom* (New York, NY: Routledge, 2005), p. 28. First published in 1944.

[115] Walter Lippmann, *The Good Society* (New Brunswick, NJ: Transaction Publications, 2005), p. 89. First published in 1937.

[116] Walter Lippmann, *A Preface to Morals* (New Brunswick, NJ: Transaction Publishers, 1982), p. 80. First published in 1929.

[117] Aly, *Hitler's Beneficiaries*, 2005, p. 323.

[118] Adolf Hitler, "Why We Are Anti-Semites," Aug. 15, 1920 speech in Munich at the Hofbräuhaus. https://carolynyeager.net/why-we-are-antisemites-text-adolf-hitlers-1920-speech-hofbr%C3%A4uhaus.

[119]"Down with Judah!" Nazi poster from Münster that dates from shortly before the Apr. 1, 1933 boycott of the Jews. Archive of Antisemitic Publications from 1930–1945. http://research.calvin.edu/german-propaganda-archive/muenster.htm.

[120]Abram L. Harris, "Sombart and German (National) Socialism," *Journal of Political Economy*, Vol. 50, No. 6 (Dec. 1942), pp. 812–813.

[121]Ibid., pp. 808–809.

[122]Ibid., pp. 810–811.

[123]Aurel Kolnai, "Society and Economics," chap. VII in *The War Against the West* (London, UK: Victor Gol, 1938), p. 326.

[124]Abram L. Harris, "Sombart and German (National) Socialism," *Journal of Political Economy*, Vol. 50, No. 6 (Dec. 1942), p. 813.

[125]F.A. Hayek, *The Road to Serfdom* (London, UK: Routledge & Kegan Paul, 1979), p. 127.

[126]Kitchen, *A History of Modern Germany*, p. 205.

[127]Bernard N. Schumacher, ed., *A Cosmopolitan Hermit: Modernity and Tradition in the Philosophy of Josef Pieper* (The Catholic University of America Press, 2009), p. 94.

[128]Thomas Rohkrämer, *A Single Communal Faith?: The German Right from Conservatism to National Socialism*, Monographs in German History 20 (Berghahn Books, 2007), p. 130.

[129]Kitchen, *A History of Modern Germany*, p. 205.

[130]Ibid.

[131]Aurel Kolnai, "Society and Economics," chap. VII in *The War Against the West* (London, UK: Victor Gol, 1938), p. 329.

[132]Patrick Henry, ed., *The Jewish Resistance Against the Nazis* (Washington D.C.: Catholic University of America Press, 2014), p. 553.

[133]Neocleous, *Fascism*, pp. 39–40.

[134]Ibid., p. 40.

[135]Ibid.

[136]George Orwell, *My Country Right or Left, 1940–1943*, ed. Sonia Orwell and Ian Angus (Jeffrey, NH: Nonpareil Book, 1968), p. 80. His essay first published in 1941, as "The Lion and the Unicorn."

[137]Ibid.

[138]Peter Lamb, J.C. Docherty, *Historical Dictionary of Socialism*, Lanham, Maryland, UK; Oxford, England, UK, Scarecrow Press, Inc., 2006, p. 1.

[139]Heiden, *The Führer*, p. 122. Also partially quoted in Hannah Arendt, *Totalitarianism: Part Three of the Origins of Totalitarianism* (New York, NY: A Harvest Book, 1985), p. 7n.

[140]Adam Buick, "Russia was never socialist—and why ... what we said over the years," *The Socialist Standard*, published by the Socialist Party of Great Britain.

[141]Noam Chomsky, "The Soviet Union Versus Socialism," *Our Generation*, Spring/Summer, 1986.

[142]Noam Chomsky – speech on "Lenin, Trotsky and Socialism & the Soviet Union," Mar. 15, 1989. https://www.youtube.com/watch?v=yQsceZ9skQI.

[143] George Orwell, Preface to the Ukrainian edition of *Animal Farm*, as published in "The Collected Essays, Journalism, and Letters of George Orwell: As I please, 1943–1945," 1968. See http://home.iprimus.com.au/korob/Orwell.html.

[144] Victor Serge, *From Lenin to Stalin* (New York, NY: Pioneer Publishers, 1937), p. 43.

[145] Albert Speer, *Spandau: The Secret Diaries* (New York, NY: Pocket Books, 1977), p. 84.

[146] Kitchen, *A History of Modern Germany*, p. 205.

[147] *Die Rote Fahne*, June 21, 1923. Voigt, *Unto Caesar*, pp. 141–142.

[148] Nazi poster: The Winter Aid (*Winterhilfswerk*) 1934/35.

[149] Lane and Rupp, *Nazi Ideology Before 1933*, p. xxi.

[150] Deverlein, *Aufstieg*, p. 60, Joachimsthaler, *Weg*, p. 252, and diary of Gottfried Feder, Weber, *Becoming Hitler*, p. 112.

[151] Heiden, *A History of National Socialism*, p. 7.

[152] Ibid.

[153] Ibid., p. 10.

[154] Hitler's speech of Apr. 12, 1922, Munich.

[155] Calic, *Secret Conversations with Hitler*, p. 22. Also published under the title *Unmasked: Two Confidential Interviews with Hitler in 1931*, Chatto & Windus, 1971.

[156] Ibid., p. 33.

[157] Wagener, *Hitler—Memoirs of a Confidant*, p. 14.

[158] A movement started by Louis Auguste Blanqui (1805–1881) called "blanquism" that sought to incite a temporary dictatorship by force—a sort of "putschism" that would overturn the bourgeois social order.

[159] Karl Marx: Letter to Engels, July 13, 1851. Schwarzschild, *Karl Marx: The Red Prussian*, pp. 187–188.

[160] Gustav Mayer, *Friedrich Engels, A Biography*, (American Edition), p. 127. Schwarzschild, *Karl Marx: The Red Prussian*, p. 187.

[161] Peter D. Stachura, *Gregor Strasser and the Rise of Nazism* (New York, NY: Routledge, 2015), p. 3.

[162] Strasser, *Hitler and I*, p. 3.

[163] Ibid., p. 2.

[164] John Hellman, *Communitarian Third Way: Alexandre Marc and Ordre Nouveau, 1930–2000* (McGill-Queen's University Press, 2002), p. 52.

[165] Thomas Childers, *The Third Reich: A History of Nazi Germany* (New York, NY: Simon & Schuster, 2017), p. 84. Nov. 1925 speech.

[166] Gerhard Hirschfeld, "Nazi Germany and Eastern Europe," chap. 4 in *Germany and the European East in the Twentieth Century*, ed. Mühle Eduard (Oxford, UK: Berg Publishers, 2003), p. 71.

[167] "Combat Publishing"—published from 1926 to 1930.

[168] Kershaw, *Hitler 1889–1936: Hubris*, p. 326.

[169] Ibid., p. 325.

[170] Burleigh, *The Third Reich*, p. 246. Campaign speech to the Krupp Locomotive factory workers in Essen, Mar. 27, 1936.

[171] "*Einbeitsfront*," *Der Angriff* editorial, May 27, 1929. Schoenbaum, *Hitler's Social Revolution*, p. 25.

[172] Gerhard Hirschfeld, "Nazi Germany and Eastern Europe," chap. 4 in *Germany and the European East in the Twentieth Century*, ed. Mühle Eduard (Oxford, UK: Berg Publishers, 2003), p. 71.

[173] Ibid.

[174] Nolte, *Three Faces of Fascism*, p. 336.

[175] Ian Kershaw, *Hitler: A Profile in Power* (London, UK, 1991). See especially chapter III, first section.

[176] John B. Thompson, *Studies in the Theory of Ideology* (University of California Press, 1984), p. 215.

[177] Heiden, *The Führer*, p. 467.

[178] Shirer, *The Rise and Fall of the Third Reich*, p. 205.

[179] Ibid.

[180] Daniel Allen Butler, *Field Marshal: The Life and Death of Erwin Rommel* (Philadelphia, PA and Oxford, UK: Casemate Publishers, 2015), p. 117.

[181] Nick Pinfield, *Quest for Political Stability: Germany 1871–1991* (Cambridge University Press, 2015), p. 105.

[182] Hitler's speech July 6, 1933, to the Official End of the National-Socialist Revolution.

[183] *Manifesto of the Communist Party*, Chapter I. "Bourgeois and Proletarians," 1848. Also known as *The Communist Manifesto*.

[184] Horace B. Davis, *Nationalism and Socialism: Marxist and Labor Theories of Nationalism to 1917* (New York, NY: Monthly Review Press, 2009), p. 69.

[185] Glenn E. Curtis, ed., *Russia: A Country in Study* (Library of Congress, Federal Research Division, 1998), p. 300.

[186] Lenny Flank, *Rise and Fall of the Leninist State: A Marxist History of the Soviet Union* (Red and Black Publishers, 2008).

[187] Hitler's "Barbarossa" Proclamation, June 22, 1941, "*Der Führer an das deutsche Volk 22. Juni 1941*," in Philipp Bouhler, edit., *Der großdeutsche Freiheitskampf. Reden Adolf Hitlers, Vol. 3*, Munich: Franz Eher, 1942, pp. 51–61.

[188] Joseph W. Bendersky, *A Concise History of Nazi Germany* (Lanham, MD and Plymouth, UK: Rowman & Littlefield Publishers, Inc., 2007), p. 96.

[189] Joseph W. Bendersky, *A History of Nazi Germany: 1919–1945*, second ed. (Burnham Publishers, 2000), pp. 58–59.

[190] Ernst Röhm, *Die Geschichte eines Hochverräters* ("The Story of a High Traitor" – Röhm's autobiography), Munich, Verlag Frz. Eher Nachf. GmbH, 1933, Volksausgabe, p. 273.

[191] Shirer, *The Rise and Fall of the Third Reich*, p. 120.

[192] Lothar Machtan, *The Hidden Hitler* (Basic Books, 2002), p. 107.

[193] Frank Rector, *The Nazi Extermination of Homosexuals* (Stein & Day Publications, 1981), p. 80.

[194] Walter Reich, "All the Führer's Men," *New York Times*, book review of Lothar Machtan's *The Hidden Hitler*, Dec. 16, 2001.

[195] Heiden, *Hitler: A Biography*, p. 390.

[196] Ibid.

[197] Brown, *Weimar Radicals*, p. 2.

[198] Payne, *A History of Fascism, 1914–1945*, p. 126.

[199] Brown, *Weimar Radicals*, p. 3.

[200] Ibid.

[201] Maya Jaggi, "A Question of Faith," *The Guardian* newspaper, Sept. 14, 2002. https://www.theguardian.com/books/2002/sep/14/biography.history/.

[202] "Shaw Praises Hitler as Able Statesman; But Chancellor Erred, He Says, by Not Urging Intermarriage With Jews," *New York Times*, Nov. 24, 1933. Also in "Shaw Heaps Praise upon the Dictators: While Parliaments Get Nowhere, He Says, Mussolini and Stalin Do Things," *New York Times*, Dec. 10, 1933, Shaw's lecture before the Fabian Society in London called "The Politics of Unpolitical Animals," Nov. 23, 1933.

[203] David Dunn, "A Good Fabian fallen among the Stalinists," *Survey* 28, No. 4 (winter 1984); p. 28.

[204] Vera Micheles Dean, *Europe in Retreat*, revised ed. (New York, NY: Alfred A. Knopf, Inc., 1939), p. 87; Furet, *The Passing of an Illusion*, p. 153; David Dunn, "A Good Fabian fallen among the Stalinists," *Survey* 28, No. 4 (winter 1984); p. 28.

[205] Furet, *The Passing of an Illusion*, p. 207.

[206] Ibid., pp. 205–206.

[207] "Editorial: The Russian Betrayal," *New York Times*, Sept. 18, 1939.

[208] *Wall Street Journal*, June 25, 1941.

[209] Norman Thomas, "Which Way America—Fascism, Communism, Socialism or Democracy?" *Town Meeting Bulletin*, XIII, Mar. 16, 1948, pp. 19–20.

[210] Les K. Adler and Thomas G. Paterson, "Red Fascism: The Merger of Nazi Germany and Soviet Russia in the American Image of Totalitarianism, 1930s–1950s," *American Historical Review* 75, no. 4 (Apr. 1970): p. 1046n4.

[211] Adolf Hitler, speech delivered on Feb. 24, 1941. *The Bulletin of International News* (London), XVIII, No. 5 (Mar. 8, 1941) p. 269, published by the Royal Institute of International Affairs. Pipes, *Russia Under the Bolshevik Regime*, p. 259. Apparently, this quote is not found in Hitler's speech as posted online, but nonetheless appears in *The Bulletin of International News*.

[212] Brown, *Weimar Radicals*, p. 136.

[213] Peter H. Merkl, *Political Violence Under the Swastika: 581 Early Nazis* (Princeton University Press, 1975), p. 484.

[214] Adelheid von Saldern, *The Challenge of Modernity: German Social and Cultural Studies, 1890–1960* (University of Michigan Press, 2002), p. 78.

[215] Mike Schmeitzner, *Totalitarismuskritik von links Deutsche Diskurse Im 20. Jahrhundert* (Vandenhoeck & Ruprecht, 2007), p. 255.

[216] Patrick Major, *The Death of the KPD: Communism and Anti-Communism in West Germany, 1945–1956* (Clarendon Press [Oxford University Press], 2004), p. 43.

[217] Kershaw, *Hitler 1889–1936: Hubris*, pp. 390–391.

[218] Adelheid von Saldern, *The Challenge of Modernity: German Social and Cultural Studies, 1890–1960* (University of Michigan Press, 2002), p. 78.

[219] Rob Sewell, "Fascism's Rise to Power," chap. 7 in *Germany: From Revolution to Counter-Revolution* (Fortress Books, 1988).

[220] Kershaw, *Hitler 1889–1936: Hubris*, pp. 390–391.

[221] Ibid., p. 390.

[222] Ibid., p. 391.

[223] Childers, *The Nazi Voter*, p. 153.

[224] Ibid.

[225] Ibid., p. 154; *Hitler Kern: Sowjetstern*, DDP leaflet, 1930, BA ZSg.I, 27/20 (2).

[226] Ibid., p. 154.

[227] Ibid., p. 154; *Rettet Deutschland!* DVP leaflet, 1930, BA ZSg.I, 42/8 (2).

[228] Kershaw, *Hitler 1889–1936: Hubris*, p. 412.

[229] Ibid.

[230] Back, *The Fateful Alliance*, pp. 72–75.

[231] Ibid., p. 75.

[232] Ibid., p. 84.

[233] Childers, *The Nazi Voter*, p. 111.

[234] J.V. Stalin, "Concerning the International Situation," *Works*, Vol. 6, Jan.–Nov. 1924, pp. 293–314.

[235] Report to the 10th Plenum of ECCI, in International Press Correspondence, Vol. 9, No. 40, Aug. 20, 1929, p. 848.

[236] J.V. Stalin, "Concerning the International Situation," *Works*, Vol. 6, Jan.–Nov. 1924, pp. 293–314.

[237] Weber, *Becoming Hitler*, pp. 66–67.

[238] Ibid., p. 65.

[239] Ibid.

[240] Heather M. Campbell, ed., *The Britannica Guide to Political and Social Movements That Changed the Modern World* (New York, NY: Britannica Educational Publishing, 2010), p. 141.

[241] Ibid.

[242] Jäckel, *Hitler: Sämtliche Aufzeichnungen 1905–1924*, p. 448.

[243] Kershaw, *Hitler 1889–1936: Hubris*, p. 118.

[244] Heiden, *Hitler: A Biography*, p. 54.

[245] Weber, *Becoming Hitler*, p. 66.

[246] Weber, *Becoming Hitler*, pp. 66–67. Additional source: IFZ, ZS89/2, Friedrich Krohn, *Fragebogen über Adolf Hitler*, 1952.

[247] Weber, *Becoming Hitler*, p. 75. Additional source: Quote came from Anton Joachimsthaler, *Hitlers Weg begann in München 1913–1923*, (*Hitler's Path Began in Munich 1913–1923*), Munich, 2003, p. 203.

[248] Ibid., p. 64.

[249] Ibid., p. 83.

[250] Ibid., p. 73.

[251] Kershaw, *Hitler 1889–1936: Hubris*, p. 118.

[252] Ibid., p. 119.

[253] Ibid.

[254] Weber, *Becoming Hitler*, p. 47.

[255] Kershaw, *Hitler 1889–1936: Hubris*, p. 119.

[256] Ibid.

[257] Rob Sewell, "Fascism's Rise to Power," chap. 7 in *Germany: From Revolution to Counter-Revolution* (Fortress Books, 1988).

[258] Uwe Klußmann, "Conquering the Capital: The Ruthless Rise of the Nazis in Berlin, Part 2: Battling All Sides, but Mostly Left," *Spiegel Online International*, Nov. 29, 2012.

[259] Jane Degras, ed., *The Communist International 1919–1943: Documents, Vol. 3, 1929–1943* (London, UK: Routledge, 2014), p. 120.

[260] Ibid., p. 121.

[261] Back, *The Fateful Alliance*, pp. 78–79.

[262] Stephen P. Halbrook, "How the Nazis Used Gun Control," *National Review*, Dec. 2, 2013. https://nationalreview.com/2013/12/how-nazis-used-gun-control-stephen-p-halbrook/.

[263] Rauschning, *The Voice of Destruction*, p. 187.

[264] *The Nation*, Vol. 107, No. 2789, July 1, 1918, to Dec. 30, 1918, p. 722.

[265] Allan Mitchell, *Revolution in Bavaria, 1918–1919: The Eisner Regime and the Soviet Republic* (Princeton University Press, 1965), p. 140.

[266] Ibid., p. 99.

[267] Ibid., p. 100.

[268] Weber, *Becoming Hitler*, p. 31.

[269] Jäckel, *Hitler: Sämtliche Aufzeichnungen 1905–1924*, p. 448.

[270] Weber, *Becoming Hitler*, pp. 33–34, Lotter's Putsch is also referred to as the "Sailor's Putsch."

[271] Ibid., Allan Mitchell, *Revolution in Bavaria, 1918–1919: The Eisner Regime and the Soviet Republic* (Princeton University Press, 1965), p. 139.

[272] Ibid., p. 138.

[273] Chris Harman, *The Lost Revolution: Germany 1918 to 1923* (Bookmarks, 1982), pp. 129–130.

[274] Weber, *Hitler's First War*, p. 253.

[275] "Hitler's First War by Thomas Weber," *Military History Monthly*, Oct. 1, 2010.

[276] Weber, *Becoming Hitler*, p. 38.

[277] Alastair Hamilton, *The Appeal of Fascism: A Study of Intellectuals and Fascism 1919–1945* (London, UK: Anthony Blond, 1971), p. 166.

[278] Gompers and Walling, *Out of Their Own Mouths*, p. 76.

[279] Klaus Hildebrand, *The Third Reich* (London, UK: Routledge, 1991), p. 106.

[280] Weber, *Hitler's First War*, p. 251. Original source: Knopp and Remy, *Hitler*, Episode 1.

[281] *Hitler: A Profile* 1 of 6, "The Private Man" written and produced by Guido Knopp and Maurice Philip Remy, produced by ZDF (Germany) in association with A&E Home Video and The History Channel, 1995. https://www.youtube.com/watch?v=e1RJY-O03bY&t=14s.

[282] Weber, *Hitler's First War*, p. 251.

[283] Ibid.

[284] Weber, *Becoming Hitler*, pp. 39–40. The State Library of Bavaria now owns the photo.

[285] Evans, *The Coming of the Third Reich*, p. 161.

[286] Kershaw, *Hitler 1889–1936: Hubris*, p. 120.

[287] Anton Joachimsthaler, *Korrektur einer Bibliographie, Adolf Hitler 1908–1920, (Correction of a Biography, Adolf Hitler 1908–1920)* (Munich, 1989), pp. 125, 188, 197–198; Werner Maser, *Adolf Hitler: Das Ende der Führer-Legende* (Düsseldorf, Vienna, 1980), p. 263n. (citing remarks made to him in the early 1950s by Otto Strasser and Hermann Esser); Hans-Jürgen Eitner, *'Der Führer': Hitlers Persönlichkeit und Charakter* (Munich and Vienna, 1981), p. 66.

[288] Weber, *Hitler's First War*, p. 250.

[289] Weber, *Becoming Hitler*, pp. 50–51.

[290] Ibid., p. 52.

[291] Ibid., p. 42.

[292] Ibid. Additional Source: Anton Joachimsthaler, *Weg*, pp. 198–218.

[293] Weber, *Becoming Hitler*, p. 31.

[294] Stefan Vogt, *Nationaler Sozialismus und Soziale Demokratie: Die sozialdemokratische Junge Rechte 1918–1945* (Bonn, Germany: Dietz Verlag, 2006).

[295] Weber, *Hitler's First War*, p. 253.

[296] Noam Chomsky – speech on "Lenin, Trotsky and Socialism & the Soviet Union," Mar. 15, 1989. https://www.youtube.com/watch?v=yQsceZ9skQI.

[297] Weber, *Hitler's First War*, p. 253.

[298] Weber, *Becoming Hitler*, p. 53.

[299] Eugenio Pacelli Edition, report, Pacelli to Pietro Gasparri, Apr. 30, 1919.

[300] Burleigh, *The Third Reich*, p. 40.

[301] Weber, *Hitler's First War*, p. 251.

[302] Norman Stone, "The Fuhrer In the Making," *Wall Street Journal*, Oct. 30, 2012.

[303] Kershaw, *Hitler 1889–1936: Hubris*, p. 118. Archival material: BHStA, Abt.IV, 2.I.R., Batl. Anordnungen, Bl.1505, 1516; Joachimsthaler, pp. 212–213, 217.

[304] Weber, *Becoming Hitler*, pp. 49–50. "Archival Collections & Private Papers and Interviews," files of: 6th Bavarian Reserve Division (RD6), 16 Bavarian Reserve Infantry Regiment (RIR16), 17 Bavarian Reserve Infantry Regiment (RIR17), from Bayerisches Hauptstaatsarchiv, Munich, pp. 391–392.

[305] Ibid., p. 45.

[306] Ibid., p. 40.

[307] Ibid., p. 64.

[308] Weber, *Hitler's First War*, p. 251.

[309] Kershaw, *Hitler 1889–1936: Hubris*, p. 120.

[310] Strasser, *Hitler and I*, p. 12.

[311] Kershaw, *Hitler 1889–1936: Hubris*, p. 114. Kershaw estimated the death total in battle at 606.

[312] Weber, *Becoming Hitler*, p. 70.

[313] Ibid.

[314] Ibid.

[315] Ibid., p. 62.

[316] Ibid., p. 56.

[317] Ibid., pp. 56, 70–72.

[318] Ibid., p. 72.

[319] Ibid.

[320] Ibid.

[321] Léon Poliakov, *The History of Anti-Semitism, Volume Four: Suicidal Europe, 1870–1933* (University of Pennsylvania Press, 2003), p. 24.

[322] Toland, *Adolf Hitler: The Definitive Biography*, p. 315.

[323] Hitler, *Mein Kampf, Vol. Two*, chap. IV, "Personality and the Conception of the Völkisch State."

[324] Hitler, *Mein Kampf, Vol. Two*, chap. VII, "The Struggle with the Red Front."

[325] Toland, *Adolf Hitler: The Definitive Biography*, p. 105.

[326] Zeev Sternhell, "Fascist Ideology," chap. 6 in *Fascism: Critical Concepts in Political Science*, eds. Roger Griffin and Matthew Feldman (New York, NY: Routledge, 2004), p. 112.

[327] Jackson J. Spielvogel, *Western Civilization: A Brief History, Vol. II: Since 1550*, 4th ed. (Wadsworth, 1999), p. 502.

[328] Fritzsche, *Life and Death in the Third Reich*, p. 38.

[329] Michael Wildt, *Hitler's Volksgemeinschaft and the Dynamics of Racial Exclusion, Germany* (Berghahn Books, 2012), p. 35.

[330] Steber and Gotto, *Visions of Community in Nazi Germany*, p. 7.

[331] Fritzsche, *Life and Death in the Third Reich*, p. 39.

[332] Grunberger, *The 12-Year Reich*, p. 46.

[333] "Chronology of the Nazi Record: 1933–1943," *The Ukrainian Weekly* (Jersey City, NJ), Jan. 30, 1943.

[334] Robert Wilde, "What Was the Nazi Idea of Volksgemeinschaft?" *ThoughtCo.*, Mar. 6, 2017. https://www.thoughtco.com/what-was-volksgemeinschaft-1221370/.

[335] Martin Rein, Gøsta Esping-Andersen, and Lee Rainwater, eds., *Stagnation and Renewal in Social Policy: The Rise and Fall of Policy Regimes* (Armonk, NY: M.E. Sharpe, Inc., 1987), p. 63.

[336] Redman, *Ezra Pound and Italian Fascism*, p. 114. From a Mar. 24, 1924, speech on the 5th anniversary of the Combat Leagues.

[337] Max Domarus, *The Essential Hitler: Speeches and Commentary* (Bolchazy-Carducci, 2007), pp. 171, 172–173.

[338] Schoenbaum, *Hitler's Social Revolution*, p. 57. Hitler interview by Hanns Johst, in *Frankfurter Volksblatt*, Jan. 27, 1934.

[339] John J. White and Ann White, *Bertolt Brecht's Furcht Und Elend Des Dritten Reiches: A German Exile Drama in the Struggle against Fascism* (Rochester, NY: Camden Press, 2010), p. 60.

[340] Ibid.

[341] Fritzsche, *Life and Death in the Third Reich*, p. 45.

[342] Richard Pipes, *Property and Freedom* (New York, NY: Alfred A. Knopf, 1999), p. 220.

[343] Lane and Rupp, *Nazi Ideology Before 1933*, p. 43.

[344] Arthur M. Schlesinger, Jr., *The Vital Center: The Politics of Freedom* (New Brunswick, NJ: Transaction Publishers, 1998), p. 56. First printed in 1949. Second Speech Delivered at the Presidium of the ECCI on the American Question, May 14, 1929.

[345] Watson, *The Lost Literature of Socialism*, p. 80.

[346] Ibid.

[347] Ibid., p. 78.

[348] V.I. Lenin, "Lessons of the Moscow Uprising," Proletary, No. 2, Aug. 29, 1906. *Lenin Collected Works*, Moscow, Progress Publishers, 1965, Vol. 11, pp. 171–178.

[349] David F. Kelly, Gerard Magill, and Henk ten Have, *Contemporary Catholic Health Care Ethics*, 2nd ed. (Washington D.C.: Georgetown University Press, 2013), p. 54.

[350] Robert Conquest, *Reflections on a Ravaged Century* (W.W. Norton & Company, 2001), p. 94.

[351] David Rubinstein, *Culture, Structure, and Agency: Toward a Truly Multidimensional Sociology* (SAGE Publications, 2001), p. 69.

[352] Kershaw, *Hitler 1889–1936: Hubris*, p. 135.

[353] Adolf Hitler's Aug. 15, 1920, speech entitled "Why We Are Anti-Semites." It was apparently delivered several times in Aug. 1920. Due to different translations, this speech is also known as "Why Are We Anti-Semites?"

[354] Ibid.

[355] Philip Mendes, *Jews and The Left: The Rise and Fall of a Political Alliance* (Houndmills, UK and New York, NY: Palgrave Macmillan, 2014), p. 47.

[356] Friedrich Engels, "The Magyar Struggle," *Neue Rheinische Zeitung*, No. 194, Jan. 13, 1849. Some translations use "ethnic trash" instead of "trash races."

[357] Friedrich Engels, *Neue Rheinische Zeitung*, Apr. 29, 1849.

[358] Karl Marx, "Forced Emigration," first published in the *New York Daily Tribune* of Mar. 22, 1853 and republished in the *People's Paper* of Apr. 16, 1853.

[359] Pipes Richard, ed., *The Unknown Lenin: From the Secret Archive*, trans. Catherine A. Fitzpatrick (Yale University Press, 1996), p. 77.

[360] Pipes, *Russia Under the Bolshevik Regime*, p. 363. Original source: Nora Levin, *The Jews in the Soviet Union since 1917* (New York, NY: NYU Press, 1988), p. 57.

[361] Zvi Gitelman, *A Century of Ambivalence: The Jews of Russia and the Soviet Union, 1881 to the Present* (New York, NY: Schocken, 1988), p. 118.

[362] Benjamin Pinkus, *The Soviet Government and the Jews: A Documented Study, 1948–1967* (Cambridge University Press, 1984), p. 13.

[363] Yaacov Ro'i, *Jews and Jewish Life in Russia and the Soviet Union* (Routledge, 1995), pp. 103–106.

[364] Miklós Kun, *Stalin: An Unknown Portrait* (Central European University Press, 2003), p. 287.

[365] Furet, *The Passing of an Illusion*, pp. 191–192.

[366] Eugene Lyons, *Workers' Paradise Lost: Fifty Years of Soviet Communism: A Balance Sheet* (Funk & Wagnalls, 1967), p. 287.

[367] Friedrich Engels, "Telegraph für Deutschland," No. 5, Jan. 1841.

[368] Engel's letter to Marx, May 23, 1851. Schwarzschild, *Karl Marx: The Red Prussian*, p. 193.

[369] Marx's letter to Engels, Jan. 13, 1869.

[370] Marx's letter to Engels, Dec. 17, 1869. Schwarzschild, *Karl Marx: The Red Prussian*, p. 353.

[371] Ibid., Leopold Schwarzschild, p. 364.

[372] Christopher Hollis, M.P., "II: Marx, the Father of Hitler," *The Tablet*, International Catholic News Weekly, Apr. 9, 1949, p. 231.

[373] "Demands of the Communist Party in Germany," *Marx-Engels Collected Works*, Vol. 7, pp. 3ff, Progress Publishers: 1975–2005.

[374] *Marx-Engels Gesamt-Ausgabe, Erste Abteilung*, Vol. 7, Mar. to Dec. 1848, p. 304. Schwarzschild, *Karl Marx: The Red Prussian*, p. 202.

[375] Robert C. Tucker, *Stalin in Power: The Revolution from Above, 1928–1941* (New York and London: W.W. & Company, 1992), p. 41.

[376] Ibid., p. 359.

[377] Dorothy Thompson, *The New Russia* (New York, NY: Henry Holt and Company, 1928), pp. 27–28.

[378] Karl Marx, "On the Jewish Question," *Deutsch-Französische Jahrbücher*, Feb. 1844.

[379] Karl Marx, "The Russian Loan," *New-York Daily Tribune*, Jan. 4, 1856. Quoted in Nathaniel Weyl, *Karl Marx: Racist* (New York, NY: Arlington House, 1979), p. 90.

[380] Karl Marx to Friedrich Engels (Letter, July 1862) in reference to his socialist political competitor, Ferdinand Lassalle. Slightly different translation of this quote found quoted in William Otto Henderson, *Marx And Engels and the English Workers: And Other Essays* (Psychology Press, 1989), p. 71.

[381] Friedrich Engels, Letter to Marx, Feb. 13, 1851.

[382] *Marx-Engels Gesamtausgabe*, Abteilung 3, Vol. 1, p. 121.

[383] Karl Marx: Letter to Engels, Feb. 10, 1851.

[384] Karl Marx: Letter to Engels, Dec. 9, 1851.

[385] Karl Marx: Letter to Engels, Dec. 1, 1851. Schwarzschild, *Karl Marx: The Red Prussian*, p. 245.

[386] Friedrich Engels: Letter to Marx, Jan. 14, 1848.

[387] Friedrich Engels: Letter to Marx, Sept. 18, 1846.

[388] Friedrich Engels: Letter to Marx, Jan. 14, 1846. Schwarzschild, *Karl Marx: The Red Prussian*, p. 147.

[389] Friedrich Engels, "Democratic Pan-Slavism," Feb. 14, 1849, K. Marx and F. Engels. Can be found in P.W. Blackstock and B.F. Hoselitz, eds., *The Russian Menace to Europe* (Glencoe: Free Press, 1952), p. 71.

[390] Jorge Larrain, *Ideology and Cultural Identity: Modernity and the Third World Presence* (Cambridge, UK: Polity Press, 1994), p. 20. Original source: Karl Marx, letter to F. Engels, Dec. 2, 1854, in K. Marx and F. Engels, *Materiales para la Historia de America Latina, Mexico: Cuadernos de Pasado y Presente*, 1980, pp. 203–204.

[391] *Anthony Bourdain: Parts Unknown*, Cuba, *CNN*, season 6/episode 1, 2015.

[392] Karl Marx to Pavel Vasilyevich Annenkov, Letter, Dec. 28, 1846. Rue d'Orleans, 42, Faubourg Namur, *Marx Engels Collected Works* Vol 38, p. 95; International Publishers (1975). First Published: in full in the French original in *M.M. Stasyulevich i yego sovremenniki v ikh perepiske*, Vol. III, 1912.

[393] Christopher Hollis, M.P., "II: Marx, the Father of Hitler," *The Tablet*, International Catholic News Weekly, Apr. 9, 1949, p. 231.

[394] Horace B. Davis, *Nationalism and Socialism: Marxist and Labor Theories of Nationalism to 1917* (New York, NY: Monthly Review Press, 2009), p. 72. Original: Marx, "Zur Judenfrange" in *Werke*, I, (1843) pp. 374–376.

[395] Tyler Cowen, "The Socialist Roots of Modern Anti-Semitism: Socialist Economies Breed Intolerance and Persecution," *FEE* magazine, Jan. 1, 1997. https://fee.org/articles/the-socialist-roots-of-modern-anti-semitism/.

[396] Rauschning, *The Voice of Destruction*, p. 235.

[397] *The Soviet Story*, Edvins Snore, writer/director, 85-minute documentary, 2008.

[398] The arrest was related to her second husband.

[399] Margarete Buber-Neumann, *Under Two Dictators: Prisoner of Stalin and Hitler* (London, UK: Pimlico, 2008), p. 300. First published in 1949.

[400] *The Soviet Story*, Edvins Snore, writer/director, 85-minute documentary, 2008.

[401] Gregor, *The Fascist Persuasion in Radical Politics*, p. 119.

[402] Alf Lüdtke, "The 'Honor of Labor': Industrial Workers and the Power of Symbols under National Socialism," in *Nazism and German Society, 1933–1945*, ed. David F. Crew (New York, NY: Routledge, 1994), pp. 67–109.

[403] Sternhell, Sznajder, and Asheri, *The Birth of Fascist Ideology*, p. 5.

[404] Robert Soucy, *French Fascism: The Second Wave, 1933–1939* (Yale University Press, 1995), p. 54.

[405] Zeev Sternhell, "Les convergences fascists," in *Nouvelle histoire des idées politiques* (in French), ed. Pascal Ory (Pluriel Hachette, 1987), pp. 533–556.

[406] Roger Griffin and Matthew Feldman, eds., *Fascism: Critical Concepts in Political Science* (New York, NY: Routledge, 2004), p. 102.

[407] Ibid.

[408] Sternhell, *Neither Right nor Left*, p. 226. Quotes come from Drieu's book *Socialisme Fasciste*.

[409] Ibid.

[410] Thierry Maulnier, "*Le Seul Combat Possible,*" 1936, *Combat.*

[411] Robert Soucy, *French Fascism: The Second Wave, 1933–1939* (Yale University Press, 1995), p. 53.

[412] Richard J. Golsan, ed., *Fascism's Return: Scandal, Revision and Ideology since 1980* (University of Nebraska Press, 1998), p. 135.

[413] Yohanon Cohen, *Small Nations in Times of Crisis and Confrontation* (SUNY Press, 1989), p. 110.

[414] "Russia: Arms & Art," *Time* magazine, Sept. 11, 1939.

[415] Fulton John Sheen, *Communism and the Conscience of the West* (Bobbs-Merrill, 1948), p. 115.

[416] *The Soviet Story,* Edvins Snore, writer/director, 85-minute documentary, 2008.

[417] Toland, *Adolf Hitler: The Definitive Biography,* p. 80.

[418] Ibid., p. 314.

[419] Overy, *War and Economy in the Third Reich,* pp. 1–2.

[420] Eugen Weber, *Varieties of Fascism: Doctrines of Revolution in the Twentieth Century* (D. Van Nostrand, 1964), p. 47.

[421] Overy, *War and Economy in the Third Reich,* p. 66.

[422] Shirer, *The Rise and Fall of the Third Reich,* p. 261.

[423] Reimann, *The Vampire Economy,* p. 18.

[424] Barkai, *Nazi Economics,* p. 169. Source: Bernhard Köhler, *Unser Wille and Weg* 2 (1932): p. 132.

[425] A. Holtz, "Sozialistische Wirtschaft," *Der Aufbau* 4, No. 17, (1936): pp. 6–7.

[426] Martin Dean, Constantin Goschler, and Philipp Ther, edit., *Robbery and Restitution: The Conflict over Jewish Property in Europe,* Vol. 9, New York and Oxford, Berghahn Books, 2007, Part II, Martin Dean, "The Seizure of Jewish Property in Europe, Comparative Aspects of Nazi Methods and Local Responses," p. 22.

[427] Derek Scally, "Germany's duty: a damning portrait," *The Irish Times,* Nov. 9, 2013.

[428] Tony F. Freyer, *Anti-Trust and Global Capitalism, 1930–2004* (Cambridge University Press, 2009), p. 64.

[429] Aly, *Hitler's Beneficiaries,* 2005, p. 7.

[430] Ibid., p. 311.

[431] "Chronology of the Nazi Record: 1933–1943," *The Ukrainian Weekly* (Jersey City, NJ), Jan. 30, 1943.

[432] Otto Koellreuther, ed., *Jahrbuch des Oeffentlichen Rechtes der Gegenwart,* 1935, p. 267. Reimann, *The Vampire Economy,* p. 12.

[433] Aly, *Hitler's Beneficiaries,* 2005, p. 71.

[434] Ibid., p. 55.

[435] Head, Financial Office, Grevenbroich, to OFP (chief financial officer), Düsseldorf, Dec. 1, 1939. Published in Aly, *Hitler's Beneficiaries,* 2005, p. 55.

[436] Steber and Gotto, *Visions of Community in Nazi Germany,* pp. 92–93.

[437] Hitler's speech to workers at Berlin's Rheinmetall-Borsig factory, Oct. 10, 1940. Published in Aly, *Hitler's Beneficiaries*, 2007, p. 13.

[438] Dagmar Herzog, "Handouts From Hitler," *New York Times*, Feb. 18, 2007, Sunday book review. https://www.nytimes.com/2007/02/18/books/review/Herzog.t.html.

[439] Aly, *Hitler's Beneficiaries*, 2005, p. 61.

[440] Ibid., p. 62.

[441] Adam Tooze, *The Wages of Destruction: The Making and Breaking of the Nazi Economy* (New York, NY: Penguin, 2006), p. 37.

[442] Aly, *Hitler's Beneficiaries*, 2005, p. 50.

[443] Evans, *The Third Reich in Power, 1933–1939*, p. 411.

[444] Fohlin, *Finance Capitalism and Germany's Rise to Industrial Power*, p. 301.

[445] Ibid.

[446] Ibid., p. 302.

[447] Ibid.

[448] Ibid., pp. 302–303.

[449] Harold James, *The Deutsche Bank and the Nazi Economic War Against the Jews: The Expropriation of Jewish-Owned Property* (Cambridge University Press, 2001), p. 21.

[450] Ibid.

[451] Fritz Nummenbruch, *Die Dynamische Wirtschaft* (Munich, "Centralverlag der N.S.D.A.P.," 1936, p. 114 and p. 119). Reimann, *The Vampire Economy*, p. 13.

[452] Shirer, *The Rise and Fall of the Third Reich*, p. 144.

[453] Ibid.

[454] "Germany: Death of the States," *Time* magazine, Feb. 12, 1934.

[455] Fohlin, *Finance Capitalism and Germany's Rise to Industrial Power*, p. 302.

[456] "Chronology of the Nazi Record: 1933–1943," *The Ukrainian Weekly* (Jersey City, NJ), Jan. 30, 1943.

[457] Evans, *The Coming of the Third Reich*, p. 381.

[458] Maiken Umbach, ed., *German Federalism: Past, Present, Future* (Palgrave Macmillan, 2002), p. 207.

[459] Shirer, *The Rise and Fall of the Third Reich*, p. 262.

[460] Ibid.

[461] Fohlin, *Finance Capitalism and Germany's Rise to Industrial Power*, p. 303.

[462] Evans, *The Coming of the Third Reich*, p. 384.

[463] Ibid.

[464] Ibid., pp. 384–385.

[465] Schoenbaum, *Hitler's Social Revolution*, p. 118. Reported in the Nazi journal *Völkischer Beobachter* on July 20, 1934. The *Völkischer Beobachter* (*Völkisch Observer*) was the newspaper of the National Socialist German Workers' Party (NSDAP) starting in 1920.

[466] Ibid., p. 125.

[467] Ibid., pp. 130–131.

[468] Ibid., p. 124.

[469]"*Die geistigen Grundlagen der nationalsozialistischen Wirtschaftslehre,*" *Völkischer Beobachter,* Apr. 4, 1933.

[470]R.J. Overy, *The Dictators: Hitler's Germany, Stalin's Russia* (New York/London: W.W. Norton & Company, 2004), p. 392.

[471]Ibid., p. 393.

[472]Ibid., p. 395.

[473]Ibid., p. 399.

[474]Ibid., p. 230.

[475]*Kritika: Explorations in Russian and Eurasian History,* Vol. 7, Issue 4, Slavica Publishers, 2006, p. 922.

[476]Adolf Hitler, speech at the Berlin Sportpalast on the opening of the *Kriegswinterhilfswerk,* Sept. 4, 1940.

[477]Hitler, *Mein Kampf, Vol. Two,* chap. VII, "The Struggle with the Red Front."

[478]Payne, *A History of Fascism, 1914–1945,* pp. 463–464. Mussolini boasted that three-fourths of Italy's industries were owned by the state by 1934.

[479]Childers, *The Nazi Voter,* p. 111.

[480]Adolf Hitler, "Adolf Hitler's Order of the Day Calling for Invasion of Yugoslavia and Greece," Berlin, (Apr. 6, 1941), *New York Times,* Apr. 7, 1941.

[481]Jeff Rutherford, *Combat and Genocide on the Eastern Front: The German Infantry's War, 1941–1944* (Cambridge University Press, 2014), p. 80.

[482]Childers, *The Nazi Voter,* p. 105.

[483]The 11th plank of the Nazi 25-Point Program of 1920.

[484]Howard Richards and Joanna Swanger, *The Dilemmas of Social Democracies: Overcoming Obstacles to a More Just World* (Lanham, MD: Lexington Books, 2006), p. 192.

[485]Drucker, *The End of Economic Man,* p. 149.

[486]Bruce Walker, "Nazis were Marxists," *The American Thinker,* Nov. 25, 2007. https://www.americanthinker.com/articles/2007/11/the_nazis_were_maxists.html.

[487]David Skeel, "Mortgage Settlement Or Mortgage Shakedown?" *Wall Street Journal,* Feb. 21, 2012.

[488]William D. Cohan, "How Wall Street's Bankers Stayed Out of Jail," *The Atlantic,* Sept. 2015.

[489]Ibid.

[490]"The Morgan Shakedown: A landmark that shows how much politicians now control U.S. finance," *Wall Street Journal,* Oct. 20, 2013. https://www.wsj.com/articles/the-morgan-shakedown-1382312647.

[491]Raffael Scheck, *Germany, 1871–1945: A Concise History* (Berg Publishers, 2008), p. 167.

[492]Adam Young, "Nazism is Socialism," *The Free Market,* Sept. 1, 2001. https://mises.org/library/nazism-socialism.

[493]Berman, *The Primacy of Politics,* p. 146.

[494]Ibid.

[495] Gustav Stolper, *The German Economy: 1870 to the Present* (Weidenfield & Nicolson, 1967), p. 137.

[496] Kitchen, *A History of Modern Germany*, p. 287.

[497] Shirer, *The Rise and Fall of the Third Reich*, p. 264.

[498] Michael C. Thomsett, *The German Opposition to Hitler: The Resistance, the Underground, and Assassination Plots, 1938–1945* (Jefferson, NC: McFarland & Company, 1997), p. 81.

[499] Shirer, *The Rise and Fall of the Third Reich*, p. 264.

[500] Kershaw, *Hitler 1889–1936: Hubris*, p. 448.

[501] Newton, *The Path to Tyranny*, p. 208.

[502] Llewellyn H. Rockwell Jr., "Hitler's Economics," *Mises Daily*, June 28, 2012. https://mises.org/library/hitlers-economics.

[503] Nicholas Crafts and Peter Fearon, eds., *The Great Depression of the 1930s: Lessons for Today* (Oxford University Press, 2013), p. 118.

[504] Kitchen, *A History of Modern Germany*, p. 284.

[505] Hans-Joachim Braun, *The German Economy in the Twentieth Century* (New York, NY: Routledge, 1990), p. 78.

[506] John K. Galbraith, *The Age of Uncertainty* (Boston, MA: Houghton Mifflin Co., 1977), pp. 213–214.

[507] Stephen Roberts, *The House Hitler Built* (London and New York: Harper & Brothers Publishers, 1938), p. 162.

[508] Dan P. Silverman, *Hitler's Economy: Nazi Work Creation Programs, 1933–1936* (Harvard University Press, 1998).

[509] Michael McMenamin, "Nazi Economics," *Reason* magazine, Aug. 1, 1999. https://reason.com/archives/1999/08/01/nazi-economics.

[510] J. Bradford DeLong, *Slouching Towards Utopia? The Economic History of the Twentieth Century*, "XV. Nazis and Soviets," Feb. 1997. https://web.archive.org/web/20080511190923/http://econ161.berkeley.edu/TCEH/Slouch_Purge15.html.

[511] Richard Gaettens. *Geschichte der Inflationen Von Altertum bis zum Gegenwart* (*German: History of Inflations from Old Ages to the Present*), and *Die preisgestoppte Deutsche Inflation von 1936 bis 1948* (*The Price-Stopped German Inflation from 1936 to 1948*), pp. 279–298.

[512] Evans, *The Third Reich in Power, 1933–1939*, p. 411.

[513] "Wotan's Nazis: Germans Tighten Belts to Slogan, Guns Instead of Butter," *The Literary Digest*, Jan. 2, 1937, p. 12. http://www.oldmagazinearticles.com/food-rationing_in_Pre-World_War_Two_Germany.

[514] Ibid.

[515] Ian Kershaw, *Hitler 1936–1945: Nemesis* (New York, NY: W.W. Norton & Company, 2000), p. 9.

[516] Ibid.

[517] Lucy Dawidowicz, ed., *A Holocaust Reader* (New York, NY: Behrman House, 1976), p. 32.

[518] Aly, *Hitler's Beneficiaries*, 2005, p. 44.

[519] Hans-Joachim Braun, *The German Economy in the Twentieth Century* (New York, NY: Routledge, 1990), p. 85.

[520] James Dunnigan and Raymond M. Macedonia, *Getting It Right: American Military Reforms After Vietnam to the Gulf War and Beyond* (William Morrow & Co., 1993), p. 384.

[521] Gordon Martel, ed., *The Origins of the Second World War Reconsidered*, second ed. (New York, NY: Routledge, 2014), p. 109.

[522] Berman, *The Primacy of Politics*, p. 146.

[523] Ibid., p. 147.

[524] Ibid.

[525] Peter Temin, "Soviet and Nazi Economic Planning in the 1930s," *The Economic History Review*, New Series, Vol. 44, No. 4, Nov. 1991, pp. 573–593.

[526] Overy, *War and Economy in the Third Reich*, p. 16.

[527] Germà Bel, "Against the mainstream: Nazi privatization in 1930s Germany," Departament de Política Econòmica i EEM. Torre 6, planta 3, Barcelona, Spain, 2004, p. 11. http://www.ub.edu/graap/nazi.pdf.

[528] Panikos Panayi, ed., *Weimar and Nazi Germany: Continuities and Discontinuities* (New York, NY: Routledge, 2014), p. 44.

[529] Albert Speer, *Inside the Third Reich: Memoirs* (New York, NY: Simon and Schuster, 1970), p. 359.

[530] Martin Kitchen, *Speer: Hitler's Architect* (New Haven, CT and London, UK: Yale University Press, 2015), p. 202.

[531] Evans, *The Third Reich in Power, 1933–1939*, p. 372.

[532] Overy, *War and Economy in the Third Reich*, p. 146.

[533] Ibid., p. 107.

[534] Ibid., p. 17.

[535] Berend, *An Economic History of Twentieth-Century Europe*, p. 93.

[536] Ibid., p. 90.

[537] Overy, *War and Economy in the Third Reich*, pp. 1–2.

[538] Ibid., p. 118.

[539] Ibid., p. 1.

[540] Ibid., p. 17.

[541] Adam Tooze, *The Wages of Destruction: The Making and Breaking of the Nazi Economy* (New York, NY: Penguin, 2006), pp. 658–660.

[542] Barkai, *Nazi Economics*, p. 10.

[543] Otto Nathan, *The Nazi Economic System. Germany's Mobilization for War* (Cambridge, MA: National Bureau of Economic Research, 1944), p. 5.

[544] Aly, *Hitler's Beneficiaries*, 2005, pp. 65–66.

[545] Ibid., p. 2.

[546] Ibid., p. 7.

[547] Michael C. Moynihan, "Hitler's Handouts Inside the Nazis' Welfare State," *Reason* magazine, Aug./Sept. 2007. https://reason.com/archives/2007/08/15/hitlers-handouts.

[548] Hallett, *The Social Economy of West Germany*, p. 15.

[549] Ibid., p. 16.

[550] Dan Michman, *The Emergence of Jewish Ghettos during the Holocaust* (Cambridge University Press, 2011), p. 32.

[551] Burleigh, *The Third Reich*, p. 219.

[552] Victor Klemperer, *I Will Bear Witness: A Diary of the Nazi Years, 1942–1945*, vol. 2 (Random House, Inc., 2001), p. 317; Goebbels' "Our Socialism" editorial, written on Apr. 30, 1944.

[553] Evans, *The Third Reich in Power, 1933–1939*, pp. 489–491.

[554] Steber and Gotto, *Visions of Community in Nazi Germany*, p. 2.

[555] Michael Geyer and Sheila Fitzpatrick, *Beyond Totalitarianism: Stalinism and Nazism Compared* (Cambridge University Press, 2009), p. 147.

[556] Ibid., p. 147.

[557] Steber and Gotto, *Visions of Community in Nazi Germany*, p. 92.

[558] Berman, *The Primacy of Politics*, p. 147.

[559] Steber and Gotto, *Visions of Community in Nazi Germany*, p. 93.

[560] Ibid., pp. 93–94.

[561] Aly, *Hitler's Beneficiaries*, 2005, p. 163.

[562] Burleigh, *The Third Reich*, pp. 221–222.

[563] Interview of Hitler by Louis Lochner, *Associated Press* correspondent in Berlin. Quote from Burleigh, *The Third Reich*, p. 247.

[564] Peter Temin, *Lessons from the Great Depression*, (Lionel Robbins lectures), (Cambridge, MA: MIT Press, 1989), p. 111. Note that the Nazi welfare system excluded Jews and other minorities, who were deprived of their German citizenship, something that occurred with unpopular minorities under communist dictatorships as well.

[565] Christoph Buchheim and Jonas Scherner, "The Role of Private Property in the Nazi Economy: The Case of Industry," *The Journal of Economic History*, Vol. 66, No. 2, June 2006, pp. 392–393.

[566] Stephens J. Lee, *Hitler and Nazi Germany* (London and New York: Routledge, 2000), p. 70.

[567] Aly, *Hitler's Beneficiaries*, 2005, p. 39.

[568] Henry Ashby Turner, *German Big Business and the Rise of Hitler* (Oxford University Press, 1985), p. 114.

[569] Wagener, *Hitler—Memoirs of a Confidant*, p. 288.

[570] Overy, *War and Economy in the Third Reich*, p. 12.

[571] Watson, *The Lost Literature of Socialism*, p. 76.

[572] Norman Thomas, *A Socialist's Faith* (W.W. Norton, 1951), p. 53.

[573] Ibid., p. 55.

[574] Kershaw, *Hitler 1889–1936: Hubris*, p. 359.

[575] Heiden, *Hitler: A Biography*, p. 58.

[576] Barkai, *Nazi Economics*, p. 26.

[577] Orlow, *The Nazi Party 1919–1945*, p. 61. Hitler at the May 1927 NSDAP provincial congress in Stuttgart.

[578] Cris Whetton, *Hitler's Fortune* (Yorkshire, UK: Pen & Sword Books, 2004), pp. 141–142.

[579] Ibid., p. 140.

[580] Hermann Rauschning, *The Revolution of Nihilism: Warning to the West* (New York, NY: Alliance Books Corporation, 1939), p. 88.

[581] Dorothy Thompson, "On the Record," *Harrisburg Telegraph* (Harrisburg, PA), Mar. 6, 1939, p. 7.

[582] Orlow, *The Nazi Party 1919–1945*, p. 61, referring to the 1926–1927 time period.

[583] Calic, *Secret Conversations with Hitler*, p. 36.

[584] Ibid., p. 31. "Public companies" refers to publicly-traded companies (corporations) listed on stock exchanges.

[585] Ibid., p. 32.

[586] Ibid., pp. 14–15.

[587] Reimann, *The Vampire Economy*, p. 6.

[588] Ibid., p. 7.

[589] Ibid., p. 12.

[590] Ibid., p. 84.

[591] Ibid., p. 31.

[592] Ibid., p. 33.

[593] Nathan Stoltzfus, *Resistance of the Heart: Intermarriage and the Rosenstrasse Protest in Nazi Germany* (Rutgers University Press, 2001), p. 84.

[594] Reimann, *The Vampire Economy*, pp. 31–32.

[595] Vera Micheles Dean, *Europe in Retreat*, revised ed. (New York, NY: Alfred A. Knopf, Inc., 1939), p. 206.

[596] Ibid., p. 207.

[597] Calic, *Secret Conversations with Hitler*, pp. 31–32.

[598] Arvind Sivaramakrishnan, "Hugo Chávez: Death of a socialist," *The Hindu*, Mar. 6, 2013. https://www.thehindu.com/news/international/world/hugo-chvez-death-of-a-socialist/article4481169.ece.

[599] Victor Salmerón, *"Plan Chávez prevé crear 30 mil empresas de propiedad social,"* *El Universal* (in Spanish), June 13, 2012.

[600] Trotsky, *The Revolution Betrayed*, p. 241.

[601] Leonard Peikoff, *The Ominous Parallels: The End of Freedom in America* (New York, NY: Meridian Book, 1993), p. 18. First published 1982.

[602] David Boaz, "Hitler, Mussolini, Roosevelt: What FDR had in common with the other charismatic collectivists of the 30s," *Reason* magazine, Oct. 2007. http://reason.com/archives/2007/09/28/hitler-mussolini-roosevelt.

[603] David Nicholls, *Adolf Hitler: A Biographical Companion* (Santa Barbara, CA: ABC-CLIO, 2000), p. 245.

[604] Ibid.

[605] Grunberger, *The 12-Year Reich*, p. 47. Published in the Nazi Party official newspaper, *Völkischer Beobachter*, Nov. 21, 1936.

[606] Shirer, *The Rise and Fall of the Third Reich*, p. 263.

[607] Payne, *A History of Fascism, 1914–1945*, p. 192.

[608] Leon Degrelle, "How Hitler Consolidated Power in Germany and Launched a Social Revolution," chap. VI. "The Social Revolution," *Journal of Historical Review*, Vol. 12, No. 3, (Fall 1992). Note: The *Journal of Historical Review* was infamous for publishing articles denying the Holocaust, but there is no reason to doubt Leon Degrelle's details about the socioeconomic and labor policies of Nazi Germany.

[609] Interview of Hitler by Louis P. Lochner, Berlin Correspondent of the *Associated Press*, Feb. 23, 1933.

[610] Shirer, *The Rise and Fall of the Third Reich*, p. 264.

[611] Ibid., p. 265.

[612] Ibid.

[613] T.W. Mason, *Social Policy in the Third Reich: The Working Class and the "National Community," 1918–1939* (Oxford, UK: Berg Publishers, 1993), p. 160. *Völkischer Beobachter*, Nov. 21, 1936.

[614] Shelly Baranowski, *Strength through Joy: Consumerism and Mass Tourism in The Third Reich* (Cambridge University Press, 2004), p. 1.

[615] Hasso Spode, "Some Quantitative Aspects of Kraft Durch Freude Tourism, 1934–1939," in *European Tourism and Culture*, ed. Margarita Dritsas (Athens: Livanis Publishing Organization, 2007), p. 125.

[616] Louis P. Lochner, *What About Germany?* (New York, NY: Dodd, Mead & Company, 1942), p. 32.

[617] Ibid.

[618] Hasso Spode, "Some Quantitative Aspects of Kraft Durch Freude Tourism, 1934–1939," in *European Tourism and Culture*, ed. Margarita Dritsas (Athens: Livanis Publishing Organization, 2007), p. 123.

[619] Shelly Baranowski, *Strength through Joy: Consumerism and Mass Tourism in The Third Reich* (Cambridge University Press, 2004), p. 156.

[620] Richard Bessel, *Nazism and the War* (New York, NY: Modern Library, 2006), p. 67.

[621] Shirer, *The Rise and Fall of the Third Reich*, p. 266.

[622] Richard Bessel, *Nazism and the War* (New York, NY: Modern Library, 2006), p. 67.

[623] Michael T. Florinsky, *Fascism and National Socialism: A Study of the Economic and Social Policies of the Totalitarian State* (New York, NY: Macmillan, 1936).

[624] Karl Hardach, *The Political Economy of Germany in the Twentieth Century* (University of California Press, 1980), p. 61.

[625] Salvemini, *The Fate of Trade Unions Under Fascism*, p. 35.

[626] *Russian Since 1917: Socialist Views of Bolshevik Policy*, 1948, reprints of past articles in the Socialist Party of Great Britain's journal, *The Socialist Standard* (1915 to 1948), Chapter Eight: "Economic Policy and Development."

[627] Emily Atkin, "Bernie Sanders Just Delivered 'The Most Important Speech' Of His Presidential Campaign," *ThinkProgress*, Nov. 19, 2015. https://thinkprogress.

org/bernie-sanders-just-delivered-the-most-important-speech-of-his-presidential-campaign-64263eadae89/.

[628] Leszek Kołakowski, *Main Currents of Marxism: The Founders - The Golden Age - The Breakdown* (New York, NY: W.W. Norton & Company, 2005), p. 683.

[629] Ibid.

[630] Luxemburg's best-known attack on Lenin's views are her 1904 "Organizational Questions of the Russian Social Democracy, or, Leninism or Marxism?" and her 1918 "The Russian Revolution."

[631] Denis Mack Smith, *Mussolini: A Biography* (New York, NY: Vintage Books, 1983), p. 41. Original source: *Opera Omnia di Benito Mussolini*, E. and D. Susmel, edit., Florence, 1951–, 13/168, June 4, 1919, *Opera Omnia di Benito Mussolini*, E. and D. Susmel, edit., Florence, 1951–, 15/220, Sept. 20, 1920.

[632] Strasser, *Hitler and I*, p. 59.

[633] Ibid., p. 93.

[634] Joseph Goebbels, *The Goebbels Diaries 1939–1941*, ed. and trans. Fred Taylor (New York, NY: G.P. Putnam's Sons, 1983), p. 77. Entry: Dec. 29, 1939.

[635] Ernst Hanfstaengl, *Hitler: The Memoir of a Nazi Insider Who Turned Against the Führer* (New York, NY: Arcade Publishing, 2011), p. 69.

[636] Heiden, *A History of National Socialism*, p. 89.

[637] Alan Bullock, *Hitler: A Study in Tyranny* (New York, NY: Harper Perennial, 1991), p. 219.

[638] William L. Shirer, *The Nightmare Years: 1930–1940* (Boston, MA: Little, Brown and Company, 1984), p. 152.

[639] Adolf Hitler, *Hitler's Table Talk, 1941–1944*, ed. Hugh Trevor-Roper, trans. N. Cameron and R.H. Stevens, 3rd ed. (New York, NY: Engima Books, 2000), pp. 6–7, Night of July 11–12, 1941.

[640] Geoffrey Blainey, *A Short History of Christianity* (Viking, 2011), pp. 495–496.

[641] "Chronology of the Nazi Record: 1933–1943," *The Ukrainian Weekly* (Jersey City, NJ), Jan. 30, 1943.

[642] Ibid.

[643] Schoenbaum, *Hitler's Social Revolution*, p. 65. Original source: Max Domarus, *Hitler: Reden und Proklamationen, 1932–1938* (Würzburg, 1962), p. 525.

[644] Burleigh, *The Third Reich*, p. 255.

[645] Ibid., p. 256.

[646] Albert Speer, *Inside the Third Reich: Memoirs* (New York, NY: Simon and Schuster, 1970), p. 96.

[647] Shirer, *The Rise and Fall of the Third Reich*, p. 240.

[648] Jochen von Lang, *The Secretary: Martin Bormann, The Man Who Manipulated Hitler* (New York, NY: Random House, 1979), p. 221.

[649] Paul Berben, *Dachau, 1933–1945: The Official History* (Norfolk Press, 1975), pp. 276–277.

[650] Rabbi David G. Dalin, *The Myth of Hitler's Pope: How Pope Pius XII Rescued from the Nazis* (Washington D.C.: Regnery Publishing, 2005), pp. 76–77.

[651] Grunberger, *The 12-Year Reich*, p. 442, (Dokument PS 3751).

[652] Ibid.

[653] Alan Bullock, *Hitler: A Study in Tyranny* (New York, NY: Harper Perennial Edition, 1991), p. 218.

[654] Roger Griffin, "Fascism's relation to Religion," in *World Fascism: A Historical Encyclopedia, Vol. 1*, ed. Cyprian Blamires (Santa Barbara, CA: ABC-CLIO, 2006), p. 10.

[655] Anton Gill, *An Honourable Defeat; A History of the German Resistance to Hitler* (London, UK: Heinemann, 1994), pp. 14–15.

[656] Robert Anthony Krieg, *Catholic Theologians in Nazi Germany* (Continuum, 2004), p. 4.

[657] Joseph Goebbels, diary entry for Oct. 16, 1928. *PBS American Experience* series: "The Man Behind Hitler," Directed by Lutz Hachmeister, Season 13, aired May 22, 2006. Found at: http://www.pbs.org/wgbh/amex/goebbels/filmmore/pt.html.

[658] Evans, *The Third Reich in Power, 1933–1939*, pp. 239–240.

[659] Lauren Faulkner Rossi, *Wehrmacht Priests: Catholicism and the Nazi War of Annihilation* (Harvard University Press, 2015), p. 41.

[660] Evans, *The Third Reich in Power, 1933–1939*, p. 239.

[661] Ibid., p. 241.

[662] Ibid., p. 244.

[663] Adolf Hitler, quoted in Richard Dawkins, *The God Delusion* (Boston and New York: Houghton Mifflin Co., 2006), p. 276. Original source is *Hitler's Table Talk*, night Oct. 19, 1941, an entry in *Bormann Vermerke*, but not in Henry Picker's notebook.

[664] Dr. Louis Bauman, "Editorially Speaking," *The Brethren Mission Herald*, Vol. 6, No. 1, Jan. 1, 1944, p. 5.

[665] Margaret Brearley, "Hitler and Wagener: The Leader, the Master and the Jews," Patterns of Prejudice, 22/2, Institute of Jewish Affairs, Summer 1988. Also cited in Richard Harries, *After the Evil: Christianity and Judaism in the Shadow of the Holocaust* (Oxford University Press, 2003), p. 14.

[666] Alan Bullock, *Hitler: A Study in Tyranny*, trans. N. Cameron and R.H. Stevens (New York, NY: Konecky & Konecky Bullock, 1999), p. 389.

[667] Adolf Hitler, *Hitler's Table Talk, 1941–1944*, ed. Hugh Trevor-Roper, trans. N. Cameron and R.H. Stevens, 3rd ed. (New York, NY: Engima Books, 2000), pp. 58–60, midday Oct. 14, 1941.

[668] Speech by President Franklin D. Roosevelt, "Navy and Total Defense Day Address," Oct. 27, 1941, Roosevelt, D. Franklin, *Public Papers of the Presidents of the United States*, 1941, Vol. 10, p. 440.

[669] Wagener, *Hitler—Memoirs of a Confidant*, p. 59.

[670] Thomas Childers, "Lecture 5: The Nazi Breakthrough." A History of Hitler's Empire, 2nd edition, lecture series published by The Teaching Company, Chantilly, VA, 2001, minutes 5–6.

5. Proslavery and Socialist Roots of the Modern Left

> Of all tyrannies, a tyranny sincerely exercised for the good of its victim may be the most oppressive. It may be better to live under robber barons than under omnipotent moral busybodies. The robber baron's cruelty may sometimes sleep, his cupidity may at some point be satiated, but those who torment us for our own good will torment us without end for they do so with the approval of their own conscience.
>
> —C.S. Lewis, *God in the Dock*

Today's modern, statist Left has covertly hidden their ancestors' advocacy of involuntary servitude and its sidekick, coercive socialism. Only recently has it been established that the forefathers of collectivism had merged the system of chattel slavery with socialist principles. Moreover, not only did they espouse socioeconomic and institutionalized slavery, but they voiced hostility towards the type of free capitalistic society that had ushered in the age of Enlightenment and later, the American Revolution.

Of course, this background of authoritarian socialism and slavocratic plantation life had to be concealed for clear reasons. If the ugly institution of slavery were ever to be publicly associated with socialism and communism, the modern left's house of cards would tumble into the garbage pail of history. The public would quickly realize that Progressive political leaders have been crafting legislation and bureaucratic excesses to compel people to strictly obey the government, and by doing so, have made the public dependent upon the largesse of these egalitarian-sounding slave masters. In the statist Left's reactionary crusade against liberal polity, the peddlers of involuntary servitude have engaged in political agendas where the state seeks power *over* people, not power *from* people.

This kinship to socialism and slavery dates back to the era of Karl Marx and Friedrich Engels, both of whom regularly twisted the meaning of liberty, democracy, and equality to pander an authoritarian socioeconomic agenda. For instance, Marx supported slavery in America, writing in 1846 that:

> Without slavery there would be no cotton, without cotton there would be no modern industry. It is slavery which has given value to the colonies... Slavery is therefore an economic category of paramount importance. Without slavery, North America, the most progressive nation, would be transformed into a patriarchal country.[1]

Engels, Marx's collaborator, contorted the meanings of "liberty" and "democracy" to suggest that they can arise only from autocratic states. He dismissed democracy and political liberty as a sham that would beget "the worst possible slavery." Apparently, Marx's and Engels's distortion of language preceded George Orwell's doublespeak, wherein "slavery is freedom." A professional at linguistic tricksterism, Engels believed that only the act of imposing communism would break workers' chains of exploitation. He wrote:

> Political liberty is sham-liberty, the worst possible slavery; the appearance of liberty, and therefore the reality of servitude. Political equality is the same; therefore democracy, as well as every other form of government, must ultimately break to pieces: hypocrisy cannot subsist, the contradiction hidden in it must come out; we must have either a regular slavery—that is, an undisguised despotism, or real liberty, and real equality—that is, Communism.[2]

Engels added another dimension to his beloved socialization of society. Servitude to the public collective was not optional; everyone had to forcibly follow his value system (moral valuism). Everyone had to conform and behave under an ambiguous schema of democratic dictatorship, effectively hogtying individuals to each other, as if mere beasts of burden, herded under heavy guard. To bring about this life-long "communal yokism,"[3] an authoritarian, socialist framework had to be established. Similar to how blacks were treated under a plantation-dominated society, the general populace had to be ruled and disciplined, and they were obliged to obey the plantation's communal overseer. These allegedly enlightened overseers were empowered to rule everyone, because rights were seen as social and collective, not individual. To collectivists, one must be confined by communal values and needs. Here, individual choice has no role, and individual lives must be superseded by a compulsory, communal solidarity, on the communist-servant plantation.

Engels made it crystal clear that Marxists were not fanciers of liberty or democratic-republicanism, but were determined to wield the implements of revolutionary force and terror to achieve socialist ends. He wrote:

> Revolution is certainly the most authoritarian thing there is; it is the act whereby one part of the population imposes its will upon the other part by means of rifles, bayonets and cannon... it must maintain this rule by means of the terror. ...[4]

The violence and terror of thralldom have become the legacy of the statist Left. Under Marxist socialism, the state apparatus has the authority to control and coerce the populace, because individual rights to property, life, and self-ownership have been abrogated. These socialist intellectuals revered dictatorship of the group and expected the socialist overseers to usher in classless equality and a bounty of free welfare benefits: shelter, food, clothes, and medical care. Yet, this socioeconomic structure matches the horrors of black enslavement that were instituted in the antebellum Old South, where the slaves were equally poor, subservient, and dependent. Of course, they were free of material want, but incapable of exercising their rights without permission from a master.

One of the most astute articles to reveal the collectivistic ancestry of slavery, socialism, racism, and other detestation is Jarrett Stepman's essay, "'The Very Best Form of Socialism': The Pro-Slavery Roots of the Modern Left."[5] Stepman introduces three major contentions that provide evidence to expose this long-standing political shell game.

First, the antebellum proslavery school attempted to quash the individual-liberty premises of the Founders and the free-Left roots of classical liberalism. They dismissed the Founders' embrace of John

Locke's social contract and natural rights where governing entities "grow organically out of community." These slavery apologists claimed that the state, not the untrustworthy "people," should be the holder and grantor of all rights.

Second, the American revolutionaries in both in the North and the South viewed slavery as a wrong, a fading wickedness, perhaps necessary in the short term, but a moral and political evil to eventually abolish. Latter-day slavers of the 1830s and beyond, however, considered this anti-slavery attitude outdated. One man who wholeheartedly believed in the virtues of slavery and who popularized the righteousness of slavery was US Senator John C. Calhoun (1782–1850). In 1838 he stated:

> Many in the South once believed that slavery was a moral and political evil. That folly and delusion are gone. We see it now in its true light, and regard it as the most safe and stable basis for free institutions in the world.[6]

Pro-slavery intellectuals contended that chattel slavery was a positive good, under the theory that superior people should rule (supremacism), and that it was the duty of the state-sanctioned slaveholder to care and manage the lives of the unfit and inferior (paternalism). So, to make their case and protect the institution of enslavement, the pro-slavers found it necessary to justify the ideological integrity of institutionalized thralldom. They touted bondage as a panacea for most social ills, wherein not only would society provide for the welfare of its less fortunate and unfit members but would place them into protective custody. The proponents of the South's slavocracy rationalized such treatment as humane—righteously taking a stand to faithfully fulfill society's obligation to protect and aid those unable to provide for themselves.

This theory allowed early Democratic Party leaders and mostly southern plantation owners to forge a distinct division between the privileged superior and the less-privileged inferior, between the indolent and the industrious. They saw this division as a recipe for a great civilization, which included John C. Calhoun. He believed that the superior man brought order; the inferior man instigated chaos. In fact, the proslavery doctrinaires emphasized order as being far more important than freedom, and that individual rights were not something bestowed by God or nature.

Last and most importantly, the guardians of slavery and early proto-socialism opposed the concept of equality framed in the Declaration of Independence. Instead of equality of opportunity or equality under the law, proslavery apostles argued that society was based on the principle of human inequality in accordance to the "new scientific" knowledge about human nature and the organization of government. In other words, political elite in government should assume the role of arbitrators in determining who or what would be free and equal. The ideals of free choice and self-ownership did not fit well with those who wanted to micromanage the personal and economic behavior of society. They viewed rights as something granted by a wise and benevolent government, who had the omniscience to care for the public good. For instance, Calhoun did not consider humans as autonomous individuals, but that "instead of being born free and equal, [people] are born subject, not only to parental authority, but to the laws and institutions of the country..."[7] As for "political rights," Calhoun took the position that they "derive from the collective will of the people and are not natural."[8]

Proslavery Link to Socialism

Once this proslavery link to socialism was detected in recent years, scholars began to piece together the modern-statist Left's nefarious past. As it turns out, historically, the roots of the slavocracy Left are traceable to the forbears of the Democratic Party, who actively supported enslavement, lynching, segregation, racism, welfarism, proto-socialism, paternalism, and white supremacy before and after the American Civil War. In this sense, the beginning of the Democratic Party in the late 1820s represents the start of an anti-Founders movement initiated to invalidate the original intent of the creators of liberal capitalism and self-ownership. Nevertheless, most Democrat Party members are unaware of this slavery-socialist origin of their own party. Many of these rank-and-file members are more in tune with the traditional sentiments of tax-cutting, civil rights, and the soft classical liberalism of President John F. Kennedy.

Some scholars now refer to the Democratic Party's longtime support of slavery and supremacy as the epitome of a "thievery society," where the societal collectives own and control everything, even people. Such a thievery polity would bestow on governing bodies the authority to steal anything with immunity, for whatever noble or ignoble purpose. Perhaps this is why William Lloyd Garrison (1805–1879), the most prominent abolitionist in the United States, denounced slavery as an institution of "man-stealing," writing: "Every slave is a stolen man; every slave-holder is a man-stealer."[9] The concept of self-ownership, which dates from John Locke, opposes slavery, socialism, and authoritarianism, because they would inhibit or prohibit individuals from pursuing ownership of property.[10] In this way, any borg-like collective would have the authority, often over the wishes of individual citizens, to bar people from running their own lives as they see fit—literally making slaves of the populace.

Furthermore, it was these early Democrats who set in motion a movement to discredit the classical liberalism of the founders, abolitionists and those engaged in commercial trade. Lo and behold, the first notable public figure discovered to have heavily influenced the dissemination of proslavery ideology was John C. Calhoun, who, as a political theorist and Southern protagonist, tried to redefine "republicanism" as a species favorable to a positive view of slavery. A war hawk who agitated in Congress to declare war on Great Britain (War of 1812), Calhoun and his disciples rejected the Lockean view of the natural rights of all men, a free and open press, and free-market capitalism.

Such muddled thinking should not be surprising. Calhoun was one of the earliest Democrats, and he served under the first Democratic president, Andrew Jackson (1767–1845), who owned as many as 300 slaves during his lifetime. Not only did Jackson instruct the US Postmaster General to obstruct anti-slavery literature from being delivered, but introduced the corruptive "spoils system" to American politics. Jackson also spearheaded the Indian Removal Act of 1830 that forcibly relocated many tribes to the Indian Territory (now Oklahoma), which resulted in more than 10,000 deaths. In *What Hath God Wrought*, historian Daniel Walker Howe wrote:

> The Jacksonian movement in politics, although it took the name of the Democratic Party, fought so hard in favor of slavery and white supremacy, and opposed the inclusion of non-whites

and women within the American civil polity so resolutely, that it makes the term "Jacksonian Democracy" all the more inappropriate as a characterization of the years between 1815 and 1848.[11]

President Jackson's influence upon the modern, statist Left is now recognized as substantial. According to Andrew Jackson's biographer Robert V. Remini,

> Jacksonian Democracy... inspired much of the dynamic and dramatic events of the nineteenth and twentieth centuries in American history—Populism, Progressivism, the New and Fair Deals, and the programs of the New Frontier and Great Society.[12]

This is what historian Arthur Schlesinger, Jr., discovered in research for his 1945 classic, *The Age of Jackson*: modern liberalism's pedigree dates back to Jackson, a major branch in the family tree of FDR's New Deal.

But it was Calhoun who was the leading intellectual protagonist for the institution of slavery. Growing up in a household of slaves in South Carolina, Calhoun believed that slavery improved society by diminishing the potential for private gain and by nurturing civic-mindedness. In his 1851 political treatise, "A Disquisition on Government," John C. Calhoun wrote:

> It follows, from what has been stated, that it is a great and dangerous error to suppose that all people are equally entitled to liberty. It is a reward to be earned, not a blessing to be gratuitously lavished on all alike;—a reward reserved for the intelligent, the patriotic, the virtuous and deserving;—and not a boon to be bestowed on a people too ignorant, degraded and vicious, to be capable either of appreciating or of enjoying it.[13]

In other words, Calhoun proposed that government should be the mediator in decisions over who gets rights and privileges, and who gets to wear leg irons. Under Calhoun's political theories, the Lockean principle of the "consent of the governed" was readily dismissed, as only certain people were deemed worthy of representative self-governance. Equality could exist and be exercised, but only for those deemed worthy of being equal. It was as though inequality was the new equality, mirroring George Orwell's allegory in *Animal Farm*, where "all animals are equal, but some animals are more equal than others." This perspective illustrates the hypocrisy of governmentalists who juxtapose the inequality of the lesser citizens with the equality of the more privileged.

To the dominant slaveholders, liberty was seen as a "reward of the races or individuals properly qualified for its possession."[14] Under this slavery-socialism axis, individual rights did not reside within every individual. Instead, rights were reserved only for those who were regarded as "intelligent, the patriotic, the virtuous and deserving," as claimed by Calhoun. This interpretation voided the essence of the Declaration of Independence, where the Founders affirmed that "all men are created equal, that they are endowed by their Creator with certain unalienable Rights. ..."

Because Calhoun treated the conferring of individual rights as a power reserved for officials of the state, anybody could be legally downgraded to unworthiness and be subjected to governmental or private bondage and dependency. Like most proslavery adherents, Calhoun's two main ideological pillars on which to promote slavery were white supremacy and paternalism. The concept of paternalism was employed extensively in the antebellum South to justify the legitimacy of slavery. Interestingly, Southern white women not only offered material goods to plantation slaves, but provided a type of maternal care towards Negroes, beholding them as a primitive race endowed with childlike qualities. They saw themselves as protectors of their slave family. This attitude included efforts to convince slaves that they lived under better conditions than the blacks and white factory workers in the North.[15]

In fact, under Calhoun's vision of governance, an individual of any race or group could be designated a slave—even unfit whites. Again, this argument was alien to the Founders, who saw slavery as a short-term necessary evil that was destined to be extinguished. Calhoun regarded the institution of slavery as not only good for the slave owner, but also for the slave. In his famous "Slavery a Positive Good" speech of 1837, Calhoun declared that slavery is "instead of an evil, a good—a positive good." Calhoun envisioned slavery as a time-honored tradition that made society prosper and civilizations progress. In essence, if it was good enough for the Greek and Roman civilizations, it had to be a worthy institution for America.

After the Confederate States of America lost the Civil War in 1865, it was the Democratic Party which took center stage in opposing any civil rights protections for blacks. They opposed the Civil Rights Act of 1866, which the Republican Congress passed, over President Andrew Johnson's veto. The law was simple and pertinent; it was "designed to provide blacks with the right to own private property, sign contracts, sue and serve as witnesses in a legal proceeding."[16]

Worse still, it was the Democratic Party which founded the Ku Klux Klan in order to keep blacks suppressed and to keep them from owning guns. According to Eric Foner, professor of history at Columbia University:

> In effect, the Klan was a military force serving the interests of the Democratic party, the planter class, and all those who desired the restoration of white supremacy. It aimed to destroy the Republican party's infrastructure, undermine the Reconstruction state, reestablish control of the black labor force, and restore racial subordination in every aspect of Southern life.[17]

Likewise, Allen W. Trelease, professor emeritus of history at the University of North Carolina, documented the same offensive history, writing that during this period, "the Klan became in effect a terrorist arm of the Democratic party."[18]

Racism and Powerlessness

Collectivists have never trusted people to do the right thing—whatever that is. They see themselves as the policemen of society. For instance, they abhor the free use of firearms in the hands of ordinary people, because it could empower the general populace and downtrodden minorities by threatening the state's grip on power. The statist Left, despite its projected high-minded pretentiousness, has always been an intolerant, anti-liberal movement with authoritarian overtones and Orwellian doublethink which must, at all costs, service its ideology. Ever since the second stage of the French Revolution, they have represented the self-righteous torchbearers of the bully state.

In comparison, the statist Right was almost devoid of any serious ideological underpinnings. Its authoritarian stance was not generally ideologically driven, but predicated on the past traditionalism of obeying kings, nobles, church officials, elders, and parents—those with community status or aged with experience. Obedience to superiors was paramount. The people were told that they had a duty to obey their king, and children had an obligation to obey their parents and elders. The structure was compartmentalized and systemized, ruled as a dictatorship of status, a pecking order that supposedly promoted stability, order, and morality. For instance, Francisco Franco (1892–1975) was the quintessential statist-Right dictator due to his support for the Spanish monarchy and the Catholic Church. He was a military dictator, but not a fascist. He never joined the fascist Falange party of Spain due to its atheist and socialist tendencies.

Still, when it came to the Southern proslavery defenders, they sought government authority to defend their power by making it illegal for the disenfranchised and powerless to rise up and take back their liberty. Throughout the 1800s, the Southern States took legal measure to circumvent the Second Amendment for African-Americans. For instance, the state of Tennessee inserted "free white men" into their constitution after the Nat Turner rebellion of 1831, changing it only to read "free white men of this state have a right to keep and to bear arms for their common defence." According to Adam Winkler in *Gunfight: The Battle Over the Right to Bear Arms in America*, there was

> constant pressure among white racists to keep guns out of the hands of African-Americans, because they would rise up and revolt... The KKK began as a gun-control organization. Before the Civil War, blacks were never allowed to own guns... White racists do things like pass laws to disarm them, but that's not really going to work. So, they form these racist posses [sic] all over the South to go out at night in large groups to terrorize blacks and take those guns away.[19,20]

Without guns, blacks were defenseless against racist vigilantes and extra-judicial executions.

Ida B. Wells (1862–1931), the black journalist who led a crusade against lynching, wrote that "the only times an Afro-American who was assaulted got away has been when he had a gun and used it in self-defense." Wells' advice was forthright: "A Winchester rifle should have a place of honor in every black home, and it should be used for that protection which the law refuses to give."[21] As author Gary Kleck pointed out in *Point Blank: Guns and Violence in America*, gun-control laws were mostly an anti-liberal movement that targeted "blacks in the south and the foreign-born in the north" during the 19th and early 20th centuries.[22]

No dictator or single-party oligarchy wants an armed populace, especially not a subjugated minority who holds resentments. Adolf Hitler made this clear in 1942, warning:

> The most foolish mistake we could possibly make would be to allow the subject races to possess arms. History shows that all conquerors who have allowed their subject races to carry arms have prepared their own downfall by so doing.[23]

Until the 1980s, the movement for gun control was mainly propelled by white southern Democrats in an attempt to prevent African Americans from owning firearms, through laws referred to as "Black Codes." For over a century, gun control was a form of racist domination devised to disarm blacks, making them easy prey for mob lynchings, white terrorism, and persecution by hate groups. In some states it was a crime for whites to loan firearms to black citizens.[24]

Obviously, collectivism, which has deep roots in racism, was a determining factor, which eventually drove the statist Left to take over the anti-gun issue from white supremacists. This change is most revealing, as it highlights the collectivist Left's reactionary mindset, which reflected the racists' fear of the inability to control inferiors. This fear led, in turn, to the idea that everyone in society should be disarmed in order to secure obedience to state authority.

The Proslavery Socialism of George Fitzhugh

Not long after Calhoun's death, another slavery advocate came to promi-
nence, flagrantly and publicly declaring the ideas of slavery and socialism
were interchangeable. A planter, lawyer, and Democrat from Virginia,
this socialist intellectual was author George Fitzhugh (1806–1881),
who ardently supported collectivism, racism, and involuntary servitude.
Through the writings of Horace Greely, Fitzhugh discovered the ideals
of French utopian socialist Charles Fourier, whose "phalanstery" theories about self-contained, mutual-benefit communities clearly described
plantation life. Fitzhugh, like other pro-slavery socialists, was pushing
for a cradle-to-the-grave plantation welfare system enforced by strict
supervision, corporal punishment, and the whip.

A social theorist who practiced law, Fitzhugh asserted that the Negro
was merely "a grown-up child" who required the economic and social
protection of slavery. In a time before politically correct speech, Fitzhugh spoke his mind freely; he was a strong supporter of socialism and
an opponent of free-market capitalism because it causes "a war of the
rich with the poor, and the poor with one another"—a form of class
struggle that was popularized by Karl Marx. To Fitzhugh, the capitalist,
free-labor society was "diseased" in that it exploited workers.

In *Sociology for the South, Or the Failure of Free Society* (1854), Fitzhugh wrote that society needed slavery for security and morality and that
it was not only good for blacks, but also for poor whites. He proclaimed:
"Slavery is a form, and the very best form, of socialism," and that "socialism is the new fashionable name of slavery."[25] Fitzhugh attempted to
remake plantation life into an "agricultural collective and slavery into a
benign condition" of government dependence,[26] and many Southerners
supported him.

Some of Fitzhugh's harshest criticism was reserved for the evils of a
free society. He considered free societies of open capitalism and economic mobility recipes for failure. He argued in his books and pamphlets
that society required socialism and slavery so that man's greedy human
nature would be destroyed. In justifying slavery, Fitzhugh's wrote:

> Free society is a failure. We slaveholders say you must recur to
> domestic slavery, the best and most common form of Socialism.

> The new schools of Socialism promise something better, but admit, to obtain that something, they must first destroy and eradicate man's human nature.[27]

In an era devoid of political correctness, Fitzhugh felt perfectly justified in affirming that the slaves were better off than the free laborers in the North. He wrote: "The slaves are all well fed, well clad, have plenty of fuel, and are happy. They have no dread of the future—no fear of want."[28] This proud Democratic Party member even referred to his slavery-socialist movement as communistic—writing in his second book that "Slavery is a form of communism."

Not only did Fitzhugh dub free society "a monstrous abortion," but he criticized the Declaration of Independence as "exuberantly false and arborescently fallacious." He opposed letting people handle their own affairs and believed that people should be unequal before the law. He asserted that "the bestowing upon men equality of rights, is but giving license to the strong to oppress the weak."[29] Alongside his socialistic and self-avowed "communist" disposition, Fitzhugh took the position that liberty and free competition encourage the "strong to master the weak" and therefore secure the success of the wealthy.[30]

Furthermore, he entertained the idea to restrict or "banish the use of money," writing that "money is a great weapon in a free, equal and competitive society," which "exploitate and oppress the poor, the improvident, and the weak-minded."[31] Fitzhugh was also noted for fervently opposing private property. Arguing that "slavery is a form of communism," he believed that "private property has monopolized the earth and destroyed both his liberty and equality."[32] He even concluded that society owned every individual's money, labor, and property, a rather obvious socialist position which also led him to justify a slave society.

In *Cannibals All! or Slaves Without Masters* (1857), Fitzhugh paraded his hardcore socialist colors by coming out against the "wages is slavery" mantra, which he accused the Yankee capitalists of imposing on the people in the North. Fitzhugh wrote: "The unrestricted exploitation of so-called free society is more oppressive to the laborer than domestic slavery."[33] Considered as an early sociologist, Fitzhugh argued that the chattel slavery system was essential, in order to replace the un-

caring wage-slavery of the capitalists, trapped by the oppression of capitalists' exploitation, while slaves in the South were actually freer.[34] In
typical socialist fashion, Fitzhugh urged compensation for the victims of
inequality found in free societies that allowed laborers to sell their labor
to the highest bidder. His solution was to stop "wage slavery," and end
capitalist-spawned social inequality by establishing a system of universal
slavery, arguing that "nineteen out of every twenty individuals have... a
natural and inalienable right to be slaves."[35]

He worried about the plight of weaker members of society, writing:
"'It is the duty of society to protect the weak;' but protection cannot
be efficient without the power of control; therefore, 'It is the duty of
society to enslave the weak.'"[36] An advocate of women's right to vote,
Fitzhugh is considered a leading non-Marxist socialist with both egalitarian and anti-egalitarian undertones whose rants were said to have angered
Abraham Lincoln more than any other defender of a slave society. Nevertheless, Fitzhugh's first book greatly influenced Lincoln's commitment
against the institution of slavery. He found Fitzhugh's slavery-based sociological theories horrifying in that they seemed to justify slavery in every
possible way. According to Lincoln's law partner, William Henry Hern-
don, Fitzhugh's writings "aroused the ire of Lincoln more than most
pro-slavery books."[37]

Southerners like Fitzhugh pushed the Democratic Party towards a
socialist-slavery plantation society that would impose a dependency on
government largesse under the shadow of paternalistic racism. His was a
popular voice in justifying slavery, finding support among many southern politicians, slaveholders, and newspapers.

The influential *Richmond Enquirer* agreed with Fitzhugh's proslavery sentiment, writing that the defense of slavery could now be seen as
more than "mere negro slavery," that "slavery is a right, natural and necessary."[38] Many Southerners came to agree with Fitzhugh's sentiments
and "declared slavery the system that best ensured the rights of man."[39]

What makes this even more surprising is that in the 1820s, the "slave
states contained a great many more anti-slavery societies than the free
states and furnished leadership for the movement in the country."[40] A
decade later, the situation had radically changed, mostly because of the
proslavery intelligentsia who sought to justify slavery under a paternal-

istic and socialist relationship that also demanded reciprocal obligations from the enslaved. Comparable to the Nazis' concept of "Völkisch equality," slaveholders began to expect their chattel to live under a collective plantation society where each person had to uphold certain duties and obligations. Likewise, the plantation's managers were expected to be responsible for their slaves' safety, health, material well-being, and conduct. Ironically, many collectivistic governments behave in the same way: they treat their populace under the same citizen-slave paradigm, molding their citizenry under a compulsory structure of supposedly loving-care plantation welfarism, strictly enforced and taxed and which values the collective over the individual.

Slavery was rationalized as a common good, as Calhoun described it; something that was beneficial to the whole community, for both slaveholders and slaves alike.[41] Southerners began to favor slavery as a mutually beneficial system designed to help those unfit to take care of themselves, which is clearly comparable to a utopian plantation society, but placed under the ruling yoke of authoritarian socialism. Under this slavocracy model, citizen-slaves were governed as if they had no capacity for self-government, and therefore the rights of individuals became subservient to their social obligations and to the rights of the collective. This analogy holds true for any individual of any race or ethnicity living under a government that has abrogated the individual rights of free choice and mobility.

This sentiment makes logical sense—in a twisted, deranged way. The development of slavery in the southern states of America is comparable to "black socialism." Think about it. Plantation slaveholders believed that they were being good shepherds toward their Negro flock when they lodged their slaves under the control, but also under the care, of the slaveholder. They gave their human chattel free medical care, housing, clothing, and food, along with having few concerns over financial, health, or security worries. They would be supported by a slave-master state, a slavocracy ensured to provide a welfare-based safety net to the chattel laborers. As for equality, everyone was supposed to have the same amount of material goods—which wasn't much. Of course, there was just one small problem: none of the laborers could leave the plantation without permission.

Even today, there is a common perception that African-Americans are still living under a plantation-style life of misery. Barack Obama in his *Dreams from My Father* acknowledged what African-Americans disdainfully called their black ghettos—"economic plantations" and "plantation politics," where they lamented over being poor, despairing, and second-class citizens. Here, Obama echoed their sentiment of injustice, writing:

> Black people in the worst jobs. The worst housing. Police brutality rampant. But when the so-called black committeemen came around election time, we'd all line up and vote the straight Democratic ticket. Sell our soul for a Christmas turkey.[42]

George Fitzhugh's collectivistic bent went a bit further than just advocating socialism and slavery. He also seemed to have a fetish for medieval feudalism. He justified a return to feudalism and involuntary servitude by arguing that one's position in life is stationary and set at birth. Such a closed system of hereditary dominance prevented a person's status in life from changing, forcing children to pursue the career of their parents. The feudal king, for instance, became the king not because of his talents or skills, but by an accident of birth. Fitzhugh explained that in a feudal-socialist society of the privileged few, some people were "born with saddles on their back, and others booted and spurred to ride them—and the riding does them good."[43] To the classical liberals and Jeffersonians, human equality meant that no one was born to serve others. Similar to Nietzsche's "neither a master, nor a slave" aphorism, the Founding Fathers understood that nobody was born to rule nor born into servitude.

The Good Works of Servitude and Violence

But servitude and good works seem to be the calling card of many socialists. In 2015, I had a conversation with a socialist from a peace organization that I supported. He felt compelled to defend Che Guevara, Fidel Castro, and the Cuban Revolution. At first, the conflict was over violence. This particular socialist believed it was perfectly acceptable for Che Guevara to shoot people in the head and engage in extrajudicial executions of up to 500 inmates at La Cabaña fortress prison. The reason provided suggested that since the former evil and corrupted dictator, Fulgencio Batista, had done the same with past state-defined criminals, so could the "enlightened" leaders of the Cuban Revolutions.

But Che Guevara's advocacy of violence was also justified due to his good works. It was pointed out that Guevara had fought against racial injustice and had helped to provide a good educational system for the Cuban people. Somehow such social justice practices warranted mass murder, violence, and executions without trials, without juries. I felt obliged to point out that Mussolini, a former schoolteacher, had built thousands of schools in Italy along with a vast and encompassing welfare system. Why not give Mussolini the same consideration? In fact, the Italian Fascists also promoted social revolution and "social justice" during their reign. Alas, my social justice peacenik failed to see the parallels.

This exchange, however, refocused us on the issue of slavery. I asked my socialist colleague, "What is the difference between a slave plantation and Castro's Cuba?" After all, under the plantation structure, slaves got all of their supplies and services for free. The slave owner provided an expansive welfare system, while workers supplied unpaid labor, which is a defining feature of government ownership of people. He simply ignored the question.

I admitted that the promise of ample freebies sounded great—at least until someone gets a hankering to travel beyond the barbed-wire fence, but such unescorted excursions are usually not permitted in a welfare-driven slavocracy. Only the commandant can leave the plantation without authorization, and since slaves are viewed as too inferior to take care of themselves, slavery apologists concluded that the liberty inherent in self-governance is unacceptable. Like the East German populace behind the Berlin Wall, the state-owned people are trapped under a structure of disempowerment and subjugation. The antebellum slaveholders had exploited the legal system and acquired the authority (state slavery laws) to behave like a tyrannical government in order to get free, unpaid work from their chattel. Compulsory socialism is just another version of plantation-based slave society.

Southern apologists for slavery were simply applying hardcore socialist principles to justify enslavement. Socialists treat the general populace in the same way, arguing that people are incapable of self-rule, unfit to take care of themselves, irresponsible, and shiftless. Under their utopian vision, central planners and technocrats are required to usher in a more equalitarian life of plenty and joy. Except they always seem to fail to mention that their *modus operandi* is geared to re-engineer mankind in the overlord's image, something the Nazis attempted to do with their extensive welfare system, but excluding minorities and dissenters from receiving public welfare.

Of course, this cradle-to-grave slavery-socialism results in paradoxical side effects. Slavery has a habit of making the enslaved dependent upon their masters, which usually sabotages the nurturing care required to make someone self-sufficient and able-bodied. Then again, what overlord wants their chattel to actually declare their independence?

In 2017 a movement emerged to demand the removal of all Confederate statues and monuments across the South, which many contend symbolize the evils of slavery, racism and white supremacy. Good enough, but something was forgotten. Ironically, where was the outcry to sweep away the Confederate perpetrators who established, financed and fought to preserve those iron shackles of slavery? Where was the demand to depose the political party that has been synonymous with such racist, antiquated views for so long—the Democratic Party? Why aren't the Democrats included in this noble campaign to consign race-based subjugation to the dustbin of history? This is the real atrocity: toppling the statues of racists, but not those who built them.

The Warranteeism of Henry Hughes

Sociologist Henry Hughes (1829–1862), another pro-thralldom intellectual, came up with a modified version of slavery and welfarism: "warranteeism." Under Hughes's ideas, a powerful, central government would warranty work for everyone, in a society where he assured that "want is eliminated. There are no poor; all have competence."[44] That right to a job would be *compulsory*—similar to what was mandated in the Soviet Union, where citizens either had to work or they were subject to punishment. After all, Lenin once proclaimed: "He who does not work shall not eat."[45] And if not enough work can be found, Keynesian make-work jobs could be instigated—dig a hole in the ground and then fill it up—so that incomes would be artificially boosted, and the economy temporarily stimulated. Further, this economic rigidity would apply to both employee and employer, letting government overseers engage in such practices so that "both masters and slaves were 'servants of the social order.'"[46]

Under Hughes's world of subservience, the government would become the plantation taskmaster, wielding a rawhide whip in one hand and free goodies in the other. Under Hughes's minimum-wage laws, the warrantee-laborer would get food, housing, transportation, legal services, insurance, and medical care, as prescribed by the state.[47] As an early social-welfare activist who also supported unemployment compensation, Hughes saw the role of government as guaranteeing "substance and order." It was Hughes who came up with the aphorism that there should be "a chicken in every man's pot."

Antebellum historian William H. Freehling puts Hughes's advocacy into a wider context, writing: "Just as Hughes wished Southern government to warrant a chicken for every slave, so he wanted northern government to warrant a meal for every free laborer."[48] Again, this mixture of serfdom with plantation socialism could easily allow some to justify the subjugation of an unequal inferior to an equal superior.

A colonel in the Confederate Army from Mississippi, Hughes supported the re-establishment of the African slave trade. He proposed to repatriate (in effect, deport) slaves to Africa, and exchange them for fresh new African "warrantees," who would recognize the duty of work in order to serve the state, as opposed to traditional, old-fashioned slavery that had no written contract.[49] Naturally, Hughes had no use for *laissez-faire* capitalism so readily found in the free-labor markets up North, which embraced the individuality of human potential. In fact, he called a free and independent labor society "a live murder machine. It is organized homicide." Like Hughes, most proslavery writers contended that plantation servitude was fair and gentle, when compared to the dirty and disorderly labor of free individuals in the more industrialized North.

Hughes's backing for big-government interventionism was predicated on the notions that not only were blacks inferior but that most individuals, no matter the race, were incapable of self-governance. This mistrust of unbridled and free-wheeling people compelled pro-slavery and pro-socialist intellectuals to conclude that involuntary servitude and dependency upon the state would lead to better and happier citizens. They considered involuntary servitude and social welfare as meritorious, because laborers need to live under a master who takes on the burden of society's responsibility of paternalistically providing care. The socialist-slavery defenders deduced that most people "were permanently incapable of self-government and were better off enslaved."[50]

Furthermore, Hughes upheld the anti-capitalist notion that the enslavement of inferior people provided a social justice tool to fix the inequalities of economic distribution. Concerned over the inequality of the economic status of the people, Hughes favored a welfare-slavery duality so that "injustice in the distribution shall be eliminated."

Surprisingly, Hughes gained some notoriety in the 20th century. His concept of a government-mandated distribution of warrantees influenced President Franklin D. Roosevelt's Keynesian economic policies, especially FDR's Second Bill of Rights that called for government to provide adequate food, clothing, education, home, medical care, and so forth,[51] arguing that people had a right to such material goods. In other words, FDR's Second Bill of Rights has roots in the pro-slavery and pro-socialist intelligentsia from the epoch of the Confederacy that promoted a plantation society. Worst of all, this same concept of government welfarism, socialism, and dependency on governmental entitlements were to accrete into Russian Sovietism, Italian Fascism, and German National Socialism.

Racist and Fascist Elements Confronting Democrats

Interestingly, this was the same FDR who, according to Jesse Owens, the black athlete of track-and-field fame, snubbed him after he had won four gold medals at the 1936 World Olympic Games in Hitler's Germany. The most successful athlete at the games, Owens said: "Hitler didn't snub me; it was our president who snubbed me. The president didn't even send a telegram."[52,53,54] Revealing the Democratic Party's deep roots in racial inequality, FDR invited every white US Olympian to a special gathering in the White House, but not Owens.[55]

There are also incidents that have raised questions about the FDR administration's attitude towards Asians. Through a 1941 executive order, FDR authorized more than 100,000 American citizens of Japanese ancestry to be forcibly relocated to concentration camps, without due process. Further, anyone with as little as 1/16 Japanese heritage could be interned in the camps, which some claim demonstrated a racist component to their treatment. Strangely, Americans of German and Italian descent were not incarcerated in internment camps, except for the very few classified as enemy aliens.

But one of the darkest legacies of FDR's early administration was Franklin Roosevelt's admiration for Mussolini, shared by many in America at the time, including his Brain Trust advisors. FDR wrote that he was "deeply impressed by what [Mussolini] has accomplished."[56] He sent members of his staff to Italy to review the socioeconomic policies of Fascist Italy. One of FDR's closest Brain Trust advisers, Rexford Guy Tugwell, traveled to the USSR and Fascist Italy, and credited Mussolini's fascism as "the cleanest, neatest, most efficiently operating piece of social machinery I've ever seen. It makes me envious."[57] Not surprisingly, Tugwell also heaped praise upon the Soviet Union's centralized planned economy. The Brain Trust's fascination for fascism went much deeper. At FDR's first 1933 Cabinet meeting, books by Giovanni Gentile were distributed to every member, and they were asked to study it. Gentile repeatedly described himself as "the philosopher of Fascism" and was Mussolini's Minister of Public Education. According to socialist historian George Rawick:

> ... the financier and adviser to Roosevelt, Bernard Baruch, and Baruch's friend General Hugh Johnson, who was to become the head of the National Recovery Administration, came in with a copy of a book by Gentile, the Italian Fascist theoretician, for each member of the Cabinet, and we all read it with great care.[58,59]

Obviously, Franklin D. Roosevelt's administration was heavily influenced by Mussolini's Fascism, especially the National Recovery Administration (NRA) originally headed by Hugh Johnson. Even the six-time Socialist Party candidate for US president, Norman Thomas, recognized that FDR's economic policies drifted towards national socialism, writing: "The similarities of the economics of the New Deal to the economics of Mussolini's corporative state or Hitler's totalitarian state are both close and obvious."[60] That influence began to wane after Mussolini ordered an unprovoked attack and invasion of Ethiopia in 1935.

A prolific writer himself, even after ascending to dictatorship, Mussolini gave a sparkling review of Roosevelt's book, *Looking Forward* (1933). From his reading of FDR's book, Mussolini saw "reminiscent of fascism ... the principle that the state no longer leaves the economy to its own devices."[61] In addition, he praised the soft fascism of the New Deal as "boldly... interventionist in the field of economics."[62] Many prestigious magazines echoed similar language in connecting Mussolini's social policies to the New Deal, including *Fortune* magazine, which editorialized: "The Corporate State is to Mussolini what the New Deal is to Roosevelt."[63]

Even the Nazis found much to like about FDR and his New Deal. The German National Socialist Party newspaper, the *Völkischer Beobachter*,

> stressed "Roosevelt's adoption of National Socialist strains of thought in his economic and social policies," praising the president's style of leadership as being compatible with Hitler's own dictatorial *Führerprinzip*.[64]

The British journalist and television broadcaster, Alistair Cooke (1908–2004), once remarked that under FDR's administration,

> America had a fling at National Socialism. Roosevelt was for all administration purposes a dictator, but a benevolent one, and the country loved it.[65]

Even the knight of Camelot, John F. Kennedy, could not hide from the Democratic Party's legacy of obstructing civil rights for blacks. The young US senator from Massachusetts led the congressional opposition to Eisenhower's Civil Rights Act of 1957. Some argue that the final version of the bill was weak and ineffectual, but that was because the bill had had to be watered down because it had so little support among Democrats. Notwithstanding, it was the first civil rights law since 1875, and it kick-started the birth of the new movement for civil rights.

Kennedy's vice president, Lyndon Baines Johnson (1908–1973), who assumed the presidency in 1963, had a habit of using the word "nigger." According to Adam Serwer from MSNBC:

> Lyndon Johnson said the word "nigger" a lot. In Senate cloak-rooms and staff meetings, Johnson was practically a connoisseur of the word. According to Johnson biographer Robert Caro, Johnson would calibrate his pronunciations by region, using "ni-gra" with some southern legislators and "negra" with others.[66]

A Texas native, Johnson repeatedly stonewalled civil rights legislation to help the Democratic Party keep hold of their segregation and white power authority. Not satisfied with just overseeing ill-treatment of blacks, he was noted in the 1940s for his opposition to the "hordes of barbaric yellow dwarves" in East Asia. In the Johnson biography *Flawed Giant*, author Robert Dallek tells the story of Johnson's decision to nominate Thurgood Marshall to the Supreme Court. Johnson said that the reason he did not nominate a possibly more qualified, but less famous black to that bench was that, "When I appoint a nigger to the bench, I want everybody to know he's a nigger."[67] Johnson was indeed instrumental in the passage of the Civil Rights Act of 1964, but it was not for racial-egalitarian principles, but more in line with political expediency.

The Democratic Party's legacy of racism even spilled over into the twenty-first century. In 2010, when US Sen. Robert Byrd died, Hillary Clinton was quick to lavish praise on her old KKK comrade. In a fondly commemorative speech, Hillary said: "Today our country has lost a true American original, my friend and mentor Robert C. Byrd."[68] Personally leading a marathon filibuster of the Civil Rights Act of 1964 for 14 hours, Byrd had been an officer and recruiter for the KKK in the Sophia, the West Virginia chapter. He eventually recanted his ties to the KKK, but was still using the word "nigger" ("white nigger") up until 2001.[69]

Even up to 2017, Donna Brazile, the unpaid former Democratic National Committee chair, referred to her treatment by Hillary Clinton's presidential campaign staff as comparable to slavery. "I'm not Patsey the slave," Brazile told senior campaign officials at the time, referencing the black character played by Lupita Nyong'o in the movie, *12 Years a Slave*. "Y'all keep whipping me and whipping me and you never give me any money or any way to do my damn job. I am not going to be your whipping girl!"[70] This may be somewhat of a labored metaphor, but with a mostly white Hillary campaign staff, who can say whether racial discrimination was not a factor in the poor behavior towards Brazile? After all, the specter of racism has haunted the Democratic Party since its inception back in the 1820s.

It should be pointed out that slavery comes in many forms, even intruding upon the realm of economics. If an authority gains the upper hand in seizing citizens' money at almost any time for almost any reason, a form of slavery has been established. Under a political slavocracy, proponents of unfettered taxation argue that citizens' property and assets already belong to the state, often grumbling over the loss of revenue to governmental bodies if a reduction in taxation is proposed. This sentiment is a relic from the era when African Americans were legally owned by masters who stole the self-ownership and property rights from those too weak to resist.

Under this type of authoritarian subjugation, the state becomes the collective owner of the people. Within this archaic context, plebeians are owned by the state because they supposedly owe their very lives to the nation, a concept championed by Socrates in a lecture to his friend Crito. The people are supposedly mere servants of the political structure because what the state gives, "it actually lends; what it lends, it can take back."[71] This is why there can be no property or individual rights under a slavocracy; nothing can ever be owned by individuals. Only through the consent of a people endowed with *inalienable* rights of life, liberty, and property can the people be seen as owners within their democratic-republican government.

In their endeavor to preserve poor and obedient serfs, the progressive-statist Left has backed laws that impose a compulsory-service structure upon society, eager to control, own, regulate, and dictate the lives of every politically connected or unconnected citizen, essentially making automatons of most societal members. It has reached the point where—as the slaves experienced in the old South—almost every human activity has been rendered illegal at some local, state or national level. But it is their motivations that are highly reminiscent of slavery, predicating their control of society on paternalistic and "altruistic motives" that were also employed by the Southern whites to justify the legitimacy of enslavement. To most slaveholders, especially southern white women, there was a sense of duty to care for the unfit and impoverished masses on their plantation.[72] In other words, the Southern paternalistic hierarchy of thralldom was put in place to promote the slaves' own good, whether they liked it or not.

Today in America, the slave master is now the state. This dedication to socioeconomic servitude and welfarism is the legacy of the statist Left, and of the current leadership of the Progressives and of the Democratic Party in the United States. These groups are averse to the concept of inalienable rights, even the gun rights for blacks to protect themselves from racist aggressors and police brutality. To the statist Left, the enslavement of African-Americans was just the beginning stage of a collective process not only to dominate minorities, but to extend state ownership equally to everyone.

For instance, a number of progressive academicians have recently displayed their true colors over the issue of being either a "free agent" or one subject to public ownership. Ironically, one of them was an African-American professor at Tulane University, Melissa Harris-Perry, who favored the idea of human ownership by the state, declaring as an MSNBC television host: "We have to break through our kind of private idea that kids belong to their parents or kids belong to their families and recognize that kids belong to whole communities."[73] Adolf Hitler, another collectivist beholden to the *Volksgemeinschaft* ("people's community"), echoed a similar theme to abrogate parental rights, proclaiming: "Your child belongs to us already... In a short time they will know nothing else but this new community."[74]

One journalist who was not fooled for long by the statist Left's antiliberal populism, was Walter Lippmann, a two-time Pulitzer Prize winner. Later in life, he became alarmed over America's march toward a nightmarish future under FDR's New Deal and the Progressive movement. He referred to it as a "collectivist heresy." In his 1937 book, *An Inquiry into the Principles of the Good Society*, Walter Lippmann warned that America was heading towards a regimented economy that had all the makings of a totalitarian state. Combined with gradual collectivism and a nation captained by an irresponsible executive, Lippmann saw government veering from a market economy and law to an arbitrary state absent of principles and concerns for liberty.

The Democratic Party still seems to attract racists and admirers of Hitler's military and economic accomplishments, even if they are of African descent. Louis Farrakhan, head of the Nation of Islam, has been denounced as anti-Semitic and racist by the Southern Poverty Law Center, but still commands a popular following among many Democrats.[75] Not only has Farrakhan expressed racial hatred of whites and Jews, but was impressed by Hitler, once declaring that "Hitler was a very great man."[76] On February 25, 2018, Farrakhan peppered his speech with bigoted comments, proclaiming: "White folks are going down. And Satan is going down. And Farrakhan, by God's grace, has pulled the cover off of that Satanic Jew, and I'm here to say your time is up, your world is through," and that "the powerful Jews are my enemy."[77]

Farrakhan does not reserve his wrath only for Jews, but also takes potshots at other races. In a Reuters Television interview on October 4, 1994, Farrakhan stated:

> Many of the Jews who owned the homes, the apartments in the black community, we considered them bloodsuckers because they took from our community and built their community. But they didn't offer anything back to the community. And when the Jews left, the Palestinian Arabs came, Koreans came, Vietnamese and other ethnic and racial groups came. And so this is a type, and we call them bloodsuckers.[78]

As the organizer of the 1995 Washington D.C. Million Man March, Farrakhan announced his support for Barack Obama during his 2008 Presidential campaign. Obama was quick to distance himself from Farrakhan's praise at the time, but in 2018 a photo came to light showing Obama standing next to Farrakhan, taken in 2005 with the Congressional Black Caucus by journalist Askia Muhammad.[79] The photo was kept a secret for over a decade so it would not damage Obama's candidacy.

Farrakhan did more than just have his photo taken with a smiling Obama. Farrakhan revealed in a 2016 mosque sermon that he had secret meetings at his home with Obama.[80] Farrakhan boasted to his congregation that he and his Islamic organization gave Obama financial backing to help him get elected to public office. "We supported him when he was a community organizer," Farrakhan disclosed. "We backed him with money and with the help of the [Fruit of Islam] to get him elected."[81]   Apparently, Obama was taking campaign money from a man widely known as a blatant anti-Semite, racist and homophobe. In fact, according to *Rolling Stone* magazine, Farrakhan and his Nation of Islam, have "denied the Holocaust," believe that Jews "control" the government and entertainment industry, and that Jews seek to oppress black Americans.[82]

Imagine what would happen to any politician who took campaign money from the American white supremacist, Holocaust denier and anti-Semite David Duke. Many Democrats, Progressives and Women's March leaders in 2018 have refused or hesitated to rebuke Farrakhan's reactionary views. The hypocrisy of Democrats who allegedly promote a no-tolerance view of bigotry is deafening. Apparently, the Democrat apple does not fall far from the racial prejudice tree.

However, the Democratic Party began to tone down their supremacy-of-race ideology since the Civil Rights movement gained ground in the mid-1950s. As the belief in white people's superiority continued to grow unpopular, the Democratic Party leadership realized that they were going to lose a huge influx of newly registered black voters. Embracing the superiority of white people became a dead end in the battle for power, which they saw as political suicide.

The Democratic leaders had to devise another scheme to obtain votes from both white and black citizens while still subjecting them to the plantation bullwhip of paternalism and socialism. To accomplish this, the Democrats had to replace white supremacy with "state supremacy," which recast the state as the new slave master and societal overlord, regardless of race. This should not be surprising since Democrat Party ideological foundations were originally based on the "man-stealing" premise of domination and submission.

Intellectual Forebears of the Modern Left: The Early Progressives

Today, it is no wonder that Calhoun and a slew of proslavery theorists are being identified as "intellectual forebears of the political philosophy of Woodrow Wilson, FDR, and the modern left."[83]   The core idealism of pre-Civil War slavery, especially their anti-capitalist economic policies, still resonates on the socialist and collective left that rose during the first "Progressive Era" (the 1890s–1920s). Historian William Leuchtenburg described this period:

> The Progressives believed in the Hamiltonian concept of positive government, of a national government directing the destinies of the nation at home and abroad. They had little but contempt for the strict construction of the Constitution by conservative judges, who would restrict the power of the national government to act against social evils and to extend the blessings of democracy to less favored lands.[84]

But other scholars have been far less generous about what the progressives actually represented. Many saw the early Progressive movement as the ancient regressive impulses of domination, power-lusting and the collective hatred for divergent groups. In a *Reason* magazine book review, "When Bigots Become Reformers: The Progressive Era's shameful record on race," Damon Root wrote:

> Yet the Progressive Era was also a time of vicious, state-sponsored racism. In fact, from the standpoint of African-American history, the Progressive Era qualifies as arguably the single worst period since Emancipation. The wholesale disfranchisement of Southern black voters occurred during these years, as did the rise and triumph of Jim Crow. Furthermore, as the Westminster College historian David W. Southern notes in his recent book, *The Progressive Era and Race: Reform and Reaction, 1900–1917*, the very worst of it—disfranchisement, segregation, race baiting, lynching—"went hand-in-hand with the most advanced forms of southern progressivism." Racism was the norm, not the exception, among the very crusaders romanticized by today's activist left.[85]

Obviously, the first Progressive movement in America was pockmarked with a face full of unsightly lesions and regressive deformities. Even when the popular and progressive Theodore Roosevelt was elected president in 1904, he was "openly opposed to civil rights and suffrage for blacks" and averse to voting rights for blacks.[86]

Considered by many as a key founder of "modern liberalism," Democrat-elected President Woodrow Wilson (1856–1924) is today considered an outright racist, reactionary, and anglophile, who pushed for restrictive and discriminatory immigration laws. Not only did Wilson praise the wildly racist 1915 silent film, *The Birth of a Nation*, but was overjoyed to see one of his own book's excerpts flickering on the screen in an intertitle (text on the screen) to introduce the Reconstruction section of the film, which was inserted to glorify the activities of the Ku Klux Klan. Wilson's text read: "The white men were roused by a mere instinct of self-preservation... until at last there had sprung into existence a great Ku Klux Klan, a veritable empire of the South, to protect the Southern country."[87]

Resisting repeated efforts to enact federal anti-lynching laws that could have mitigated widespread vigilante justice in the South, Wilson had no qualms about pushing for segregation at the federal level. In fact, Wilson set back race relations by firing most black postal workers while re-segregating the US military. Some federal offices set up screens or cages to separate the races, but most simply fired the blacks.[88] Many of Wilson's unprecedented policies were more akin to white supremacy than to progressive advancement. In the margins of one of his manuscripts, Wilson took time to explain that Reconstruction in the South was detestable "not because the Republican Party was dreaded but because the dominance of an ignorant and inferior race was justly dreaded."[89]

In 1914 Wilson freely flaunted his pro-segregation sentiments to a delegation of black leaders, hostilely declaring: "Segregation is not humiliating, but a benefit, and ought to be so regarded by you gentlemen." Then he immediately showed them the door.[90] After lavishing praise on Wilson for almost 100 years, *The New York Times* finally admitted in an editorial that he was an "unapologetic racist" who "purged black workers from influential jobs and transformed the government into an instrument of white supremacy."[91] Not only that, but Wilson "believed that black Americans were unworthy of full citizenship and admired the Ku Klux Klan for the role it had in terrorizing African-Americans to restrict their political power."[92]

Not surprisingly, Wilson also had a soft spot for socialism and a heart hardened against individual liberty, stating that

> In fundamental theory socialism and democracy are almost if not quite one and the same. They both rest at bottom upon the absolute right of the community to determine its own destiny and that of its members. Men as communities are supreme over men as individuals.[93]

Once mocking the Fourth of July sentiments of those who still believed in the ideals of the Founders, Wilson wrote:

> No doubt a lot of nonsense has been talked about the inalienable rights of the individual, and a great deal that was mere vague sentiment and pleasing speculation has been put forward as fundamental principle.[94]

Wilson believed that the founding ideas of the United States were obsolete, penning: "we are not bound to adhere to the doctrine held by the signers of the Declaration of Independence."[95]

Another, less-than-progressive approach was Wilson's willingness to use "gunboat diplomacy," alongside bouts of imperialism and foreign regime changes, always insisting that invasions of less-free nations would advance democracy. Besides the suppression of dissenters during World War I, warrantless arrests and detainees held without trial, Wilson's checkered background should not qualify him as the leading force in a so-called Progressive movement. But John Milton Cooper, author of *Woodrow Wilson: A Biography*, ranked him as "among the greatest legislative presidents in the twentieth century" who passed some of the most progressive legislation. "His only rivals would be Franklin Roosevelt with the New Deal in the 1930s and Lyndon Johnson with the Great Society in the 1960s."[96] It is hard to fathom how anyone could proclaim President Wilson as the major leader of left-wing progressivism or modern liberalism, but then again, modern, social liberalism was never modern, liberal, or progressive.

As historian Julian E. Zelizer explained: "The irony here is that Wilson really is the architect of a lot of modern liberalism." He started a "tradition that runs through F.D.R. to L.B.J. and Obama really starts with his administration."[97] Still, Wilson has liberal progressive defenders like David Greenberg, a historian at Rutgers University, who said, "Going to the mat for Wilson should not be hard... If your standards are liberal progressive values in general, Wilson deserves to be celebrated."[98]

In other issues, the early Progressives were also instrumental in enacting the Eighteenth Amendment, which prohibited the manufacture, transportation, and sale of alcoholic beverages. Still, in a political attempt to depict a sense of liberty, the federally passed Volstead Act was written in a way that made alcohol consumption, *per se*, not illegal. Consumers could legally drink alcohol, but nobody could provide it.

Other so-called progressives, mostly unsuccessful business competitors, sought more government controls over the marketplace. One strand of progressive intelligentsia got caught up in the social Darwinism of eugenics to eliminate undesirable genetic traits, to "assist the race toward the elimination of the unfit," where science could beget the perfect race, so as to breed a better voter. Many Southern states with racist intentions gave their support wholeheartedly to the science of eugenics and imposed mandatory sterilization of blacks they saw as unfit. Furthermore, many progressives and Democratic leaders promoted forced sterilization and worked to stop immigrants of particular races from entering America.

Like many progressives and socialists, the science fiction writer H.G. Wells also dabbled in hardcore eugenics. He once defined the categories of those who would be put to death in his utopian state. He wrote in his 1901 book *Anticipations* that his New Republic would have no use for

> a multitude of contemptible and silly creatures, fear-driven and helpless and useless, unhappy or hatefully happy in the midst of squalid dishonour, feeble, ugly, inefficient, born of unrestrained lusts, and increasing and multiplying through sheer incontinence and stupidity.[99]

The type of nondemocratic government he envisioned was one that was ruled by a "self-selected caste of enlightened technicians, who would rule according to the dictates of science."[100] Later in his writings and speeches, the people he thought could rule the world better were the "Italian Fascists and especially the Soviet Communist Party."[101]

In *Anticipations*, with its socialist "Utopian World State,"[102] Wells detailed the new ethics of death. This new, progressive society embraced government-directed euthanasia, where it would be the duty of the "more efficient peoples to conquer the weaker ones." The inferior "people of the Abyss," as Wells called them, included blacks, Jews, the mentally ill, and the diseased—and anyone else who did not fit a noble classification of society—a society to be populated only by "white English-speaking peoples," whom he saw as the superior, scientific elite.

This policy to exterminate the unfit was popular among socialist intellectuals. As stated by George Watson in *The Lost Literature of Socialism*,

> Ethnic cleansing was orthodox socialism for a century or more. ...
> So the socialist intelligentsia of the western world entered World
> War I publicly committed to racial purity and white domination,
> and no less committed to violence.[103]

The program of socialist genocide in the futuristic New Republic that Wells depicted in *Anticipations* caused some critics, like Lovat Dickson, to suggest that the novel "carries a suggestion of 'strong-arm fascism.'"[104] Obviously, Wells' writing shows how socialists' rationale can easily detour into racist attitudes when they try to determine just what is to be done with those backward people who are remnants of the feudal system, or what Friedrich Engels called the "racial trash." Although his book was wildly popular, Wells eventually backpedaled, apologizing for his poor choice of words.

Many idealistic reformers favored legislation to institute a progressive taxation structure—a national income tax—which mocked freedom of action (*laissez-faire*) and the anti-tax Founders. Then came their *pièce de résistance*: wealthy progressives resurrected a private-public central bank, the Federal Reserve Bank. Ironically, the demand for a strongly progressive tax on capital, women's voting rights, and state-imposed minimum wages laws with a 40-hour work week were championed not only by progressives in America, but also by Mussolini's Fascist Revolutionary Party.

Along with a strong centralized government, the specter of racism also shadowed the Progressives. One American socialist author, Edward

Bellamy, like other Progressives, was concerned about human and racial perfection as well. He took the view that social society could be advanced through eugenics, sterilization, and science. In his bestselling novel *Looking Backward, 2000–1887*, Edward Bellamy fantasized over "racial purification" as well as the nationalization of private property. After the book's release, at least 165 Nationalist Clubs were created to promote nationalization. The clubs grew from socialist political associations to networks which prodded the government to confiscate private property and to nationalize educational institutions. Both Bellamy and his cousin, Francis Bellamy, believed that schools should be both militarized and segregated by race.

Edward Bellamy is characterized in one of two ways. Some refer to him as a utopian socialist who advocated the militarization of labor under a centrally planned and command-based economy with all industries owned by the nation, and who believed that economic inequality would thus vanish. Other critics view him as an early national socialist. Donald F. Busky, an adjunct professor of history and political science, painted him as a fascist, writing, "Bellamy's ideas could be called state capitalism, rather than utopian socialism, since his economic ideas of nationalism had more in common with fascism than socialism."[105]

As for the rise of nationalism, Herbert Croly (1869–1930), the co-founder of the *New Republic* magazine, was a prominent and popular progressive who embraced a tougher nationalism. He referred to himself and his followers as "the new nationalists." In his book, *The Promise of American Life* (1909), Croly turned to the ideas of Alexander Hamilton, believing that stronger nationalism was an antidote to cure the relatively weak national institutions. Under this new nationalism, the army and navy would be stronger. Pacifism and non-interventionism would be shunned. Considered as one of the founders of modern social liberalism, Croly took an anti-capitalistic position and believed that only through "syndicalistic" reforms would social ills be resolved. Of course, these national reforms closely matched Mussolini's fascist policies of revolutionary and national syndicalism (trade unionism), nationalism, and the collectivist-corporate state. Croly's theories not only influenced President Teddy Roosevelt but also Franklin D. Roosevelt's New Deal polices.

Taking a cue from the *Volksgemeinschaft* (people's community) of German National Socialism, Croly defined democracy not as a government dedicated to equal rights or limited government with checks and balances, but as a government "bestowing a share of the responsibility and the benefits, derived from political economic association, upon the whole community."[106] In order to reinvigorate the country, he proposed nationalizing American democracy—a sort of "democratic nationalism."[107]

Having little sympathy for the business community, Croly sought the nationalization of large corporations, the bolstering of labor unions, and a central government adorned with almost unlimited power. Like many in the Progressive movement, he was enthralled with installing ruling elites to make quick changes to a "living constitution" that could be easily altered. To him, democracy in America had a greater role than ensuring "rights," resulting in his work being pilloried for exhibiting "totalitarian implications" and a "taint of fascism."[108]

Croly actually sought to eradicate liberal individualism and individual rights so as to create a national political community, with a strong nationalist government entrenched with welfare benefits and socialism.[109] These utopian notions, which also mimicked Edward Bellamy's theories, are now being singled out as carrying underlying tones akin to National Socialism and Italian Fascism. In fact, a number of scholars have pointed to modern-day leftism as old, recycled fascism where Mussolini would qualify as one of its major predecessors.

As might be expected, many progressive and socialist movements overran Europe with astonishing rapidity. One of the more famous was the Fabian Society founded in Britain in 1884. Not only did the Fabians promote a socialist and Keynesian economic system through gradualist and reformist means, but they turned into hardcore promoters of British imperialism as a progressive and modernizing force.[110] Their socialist goal was to re-engineer the behavior of unwitting human beings; the Fabians referred to this plan as the "Third Way," the same term used by Mussolini and Hitler to describe their strategy for the central planning of their economy. In fact, because Keynesianism was embraced by most Fabians as well as by Mussolini, it could be deduced "that a hairline separates the two collectivisms."[111]

Considering that prominent Fabians often embraced socialism, centralized statism, proletariat nationalism,[112] imperialism, and racism,[113] the American journalist and author John T. Flynn could not help but notice similarities between Fabians and fascists. Flynn wrote in 1949: "The line between fascism and Fabian socialism is very thin. Fabian socialism is the dream. Fascism is Fabian socialism plus the inevitable dictator."[114] One glaring example is the Fabian, Oswald Mosley, who not only associated with the Nazis, but founded the British Union of Fascists in 1932. His creed was typically socialist and anti-Semitic, calling for state nationalization of key industries, high tariffs, more public-works projects, and the spending of public funds to promote industrial expansion. His economic vision was to build a "Keynesian economic state, with an emphasis on deficit spending."[115] This was in sharp contrast to the Fabians' strong objections to "Gladstonian liberalism," which epitomized the classical liberal notions of individualism at home and *laissez-faire* economics of friendly, free trade internationally.

Such ideological movements as the Fabian Society were built to emasculate free societies, liberal democracy, parliamentarianism, market capitalism, and limited government. One of the early members of the Fabian Society was George Bernard Shaw (1856–1950), who hated classical liberalism and the US Constitution. In a 1931 newsreel, Shaw displayed his allegiance to unfettered government and Franklin D. Roosevelt:

> Well, I tell you again to get rid of your Constitution. But I suppose you won't do it. You have a good President and you have a bad Constitution, and the bad Constitution gets the better of the good President all the time. The end of it will be is that you might as well have an English Prime Minister.[116]

But Shaw was consumed by a darker side that underscored his socialist perspectives. He was not only hobnobbing with socialists, dictators, social democrats, and other progressives but gave glowing reviews of Hitler, Mussolini and Stalin. He was drawn to anti-democratic ideologies as well as bellicose men sporting iron nerves and "communal being" convictions. Acting like a fanboy of Hitler, Shaw wrote in 1925, "The Nazi movement is in many respects one which has my warmest sympathy."[117] Not only did he sing praises of the National Socialists, but lauded dictators in general when lecturing at the annual Fabian Society gathering in 1933.[118] Yet his undying praise for the Soviet Union was far more alarming. As for Mussolini, again Shaw praised him and suggested that *Il Duce* was forging the sort of socialist society prescribed by the Fabians.

During his ten-day visit to the Soviet Union in 1931, Shaw eagerly displayed his admiration for the "great Communist experiment." Trying to impress his hosts, Shaw was "concerned precisely with establishing himself as the grand old man of socialism who had always been a defender of the Bolshevistic Revolution and who had known and corresponded with Lenin."[119] During his VOKS-sponsored speech in Russia (June 26, 1931), Shaw belittled Western countries for not following in the Soviets' revolutionary footsteps. He even joked about the rumored torture, liquidation of undesirables, and government-directed famine.

Despite his undying words of admiration for Stalin's Soviet Union, even up to 1944, Shaw insisted that he had preceded Hitler in being a National Socialist.[120] He supported Oswald Mosley, also a Fabian, who spearheaded the British Union of Fascists (BUF) in 1932. In one infamous quote, Shaw came to the defense of both Fascism and Oswald Mosley, writing: "As a red-hot Communist I am in favour of fascism. The only drawback to Sir Oswald's movement is that it is not quite British enough."[121] In addition, Shaw declared that the Nazis, "as socialist[s], using Bolshevik doctorial tactics," had "the sympathy of Russia in spite of the rivalry of Fascism and Communism."[122] Shaw was indeed endowed with a Fascist-Marxist mindset that influenced many thinkers and writers.

With such reverence for both communism and fascism, Shaw could be categorized as a "fascist communist," although he had a habit of flip-flopping—denying what he had once supported and supporting what he had once denied. Eventually, he turned against both Hitler and Mussolini. Nevertheless, most historians agree that Shaw's praise for communism and for Stalin rarely wavered.

George Orwell took note of Shaw's *ménage à trois* with both communism and fascism in a 1946 essay, "James Burnham and the Managerial Revolution," writing:

> English writers who consider Communism and Fascism to be the same thing invariably hold that both are monstrous evils which must be fought to the death; on the other hand, any Englishman

who believes Communism and Fascism to be opposites will feel that he ought to side with one or the other... The only exception I am able to think of is Bernard Shaw, who, for some years at any rate, declared Communism and Fascism to be much the same thing, and was in favour of both of them.[123]

Eugenics, Social Darwinism, anti-Semitism, and Colonialism

Shaw suffered other social, political, and moral maladies, and he appeared to be one of the most fervent cheerleaders for state-imposed eugenics to cleanse society of the less fit. His agenda of purification was more equalitarian than racist, meaning that everyone should be subjected to chopping block of the eugenics craze. Whether one was Jewish, black, or otherwise unappealing, Shaw believed that every citizen should have the same opportunity to be exterminated by the state, if diagnosed unsuitable. In a 1931 "Paramount Sound News Exclusive" newsreel, he displayed a smug grin and announced that everybody should "come before a properly appointed board, just as he might come before the income-tax commissioners," to basically justify their existence. In the filmed interview, Shaw declared:

> I don't want to punish anybody, but there are an extraordinary number of people who I might want to kill. ... I think it would be a good thing to make everybody come before a properly appointed board just as he might come before the income tax commissioner and say every 5 years or every 7 years... just put them there and say, "Sir or madam will you be kind enough to justify your existence... if you're not producing as much as you consume or perhaps a little bit more, then clearly we cannot use the big organization of our society for the purpose of keeping you alive. Because your life does not benefit us and it can't be of very much use to yourself."[124]

Shaw's alarming words reflected an example of the modern, leftist, socialist, secret obsession with social Darwinism, which holds that the weak and unfit have no right to live at the expense of society. This is similar to the communist Khmer Rouge declaration to the general public during Pol Pot's rule: "To keep you is no benefit, to destroy you is no loss." The early eugenicists were convinced that science would engender a virtuous breed of man per "survival of the fittest." Amidst this backdrop, the human race would be altered through sterilization, abortion, or extermination, in order to eliminate the unfit, unproductive, and undesirable—methods practiced during Stalin's Soviet Union (new Soviet Man) and Hitler's Germany (new Aryan Man). These Holocaust and Holodomor episodes were either race- or class-based eradications, imposed on society by those who believed that only an antidemocratic state had the will power to instill "equality of outcome." And yet, the irony of ironies is that socialist eugenicists would regard the state-mandated killings of millions of so-called "unfit" lives as a mere statistic in their quest to forge the new utopian man. Nevertheless, if one so-called unfit life was ended by natural causes, through coldness or hunger, socialist eugenicists would instead regard the loss as a horrendous tragedy perpetrated by reactionary and capitalistic forces.

A few years after proclaiming that government officials should decide who lives and dies, Shaw espoused another chilling remark in an effort to discover better-performing exterminations. Shaw suggested that scientists should invent a "humane gas" to kill people. He declared in 1934: "I appeal to the chemists to discover a humane gas that will kill instantly and painlessly. In short, a gentlemanly gas—deadly by all means, but humane not cruel."[125]

Actually, Shaw did not have to wait long. The Nazi government eventually developed a system to speed up the process of murdering enemy-of-the-state Jews, the ungovernable, and undesirables, with the use of lethal gas (Zyklon B) and death chambers. Nonetheless, it can be argued that Shaw meant gassing only convicted criminals, but under Shaw's utopian socialist world, criminal convictions by the state could include almost any human activity. Just examine Shaw's rather authoritarian and slavish approach towards imposing his socialist and welfarism agenda on the public. In *The Intelligent Woman's Guide: To Socialism, Capitalism, Sovietism and Fascism*, Shaw wrote: "Under Socialism, you would not be allowed to be poor. You would be forcibly fed, clothed, lodged, taught, and employed whether you liked it or not...”[126]

So, if recalcitrant citizens disobeyed Shaw's socialism-based laws, they would be classified as lawbreakers so might become likely candidates to be “executed in a kindly manner.” Isn't this what happened to the Jews in Germany? They broke the Nazi law of being Jewish. The state acquired the authority to turn anyone into a criminal, whether to punish or eradicate those of different cultural, religious, or political standpoints. In truth, nobody is safe from a dogmatic regime wielding the power of involuntary servitude and the executioner's axe. In fact, they were no safer than during the “Reign of Terror” of Robespierre, who attempted to establish a virtuous society via guillotine executions. What progressives and socialists have failed to understand is that any inhumane act can be justified by political ideologues who believe they have been anointed to impose their value system upon others. This is why Shaw praised eugenics as the means by which the state could get rid of unwanted people. He blatantly spread this social Darwinian message to the political, socialist, and Fabian intelligentsia, lecturing to eugenicists that

> A part of eugenic politics would finally land us in an extensive use of the lethal chamber. A great many people would have to be put out of existence simply because it wastes other people's time to look after them.[127]

Besides fervid support for state-imposed eugenics, Shaw had a few issues with Jews. In a letter to sociologist Beatrice Webb, he managed to combine both eugenics and the Final Solution involving apparently unfit Jews. He wrote: “I think we ought to tackle the Jewish Question by admitting the right of the States to make eugenic experiments by weeding out any strains they think undesirable. ...”[128] Shaw even instructed Hitler as to what he should do about the Jews, stating:

> What Hitler should have done was not to drive the Jews out, what he ought to have said was, “I will tolerate the Jews to any extent on condition that no Jew marries a Jewess, on condition that he marries a German.”[129]

This was exactly the same eugenic policy that the Soviet Union used in their attempt to gradually snuff out the Jewish race, language and culture.

Shaw also demonstrated a strong Eurocentric bias against African tribes in Ethiopia, declaring that Italy had the right to spread civilization through Western colonization. Enthralled with Mussolini's bold adventurism in foreign policy, Shaw backed Mussolini's brutal invasion of Ethiopia in 1935. Not only did he support the Italy's invasion, but clearly stated that it must involve violence and "even the extermination of the uncivilized."[130] In an article in the *Times* of London, Shaw revealed his true imperialistic traits, portraying the struggle as a battle between the Danakil tribesmen and the civilizing effect of Italian engineers who would bring about modern trade and communications. Another example of his Eurocentric preference appeared in the *Times and Tide*. Shaw wrote: "The Italians must allow us to slaughter the Momands, because, if we do not kill the warlike hillmen, they will kill us. And we must allow the Italians to slaughter the Danakils for the same reason."[131]

Actually, there were many other intellectuals who heralded various socialist ideologies or bouts of racism, anti-Semitism, and social Darwinism. Some, like progressive Margaret Sanger, whose birth-control organization evolved into Planned Parenthood, had issues with blacks. Considered as a proponent of negative eugenics, Sanger penned: "We do not want word to go out that we want to exterminate the Negro population and the minister is the man who can straighten out that idea if it ever occurs to any of their more rebellious members."[132] She claimed that eugenics would "assist the race toward the elimination of the unfit."[133]

Even economist John Maynard Keynes, a favorite of Mussolini, found Jews to be unpalatable, although he had Jewish friends. He stated: "It is not agreeable to see a civilization so under the thumbs of its impure Jews who have all the money and the power and the brains. ..."[134] As for Hitler, by the early 1930s, Nazi economists were developing policies paralleling Keynesianism, determined to incur "large budget deficits, public works programs and easy credit."[135] In fact, the economist John Kenneth Galbraith, argued in his 1977 book *The Age of Uncertainty* that Hitler "was the true protagonist of the Keynesian ideas."

Another candidate was H.G. Wells, who also seemed to exhibit many of these traits. A Fabian Society member, Wells in 1932 urged the University of Oxford Young Liberals that progressive leaders should transform themselves into "Liberal *fascisti*" and "enlightened Nazis."[136] Wells took the position that the old classical liberalism that embraced individualism was too weak to work in the collectivistic age.

Interestingly, the economic policies of Mussolini and Hitler are almost indistinguishable from the modern liberalism currently found in England, Canada, and the United States. When H.G. Wells spoke favorably of "liberal fascism," he was referring not to the original liberalism of John Locke, but to the bastardized progressive version of modern social liberalism that had been hijacked by statist philosophers looking for a better way to sell their autocratic snake oil. But for H.G. Wells and his socialist colleagues, fascism had become the new socialist movement on the block.

Discouraged, H.G. Wells eventually left the Fabian Society, saying that it was not radical enough. Idealizing Lenin as a forceful leader, Wells also offered kind words for Stalin, whom he interviewed in 1934, telling the Soviet dictator that "I am more to the Left than you, Mr. Stalin."[137] In that interview, Wells debated with Stalin over the merits of reformist socialism versus Marxism-Leninism. Later, in his 1934 book, *Experiment in Autobiography*, Wells gave particular praise for Stalin:

> I have never met a man more candid, fair and honest, and to these qualities it is, and to nothing occult and sinister, that he owes his tremendous undisputed ascendancy in Russia.[138]

Wells also nurtured an anti-Semitism streak. Some scholars overlook this shortcoming, because "Wells belonged to a different anti-Semitic tradition: not of the nationalist right but of the progressive left."[139] Wells blamed the Jews for inventing nationalism via Zionism, and stubbornly clinging to their "parochial identity." The Bolsheviks were also opposed to the independent-minded Jewish culture. Starting in 1918, Soviet leadership established a Jewish section under Communist Russia's Information and Propaganda Department to decimate the Jewish language and culture, known as "*Yevsektsiya*." The Bolsheviks' stated mission was the "destruction of traditional Jewish life, the Zionist movement, and Hebrew culture."[140]

According to David Lodge, author of *A Man of Parts*, Wells saw Nazism as merely an "inverted Judaism." Incredibly, Wells had the audacity to blame the rise of Hitlerism on the "Jewish refusal to assimilate."[141] In his 1939 book *The Fate of Homo Sapiens*, Wells criticizes the worldwide Jewish influence as an "aggressive and vindictive conspiracy."[142]

Considering that a slew of well-known left-wing socialist and progressive stalwarts defended imperialism, antidemocratic movements, Italian fascism, enlightened Nazism, white supremacy, anti-Semitism, social Darwinism, Eurocentric racism, and eugenics policies to purify unfit and inferior individuals, one would naturally expect that this motley crew permeated right-wing extremism. However, history recorded it much differently, identifying them as card-carrying leftists with socialist and progressive credentials. So, the question begs the answer: how can political scientists and historians distinguish the left from the right? If George Bernard Shaw shared most of the same opinions held by Hitler, Mussolini, and Stalin, why is he classified as an apostle of the socialist Left? What about the numerous Marxists and communist leaders, such as Nicola Bombacci, who simultaneously supported Mussolini's Fascism and Stalin's Communism? That would make them Fascist-Marxists. So, are they on the left or right side of the aisle? And who gets the license to delineate where someone's political opinions reside? Or is the left-right political spectrum simply a scheme to confuse the public, as a phony dichotomy perpetrated for some political end?

After all, left or right gradations are predicated on where someone's relative and changing positions lie. In truth, the political spectrum has meaning only in relation to another person's relative position. Political dichotomies are not absolute; they are all comparative, and each node within them exists in relation to other nodes. Left and right classifications depend upon where a person's political position stands—or rather, rests. To hardcore Marxists, everyone occupies the right side of the political spectrum, including moderate or reformist Marxists.

The Fascism and Social Justice of Father Charles Coughlin

Another famous social collectivist who hobnobbed with progressives and followed in lockstep with the socialist-slavery tradition was Father Charles Edward Coughlin (1891–1979), a left-wing populist theocrat whose favorite villains were the international bankers and capitalists. A Roman Catholic priest, Coughlin became a pioneer in radio broadcasting in the 1930s, using his weekly program to reach a mass audience of up to thirty million listeners. After having been an early supporter of Franklin D. Roosevelt's New Deal proposals, he changed his position and denounced Roosevelt for his cozy relationship with bankers and his refusals to make radical social reforms.[143]

To counter Roosevelt's refusal to support more socialistic policies, Coughlin established the National Union for Social Justice in 1934, a nationalistic workers' rights organization. His platform called for monetary reforms, the nationalization of major industries and railroads, income guarantees, a minimum annual wage, wealth redistribution by heavy taxation of the wealthy, curtailing property rights to allow for more government control of the economy, and protection of the rights of labor.[144] Coughlin proclaimed that "Capitalism is doomed and is not worth trying to save," while he simultaneously took a stand supporting a form of socialized or "state capitalism,"[145] which he thought could ensure a greater equitable distribution of goods and services—which ideologically, exhibited both Leninist-Marxist and fascist overtones.

Coughlin was a fervent anti-capitalist and socialistic leftist, who stated:

> We maintain the principle that there can be no lasting prosperity if free competition exists in industry. Therefore, it is the business of government not only to legislate for a minimum annual wage and maximum working schedule to be observed by industry, but also to curtail individualism that, if necessary, factories shall be licensed and their output shall be limited.[146]

Offering his policies as an antidote to communism, Coughlin began to sympathize with Hitler's and Mussolini's governments after America's 1936 election.[147] After claiming that Jewish bankers had financed the Russian Revolution, Coughlin began airing programs that many considered as anti-Semitic commentary. The broadcasts have been termed as "a variation of the Fascist agenda applied to American culture."[148] In 1936, he began publishing his weekly magazine, *Social Justice*, which became controversial for printing anti-Semitic polemics such as the 1903 fabricated document, *The Protocols of the Elders of Zion*.[149] One of Coughlin's articles in *Social Justice* plagiarized much of the verbiage from the September 13, 1935 speech made by Joseph Goebbels, Reich Minister of Propaganda in Nazi Germany. Whole sections of Coughlin's article had been filched from Goebbels' speech verbatim.

After the outbreak of World War II, the Roosevelt administration eventually forced the cancellation of Coughlin's radio show. Through the administration's political maneuvers, including exerting pressure on the Postmaster General and the Catholic Church, Coughlin was forbidden to disseminate his *Social Justice* newspaper—and thus his views it contained—through the post office.[150]

Obviously, Coughlin was a National Socialist sympathizer who favored social justice, radical social reforms, wealth redistribution, trade unionism, limited nationalization, restricted property rights for the public good, and anti-capitalist ideology.[151] This type of statist Left personality is pervasive within both the fascist and communist constructs. They are utopian taskmasters who don't bare their exacting fangs until it is too late. In the long run, their socioeconomic impacts devolve into the type of authoritarian socialism that emulates a plantation-life slavocracy, while simultaneously purporting to provide all the blessings of equality, liberty, and social justice.

Mussolini and other Italian Fascists also applied the term "social justice" in the 1930s and 1940s in their desire to foment social revolution. After Mussolini's Italy became a puppet government of Nazi Germany, he attempted to spend even more lavishly on elaborate social welfare programs which were "motivated by the 'moral' concern with abstract 'social justice.'"[152]

* * * * *

Interestingly, my first encounter with the debate over benign slavery versus rugged individualism was as a teenager, while watching an episode from the original 1966 "Star Trek" television series. I was impressed with "The Menagerie, Part II," which focused on the enslavement of several starship Enterprise officers who were promised a good-but-fantasy life if they remained on the planet for the purpose of becoming a breeding stock. Captain Kirk and his officers resisted. Eventually, one of the female officers threatened to kill herself by detonating a phaser if they were not released. The dumbfounded alien, a Talosian magistrate, exclaimed: "The customs and history of your race show a unique hatred of captivity; even when it's pleasant and benevolent, you prefer death!" That was the episode's core message. Death is preferable to a paradise without liberty. It was no secret that Gene Roddenberry, the creator of "Star Trek," had been heavily influenced by the individualistic philosophy of novelist and philosopher Ayn Rand. Roddenberry once remarked: "I read *The Fountainhead* four or five times, *Atlas Shrugged*, but also some of her nonfiction..."[153] Libertarians and science fiction have always had a close relationship, especially when the writer delves into dystopian societies.

In sharp contrast, as mentioned before, William Lloyd Garrison, the classical liberal abolitionist and voluntaryist, was the key proponent of self-ownership. A co-founder of the American Anti-Slavery Society, Garrison fought slavery by advocating for the sovereignty of the individual. He and many abolitionists asserted that the involuntary servitude of men was "theft on a grand scale because the slaveowner expropriated from the slave that which was properly his own—namely his body, labor and their fruits."[154] In fact, President Lincoln made this connection between theft and slavery in many of his anti-slavery speeches—regarding slavery as theft. According to the American historian Eric Foner, "Essentially what Lincoln said is slavery is a form of theft, the theft of labor, one person stealing another person's labor without that person's permission."[155] This point cannot be overstated. Broken down to its simplest core element, autocratic socialism is based on the "sanctity of theft," whereby societal elites are licensed to steal anything from anybody and then redistribute the loot to the politically deserving. Nothing is private, nothing can be owned by individuals, nobody owns themselves, and all things are controlled and owned by the politically powerful. Collectivized theft and aggression is the perfection of a slave state.

A state of thievocracy is promoted because it permits politically connected taskmasters to redirect wealth to those deemed worthier by the state. In this sense, slavery is the socialization of labor and property, imposed to make the populace subservient to an institutionalized authority that often preaches equalitarianism and altruism but practices a slavery-enriched militarism. To the far statist Left and their slavocracy comrades, individuals have no ownership rights—so humans can be beasts of burden or simply be exterminated in cleansing bouts of genocide. Many leaders of the Democratic Party are still tied to this slavocracy-socialist tradition as a means to steal wages and assets from the citizenry as well as corrode free speech, due process and the presumption of innocence.

Collectivists have employed ideology, illusions, metaphors, and sweet-sounding jargon to mask the ugly face of control, supremacism, and enslavement. They are determined to become both the caretakers and gravediggers of society, consumed by ignoble, anti-liberal, and socialist chicanery to transfer people's wealth and energy to taskmasters of a plantocracy. This is the dismal history of dictatorial socialism, steeped in the *Volksgemeinschaft* of bondage and kleptomania, which inevitably culminates in the tyranny of the politically privileged, crony fat cats, and socialist party elites.

The old parable about trapping wild pigs in the forest is prophetic. To capture and control the wild and free, one needs only to lay out a spread of free food while secretly constructing a sturdy fence around the perimeter. Every day, as the animals munch on freebies, the fence's length expands until it has surrounded the oblivious victims. Once the trap is sprung, it is the trapper who feasts on the foolish. This anecdote illustrates how coercive socialism works to enslave a populace through perennial promises of "free stuff." Yet, as an economic principle asserts, it is almost impossible to get something for nothing. Nothing is actually free; everything has its cost. The price may be hidden, but someone must pay the final bill at the checkout counter. Someone must give up something. That someone is usually the general public, who are often duped into swapping their very right to live free for an allegedly costless buffet of social provisions.

Notes

[1] Karl Marx to Pavel Vasilyevich Annenkov, (Letter, Dec. 28, 1846.) Published in *Marx/Engels Collected Works Vol. 38*, International Publishers, 1975, p. 95.

[2] Friedrich Engels, "Progress of Social Reform on the Continent," first published in *The New Moral World*, 3rd Series, Nos. 19, Nov. 4, 1843.

[3] This is my coinage for defining collective enslavement.

[4] Friedrich Engels, "On Authority," written in 1872, first published 1874 in the Italian, *Almanacco Republicano*. Also published in Robert C. Tucker, ed., *The Marx-Engels Reader*, second ed. (New York, NY: W.W. Norton and Co., 1978), pp. 730–733. First edition was published in 1972.

[5] Jarrett Stepman, "'The Very Best Form of Socialism': The Pro-Slavery Roots of the Modern Left," *Breitbart.com*, Aug. 6, 2013. https://www.breitbart.com/politics/2013/08/06/the-pro-slavery-roots-of-the-modern-left/.

[6] William C. Davis, *Brother Against Brother: The War Begins*, vol. 1, The Civil War (New York, NY: Time-Life Books, 1983), p. 40. Quote from 1838.

[7] John C. Calhoun, "Disquisition on Government," 1840.

[8] Eugene D. Genovese, *The Southern Tradition: The Achievement and Limitations of an American Conservatism* (President and Fellows of Harvard College, 1994), p. 53.

[9] William Lloyd Garrison, "No Compromise with the Evil of Slavery," 1854 essay.

[10] John Locke's quote on self-ownership, "yet every Man has a Property in his own Person. Thus no Body has any Right to but himself." *Second Treatise of Government*, Ch. V, sec. 27.

[11] Daniel Walker Howe, *What Hath God Wrought* (Oxford University Press, 2007), p. 4.

[12] Robert V. Remini, *The Life of Andrew Jackson* (Harper Perennial, 2011), p. 307.

[13] John C. Calhoun, *A Disquisition on Government* was written in 1849 after six years of writing. This essay was published posthumously in 1851, Charleston, South Carolina, Press of Walker and James.

[14] Thomas L. Krannawitter, *Vindicating Lincoln: Defending the Politics of Our Greatest President* (Lanham, MD: Rowman & Littlefield Publishers, 2010), p. 297.

[15] Erin R. Mulligan, "Paternalism and the Southern Hierarchy: How Slaves Defined Antebellum Southern Women," Armstrong Undergraduate *Journal of History* 2, No. 2, Aug. 2012.

[16] Jeffrey Lord, "The Democrats' Missing History," *Wall Street Journal*, Aug. 13, 2008. https://www.wsj.com/articles/SB121856786326834083.

[17] Eric Foner, *A Short History of Reconstruction* (New York, NY: Harper & Row Publishers, Inc., 1990), p. 184.

[18] Allen W. Trelease, introduction to *White Terror: The Ku Klux Klan Conspiracy and Southern Reconstruction* (Praeger, 1979), p. xlvii.

[19] Barbara Chai, "Love Your Gun? Thank the Black Panthers, Says New Book,"

Wall Street Journal, Sept. 21, 2011. https://blogs.wsj.com/speakeasy/2011/09/21/love-your-gun-thank-the-black-panthers-says-new-book/.

[20] Charles M. Blow, "Gun Control and White Terror," *New York Times*, Jan. 7, 2016. https://www.nytimes.com/2016/01/07/opinion/gun-control-and-white-terror.html.

[21] Ida B. Wells, "Self Help," chap. VI in *Southern Horrors: Lynch Law in All Its Phases*, 1892.

[22] Gary Kleck, *Point Blank: Guns and Violence in America* (Aldine Transaction Publishers, 2009), p. 5. Robert Farago, "Gun Rights Are Racist," *Atlantic* magazine, Oct. 1, 2015. https://www.thetruthaboutguns.com/2015/10/robert-farago/atlantic-magazine-gun-rights-are-racist/.

[23] Adolf Hitler, *Hitler's Table Talk, 1941–44: His Private Conversations*, ed. Hugh Trevor-Roper, trans. Norman Cameron and R.H. Stevens, 2nd ed. (London, UK: Weidenfeld and Nicolson, 1973), pp. 425–426, dinner talk on Apr. 11, 1942.

[24] Robert J. Cottrol and Raymond T. Diamond, *The Second Amendment: Toward an Afro-Americanist Reconsideration*, 1991, p. 345n178.

[25] Fitzhugh, *Sociology for the South*, first quote pp. 27–28, second quote p. 42.

[26] Mason I. Lowance Jr., ed., *A House Divided: The Antebellum Slavery Debates 1776–1865* (Princeton, NJ: Princeton University Press, 2003), p. 130.

[27] Fitzhugh, *Sociology for the South*, p. 72.

[28] Ibid., p. 246.

[29] Ibid., p. 233.

[30] Ibid., p. 179.

[31] Fitzhugh, *Cannibals All!*, p. 303.

[32] Ibid., p. 324.

[33] Ibid., Preface, p. ix.

[34] C. Vann Woodward, "A Southern War Against Capitalism," in *American Counterpoint: Slavery and Racism in the North-South Dialogue* (Boston, MA: Little, Brown and Company, 1964), pp. 107–139.

[35] Fitzhugh, *Cannibals All!*, p. 102.

[36] Ibid., p. 278.

[37] Sidney Blumenthal, "How Abraham Lincoln Found his Anti-Slavery Voice," *Newsweek* magazine, May 20, 2017.

[38] J. Watson Webb, *Speech of General J. Watson Webb, at the Great Mass Meeting on the Battle Ground of Tippecanoe, 60,000 Freeman in Council*, 3rd ed. (New York, NY, 1856), p. 57.

[39] Wolfgang Schivelbusch, *The Culture of Defeat: On National Trauma, Mourning, and Recovery* (New York, NY: Picador: A Metropolitan Book, 2004), p. 45.

[40] Ibid., p. 44.

[41] Stephen M. Feldman, *Free Expression and Democracy in America: A History* (University of Chicago Press, 2008), p. 145.

[42] Barack Obama, *Dreams from My Father: A Story of Race and Inheritance* (New York, NY: Times Books, 1995), p. 147.

[43] George Brown Tindall, *America: A Narrative History*, 2nd ed., vol. 1 (New York, NY: W.W. Norton & Co., 1988), pp. 595–596.

[44] Henry Hughes, *A Treatise on Sociology, the Theoretical and Practical* (Philadelphia, PA: Lippincott, Grambo, 1854), p. 287.

[45] Vladimir Lenin, *The State and Revolution* (Chicago, IL: Haymarket Books, 2014), p. 132. First published in 1917.

[46] Jeffrey P. Sklansky, *The Soul's Economy: Market Society and Selfhood in American Thought, 1820–1920* (Chapel Hill, NC: University of North Carolina Press, 2002), pp. 95–103.

[47] Henry Hughes, *A Treatise on Sociology, the Theoretical and Practical* (Philadelphia, PA: Lippincott, Grambo, 1854), pp. 169–170.

[48] William H. Freehling, *The Road to Disunion, Volume II: Secessionists Triumphant, 1854–1861* (Oxford University Press, 2007), p. 52.

[49] Stanford M. Lyman and Arthur J. Vidich, eds., *Selected Works of Herbert Blumer: A Public Philosophy for Mass Society* (Champaign, IL: University of Illinois Press, 2000), pp. 14–19.

[50] Jarrett Stepman, "'The Very Best Form of Socialism': The Pro-Slavery Roots of the Modern Left," *Breitbart.com*, Aug. 6, 2013.

[51] Stanford M. Lyman and Arthur J. Vidich, eds., *Selected Works of Herbert Blumer: A Public Philosophy for Mass Society* (Champaign, IL: University of Illinois Press, 2000), pp. 14–19.

[52] Lawrence W. Reed, "Hitler Didn't Snub Me – It Was Our President," *FEE* magazine, Aug. 21, 2015. https://fee.org/articles/hitler-didn-t-snub-me-it-was-our-president/.

[53] "'SNUB' FROM ROOSEVELT," *St. Joseph News-Press*, Oct. 16, 1936.

[54] Jeremy Schaap, *Triumph: The Untold Story of Jesse Owens and Hitler's Olympics* (New York, NY: Houghton Mifflin Harcourt, 2007), p. 211.

[55] Burton W. Folsom, *New Deal Or Raw Deal?: How FDR's Economic Legacy Has Damaged America* (Simon and Schuster, 2009), p. 210.

[56] Franklin D. Roosevelt to US Ambassador to Italy Breckinridge Long, Schivelbusch, *Three New Deals*, p. 31.

[57] Michael A. Ledeen, *Accomplice to Evil: Iran and the War Against the West* (New York, NY: St. Martin's Press, 2009), p. 33.

[58] George Rawick, "Working Class Self-Activity," *Radical America*, Vol. 3, No.2, Mar.–Apr. 1969, pp. 23–31. Rawick recounts what Francis Perkins, FDR's Secretary of Labor, told him.

[59] Antony C. Sutton, *Wall Street and FDR: The True Story of How Franklin D. Roosevelt Colluded with Corporate America* (Clairview Books, 2013), p. 170. First published 1975.

[60] Schivelbusch, *Three New Deals*, pp. 28–29.

[61] Ibid., pp. 23–24.

[62] Stuart K. Hayashi, *Hunting Down Social Darwinism: Will This Canard Go Extinct?* (Lanham, MD: Lexington Books, 2015), p. 190.

[63] Diggins, *Mussolini and Fascism*, p. 164.

[64] Schivelbusch, *Three New Deals*, p. 190.

[65] Alistair Cooke, *Alistair Cooke's America* (New York, NY: Alfred A. Knopf, Inc., 1973), p. 329.

[66] Adam Serwer, "Lyndon Johnson Was a Civil Rights Hero. But Also a Racist," *MSNBC*, Apr. 12, 2014. https://msnbc.com/msnbc/lyndon-johnson-civil-rights-racism.

[67] Ibid.

[68] Reid Pillifant, "Hillary Clinton Remembers 'Friend and Mentor' Robert Byrd," *Observer.com*, June 28, 2010. https://www.youtube.com/watch?v=p4wo9nqWrwE.

[69] Interview with Tony Snow, Mar. 4, 2001.

[70] Philip Rucker, "Donna Brazile: I considered replacing Clinton with Biden as 2016 Democratic nominee," *Washington Post*, Nov. 4, 2017. https://www.washingtonpost.com/politics/brazile-i-considered-replacing-clinton-with-biden-as-2016-democratic-nominee/2017/11/04/f0b75418-bf4c-11e7-97d9-bdab5a0ab381_story.html.

[71] George Kateb, "On Patriotism," *Cato Unbound*, Mar. 10, 2008. https://www.cato-unbound.org/2008/03/10/george-kateb/patriotism.

[72] Erin R. Mulligan, "Paternalism and the Southern Hierarchy: How Slaves Defined Antebellum Southern Women," Armstrong Undergraduate *Journal of History* 2, No. 2, Aug. 2012.

[73] "It Takes A Village Idiot to Say Kids Belong to State," editorial, *Investor's Business Daily*, Apr. 9, 2013. https://www.investors.com/politics/editorials/msnbc-host-says-children-belong-to-state/.

[74] Adolf Hitler, on Public Education, speech on Nov. 6, 1933. William L. Shirer, *The Rise of the Third Reich: A History of Nazi Germany* (Simon & Schuster, 2011), p. 249.

[75] SPLC website, https://splcenter.org/fighting-hate/extremist-files/individual/louis-farrakhan.

[76] "Farrakhan Again Describes Hitler as a 'Very Great Man,'" *New York Times*, July 17, 1984; broadcast of speech on a Chicago radio station, Mar. 11, 1984.

[77] Sophie Tatum, "The Nation of Islam leader Farrakhan delivers anti-Semitic speech," *CNN Politics*, Mar. 1, 2018.

[78] Charles Bierbauer, "Its goal more widely accepted than its leader," CNN, Oct. 17, 1995, Farrakhan told Reuters Television in an interview recorded on Oct. 4, 1995.

[79] Jonah Engel Bromwich, "Why Louis Farrakhan Is Back in the News," *New York Times*, Mar. 9, 2018.

[80] Chuck Ross, "Louis Farrakhan Shares Details of Private Meeting with Obama [VIDEO]," *The Daily Caller*, Nov. 10, 2016. https://dailycaller.com/2016/11/10/louis-farrakhan-shares-details-of-private-meeting-with-obama-video/.

[81] Ibid.

[82] Briahna Joy Gray, "On the Dangers of Following Louis Farrakhan," *Rolling Stone*, Mar. 13, 2018. https://www.rollingstone.com/politics/politics-news/on-the-dangers-of-following-louis-farrakhan-2-197347/.

[83]Jarrett Stepman, "'The Very Best Form of Socialism': The Pro-Slavery Roots of the Modern Left," *Breitbart.com*, Aug. 6, 2013.

[84]William Leuchtenburg, "Progressivism and Imperialism: The Progressive Movement and American Foreign Policy, 1898–1916," *The Mississippi Valley Historical Review* 39, no. 3 (Dec. 1952): pp. 483–485.

[85]Damon Root, "When Bigots Become Reformers: The Progressive Era's shameful record on race," *Reason* magazine, May 2006. https://reason.com/archives/2006/05/05/when-bigots-become-reformers/.

[86]Tsahai Tafari, "The Rise and Fall of Jim Crow," the series material for the PBS four-part TV documentary, 2002.

[87]Woodrow Wilson quotation in the 1915 film *The Birth of a Nation*. Originally from Wilson's *A History of the American People*, Volume 9, (New York and London: Harper & Brothers Publishers, 1918), p. 60, first published in 1902.

[88]W.E.B. Du Bois, "Another Open Letter to Woodrow Wilson," Sept. 1913.

[89]Ronald J. Pestritto, *Woodrow Wilson and the Roots of Modern Liberalism* (Rowman & Littlefield Publishers, Inc., 2005), p. 45.

[90]Wilson's argument in defending the re-segregation of federal offices during a conference with members of the National Association for Equal Rights, Nov. 1914. William R. Keylor, "Should we scrub all memorials to Woodrow Wilson?" *CNN*, Nov. 20, 2015.

[91]"The Case Against Woodrow Wilson," *New York Times*, editorial opinion, Nov. 24, 2015, p. A30.

[92]Ibid.

[93]Woodrow Wilson, "Socialism and Democracy," essay first published, Aug. 22, 1887. Reproduced in Arthur S. Link, ed., *The Papers of Woodrow Wilson*, vol. 5 (Princeton University Press, 1968), pp. 559–562.

[94]Woodrow Wilson, *Constitutional Government in the United States* (New York, NY: Columbia University Press, 1908), p. 16.

[95]Woodrow Wilson, "The Author and Signers of the Declaration," July 1907, *The Papers of Woodrow Wilson (PWW)*, 17:251.

[96]John Milton Cooper, *Woodrow Wilson: A Biography* (New York, NY: Vintage, 2009), p. 213.

[97]Jennifer Schuessler, "Woodrow Wilson's Legacy Gets Complicated," *New York Times*, Nov. 29, 2015. https://nytimes.com/2015/11/30/arts/woodrow-wilsons-legacy-gets-complicated.html.

[98]Ibid.

[99]Adam Kirsch, "Utopian Pessimist: The Works, World View, and Women of H.G. Wells," *The New Yorker*, Oct. 17, 2011. https://www.newyorker.com/magazine/2011/10/17/utopian-pessimist.

[100]Ibid.

[101]Ibid.

[102]"Literature: A Modern Utopia," book review of *Anticipations, The Athenæum* publication, No. 4044, Apr. 29, 1905, p. 519.

[103] Watson, *The Lost Literature of Socialism*, pp. 78–79.

[104] Michael Sherborne, *H.G. Wells: Another Kind of Life* (London/Chicago: Peter Owen, 2010), p. 150.

[105] Donald F. Busky, *Communism in History and Theory: From Utopian Socialism to the Fall of the Soviet Union* (Westport, CT: Praeger Publishers, 2002), pp. 99–100.

[106] Herbert Croly, *The Promise of American Life* (New York, NY: The Macmillan Company, 1911), p. 194.

[107] Charles Forcey, *The Crossroads of Liberalism: Croly, Weyl, Lippmann, and the Progressive Era, 1900–1925* (New York, NY: Oxford University Press, 1961), p. 37.

[108] Ibid.

[109] David K. Nichols, "The promise of progressivism: Herbert Croly and the progressive rejection of individual rights," 1987, Oxford University Press, *Publius*, Vol. 17, No. 2, Spring 1987, pp. 27–39.

[110] Richard B. Day and Daniel Gaido, trans., *Discovering Imperialism: Social Democracy to World War I* (Historical Materialism Book, 2011), p. 249.

[111] Zygmund Dobbs, "Fascism—Keynesianism—Socialism," chap. VII in *Keynes at Harvard: Economic Deception as a Political Credo* (Probe Research, Inc., 1969). Dobbs was reared in a communist family, became an active Trotskyite, then abandoned his earlier convictions to actively oppose communism.

[112] Alberto Spektorowski and Liza Ireni-Saban, *Politics of Eugenics: Productionism, Population, and National Welfare (Extremism and Democracy)* (New York, NY: Routledge, 2013), p. 45.

[113] Jonathan Schneer, *London 1900: The Imperial Metropolis, New Haven and London* (Yale University Press, 2001), p. 169.

[114] John T. Flynn, *The Road Ahead: America's Creeping Revolution* (The Devin-Adair Company, 1949), p. 149.

[115] Bret Rubin, "The Rise and Fall of British Fascism: Sir Oswald Mosley and the British Union of Fascists," *Intersections*, (*Journal of the Comparative History of Ideas*), University of Washington, Seattle, Vol. 11, No. 2, Autumn 2010, pp. 323–380. https://depts.washington.edu/chid/intersections_Autumn_2010/Rubin.html.

[116] Various Scenes with George Bernard Shaw, 1933, Fox Movietone Newsreel, Clip at: https://www.youtube.com/watch?v=a0Pk0NUiw2o.

[117] *London Morning Post*, Dec. 3, 1925.

[118] "Shaw Praises Hitler as Able Statesman; But Chancellor Erred, He Says, by Not Urging Intermarriage With Jews," *New York Times*, Nov. 24, 1933.

[119] Michael David-Fox, *Showcasing the Great Experiment* (Oxford University Press, 2012), p. 213.

[120] Leslie Evans, "George Bernard Shaw: Can His Reputation Survive His Dark Side?" *Boryana Books*, Feb. 1, 2012. http://boryanabooks.com/?p=1042.

[121] Griffith, *Socialism and Superior Brains*, p. 264. Original source: "The Blackshirt Challenge," *The News Chronicle*, Jan. 17, 1934.

[122] Ibid., p. 266. Original source: "Shaw sees America as Speech of Future," *New York Times*, Apr. 4, 1933.

[123] George Orwell, "Second Thoughts on James Burnham," *Polemic* No. 3, May 1946. It appeared in various essay collections, as "James Burnham and the Managerial Revolution," starting in the summer of 1946. The last section of his quotes comes from footnote 3.

[124] "George Bernard Shaw reopens capital punishment controversy," Paramount British Pictures, Mar. 5, 1931. https://www.youtube.com/watch?v=FQXAqP6ReqY.

[125] George Bernard Shaw, *The Listener*, Feb. 7, 1934.

[126] George Bernard Shaw, *The Intelligent Woman's Guide: To Socialism and Capitalism* (New York, NY: Brentano, 1928), p. 670. Book title was changed by Shaw in the 1930s to *The Intelligent Woman's Guide to Socialism, Capitalism, Sovietism, and Fascism*.

[127] Bernard Shaw's Lecture to the London's Eugenics Education Society, reported in *The Daily Express*, Mar. 4, 1910. Evelyn Cobley, *Modernism and the Culture of Efficiency: Ideology and Fiction* (University of Toronto Press, 2009), p. 159.

[128] Shaw's correspondence to English sociologist Beatrice Webb, Feb. 6, 1938. Bryan Cheyette, *Construction of 'the Jew' in English Literature and Society: Racial Representation 1875–1945* (Cambridge University Press, 1993), p. 115.

[129] "Shaw Heaps Praise upon the Dictators: While Parliaments Get Nowhere, He Says, Mussolini and Stalin Do Things," *New York Times*, Dec. 10, 1933, from Shaw's lecture before the Fabian Society in London called "The Politics of Unpolitical Animals," Nov. 23, 1933.

[130] Griffith, *Socialism and Superior Brains*, p. 267.

[131] Ibid.

[132] Commenting on the 'Negro Project' in a letter to Dr. Clarence Gamble, Dec. 10, 1939. Sanger manuscripts, Sophia Smith Collection, Smith College, Northampton, Massachusetts. Also described in Linda Gordon, *Woman's Body, Woman's Right: A Social History of Birth Control in America* (New York, NY: Grossman Publishers, 1976).

[133] Margaret Sanger, "Birth Control and Racial Betterment," *The Birth Control Review*, Feb. 1919 (New York, NY), p. 11.

[134] John Maynard Keynes, *The Collected Writings of John Maynard Keynes*, vol. 10 (Royal Economic Society/Cambridge University Press, 2010), p. 383. Notes after a meeting with Albert Einstein in 1926. First published 1933.

[135] Bruce Bartlett, "Hitler and Keynes," *Townhall.com*, Jan. 16, 2004. https://townhall.com/columnists/brucebartlett/2004/01/16/hitler-and-keynes-n1357780.

[136] Mark Mazower, *Dark Continent: Europe's Twentieth Century*, new ed. (New York, NY: Penguin Group, 1999), p. 23.

[137] H.G. Wells: "It seems to me that I am more to the Left than you, Mr. Stalin," *New Statesman*, Oct. 27, 1934.

[138] H.G. Wells, *Experiment in Autobiography: Discoveries and Conclusions of a Very Ordinary Brain* (Victor Gollancz LTD., 1934), p. 806.

[139] Adam Kirsch, "Utopian Pessimist: The Works, World View, and Women of H.G. Wells," *The New Yorker*, Oct. 17, 2011.

[140] Pipes, *Russia Under the Bolshevik Regime*, p. 363. Original source: Nora Levin, *The Jews in the Soviet Union since 1917* (New York, NY: NYU Press, 1988), p. 57.

[141] Robert S. Wistrich, *From Ambivalence to Betrayal: The Left, the Jews, and Israel* (University of Nebraska Press, 2012), p. 539.

[142] H.G. Wells, *The Fate of Homo Sapiens* (London, UK: Secker and Warburg, 1939), p. 128.

[143] "President Roosevelt and Social Justice!" speech on Jan. 6, 1935. Posted on "Social Security History: Father Charles E. Coughlin," US Social Security Administration. http://www.ssa.gov/history/cough.html.

[144] Alan Brinkley, *Voices of Protest: Huey Long, Father Coughlin, and the Great Depression* (New York, NY: Knopf Publishing Group, 1982), pp. 287–288. Brinkley's source was the Principles of the National Union for Social Justice.

[145] Chip Berlet and Matthew Nemiroff Lyons, *Right-Wing Populism in America: Too Close for Comfort* (New York, NY: The Guilford Press, 2000), p. 140.

[146] Charles A. Beard and George H.E. Smith, eds., *Current Problems of Public Policy: A Collection of Materials* (New York, NY: The Macmillan Company, 1936), p. 54.

[147] Sheldon Marcus, *Father Coughlin: The Tumultuous Life of the Priest of the Little Flower* (Boston, MA: Little, Brown and Co., 1972), pp. 189–190.

[148] Lawrence DiStasi, ed., *Una Storia Segreta: The Secret History of Italian American Evacuation and Internment During World War II* (Heyday Books, 2001), p. 163.

[149] "The Protocols of the Elders of Zion" was an anti-Semitic canard that was determined to be a hoax by the *Times* of London in 1921. First published in Russian in 1903, it purported that a Jewish conspiracy would achieve global domination, publisher: Znamya.

[150] David B. Woolner and Richard G. Kurial, eds., *Franklin D. Roosevelt, the Vatican, and the Roman Catholic Church in America, 1933–1945* (Palgrave Macmillan, 2003), p. 275.

[151] Alan Brinkley, "Principles of the National Union for Social Justice," in *Voices of Protest: Huey Long, Father Coughlin, and the Great Depression* (New York, NY: Knopf Publishing Group, 1982), pp. 287–288.

[152] Gregor, *Italian Fascism and Developmental Dictatorship*, p. 257.

[153] Ronald E. Merrill, *Ayn Rand Explained: From Tyranny to Tea Party* (Open Court, 2013), p. 9. This book was Revised and updated by Marsha Familaro Enright. Original source: Jacqueline Lichtenberg, Sondra Marshak, and Joan Winston, *Star Trek Lives!* (Bantam Books, 1975).

[154] Ronald Hamowy, editor-in-chief, "Abolitionism," in *The Encyclopedia of Libertarianism* (London, UK: Sage Publishing, Inc., 2008), p. 1.

[155] Eric Foner quoted in "Lincoln's Nuanced View of Slavery Explained by Renowned Historian," Michelle Merlin, *The Register Citizen*, Aug. 9, 2012.

6. Past Political Commentaries

Don't Be an Accessory to Murder[1]

What would happen if someone in your vehicle pulled out a gun and shot someone in an adjacent vehicle? It's highly likely that the police would charge everyone in the vehicle with murder.

In the case of taxation, most people are putting money into the federal tax pot. A sizable portion of that money is being spent to fight a so-called preemptive-strike war in Iraq—a nation that has neither attacked nor directly threatened the sovereignty of the United States. And although it is common knowledge that thousands of innocent Iraqi citizens have died at the hands of US troops, many American citizens still support and willingly pay taxes to the US government.

According to research from Johns Hopkins University, over 100,000 innocent Iraqi citizens, mostly women and children, have died as a result of the war in Iraq. The study surveyed mortality rates in Iraq from 15 months before the war and from 18 months after the March 2003 invasion. The researchers actually visited Iraqi cities and tallied the number of deaths in many war-torn neighborhoods. Other sources have reported lower death totals, from 14,000 to 16,000.

Whether the body count is higher or lower, this collateral damage means that most US citizens paying federal taxes have blood on their hands. Applying the logic of how the law would treat a drive-by shooting situation, technically, any taxpayer paying federal taxes can be considered an accessory to murder.

Again, the war in Iraq is not a defensive war. Iraq did not threaten the United States with military action, nor did Iraq amass troops near the border of the United States for a planned attack. Iraq had no intercontinental missiles, no nuclear bombs, and no weapons of mass destruction, although the United States gave them the technology to make weapons of mass destruction (WMD) from anthrax. This means that the US government drew the first blood in the Iraq conflict. It is the aggressor, that sole gunman firing into an adjacent vehicle, killing one of its occupants. Under criminal law, anyone funding criminal activity or withholding knowledge of the criminal act can be charged as an accessory to the crime, before or after the fact.

To the libertarian, the best way to stop criminal activity is to refuse to support it financially. Without an ample supply of money coerced from citizens, the war of empire-building and its murderous consequences cannot be sustained.

As Supreme Court Justice John Marshall wrote in 1819, "The power to tax is the power to destroy." We must stop this destructive taxing and warring apparatus of the state if we wish to preserve human life and liberty.

Can Only Democrats Engage in Wars of Aggression?[2]

Can Democrats support war without getting shot down in a hail of flak by the media and progressives? That question has proven to be a thorny issue, but evidence keeps accumulating to suggest that this is indeed the case. One example surfaced in the Monterey Peninsula area of California.

As a representative of Libertarians for Peace and a member of the Peace Coalition of Monterey County, I introduced the "Give It Back" resolution in September 2011. The resolution called upon President Obama to return his Nobel Peace Prize because his foreign policies have "continued old wars and engaged in new ones." It was a simple, clear, one-sentence resolution, but few took it that way.

In the last few years, a dirty little secret behind the peace movement has emerged: there is a double standard regarding which political party can conduct foreign wars of aggression. For a number of reasons, it appears that Democratic presidents can go to war with impunity, escalate troop strength, engage in torture, rendition, illegal wiretapping, harassment of whistleblowers, and so forth, but Republican presidents cannot employ the same policies. My "Give It Back" resolution brought this controversy to the forefront.

When the resolution was first presented, a murmur of support rippled through the air. Many coalition members seemed pleased with the "Give It Back" proposal. But within days of its submission, the chairman of the Peace Coalition began to show his true colors. He objected to Obama's returning the Nobel Peace Prize, arguing that the resolution would be "demeaning" to the president and "frivolous."

Of course, nobody in the Peace Coalition would have opposed this resolution if President Bush had been the Peace Prize recipient in question. In fact, I would wager that peace movement activists would have lined up around the block to sign a petition demanding that Bush return any peace prize immediately. But do most peace activists have an unbiased eye when they are also involved in partisan politics? Do they favor "principle over party," or do they play favorites and look the other way when Obama acts like Bush on steroids? I was almost afraid to ask that question.

Having spent years in the Peace Coalition organizing dozens of peace rallies and "impeach Bush and Cheney" demonstrations, I was sure I would get a good deal of support for the resolution, even if it failed to gain the required 100 percent consensus. My feeling was that most peace activists saw beyond party policies, that it did not matter which group of politicians was behaving like warmongers. A number of them told me that principles did indeed trump party politics and that they were not beholden to the Democratic Party. Still, something was wrong, somewhere, because the participants failed to live up to their denial of party alignment.

The first roadblock erected against the resolution was a procedural maneuver. The Peace Coalition chairman refused to put the resolution on the next meeting's agenda. His excuse? That all 20 member organizations that composed the Peace Coalition had to be in attendance. This was a silly argument because the coalition had frequently passed all sorts of endorsements for rallies, speeches, and events with barely a quorum. This was a bogus requirement and frivolous objection. Finally, this conflict was resolved through the diplomatic skills of Prof. David Henderson, a Libertarians for Peace leader and a board member of the libertarian faction within the Monterey County Tea Party.

The resolution was grudgingly added to the agenda a day or so before the meeting.

And the result? Disappointing. Not a single peace organization in attendance would give the resolution a thumbs-up. There was not even a vote. Both Veterans for Peace and the Green Party immediately came out against it. The National Lawyers Guild said that they might agree to it, if some minor wording changes were made. The local Quaker organization explicitly abstained. The other peace group leaders just sat silently and watched. The resolution never had a chance.

I had heard a number of complaints that the Peace Coalition had a strong bias toward the Democratic Party, so in retrospect, I suppose I was testing whether my suspicions were correct. Since the election of President Obama, the Coalition had sponsored only three peace rallies, compared to a dozen or more during the Bush administration. Of the three antiwar rallies the coalition sponsored, two were spearheaded by Libertarians for Peace. I had to take charge of one rally when nobody else would volunteer to do it. As this lack of activity became more apparent, some of the more Libertarian peace activists began to wonder whether the Peace Coalition was actually putting party before principles. They worried that if antiwar leaders were to protest too loudly against President Obama's administration, he might lose re-election.

After my resolution failed, the chairman told me to contact each organization separately and try to convince them of my resolution's merit. I asked for a roll-call vote so as to have an official record of who favored or opposed the resolution—because so many members had remained silent. That request was denied. I had a feeling that the chairman wanted no record of who opposed the resolution, as it might someday become an embarrassment.

It was now apparent that many of the Peace Coalition members were willing to let Democratic President Obama get away with whatever pro-war policies he wanted to pursue. This bias shows, in essence, that Democrats in power are exempt from normal antiwar criticism, and that *their* wars of aggression are permissible. I wish this partisan favoritism were not true, but through their actions, these folks have demonstrated all too clearly what their words have denied.

The lack of support for the "Give It Back" resolution answered my questions. A large percentage of peace activists are indeed beholden to their partisan politics, and this is an indictment of those who *proclaim* to support the values of peace and non-violence.

Tea Party Purge: A Cause without a Rebel[3]

The Tea Party movement has reconnected the cooperation between conservatives and libertarians that harks back to their mutual opposition to FDR's big-government days. Despite that, a host of these newly-forged alliances have failed to take hold. There is an undercurrent of ill-fitting philosophies and anti-intellectual clashes that suggest freedom is not always brewing at many Tea Parties. One example of a Tea Party organization divorcing its libertarian brethren recently occurred in Monterey, California.

I helped establish a nine-member board for the Monterey County (M.C.) Tea Party after a tax-day demonstration (on April 15, 2009) that had attracted 600 sign-waving protestors. We seemed to be a perfect match made in heaven. We all agreed on a mission statement that supported smaller government, lower taxes, and the US Constitution and Bill of Rights. The libertarians wanted to include a non-interventionist plank, but, under pressure, were willing to forgo it for the sake of a peaceful alliance.

But after a successful Fourth of July Tea Party parade and Freedom Rally in Monterey, the fissures in the alliance split wide open. I was accused of belonging to too many leftist organizations. In fact, I am co-chair of the local Libertarians for Peace, which joined the 27-member Monterey County Peace Coalition to protest the wars in Iraq and Afghanistan. Libertarians for Peace is *neither* left nor right and stands only to promote peace.

Looking back, the fur first hit the fan when Monterey CodePink asked to co-sponsor the Tea Party Freedom Rally. I loved the idea of bringing together the antiwar and anti-tax crowds, but this possible alliance alarmed the conservatives. The left and right dehumanize each other daily on talk radio and cable news, so I should not have been surprised by their fierce determination to share no common ground with any leftist organization. To calm their fears, I tried to put the issue in perspective. Nationwide, CodePink follows a socialist agenda—no argument there. But the Monterey branch of CodePink has worked with libertarians on both antiwar and anti-tax issues for years. In fact, the local Monterey CodePink leader was one of the most active signature-gathers in an attempt to abolish the utility tax in the city of Seaside.

Next, I was accused of being too involved with the Libertarian Party, as though it was the Libertarians who were responsible for the financial meltdown, bailouts, and stimulus packages. To their credit, the conservative flock wanted no association with Republicans or Democrats, either, saying that both of the dominant political parties had caused our current problems. But somehow, they were upset with the M.C. Tea Party board members who also held leadership roles in the Libertarian Party. It did not seem to matter to them that libertarians were heavily involved in *starting* the Tea Party movement back in 2008, nor that the original 1773 tea partiers at Boston Harbor were libertarian (classical liberals), not Tories or conservatives.

Obviously, the Tea Party conservatives were neophytes; never before had they been involved in political activism. Some had never heard of Congressman Ron Paul. Prof. David R. Henderson, one of the libertarian MC Tea Party board members, described this curious phenomenon as "activism without ideals." I dubbed it "a cause without a rebel." In fact, as demands to purge the libertarians intensified, we got the distinct feeling that the purgers fit the category of "reactionary," because they seemed to know only what they opposed, not what they favored. Amazingly, they never pointed out any philosophical differences that they found objectionable. It was as though they were devoid of ideas, marooned with empty rhetoric and no real solutions.

One of my major "crimes" was passing out several copies of my book, *The Facets of Liberty*. This occurred at a Tea Party event billed as a "mixer." A few days later, I was told that I should have neither passed out educational material nor mixed with the crowd. The libertarians soon labeled this misnamed event the "non-mixer mixer."

In retrospect, it did not help our case when we asked these rookies embarrassing questions. We asked them why they had done nothing when President Bush bailed out the banks and auto companies, spent money like a drunken sailor, bashed civil liberties, and advanced socialized medicine with the Medicare Prescription Drug, Improvement, and Modernization Act of 2003, a program that some in Congress estimated will have a price tag of $1.2 trillion by 2016. I suppose our questioning merely rubbed their noses too deeply in their ignorance.

Whatever the reasons, the Monterey County Tea Party purged the libertarians by dissolving the entire organization. That failed to stop us. The libertarians quickly formed the Liberty Tea Party and, in an effort to set up a large tent, invited everyone to join a "more enlightened" Tea Party.

Evicting Libertarian Party Principles: The Portland Purge[4]

"Portland, we have a problem."

The July 1–2, 2006, Libertarian Party National Convention held in Portland, Oregon, is over, but the repercussions will be felt for years. A small, well-organized group of pragmatists and conservatives—the Libertarian Party (LP) Reform Caucus—attempted to oust the original heirs of the Libertarian Party.

First, the usurpers attempted to abolish the Libertarian Party pledge: "I hereby certify that I do not believe in or advocate the initiation of force as a means of achieving political or social goals." They argued that it was simply too shocking for the general public. They failed to abolish it, but barely. Next, through a parliamentary procedure, the Reform Caucus successfully gutted the platform from over 60 planks to about a dozen. Little remains, however, not even the venerable plank opposing foreign interventionism.

With typical political thinking, this small, discordant group dismisses anyone favorable to the platform as "anarchistic," predisposed to stopping any "Big Tent Libertarian" outreach ventures. Unable to abolish every plank in one full sweep, the reformers planned to recruit new LP members from the ranks of other political parties, specifically from the religious-right Constitution Party. With these people as card-carrying LP members, they hoped to finish off the remaining platform and pledge at the 2008 convention.

So, what did these reformers want? They desperately wanted to win elections. They believed that by watering down or abolishing the LP platform, the voting public would empower the Libertarian Party with greater vote totals. Whether this strategy would ever succeed is questionable. The Green Party has changed their platform to be far more acceptable to the general public, but with little electoral success. Their 2004 presidential candidate, David Cobb, received only 118,000 votes, compared with Libertarian candidate Michael Badnarik's 400,000.

So, what are the principles that they believed must go? First and foremost is the non-aggression principle, considered the main threat to an election-oriented populism. If Libertarians would simply throw away their core idea to oppose the initiation of aggression, then, like dominoes, the rest of the LP policies—on taxation, the drug war, foreign policy, and military intervention—would disappear, making the LP candidates more electable. Moreover, the LP would be free to advocate all sorts of government programs and interventions, as taxation would no longer be considered a violation of human rights. Voters would no longer fear that someone out there actually believes an individual's property does not belong to the state.

The reformers even want to "dumb down" the drug issue. One member of the Reform Caucus suggested that if they could not get rid of the drug-war plank, which survived the Portland purge, it could be watered down to "drug laws can hurt minorities and low-income citizens." This would eliminate any suggestion of the conviction that individuals have a right to drug use—but such an honest consistency might obviously frighten voters.

These reformers are attempting to make the LP more palatable to the vote-getting political mainstream. And yet, the founder of the Libertarian Party, David Nolan, has repeatedly said that he and the early founders were more interested in the educational opportunities available through a campaign for office. To them, actually winning an election was secondary.

Should the Libertarian Party base its success solely on achieving political power? Should we seek political power as the end-all? One Reform Caucus leader echoed this sentiment in arguing that the LP must "win elections at any cost," which comes close to the Machiavellian notion that the "ends justify the means." To him, libertarian principles were an impediment to greater LP election victories.

What would happen to the Libertarian Party should it attempt to fool voters about what Libertarians really believe? Would voters reward our "deceptive campaigning" by electing more of our candidates? Would diluting and hiding our message increase membership? Or would it open the floodgates to more conservative, religious-right, and pragmatic members who have little understanding of our philosophy? Furthermore, what would happen if other reformers in later years might pressure the LP to dilute our message, again, to gain an even greater share of the popular vote? Where would this erosion of principles end?

It was troubling that the Reform Caucus wanted the Libertarian Party to make a grab for more political power, as if Libertarian politicians would impose Libertarianism on the public. This has traditionally been unappealing to even moderate Libertarians. Most Libertarians run for office to decrease government power, not to increase it. They take a defensive posture. They do not run to gain power; they run to defend citizens against coercive powers, oppressive taxation, and government interference in everyone's lives. Of course, in the realm of the political elite, this is as popular as a mosquito in a nudist colony.

If Libertarians discard or hide their principles, they will have no map to guide them to where they had set out to go. They will be ideologically naked in a political world that has little regard for individual autonomy. Like clothes, principles provide a fabric with which to cover one's vulnerable parts. Without them, most people would be susceptible to the seductive, corrupting influence of a political system interested only in its own survival, at the expense of taxpayers. Any electoral victory by a non-principled, "big tent" Libertarian would be hollow and meaningless. He or she would simply become part of the systemic problem of government overreach.

True libertarians must retain unyielding principles. They can compromise on specific issues and differ on their choice of policies to make government smaller, but they must not compromise on their core belief in free choice, non-aggression, and self-ownership.

The Reform Caucus's attempt to highjack the Libertarian Party is a sad tale of a post-9/11 retreat from core principles. Without strong moral guidelines, the Libertarian Party might as well as change its name to "Conservative Party" or "Reform Party." If the Libertarian Party wishes to remain the "party of principle," it must have some.

Notes

[1] A version of this article was posted on *Antiwar.com*, Feb. 21, 2006. https://original.antiwar.com/lawrence-samuels/2006/02/21/dont-be-an-accessory-to-murder/.

[2] A version of this article was posted on *Antiwar.com*, Sept. 24, 2011. http://original.antiwar.com/lawrence-samuels/2011/09/23/can-only-democrats-engage-in-wars-of-aggression/.

[3] A version of this article was originally posted on *Hollywood Investigator* on Oct. 7, 2009.

[4] A version of this article was originally posted on *LewRockwell.com*, July 7, 2006. https://lewrockwell.com/2006/07/lk-samuels/evicting-libertarian-party-principles-theportlandpurge/.

7. Comparison Chart – Political Spectrum

I have redrawn the political spectrum into two charts. Both charts group authoritarians on one side of the political divide and the original liberals on the other. I believe this more precise interpretation will clear up the confusion.

Chart A[a], which is the original political spectrum from first stage of the French Revolution, has both Classical Liberals and Libertarians can be considered the "Free Left."

Chart B[b,c] is the result from Socialists and Marxists stealing the "Left-wing" political designation from classical liberals and condemning any opponent as "right-wing". According to Mussolini in his 1933 "Political and Social Doctrine of Fascism," Fascism was on the "Left." He had been an avowed Marxist for almost two decades.

---

[a] Both Classical Liberals and Libertarians can be considered the "Free Left."

[b] Doyle, *The Oxford History of the French Revolution*, p. 422.

[c] Mussolini wrote in his 1933 "Political and Social Doctrine of Fascism" that Fascism was on the "Left." He had been an avowed Marxist for almost two decades. Hitler was a red-armband wearing communist and later promoted "national Social Democracy" in 1919. (Weber, *Becoming Hitler*, pp. 66–67)

Chart A: Left-Right Spectrum

The original political spectrum from first stage of the French Revolution

The LEFT
(Open,
Individual Liberty)

← No Government

← Free Left

The RIGHT
(Closed,
Authoritarian)

Total Government →

| Anarchism | Libertar-ianism | Classical Liberalism* | Conser-vatism | Modern Liberalism | Social Democracy | Fascism/ National Socialism | Communism |

Chart B: Right-Left Spectrum

The result from Socialists and Marxists stealing the "Left-wing" political designation from classical liberals and condemning any opponent as "right-wing"*

**The RIGHT
(Open,
Individual Liberty)**

**The LEFT
(Closed,
Authoritarian)**

← No Government

Total Government →

				Statist Left →			
Anarchism	Libertar-ianism	Classical Liberalism	Conser-vatism	Modern Liberalism	Social Democracy	Fascism/ National Socialism**	Communism

The Comparison

This chart compares German National Socialism, Italian Fascism and Russian Sovietism with each other.

	German National Socialism (Nazi)	Italian Fascism	Russian Sovietism
Anti-bourgeois sentiment	Yes[1]	Yes[2]	Yes
Anti-capitalism	Yes[3,4,5]	Yes[6,7]	Yes
Anti-clericalism	Yes[8]	Yes[9]	Yes
Anti-individualism	Yes	Yes	Yes
Anti-Semitic	Yes	No, not until 1938	Yes[10]
Authoritarianism	Yes	Yes[11]	Yes
Banned independent unions	Yes	Yes	Yes
Banned worker strikes	Yes[12]	Yes[13]	Yes[14]
Classless society	Yes[15,16]	Yes[17]	Yes
Civil Liberties	No	No	No
Collectivism	Yes[18]	Yes[19]	Yes
Equality	Yes, in theory[20,21,22]	Partially[23]	Yes, in theory
Free trade (Protectionism known as "autarky")	Yes	Yes	Yes
Freedom of Speech	No	No	No

	German National Socialism (Nazi)	Italian Fascism	Russian Sovietism
Genocide	Yes	No	Yes
Gold standard	No	No	No
Govt. healthcare	Yes	Yes	Yes
Govt. ownership of banks	Yes[24]	Yes[25]	Yes
Govt.-provided retirement (social security)	Yes	Yes	Yes
Govt. welfare	Yes[26,27]	Yes[28]	Yes
High govt. borrowing	Yes	Yes	Yes
High spending, deficits	Yes	Yes	Yes
High taxation	Yes[29]	Yes	Complex
Imperialistic foreign policies	Yes	Yes	Yes
Internationalism	No	No	Mostly in theory[30]
Left-wing label	Somewhat[31,32,33,34]	Yes[35,36]	Yes
Mandatory trade unions	Yes[37]	Yes[38,39]	Yes[40]
Marxism	Partial[41,42,43] (Acknowledged Marxist influence)	Mostly[44] (Mussolini: an avowed Marxist for two decades)	Yes
Massive public works	Yes	Yes	Yes
Militarism	Yes	Yes	Yes

	German National Socialism (Nazi)	Italian Fascism	Russian Sovietism
Nationalism	Yes[45]	Yes	Mostly[46,47]
Nationalization	Partial[48,49] (Nationalized 500-plus companies)	Yes (Nationalized 3/4 of economy by 1939)[50]	Yes (Total Nationalization)
Opposed Gun Rights	Yes	Yes	Yes
Relatively high inflation	Yes	Yes[51]	Yes
Rent controls	Yes[52]	Yes, in later years	Yes
Roots in the French Revolution	Yes	Yes	Yes
Social engineering	Yes[53]	Yes[54]	Yes
Socialism	Yes[55,56,57]	Yes[58,59]	Yes
Social justice	Yes[60,61,62]	Yes[63,64]	Yes
State-owned education	Yes[65,66]	Yes	Yes
State rights, federalism	No[67]	No	No
Totalitarian state	Yes	Yes[68]	Yes
Wage and price controls	Yes[69,70]	Yes	Yes
Warfare state	Yes	Yes	Yes

Notes

[1] Adolf Hitler: "[W]e will do what we like with the bourgeoisie. ... We give the orders; they do what they are told. Any resistance will be broken ruthlessly." Hitler's interview with Richard Breiting, 1931, published in Calic, *Secret Conversations with Hitler*, chapter "First Interview with Hitler," p. 36.

[2] Benito Mussolini: "If the bourgeoisie," I said then, "think that they will find lightning-rods in us, they are deluding themselves;..." Mussolini, *The Political and Social Doctrine of Fascism*, p. 9.

[3] "Hitler called the bourgeois capitalist exploitative profiteers and cowardly shits." *Kritika: Explorations in Russian and Eurasian History*, Vol. 7, Issue 4, Slavica Publishers, 2006, p. 922.

[4] Adolf Hitler: "We are socialists, we are enemies of today's capitalistic economic system for the exploitation of the economically weak, ..." Toland, *Adolf Hitler: The Definitive Biography*, p. 224. Hitler's speech on May 1, 1927. Hitler plagiarized part of Gregor Strasser one-page talking-points from 1926. Gregor Strasser was the leader of the Nazi party's national organization.

[5] In an Apr. 6, 1941, statement, Hitler pinpointed the exact enemy of the Nazis. Bragging about his victorious 45-day battle against the western Allies, Hitler declared that, "It is already war history how the German Armies defeated the legions of capitalism and plutocracy." Adolf Hitler, "Adolf Hitler's Order of the Day Calling for Invasion of Yugoslavia and Greece," Berlin, (Apr. 6, 1941), *New York Times*, Apr. 7, 1941.

[6] Benito Mussolini: "This is what we propose now to the Treasury: either the property owners expropriate themselves, or we summon the masses of war veterans to march against these obstacles and overthrow them." Daniel Guerin, *Fascism and Big Business* (New York, NY: Monad Press, 1973), p. 83. First edition published in 1939. Originally from Mussolini's article in his fascist newspaper *Il Popolo d'Italia*, June 19, 1919.

[7] "Fascism and National Socialism had certain things in common: They were anticapitalist as well as anti-Communist." John Luckacs, *The Last European War: September 1939–December 1941* (New Haven and London, Yale University Press, 2001), p. 309.

[8] Adolf Hitler: "Nothing will prevent me from tearing up Christianity, root and branch. ... We are not out against a hundred-to-one different kinds of Christianity, but against Christianity itself." *The Brethren Mission Herald*, "Editorially Speaking," Dr. Louis Bauman, Vol. 6, No. 1, Jan. 1, 1944, p. 5.

[9] Benito Mussolini: "God does not exist—religion in science is an absurdity, in practice an immorality and in men a disease." "Religion: Benito a Christian?" *Time* magazine, Aug. 25, 1924.

[10] Karl Marx: "What is the worldly religion of the Jew? Huckstering. What is his worldly God? Money... Money is the jealous god of Israel, in face of which no other god may exist." Karl Marx, "On the Jewish Question," *Deutsch-Französische Jahrbücher*, Feb. 1844.

[11] Benito Mussolini: "Everything within the state, nothing outside the state, nothing against the state." Gregor, *Marxism, Fascism & Totalitarianism*, p. 268.

[12] "In [Fascist] Italy and [Nazi] Germany the official unions have been made compulsory by law, while in the United States, the workers are not legally obligated to join the company unions but may even, if they so wish, oppose them." Salvemini, *The Fate of Trade Unions Under Fascism*, p. 35.

[13] Ibid., p. 35.

[14] Lenin and Trotsky abolished the right to strike and implemented compulsory labor (mandatory overtime) that saw workers labor up to 80 hours a week. Gompers and Walling, *Out of Their Own Mouths*, p. 76.

[15] Adolf Hitler: "We want a society with neither castes nor ranks and you must not allow these ideas to grow within you!" Hitler speech in the 1935 Nazi-produced *Triumph of the Will* propaganda film.

[16] Adolf Hitler: "There are no such things as classes: they cannot be." Apr. 12, 1922, Hitler Speech, Munich.

[17] Benito Mussolini: "Fascism was not the protector of any one class, but a supreme regulator of the relations between all citizens of a state." Mussolini, *My Autobiography*, p. 280.

[18] Adolf Hitler: "Our Socialism goes far deeper. ... Why need we trouble to socialize banks and factories? We socialize human beings." Hitler, as quoted by Rauschning, *The Voice of Destruction*, pp. 191–193.

[19] Benito Mussolini: "For if the nineteenth century was the century of individualism (Liberalism always signifying individualism) it may be expected that this will be the century of collectivism, and hence the century of the State." Mussolini, *The Political and Social Doctrine of Fascism*, p. 20.

[20] Adolf Hitler: "The National Socialist State recognizes no 'classes.' But, under the political aspect, it recognizes only citizens with absolutely equal rights and equal obligations corresponding thereto." Hitler, *Mein Kampf, Vol. Two*, chap. XII, "The Trade-Union Question."

[21] "By exploiting material wealth confiscated and plundered in a racial war, Hitler's National Socialism achieved an unprecedented level of economic equality and created vast new opportunities for upward mobility for the German people." Aly, *Hitler's Beneficiaries*, 2007, pp. 7–8.

[22] Adolf Hitler: "All citizens must have equal rights and obligations." Speech by Hitler on Feb. 24, 1920, 25-point Programme of the NSDAP.

[23] Benito Mussolini: "Fascism establishes the real equality of individuals before the nation..." Mussolini, *Four Speeches on the Corporate State*, pp. 39–40. Eric Jabbari, *Pierre Laroque and the Welfare State in Postwar France* (Oxford University Press, 2012), p. 46.

[24] "There were already state-owned banks, such as the Reichs-Kredit-Gesellschaft, and the Nazis added more for particular investment in connection with the new military and economic priorities." Harold James, *The Deutsche Bank and the Nazi Eco-*

nomic War Against the Jews: The Expropriation of Jewish-Owned Property (Cambridge University Press, 2001), p. 21.

[25] "Institute for Industrial Reconstruction (IRI)" [had] "became the owner not only of the three most important Italian banks, which were clearly too big to fail, but also of the lion's share of the Italian industries." Costanza A. Russo, "Bank Nationalizations of the 1930s in Italy: The IRI Formula," *Theoretical Inquiries in Law*, Vol. 13:407, 2012, p. 408.

[26] Joseph Goebbels: "We and we alone [the Nazis] have the best social welfare measures. Everything is done for the nation..." "Our Socialism" editorial, written on Apr. 30, 1944. Victor Klemperer, *I Will Bear Witness: A Diary of the Nazi Years, 1942–1945*, vol. 2 (Random House, Inc., 2001), p. 317.

[27] "All the modern twentieth-century European dictatorships of the right, both fascist and authoritarian, were welfare states." Robert O. Paxton, "Vichy Lives! – In a way," *The New York Review of Books*, Apr. 25, 2013.

[28] "Fascist social welfare legislation compared favorably with the more advanced European nations and in some respect was more progressive." Gregor, *Italian Fascism and Developmental Dictatorship*, p. 263.

[29] German businessmen were "Buried under mountains of red tape, directed by the State as to what they could produce, how much and at what price, burdened by increasing taxation and milked by steep and never ending 'special contributions' to the party, ..." Shirer, *The Rise and Fall of the Third Reich*, p. 261.

[30] Stalin took a nationalistic position called "Socialism in One Country."

[31] Schoenbaum, *Hitler's Social Revolution*, p. 57. Hitler interview by Hanns Johst, in *Frankfurter Volksblatt*, Jan. 27, 1934. Hitler responded in the interview that Nazism did not favor any particular class, neither the left nor the right. Max Domarus, *The Essential Hitler: Speeches and Commentary* (Bolchazy-Carducci, 2007), pp. 171, 172–173.

[32] "Another source of the Nazi Party's popularity was its liberal borrowing from the intellectual tradition of the socialist left. Many of the men who would become the movement's leaders had been involved in communist and socialist circles." Aly, *Hitler's Beneficiaries*, 2007, p. 16.

[33] Joseph Goebbels: "the NSDAP [Nazi Party] is the German Left. We despise bourgeois nationalism." *Der Angriff* (*The Attack*), Dec. 6, 1931. *Der Angriff* was the official newspaper of the Nazi-Sozi party in Berlin, Germany. First published on July 4, 1927 by the Angriff Press under Joseph Goebbels.

[34] Adolf Hitler: "In our movement the two extremes come together: the Communists from the Left and the officers and students from the Right. These two have always been the most active elements, and it was the greatest crime that they used to oppose each other in street fights. ... Our party has already succeeded in uniting these two utter extremes within the ranks of our storm troops. They will form the core of the great German liberation movement, in which all without distinction will stand together when the day comes to say: The Nation arises, the storm is breaking!" Quoted from Heiden, *The Führer*.

[35]"... it may rather be expected that this will be a century of authority, a century of the Left, a century of Fascism." Mussolini, *The Political and Social Doctrine of Fascism*, p. 20. According to George Bernard Shaw, a leading member of the socialist Fabian Society, Mussolini was "farther to the Left in his political opinions than any of his socialist rivals."

[36] Applauding his domestic policies, Shaw pointed out that Mussolini was "farther to the Left in his political opinions than any of his socialist rivals." Shaw made this statement in the *Manchester Guardian* in 1927. Griffith, *Socialism and Superior Brains*, p. 253.

[37]"In [Fascist] Italy and [Nazi] Germany the official unions have been made compulsory by law, while in the United States, the workers are not legally obligated to join the company unions but may even, if they so wish, oppose them." Salvemini, *The Fate of Trade Unions Under Fascism*, p. 35.

[38] Ibid., Benito Mussolini: "I declare that henceforth capital and labor shall have equal rights and duties as brothers in the fascist family."

[39] Ibid., Mussolini started out as a revolutionary syndicalist.

[40]"Stalin government" brought "the unions under complete State control. In the 1930s the unions became organs of the State whose function was not to try to improve wages and working conditions but rather to reduce cost, keep wages down and increase production." *Russian Since 1917: Socialist Views of Bolshevik Policy*, 1948, reprints of past articles in the Socialist Party of Great Briton's journal "The Socialist Standard" (1915 to 1948), Chapter Eight: "Economic Policy and Development."

[41] Adolf Hitler: "I have learned a great deal from Marxism as I do not hesitate to admit..." Quoted by Rauschning, *The Voice of Destruction*, p. 186.

[42] Adolf Hitler: "National Socialism derives from each of the two camps the pure idea that characterizes it, national resolution from bourgeois tradition; vital, creative socialism from the teaching of Marxism." Schoenbaum, *Hitler's Social Revolution*, p. 57, Hitler interview by Hanns Johst, in *Frankfurter Volksblatt*, Jan. 27, 1934.

[43] Adolf Hitler: "What Marxism, Leninism and Stalinism failed to accomplish, we shall be in a position to achieve." Quoted from Wagener, *Hitler—Memoirs of a Confidant*, p. 149.

[44]"Mussolini told the young man of his admiration for Communism—'Fascism is the same thing' [as Communism]." Quoted in Arthur M. Schlesinger Jr., *The Politics of Upheaval: 1935–1936 (The Age of Roosevelt, Vol. III)* (New York, NY: Mariner Book: Houghton Mifflin Co., 2003), p. 147. Mussolini's 1931 statement to Alfred Bingham, the son of a US Republican Senator.

[45] Adolf Hitler: "There comes a time when it will be obvious that socialism can only be carried out accompanied by nationalism and antisemitism." Hitler's speech "Why We Are Anti-Semites," Aug. 15, 1920 in Munich at the Hofbräuhaus. Hitler gave this speech a number of times in Aug. 1920 to members of the National Socialist German Workers Party. Speech is also known as "Why Are We Anti-Semites?" Translated from *Vierteljahrshefte für Zeitgeschichte*, 16. Jahrg., 4. H. (Oct. 1968), pp. 390–420. Edited by Carolyn Yeager.

[46]Stalin's regime adopted the state policy of "Socialism in One Country," thereby abandoning the Marxist idea of international communism. Starting in 1924, Stalin shifted towards a form of "national communism," while opposing Trotsky's theory of permanent revolution.

[47]*Die Rote Fahne*, the Communist Party of Germany's mouthpiece, which is usually obedient to Moscow directives, stated: "Strongly to emphasize the nation is a revolutionary deed." *Die Rote Fahne*, June 21, 1923. Voigt, *Unto Caesar*, pp. 141–142.

[48]"[D]uring the Third Reich state ownership expanded into the productive sectors, based on the strategic industries, aviation, aluminum, synthetic oil and rubber, chemicals, iron and steel, and army equipment. Government finances for state-owned enterprises rose from RM 4,000m in 1933 to RM 16,000m 10 years later; the capital assets of state-owned industry doubled during the same period; the number of state-owned firms topped 500." Overy, *War and Economy in the Third Reich*, p. 16.

[49]Adolf Hitler: "We demand the nationalisation of all (previous) associated industries (trusts)." Speech by Hitler on Feb. 24, 1920, 25-point Program of the NSDAP.

[50]Benito Mussolini: "Three-fourths of the Italian economy, industrial and agricultural, is in the hands of the state. And if I dare to introduce to Italy state capitalism or state socialism, which is the reverse side of the medal, I will have the necessary subjective and objective conditions to do it." Toniolo, *The Oxford Handbook of the Italian Economy Since Unification*, p. 59. Mussolini's speech to the Chamber of Deputies on May 26, 1934.

[51]One historian and writer, Gaetano Salvemini, suspected that Mussolini's figures were wrong and estimated Italy's national debt at 148,646,000,000 lire by 1934. It was only 93 billion lire in 1922. Flynn, *As We Go Marching*, p. 51. Also see "Twelve Years of Fascist Finance," by Dr. Gaetano Salvemini, *Foreign Affairs* 13, no. 3 (Apr. 1935), p. 463.

[52]Hallett, *The Social Economy of West Germany*, p. 15.

[53][*Volksgemeinschaft* became the] "unifying blueprint for National Socialist social engineering initiatives at all sorts of levels." Steber and Gotto, *Visions of Community in Nazi Germany*, p. 7.

[54]"The war in Africa [Ethiopia] was to provide a new context for Fascism's scheme of social engineering." Davide Rodogno, *Fascism's European Empire: Italian Occupation during the Second World War* (Cambridge University Press, 2006), p. 44.

[55]Adolf Hitler: "[T]here is a difference between the theoretical knowledge of socialism and the practical life of socialism. People are not born socialists, but must first be taught how to become them." "German *Volksgenossen!*" Hitler's opening speech at the new Winterhilfswerk, Deutschlandhalle, Berlin, Oct. 5, 1937.

[56]Adolf Hitler: "Since we are socialists, we must necessarily also be antisemites because we want to fight against the very opposite: materialism and mammonism... How can you not be an antisemite, being a socialist!"

Hitler, "Why We Are Anti-semites," Aug. 15, 1920 speech in Munich at the Hofbräuhaus. Hitler gave this speech a number of times in Aug. 1920 to members of the National Socialist German Workers Party. Translated from *Vierteljahrshefte für Zeitgeschichte*, 16. Jahrg., 4. H. (Oct. 1968), pp. 390–420. Edited by Carolyn Yeager. https://carolynyeager.net/why-we-are-antisemites-text-adolf-hitlers-1920-speech-hofbr%C3%A4uhaus.

[57]Joseph Goebbels: "England is a capitalist democracy. Germany is a socialist people's state." "Englands Schuld," *Illustrierter Beobachter, Sondernummer*, p. 14. The article is not dated, but is from the early months of the war, likely late fall of 1939. Goebbels' speech was titled "England's Guilt."

[58]Benito Mussolini: "Some still ask of us: what do you want? We answer with three words that summon up our entire program. Here they are... Italy, Republic, Socialization... Socialization is no other than the implantation of Italian Socialism..." Mussolini quoted in Norling, *Revolutionary Fascism*, pp. 119–120. Speech was given by Mussolini to a group of Milanese Fascist veterans and Black Brigade "Resega" officers on Oct. 14, 1944.

[59]Benito Mussolini: "For this I have been and am a socialist. The accusation of inconsistency has no foundation. My conduct has always been straight in the sense of looking at the substance of things and not to the form. I adapted *socialisticamente* to reality." Quote by Mussolini in "Soliloquy for 'freedom' Trimellone island," on the Italian Island of Trimellone, journalist Ivanoe Fossani, one of the last interviews by Mussolini, Mar. 20, 1945, *Opera Omnia*, Vol. 32. Interview is also known as "Testament of Benito Mussolini," or *Testamento di Benito Mussolini*. Also published under "Mussolini confessed to the stars," Publishing House "Latinitas," Rome, 1952, *Intervista di Ivanoe Fossani, Soliloquio in "libertà" all'isola Trimellone, Isola del Trimellone, 20 marzo 1945*.

[60]Adolf Hitler: "[T]he creation of a socially just state, a model society that would continue to eradicate all social barriers." Aly, *Hitler's Beneficiaries*, 2007, p. 13. Hitler's speech to workers at Berlin's Rheinmetall-Borsig factory, Oct. 10, 1940.

[61]Adolf Hitler: "[W]e do not believe that there could ever exist a state with lasting inner health if it is not built on internal social justice..." "Why We Are Anti-Semites," Aug. 15, 1920 speech in Munich at the Hofbräuhaus. Hitler presented this speech a number of times in Aug. 1920. Translated from *Vierteljahrshefte für Zeitgeschichte*, 16. Jahrg., 4. H. (Oct. 1968), pp. 390–420. Edited by Carolyn Yeager. Source: https://carolynyeager.net/why-we-are-antisemites-text-adolf-hitlers-1920-speech-hofbr%C3%A4uhaus.

[62]Adolf Hitler: "Ultimately we shall live to see the kingdom of freedom, honour and social justice. Long live Germany!" Hitler's Speech at the Lustgarten in Berlin, Apr. 4, 1932. Thomas Friedrich, *Hitler's Berlin: Abused City*, trans. Stewart Spencer (Yale University Press, 2012), p. 272.

[63]Benito Mussolini: "We are fighting to impose a higher social justice. The others are fighting to maintain the privileges of caste and class. We are proletarian nations that rise up against the plutocrats." Quote by Mussolini in "Soliloquy for 'freedom' Trimellone island," on the Italian Island of Trimellone, journalist Ivanoe Fossani, one of the last interviews by Mussolini, Mar. 20, 1945, *Opera Omnia*, Vol. 32. Interview is also known as "Testament of Benito Mussolini," or *Testamento di Benito Mussolini*.

Also published under "Mussolini confessed to the stars," Publishing House "Latinitas," Rome, 1952. (*Intervista di Ivanoe Fossani, Soliloquio in "libertà" all'isola Trimellone, Isola del Trimellone, 20 marzo 1945*)

[64] Italy spent considerable funds on elaborate social welfare programs which were "motivated by the 'moral' concern with abstract 'social justice.'" Gregor, *Italian Fascism and Developmental Dictatorship*, p. 257.

[65] Adolf Hitler: "By educating the young generation along the right lines, the People's State will have to see to it that a generation of mankind is formed which will be adequate to this supreme combat that will decide the destinies of the world." Hitler, *Mein Kampf, Vol. Two*, chap. II, "The State."

[66] Adolf Hitler: "When an opponent declares, 'I will not come over to your side,' I calmly say, 'Your child belongs to us already... What are you? You will pass on. Your descendants, however, now stand in the new camp. In a short time they will know nothing else but this new community.'" Hitler, on Public Education, speech in Nov. 1933.

[67] By 1934 Hitler's administration had "transferred many functions of individual states (*Länder*) to the Reich." Fohlin, *Finance Capitalism and Germany's Rise to Industrial Power*, p. 302.

[68] Benito Mussolini: "Everything within the state, nothing outside the state, nothing against the state." Pipes, *Russia Under the Bolshevik Regime*, p. 243. Speech to Chamber of Deputies on Dec. 9, 1928.

[69] To gain popularity among the people during the early years of Hitler's dictatorship, the Nazis froze wages, prices and rents. Hallett, *The Social Economy of West Germany*, p. 15.

[70] George Orwell: "the State, which is simply the Nazi Party, is in control of everything. It controls investment, raw materials, rates of interest, working hours, wages." George Orwell, *My Country Right or Left, 1940–1943*, ed. Sonia Orwell and Ian Angus (Jeffrey, NH: Nonpareil Book, 1968), p. 80. His essay first published in 1941, as "The Lion and the Unicorn."

Selected Bibliography

Adler, Franklin Hugh. *Italian Industrialists from Liberalism to Fascism: The Political Development of the Industrial Bourgeoisie, 1906–1934.* Cambridge University Press, 1995.

Aly, Götz. *Hitler's Beneficiaries: Plunder, Racial War, and the Nazi Welfare State.* New York, NY: A Holt Paperback, 2005.

———. *Hitler's Beneficiaries: Plunder, Racial War, and the Nazi Welfare State.* New York, NY: Metropolitan Books, 2007.

Barkai, Avraham. *Nazi Economics: Ideology, Theory, and Policy.* Yale University Press, 1990.

Beck, Hermann. *The Fateful Alliance: German Conservatives and Nazis in 1933: The Machtergreifung in a New Light.* New York and Oxford: Berghahn Books, 2008.

Berend, Ivan T. *An Economic History of Twentieth-Century Europe: Economic Regimes from Laissez-Faire to Globalization.* Cambridge University Press, 2006.

Berman, Sheri. *The Primacy of Politics: Social Democracy and the Making of Europe's Twentieth Century.* Cambridge University Press, 2006.

Blamires, Cyprian P., ed. *World Fascism: A Historical Encyclopedia.* Vol. 1. Santa Barbara, CA: ABC-CLIO, Inc., 2006.

Bosworth, R.J.B. *Mussolini's Italy: Life Under the Fascist Dictatorship, 1915–1945.* New York, NY: The Penguin Press, 2006.

Brown, Timothy S. *Weimar Radicals: Nazis and Communists Between Authenticity and Performance.* New York, NY: Berghahn Books, 2009.

Burleigh, Michael. *The Third Reich: A New History.* New York, NY: Hill and Wang, 2000.

Calic, Edouard, ed. *Secret Conversations with Hitler: The Two Newly-Discovered 1931 Interviews.* Translated by Richard Barry. New York, NY: John Day Co., 1971.

Chen, Cheng. *The Prospects for Liberal Nationalism in Post-Leninist States*. University Park, PA: Pennsylvania State University Press, 2007.

Childers, Thomas. *The Nazi Voter: The Social Foundations of Fascism in Germany, 1919–1933*. Chapel Hill, NC and London, UK: University of North Carolina Press, 1983.

De Grand, Alexander J. *Fascist Italy and Nazi Germany: The "Fascist" Style of Rule*. New York, NY: Routledge, 1995.

———. *Italian Fascism: Its Origins & Development*. Lincoln, NE: University of Nebraska Press, 1982.

Delzell, Charles F., ed. *Mediterranean Fascism 1919–1945*. New York, NY: Walker and Company, 1971.

Diggins, John P. *Mussolini and Fascism: The View from America*. Princeton University Press, 1972.

Doyle, William. *The Oxford History of the French Revolution*. Oxford University Press, 2002.

Drucker, Peter. *The End of Economic Man: The Origins of Totalitarianism*. New Brunswick and London: Transaction Publishers, 1995. First published in 1939.

Elazar, Dahlia S. *The Making of Fascism: Class, State, and Counter-Revolution, Italy 1919–1922*. Westport, CT: Praeger, 2001.

Evans, Richard J. *The Coming of the Third Reich*. New York, NY: Penguin Press, 2004.

———. *The Third Reich in Power, 1933–1939*. New York, NY: Penguin Press, 2005.

Fitzhugh, George. *Cannibals All! Or Slaves Without Masters*. Richmond, VA: A. Morris Publisher, 1857.

———. *Sociology for the South, Or the Failure of Free Society*. Richmond, VA: A. Morris Publisher, 1854.

Flynn, John T. *As We Go Marching*. New York, NY: Doubleday and Company, Inc., 1944.

Fohlin, Caroline. *Finance Capitalism and Germany's Rise to Industrial Power*. Cambridge University Press, 2007.

Furet, François. *The Passing of an Illusion: The Idea of Communism in the Twentieth Century*. Chicago, IL: University of Chicago Press, 1999.

Fritzsche, Peter. *Life and Death in the Third Reich*. President and Fellows of Harvard College, 2008.

Goldberg, Jonah. *Liberal Fascism: The Secret History of the American Left, From Mussolini to the Politics of Change*. New York, NY: Three Rivers Press, 2009.

Gompers, Samuel, and William English Walling. *Out of Their Own Mouths: A Revelation and an Indictment of Sovietism*. New York, NY: E.P. Dutton and Company, 1921.

Gregor, A. James. *Italian Fascism and Developmental Dictatorship*. Princeton, NJ: Princeton University Press, 1979.

———. *Marxism, Fascism & Totalitarianism: Chapters in the Intellectual History of Radicalism*. Stanford, CA: Stanford University Press, 2009.

———. *The Faces of Janus: Marxism and Fascism in the Twentieth Century*. New Haven, CT: Yale University Press, 2000.

———. *The Fascist Persuasion in Radical Politics*. Princeton, NJ: Princeton University Press, 1974.

———. *The Ideology of Fascism: The Rationale of Totalitarianism*. New York, NY: The Free Press, 1969.

Griffith, Gareth. *Socialism and Superior Brains: The Political Thought of Bernard Shaw*. Routledge, 2002.

Grunberger, Richard. *The 12-Year Reich: A Social History of Nazi Germany 1933–1945*. New York, NY: Holt, Rinehart and Winston, 1971.

Hallett, Graham. *The Social Economy of West Germany*. Palgrave Macmillan, 1973.

Heiden, Konrad. *A History of National Socialism*. London, UK: Methuen & Company, LTD, 1934.

———. *Hitler: A Biography*. London, UK: Constable & Co. LTD, 1938.

———. *The Führer*. New York, NY: A Herman Graf Book—Skyhorse Publishing, 2012. First published in 1944.

Hibbert, Christopher. *Mussolini: The Rise and Fall of Il Duce*. New York, NY: St. Martin's Press, 2008.

Hitler, Adolf. *Mein Kampf, Volume One: A Reckoning*. 1925.

———. *Mein Kampf, Volume Two: The National Socialist Movement*. 1926.

Jäckel, Eberhard, and Axel Kuhn, eds. *Hitler: Sämtliche Aufzeichnungen 1905–1924*. Stuttgart: Deutsche Verlags-Anstalt, 1980.

Johnson, Paul. *Modern Times: The World from the Twenties to the Eighties*. New York, NY: Harper and Row, Publishers, 1983.

Kemechey, L. *Il Duce: The Life and Work of Benito Mussolini*. Translated by Magda Vamos. New York, NY: Richard R. Smith, 1930.

Kershaw, Ian. *Hitler 1889–1936: Hubris*. New York and London: W.W. Norton & Company, 1999.

———. *Hitler 1936–1945: Nemesis*. New York, NY: W.W. Norton & Company, 2000.

Kitchen, Martin. *A History of Modern Germany, 1800–2000*. Malden, MA and Oxford, UK: Blackwell Publishing, LTD., 2006.

Knight, Patricia. *Mussolini and Fascism: Questions and Analysis in History*. New York, NY: Routledge, 2003.

Lane, Barbara Miller, and Leila J. Rupp, trans. *Nazi Ideology Before 1933: A Documentation*. Manchester University Press, 1978.

Ludwig, Emil. *Talks with Mussolini*. Boston, MA: Little, Brown and Company, 1933.

Mises, Ludwig von. *Human Action: A Treatise on Economics*. Scholar's Edition. Auburn, AL: Ludwig von Mises Institute, 1998. Originally printed in 1949 by Yale University Press.

———. *Planned Chaos*. Irvington-on-Hudson, NY: Foundation for Economic Education, 1970.

Morgan, Philip. *Fascism in Europe, 1919–1945*. New York, NY: Routledge, 2003.

Muravchik, Joshua. *Heaven on Earth: The Rise and Fall of Socialism*. New York, NY: Encounter Books, 2002.

Mussolini, Benito. *My Autobiography*. New York, NY: Charles Scribner's Sons, 1928.

———. *Four Speeches on the Corporate State*. Roma: Laboremus, 1935.

———. *The Political and Social Doctrine of Fascism*. Translated by Jane Soames. London W.C.: Leonard and Virginia Woolf (Hogarth Press), 1933.

Neocleous, Mark. *Fascism*. Minneapolis, MN: Open University Press/University of Minnesota Press, 1997.

Newton, Michael E. *The Path to Tyranny: A History of Free Society's Descent into Tyranny.* New York, NY: Routledge, 1994.

Nimni, Ephraim. *Marxism and Nationalism: Theoretical Origins of a Political Crisis.* London, UK: Pluto Press, 1994.

Nitti, Francesco Saverio. *Bolshevism, Fascism and Democracy.* Translated by Margaret M. Green. London, UK: George Allen & Unwin, LTD., 1927.

Nolte, Ernst. *Three Faces of Fascism: Action Française, Italian Fascism, National Socialism.* Translated by Leila Vennewitz. Holt, Rinehart and Winston, 1966.

Norling, Erik. *Revolutionary Fascism.* Lisbon: Finis Mundi Press, 2011.

Orlow, Dietrich. *The Nazi Party 1919–1945: A Complete History.* Enigma Books, 2010.

Overy, R.J. *War and Economy in the Third Reich.* Oxford, UK: Clarendon Press (Oxford University Press), 1994.

Paxton, Robert O. *The Anatomy of Fascism.* New York, NY: Alfred A. Knopf, 2004.

Payne, Stanley G. *A History of Fascism, 1914–1945.* Madison, WI: University of Wisconsin Press, 1995.

Pipes, Richard. *Russia Under the Bolshevik Regime.* New York, NY: Vintage Books, 1995.

Prager, Dennis, and Joseph Telushkin. *Why the Jew?: The Reason for Antisemitism.* New York, NY: Touchstone, 2003.

Rauschning, Hermann. *The Voice of Destruction.* New York, NY: G.P. Putnam's Sons, 1940. Also published under the title *Hitler Speaks.*

Read, Anthony. *The Devil's Disciples: Hitler's Inner Circle.* New York, NY and London, UK: W.W. Norton & Company, Inc., 2004.

Redman, Tim. *Ezra Pound and Italian Fascism.* Cambridge University Press, 1991.

Reimann, Günter. *The Vampire Economy: Doing Business Under Fascism.* Mises Institute, 2014. First published in 1939.

Richman, Sheldon. "Fascism." In *The Concise Encyclopedia of Economics*, 2nd ed. Indianapolis, IN: Liberty Fund, 2008.

Roberts, David D. *The Syndicalist Tradition and Italian Fascism.* University of Northern Carolina Press, 1979.

Rummel, R.J. *The Blue Book of Freedom: Ending Famine, Poverty, De-mocide, and War*. Nashville, TN: Cumberland House Publishing, 2007.

Salvemini, Gaetano. *The Fate of Trade Unions Under Fascism*. New York, NY: Anti-Fascist Literature Committee, 1937. See esp. chap. 3, "Italian Trade Unions Under Fascism."

———. *Under the Axe of Fascism*. London, UK: Victor Gollancz, LTD, 1936.

Sarfatti, Margherita. *The Life of Benito Mussolini*. London, UK: Thornton Butterworth, LTD., 1925.

Schivelbusch, Wolfgang. *Three New Deals: Reflections on Roosevelt's America, Mussolini's Italy, and Hitler's Germany, 1933–1939*. Metropolitan Books, 2006.

Schnapp, Jeffrey T., ed. *A Primer of Italian Fascism*. Translated by Jeffrey T. Schnapp, Olivia E. Sears, and Maria G. Stampino. University of Nebraska Press, 2000.

Schoenbaum, David. *Hitler's Social Revolution: Class and Status in Nazi Germany, 1933–1939*. New York, NY: W.W. Norton & Company, 1997.

Schwarzschild, Leopold. *Karl Marx: The Red Prussian*. New York, NY: The Universal Library, Grosset & Dunlap, 1947.

Shirer, William L. *The Rise and Fall of the Third Reich: A History of Nazi Germany*. Simon & Schuster, 2011. First published in 1960.

Smith, Denis Mack. *Modern Italy: A Political History*. University of Michigan Press, 1979. First published in 1959.

———. *Mussolini*. New York, NY: Vintage Books, 1983.

Steber, Martina, and Bernhard Gotto. *Visions of Community in Nazi Germany: Social Engineering and Private Lives*. Oxford, UK: Oxford University Press, 2014.

Sternhell, Zeev. *Neither Right nor Left: Fascist Ideology in France*. Translated by David Maisel. Princeton, NJ: Princeton University Press, 1996.

Sternhell, Zeev, Mario Sznajder, Maia Asheri. *The Birth of Fascist Ideology: From Cultural Rebellion to Political Revolution*. Translated by David Maisel. Princeton University Press, 1994.

Stoker, Donald J., Jr. *Girding for Battle: The Arms Trade in a Global Perspective, 1815–1940*. Edited by Jonathan A. Grant. Westport, CT: Praeger Publishers, 2003.

Strasser, Otto. *Hitler and I*. Translated from French by Gwenda David and Eric Mosbacher. Boston, MA: Houghton Mifflin Company, 1940.

Toland, John. *Adolf Hitler: The Definitive Biography*. New York, NY: Anchor Books (Doubleday), 1976.

Toler, Pamela D. *The Everything Guide to Understanding Socialism: The Political, Social, and Economic Concepts Behind This Complex Theory*. Avon, MA: Adams Media, 2011.

Toniolo, Gianni, ed. *The Oxford Handbook of the Italian Economy Since Unification*. Oxford, UK: Oxford University Press, 2013.

Townley, Edward, ed. *Mussolini and Italy*. Oxford, UK: Heinemann Educational Publishers, 2002.

Trotsky, Leon. *The Revolution Betrayed: What Is the Soviet Union and Where Is It Going?*, translated by Max Eastman. Detroit, MI: Labor Publications, Inc., 1991. First published in 1937. See esp. chap. 11, "Whither the Soviet Union."

Voigt, Frederick Augustus. *Unto Caesar*. New York, NY: G.P. Putnam's Sons, 1938.

Wagener, Otto. *Hitler—Memoirs of a Confidant*. Edited by Henry Ashby Turner Jr. Translated by Ruth Hein. New Haven, CT: Yale University Press, 1985.

Watson, George. *The Lost Literature of Socialism*. Cambridge, England: The Lutterworth Press, 1998.

Weber, Thomas. *Becoming Hitler: The Making of a Nazi*. New York, NY: Basic Books, 2017.

———. *Hitler's First War: Adolf Hitler, the Men of the List Regiment, and the First World War*. Oxford, UK: Oxford University Press, 2011.

Whalen, Grover A. *Mr. New York: The Autobiography of Grover A. Whalen*. New York, NY: G.P. Putnam's Sons, 1955.

Index

Printed in Great Britain
by Amazon

20172613R00337